ECONOMIC THOUGHT BEFORE ADAM SMITH

Economic Thought before Adam Smith

An Austrian Perspective on the
History of Economic Thought
Volume I

Murray N. Rothbard

Professor of Economics
University of Nevada
Las Vegas, US

Edward Elgar

Published by
Edward Elgar Publishing Limited
Gower House
Croft Road
Aldershot
Hants GU11 3HR
England

Edward Elgar Publishing Company
Old Post Road
Brookfield
Vermont 05036
USA

British Library Cataloguing in Publication Data
Rothbard, Murray N.
  Economic Thought Before Adam Smith:
  Austrian Perspective on the History of
  Economic Thought. – Vol. 1
  I. Title
  330.1509

Library of Congress Cataloguing in Publication Data
Rothbard, Murray Newton, 1926–
    An Austrian perspective on the history of
economic thought.
    Includes bibliographical references.
    Contents: v. 1. Economic thought before
Adam Smith — v. 2. Classical economics.
    1. Economics–History.   2. Austrian
school of economists.   I. Title.
HB75.R6726   1995   330'.09   94–15922

ISBN 1 85278 961 1

Printed and Bound in Great Britain by
Hartnolls Limited, Bodmin, Cornwall.

Contents

Introduction

As the subtitle declares, this work is an overall history of economic thought from a frankly 'Austrian' standpoint: that is, from the point of view of an adherent of the 'Austrian School' of economics. This is the only such work by a modern Austrian; indeed, only a few monographs in specialized areas of the history of thought have been published by Austrians in recent decades.[1] Not only that: this perspective is grounded in what is currently the least fashionable though not the least numerous variant of the Austrian School: the 'Misesian' or 'praxeologic'.[2]

But the Austrian nature of this work is scarcely its only singularity. When the present author first began studying economics in the 1940s, there was an overwhelmingly dominant paradigm in the approach to the history of economic thought – one that is still paramount, though not as baldly as in that era. Essentially, this paradigm features a few Great Men as the essence of the history of economic thought, with Adam Smith as the almost superhuman founder. But if Smith was the creator of both economic analysis and of the free trade, free market tradition in political economy, it would be petty and niggling to question seriously any aspect of his alleged achievement. Any sharp criticism of Smith as either economist or free market advocate would seem only anachronistic: looking down upon the pioneering founder from the point of view of the superior knowledge of today, puny descendants unfairly bashing the giants on whose shoulders we stand.

If Adam Smith created economics, much as Athena sprang full-grown and fully armed from the brow of Zeus, then his predecessors must be foils, little men of no account. And so short shrift was given, in these classic portrayals of economic thought, to anyone unlucky enough to precede Smith. Generally they were grouped into two categories and brusquely dismissed. Immediately preceding Smith were the mercantilists, whom he strongly criticized. Mercantilists were apparently boobs who kept urging people to accumulate money but not to spend it, or insisting that the balance of trade must 'balance' with each country. Scholastics were dismissed even more rudely, as moralistic medieval ignoramuses who kept warning that the 'just' price must cover a merchant's cost of production plus a reasonable profit.

The classic works in the history of thought of the 1930s and 1940s then proceeded to expound and largely to celebrate a few peak figures after Smith. Ricardo systematized Smith, and dominated economics until the 1870s; then the 'marginalists', Jevons, Menger and Walras, marginally corrected Smith–

Ricardo 'classical economics' by stressing the importance of the marginal unit as compared to whole classes of goods. Then it was on to Alfred Marshall, who sagely integrated Ricardian cost theory with the supposedly one-sided Austrian–Jevonian emphasis on demand and utility, to create modern neoclassical economics. Karl Marx could scarcely be ignored, and so he was treated in a chapter as an aberrant Ricardian. And so the historian could polish off his story by dealing with four or five Great Figures, each of whom, with the exception of Marx, contributed more building blocks toward the unbroken progress of economic science, essentially a story of ever onward and upward into the light.[3]

In the post-World War II years, Keynes of course was added to the Pantheon, providing a new culminating chapter in the progress and development of the science. Keynes, beloved student of the great Marshall, realized that the old man had left out what would later be called 'macroeconomics' in his exclusive emphasis on the micro. And so Keynes added macro, concentrating on the study and explanation of unemployment, a phenomenon which everyone before Keynes had unaccountably left out of the economic picture, or had conveniently swept under the rug by blithely 'assuming full employment'.

Since then, the dominant paradigm has been largely sustained, although matters have recently become rather cloudy. For one thing, this kind of Great Man ever-upward history requires occasional new final chapters. Keynes's *General Theory*, published in 1936, is now almost sixty years old; surely there must be a Great Man for a final chapter? But who? For a while, Schumpeter, with his modern and seemingly realistic stress on 'innovation', had a run, but this trend came a cropper, perhaps on the realization that Schumpeter's fundamental work (or 'vision', as he himself perceptively put it) was written more than two decades before the *General Theory*. The years since the 1950s have been murky; and it is difficult to force a return to the once-forgotten Walras into the Procrustean bed of continual progress.

My own view of the grave deficiency of the Few Great Men approach has been greatly influenced by the work of two splendid historians of thought. One is my own dissertation mentor Joseph Dorfman, whose unparalleled multi-volume work on the history of American economic thought demonstrated conclusively how important allegedly 'lesser' figures are in any movement of ideas. In the first place, the stuff of history is left out by omitting these figures, and history is therefore falsified by selecting and worrying over a few scattered texts to constitute The History of Thought. Second, a large number of the supposedly secondary figures contributed a great deal to the development of thought, in some ways more than the few peak thinkers. Hence, important features of economic thought get omitted, and the developed theory is made paltry and barren as well as lifeless.

Furthermore, the cut-and-thrust of history itself, the context of the ideas and movements, how people influenced each other, and how they reacted to and against one another, is necessarily left out of the Few Great Men approach. This aspect of the historian's work was particularly brought home to me by Quentin Skinner's notable two-volume *Foundations of Modern Political Thought*, the significance of which could be appreciated without adopting Skinner's own behaviourist methodology.[4]

The continual progress, onward-and-upward approach was demolished for me, and should have been for everyone, by Thomas Kuhn's famed *Structure of Scientific Revolutions*.[5] Kuhn paid no attention to economics, but instead, in the standard manner of philosophers and historians of science, focused on such ineluctably 'hard' sciences as physics, chemistry, and astronomy. Bringing the word 'paradigm' into intellectual discourse, Kuhn demolished what I like to call the 'Whig theory of the history of science'. The Whig theory, subscribed to by almost all historians of science, including economics, is that scientific thought progresses patiently, one year after another developing, sifting, and testing theories, so that science marches onward and upward, each year, decade or generation learning more and possessing ever more correct scientific theories. On analogy with the Whig theory of history, coined in mid-nineteenth century England, which maintained that things are always getting (and therefore must get) better and better, the Whig historian of science, seemingly on firmer grounds than the regular Whig historian, implicitly or explicitly asserts that 'later is always better' in any particular scientific discipline. The Whig historian (whether of science or of history proper) really maintains that, for any point of historical time, 'whatever was, was right', or at least better than 'whatever was earlier'. The inevitable result is a complacent and infuriating Panglossian optimism. In the historiography of economic thought, the consequence is the firm if implicit position that every individual economist, or at least every school of economists, contributed their important mite to the inexorable upward march. There can, then, be no such thing as gross systemic error that deeply flawed, or even invalidated, an entire school of economic thought, much less sent the world of economics permanently astray.

Kuhn, however, shocked the philosophic world by demonstrating that this is simply not the way that science has developed. Once a central paradigm is selected, there is no testing or sifting, and tests of basic assumptions only take place after a series of failures and anomalies in the ruling paradigm has plunged the science into a 'crisis situation'. One need not adopt Kuhn's nihilistic philosophic outlook, his implication that no one paradigm is or can be better than any other, to realize that his less than starry-eyed view of science rings true both as history and as sociology.

But if the standard romantic or Panglossian view does not work even in the hard sciences, *a fortiori* it must be totally off the mark in such a 'soft science' as economics, in a discipline where there can be no laboratory testing, and where numerous even softer disciplines such as politics, religion, and ethics necessarily impinge on one's economic outlook.

There can therefore be no presumption whatever in economics that later thought is better than earlier, or even that all well-known economists have contributed their sturdy mite to the developing discipline. For it becomes very likely that, rather than everyone contributing to an ever-progressing edifice, economics can and has proceeded in contentious, even zig-zag fashion, with later systemic fallacy sometimes elbowing aside earlier but sounder paradigms, thereby redirecting economic thought down a total erroneous or even tragic path. The overall path of economics may be up, or it may be down, over any give time period.

In recent years, economics, under the dominant influence of formalism, positivism and econometrics, and preening itself on being a hard science, has displayed little interest in its own past. It has been intent, as in any 'real' science, on the latest textbook or journal article rather than on exploring its own history. After all, do contemporary physicists spend much time poring over eighteenth century optics?

In the last decade or two, however, the reigning Walrasian–Keynesian neoclassical formalist paradigm has been called ever more into question, and a veritable Kuhnian 'crisis situation' has developed in various areas of economics, including worry over its methodology. Amidst this situation, the study of the history of thought has made a significant comeback, one which we hope and expect will expand in coming years.[6] For if knowledge buried in paradigms lost can disappear and be forgotten over time, then studying older economists and schools of thought need not be done merely for antiquarian purposes or to examine how intellectual life proceeded in the past. Earlier economists can be studied for their important contributions to forgotten and therefore new knowledge today. Valuable truths can be learned about the content of economics, not only from the latest journals, but from the texts of long-deceased economic thinkers.

But these are merely methodological generalizations. The concrete realization that important economic knowledge had been lost over time came to me from absorbing the great revision of the scholastics that developed in the 1950s and 1960s. The pioneering revision came dramatically in Schumpeter's great *History of Economic Analysis*, and was developed in the works of Raymond de Roover, Marjorie Grice-Hutchinson and John T. Noonan. It turns out that the scholastics were not simply 'medieval', but began in the thirteenth century and expanded and flourished through the sixteenth and into the seventeenth century. Far from being cost-of-production moralists, the scholastics believed that the just price was whatever price was established on the 'common estimate' of the free market. Not only that: far from being naive labour or cost-of-production value theorists, the scholastics may be considered 'proto-Austrians', with a sophisticated subjective utility theory of value and price. Furthermore, some of the scholastics were far superior to current formalist microeconomics in developing a 'proto-Austrian' dynamic theory of entrepreneurship. Moreover, in 'macro', the scholastics, beginning with Buridan and culminating in the sixteenth century Spanish scholastics, worked out an 'Austrian' rather than monetarist supply and demand theory of money and prices, including interregional money flows, and even a purchasing-power parity theory of exchange rates.

It seems to be no accident that this dramatic revision of our knowledge of the scholastics was brought to American economists, not generally esteemed for their depth of knowledge of Latin, by European-trained economists steeped in Latin, the language in which the scholastics wrote. This simple point emphasizes another reason for loss of knowledge in the modern world: the insularity in one's own language (particularly severe in the English-speaking countries) that has, since the Reformation, ruptured the once Europe-wide community of scholars. One reason why continental economic thought has often exerted minimal, or at least delayed, influence in England and the United States is simply because these works had not been translated into English.[7]

For me, the impact of scholastic revisionism was complemented and strengthened by the work, during the same decades, of the German-born 'Austrian' historian, Emil Kauder. Kauder revealed that the dominant economic thought in France and Italy during the seventeenth and especially the eighteenth centuries was also 'proto-Austrian', emphasizing subjective utility and relative scarcity as the determinants of value. From this groundwork, Kauder proceeded to a startling insight into the role of Adam Smith that, however, follows directly from his own work and that of the scholastic revisionists: that Smith, far from being the founder of economics, was virtually the reverse. On the contrary, Smith actually took the sound, and almost fully developed, proto-Austrian subjective value tradition, and tragically shunted economics on to a false path, a dead end from which the Austrians had to rescue economics a century later. Instead of subjective value, entrepreneurship, and emphasis on real market pricing and market activity, Smith dropped all this and replaced it with a labour theory of value and a dominant focus on the unchanging long-run 'natural price' equilibrium, a world where entrepreneurship was assumed out of existence. Under Ricardo, this unfortunate shift in focus was intensified and systematized.

If Smith was not the creator of economic theory, neither was he the founder of *laissez-faire* in political economy. Not only were the scholastics analysts of, and believers in, the free market and critics of government intervention; but the French and Italian economists of the eighteenth century were even more *laissez-faire*-oriented than Smith, who introduced numerous waffles and qualifications into what had been, in the hands of Turgot and others, an almost pure championing of *laissez-faire*. It turns out that, rather than someone who should be venerated as creator of modern economics or of *laissez-faire*, Smith was closer to the picture portrayed by Paul Douglas in the 1926 Chicago commemoration of the *Wealth of Nations*: a necessary precursor of Karl Marx.

Emil Kauder's contribution was not limited to his portrayal of Adam Smith as the destroyer of a previously sound tradition of economic theory, as the founder of an enormous 'zag' in a Kuhnian picture of a zig-zag history of economic thought. Also fascinating if more speculative was Kauder's estimate of the essential *cause* of a curious asymmetry in the course of economic thought in different countries. Why is it, for example, that the subjective utility tradition flourished on the Continent, especially in France and Italy, and then revived particularly in Austria, whereas the labour and cost of production theories developed especially in Great Britain? Kauder attributed the difference to the profound influence of religion: the scholastics, and then France, Italy and Austria were Catholic countries, and Catholicism emphasized consumption as the goal of production and consumer utility and enjoyment as, at least in moderation, valuable activities and goals. The British tradition, on the contrary, beginning with Smith himself, was Calvinist, and reflected the Calvinist emphasis on hard work and labour toil as not only good but a great good in itself, whereas consumer enjoyment is at best a necessary evil, a mere requisite to continuing labour and production.

On reading Kauder, I considered this view a challenging insight, but essentially an unproven speculation. However, as I continued studying economic thought and embarked on writing these volumes, I concluded that Kauder was being confirmed many times over. Even though Smith was a 'moderate' Calvinist, he was a staunch one nevertheless, and I came to the conclusion that the Calvinist emphasis could account, for example, for Smith's otherwise puzzling championing of usury laws, as well as his shift in emphasis from the capricious, luxury-loving consumer as the determinant of value, to the virtuous labourer embedding his hours of toil into the value of his material product.

But if Smith could be accounted for by Calvinism, what of the Spanish–Portuguese Jew-turned-Quaker, David Ricardo, surely no Calvinist? Here it seems to me that recent research into the dominant role of James Mill as mentor of Ricardo and major founder of the 'Ricardian system' comes strongly into play. For Mill was a Scotsman ordained as a Presbyterian minister and steeped in Calvinism; the fact that, later in life, Mill moved to London and became an agnostic had no effect on the Calvinist nature of Mill's basic attitudes toward life and the world. Mill's enormous evangelical energy, his crusading for social betterment, and his devotion to labour toil (as well as the cognate Calvinist virtue of thrift) reflected his lifelong Calvinist world-out-look. John Stuart Mill's resurrection of Ricardianism may be interpreted as his fileopietist devotion to the memory of his dominant father, and Alfred Marshall's trivialization of Austrian insights into his own neo-Ricardian schema also came from a highly moralistic and evangelical neo-Calvinist.

Conversely, it is no accident that the Austrian School, the major challenge to the Smith–Ricardo vision, arose in a country that was not only solidly Catholic, but whose values and attitudes were still heavily influenced by Aristotelian and Thomist thought. The German precursors of the Austrian School flourished, not in Protestant and anti-Catholic Prussia, but in those German states that were either Catholic or were politically allied to Austria rather than Prussia.

The result of these researches was my growing conviction that leaving out religious outlook, as well as social and political philosophy, would disastrously skew any picture of the history of economic thought. This is fairly obvious for the centuries before the nineteenth, but it is true for that century as well, even as the technical apparatus takes on more of a life of its own.

In consequence of these insights, these volumes are very different from the norm, and not just in presenting an Austrian rather than a neoclassical or institutionalist perspective. The entire work is much longer than most since it insists on bringing in all the 'lesser' figures and their interactions as well as emphasizing the importance of their religious and social philosophies as well as their narrower strictly 'economic' views. But I would hope that the length and inclusion of other elements does not make this work less readable. On the contrary, history necessarily means narrative, discussion of real persons as well as their abstract theories, and includes triumphs, tragedies, and conflicts, conflicts which are often moral as well as purely theoretical. Hence, I hope that, for the reader, the unwonted length will be offset by the inclusion of far more human drama than is usually offered in histories of economic thought.

Murray N. Rothbard
Las Vegas, Nevada

Notes

1. Joseph Schumpeter's valuable and monumental *History of Economic Analysis* (New York: Oxford University Press, 1954), has sometimes been referred to as 'Austrian'. But while Schumpeter was raised in Austria and studied under the great Austrian Böhm-Bawerk, he himself was a dedicated Walrasian, and his *History* was, in addition, eclectic and idiosyncratic.
2. For an explanation of the three leading Austrian paradigms at the present time, see Murray N. Rothbard, *The Present State of Austrian Economics* (Auburn, Ala.: Ludwig von Mises Institute, 1992).
3. When the present author was preparing for his doctoral orals at Columbia University, he

had the venerable John Maurice Clark as examiner in the history of economic thought. When he asked Clark whether he should read Jevons, Clark replied, in some surprise: 'What's the point? The good in Jevons is all in Marshall'.

4. Joseph Dorfman, *The Economic Mind in American Civilization* (5 vols, New York: Viking Press, 1946–59); Quentin Skinner, *The Foundations of Modern Political Thought* (2 vols, Cambridge: Cambridge University Press, 1978).

5. Thomas S. Kuhn, *The Structure of Scientific Revolutions* (1962, 2nd ed., Chicago: University of Chicago Press, 1970).

6. The attention devoted in recent years to a brilliant critique of neoclassical formalism as totally dependent on obsolete mid-nineteenth century mechanics is a welcome sign of this recent change of attitude. See Philip Mirowski, *More Heat than Light* (Cambridge: Cambridge University Press, 1989).

7. At the present time, when English has become the European *lingua franca*, and most European journals publish articles in English, this barrier has been minimized.

Acknowledgements

These volumes were directly inspired by Mark Skousen, of Rollins College, Florida, who urged me to write a history of economic thought from an Austrian perspective. In addition to providing the spark, Skousen persuaded the Institute for Political Economy to support my research during its first academic year. Mark first envisioned the work as a standard Smith-to-the-present moderately sized book, a sort of contra-Heilbroner. After pondering the problem, however, I told him that I would have to begin with Aristotle, since Smith was a sharp decline from many of his predecessors. Neither of us realized then the scope or length of the ensuing research.

It is impossible to list all the persons from whom I have learned in a lifetime of instruction and discussion in the history of economics and all its cognate disciplines. Here I shall have to slight most of them and single out a few. The dedication acknowledges my immense debt to Ludwig von Mises for providing a mighty edifice of economic theory, as well as for his teaching, his friendship, and for the inspiring example of his life. And to Joseph Dorfman for his path-breaking work in the history of economic thought, his stress on the importance of the stuff of history as well as of the theories themselves, and his painstaking instruction in historical method.

I owe a great debt to Llewellyn H. Rockwell Jr for creating and organizing the Ludwig von Mises Institute, establishing it at Auburn University, and building it, in merely a decade, into a flourishing and productive centre for advancing and instructing people in Austrian economics. Not the least service to me of the Mises Institute was attracting a network of scholars from whom I could learn. Here again I must single out Joseph T. Salerno, of Pace University, who has done remarkably creative work in the history of economic thought; and that extraordinary polymath and scholar's scholar, David Gordon of the Mises Institute, whose substantial output in philosophy, economics and intellectual history embodies only a small fraction of his erudition in these and many other fields. Also thanks to Gary North, head of the Institute for Christian Economics in Tyler, Texas, for leads into the extensive bibliography on Marx and on socialism generally, and for instructing me in the mysteries of varieties of millennialism, a-, pre- and post. None of these people, of course, should be implicated in any of the errors herein.

Most of my research was conducted with the aid of the superb resources of Columbia and Stanford University libraries, as well as the library at the University of Nevada, Las Vegas, supplemented by my own book collection accumulated over the years. Since I am one of the few scholars remaining who stubbornly cleave to low-tech typewriters rather than adopt word processors/computers, I have been dependent on the services of a number of typists/word processors, among whom I would particularly mention Janet Banker and Donna Evans of the University of Nevada, Las Vegas.

In addition the author and publishers wish to thank the following who have kindly given permission for the use of copyright material.

Groenewegen, P.D. (ed.), *The Economics of A.R.J. Turgot*. Copyright 1977, by Martinus Nijhoff, The Hague. Reprinted by permission of Kluwer Academic Publishers.

Rothkrug, Lionel, *Opposition to Louis XIV*. Copyright 1965, renewed 1993, by the Princeton University Press. Reprinted by permission of Princeton University Press.

The author would particularly like to express his appreciation for the efficiency and graciousness of Mrs Berendina van Straalen, of the Rights and Permission Dept, Kluwer Academic Publishers, Dordrecht, The Netherlands.

1 The first philosopher–economists: the Greeks

It all began, as usual, with the Greeks. The ancient Greeks were the first civilized people to use their reason to think systematically about the world around them. The Greeks were the first philosophers (*philo sophia* – lovers of wisdom), the first people to think deeply and to figure out how to attain and verify knowledge about the world. Other tribes and peoples had tended to attribute natural events to arbitrary whims of the gods. A violent thunderstorm, for example, might be ascribed to something that had irritated the god of thunder. The way to bring on rain, then, or to curb violent thunderstorms, would be to find out what acts of man would please the god of rain or appease the thunder god. Such people would have considered it foolish to try to figure out the natural causes of rain or of thunder. Instead, the thing to do was to find out what the relevant gods wanted and then try to supply their needs.

The Greeks, in contrast, were eager to use their reason – their sense observations and their command of logic – to investigate and learn about their world. In so doing, they gradually stopped worrying about the whims of the gods and to investigate actual entities around them. Led in particular by the great Athenian philosopher Aristotle (384–322 B.C.), a magnificent and creative systematizer known to later ages as The Philosopher, the Greeks evolved a theory and a method of reasoning and of science which later came to be called the *natural law*.

1.1   The natural law

Natural law rests on the crucial insight that *to be* necessarily means to be *something*, that is, some particular thing or entity. There is no Being in the abstract. Everything that *is*, is some particular thing, whether it be a stone, a cat, or a tree. By empirical fact there is more than one kind of thing in the universe; in fact there are thousands, if not millions of kinds of things. Each thing has its own particular set of properties or attributes, its own *nature*, which distinguishes it from other kinds of things. A stone, a cat, an elm tree; each has its own particular nature, which man can discover, study and identify.

Man studies the world, then, by examining entities, identifying similar kinds of things, and classifying them into categories each with its own properties and nature. If we see a cat walking down the street, we can immediately include it into a set of things, or animals, called 'cats' whose nature we have already discovered and analysed.

If we can discover and learn about the natures of entities X and Y, then we can discover what happens when these two entities *interact*. Suppose, for example, that when a certain amount of X interacts with a given amount of Y we get a certain quantity of another thing, Z. We can then say that the effect, Z, has been *caused* by the interaction of X and Y. Thus, chemists may discover that when two molecules of hydrogen interact with one molecule of oxygen, the result is one molecule of a new entity, water. All these entities –

hydrogen, oxygen and water – have specific discoverable properties or natures which can be identified.

We see, then, that the concepts of *cause* and *effect* are part and parcel of natural law analysis. Events in the world can be traced back to the interactions of specific entities. Since natures are given and identifiable, the interactions of the various entities will be replicable under the same conditions. The same causes will always yield the same effects.

For the Aristotelian philosophers, logic was not a separate and isolated discipline, but an integral part of the natural law. Thus, the basic process of identifying entities led, in 'classical' or Aristotelian logic, to the Law of Identity: a thing is, and cannot be anything other than, what it is: *a* is *a*.

It follows, then, that an entity cannot be the negation of itself. Or, put another way, we have the Law of Non-Contradiction: a thing cannot be both *a* and *non-a*. *a* is not and cannot be *non-a*.

Finally, in our world of numerous kinds of entities, anything must be either *a* or it won't be; in short, it will either be *a* or *non-a*. Nothing can be both. This gives us the third well-known law of classical logic: the Law of the Excluded Middle: everything in the universe is either *a* or *non-a*.

But if every entity in the universe – if hydrogen, oxygen, stone, or cats – can be identified, classified, and its nature examined, then so too can man. Human beings must also have a specific nature with specific properties that can be studied, and from which we can obtain knowledge. Human beings are unique in the universe because they can and do study themselves, as well as the world around them, and try to figure out what goals they should pursue and what means they can employ to achieve them.

The concept of 'good' (and therefore of 'bad') is only relevant to *living* entities. Since stones or molecules have no goals or purposes, any idea of what might be 'good' for a molecule or stone would properly be considered bizarre. But what might be 'good' for an elm tree or a dog makes a great deal of sense: specifically, 'the good' is whatever conduces to the life and the flourishing of the living entity. The 'bad' is whatever injures such an entity's life or prosperity. Thus, it is possible to develop an 'elm tree ethics' by discovering the best conditions: soil, sunshine, climate, etc., for the growth and sustenance of elm trees; and by trying to avoid conditions deemed 'bad' for elm trees: elm blight, excessive drought, etc. A similar set of ethical properties can be worked out for various breeds of animals.

Thus, natural law sees ethics as living-entity- (or *species-*) relative. What is good for cabbages will differ from what is good for rabbits, which in turn will differ from what is good or bad for man. The ethic for each species will differ according to their respective natures.

Man is the only species which can – and indeed must – carve out an ethic for himself. Plants lack consciousness, and therefore cannot choose or act.

The consciousness of animals is narrowly perceptual and lacks the conceptual: the ability to frame concepts and to act upon them. Man, in the famous Aristotelian phrase, is uniquely the *rational animal* – the species that uses reason to adopt values and ethical principles, and that acts to attain these ends. Man *acts*; that is, he adopts values and purposes, and chooses the ways to achieve them.

Man, therefore, in seeking goals and ways to attain them, must discover and work within the framework of the natural law: the properties of himself and of other entities and the ways in which they may interact.

Western civilization is in many ways Greek; and the two great philosophic traditions of ancient Greece which have been shaping the Western mind ever since have been those of Aristotle and his great teacher and antagonist Plato (428–347 BC). It has been said that every man, deep down, is either a Platonist or an Aristotelian, and the divisions run throughout their thought. Plato pioneered the natural law approach which Aristotle developed and systematized; but the basic thrust was quite different. For Aristotle and his followers, man's existence, like that of all other creatures, is 'contingent', i.e. it is not necessary and eternal. Only God's existence is necessary and transcends time. The contingency of man's existence is simply an unalterable part of the natural order, and must be accepted as such.

To the Platonists, however, especially as elaborated by Plato's follower, the Egyptian Plotinus (204–270 AD), these inevitable limitations of man's natural state were intolerable and must be transcended. To the Platonists, the actual, concrete, temporal factual existence of man was too limited. Instead, this existence (which is all that any of us has ever seen) is a fall from grace, a fall from the original non-existent, ideal, perfect, eternal being of man, a god-like being perfect and therefore without limits. In a bizarre twist of language, this perfect and never-existent being was held up by the Platonists as the *truly* existent, the true essence of man, from which we have all been alienated or cut off. The nature of man (and of all other entities) in the world is to be *some thing* and to exist in time; but in the semantic twist of the Platonists, the *truly* existent man is to be eternal, to live outside of time, and to have no limits. Man's condition on earth is therefore supposed to be a state of degradation and alienation, and his purpose is supposed to be to work his way back to the 'true' limitless and perfect self alleged to be his original state. Alleged, of course, on the basis of no evidence whatever – indeed, evidence itself identifies, limits, and therefore, to the Platonic mind, corrupts.

Plato's and Plotinus's views of man's allegedly alienated state were highly influential, as we shall see, in the writings of Karl Marx and his followers. Another Greek philosopher, emphatically different from the Aristotelian tradition, who prefigured Hegel and Marx was the early pre-Socratic philosopher Heraclitus of Ephesus (c.535–475 BC). He was pre-Socratic in the sense of predating Plato's great teacher Socrates (470–399 BC), who wrote nothing but has come down to us as interpreted by Plato and by several other follow-ers. Heraclitus, who was aptly given the title 'The Obscure' by the Greeks, taught that sometimes opposites, *a* and *non-a*, can be identical, or, in other words, that *a* can be *non-a*. This defiance of elemental logic can perhaps be excused in someone like Heraclitus, who wrote before Aristotle developed classical logic, but it is hard to be so forbearing to his later followers.

1.2   The politics of the *polis*

When man turns the use of his reason from the inanimate world to man himself and to social organization, it becomes difficult for pure reason to avoid giving way to the biases and prejudices of the political framework of the age. This was all too true of the Greeks, including the Socratics, Plato and Aristotle. Greek life was organized in small city-states (the *polis*) some of which were able to carve out overseas empires. The largest city-state, Athens, covered an area of only about one thousand square miles, or half the size of modern Delaware. The key facet of Greek political life was that the city-state was run by a tight oligarchy of privileged citizens, most of whom were large landowners. Most of the population of the city-state were slaves or resident foreigners, who generally performed the manual labour and commercial enterprise respectively. The privilege of citizenship was reserved to descendants of citizens. While Greek city-states fluctuated be-tween outright tyrannies and democracies, at its most 'democratic' Athens, for example, reserved the privileges of democratic rule to 7 per cent of the population, the rest of whom were either slaves or resident aliens. (Thus, in Athens of the fifth century BC, there were approximately 30 000 citizens out of a total population of 400 000.)

As privileged landowners living off taxes and the product of slaves, Athe-nian citizens had the leisure for voting, discussion, the arts and – in the case of the particularly intelligent – philosophizing. Although the philosopher Socrates was himself the son of a stonemason, his political views were ultra-elitist. In the year 404 BC, the despotic state of Sparta conquered Athens and established a reign of terror known as the Rule of the Thirty Tyrants. When the Athenians overthrew this short-lived rule a year later, the restored democ-racy executed the aged Socrates, largely on suspicion of sympathy with the Spartan cause. This experience confirmed Socrates's brilliant young disciple, Plato, the scion of a noble Athenian family, in what would now be called an 'ultra-right' devotion to aristocratic and despotic rule.

A decade later, Plato set up his Academy on the outskirts of Athens as a think-tank not only of abstract philosophic teaching and research, but also as a fountainhead of policy programmes for social despotism. He himself tried three times unsuccessfully to set up despotic regimes in the city state of

Syracuse, while no less than nine of Plato's students succeeded in establishing themselves as tyrants over Greek city-states.

While Aristotle was politically more moderate than Plato, his aristocratic devotion to the *polis* was fully as evident. Aristotle was born of an aristocratic family in the Macedonian coastal town of Stagira, and entered Plato's Academy as a student at the age of 17, in 367 BC. There he remained until Plato's death 20 years later, after which he left Athens and eventually returned to Macedonia, where he joined the court of King Philip and tutored the young future world conqueror, Alexander the Great. After Alexander ascended the throne, Aristotle returned to Athens in 335 BC and established his own school of philosophy at the Lyceum, from which his great works have come down to us as lecture notes written by himself or transcribed by his students. When Alexander died in 323 BC, the Athenians felt free to vent their anger at Macedonians and their sympathizers, and Aristotle was ousted from the city, dying shortly thereafter.

Their aristocratic bent and their lives within the matrix of an oligarchic *polis* had a greater impact on the thought of the Socratics than Plato's various excursions into theoretical right-wing collectivist Utopias or in his students' practical attempts at establishing tyranny. For the social status and political bent of the Socratics coloured their ethical and political philosophies and their economic views. Thus, for both Plato and Aristotle, 'the good' for man was not something to be pursued by the individual, and neither was the individual a person with rights that were not to be abridged or invaded by his fellows. For Plato and Aristotle, 'the good' was naturally not to be pursued by the individual but by the *polis*. Virtue and the good life were *polis*- rather than individual-oriented. All this means that Plato's and Aristotle's thought was statist and elitist to the core, a statism which unfortunately permeated 'classical' (Greek and Roman) philosophy as well as heavily influencing Christian and medieval thought. Classical 'natural law' philosophy therefore never arrived at the later elaboration, first in the Middle Ages and then in the seventeenth and eighteenth centuries, of the 'natural rights' of the individual which may not be invaded by man or by government.

In the more strictly economic realm, the statism of the Greeks means the usual aristocratic exaltation of the alleged virtues of the military arts and of agriculture, as well as a pervasive contempt for labour and for trade, and consequently of money-making and the seeking and earning of profit. Thus Socrates, openly despising labour as unhealthy and vulgar, quotes the king of Persia to the effect that by far the noblest arts are agriculture and war. And Aristotle wrote that no good citizens 'should be permitted to exercise any low mechanical employment or traffic, as being ignoble and destructive to virtue.'

Furthermore, the Greek elevation of the *polis* over the individual led to their taking a dim view of economic innovation and entrepreneurship. The entrepreneur, the dynamic innovator, is after all the locus of individual ego and creativity, and is therefore the harbinger of often disturbing social change, as well as economic growth. But the Greek and Socratic ethical ideal for the individual was not an unfolding and flowering of inner possibilities, but rather a public/political creature moulded to conform to the demands of the *polis*. That kind of social ideal was designed to promote a frozen society of politically determined status, and certainly not a society of creative and dynamic individuals and innovators.

1.3   The first 'economist': Hesiod and the problem of scarcity

No one should be misled into thinking that the ancient Greeks were 'economists' in the modern sense. In the course of pioneering in philosophy, their philosophizing on man and his world yielded fragments of politico-economic or even strictly economic thoughts and insights. But there were no modern-style treatises on economics *per se*. It is true that the term 'economics' is Greek, stemming from the Greek *oikonomia*, but *oikonomia* means not economics in our sense but 'household management', and treatises on 'economics' would discuss what might be called the technology of household management – useful perhaps, but certainly not what we would regard today as economics. There is furthermore a danger, unfortunately not avoided by many able historians of economic thought, of eagerly reading into fragments of ancient sages the knowledge gained by modern economics. While we surely should not overlook any giants of the past, we must also avoid any 'presentist' seizing upon a few obscure sentences to hail alleged but non-existent forerunners of sophisticated modern concepts.

The honour of being the first Greek economic thinker goes to the poet Hesiod, a Boeotian who lived in the very early ancient Greece of the middle of the eighth century BC. Hesiod lived in the small, self-sufficient agricultural community of Ascra, which he himself refers to as a 'sorry place...bad in winter, hard in summer, never good'. He was therefore naturally attuned to the eternal problem of scarcity, of the niggardlinesss of resources as contrasted to the sweep of man's goals and desires. Hesiod's great poem, *Works and Days*, consisted of hundreds of verses designed for solo recitation with musical accompaniment. But Hesiod was a didactic poet rather than a mere entertainer, and he often broke out of his story line to educate his public in traditional wisdom or in explicit rules for human conduct. Of the 828 verses in the poem, the first 383 centred on the fundamental economic problem of scarce resources for the pursuit of numerous and abundant human ends and desires.

Hesiod adopts the common religious or tribal myth of the 'Golden Age', of man's alleged initial state on earth as an Eden, a Paradise of limitless abundance. In this original Eden, of course, there was no economic problem, no problem of scarcity, because all of man's wants were instantaneously fulfilled. But now, all is different, and 'men never rest from labour and sorrow by day and from perishing by night.' The reason for this low state is an all-encompassing scarcity, the result of man's ejection from Paradise. Because of scarcity, notes Hesiod, labour, materials and time have to be allocated efficiently. Scarcity, moreover, can only be partially overcome by an energetic application of labour and of capital. In particular, labour – work – is crucial, and Hesiod analyses the vital factors which may induce man to abandon the god-like state of leisure. The first of these forces is of course basic material need. But happily, need is reinforced by a social disapproval of sloth, and by the desire to emulate the consumption standards of one's fellows. To Hesiod, emulation leads to the healthy development of a spirit of competition, which he calls 'good conflict', a vital force in relieving the basic problem of scarcity.

To keep competition just and harmonious, Hesiod vigorously excludes such unjust methods of acquiring wealth as robbery, and advocates a rule of law and a respect for justice to establish order and harmony within society, and to allow competition to develop within a matrix of harmony and justice. It should already be clear that Hesiod had a far more sanguine view of economic growth, of labour and of vigorous competition, than did the far more philosophically sophisticated Plato and Aristotle three and a half centuries later.

1.4 The pre-Socratics

Man is prone to error and even folly, and therefore a history of economic thought cannot confine itself to the growth and development of economic truths. It must also treat influential error, that is, error that unfortunately influenced later developments in the discipline. One such thinker is the Greek philosopher Pythagoras of Samos (c.582–c.507 BC) who, two centuries after Hesiod, developed a school of thought which held that the *only* significant reality is *number*. The world not only *is* number, but each number even embodies moral qualities and other abstractions. Thus justice, to Pythagoras and his followers, *is* the number four, and other numbers consisted of various moral qualities. While Pythagoras undoubtedly contributed to the development of Greek mathematics, his number-mysticism could well have been characterized by the twentieth century Harvard sociologist Pitirim A. Sorokin as a seminal example of 'quantophrenia' and 'metromania'. It is scarcely an exaggeration to see in Pythagoras the embryo of the burgeoning and overweeningly arrogant mathematical economics and econometrics of the present day.

Pythagoras thus contributed a sterile dead-end to philosophy and economic thought, one that later influenced Aristotle's pawky and fallacious attempts to develop a mathematics of justice and of economic exchange. The next important positive development was contributed by the pre-Socratic (actually contemporary of Socrates) Democritus (c.460–c.370 BC).

This influential scholar from Abdera was the founder of 'atomism' in cosmology, that is, the view that the underlying structure of reality consists of interacting atoms. Democritus contributed two important strands of thought to the development of economics. First, he was the founder of subjective value theory. Moral values, ethics, were absolute, Democritus taught, but economic values were necessarily subjective. 'The same thing', Democritus writes, may be 'good and true for all men, but the pleasant differs from one and another'. Not only was valuation subjective, but Democritus also saw that the usefulness of a good will fall to nothing and become negative if its supply becomes superabundant.

Democritus also pointed out that if people restrained their demands and curbed their desires, what they now possess would make them seem relatively wealthy rather than impoverished. Here again, the relative nature of the subjective utility of wealth is recognized. In addition, Democritus was the first to arrive at a rudimentary notion of time preference: the Austrian insight that people prefer a good at present to the prospect of the good arriving in the future. As Democritus explains, 'it is not sure whether the young man will ever attain old age; hence, the good on hand is superior to the one still to come'.

In addition to the adumbration of subjective utility theory, Democritus's other major contribution to economics was his pioneering defence of a system of private property. In contrast to Oriental despotisms, in which all property was owned or controlled by the emperor and his subordinate bureaucracy, Greece rested on a society and economy of private property. Democritus, having seen the contrast between the private property economy of Athens and the oligarchic collectivism of Sparta, concluded that private property is a superior form of economic organization. In contrast to communally owned property, private property provides an incentive for toil and diligence, since 'income from communally held property gives less pleasure, and the expenditure less pain'. 'Toil', the philosopher concluded, 'is sweeter than idleness when men gain what they toil for or know that they will use it'.

1.5   Plato's right-wing collectivist utopia

Plato's search for a hierarchical, collectivist utopia found its classic expression in his most famous and influential work, *The Republic*. There, and later in *The Laws*, Plato sets forth the outline of his ideal city-state: one in which right oligarchic rule is maintained by philosopher–kings and their philosophic colleagues, thus supposedly ensuring rule by the best and wisest in the community. Underneath the philosophers in the coercive hierarchy are the 'guardians' – the soldiers, whose role is to aggress against other cities and lands and to defend their *polis* from external aggression. Underneath them are to be the body of the people, the despised producers: labourers, peasants and merchants who produce the material goods on which the lordly philosophers and guardians are to live. These three broad classes are supposed to reflect a shaky and pernicious leap if there ever was one – the proper rule over the soul in each human being. To Plato, each human being is divided into three parts: 'one that craves, one that fights, and one that thinks', and the proper hierarchy of rule within each soul is supposed to be reason first, fighting next, and finally, and the lowest, grubby desire.

The two ruling classes – the thinkers and the guardians – that really count are, in Plato's ideal state, to be forced to live under pure communism. There is to be no private property whatsoever among the elite; all things are to be owned communally, including women and children. The elite are to be forced to live together and share common meals. Since money and private possessions, according to the aristocrat Plato, only corrupt virtue, they are to be denied to the upper classes. Marriage partners among the elite are to be selected strictly by the state, which is supposed to proceed according to the scientific breeding already known in animal husbandry. If any of the philosophers or guardians find themselves unhappy about this arrangement, they will have to learn that their personal happiness means nothing compared to the happiness of the *polis* as a whole – a rather murky concept at best. In fact, those who are not seduced by Plato's theory of the essential reality of ideas will not believe that there *is* such a real living entity as a *polis*. Instead, the city-state or community consists only of living, choosing *individuals*.

To keep the elite and the subject masses in line, Plato instructs the philosopher–rulers to spread the 'noble' lie that they themselves are descended from the gods whereas the other classes are of inferior heritage. Freedom of speech or of inquiry was, as one might expect, anathema to Plato. The arts are frowned on, and the life of the citizens was to be policed to suppress any dangerous thoughts or ideas that might come to the surface.

Remarkably, in the very course of setting forth his classic apologia for totalitarianism, Plato contributed to genuine economic science by being the first to expound and analyse the importance of the division of labour in society. Since his social philosophy was founded on a necessary separation between classes, Plato went on to demonstrate that such specialization is grounded in basic human nature, in particular its diversity and inequality. Plato has Socrates say in *The Republic* that specialization arises because 'we are not all alike; there are many diversities of natures among us which are adapted to different occupations'.

Since men produce different things, the goods are naturally traded for each other, so that specialization necessarily gives rise to exchange. Plato also points out that this division of labour increases the production of all the goods. Plato saw no problem, however, in morally ranking the various occupations, with philosophy of course ranking highest and labour or trade being sordid and ignoble.

The use of gold and silver as money greatly accelerated with the invention of coinage in Lydia in the early seventh century BC and coined money quickly spread to Greece. In keeping with his distaste for money-making, trade and private property, Plato was perhaps the first theorist to denounce the use of gold and silver as money. He also disliked gold and silver precisely because they served as international currencies accepted by all peoples. Since these precious metals are universally accepted and exist apart from the imprimatur of government, gold and silver constitute a potential threat to economic and moral regulation of the *polis* by the rulers. Plato called for a government fiat currency, heavy fines on the importation of gold from outside the city-state, and the exclusion from citizenship of all traders and workers who deal with money.

One of the hallmarks of an ordered utopia sought by Plato is that, to remain ordered and controlled, it must be kept relatively static. And that means little or no change, innovation or economic growth. Plato anticipated some present-day intellectuals in frowning on economic growth, and for similar reasons: notably, fear of collapse of the domination of the state by the ruling élite. Particularly difficult in trying to freeze a static society is the problem of population growth. Quite consistently, therefore, Plato called for freezing the size of the population of the city-state, keeping the number of its citizens limited to 5 000 agricultural landlord families.

1.6   Xenophon on household management

A disciple and contemporary of Plato was the Athenian landed aristocrat and army general, Xenophon (430–354 BC). Xenophon's economic writings were scattered throughout such works as an account of the education of a Persian price, a treatise on how to increase government revenue, and a book on 'economics' in the sense of thoughts on the technology of household and farm management. Most of Xenophon's adumbrations were the usual Hellenic scorn for labour and trade, and admiration for agriculture and the military arts, coupled with a call for a massive increase in government operations and interventions in the economy. These included improving the port of Athens, building markets and inns, establishing a governmental merchant fleet and greatly expanding the number of government-owned slaves.

Interspersed in this roll of commonplace bromides, however, were some interesting insights into economic matters. In the course of his treatise on household management, Xenophon pointed out that 'wealth' should be defined as a resource that a person can use and knows how to use. In this way, something that an owner has neither the ability nor the knowledge to use cannot really constitute part of his wealth.

Another insight was Xenophon's anticipation of Adam Smith's famous dictum that the extent of the division of labour in society is necessarily limited by the extent of the market for the products. Thus, in an important addition to Plato's insights on the division of labour, written 20 years after *The Republic*, Xenophon says that 'In small towns the same workman makes chairs and doors and plows and tables, and often the same artisan builds houses...' whereas in the large cities 'many people have demands to make upon each branch of industry', and therefore 'one trade alone, and very often even less than a whole trade, is enough to support a man'. In large cities', we find one man making men's boots only; and another, women's only'... one man lives by cutting out garments, another by fitting together the pieces'.

Elsewhere, Xenophon outlines the important concept of general equilibrium as a dynamic tendency of the market economy. Thus, he states that when there are too many coppersmiths, copper becomes cheap and the smiths go bankrupt and turn to other activities, as would happen in agriculture or any other industry. He also sees clearly that an increase in the supply of a commodity causes a fall in its price.

1.7   Aristotle: private property and money

The views of the great philosopher Aristotle are particularly important because the entire structure of his thought had an enormous and even dominant influence on the economic and social thought of the high and late Middle Ages, which considered itself Aristotelian.

Although Aristotle, in the Greek tradition, scorned moneymaking and was scarcely a partisan of *laissez-faire*, he set forth a trenchant argument in favour of private property. Perhaps influenced by the private-property arguments of Democritus, Aristotle delivered a cogent attack on the communism of the ruling class called for by Plato. He denounced Plato's goal of the perfect unity of the state through communism by pointing out that such extreme unity runs against the diversity of mankind, and against the reciprocal advantage that everyone reaps through market exchange. Aristotle then delivered a point-by-point contrast of private as against communal property. First, private property is more highly productive and will therefore lead to progress. Goods owned in common by a large number of people will receive little attention, since people will mainly consult their own self-interest and will neglect all duty they can fob off on to others. In contrast, people will devote the greatest interest and care to their own property.

Second, one of Plato's arguments for communal property is that it is conducive to social peace, since no one will be envious of, or try to grab the property of, another. Aristotle retorted that communal property would lead to continuing and intense conflict, since each will complain that he has worked harder and obtained less than others who have done little and taken more from the common store. Furthermore, not all crimes or revolutions, declared Aristotle, are powered by economic motives. As Aristotle trenchantly put it, 'men do not become tyrants in order that they may not suffer cold'.

Third, private property is clearly implanted in man's nature: His love of self, of money, and of property, are tied together in a natural love of exclusive ownership. Fourth, Aristotle, a great observer of past and present, pointed out that private property had existed always and everywhere. To impose communal property on society would be to disregard the record of human experience, and to leap into the new and untried. Abolishing private property would probably create more problems than it would solve.

Finally, Aristotle wove together his economic and moral theories by providing the brilliant insight that only private property furnishes people with the opportunity to act morally, e.g. to practise the virtues of benevolence and philanthropy. The compulsion of communal property would destroy that opportunity.

While Aristotle was critical of money-making, he still opposed any limitation – such as Plato had advocated – on an individual's accumulation of private property. Instead, education should teach people voluntarily to curb their rampant desires and thus lead them to limit their own accumulations of wealth.

Despite his cogent defence of private property and opposition to coerced limits on wealth, the aristocrat Aristotle was fully as scornful of labour and trade as his predecessors. Unfortunately, Aristotle stored up trouble for later centuries by coining a fallacious, proto-Galbraithian distinction between 'natural' needs, which should be satisfied, and 'unnatural' wants, which are limitless and should be abandoned. There is no plausible argument to show why, as Aristotle believes, the desires filled by subsistence labour or barter are 'natural', whereas those satisfied by far more productive money exchanges are artificial, 'unnatural' and therefore reprehensible. Exchanges for monetary gain are simply denounced as immoral and 'unnatural', specifically such activities as retail trade, commerce, transportation and the hiring of labour. Aristotle had a particular animus toward retail trade, which of course directly serves the consumer, and which he would have liked to eliminate completely.

Aristotle is scarcely consistent in his economic lucubrations. For although monetary exchange is condemned as immoral and unnatural, he also praises such a network of exchanges as holding the city together through mutual and reciprocal give-and-take.

The confusion in Aristotle's thought between the analytic and the 'moral' is also shown in his discussion of money. On the one hand, he sees that the growth of money greatly facilitated production and exchange. He sees also that money, the medium of exchange, represents general demand, and 'holds all goods together'. Also money eliminates the grave problem of 'double coincidence of wants', where each trader will have to desire the other man's goods directly. Now each person can sell goods for money. Furthermore, money serves as a store of values to be used for purchases in the future.

Aristotle, however, created great trouble for the future by morally condemning the lending of money at interest as 'unnatural'. Since money cannot be used directly, and is employed only to facilitate exchanges, it is 'barren' and cannot itself increase wealth. Therefore the charging of interest, which Aristotle incorrectly thought to imply a direct productivity of money, was strongly condemned as contrary to nature.

Aristotle would have done better to avoid such hasty moral condemnation and to try to figure out why interest is, *in fact*, universally paid. Might there not be something 'natural', after all, about a rate of interest? And if he had discovered the economic reason for the charging – and the paying – of interest, perhaps Aristotle would have understood why such charges are moral and not unnatural.

Aristotle, like Plato, was hostile to economic growth and favoured a static society, all of which fits with his opposition to money-making and the accumulation of wealth. The insight of old Hesiod into the economic problem as the allocation of scarce means for the satisfying of alternative wants was virtually ignored by both Plato and Aristotle, who instead counselled the virtue of scaling down one's desires to fit whatever means were available.

1.8   Aristotle: exchange and value

Aristotle's difficult but influential discussion of exchange suffered grievously from his persistent tendency to confuse analysis with instant moral judgement. As in the case of charging interest, Aristotle did not remain content to complete a study of why exchanges take place in real life before leaping in with moral pronouncements. In analysing exchanges, Aristotle declares that these mutually beneficial transactions imply a 'proportional reciprocity', but it is characteristically ambivalent in Aristotle whether *all* exchanges are by nature marked by reciprocity, or whether only proportionately reciprocal exchanges are truly 'just'. And of course Aristotle was never one to raise the question: why do people voluntarily engage in 'unjust' exchanges? In the same way, why should people voluntarily pay interest charges if they are really 'unjust'?

To muddle matters further, Aristotle, under the influence of the Pythagorean number-mystics, introduced obscure and obfuscating mathematical terms into what could have been a straightforward analysis. The only dubious benefit of this contribution was to give many happy hours to historians of economic thought attempting to read sophisticated modern analysis into Aristotle. This problem has been aggravated by an unfortunate tendency among historians of thought to regard great thinkers of the past as necessarily consistent and coherent. That of course is a grievous historiographic error; however great they may have been, any thinkers can slip into error and inconsistency, and even write gibberish on occasion. Many historians of thought do not seem able to recognize that simple fact.

Aristotle's famous discussion of reciprocity in exchange in Book V of his *Nichomachean Ethics* is a prime example of descent into gibberish. Aristotle talks of a builder exchanging a house for the shoes produced by a shoemaker. He then writes: 'The number of shoes exchanged for a house must therefore correspond to the ratio of builder to shoemaker. For if this be not so, there will be no exchange and no intercourse'. Eh? How can there possibly be a ratio of 'builder' to 'shoemaker'? Much less an equating of that ratio to shoes/houses? In what *units* can men like builders and shoemakers be expressed?

The correct answer is that there is no meaning, and that this particular exercise should be dismissed as an unfortunate example of Pythagorean quantophrenia. And yet various distinguished historians have read tortured constructions of this passage to make Aristotle appear to be a forerunner of the labour theory of value, of W. Stanley Jevons, or of Alfred Marshall. The labour theory is read into the unsupportable assumption that Aristotle 'must have meant' labour hours put in by the builder or shoemaker, while Josef Soudek somehow sees here the respective skills of these producers, skills which are then measured by their products. Soudek eventually emerges with Aristotle as an ancestor of Jevons. In the face of all this elaborate wild goose chase, it is a pleasure to see the verdict of gibberish supported by the economic historian of ancient Greece, Moses I. Finley, and by the distinguished Aristotelian scholar H.H. Joachim, who has the courage to write, 'How exactly the values of the producers are to be determined, and what the ratio between them can mean is, I must confess, in the end unintelligible to me'.[1]

Another grave fallacy in the same paragraph in the *Ethics* did incalculable damage to future centuries of economic thought. There Aristotle says that in order for an exchange (*any* exchange? a *just* exchange?) to take place, the diverse goods and services 'must be equated', a phrase Aristotle emphasizes several times. It is this necessary 'equation' that led Aristotle to bring in the mathematics and the equal signs. His reasoning was that for A and B to exchange two products, the value of both products must be equal, otherwise an exchange would not take place. The diverse goods being exchanged for one another must be made equal because only things of equal value will be traded.

The Aristotelian concept of equal value in exchange is just plain wrong, as the Austrian School was to point out in the late nineteenth century. If A trades shoes for sacks of wheat owned by *B*, *A* does so because he prefers the wheat to the shoes, while *B*'s preferences are precisely the opposite. If an exchange takes place, this implies not an equality of values, but rather a *reverse inequality* of values in the two parties making the exchange. If I buy a newspaper for 30¢ I do so because I prefer the acquisition of the newspaper to keeping the 30 cents, whereas the newsagent prefers getting the money to keeping the newspaper. This double inequality of subjective valuations sets the necessary precondition for any exchange.

If the equation of ratio of builder to labourer is best forgotten, other parts of Aristotle's analysis have been seen by some historians as predating parts of the economics of the Austrian School. Aristotle clearly states that money represents human need or demand, which provides the motivation for exchange, and 'which holds all things together'. Demand is governed by the use-value or desirability of a good. Aristotle follows Democritus in pointing out that after the quantity of a good reaches a certain limit, after there is 'too much', the use value will plummet and become worthless. But Aristotle goes beyond Democritus in pointing out the other side of the coin: that when a good becomes scarcer, it will become subjectively more useful or valuable. He states in the *Rhetoric* that 'what is rare is a greater good than what is plentiful. Thus gold is a better thing than iron, though less useful'. These statements provide an intimation of the correct influence of different levels of supply on the value of a good, and at least a hint of the later fully formed Austrian marginal utility theory of value, and its solution of the 'paradox' of value.

These are interesting allusions and suggestions; but a few fragmentary sentences scattered throughout different books hardly constitute a fully fledged precursor of the Austrian School. But a more interesting harbinger of Austrianism has only come to the attention of historians in recent years: the groundwork for the Austrian theory of marginal productivity – the process by which the value of final products is imputed to the means, or factors, of production.

In his little-known work, the *Topics*, as well as in his later *Rhetoric*, Aristotle engaged in a philosophical analysis of the relationship between human ends and the means by which people pursue them. These means, or 'instruments of production', necessarily derive their value from the final products useful to man, 'the instruments of action'. The greater the desirability, or subjective value, of a good, the greater the desirability, or value of the means to arrive at that product. More important, Aristotle introduces the marginal element into this imputation by arguing that if the acquisition or addition of a good *A* to an already desirable good *C* creates a more desirable result than the addition of good *B*, then *A* is more highly valued than *B*. Or, as Aristotle put it: 'judge by means of an addition, and see if the addition of A to the same thing as B makes the whole more desirable than the addition of B'. Aristotle also introduces an even more specifically pre-Austrian, or pre-Böhm-Bawerkian, concept by stressing the differential value of the *loss*, rather than the addition of a good. Good *A* will be more valuable than *B*, if the loss of *A* is considered to be worse than the loss of *B*. As Aristotle clearly phrased it: 'That is the greater good whose contrary is the greater evil, and whose loss affects us more.'

Aristotle also took note of the importance of the complementarity of economic factors of production in imputing their value. A saw, he pointed out, is more valuable than a sickle in the art of carpentry, but it is not more valuable everywhere and in all pursuits. He also pointed out that a good with many potential uses will be more desirable, or valuable, than a good with only one use.

Critics of the economic importance of Aristotle's analysis charge that, with the exception of the saw-and-sickle passage, Aristotle made no economic application of his broad philosophical treatment of imputation. But this charge misses the crucial Austrian point – made with particular force and elaboration by the twentieth century Austrian economist Ludwig von Mises – that economic theory is but a part, a subset, of a broader, 'praxeological' analysis of human action. By analysing the logical implications of the employment of means to the pursuit of ends in all human action, Aristotle brilliantly began to lay the groundwork for the Austrian theory of imputation and marginal productivity over two millennia later.

1.9   The collapse after Aristotle

It is remarkable that the great burst of economic thinking in the ancient world covered only two centuries – the fifth and the fourth BC – and only in one country, Greece. The rest of the ancient world, and even Greece before and after these centuries, was essentially a desert of economic thought. Nothing of substance came out of the great ancient civilizations in Mesopotamia and India, and very little except political thought in the many centuries-long civilization of China. Remarkably, little or no economic thought emerged out of those civilizations, even though the economic institutions: trade, credit, mining, crafts, etc. were often far advanced, and even more so than in Greece. Here is an important indication that, contrary to Marxists and other economic determinists, economic thought and ideas do not simply emerge as a reflex of the development of economic institutions.

There is no way that historians of thought can ever completely penetrate the mysteries of creativity in the human soul, and thus completely explain this relatively brief flowering of human thought. But it is surely no accident that it was the Greek philosophers who provided us with the first fragments of systematic economic theory. For philosophy, too, was virtually non-existent in the rest of the ancient world or before this era in Greece. The essence of philosophic thought is that it penetrates the *ad hoc* vagaries of day-to-day life in order to arrive at truths that transcend the daily accidents of time and place. Philosophy arrives at truths about the world and about human life that are absolute, universal and eternal – at least while the world and humanity last. It arrives, in short, at a system of natural laws. But economic analysis is a subset of such investigation, because genuine economic theory can only advance beyond shifting day-to-day events by penetrating truths about human action which are absolute, unchanging and eternal, which are unaffected by changes of time and place. Economic thought, at least correct economic thought, is itself a subset of natural laws in its own branch of investigation.

If we remember the snatches of economic thought contributed by the Greeks: Hesiod on scarcity, Democritus on subjective value and utility, the influence of supply and demand on value, and on time-preference, Plato and Xenophon on the division of labour, Plato on the functions of money, Aristotle on supply and demand, money, exchange, and the imputation of value from ends to means, we see that all of these men were focusing on the logical implications of a few broadly empirical axioms of human life: the existence of human action, the eternal pursuit of goals by employing scarce means, the diversity and inequality among men. These axioms are certainly empirical, but they are so broad and pervasive that they apply to all of human life, at any time and place. Once articulated and set forth, they impel assent to their truth by a shock of recognition: once articulated, they become *evident* to the human mind. Since these axioms are then established as certain and apodictic, the processes of logic – themselves universal and apodictic and transcending time and place – can be used to arrive at absolutely true conclusions.

While this method of reasoning – of philosophy and of economics – is both empirical, being derived from the world, and true, it runs against the grain of modern philosophies of science. In modern positivism, or neopositivism, for example, 'evidence' is much narrower, fleeting and open to change. In much of modern economics, using the positivist method, 'empirical evidence' is a congeries of isolated and narrow economic events, each of which is conceived as homogeneous bits of information, supposedly used to 'test', to confirm or refute, economic hypotheses. These bits, like laboratory experiments, are supposed to result in 'evidence' to test a theory. Modern positivism is unequipped to understand or handle a system of analysis – whether classical Greek philosophy or economic theory – grounded on deductions from fundamental axioms so broadly empirical as to be virtually self-evident – evident to the self – once they are articulated. Positivism fails to understand that the results of laboratory experiments are only 'evidence' because they too *make evident* to the scientists (or to others who follow the experiments), that is, make evident *to the self*, facts or truths not evident before. The deductive processes of logic and mathematics do the same thing: they compel assent by making things evident to people which were not evident before. Correct economic theory, which we have named as 'praxeological' theory, is another way by which truths are made evident to the human mind.

Even politics, which some scoff at as not purely or strictly economics, impinges heavily on economic thought. Politics is of course an aspect of human action, and much of it has a crucial impact on economic life. Eternal natural law truths about economic aspects of politics may be and have been arrived at, and cannot be neglected in a study of the development of economic thought. When Democritus and Aristotle defended a regime of private property and Aristotle demolished Plato's portrayal of an ideal communism, they were engaging in important economic analysis of the nature and consequences of alternative systems of control and ownership of property.

Aristotle was the culmination of ancient economic thought as he was of classical philosophy. Economic theorizing collapsed after the death of Aristotle, and later Hellenistic and Roman epochs were virtually devoid of economic thought. Again, it is impossible to explain fully the disappearance of economic thought, but surely one reason must have been the disintegration of the once proud Greek *polis* after the time of Aristotle. The Greek city-states were subjected to conquest and disintegration beginning with the empire of Alexander the Great during the life of his former mentor Aristotle. Eventually Greece, much diminished in wealth and economic prosperity, became absorbed by the Roman Empire.

Small wonder, then, that the only references to economic affairs should be counsels of despair, with various Greek philosophers futilely urging their followers to solve the problem of aggravated scarcity by drastically curbing their wants and desires. In short, if you're miserable and poverty-stricken, accept your lot as man's inevitable fate and try to want no more than you have. This counsel of hopelessness and despair was preached by Diogenes (412–323 BC) the founder of the school of Cynics, and by Epicurus (343–270 BC), the founder of the Epicureans. Diogenes and the Cynics pursued this culture of poverty to such length as to adopt the name and the life of dogs; Diogenes himself made his home in a barrel. Consistent with his outlook, Diogenes denounced the hero Prometheus, who in Greek myth stole the gift of fire from the gods and thus made possible innovation, the growth of human knowledge, and the progress of mankind. Prometheus, wrote Diogenes, was properly punished by the gods for this fateful deed.

As Bertrand Russell summed up:

> ...Aristotle is the last Greek philosopher who faces the world cheerfully; after him, all have, in one form or another, a philosophy of retreat. The world is bad; let us learn to be independent of it. External goods are precarious; they are the gift of fortune, not the reward of our own efforts.

The most interesting and influential school of Greek philosophers after Aristotle was the Stoics, founded by Zeno of Clitium (c.336–264 BC), who appeared about the year 300 BC in Athens to teach at a painted porch (*stoa poikile*) after which he and his followers were called Stoics. While the Stoics began as an offshoot of Cynicism, preaching the quenching of desire for worldly goods, it took on a new and more optimistic note with Stoicism's second great founder, Chrysippus (281–208 BC). Whereas Diogenes had preached that the love of money was the root of all evil, Chrysippus countered with the quip that the 'wise man will turn three somersaults for an adequate fee'. Chrysippus was also sound on the inherent inequality and diversity of man: 'Nothing', he pointed out, 'can prevent some seats in the theatre from being better than others'.

But the most important contribution of Stoic thought was in ethical, political and legal philosophy, for it was the Stoics who first developed and systematized, especially in the legal sphere, the concept and the philosophy of natural law. It was precisely because Plato and Aristotle were circumscribed politically by the Greek *polis* that their moral and legal philosophy became closely intertwined with the Greek city-state. For the Socratics, the city-state, not the individual, was the locus of human virtue. But the destruction or subjugation of the Greek *polis* after Aristotle freed the thought of the Stoics from its admixture with politics. The Stoics were therefore free to use their reason to set forth a doctrine of natural law focusing not on the *polis* but on each individual, and not on each state but on all states everywhere. In short, in the hands of the Stoics, natural law became absolute and universal, transcending political barriers or fleeting limitations of time and place. Law and ethics, the principles of justice, became transcultural and transnational, applying to all human beings everywhere. And since every man possesses the faculty of reason, he can employ right reason to understand the truths of the natural law. The important implication for politics is that the natural law, the just and proper moral law discovered by man's right reason, can and should be used to engage in a moral critique of the positive man-made laws of any state or *polis*. For the first time, positive law became continually subject to a transcendent critique based on the universal and eternal nature of man.

The Stoics were undoubtedly aided in arriving at their cosmopolitan disregard for the narrow interests of the *polis* by the fact that most of them were Easterners who had come from outside the Greek mainland. Zeno, the founder, described as 'tall, gaunt, and swarthy', came from Clitium on the island of Cyprus. Many, including Chrysippus, came from Tarsus, in Cilicia, on the Asia Minor mainland near Syria. Later Greek Stoics were centred in Rhodes, an island off Asia Minor.

Stoicism lasted 500 years, and its most important influence was transmitted from Greece to Rome. The later Stoics, during the first two centuries after the birth of Christ, were Roman rather than Greek. The great transmitter of Stoic ideas from Greece to Rome was the famous Roman statesman, jurist, and orator Marcus Tullius Cicero (106–43 BC). Following Cicero, Stoic natural law doctrines heavily influenced the Roman jurists of the second and third centuries AD, and thus helped shape the great structures of Roman law which became pervasive in Western civilization. Cicero's influence was assured by his lucid and sparkling style, and by the fact that he was the first Stoic to write in Latin, the language of Roman law and of all thinkers and writers in the West down to the end of the seventeenth century. Moreover, Cicero's and other Latin writings have been far better preserved than the fragmentary remains we have from the Greeks.

Cicero's writings were heavily influenced by the Greek Stoic leader, the aristocratic Panaetius of Rhodes (c.185–110 BC) and as a young man he travelled there to study with his follower, Posidonius of Rhodes (135–51 BC), the greatest Stoic of his age. There is no better way to sum up Cicero's Stoic natural law philosophy than by quoting what one of his followers called his 'almost divine words'. Paraphrasing and developing the definition and insight of Chrysippus, Cicero wrote:

> There is a true law, right reason, agreeable to nature, known to all men, constant and eternal, which calls to duty by its precepts, deters from evil by its prohibition … This law cannot be departed from without guilt … Nor is there one law at Rome and another at Athens, one thing now and another afterward; but the same law, unchanging and eternal, binds all races of man and all times; and there is one common, as it were, master and ruler – God, the author, promulgator and mover of this law. Whoever does not obey it departs from [his true] self, contemns the nature of man and inflicts upon himself the greatest penalties…

Cicero also contributed to Western thought a great anti-statist parable which resounded through the centuries, a parable that revealed the nature of rulers of state as nothing more than pirates writ large. Cicero told the story of a pirate who was dragged into the court of Alexander the Great. When Alexander denounced him for piracy and brigandage and asked the pirate what impulse had led him to make the sea unsafe with his one little ship, the pirate trenchantly replied, 'the same impulse which has led you [Alexander] to make the whole world unsafe'.

But despite their important contributions to moral and legal philosophy, neither the Stoics nor other Romans contributed anything else of significance to economic thought. Roman law, however, heavily influenced and pervaded later legal developments in the West. Roman private law elaborated, for the first time in the West, the idea of property rights as absolute, with each owner having the right to use his property as he saw fit. From this stemmed the right to make contracts freely, with contracts interpreted as transfers of titles to property. Some Roman jurists declared that property rights were required by the natural law. The Romans also founded the law merchant, and Roman law strongly influenced the common law of the English-speaking countries and the civil law of the continent of Europe.

1.10 Taoism in ancient China

The only other body of ancient thought worth mentioning is the schools of political philosophy in ancient China. Though remarkable for its insights, ancient Chinese thought had virtually no impact outside the isolated Chinese Empire in later centuries, and so will be dealt with only briefly.

The three main schools of political thought: the Legalists, the Taoists, and the Confucians, were established from the sixth to the fourth centuries BC. Roughly, the Legalists, the latest of the three broad schools, simply believed in maximal power to the state, and advised rulers how to increase that power. The Taoists were the world's first libertarians, who believed in virtually no interference by the state in economy or society, and the Confucians were middle-of-the-roaders on this critical issue. The towering figure of Confucius (551–479 BC), whose name was actually Ch'iu Chung-ni, was an erudite man from an impoverished but aristocratic family of the fallen Yin dynasty, who became Grand Marshal of the state of Sung. In practice, though far more idealistic, Confucian thought differed little from the Legalists, since Confucianism was largely dedicated to installing an educated philosophically minded bureaucracy to rule in China.

By far the most interesting of the Chinese political philosophers were the Taoists, founded by the immensely important but shadowy figure of Lao Tzu. Little is known about Lao Tzu's life, but he was apparently a contemporary and personal acquaintance of Confucius. Like the latter he came originally from the state of Sung and was a descendant of lower aristocracy of the Yin dynasty. Both men lived in a time of turmoil, wars and statism, but each reacted very differently. For Lao Tzu worked out the view that the individual and his happiness was the key unit of society. If social institutions hampered the individual's flowering and his happiness, then those institutions should be reduced or abolished altogether. To the individualist Lao Tzu, government, with its 'laws and regulations more numerous than the hairs of an ox', was a vicious oppressor of the individual, and 'more to be feared than fierce tigers'. Government, in sum, must be limited to the smallest possible minimum; 'inaction' became the watchword for Lao Tzu, since only inaction of government can permit the individual to flourish and achieve happiness. Any intervention by government, he declared, would be counterproductive, and would lead to confusion and turmoil. The first political economist to discern the systemic effects of government intervention, Lao Tzu, after referring to the common experience of mankind, came to his penetrating conclusion: 'The more artificial taboos and restrictions there are in the world, the more the people are impoverished... The more that laws and regulations are given prominence, the more thieves and robbers there will be'.

The worst of government interventions, according to Lao Tzu, was heavy taxation and war. 'The people hunger because their superiors consume an excess in taxation' and, 'where armies have been stationed, thorns and brambles grow. After a great war, harsh years of famine are sure to follow'.

The wisest course is to keep the government simple and inactive, for then the world 'stabilizes itself'.

As Lao Tzu put it: 'Therefore, the Sage says: I take no action yet the people transform themselves, I favor quiescence and the people right themselves, I take no action and the people enrich themselves...'

Deeply pessimistic, and seeing no hope for a mass movement to correct oppressive government, Lao Tzu counselled the now familiar Taoist path of withdrawal, retreat, and limitation of one's desires.

Two centuries later, Lao Tzu's great follower Chuang Tzu (369–c.286 BC) built on the master's ideas of *laissez-faire* to push them to their logical conclusion: individualist anarchism. The influential Chuang Tzu, a great stylist who wrote in allegorical parables, was therefore the first anarchist in the history of human thought. The highly learned Chuang Tzu was a native of the state of Meng (now probably in Honan province), and also descended from the old aristocracy. A minor official in his native state, Chuang Tzu's fame spread far and wide throughout China, so much so that King Wei of the Ch'u kingdom sent an emissary to Chuang Tzu bearing great gifts and urging him to become the king's chief minister of state. Chuang Tzu's scornful rejection of the king's offer is one of the great declarations in history on the evils underlying the trappings of state power and the contrasting virtues of the private life:

> A thousand ounces of gold is indeed a great reward, and the office of chief minister is truly an elevated position. But have you, sir, not seen the sacrificial ox awaiting the sacrifices at the royal shrine of state? It is well cared for and fed for a few years, caparisoned with rich brocades, so that it will be ready to be led into the Great Temple. At that moment, even though it would gladly change places with any solitary pig, can it do so? So, quick and be off with you! Don't sully me. I would rather roam and idle about in a muddy ditch, at my own amusement, than to be put under the restraints that the ruler would impose. I will never take any official service, and thereby I will [be free] to satisfy my own purposes.

Chuang Tzu reiterated and embellished Lao Tzu's devotion to *laissez-faire* and opposition to state rule: 'There has been such a thing as letting mankind alone; there has never been such a thing as governing mankind [with success]'. Chuang Tzu was also the first to work out the idea of 'spontaneous order', independently discovered by Proudhon in the nineteenth century, and developed by F.A. von Hayek of the Austrian School in the twentieth. Thus, Chuang Tzu: 'Good order results spontaneously when things are let alone'.

But while people in their 'natural freedom' can run their lives very well by themselves, government rules and edicts distort that nature into an artificial Procrustean bed. As Chuang Tzu wrote, 'The common people have a constant nature; they spin and are clothed, till and are fed...it is what may be called their "natural freedom"'. These people of natural freedom were born and died themselves, suffered from no restrictions or restraints, and were neither quarrelsome nor disorderly. If rulers were to establish rites and laws to govern the people, 'it would indeed be no different from stretching the short legs of the duck and trimming off the long legs of the heron' or 'haltering a horse'. Such rules would not only be of no benefit, but would work great harm. In short, Chuang Tzu concluded, the world 'does simply not need governing; in fact it should not be governed'.

Chuang Tzu, moreover, was perhaps the first theorist to see the state as a brigand writ large: 'A petty thief is put in jail. A great brigand becomes a ruler of a State'. Thus, the only difference between state rulers and out-and-out robber chieftains is the size of their depredations. This theme of ruler-as-robber was to be repeated, as we have seen, by Cicero, and later by Christian thinkers in the Middle Ages, though of course these were arrived at independently.

Taoist thought flourished for several centuries, culminating in the most determinedly anarchistic thinker, Pao Ching-yen, who lived in the early fourth century AD, and about whose life nothing is known. Elaborating on Chuang-Tzu, Pao contrasted the idyllic ways of ancient times that had had no rulers and no government with the misery inflicted by the rulers of the current age. In the earliest days, wrote Pao 'there were no rulers and no officials. [People] dug wells and drank, tilled fields and ate. When the sun rose, they went to work; and when it set, they rested. Placidly going their ways with no encumbrances, they grandly achieved their own fulfillment'. In the stateless age, there was no warfare and no disorder:

> Where knights and hosts could not be assembled there was no warfare afield...Ideas of using power for advantage had not yet burgeoned. Disaster and disorder did not occur. Shields and spears were not used; city walls and moats were not built...People munched their food and disported themselves; they were carefree and contented.

Into this idyll of peace and contentment, wrote Pao Ching-yen, there came the violence and deceit instituted by the state. The history of government is the history of violence, of the strong plundering the weak. Wicked tyrants engage in orgies of violence; being rulers they 'could give free rein to all desires'. Furthermore, the government's institutionalization of violence meant that the petty disorders of daily life would be greatly intensified and expanded on a much larger scale. As Pao put it:

> Disputes among the ordinary people are merely trivial matters, for what scope of consequences can a contest of strength between ordinary fellows generate? They have no spreading lands to arouse avarice...they wield no authority through which they can advance their struggle. Their power is not such that they can assemble mass followings, and they command no awe that might quell [such gatherings] by their opponents. How can they compare with a display of the royal anger, which can deploy armies and move battalions, making people who hold no enmities attack states that have done no wrong?

To the common charge that he has overlooked good and benevolent rulers, Pao replied that the government itself is a violent exploitation of the weak by the strong. The system *itself* is the problem, and the object of government is not to benefit the people, but to control and plunder them. There is no ruler who can compare in virtue with a condition of non-rule.

Pao Ching-yen also engaged in a masterful study in political psychology by pointing out that the very existence of institutionalized violence by the state generates imitative violence among the people. In a happy and stateless world, declared Pao, the people would naturally turn to thoughts of good order and not be interested in plundering their neighbours. But rulers oppress and loot the people and 'make them toil without rest and wrest away things from them endlessly.' In that way, theft and banditry are stimulated among the unhappy people, and arms and armour, intended to pacify the public, are stolen by bandits to intensify their plunder. 'All these things are brought about because there are rulers.' The common idea, concluded Pao, that strong government is needed to combat disorders among the people, commits the serious error of confusing cause and effect.

The only Chinese with notable views in the more strictly economic realm was the distinguished second century B.C. historian, Ssu-ma Ch'ien (145– c.90 BC). Ch'ien was an advocate of *laissez-faire*, and pointed out that minimal government made for abundance of food and clothing, as did the abstinence of government from competing with private enterprise. This was similar to the Taoist view, but Ch'ien, a worldly and sophisticated man, dismissed the idea that people could solve the economic problem by reducing desires to a minimum. People, Ch'ien maintained, preferred the best and most attainable goods and services, as well as ease and comfort. Men are therefore habitual seekers after wealth.

Since Ch'ien thought very little of the idea of limiting one's desires, he was impelled, far more than the Taoists, to investigate and analyse free market activities. He therefore saw that specialization and the division of labour on the market produced goods and services in an orderly fashion:

> Each man has only to be left to utilize his own abilities and exert his strength to obtain what he wishes...When each person works away at his own occupation and delights in his own business, then like water flowing downward, goods will naturally flow ceaselessly day and night without being summoned, and the people will produce commodities without having been asked.

To Ch'ien, this was the natural outcome of the free market. 'Does this not ally with reason? Is it not a natural result?' Furthermore, prices are regulated on the market, since excessively cheap or dear prices tend to correct themselves and reach a proper level.

But if the free market is self-regulating, asked Ch'ien perceptively, 'what need is there for government directives, mobilizations of labor, or periodic assemblies?' What need indeed?

Ssu-ma Ch'ien also set forth the function of entrepreneurship on the market. The entrepreneur accumulates wealth and functions by anticipating conditions (i.e. forecasting) and acting accordingly. In short, he keeps 'a sharp eye out for the opportunities of the times.'

Finally, Ch'ien was one of the world's first monetary theorists. He pointed out that increased quantity and a debased quality of coinage by government depreciates the value of money and makes prices rise. And he saw too that government inherently tended to engage in this sort of inflation and debasement.

1.11 Note

1. H.H. Joachim, *Aristotle: The Nichomachean Ethics* (Oxford: The Clarendon Press, 1951), p. 50. Also see Moses I. Finley, 'Aristotle and Economic Analysis', in *Studies in Ancient Society* (London: Routledge and Kegan Paul, 1974), pp. 32–40.

2 The Christian Middle Ages

2.1 The Roman law: property rights and *laissez-faire*

One of the most powerful influences in the legal and political thought and institutions of the Christian West during the Middle Ages was the Roman law, derived from the Republic and Empire of ancient Rome. Roman law classically developed in the first to the third centuries AD. Private law developed the theory of the absolute right of private property and of freedom of trade and contract. While Roman public law theoretically allowed state interference in the life of the citizen, there was little such interference in the late Republic and early Empire. Private property rights and *laissez-faire* were therefore the fundamental heritage of the Roman law to later centuries, and much of it was adopted by countries of the Christian West. Though the Roman Empire collapsed in the fourth and fifth centuries, its legal heritage continued, as embodied in two great collections of the Roman law: influential in the West, the Theodosian Code, promulgated by the Emperor Theodosius in 438 AD and in the East the great four-volume *Corpus Juris Civilis*, promulgated by the Byzantine Christian Emperor Justinian in the 530s.

Both collections emphasized strongly that the 'just' price (*justum pretium*) was simply any price arrived at by free and voluntary bargaining between buyer and seller. Each man has the right to do what he wants with his property, and therefore has the right to make contracts to give away, buy, or sell such property; hence, whatever price is freely arrived at is 'just'. Thus in the *Corpus*, several leading Roman jurists of the third century quoted the early second century jurist Pomponius in a classic expression of the morality of *laissez-faire*: 'In buying and selling natural law permits the one party to buy for less and the other to sell for more than the thing is worth; thus each party is allowed to outwit the other'; and 'it is naturally permitted to parties to circumvent each other in the price of buying and selling'. The only problem here is the odd phrase, 'the thing is worth', which assumes that there is some value *other* than free bargaining that expresses some 'true worth', a phrase that would prove to be an unfortunate harbinger of the future.

More specifically, the Theodosian Code was crystal-clear: any price set by free and voluntary bargaining is just and legitimate, the only exception being a contract made by children. Force or fraud, as infringements on property rights, were of course considered illegal. The code held explicitly that ignorance of the value of a good by either buyer or seller was insufficient ground for authorities to step in and rescind the voluntarily agreed contract. The Theodosian Code was carried forward in western Europe, e.g. the Visigothic law set forth in the sixth and seventh centuries, and the Bavarian law of the early eighth century. Bavarian law added the explicit provision that a buyer may not rescind a sale because he later decides that the agreed price was too high. This *laissez-faire* aspect of the Theodosian Code later became incorporated into Christian canon law by being included in the collection of 'capitularies' (decrees) by St Benedictus Diaconus in the ninth century AD.

While the Justinian *Corpus*, promulgated in the East, was equally devoted to *laissez-faire*, it included a minor element that was later to grow and justify attacks upon free bargaining. As part of the Justinian discussion of how courts can appraise property for payment of damages, the code mentioned that if a seller has sold his property for less than half 'the just price', then he suffers 'great loss' (*laesio enormis*), and the seller is then entitled either to get back the difference between the original price and the just price from the buyer, or else get his property back at that original price. This clause was apparently meant only to apply to real estate and to compensations for damages, where authorities must somehow assess the 'true' price, and it had no influence on the laws of the next centuries. But it was to yield unfortunate effects in the future.

2.2   Early Christian attitudes towards merchants

Roman law was not the only influence on economic ideas in the Middle Ages. Ambivalent attitudes in the early Christian tradition also proved highly important.

Economic matters were of course scarcely central to either the Old or New Testament, and scattered economic pronouncements are contradictory or subject to ambivalent interpretation. Fulminations against excessive love of money do not necessarily imply hostility to commerce or wealth. One remarkable aspect of the Old Testament, however, is its repeated, almost pre-Calvinist, extolling of work for its own sake. In contrast to the contemptuous attitude toward labour of the Greek philosophers, the Old Testament is filled with exhortations in favour of work: from the 'be fruitful and multiply' of Genesis to 'Enjoy life in your toil at which you toil under the sun' of Ecclesiastes. Oddly, these calls to labour are often accompanied by admonitions against the accumulation of wealth. Later, in the second century BC, the Hebrew scribe who wrote the Apocryphal book Ecclesiasticus goes so far as to extol labour as a sacred calling. Manual workers, he writes, 'keep stable the fabric of the world, and their prayer is in the practice of their trade'. Yet the pursuit of money is condemned, and merchants are habitually treated with deep suspicion: 'A merchant can hardly keep from wrong doing, and a tradesman will not be declared innocent of sin'. And yet, in the same book of Ecclesiasticus, the reader is instructed not to be ashamed of profit or success in business.

The attitude of the early Christians, including Jesus and the Apostles, toward work and trade was coloured by their intense expectation of the imminent end of the world and of the coming of the Kingdom of God. Obviously, if one expects the impending end of the world, one is inclined to have little patience for such activities as investing or accumulating wealth; rather the tendency is to act as the lilies of the field, to follow Jesus, and forget about mundane matters. It was in this context that we must understand St Paul's famous 'the love of money is the root of all evil.'

By approximately 100 AD, however, the books of the New Testament written by St John make it clear that the Christian Church had abandoned the idea of the imminent end of the world. But the Hellenistic and the Gospel heritage fused to lead the early Church Fathers into a retreatist view of the world and its economic activities, combined with fulminations against wealth and merchants who tend to amass such wealth. The Church Fathers railed against mercantile activities as necessarily stamped with the sin of greed, and as almost always accompanied by deceit and fraud. Leading the parade was the mystical and apocalyptic Tertullian (160–240), a prominent Carthaginian lawyer who converted late in life to Christianity and eventually formed his own heretical sect. To Tertullian, attack on merchants and money-making was part and parcel of a general philippic against the secular world, which he expected at any moment to founder on the shoals of excess population, so that the earth would soon suffer from 'epidemics, famines, wars, and the earth's opening to swallow whole cities' as a grisly solution to the overpopulation problem.

Two centuries later, the fiery St Jerome (c.340–420), educated in Rome but also influenced by the eastern Fathers, took up the theme, proclaiming the fallacy that in trade, one man's gain must be achieved by means of the other man's loss: 'All riches come from iniquity, and unless one has lost, another cannot gain. Hence that common opinion seems to me to be very true, 'the rich man is unjust, or the heir of an unjust one''. And yet there was another, contradictory strain even in Jerome, who also declared that 'A wise man with riches has greater glory than one who is wise only', for he can accomplish more good things; 'wealth is not an obstacle to the rich man who uses it well'.

Probably the most intelligent attitude toward wealth and money-making among the early Church Fathers was that of the Athenian-born eastern Father Clement of Alexandria (c.150–215). While Clement counselled that property be used for the good of the community, he endorsed private property and the accumulation of wealth. He attacked as foolish the ascetic ideal of divesting oneself of one's possessions. As Clement wisely put it, employing a natural law theme:

> We must not cast away riches which can benefit our neighbor. Possessions were made to be possessed; goods are called goods because they do good, and they have been provided by God for the good of men: they are at hand and serve as the material, the instruments for a good use in the hand of him who knows how to use them.

Clement also took a hard-nosed attitude toward the rootless poor. If living without possessions was so desirable, he pointed out,

> then that whole swarm of proletarians, derelicts and beggars who live from hand to mouth, all those wretched cast out upon the streets, though they live in ignorance of God and of his justice, would be the most blessed and the most religious and the only candidates for eternal life simply because they are penniless...

The early Church Fathers culminated in the great Saint Augustine (354–430) who, living at the time of the sack of Rome in 410 and of the collapse of the Roman Empire, had to look ahead to a post-ancient world which he was greatly to influence. Born in Numidia in Africa, Aurelius Augustinus was educated in Carthage, and became a professor of rhetoric in Milan. Baptized a Christian at the age of 32, St Augustine became bishop of Hippo in his native North Africa. The Roman Empire under Constantine had embraced Christianity a century earlier, and Augustine wrote his great work, *The City of God*, as a rebuttal to the charge that the embrace of Christianity had resulted in the fall of Rome.

Augustine's economic views were scattered throughout *The City of God* and his other highly influential writings. But he definitely, and presumably independently of Aristotle, arrived at the view that people's payments for goods, the valuation they placed on them, was determined by their own needs rather than by any more objective criterion or by their rank in the order of nature. This was at least the basis of the later Austrian theory of subjective value. He also pointed out that it was the common desire of all men to buy cheap and to sell dear.

Furthermore, Augustine was the first Church Father to have a positive attitude towards the role of the merchant. Rebutting the common patristic charges against the merchants, Augustine pointed out that they perform a beneficial service by transporting goods over great distances and selling them to the consumer. Since, according to Christian principle, 'the labourer is worthy of his hire', then the merchant too deserved compensation for his activities and labour.

To the common charge of endemic deceit and fraud in the mercantile trades, Augustine cogently replied that any such lies and perjuries were the fault not of the trade but of the trader himself. Such sins originated in the iniquity of the person, not in his occupation. After all, Augustine pointed out, shoemakers and farmers are also capable of lies and perjuries, and yet the Church Fathers had not condemned *their* occupations as being *per se* evil.

Clearing the merchants of the stain of inherent evil proved enormously influential in the following centuries, and was quoted time and again in the flowering of Christian thought in the twelfth and thirteenth centuries.

A less tangible but still important contribution to social thought was St Augustine's recasting of the ancient world's view of the human personality. To the Greek philosophers, the individual personality was to be moulded to conform to the needs and desires of the *polis*. Dictation by the *polis* necessarily meant a static society, with discouragement directed towards any innovating entrepreneurs trying to break out of the contemporary mould. But St Augustine's stress was on the individual's personality unfolding itself and therefore progressing over time. Hence Augustine's profound emphasis on the individual at least set the stage indirectly for an attitude favourable to innovation, economic growth and development. That aspect of Augustine's thought, however, was not really stressed by the thirteenth century Christian theologians and philosophers who built on Augustine's thought. It is ironic that the man who set the stage for optimism and a theory of human progress should, on his death-bed, find the barbarian hordes besieging his beloved city of Hippo.

If St Augustine looked benignly on the role of the merchant, he was also favourable, though not as warmly, towards the social role of rulers of state. On the one hand, Augustine took up and expanded Cicero's parable demonstrating that Alexander the Great was simply a pirate writ large, and that the state is nothing but a large-scale and settled robber band. In his famous *City of God*, Augustine asks:

> And so if justice is left out, what are kingdoms except great robber bands? For what are robber bands except little kingdoms? The band also is a group of men governed by the orders of a leader, bound by a social compact, and its booty is divided according to a law agreed upon. If by repeatedly adding desperate men this plague grows to the point where it holds territory and establishes a fixed seat, seizes cities and subdues people, then it more conspicuously assumes the name of kingdom, and this name is now openly granted to it, not for any subtraction of cupidity, but by addition of impunity. For it was an elegant and true reply that was made to Alexander the Great by a certain pirate whom he had captured. When the king asked him what he was thinking of, that he should molest the sea, he said with defiant independence: 'The same as you when you molest the world! Since I do this with a little ship I am called a pirate. You do it with a great fleet and are called emperor'.[1]

Yet Augustine ends by approving the role of the state, even though it is a robber band on a large scale. For while he stressed the individual rather than the *polis*, in pre-Calvinist fashion Augustine emphasized the wickedness and depravity of man. In this fallen, wicked and sinful world, state rule, though unpleasant and coercive, becomes necessary. Hence, Augustine supported the forcible crushing by the Christian Church in North Africa of the Donatist heresy, which indeed believed, in contrast to Augustine, that all kings were necessarily evil.

The likening of the head of state to a large-scale brigand, however, was resurrected in its original anti-state context by the great Pope Gregory VII, in the course of his struggle with the kings of Europe over his Gregorian reforms in the late eleventh century. This strain of bitter anti-statism, then, emerges from time to time in the early Christian era and in the Middle Ages.

2.3   The Carolingians and canon law

'Canon law' was the law governing the Church, and during the early Christian era and the Middle Ages the intertwining of Church and state often meant that canon law and state law were one and the same. Early canon law consisted of papal decretals, decrees of church councils, and the writings of the Church Fathers. We have seen that later canon law also incorporated much of the Roman law. But canon law also included something else basically pernicious: the decrees and regulations ('capitularies') of the Carolingian Empire in the latter eighth and ninth centuries.

From the fifth to the tenth centuries, the economic and political chaos of the Dark Ages prevailed throughout Europe, and there was consequently little or no room for the development of political, legal or economic thought. The only exception was the activities of the Carolingian Empire, which burgeoned in western Europe. The most important Carolingian Emperor was Charlemagne (742–814) and his rule devolved on to his successors during the remainder of the ninth century. In capitulary after capitulary, Charlemagne and his successors laid down detailed regulations for every aspect of economic, political and religious life throughout the empire. Many of these regulations became incorporated into the canon law of later centuries, thereby remaining influential well after the crumbling of the Carolingian Empire itself.

Charlemagne built his despotic network of regulations on a shaky foundation. Thus the important Church council of Nicaea (325) had forbidden any clergymen from engaging in any economic activities leading to 'shameful gain' (*turpe lucrum*). In his council at Nijmegen (806) Charlemagne revived, greatly broadened and imposed the old doctrine of *turpe lucrum*. But now the prohibition was extended from the clergy to everyone, and the definition broadened from fraud to all greed and avarice, and included any disobedience of Charlemagne's extensive price regulations. Any market deviations from these fixed prices were accused of being profiteering by either buyers or sellers and hence *turpe lucrum*. As a corollary, all speculative buying and selling in foodstuffs was prohibited. Moreover, in foreshadowing the English common law prohibition of 'forestalling', any sale of goods outside and at higher prices than the regular markets was prohibited. Since the English common law was motivated, not by a misguided attempt to aid the poor but in order to confer monopoly privileges on local owners of market sites, it is highly probable that Charlemagne, too, was trying to cartelize markets and confer privileges on market owners.

Every arbitrary price decree of the Carolingian officialdom was of course revered by the Carolingians as the 'just price.' Probably this coerced price was often near what had been a customary or current price in the neighbourhood; otherwise it would be difficult to conceive how the Carolingian officials would discover what price was supposed to be just. But this meant a futile and uneconomic attempt to freeze all prices on the basis of some past market *status quo*.

The problem, then, is that later canon law incorporated the idea of the just price as being the state-decreed price. The banning of any price higher than the current market price was reimposed by the late Carolingian Emperor Carloman in 884, and incorporated into the canon law collection of Regino of Prum in 900, and over a century later into that of Burchard of Worms.

Remarkably, the two contradictory legal strains: the *laissez-faire* theme of the Theodosian Code, and the statist Carolingian *motif*, both found their way into the great collection at the basis of the medieval discipline of the canon law: that of Bishop Ivo of Chartres, at the turn of the twelfth century. There, in the same collection, we find the view that the just price is any price voluntarily arrived at by buyer and seller, *and* also the contradictory view that the just price is one decreed by the state, especially if it be the common price in general markets.

2.4   Canonists and Romanists at the University of Bologna

The High Middle Ages were established by the commercial revolution of the eleventh to thirteenth centuries, in which trade, production and finance flourished, living standards rose markedly, and the institutions of commercial capitalism developed in western Europe. With the advent of economic growth and prosperity, canon and Roman law, learning and social thought, also began to flourish once again.

The fountainhead and great centre of both canon and Roman law studies during the High Middle Ages was the University of Bologna, in Italy, flourishing from the early twelfth century to the latter part of the thirteenth. During those two centuries, both canon and Roman law, including the Justinian Code, were revived at Bologna, influenced each other, and penetrated to the rest of western Europe.

The great and definitive collection of canon law, the *Decretum*, was published around the year 1140 by the Italian monk, Johannes Gratian, who founded canon law studies at the University of Bologna. The *Decretum* was the definitive canon law work from that point on, and for the remainder of the twelfth century Bolognese scholars, known as the decretists, elaborated, discussed, and wrote glosses on Gratian's work.

Gratian himself and his early glossators took a traditional zealous anti-merchant position. Speculation, buying cheap to sell dear – purely mercantile activities – were *turpe lucrum* and inevitably involved fraud.

The first decretist to begin to take an intelligent position on the activities of the merchant was Rufinus, a professor at Bologna who later became bishop of Assisi and then archbishop of Sorrento. In his *Summa* (1157–59) to the *Decretum*, Rufinus pointed out that artisans and craftsmen could buy materials cheaply, work on them and transform them, and then sell the product at a higher price. This form of buying cheap and selling dear was justified by the craftsmen's expenses and labour, and is permissible even to the clergy as well as to the laity. However, another activity, practised by the pure merchant or speculator, who buys cheap and sells dear without transforming the product is, according to Rufinus, absolutely forbidden to the clergy. The lay merchant, however, could honourably engage in these transactions provided that he had either made heavy expenditures or was fatigued by hard labour. But a pure entrepreneurial cheap purchase to be followed by a sale when market prices were higher was condemned unconditionally by Rufinus.

This partial rehabilitation of the merchant by the decretists was included in the important *Summa* of 1188 of Huguccio, professor at Bologna, later chosen bishop of Ferrara. Huguccio repeated the views of Rufinus, but shifted the justification of the merchant from labour or expenses to actions that provide for the needs of the merchant's family. Huguccio's stress, then, was not on objective costs but on the subjective intentions of the merchant, supposing that they could be discovered: was it mere greed or was it a desire to fulfil his family's needs? Clearly, Huguccio allowed considerable room for mercantile activities.

Moreover, Huguccio began a radical reconstruction of Patristic teachings about private property. From the time of Huguccio, private property was to be considered a sacrosanct right derived from the natural law. The property of individuals and communities was, at least in principle, supposed to be free from arbitrary invasion on the part of the state. As 'moderator and arbiter' of his own goods, an individual owner could use and dispose of them as he saw fit, provided that he did not violate general legal rules. A ruler could only expropriate the property of an innocent subject if 'public necessity' required it. This, of course, was a hole in the system of rights, since 'public necessity' could be and was an elastic concept. But this concept of private property was an enormous advance over patristic teachings.

After the late twelfth century, the decretist movement in canon law gave way to the decretalists, who based themselves on a stream of papal edicts or decretals, from the late twelfth to the thirteenth century. Since the pope is supreme in the Catholic Church, the decretals pronounced by him and his

Vatican *curia* automatically became incorporated into the body of canon law. In this way, canon law came to differ from that of Gratian and the Decretists, who built the law chiefly on ancient sources. But the new decretals were scarcely arbitrary; they built on and elaborated previous canon law. The continuity of the building process was greatly aided by the fact that several of these popes were former Bolognese. Thus, Pope Alexander III (Roland Bandinelli), who initiated the new decretal process and who enjoyed a long papal reign from 1159 to 1181, had studied both law and theology at Bologna, was probably a professor there, and had direct contact with the great Gratian. A distinguished legal scholar, who himself had written an early *Summa* to Gratian's *Decretum*, Alexander became cardinal and chancellor before being elected to the papacy. Another significant papal decretalist, Pope Innocent II (Lothaire de Segni), who reigned from 1198 to 1216, had studied canon law under Huguccio at Bologna. Finally, Pope Gregory IX (Ugolino de Segni), a pontiff from 1227 to 1241, commissioned and published the momentous *Decretals* in 1234, incorporating Gratian's *Decretum* of a century before in addition to the various papal decretals. Gregory IX's *Decretals* became the standard work of canon law from that point on.

The decretalists had a far more favourable attitude towards merchants and the free market than had the early decretists. In the first place, instead of the negative patristic attitude toward merchants and trade, the decretalists, beginning with Pope Alexander III and continuing through Gregory IX, incorporated the free market attitude of the Roman law. Unfortunately, it was not the pure *laissez-faire* attitude of the Theodosian or even Justinian law. For when the Justinian Code came to Bologna and western Europe at the beginning of the twelfth century, the French author of the *Brachylogus* took up the *laesio enormis* principle of the Justinian Code and greatly changed its meaning. Instead of applying the concept of 'just price' differing from the actual price to the assessment of damages as in the Justinian Code, the *Brachylogus* expanded the concept from real estate to all goods, and from assessing damages to actual sales. In the hands of the *Brachylogus*, if any sale, even a voluntary one, had been made at less than half the 'just price', the seller could present the buyer with the choice: either pay me the difference between the sale price and the just price, or else rescind the contract, with the buyer returning the goods and the seller returning the payment. It has been pointed out that this was not a cartelizing device, since neither third parties nor the state could step in to enforce *laesio enormis*; the enforcement had to be done on a charge made by the seller himself.

The Roman law developing during the twelfth and thirteenth centuries was largely the product of the University of Bologna, where Roman law studies had been founded by Irnerius in the late eleventh century. In the mid-twelfth century, the Bolognese Roman jurists began to incorporate the broader concept of *laesio enormis* of the *Brachylogus*. About 1150, the Provençal *Lo Codi*, a popular adaptation of a recent Bolognese *Summa*, added another fateful expansion of *laesio enormis*. For the first time, this Provençal work included *buyers* as well as sellers as suffering from *laesio enormis*, when the sale price was significantly higher than the just price. In the *Lo Codi*, if a buyer had paid more than twice the true value, or just price, of a product, then the seller had the option either to pay the buyer the difference between the just and the sale price, or else rescind the contract. Remarkably, when the *Lo Codi* was translated back into Latin, this new extended restriction on *laissez-faire* was added to the Roman law, particularly by Albericus, professor of Roman law at Bologna, in his canon law collection at the end of the twelfth century.

The burgeoning principle of *laesio enormis* reached its final extension in the late twelfth century work of the Bolognese-trained Petrus Placentinus. Placentinus lowered the maximum permissible price to 1.5 times the just price, beyond which the principle of *laesio enormis* went into effect. This final expansion was incorporated into the works of the three great Bolognese Roman law professors of the thirteenth century: Azo (c.1210); Azo's highly influential student and follower Accursius (c.1228–60), a native of Florence; and the culmination of the Bolognese school in Odofredus, in the mid-thirteenth century.

While it is true that the twelfth and thirteenth century Romanists took the trivial concept of *laesio enormis* and made it a significant restriction on freedom of bargaining and *laissez-faire*, at least by the late twelfth century they also made clear that there was to be full freedom of bargaining and freedom to outwit the other, *within* the matrix of *laesio enormis*. The decretalists, beginning with Pope Alexander III, incorporated much of this developing Roman law. This meant that Church law now included not only the patristic fulminations against merchants *per se*, but also the contrasting Romanist tradition of full freedom of bargaining within the *laesio enormis* matrix. The decretalists reached their culmination, after building on and glossing the *Decretals* of Gregory IX, in the works of Cardinal Henricus Hostiensis de Segusio, first in the late 1250s and finally in 1271, the year of his death. Hostiensis had studied canon and Roman law at Bologna, had taught in England and France and was cardinal–archbishop of Ostia.

The decretalists justified speculative buying and selling, freeing it from the sin of *turpe lucrum*, by adopting and expanding the Huguccian line that speculation was permissible if the speculator was acting to fulfil the needs of his family. In the *Gloss* of the French Dominican canonist William of Rennes (c.1250), this area of freedom was broadened still further. A merchant's or speculator's actions were not considered sinful unless he was driven by 'a wanton desire for having temporal riches, not for necessary use or utility, but for curiosity, so that the fancy is charmed by such, just as a magpie or a crow is enticed by coins, which they discover and hide away'. Surely this kind of stricture, which can only apply to a few persons in the real world, had come very far from the patristic denunciations of merchants and traders *per se*.

Another loosening of restrictions came with Alanus Anglicus, an English-born professor of canon law at Bologna, writing in the first two decades of the thirteenth century. Alanus declared that no *turpe lucrum* (or usury, for that matter) could exist if the future price of a good was uncertain in the mind of the merchant. Not only is uncertainty always present in the market, but also it is impossible for outside courts or authorities to prove that a merchant did *not* feel uncertain when he bought or sold. In effect, all *turpe lucrum* restrictions on trade or speculation had now been removed.

In analysing business profits, the later thirteenth century canonists added to the older justification of profit as covering labour plus expenses. This was the element of risk, present in every business situation. Increase of price as a consequence of risk was first justified in the prominent canon law commentaries of Pope Innocent IV (Sinibaldo Fieschi), published between 1246 and 1253. Before becoming pope, Innocent had been a native of Genoa and a student of Roman and canon law at Bologna, a professor of Roman law at that university, and finally a cardinal and a famous statesman.

If transactions were to be sinful and illegal beyond a certain zone above or below the just price, then the Church and the authorities had to find some way of figuring out *what* the just price was supposed to be. This had not been a problem before the twelfth and thirteenth centuries, since the doctrine of *laesio enormis* had not really been applied before. The Romanist and canonist solution, reminiscent of Carolingian doctrine, was that the just price was the going, current, common market price (the *communis aestimatio*). This meant *either* the competitive, general market price as contrasted to single isolated transactions, *or* it could refer to prices fixed by governments or government-privileged guilds, since such controls, by strict legality, would *be* the going *de jure* price. Perhaps it would have been beneath the dignity of these jurists to sanction or even recognize any black market prices that violated such regulations.

Placentinus used this criterion in late twelfth century Roman jurisprudence, as did in particular Azo in the early thirteenth. Azo was liberal enough to refer to the price of a sale equalling that of any other comparable sale as being a 'just price', but Accursius, and after him Odofredus, explicitly referred to the general or common market price as being the standard of justice. As Accursius put it, 'a thing was valued at that for which it could be commonly sold'.

The canon lawyers adopted the same criterion for the just price. Influenced by Carolingian practice, and by hints from the sixth century Rule of St

Benedict, the late twelfth century canonist and student of Gratian, Simon of Bosignano, first described the true value of goods as the price for which they commonly sold. The same position was then taken by the decretalists in the thirteenth century. Canonists and Romanists alike were now agreed on the common price of a good as the just one.

But still the developed canonists of the thirteenth century had a problem. On the one hand, they had adopted the Roman law view that all free bargaining was legitimate except for a zone more than a certain degree above or beyond the 'just price', which they held to be the going, common market price. But on the other hand, they had inherited from the Church Fathers and the earlier decretists a hostility toward mercantile, especially speculative, transactions. How could they square this contradiction?

Partly, as we have seen, they were able to weaken the extent of shameful speculation. Also, from the thirteenth century on, the Church and its canon lawyers largely solved the problem through the highly sensible doctrine of the 'two forums' over which the Church exercised jurisdiction. The 'external forum' – the *jus fori* – judged the social activities of Christians in public ecclesiastical courts. There the courts judged offences against the Church and her common law in much the same procedures as the secular courts. On the other hand, the 'internal forum' – the *jus poli* – was the confessional, in which the priest judged individual Christians on the basis of their personal relation to God. The two forums were separate and distinct, the respective judgements on two different levels. While the Church presumed to rule over both, the one was external and social, the other private and personal.

The doctrine of the two forums enabled the canonists to resolve the seeming contradiction in canon law. The free-bargaining, *laesio enormis*, common market principle was the realm of external law and the open court, where, in other words, a roughly free market could prevail. On the other hand, the strictures against mercantile profits going beyond labour, costs, and risk were a matter not for the state and external law, but for conscience in the confessional. Even more obviously for the confessional alone were the injunctions against trade or speculation based on avarice as going beyond honourable need to support one's family. Clearly, only the man himself, internally in his conscience, could know his intentions; they were scarcely observable by external law.

2.5   The canonist prohibition of usury

The great relaxation of moral and legal restrictions and prohibitions against trade that permeated the canonists and Romanists in the Middle Ages, unfortunately did not apply to the stern prohibitions levelled against usury. Modern people think of 'usury' as very high interest rates charged on a loan, but this was by no means the meaning until recent times. Classically 'usury' means *any* rate whatsoever charged on a loan, no matter how low. The prohibition of usury was a prohibition against any interest charge on a loan.

With one exception, no one in the ancient world – whether in Greece, China, India or Mesopotamia – prohibited interest. That exception was the Hebrews who, in an expression of narrow tribal morality, permitted charging interest to non-Jews but prohibited it among Jews.

The fierce medieval Christian assault on usury is decidedly odd. For one thing, there is nothing in the Gospels or the early Fathers, despite their hostility to trade, that can be construed as urging the prohibition of usury. In fact, the parable of the talents in Matthew (25:14–30) can easily be taken as approval for earning interest on commercial loans. The campaign against usury begins with the first Church council, in Nicaea in 325, which itself prohibited only the clergy from charging interest on a loan. But the Nicene council grabbed on to one phrase of Psalm 14 in the Old Testament, 'Lord, who shall dwell in thy tabernacle? He that hath not put out his money to usury', and this was to become the favourite – and virtually the only – biblical text against usury during the Middle Ages. The Nicene injunctions were repeated in later fourth century councils at Elvira in Spain and at Carthage, and then in the fifth century Pope Leo I extended the prohibition to the laity as well, condemning lay usurers as indulging in *turpe lurcum*. Several local councils in Gaul in the seventh century repeated Leo's denunciation, as did Pope Adrian and several English church synods in the eighth century.

But the prohibition of all usury enters secular legislation for the first time in the all-embracing totalitarian regime of the Emperor Charlemagne. At the fateful imperial synod of Aachen in 789, Charlemagne prohibited usury to everyone in his realm, lay and cleric alike. The prohibition was renewed and elaborated in the later council at Nijmegen in 806, where usury is defined for the first time, as an exchange where 'more is demanded back than what is given'. So that, from the time of Charlemagne, usury was intensely held to be a special and particularly malevolent form of *turpe lucrum*, and attempts to relax this ban were fiercely resisted. The sweeping definition, 'more demanded than what is given', was repeated intact by canonists from the tenth century Regino of Prum through Ivo of Chartres to Gratian.

But oddly, though the hostility towards usury continued and was indeed greatly strengthened among the canonists, the explicit *basis* for the antagonism changed considerably. During the first centuries of the Christian era, usury was shameful as a form of avarice or lack of charity; it was not yet considered a vicious sin against justice. As commerce began to revive and flourish in eleventh century Europe, indeed, denouncing interest-taking as a form of lack of charity began to be considered wide of the mark, since charity had little to do with commercial loans. It was the Italian monk St Anselm of

Canterbury (1033–1109) who first shifted the ground of attack to rail against usury as 'theft'. This new doctrine was developed by St Anselm's disciple Anselm of Lucca, a fellow Italian and native of a city with a burgeoning textile industry. In his collection of canons, made about 1066, Anselm of Lucca explicitly condemned usury as theft and a sin against the Seventh Commandment, and demanded restitution of usuries to the borrower as 'stolen goods'. This expansion of 'theft' to a voluntary contract where no coercion was used was surely bizarre, and yet this outrageous new concept caught hold and was repeated by Hugh of St Victor (1096–1141) and by the collections of Ivo of Chartres.

In 1139, the second lateran council of the Church explicitly prohibited usury to all men, laity as well as clergy, and held all usurers to be infamous. The council vaguely declared that the Old and New Testaments mandated such a prohibition, but gave no explicit reference. Nine years later, Pope Eugene III moved against the common practice of monasteries charging interest on mortgages.

Finally, the canon law reached mature form with the *Decretum* of Gratian. Gratian hammers away against usury with whatever weapons he can find from Psalm 14 to the new view that usury is theft and therefore requires restitution. Expounding on the strict prohibition of usury, Gratian extended it to the loan of goods as well as money, so long as anything is demanded beyond the principal, and he expressly declared that, in such a case, the 'just price' was *not* the common market price but zero, i.e. the exact equivalent of the goods or money lent.

The great decretalist Pope Alexander III might have been inclined towards a free market in other areas, but on the usury question he merely deepened and extended the ban, applying the condemnation to charging higher prices for credit than for cash sales. This practice was denounced as implicit usury, even though it was not explicitly interest on a loan. The third lateran council, presided over by Pope Alexander III in 1179, condemned usury, and excommunicated and denied Christian burial to all manifest usurers. The next pope, Urban III (1185–87), in his decretal *Consoluit*, dredged up a previously unused citation from Jesus, 'Lend freely, hoping nothing thereby' (Luke 6: 35), which from then on became the centrepiece of the theological condemnation of usury as a mortal sin; and not only that: even the very *hope* of obtaining usury was supposed to be a virtually equivalent sin.

So pervasive was the canonist obsession with usury that Gratian, his predecessors and his successors, largely worked out their theories of sale, profit, or just price in terms of whether or not any particular transaction fell under the dread rubric of 'usury'. Thus, late twelfth century decretists like Simon of Bosignano in 1179 and the great Huguccio in 1188, maintained the strict prohibition of any interest charged on a loan as usury, while allowing the renting of a good or buying cheap in order to sell dear as *not* being cases of usury. Huguccio's tortured moral distinction maintained that a *commodatum* – a rental contract that transferred only the *use* of a good – was somehow morally very different from a *mutuum* – a pure loan where *ownership* was transferred for a time. Charging for a lease, a *commodatum* was all right because the owner retains ownership and charges for the use of his own good; but somehow it becomes sinful when a lender charges for the use of a good which he no longer (temporarily) owns. Profits on trade, too, could be legitimate and lawful as a reward for risk, but interest on a loan – where the risk is borne by the borrower and not the lender – was always usury.

The later decretalists, attempting to combat practices of merchants in disguising usury in various contracts, pressed on to condemn such contracts as 'implicit usury', provided, as we have seen in treatment of sales contracts, that there is no uncertainty on the future price in the minds of buyer and seller. The early thirteenth century canonist Alanus Anglicus declared that if there was uncertainty in such a contract, and buyer and seller stood equal chance to gain or lose, usury did not exist. Providing the first real, if small, loophole in the sweeping prohibition against usury, Anglicus explained that this form of implicit usury could exist only in the mind and could not be subject to legal enforcement. This uncertainty loophole was widened slightly in the *Decretals* of Gregory IX.

On the other hand, the canonists persisted in cracking down on evasions of the usury ban which the market kept creatively inventing. Contracts providing for deferred payment on a sale were treated with suspicion, and very high prices in such a contract were taken by the canonists to prove intent to commit usury beyond a reasonable doubt. The *Decretals* also went so far as to condemn creditors charging interest for loans to travelling merchants, even though the canonists realized that the interest was a direct compensation for risks. Although canonists after Innocent IV began to talk of risks justifying profits, so that a profit on risky investments was considered perfectly justified, any interest on a pure loan (or *mutuum*) was condemned as usury despite reasonably mitigating circumstances.

The usury prohibition was the tragic flaw in the economic views of medieval jurists and theologians. The prohibition was economically irrational, depriving marginal borrowers and high credit risks of any borrowed capital whatever. It had no groundwork in natural law and virtually none in Old or New Testament teachings. And yet it was clung to fiercely throughout the Middle Ages, so that jurists and theologians had to engage in ingenious and artful twists in reasoning in order to make exceptions from the prohibition and to accommodate the growing practice of lending money and charging interest on a loan. And yet the medievalists, especially the later philosophers and theologians, had a fascinating and important point: for what *was* the moral or economic justification for interest on a pure loan? As we will see, medieval scholastics came to understand full well the economic and moral justifications for almost every aspect of interest charges: as an implicit profit on risk, as an opportunity foregone for making profits on investments, and many others. But why is there still interest charged on a simple, riskless, non-opportunity-foregone loan? That answer was not to come fully until the Austrian School of the late nineteenth century. Where the scholastics were gravely lacking was in not realizing that if interest was paid as well as charged voluntarily, that in itself is sufficient moral justification. And further that there *must have been* an economic explanation, even though economic science had not yet discovered it.

The first systematic breach in the usury prohibition came with the last of the thirteenth century canonists, Cardinal Hostiensis. In addition to having been a distinguished law professor, Hostiensis was a worldly cosmopolite, having been the ambassador of Henry III to his friend Pope Innocent IV. First Hostiensis reverted to the old milder tradition that usury is uncharitable, but not a sin against justice. Then he listed no less than 13 instances in which the usury prohibition could be broken and interest charged on a loan. One is as surety required by the guarantor of a loan; another that a seller may charge a higher price for a good sold on credit than for cash, provided that there is uncertainty (as indeed there always is) about the future price of the commodity. Another important exception allowed a creditor to write a penalty clause into a loan so that the debtor would have to pay a penalty above the principal if he did not repay on the date due. This of course paved the way for covert agreement on both sides to delay payment so as to allow the 'penalty'. Another exception was that the creditor might charge for labour which he undertook in making the particular loan.

These were all some form of penalty or special payment. But, in addition, Hostiensis provided the first path-breaking argument for charging a rate of interest on a loan from the very beginning, a charge that does not involve delay or guarantees. This is *lucrum cessans* (profit ceasing), a legitimate interest charge by the creditor to compensate him for profit foregone in investing the money himself. In short, *lucrum cessans* anticipated the Austrian concept of opportunity cost, of income foregone, and applied it to the charging of interest. Unfortunately, however, Cardinal Hostiensis's use of *lucrum cessans* was limited to non-habitual lenders who lend money out of charity to a debtor. Thus lenders could not be in the business of charging money on a loan, even on the ground of *lucrum cessans*.

Another exception made by Hostiensis also provided an open channel for the charging of interest on loans. He allowed the debtor to give a free gift to the creditor, so long as the 'gift' was not required by the creditor. But in that case debtors, in particular Florentine bankers who received deposits, felt obliged to make 'gifts' to their depositors, else the depositors would shift their funds to competitors who habitually made such 'gifts'. The making of a fake gift became an important mechanism in allowing the *de facto* charging of interest.

2.6   Theologians at the University of Paris

Theology, in the Middle Ages, was the queen of the 'sciences': i.e. the intellectual disciplines offering truth and wisdom. But theology had fallen on bad times during the Dark Ages, and the Roman and canon lawyers were left to apply ethical systems to law and human affairs. Theology began to flourish again in the early twelfth century at the University of Paris, under the famous Peter Abelard. From then on, Paris was the equivalent centre for theology during the High Middle Ages that Bologna was for Roman and canon law. But during the remainder of the twelfth century, the theologians were content to ponder and work out metaphysical and ontological questions and to leave social ethics to the jurists. It was typical of twelfth century theologians when Peter of Poitiers, later to become the dominant Regent of theology at the cathedral school of Notre Dame in Paris, declared that such doubtful questions as usury should be left to the canon lawyers.

After the turn of the thirteenth century, however, when canon and Roman law theories were already far advanced, the new university-trained philosopher–theologians turned to problems of social ethics with a will. Even before the turn of the thirteenth century, such influential theologians at the University of Paris as Radulphus Ardens and the Englishman – later Cardinal – Stephen Langton, began to write on problems of justice. Unfortunately, in dealing with the concept of 'just price', the theologians did not follow the Romanists and canonists in the sensible view that the free bargaining or market price is legitimate so long as it stays within a broad zone of the 'just price'. To the Paris theologians, it was immoral, sinful and illicit for the market price to be anything other than the just price. This of course meant that the just price became a weapon of compulsion instead of a broadly held standard. Ardens included a just price as a crucial criterion of a 'just sale'. More emphatically, his colleague and author of the first constitution of the University of Paris, the Englishman and later Cardinal Robert of Courçon (d. 1219), writing about 1204, termed selling goods above the just price an illicit practice, and the eminent Stephen Langton sternly called any seller who accepts more than the just price guilty of a mortal sin.

The theologians were well aware of their profound disagreement with the jurists, but clung to their new and extreme views. Thus, William of Auxerre (1160–1229), professor of theology at Paris, in 1220 wrote that divine law, which commanded that no sale be higher than the just price, must supersede human law, which followed *laesio enormis*. And his colleague, the Englishman Thomas Chabham, also writing about 1220, fanatically insisted that divine law demanded restitution from the seller even if the seller were only mistaken, and the mistake was only a penny.

If the theologians insisted that the just price must be strictly obeyed, then what in the world *was* it? While few of the theologians addressed this critical matter directly, it is clear that what they had in mind was the same just price as the canonists and Romanists, namely the current price at the particular place, either the common market or the government-fixed price, if such a regulation existed. The late twelfth century Paris theologian Peter Cantor (d. 1197), in treating the function of royal assessors, asserted that the just value of goods is their current price. More succinctly, the great Franciscan theologian at Paris in the first half of the thirteenth century, the Englishman Alexander of Hales (1168–1245) declared concisely that a 'just estimation of the goods' is 'as it is sold commonly in that city or place in which the sale occurs'. Even more clearly, the renowned thirteenth century German Dominican professor at Paris, Saint Albert the Great (1193–1280) put it thus: 'A price is just which can equal the value of the goods sold according to the estimation of the market place at that time'.

While the theologians, in wishing to enforce the current common price, were more restrictive than the canon or Roman jurists, they did constructive work in rehabilitating the image of the merchants from the low level to which they had sunk in the writings of the Church Fathers.

As late as Peter Lombard (d. 1160), Italian professor of theology at Paris and later bishop of Paris, the theologians had held the older view that a merchant could not perform his duties without sinning. The beginning of the full rehabilitation of the merchant came in the form of commentaries on the *Sentences* of Peter Lombard (strictly, the *Sententiarum quator libri*, 1150–51). The commentators, particularly after the turn of the thirteenth century, engaged in a systematic justification of the merchant and of mercantile profit-making. In the first place, the leading *Sentence* commentators, including the Dominican professors at Paris, St Albert the Great (*Commentary*, 1244–49), Peter of Tarentaise (later Pope Innocent V, d. 1276) (*Commentary*, 1253–57), as well as the Italian theologian at Paris, St Bonaventure (1221–74) a student of Alexander of Hales, general of the Franciscan Order and later cardinal (*Commentary*, 1250–51), all declared that merchants were essential to society. This conception was strengthened by the rediscovery of the works of Aristotle by the early thirteenth century, and the incorporation of Aristotelian philosophy into theology – first by Albert the Great and most especially by his great student Thomas Aquinas. To these new Aristotelians, and also to the English Franciscan Alexander of Hales, the division of labour was necessary to society as was the concomitant mutual exchange of goods and services. This was the path of the natural law in society.

More specifically, Thomas Chabham, despite his insistence on every penny of the just price, observed correctly that merchants performed the function of taking goods from areas of abundance and distributing them to areas of deficiency. Albert the Great repeated this insight later in the thirteenth century.

If trading is a useful and even necessary activity, it follows that profits for maintaining such activity are justifiable. Hence the theologians reiterated the twelfth century doctrine of the merchant being allowed to gain profits for the support of himself and his family. To the needs justification, the twelfth century theologians added the lawful nature of making profits in order to give to charity. The Franciscan Alexander of Hales was perhaps the first to call it a just and pious motive for trading to perform works of charity and mercy. It was unworthy, however – echoing the Huguccian doctrine – to gain profits for the sake of avarice or endless and insatiable cupidity.

If the labourer in the Christian tradition was 'worthy of his hire' (Luke 10:7), then profits from the useful activities of the merchant could be justified as covering his 'labour', or rather his labour and expenses as the jurists had already declared. Aquinas considered the earnings of the merchant a stipend for labour. For the theologians, 'labour' consisted of several types: transporting goods; storage and care; and – as had come in with the thirteenth century canonists – the assumption of risk. Thus mercantile profits were a payment or reward for the merchant's labour of transportation and storage, and his assumption of risk. The risk factor was stressed particularly by Alexander of Hales and St Thomas Aquinas. It should be noted, in contrast to many later historians, that the purpose of the jurists' and theologians' discussions of labour, cost, and risk was *not* to use these factors in determining the just price (which was simply the current common price) but to justify the profits obtained by the merchant.

Robert of Courçon was the first thirteenth century theologian to add a natural law angle to the traditional though flimsily grounded theological denunciations of usury. Courçon simply appropriated the canonist Huguccio's sophistical moral distinction between a lease and a loan, with the former being licit and the latter illicit because ownership of the money had temporarily been shifted to the borrower. More influential was fellow Parisian theologian William of Auxerre, who added a string of new fallacies to the mounting intensity of the Church's assault upon usury. William ranted that usury was intrinsically evil and monstrous, without really explaining why; he also did one better on the standard likening of usury to theft by actually comparing usury to murder, to the detriment of the former. Killing, he said can sometimes be licit, since only certain forms of killing are sinful, but usury is sinful everywhere and can never be licit. Since usury, according to William of Auxerre, is sinful by its very nature, this made it a violation of the natural law in addition to its other alleged iniquities.

On *why* usury was a sin against the natural law William was unclear; one of his innovative arguments in the anti-usury parade was that a man who charges interest on a loan is trying to 'sell time', which is properly the common property of all creatures. Since time is supposed to be common and free, William of Auxerre and later theologians could therefore use this argument to condemn as 'usury' not merely a loan but also charging a higher price for credit than for cash sales. In adding the 'free time' argument, William unwittingly touched on the later Austrian solution to the problem of pure interest on a riskless loan: the sale not of 'time', to be sure, but of 'time-preference', where the creditor is selling the debtor money, a present good (a good useful now), in exchange for an IOU for the future which is a 'future good' (a good only available at some point in the future). But since everyone prefers a present good to an equivalent future good (the universal fact of time-preference), the lender will charge, and the borrower will be willing to pay, interest on a loan. Interest is, then, the price of time-preference. The failure of the scholastics to understand or arrive at the concept of time preference was to do more than anything else to discredit scholastic economics, because of its implacable hostility to and condemnation of the universal practice of 'usury'.

William of Auxerre also tried to grapple with the voluntarist argument: how could the usury charge be evil and unjust if paid voluntarily by the borrower? In surely one of the silliest arguments in the history of economic thought, William of Auxerre conceded that the borrower's payment of interest was voluntary, but added that the borrower would have preferred a free loan still more, so that in an 'absolute' rather than a 'conditional' sense, the interest charge was *not* voluntary. William somehow failed to see that the same could be said of the buyer of *any* product; since any buyer would prefer a free good to the charge of any price, we could then conclude that all free exchanges are involuntary and sinful in an 'absolute' sense.

Despite the manifest absurdity of this argument, the 'conditional' voluntary as well as the other new arguments of William of Auxerre were highly influential and immediately incorporated into the standard theological arguments against usury.

The German Dominican St Albert the Great performed the enormous service to philosophy of bringing Aristotle and Aristotelianism back to Western thought. Born in Bavaria to an aristocratic family, Albert was for a time German provincial of the Dominican Order and bishop of Regensburg, but for most of his long life he taught at the Universities of Paris and Cologne.

Unfortunately, Albert was not nearly as good an economist as he was a philosopher, and in many ways he took scholastic economics down the wrong road. It is true that he performed the service of teaching his great pupil, St Thomas Aquinas, that the just price is the common market price, and that the merchant is performing a legitimate social role. On the other hand, Albert unfortunately added the Aristotelian attack on usury as an unnatural breeding of a 'barren metal' to the accumulated hodge-podge of all the other arguments against interest. St Albert did not realise that Aristotle's attack on usury was only part and parcel of the latter's denunciation of all retail trade, since the Latin translation of Aristotle available to Albert rendered the Greek term for retail trade as a Latin word meaning 'money-changing'. Hence, Albert adopted this argument by mistake, since he would certainly not have gone along with the Aristotelian idea that all retail trade was unnatural and sinful.

Albert also did great damage to future thought in another of his misinterpretations of Aristotle's *Nichomachean Ethics*. Somehow he interpreted the Aristotelian determinant of value not as consumer needs or utility, but as 'labour and expenses', thus at least partially prefiguring the later labour theory of value.

2.7 The philosopher–theologian: St Thomas Aquinas

St Thomas Aquinas (1225–74) was the towering intellect of the High Middle Ages, the man who built on the philosophical system of Aristotle, on the concept of natural law, and on Christian theology to forge 'Thomism', a mighty synthesis of philosophy, theology and the sciences of man. This young Italian was born an aristocrat, son of Landulph, count of Aquino at Rocco Secca in the kingdom of Naples. Thomas studied at an early age with the Benedictines, and later at the University of Naples. At the age of 15 he tried to enter the new Dominican Order, a place for Church intellectuals and scholars, but was physically prevented from doing so by his parents, who kept him confined for two years. Finally, St Thomas escaped, joined the Dominicans, and then studied at Cologne and finally at Paris under his revered teacher, Albert the Great. Aquinas took his doctorate at the University of Paris, and taught there as well as at other university centres in Europe. Aquinas was so immensely corpulent that it was said that a large section had to be carved out of the round dinner table so that he could sit at it. Aquinas wrote numerous works, beginning with his *Commentary* on Peter Lombard's *Sentences* in the 1250s, and ending with his masterful and enormously influential three-part *Summa Theologica*, written between 1265 and 1273. It was the *Summa*, more than any other work, that was to establish Thomism as the mainstream of Catholic scholastic theology in centuries to come.

Until recently, historical studies of the just price typically began with St Thomas, as if the entire discussion had suddenly leapt into being in the ample person of Aquinas in the thirteenth century. We have seen, however, that Aquinas worked in a long and rich canonist, Romanist and theological tradition. It is not surprising that Aquinas followed his revered teacher, St Albert, and the other theologians of the previous century in insisting on the just price for all exchanges and, not being content with the more liberal legist creed of free bargaining up to the alleged point of *laesio enormis*, in asserting that divine law, which must take precedence over human law, demands complete virtue, or the precise just price.

Unfortunately, in discussing the just price, St Thomas stored up great trouble for the future by being vague about what precisely the just price is supposed to be. As a founder of a system built on the great Aristotle, Aquinas, following St Albert before him, felt obliged to incorporate the Aristotelian analysis of exchange into his theory, with all the ambiguities and obscurities that that entailed. St Thomas was clearly an Aristotelian in adopting the latter's trenchant view that the determinant of exchange value was the need, or utility, of consumers, as expressed in their demand for products. And so, this proto-Austrian aspect of value based on demand and utility was reinstated in economic thought. On the other hand, Aristotle's erroneous view of exchange as 'equating' values was rediscovered, along with the indecipherable shoemaker–builder ratio. Unfortunately, in the course of the *Commentary to the* (Nichomachean) *Ethics*, Thomas followed St Albert in seeming to add to utility, as a determinant of exchange value, labour plus expenses. This gave hostage to the later idea that St Thomas had either added to Aristotle's utility theory of value a cost of production theory (labour plus expenses), or even replaced utility by a cost theory. Some commentators have even declared that Aquinas had adopted a labour theory of value, capped by the notorious and triumphant sentence by the twentieth century Anglican socialist historian Richard Henry Tawney: 'The true descendant of the doctrines of Aquinas is the labour theory of value. The last of the Schoolmen is Karl Marx.'[2]

It has taken historians several decades to recover from Tawney's disastrous misinterpretation. Indeed, the scholastics were sophisticated thinkers and social economists who favoured trade and capitalism, and advocated the common market price as the just price, with the exception of the problem of usury. Even in value theory, the labour plus expenses discussion in Aquinas is an anomaly. For labour plus expenses (*never* just labour) appears only in Aquinas's *Commentary* and not in the *Summa*, his *magnum opus*.[3] Moreover, we have seen that labour plus expenses was a formula generally used in Aquinas's times to justify the profits of merchants rather than as a means of determining economic value. It is therefore likely that Aquinas was using the concept in this sense, making the sensible point that a merchant who failed in the long run to cover his costs and not to make profits would go out of business.

In addition, there are many indications that Aquinas adhered to the common view of the Churchmen of his and previous times that the just price was the common market price. If so, then he could scarcely *also* hold that the just price equalled cost of production, since the two can and do differ. Thus his conclusion in the *Summa* was that 'the value of economic goods is that which comes into human use and is measured by a monetary price, for which purpose money was invented.' Particularly revealing was a reply Aquinas made as early as 1262 in a letter to Jacopo da Viterbo (d. 1308), a lector of the Dominican monastery in Florence and later archbishop of Naples. In his letter, Aquinas referred to the common market price as the normative and just price with which to compare other contracts. Moreover, in the *Summa*, Aquinas notes the influence of supply and demand on prices. A more abundant supply in one place will tend to lower price in that place, and vice versa. Furthermore, St Thomas described without at all condemning the activities of merchants in making profits by buying goods where they were abundant and cheap, and then transporting and selling them in places where they are dear. None of this looks like a cost-of-production view of the just price.

Finally, and most charmingly and crucially, Aquinas, in his great *Summa*, raised a question that had been discussed by Cicero. A merchant is carrying grain to a famine-stricken area. He knows that soon other merchants are following him with many more supplies of grain. *Is* the merchant obliged to tell the starving citizenry of the supplies coming soon and thereby suffer a lower price, or is it all right for him to keep silent and reap the rewards of a high price? To Cicero, the merchant was duty-bound to disclose his information and sell at a lower price. But St Thomas argued differently. Since the arrival of the later merchants was a future event and *therefore* uncertain, Aquinas declared justice did not require him to tell his customers about the impending arrival of his competitors. He could sell his own grain at the prevailing market price for that area, even though it was extremely high. Of course, Aquinas went on amiably, if the merchant wished to tell his customers anyway, that would be especially virtuous, but justice did not require him to do so. There is no starker example of Aquinas's opting for the just price as the current price, determined by demand and supply, rather than the cost of production (which of course did not change much from the area of abundance to the famine area).

A piece of indirect evidence is that Giles of Lessines (d. c.1304), a student of Albert and Aquinas and a Dominican professor of theology at Paris, analysed the just price similarly, and flatly declared that it was the common market price. Giles stressed, furthermore, that a good is properly worth as much as it can be sold for without coercion or fraud.

It should come as no surprise that Aquinas, in contrast to Aristotle, was highly favourable towards the activities of the merchant. Mercantile profit, he declared, was a stipend for the merchant's labour, and a reward for shouldering the risks of transportation. In a commentary to Aristotle's *Politics* (1272),

Aquinas noted shrewdly that greater risks in sea transportation resulted in greater profits for merchants. In his *Commentary to the Sentences* of Peter Lombard, written in the 1250s, Thomas followed preceding theologians in arguing that merchants could ply their trade without committing sin. But in his later work, he was far more positive, pointing out that merchants perform the important function of bringing goods from where they are abundant to where they are scarce.

Particularly important was Aquinas's brief outline of the mutual benefit each person derives from exchange. As he put it in the *Summa*: 'buying and selling seems to have been instituted for the mutual advantage of both parties, since one needs something that belongs to the other, and conversely'.

Building on Aristotle's theory of money, Aquinas pointed out its indispensability as a medium of exchange, a 'measure' of expression of values, and a unit of account. In contrast to Aristotle, Aquinas was not frightened at the idea of the value of money fluctuating on the market. On the contrary, Aquinas recognized that the purchasing power of money was bound to fluctuate, and was content if it fluctuated, as it usually did, more stably than did particular prices.

It was the peculiar fate of the usury prohibition in the Middle Ages that every time it seemed to be weakening in the face of reality, theorists would strengthen the ban. At a time when the highly sophisticated and knowledgeable Cardinal Hostiensis was seeking to soften the prohibition, St Thomas Aquinas unfortunately tightened it once more. Like his teacher St Albert, Aquinas added the Aristotelian objection to the medieval ban on usury, except that Aquinas also inserted something new. In the medieval tradition of starting with the conclusion – the crushing of usury – and seizing any odd argument to hand which might lead to it, Aquinas added a new twist to Aristotelian doctrine. Instead of stressing the barrenness of money as a major argument against usury, Aquinas seized on the term 'measure' and stressed that since money, in terms of money, of course, has a fixed legal face value, this means that the formal nature of money must be to remain fixed. The purchasing power of money can fluctuate due to changes in the supply of goods; that is legitimate and natural. But when the holder of money sets out to produce variations in its value by charging interest, he violates the nature of money and is therefore sinful and mindless of the natural law.

That such arrant nonsense should swiftly assume a central place in all later scholastic prohibitions of usury is testimony to the way that irrationality can seize the thought of even so great a champion of reason as Aquinas (and his followers). Why the fixed legal face value of a coin should mean that its value in exchange – at least from the side of money – should not change; or why the charging of interest should be confused with a change in the purchasing power of money, simply testifies to the human propensity for fallacy, especially when prohibiting usury had already become the over-riding goal.

But Aquinas's argument against usury involved another invention of his own. Money, to him, is totally 'consumed'; it 'disappears' in exchange. Therefore money's use is equivalent to its ownership. Hence, when one charges interest on a loan, one is charging twice, for the money itself and for its use, although they are one and the same. Highlighting this odd thesis was Aquinas's discussion of why it was legitimate for an owner of money to charge rent for someone to display a coin. In that case, there is a bailment, a charge for keeping one's money in trust. But the reason why this charge is licit, for Aquinas, is that the display of money is only a 'secondary' use, a use separate from its ownership, since money is not 'consumed' or does not disappear in the process. The primary use of money is to disappear in the purchase of goods.

There are several grave problems with this new weapon invented by Aquinas with which to beat usury. First, what is *wrong* with charging 'twice', for ownership and use? Second, even if somehow wrong, this act scarcely bears the weight of sin and excommunication that the Catholic Church had loaded for centuries upon the hapless usurer. And third, if Aquinas had looked beyond the legal formalism of money, and at the goods which the borrower purchased with his loan, he might have seen that these purchased goods were in an important sense 'fruitful', so that while the money 'disappeared' in purchases, in an economic sense the goods-equivalent of money was retained by the borrower.

St Thomas's stress on consumption of money led to a curious shift on the usury question. In contrast to all theorists since Gratian, the sin now became not charging interest on a loan *per se*, but only on a good – money – that disappears. Therefore, for Aquinas, charging interest on a loan of goods in kind would not be condemned as 'usury'.

But if the usury prohibition on money was tightened with new arguments, Aquinas continued and strengthened the previous tradition of justifying investments in a partnership (*societas*). A *societas* was licit because each partner retained ownership of his money, and ran the risk of loss; hence profit on such risky investments was legitimate. In the late eleventh century, Ivo of Chartres had already briefly distinguished a *societas* from a usurious loan, and the distinction was elaborated in the early thirteenth century by the theologian Robert of Courçon (c.1204), and in John Teutonicus' *Gloss* on Gratian (1215). Courçon had made it clear that even an inactive partner risked his capital in an enterprise. This of course meant that types of inactive partnerships, such as sea loans for specific voyages, slid over into actual loans, and the lines were often fuzzy. Besides, and this was a problem that no one at the time would face, wasn't *any* lender necessarily risking his capital, since a borrower could always turn out to be unable to repay even the principal of a loan?

Aquinas now lent his enormous authority to the view that the *societas* was perfectly licit and not usurious. He succinctly declared that the investor of money does not transfer ownership to a working partner; that ownership is retained by the investor; so that he risks his money and can legitimately earn a profit on the investment. The trouble with this, however, is that Aquinas here abandons his own thesis that the ownership of money is the same thing as its use. For the use of the money was transferred to the working partner, and therefore on St Thomas's own grounds he should have condemned all partnerships, as well as the *societas*, as illicit and usurious. Confronting a thirteenth century world in which the *societas* flourished and was crucial to commercial and economic life, it was unthinkable to Aquinas that he should throw the economy into chaos by condemning this well-established instrument of trade and finance.

Instead of ownership going with the use of a consumable item, then, Aquinas now advanced the idea of ownership going with incidence of risk. The investor risks his capital; therefore, he retains ownership of his investment. A seemingly sensible way out, but flimsy; not only did Aquinas thereby contradict his own bizarre ownership theory, he also failed to realize that, after all, not *all* ownership need be particularly risky. Another problem is that the risk-taker is making a profit on the investment of money, which is supposed to be sterile. Instead of stating that all profit should go to the working partner, St Thomas explicitly says that the capitalist rightly receives the 'gain coming thence', i.e. from the use of his money, 'as from his own property.' It looks very much as if St Thomas is here treating money as fertile and productive, providing an independent reward to the capitalist.

Yet, despite the inner contradictions rife in St Thomas's treatment of usury and the *societas*, his entire doctrine continued to be dominant for 200 years.

Finally, Aquinas was a firm believer in the superiority of private to communal property and resource ownership. Private ownership becomes a necessary feature of man's earthly state. It is the best guarantee of a peaceful and orderly society, and it provides maximum incentive for the care and efficient use of property. Thus, in the *Summa*, St Thomas keenly writes: 'every man is more careful to procure what is for himself alone that that which is common to many or to all since each one would shirk the labour and leave to another that which concerns the community, as happens where there are a great number of servants'.

Furthermore, developing the Roman law theory of acquisition, Aquinas, anticipating the famous theory of John Locke, grounded the right of original acquisition of property on two basic factors: labour and occupation. The initial right of each person is to ownership over his own self, in Aquinas's view in a 'proprietary right over himself'. Such individual self-ownership is based on the capacity of man as a rational being.

Next, cultivation and use of previously unused land establishes a just property title in the land in one man rather than in others. St Thomas's theory of acquisition was further clarified and developed by his close student and disciple, John of Paris (Jean Quidort, c.1250–1306), a member of the same Dominican community of St Jacques in Paris as Aquinas. Championing the absolute right of private property, Quidort declared that lay property

> is acquired by individual people through their own skill, labour and diligence, and individuals, as individuals, have right and power over it and valid lordship; each person may order his own and dispose, administer, hold or alienate it as he wishes, so long as he causes no injury to anyone else; since he is lord.

This 'homesteading' theory of property has been held by many historians to be the ancestor of the Marxian labour theory of value. But this charge confuses two very different things: determination of the *economic value* or price of a good, and a decision on how unused resources are to go over into private hands. The Aquinas–John of Paris–Locke view is the 'labour theory' (defining 'labour' as the expenditure of human energy rather than working for a wage) of the origin of property, *not* a labour theory of value.

In contrast to his forerunner Aristotle, labour for Aquinas was scarcely to be despised. On the contrary, labour is a dictate of positive, natural and divine law. Aquinas is very much aware that God in the Bible gave the dominion over all the earth to man for his use. Man's function is to take the materials provided by nature and, by discerning natural law, to mould that reality to achieve his purposes. While Aquinas scarcely has any conception of economic growth or capital accumulation, he clearly posits man as active moulder of his life. Gone is the passive Greek ideal of conforming to given conditions or to the requirements of the *polis*.

Perhaps St Thomas's most important contribution concerned the underpinning or framework of economics rather than strictly economic matters. For in reviving and building on Aristotle, St Thomas introduced and established in the Christian world a philosophy of natural law, a philosophy in which human reason is able to master the basic truths of the universe. In the hands of Aquinas as in Aristotle, philosophy, with reason as its instrument of knowledge, became once again the queen of the sciences. Human reason demonstrated the reality of the universe, and of the natural law of discoverable classes of entities. Human reason could know about the nature of the world, and it could therefore know the proper ethics for mankind. Ethics, then, became decipherable by reason. This rationalist tradition cut against the 'fideism' of the earlier Christian Church, the debilitating idea that only faith and supernatural revelation can provide an ethics for mankind. Debilitating because if the faith is lost, then ethics is lost as well. Thomism, in contrast, demonstrated that the laws of nature, including the nature of mankind, provided the means for man's reason to discover a rational ethics. To be sure, God created the natural laws of the universe, but the apprehension of these natural laws was possible whether or not one believed in God as creator. In this way, a rational ethic for man was provided on a truly scientific rather than on a supernatural foundation.

In the subset of natural law theory that deals with rights, St Thomas led a swing back from the twelfth century concept of a right as a claim on others rather than as an inviolable area of property right, of the dominion of an individual, to be defended from all others. In a brilliant work, Professor Richard Tuck[4] points out that early Roman law was marked by an 'active' property right/dominion view of rights, while the later twelfth century Romanists at Bologna converted the concept of 'right' to the passive listing of claims on other men. This 'passive' as opposed to 'active' concept of rights reflected the network of interwoven, customary and status claims that marked the Middle Ages. This is, in an important sense, the ancestor of the modern assertion of such 'claim-rights' as 'the right to a job', the 'right to three square meals a day', etc., all of which can only be fulfilled by coercing others to obtain them.

At thirteenth century Bologna, however, Accursius began a swing back to an active property rights theory, with the property of each individual a dominion which must be defended against all others. Aquinas adopted the idea of a natural dominion without, however, going all the way to a genuine natural rights theory, which asserts that private property is natural and not a convention created by society or government. Aquinas was moved to adopt the dominion theory because of the mighty late thirteenth century ideological battles between the Dominican and Franciscan Orders. The Franciscans, committed to total poverty, claimed that their subsistence use of resources was not really private property; this pleasant fiction enabled the Franciscans to claim that, in their state of voluntary poverty, they had risen above the ownership or possession of property. They maintained oddly that purely *consumption* use of resources, such as they engaged in, did not imply the possession of property. Supposedly, the sale or giving away of a resource was necessary to qualify it as property. Self-sufficiency or isolation did not, according to the Franciscan view, allow property to exist. The rival Dominicans, including Aquinas, understandably upset by this claim, began to insist that *all use* necessarily implied dominion, the possession and control of resources, and therefore property.

2.8 Late thirteenth century scholastics: Franciscans and utility theory

The first victory in the struggle over property right concepts was won by the Franciscans, whose theory was upheld by their protector, Pope Nicholas III, in his bull *Exiit*, issued in 1279. This dominant theory was elaborated by the first great critic of Thomism, the British Franciscan scholastic John Duns Scotus (1265–1308), professor of theology at Oxford and later at Paris. Aquinas had maintained that neither private nor communal property was a necessary feature of the state of nature, so that one condition was no more natural than the other. Scotus, on the contrary, boldly maintained that in a state of natural innocence both natural and divine law decree that all resources be held in common, so that no private property or dominion may exist. In this supposedly idyllic primitive communism, each person may take what he needs from the common store.

Rights theory was scarcely the only Franciscan deviation from mainline Thomism. As fideists, the Franciscans harked back to earlier Christian tradition before it had been superseded by the rationalism of St Thomas. They began, therefore, to deprecate the idea of a rational ethics and hence of natural law.

In the matter of rights theory, at least, the Franciscans were soon smashed. Reacting against the Franciscans, Pope John XXII issued his famous bull *Quia vir reprobus* (1329). *Quia* asserted trenchantly that God's dominion over the earth was reflected in man's dominion or property over his material possessions. Property rights, therefore, were *not*, as even Aquinas had believed, a product of positive law or social convention; they were rooted in man's nature, as created by divine law. Property rights were therefore natural and coextensive with man's actions in the material world. The Franciscans were effectively routed on this point; it was now established, as Richard Tuck puts it, that property 'was a basic fact about human beings, on which their social and political concepts had to be posited'.[5]

In more strictly economic matters, Franciscans could either adhere to or deviate from the mainline Thomist concept of the just price. Scotus himself set forth a deviationist view. In his commentary on Peter Lombard's *Sentences*, Scotus elaborated a minority view that many historians have wrongly attributed to scholasticism as a whole: that the just price was the merchant's cost of production plus compensation for the industry, labour and risk involved in bringing his product to market. The compensation, furthermore, was supposed to provide adequate support for the family of the merchant. In this way, labour plus expenses plus risk, previously employed to justify whatever profits the merchant might obtain, was now transformed into the determinant of the just price. Scotus made this cost-of-production a theory of just price, in contrast to the long-standing mainstream scholastic view that the just price was the common price on the market.

Although a Franciscan, the British scholastic at the University of Paris, Richard of Middleton (c.1249–1306), followed the economic doctrine of Aquinas and stressed need and utility as the determinants of economic value. The just price, following the main scholastic line, was equivalent to the common market price determined by these needs. Middleton also underlined Aquinas's vitally important concept that both parties to an exchange benefit. Becoming more precise than Aquinas, Middleton pointed out that, say, when a horse is sold for money, both the buyer and the seller gain from the transaction, since the buyer demonstrates that he needs the horse more than the money while the seller prefers the money to the horse.

In addition to developing this crucial concept of mutual benefit, Richard of Middleton was the first to apply that concept to international trade. International trade, as well as individual exchange, brings mutual benefits. Middleton illustrated this idea by postulating two countries: country *A* which has a superabundance of grain but a dearth of wine, and country *B* which has an abundance of wine but little grain. Both countries will then benefit by exchanging their respective surpluses. The merchants will also profit by transporting grain from country *A*, where it is abundant and its price is therefore cheap, to country *B*, where it is scarce and commands a high price. Merchants will also profit by the reverse traffic: shipping wine from country *B*, where its price is low, to *A*, where its price is high. By buying and selling at current market prices, the merchants are trading at the just price, and make a profit yet exploit no one. The merchants are justly compensated for performing a useful service and for taking trouble and risks. The only point missed by Middleton in this sophisticated analysis is that the actions of the various merchants will move toward equalizing prices in the two countries.

An even more dazzling contribution to economic thought was made by a Provençal Franciscan friar, for many years lector at Florence. Pierre de Jean Olivi (1248–98), in two treatises on contracts, one on usury and the other on purchases and sales, pointed out that economic value was determined by three factors: scarcity (*raritas*); usefulness (*virtuositas*); and desirability or desiredness (*complacibilitas*). The effect of scarcity, or what we would now call 'supply', is clear: the scarcer a product the more valuable it is, and therefore the higher the price. The more abundant the product (the greater the supply), on the other hand, the lower the value and the price.

Olivi's remarkable contribution was to investigate the previously vague concept of need or utility. Aquinas's student and disciple, the Dominican Giles of Lessines, teaching at the University of Paris, had taken the utility concept a step further by stating that goods are more or less valuable on the market according to the degree of their utility. But now Olivi separated utility into two parts. One was *virtuositas*, or the objective utility of a good, the objective power it has to satisfy human wants. But, as Olivi explains, the important factor in determining price is *complacibilitas*, or subjective utility, the subjective desirability of a product to the individual consumers.

Furthermore, Olivi squarely confronted the 'paradox of value' which would later confound Adam Smith and the classical economists, and did far better than they at solving it. The 'value paradox' is that a good such as water or bread, essential to life and therefore, according to the classical economists, having a high 'use-value', should be very cheap and have a low value on the market. At the same time, in contrast, gold or diamonds, non-essential luxuries and therefore of far lower use-value, have far higher exchange value on the market. The classical economists of the eighteenth and nineteenth centuries simply threw up their hands at this paradox and unsatisfactorily posed a sharp dichotomy between use- and exchange-value. Olivi, on the other hand, pointed to the solution: water, though necessary to human life, is so highly abundant and easily available that it commands a very low price on the market, while gold is far more scarce and therefore more valuable. Utility, in the determination of price, is relative to supply and not absolute. The complete solution to the value paradox had to wait for the Austrian School of the late nineteenth century: the 'marginal utility' – the value of each unit of a good – diminishes as its supply increases. Thus a superabundant good such as bread or water will have a low marginal utility, while a rare good such as gold will have a high one. The value of a good on the market, and therefore its price, is determined by its *marginal* utility, not the philosophical utility of the good as a whole or in the abstract. But, of course, before the Austrians, the marginal concept was lacking.

The marketplace for Olivi, then, was an arena in which prices for goods are formed out of the interaction of individuals with differing subjective utilities and valuations of the good. Just market prices, then, are not determined by referring to the objective qualities of the good, but by the interaction of subjective preferences on the market.

In addition to his monumental achievement in being the first to discover subjective utility theory, Olivi was the first to bring into economic thought the concept of capital (*capitale*) as a fund of money invested in a business venture. The term 'capital' had appeared in numerous business records since the mid-twelfth century, but this is the first time it was conceptualized. The concept of capital was used by Olivi to show that it was possible to use money in a fruitful way, to gain a profit. Olivi retained the usury ban where capital was invested without being altered in some way by the labour and industry of the investor. However, Olivi was one of the minority of scholastics to adopt the Hostiensis allowance of *lucrum cessans* – permitting an interest charge on a loan wherever the profit on an investment was foregone in the process. Unfortunately, Olivi continued Hostiensis' careful limitation of confining *lucrum cessans* to loans granted out of charity, so that the activities of a professional money-lender could still in no way be justified.

It is a notable irony in the history of economic thought that the discoverer of the subjective utility theory, a highly sophisticated analyst of how the market economy worked, a believer in the just price as the common market price, the initiator of the concept of capital, and a defender of at least the partial use of *lucrum cessans* as a way of justifying interest: that this great market thinker should have been the leader of the rigourist wing of the Franciscan order that believed in living in extreme poverty. Perhaps one explanation is that Olivi was born in the highly important market town of Narbonne. He was main intellectual leader of the Spiritual Franciscans, who believed devoutly in following faithfully the rule of total poverty laid down by the founder of the order, St Francis of Assisi (1182–1226). It is a further irony that Olivi's opponents, the Conventual Franciscans, who believed in a far laxer interpretation of the rule, hurled anathemas at Olivi and other Spirituals and managed to destroy many physical as well as intellectual traces of Olivi's work. In 1304, six years after his death, a chapter general of the Franciscan Order commanded the destruction of all Olivi's works, and 14 years later, the unfortunate Olivi's body was disinterred and his bones scattered.

Not only were many physical copies of Olivi's writings destroyed, but it became unhealthy for Franciscans, at least, to refer to his works. As a result, when, nearly a century and a half later, Olivi's forgotten work was rediscovered by the great Franciscan saint San Bernardino (St Bernardine) of Siena, Bernardino thought it prudent not even to refer to the heretic Olivi, even though he used the latter's theory of utility virtually word for word in his own work. This reticence was necessary because Bernardino belonged to the strict Observant wing of the Franciscans, in a way descendants of Olivi's Spirituals. Indeed, it has only been since the 1950s that the illuminating economic writings of Olivi, and their appropriation by San Bernardino, have come to light.

Perhaps another reason for the hysteria with which the mainstream Franciscans greeted the religious views of Pierre Olivi was his continuing dalliance with the Joachimite heresy. One of the founders of mystical Christian messianism was the Calabrian hermit and Abbot Joachim of Fiore (1145–1202). In the early 1190s Joachim adopted the thesis that there had been in history not just two ages (pre-Christian and post-Christian), but a third age, of which he himself was the prophet. The pre-Christian epoch was the age of the Father, of the Old Testament; the Christian era the age of the Son, of the New Testament. And now was coming the fulfilment, the new third age, the apocalyptic age of the Holy Spirit, in which history was soon to come to an end. The third age, which for Joachim was to be ushered in during the next half-century, in the early or mid-thirteenth century, was to be an age of pure love and freedom. The knowledge of God would be revealed directly to all men, and there would be no work or property, because human beings would possess only spiritual bodies, their material bodies having disappeared. There would be no Church or Bible or state, but only a free community of perfect spiritual beings who would spend all their time in mystical ecstasy praising God until this millennial Kingdom of the Saints would usher in the Last Days, the days of the Last Judgement.

Seemingly tiny divergences in premises often have grave social and political consequences, and such was true of disagreements among Christians on the apparently recondite question of eschatology, the science or discipline of the Last Days. Since St Augustine, the orthodox Christian view has been amillennialist, that is, that there is no special millennium or Kingdom of God in human history except the life of Jesus and the establishment of the Christian Church. This is the view of Catholics, of Lutherans, and probably of Calvin himself. The ideological or social conclusion is that Jesus will return to usher in the Last Judgement and the end of history in His own time, so that there is nothing that human beings can do to speed the Last Days. One variant of this doctrine is that after Jesus's return He will launch a thousand years of the Kingdom of God on earth before the Last Judgement; in practical terms, however, there is little of a significant difference here, since Christianity remains in place, and there is still nothing man can do to usher in the millennium.

The crucial difference comes with chiliastic ideas such as those of Joachim of Fiore, where not only was the world coming to the end soon, but man must do certain things to usher in the Last Days, to prepare the way for the Last Judgement. These are all post-millennial doctrines, that is, that man must *first* set up a Kingdom of God on earth as a necessary condition either for Jesus's return or for the Last Judgement. Generally, as we shall see further in the Protestant Reformation, post-millennial views lead to some form of theocratic coercion of society to pave the way for the culmination of history.

For Joachim of Fiore the path to the Last Days would be blazed by a new order of highly spiritual monks, from whom would come 12 patriarchs headed by a supreme teacher, who would convert the Jews to Christianity, as foretold in *Revelation*, and would lead all mankind away from the material and towards the love of things of the spirit. Then, for a brief blazing, three-and-a-half years, a secular king, the Antichrist, would chastise and destroy the corrupt Christian Church. The swift overthrow of the Antichrist would then usher in the total age of the Spirit.

In view of the radical and potentially explosive nature of Joachim's heresy, it is remarkable that no less than three contemporary popes expressed great interest in his doctrine. By the middle of the thirteenth century, however, Joachimism was neglected and little known. It is small wonder that the Joachimite heresy was revived by the Spiritual Franciscans, who were tempted to see in their own flourishing new order, and in their devotion to poverty, the very monastic order that had been foretold by Joachim to bring about the Last Days.

2.9   Notes

1. Saint Augustine, *The City of God* (Cambridge, Mass.: Loeb Classical Library/Harvard University Press, 1963), Vol. II, Book IV, IV, p. 17.
2. Richard Henry Tawney, *Religion and the Rise of Capitalism* (New York: Harcourt, Brace and World, 1937, orig. 1926), p. 36.
3. There is controversy among historians on when the *Commentary* was written. The older view, that it was written in 1266 or even earlier, would imply the simple explanation that Aquinas's views had matured from his earlier close adherence to his teacher, St Albert. The newer view, that the *Commentary* was written at the same time as the *Summa*, leaves the anomaly intact.
4. Richard Tuck, *Natural Rights Theories: Their Origin and Development* (Cambridge: Cambridge University Press, 1979).
5. Ibid., p. 24.

3 From Middle Ages to Renaissance

3.1   The great depression of the fourteenth century

Most people – historians not excepted – are tempted to think of economic and cultural progress as being continuous: in every century people are better off than in the one preceding. This comforting assumption had to be given up quite early when the Dark Ages ensued after the collapse of the Roman Empire. But it was generally held that after the 'renaissance' of the eleventh century, progress in western Europe was pretty well linear and continuous from that point to the present day. It took heroic efforts over many decades for economic historians like Professors Armando Sapori and Robert Sabatino Lopez to finally convince the historical profession that there was a grave secular decline in most of western Europe from approximately 1300 to the middle of the fifteenth century; a period which might be called the Late Middle Ages or the Early Renaissance. This secular decline, mistitled a 'depression', permeated most parts of western Europe with the exception of a few Italian city-states.

The economic decline was marked by a severe drop in population. Since the eleventh century, economic growth and prosperity had pulled up population figures. Total population in western Europe, estimated at 24 million in the year 1000 AD, had vaulted to 54 million by the year 1340. In little over a century, from 1340 to 1450, however, the western European population fell from 54 million to 37 million, a 31 per cent drop in only a century.

The successful battle to establish the fact of the great decline has done little, however, to establish the cause or causes of this debacle. Focus on the devastation caused by outbreaks of the Black Death in the mid-fourteenth century is partially correct, but superficial, for these outbreaks were themselves partly caused by an economic breakdown and fall in living standards which began earlier in the century. The causes of the great depression of western Europe can be summed up in one stark phrase: the newly imposed domination of the state. During the medieval synthesis of the High Middle Ages there was a balance between the power of Church and state, with the Church slightly more powerful. In the fourteenth century that balance was broken, and the nation-state came to hold sway, breaking the power of the Church, taxing, regulating, controlling and wreaking devastation through virtually continuous war for over a century (the Hundred Years' War, from 1337 to 1453).[1]

The first and critically most important step in the rise in the power of the state at the expense of crippling the economy was the destruction of the fairs of Champagne. During the High Middle Ages, the fairs of Champagne were the main mart for international trade, and the hub of local and international commerce. These fairs had been carefully nurtured by being made free zones, untaxed or unregulated by the French kings or nobles, while justice was swiftly and efficiently meted out by competing private and merchants' courts.

The fairs of Champagne reached their peak during the thirteenth century, and provided the centre for land-based trade over the Alps from northern Italy, bearing goods from afar.

Then, in the early fourteenth century, Philip IV, the Fair, king of France (1285–1314), moved to tax, plunder, and effectively destroy the vitally important fairs of Champagne. To finance his perpetual dynastic wars, Philip levied a stiff sales tax on the Champagne fairs. He also destroyed domestic capital and finance by repeated confiscatory levies on groups or organizations with money. In 1308, he destroyed the wealthy Order of the Templars, confiscating their funds for the royal treasury. Philip then turned to impose a series of crippling levies and confiscations on Jews and northern Italians ('Lombards') prominent at the fairs: in 1306, 1311, 1315, 1320 and 1321. Furthermore, at war with the Flemings, Philip broke the long-time custom that all merchants were welcome at the fairs, and decreed the exclusion of the Flemings. The result of these measures was a rapid and permanent decline of the fairs of Champagne and of the trading route over the Alps. Desperately, the Italian city-states began to reconstitute trade routes and sail around the Straits of Gibraltar to Bruges, which began to flourish even though the rest of Flanders was in decay.

It was particularly fateful that Philip the Fair inaugurated the system of regular taxation in France. Before then, there were no regular taxes. In the medieval era, while the king was supposed to be all-powerful in his own sphere, that sphere was restricted by the sanctity of private property. The king was supposed to be an armed enforcer and upholder of the law, and his revenues were supposed to derive from rents on royal lands, feudal dues and tolls. There was nothing that we would call regular taxation. In an emergency, such as an invasion or the launching of a crusade, the prince, in addition to invoking the feudal duty of fighting on his behalf, might ask his vassals for a subsidy; but that aid would be requested rather than ordered, and be limited in duration to the emergency period.

The perpetual wars of the fourteenth and the first half of the fifteenth centuries began in the 1290s, when Philip the Fair, taking advantage of King Edward I of England's war with Scotland and Wales, seized the province of Gascony from England. This launched a continuing warfare between England and Flanders on the one side, and France on the other, and led to a desperate need for funds by both the English and the French Crowns.

The merchants and capitalists at the fairs of Champagne might have money, but the largest and most tempting source for royal plunder was the Catholic Church. Both the English and French monarchs proceeded to tax the Church, which brought them into a collision course with the pope. Pope Boniface VIII (1294–1303) stoutly resisted this new form of pillage, and prohibited the monarchs from taxing the Church. King Edward reacted by denying justice in the royal courts to the Church, while Philip was more militant by prohibiting the transfer of Church revenue from France to Rome. Boniface was forced to retreat and to allow the tax, but his bull *Unam Sanctam* (1302) insisted that temporal authority must be subordinate to the spiritual. That was enough for Philip, who boldly seized the pope in Italy and prepared to try him for heresy, a trial only cut off by the death of the aged Boniface. At this point Philip the Fair seized the papacy itself, and brought the seat of the Roman Catholic Church from Rome to Avignon, where he proceeded to designate the pope himself. For virtually the entire fourteenth century, the pope, in his 'Babylonian captivity', was an abject tool of the French king; the pope only returned to Italy in the early fifteenth century.

In this way, the once mighty Catholic Church, dominant power and spiritual authority during the High Middle Ages, had been brought low and made a virtual vassal of the royal plunderer of France.

The decline of Church authority, then, was matched by the rise in the power of the absolute state. Not content with confiscating, plundering, taxing, crushing the fairs of Champagne, and bringing the Catholic Church under his heel, Philip the Fair also obtained revenue for his eternal wars by debasement of the coinage and thereby generated a secular inflation.

The wars of the fourteenth century did not cause a great deal of *direct* devastation: armies were small and hostilities were intermittent. The main devastation came from the heavy taxes and from the monetary inflation and borrowing to finance the eternal royal adventures. The enormous increase of taxation was the most crippling aspect of the wars. The expenses of war: recruitment of the modestly sized army; payments of its wages; supplies; and fortifications – all cost from two- to fourfold the ordinary expenses of the Crown. Add to that the high costs of tax assessment and enforcement and the cost of the loans, and the crippling burden of war taxation becomes all too clear.

The new taxes were everywhere. We have seen the grave effect of taxes on the Church; on a large monastic farm, they often absorbed over 40 per cent of the net profits of the farm. A uniform poll tax of one shilling, levied by the English Crown in 1380, inflicted great hardship on peasants and craftsmen. The tax amounted to one month's wages for agricultural workers and one week's wages for urban labourers; moreover, since many poor workers and peasants were paid in kind rather than money, amassing the money to pay the tax was particularly difficult.

Other new taxes levied were *ad valorem* on all transactions; taxes on wholesale and retail beverages; and levies on salt and wool. To combat evasion of the tax, the governments established monopoly markets for the sale of salt in France and 'staple points' for English wool. The taxes restricted supply and raised prices, crippling the critical English wool trade.

Production and trade were hampered further by massive requisitions levied by the kings, thus causing a drastic fall of income and wealth, as well as bankruptcies among the producers. In short, consumers suffered from artificially high prices and producers from low returns, with the king bleeding the economy of the differential. Government borrowing was scarcely more helpful, leading to repeated defaults by the kings and consequent heavy losses and bankruptcies among the private bankers unwise enough to lend to the government.

Originating as a response to wartime 'emergency', the new taxes tended to become permanent: not only because the warfare lasted for over a century, but because the state, always on the lookout for an increase in its income and power, seized upon the golden opportunity to convert wartime taxes into a permanent part of the national heritage.

From the middle to the end of the fourteenth century, Europe was struck with the devastating pandemic of the Black Death – the bubonic plague – which in the short span of 1348–50 wiped out fully one-third of the population. The Black Death was largely the consequence of people's lowered living standards caused by the great depression and the resulting loss of resistance to disease. The plague continued to recur, though not in such virulent form, in every decade of the century.

Such are the great recuperative powers of the human race that this enormous tragedy caused virtually no lasting catastrophic social or psychological effects among the European population. In a sense, the longest-lasting ill effect from the Black Death was the response of the English Crown in imposing permanent maximum wage control and compulsory labour rationing upon English society. The sudden decline of population and consequent doubling of wage rates was met by the government's severe imposition of maximum wage control in the Ordinance of 1349 and the Statue of Labourers of 1351. Maximum wage control was established at the behest of the employing classes: large, middle and small landlords, and master craftsmen, the former groups in particular alarmed at the rise of agricultural wage rates. The ordinance and the statute defied economic law by attempting to enforce maximum wage control at the old pre-plague levels. The inevitable result, however, was a grave shortage of labour, since at the statutory maximum wage the demand for labour was enormously greater than the newly scarce supply.

Every government intervention creates new problems in the course of vain attempts to solve the old. The government is then confronted with the choice: pile on new interventions to solve the inexplicable new problems, or repeal the original intervention. Government's instinct, of course, is to maximize its wealth and power by adding new interventions. So did the English Statute of Labourers, which imposed forced labour at the old wage rates for all men in

England under the age of 60; restricted the mobility of labour, declaring that the lord of a particular territory had first claim on a man's labour; and made it a criminal offence for an employer to hire a worker who had left a former master. In that way, the English government engaged in labour rationing to try to freeze labourers at their pre-plague occupations at pre-plague wages.

This forced rationing of labour cut against the natural inclination of men to leave for more employment at better wages, and so the inevitable rise of black markets for labour made enforcement of the statutes difficult. The desperate English Crown tried once again, in the Cambridge Statute of 1388, to make the rationing more rigorous. Labour mobility of any sort was prohibited without written permission from local justices, and compulsory child labour was imposed in agriculture. But there was continual evasion of this compulsory buyers' cartel, especially by large employers, who were particularly eager and able to pay higher wage rates. The cumbersome English judicial machinery was totally ineffective in enforcing the legislation, although the monopolistic urban guilds (monopolies enforced by government) were able to partially enforce wage control in the cities.

3.2 Absolutism and nominalism: the break-up of Thomism

Along with the rise of the absolute state, theories of absolutism arose and began to throw natural law doctrines into the shade. The adoption of natural law theory, after all, meant that the state was bound to limit itself to the dictates of the natural or the divine law. But new political theorists arose, asserting the dominance of the temporal over the spiritual, and of the state's positive law over the natural or divine order. The first and most influential of such late medieval champions of absolutism was Marsiglio of Padua (c.1275–1342), in his famous *Defensor Pacis* (*Defence of the peace*) (1324). The son of a Paduan lawyer, Marsiglio rose to become rector of the University of Paris. The state, opined Marsiglio, is supreme and must be obeyed in and for itself. This glorification of the state went hand in hand with a denial that human reason could come to know any natural law outside of positive edicts of the state. For Marsiglio, reason had to be separated from justice or human society. Justice has no rational foundation; it is purely mystical and solely a matter of faith. God's commands are purely arbitrary and mysterious, and not to be understood in terms of rational or ethical content.

As a corollary, positive law has nothing to do with right reason; it is promulgated to advance the 'life and health of the state'. According to Marsiglio, the nation is an organism, with the state functioning as its head. As Professor Rothkrug writes, 'Marsiglio says the state is a living organism not subject to reason because, like a plant, it develops in accord with inborn impulses'.[2]

The practical conclusion Marsiglio derived from his political philosophy is that the state, whether kingdom or Italian city-republic, must have absolute power within its domain, and must not be subject to any temporal check or jurisdiction by the Church. Thus, while religiously a Catholic, Marsiglio anticipated the *politiques* in France and elsewhere two centuries later by insisting that the Church may have no temporal power as against the state. Marsiglio thereby foreshadowed and helped to bring about the break-up of the medieval order in Europe.

Also destructive of the achievements of the High Middle Ages was the ideological break-up of Thomism ushered in by the fourteenth century. This decline emerged out of Franciscan fideism, begun by St Thomas's great English rival John Duns Scotus. It used to be thought that this destruction was brought to a logical conclusion by the fourteenth century Franciscan Oxford philosopher William of Ockham (c.1290–1350). Ockhamite nominalism, it has been held, denied the power of human reason to arrive at the essential truths about man and the universe, and therefore negated the power of reason to arrive at a systematic ethic for man. Only God's will, discernible by faith in revelation, could yield truths, laws, or ethics. It should be clear that nominalism paved the way for modern scepticism and positivism, for if faith in divine will is abandoned, reason no longer has the power to arrive at scientific or ethical truths. Politically, nominalism failed to provide a natural law standard to set against the state, and it therefore fitted with the growing state absolutism of the Renaissance.

Recent scholarship, however, casts grave doubt on whether Ockham and his followers were really nominalists or were rather essentialists and believers in natural law. Thus, it turns out that the eminent Augustinian contemporary of Ockham, the Italian Gregory of Rimini (d.1358) was not really a nominalist but a staunch champion of essentialism, reason and natural law. In contrast to the usual view of Ockham and his followers, Gregory held that natural law comes not from God's will but from the dictates of right reason, and he even went further towards an all-out rationalist position generally thought to have been invented three centuries later by the Dutch Protestant philosopher and jurist Hugo Grotius. This position held that, even if God did not exist, the system of natural law would be given to us by the dictates of right reason, the violation of which would still be a sin. Thus, as Gregory put it: 'If, *per impossibile*, the divine reason, or God himself did not exist, or that that reason were mistaken, still if one were to act against right reason, angelic, human or any other if such there be, he would sin'.

3.3   Utility and money: Buridan and Oresme

Being a Franciscan and a student of William of Ockham did not prevent the great French philosopher–scientist Jean Buridan de Bethune (1300–58), born in Picardy, to become rector of the University of Paris, from making the next important contribution to economic thought in the essentialist Thomist tradition. In his *Quaestiones*, a thorough commentary on Aristotle's *Ethics*, Buridan continued the Aristotle–Thomas analysis of the exchange value of goods being determined by consumer need or utility. But Buridan also pressed on to point out that a house would never exchange for one garment, since the builder would have to forego a year's worth of food for a much less valuable good. In short, Buridan was groping towards an opportunity-cost concept of cost of production and influence on supply.

More importantly, Buridan advanced beyond the initiative of Richard of Middleton in analysing the mutual benefit that each party necessarily derives from an exchange. In discussing exchange, Buridan notes that both parties benefit, and that trade is not, as many people believe, a type of warfare in which one party benefits at the expense of another. Furthermore, Buridan proceeds to a sophisticated analysis in which he dramatically shows that two parties to a two-good exchange can both benefit even if the exchange is itself immoral and is to be condemned on ethical or theological grounds. Thus Buridan poses the rather provocative hypothetical:

> Because Socrates gave his wife willingly and with her consent to Plato to commit adultery in exchange for ten books, which one of them suffered a loss and which one gained? ... Both suffered injury as far as their soul was concerned...[but] with regard to the external good, each gained since he has more than he needs.

For Buridan as for most other scholastics, the just price was the market price. Buridan also provided a sophisticated analysis of how common human need and utility resulted in market prices. The greater the need and hence the greater the demand, the greater the value; also, a reduction in the supply of a product will cause its price on the market to rise. Furthermore, a good is more expensive where it is *not* produced than where it is, since there is a greater demand for it in the former place; again, the marginal concept is all that is needed to complete the analysis of demand, supply and price. There are also intimations in Buridan of different valuations by market participants resulting in a single price, with varying consumer and producer psychic surpluses for each participant.

But the main great leap forward in economics contributed by Jean Buridan was his virtual creation of the modern theory of money. Aristotle had analysed the advantages of money, and its overcoming of the double-coincidence-of-wants problem of barter, but his outlook was clouded by his fundamental hostility to trade and money-making. To Aristotle, therefore, money was not natural but an artificial convention, and therefore basically a creature of the state or *polis*. Aquinas's theory of money was basically confined within the Aristotelian shackles. It was Jean Buridan who broke free of those shackles and founded the 'metallist' or commodity theory of money, i.e. that money originates naturally as a useful commodity on the market, and that the market will pick the medium of exchange, almost always a metal if available, possessing the best qualities to serve as a money.

Money then, for Buridan, is a market commodity, and the value of that money, just as in the case of other market commodities, 'must be measured by human need'. Just as the values of exchangeable goods 'are proportionate to human need, so they will be proportionate to money, itself proportionate to human need'. Thus, Buridan remarkably set the agenda for determining the value or price of money, on the same principles of utility that determine the market prices of goods: an agenda which would only be fulfilled six centuries later in 1912 by the Austrian Ludwig von Mises, in his *Theory of Money and Credit*.

Foreshadowing the Austrians Menger and von Mises, Buridan insisted that an effectively functioning money must be composed of a material possessing a value independent of its role as money, i.e. it must consist of a market commodity originally useful for non-monetary purposes. Buridan then went on to catalogue those qualities that lead the market to choose a commodity as a medium of exchange or money, such as portability, high value per unit weight, divisibility and durability – qualities possessed most strikingly by the precious metals gold and silver. In that way, Buridan began the classification of monetary qualities of commodities which was to constitute the first chapter of countless money and banking textbooks down to the end of the gold standard era in the 1930s.

Thus, not only did Jean Buridan found the theory of money as a market phenomenon; he thereby took money out of the mystique of being solely a creation of the state, and put it on a par with other goods as a product of the marketplace.

A not very happy modern spin-off of Buridan's theory of volition emerged in the 1930s as part of the indifference curve analysis. Buridan postulated a perfectly rational ass who found himself equidistant between two equally attractive bundles of hay. Indifferent between the two choices and therefore unable to choose, the perfectly rational ass could choose neither and thereby starved to death. What this example overlooked is that there is a third choice, which presumably the ass liked the least: starving to death. So that it was therefore 'perfectly rational' *not* to starve to death but rather to choose one of the two bundles even at random (and then to proceed to the second bundle).[3]

Until recent years, conventional texts on the history of economic thought, if they dealt with anyone at all before the mercantilists or Adam Smith, briefly mentioned only two people: St Thomas Aquinas and Nicole Oresme (1325–82). Although Oresme, a noted French mathematician, astronomer and physicist, was one of the most important European intellectuals of the fourteenth century, his contributions to economic thought scarcely deserve such exclusive attention. Oresme was a pupil and follower of Jean Buridan, a scholastic commenting on Aristotle and teaching in his turn at the University of Paris and going on to become bishop of Lisieux. Oresme was moved to write his well-known booklet, *A Treatise on the Origin, Nature, Law and Alterations of Money*, in the 1350s, applying the teachings of his hard-money mentor to the rash of monetary debasements indulged in by the kings of France in the first half of the fourteenth century. In the centuries before paper money and central banking were founded in the late seventeenth century, the only way in which kings could gain revenue through monetary manipulation was by debasement – changing the definition of the money unit by lightening its weight in terms of the basic money, gold or silver. If, for example, the money unit had been defined as 10 ounces of silver, the government could use its monopoly of the coinage to redefine the money unit as 9 silver ounces, and then pocket the difference in the course of recoinage. The extra ounces would be employed to mint new coins for the king to use in wars, for the building of palaces, and for other allegedly worthy causes.

The British currency unit, the pound sterling, got its name centuries ago by originally being defined as simply one pound of silver. The process of debasement in Britain has proceeded so far that the 'pound' is now equal to less than $1/4$ a silver ounce.

Before the advent of paper money and central banking, then, debasement was the only process by which the ruler could alter the currency to create a greater supply of money (in terms of the money unit), and thereby cause price inflation. The king was able to use his compulsory monopoly of the coinage to manipulate repeated debasements for his own gain at the expense of the rest of the public.

Oresme's most important contribution to monetary theory was to enunciate clearly, for the first time, what came to be known as 'Gresham's law', that is, the insight that if two or more moneys are legally fixed in relative value by the government, then the money overvalued by the government will drive the undervalued money out of circulation. Thus if the government decrees that, say, 1 ounce of gold is legally worth 10 ounces of silver, whereas on the free market it is worth 15, the people will stick their creditors and vendors with the legally overvalued money (silver–the 'bad' money) while they hoard the undervalued (gold – the 'good' money) or export it out of the country where it can be sold at its market value. Gresham's law has often been boiled down in common parlance into: 'bad money drives out good', but stated that way it is paradoxical and unsatisfying. For it implies that while in all other market products the good will outcompete the bad, there is some deep flaw in the free market that causes it to prefer good *money* to bad. But as Ludwig von Mises clarified in the early twentieth century, Gresham's law is the product not of the free market but of government monetary control. Its fixing of relative money value is a special case of the general consequence of any price control, i.e. shortage of a good in which maximum prices are imposed, and a 'surplus' where a minimum price is enforced. In the case of money, in our example, gold suffers a maximum price control and therefore a shortage, while the value of silver is kept up artificially and therefore goes into surplus relative to gold.

The first formulation of Gresham's law was that of the satiric ancient Greek playwright, Aristophanes, who, in *The Frogs*, states characteristically: 'In our Republic bad citizens are preferred to good, just as bad money circulates while good money disappears'.[4] Oresme, however, put the law in a cogent and correct manner, emphasizing that the monetary disruption is a function of government price-fixing: 'if the fixed legal ratio of the coins differs from the market value of the metals, the coin which is underrated entirely disappears from circulation, and the coin which is overrated alone remains current'.

In his *Treatise*, Nicole Oresme was moved to apply his mentor Buridan's metallist monetary theory to attack the debasement policy of the French kings. Oresme did not go so far as to denounce the king's coinage monopoly *per se*, but he did accomplish the feat of taking the whole matter out of the kings' carefully propounded mystique of 'sovereignty', converting the entire coinage question to a matter of practical convenience. Since the king was not entitled to cloak coinage in the mystique of royal prerogative and absolute royal will, he was duty-bound to govern according to the best interests of the community. He is therefore obliged to maintain the standards of weight and of coinage; frequent alterations in such standards 'destroy respect and breed "scandal and murmuring among the people and risk of disobedience"'. The definition of the currency unit should therefore be a fixed ordinance. Frequent alterations and debasements, Oresme pointed out, will cause money and coins to lose their character as measures of value; and internal and external trade will be crippled. Foreign merchants will be repelled, since they will no longer have good, safe money to work with, while domestic traders will no longer have any firm means of communication. Money could no longer be loaned out safely, and there would be no way of correctly valuing money incomes.

Furthermore, since debased money will have a lower value at home, gold or silver will be sent abroad where they will now have a higher market value. Thus Oresme was perhaps the first to point out that money will tend to flow to those areas and countries where its value is highest, and to leave those countries where its value is lowest.

Nicole Oresme had no illusions about the reasons for the kings' repeated debasements. As Oresme put it: if the king 'should tell the tyrant's usual lie that he applies the profit from debasement to the public advantage, he must not be believed, because he might as well take my coat and say he needed it for the public service'.

Oresme also adds to Buridan's analysis of how commodities become money on the market: he stresses easy portability, and that it should be of high value per unit weight. He also points out that after a period of gold or silver being weighed out in precise quantities for each transaction, people started to coin the precious metals, with an inscription and a head on the coin to guarantee a certain quantity of gold or silver in each coin. Gold, being a more valuable money, will generally be used for larger transactions, while silver and even copper may be used for smaller purchases.

3.4   The odd man out: Heinrich von Langenstein

One nominalist and student of Buridan, Heinrich von Langenstein the Elder (also known as Henry of Hesse) (1325–97), while an uninfluential and minor scholastic philosopher in his own and later centuries, made great mischief for modern interpretations of the history of economic thought. Langenstein, who taught first at the University of Paris and then at Vienna, began in his *Treatise on Contracts* by analysing the just price in the mainstream scholastic manner: just price is the market price, which is a rough measure of the human needs of consumers. This price will be the outcome of individuals' calculations about their wants and values, and these in turn will be affected by the relative lack or abundance of supply, as well as by the scarcity or abundance of buyers.

Having said this, Langenstein proceeded to contradict himself completely. In a highly unfortunate contribution to the history of economic thought, Langenstein urged local government authorities to step in and fix prices. Price-fixing would somehow be a better path to the just price than the interplay of the market. Other scholastics had not exactly opposed price-fixing; for them, the market price was just whether it was set by the common estimate of the market or by the government. But it was at least implicit in their writings that the free market was a better (or at the very least an equally good) path to discovering the just price. Langenstein was unique in positively advocating government price-fixing.

Moreover, Langenstein added another economic heresy. He counselled the authorities to fix the price so that each seller, whether merchant or craftsman, could maintain his status or station in life in the society. The just price was the price which maintained everyone's position in the style to which he had become accustomed – no more and no less. If a seller tried to charge a price to advance beyond his station, he was guilty of the sin of avarice.

Langenstein was the odd man out among the scholastics and late medieval thinkers. No one has been found to second the 'station in life' concept of the just price. Indeed St Thomas Aquinas himself effectively demolished this view when he trenchantly declared

> In a just exchange the medium does not vary with the social position of the persons involved, but only with regard to the quantity of the goods. For instance, whoever buys a thing must pay what the thing is worth whether he buys from a pauper or a rich man.

In short, on the market prices are the same to all, rich or poor, and furthermore this is a just method of establishing prices. In the bizarre Langenstein view, of course, a wealthy seller of the same product would be obliged to sell it for a far higher price than a poor seller, in which case it is unlikely that the wealthy man would last long in the business.

As far as can be determined, no medieval or renaissance thinker adopted the station in life theory, and only two followers adopted the price-fixing position. One was Matthew of Cracow (c.1335–1410), professor of theology at Prague and later rector at the University of Heidelberg and archbishop of Worms, and particularly Jean de Gerson (1363–1429), nominalist and French mystic who was chancellor of the University of Paris. Gerson, however, ignored the station in life notion and reverted to the thirteenth century view of John Duns Scotus that the just price is the cost of production plus compensation for labour and risk incurred by the supplier. Gerson therefore urged that the government fix prices to force them to conform to the allegedly just price. Indeed, Gerson was a fanatic on price-fixing, advocating that it be extended from its customary sphere in wheat, bread, meat, wine and beer, to embrace all commodities whatsoever. Fortunately, Gerson's view also had little influence.

Von Langenstein was scarcely important in his own or at a later day; his great importance is solely that he was plucked out of well-deserved obscurity by late nineteenth century socialist and state corporatist historians, who used his station in life fatuity to conjure up a totally distorted vision of the Catholic Middle Ages. That era, so the myth ran, was solely governed by the view that each man can only charge the just price to maintain him in his presumably divinely appointed station in life. In that way, these historians glorified a non-existent society of status in which each person and group found himself in a harmonious hierarchical structure, undisturbed by market relations or capitalist greed. This nonsensical view of the Middle Ages and of scholastic doctrine was first propounded by German socialist and state corporatist historians Wilhelm Roscher and Werner Sombart in the late nineteenth century, and it was then seized upon by such influential writers as the Anglican Socialist Richard Henry Tawney and the Catholic corporatist scholar and politician Amintore Fanfani. Finally, this view, based only on the doctrines of one obscure and heterodox scholastic, was enshrined in conventional histories of economic thought, where it was seconded by the free market but fanatically anti-Catholic economist Frank Knight and his followers in the now highly influential Chicago School.

The much-needed corrective to the older view has at last become dominant since World War II, led by the enormous prestige of Joseph Schumpeter and by the definitive research of Raymond de Roover.

3.5 Usury and foreign exchange in the fourteenth century

The charging of interest on a loan continued to be condemned totally as usury by the mainstream of scholastic writing: only a minority followed Cardinal Hostiensis and Olivi in allowing *lucrum cessans* – return on investment foregone – and then only for a charitable loan and not for professional money-lenders. Foreign exchange transactions fared no better, the mainstream of scholastics, including St Thomas, simply condemning them outright as usurers and as trying to charge interest on barren money.

By the thirteenth and fourteenth century, however, bills of exchange were coming into prominence as credit instruments, particularly in foreign exchange dealings. Sophisticated forms of foreign exchange transactions developed, in which dealers could charge and pay interest on credit, but such transactions were formally disguised as purchases or sales of foreign currencies. Again, most scholastics continued to condemn exchange dealings, but a courageous minority arose during the fourteenth century to champion these now pervasive transactions, in which the Church itself had for a long time been engaged. It started weakly with Aquinas's chief personal disciple, Giles of Lessines, who while confused about the foreign exchange market, did speak of risk as justifying these credit transactions and also showed that the exchange dealer gives something of 'more utility' to his customer than what the customer pays, entitling him to an extra charge.

The main defence of the foreign exchange market was launched by the distinguished Franciscan Alexander Bonini, also known as Alexander of Alexandria or Alexander Lombard. Bonini had an academic career at the University of Paris, then lectured at the papal court in theology, and finally served as the Franciscan provincial in his native Lombardy, the site of the most notorious usurers of the day. In his *Treatise on Usury*, a lecture given at Genoa in 1307, Alexander, while attacking usury in the usual way, presented a thoroughgoing defence of the foreign exchange transactions with which he was familiar. Attacking the Aristotelians, Alexander pointed out that money cannot have only one function, of serving as a barren medium of exchange, since there are many coins and these coins must be exchanged. The value of the coins thus traded, furthermore, is properly determined not by law but by the weight and the content of the coins. Alexander also adopted Giles of Lessines's insight that the dealer provides more utility to his customer than he receives in the money transactions. As for credit transactions in foreign exchange, Alexander Lombard did not defend them all, but provided a *lucrum cessans* defence for the changes in the value of a money between the beginning and the end of the transaction. Indeed, Alexander was one of the first to point out that the demand for money can and does vary over time, giving rise to changes in the value of money. *Lucrum cessans* provided the entering wedge for the scholastic justification of the main method by which the usury prohibition was evaded during and after the High Middle Ages.

It is illuminating that Alexander had begun his defence with the practical point that 'the Church always condemns and pursues usurers, but it does not condemn and pursue the exchange dealers, but, rather, fosters them as is apparent in the Roman Church'.

Alexander Lombard's defence of the foreign exchange market was repeated verbatim by his disciple and successor as Franciscan provincial of Lombardy: Astesanus (d. 1330). Astesanus, like his mentor, came from Lombardy, specifically from Asti, one of the principal locations of the leading international usurers. His main work was his *Summa* (1317). Like his predecessor, Astesanus was impressed by the fact that 'the Roman Church fosters the exchange dealers'. Furthermore, he adds to Alexander's reasoning a frank defence of *lucrum cessans*, which he was one of the first theologians, as distinct from canonists, to embrace.

Among the prominent fourteenth century writers we have already discussed, Heinrich von Langenstein, as we might expect, denounced all foreign exchange dealers as usurers *per se*. Even Nicole Oresme simply repeated the Aristotelian shibboleth that the trade of money for money is unnatural because money is barren. While not precisely declaring exchange transactions to be usurious *per se*, Oresme, in a flight of hate, denounced foreign exchange as 'vile', as an occupation that stains the soul just as cleaning sewers stains the body.

In contrast, however, Jean Buridan, Oresme's mentor, engaged in a defence of foreign exchange, distinguishing two kinds of exchange, one where the dealer 'gets only as much as he gives' – perfectly worthy according to the Aristotelian–Thomist tradition – and another where the dealer 'takes more than he gives'. But here Buridan makes another might leap in tearing down some of the irrational barriers that the scholastics had drawn up against monetary transactions. For even the latter kind of transaction, declared Buridan, may be legitimate, even if there is no equivalent in exchange, provided the exchange promotes the 'common good'. While not used for ordinary usury, Buridan's new concept sowed the seeds for total justification of the foreign exchange bankers.

At the turn of the fifteenth century, a thoroughgoing defence of exchange contracts was set forth by the sophisticated Florentine lay canon lawyer Lorenzo di Antonio Ridolfi (1360–1442). Ridolfi was a lecturer at the Athenaeum in Florence and was at one time ambassador of the Florentine Republic. Just as Lombard was unwilling to condemn a practice encouraged by the Church, so Ridolfi declared his unwillingness to condemn an occupation pervasive in his native Florence. Developing the insight of Lombard, Ridolfi, in his 1403 treatise on usury, emphasized that the value of money can differ from one place to another as well as over time. These differences are the result of changes in the demand for money, fluctuations of the demand relative to the supply, and alterations in the metallic content of the coinage. These variations justify foreign exchange dealings as well as credit transactions within them. Thus, Ridolfi developed the theory which showed that the value of money, like any other commodity, is determined by the interactions of its demand and supply, and that it too can vary in value over time and place.

3.6 The worldly ascetic: San Bernardino of Siena

The great mind, and the great systematizer, of scholastic economics was a paradox among paradoxes: a strict and ascetic Franciscan saint living and writing in the midst of the sophisticated capitalist world of early fifteenth century Tuscany. While St Thomas Aquinas was the systematizer of the entire range of intellectual endeavour, his economic insights were scattered in fragments throughout his theological writings. San Bernardino of Siena (1380–1444) was the first theologian after Olivi to write an entire work systematically devoted to scholastic economics. Much of this advanced thought was contributed by San Bernardino himself, and the highly advanced subjective utility theory was cribbed word for word from the Franciscan heretic of two centuries earlier: Pierre de Jean Olivi.

San Bernardino's book, written as a set of Latin sermons, was entitled *On Contracts and Usury*, and was composed during the years 1431–33. The treatise began, quite logically, with the institution and justification of the system of private property, proceeded to the system and the ethics of trade, and continued to discuss the determination of value and price on the market. In ended with a lengthy discussion of the tangled usury question.

San Bernardino's chapter on private property was nothing remarkable. Property was considered artificial rather than natural, but still vital for an efficient economic order. One of Bernardino's great contributions, however, was the fullest and most cogent discussion yet penned on the functions of the business entrepreneur. In the first place, the merchant was given an even cleaner bill of health than had been given by Aquinas. Sensibly, and in contrast to early doctrines, San Bernardino pointed out that trade, like all other occupations, could be practised either licitly or unlawfully. *All* callings, including that of a bishop, provide occasions for sin; these are scarcely limited to trade. More specifically, merchants can perform several kinds of useful service: transporting commodities from surplus to scarce regions and countries; preserving and storing goods to be available when the consumers want them; and, as craftsmen or industrial entrepreneurs, transforming raw materials into finished products. In short, the businessman can perform the useful social function of transporting, distributing, or manufacturing goods.

In his justification of trade, San Bernardino finally managed to rehabilitate the lowly retailer, who had been scorned ever since ancient Greece. Importers and wholesalers, Bernardino pointed out, buy in large quantities and then break bulk by selling by the bale or load to retailers, who in turn sell in minute quantities to consumers.

Realistically, Bernardino did not condemn profits; on the contrary, profits were a legitimate return to the entrepreneur for his labour, expenses and the risks that he undertakes.

San Bernardino then goes into his trenchant analysis of the functions of the entrepreneur. Managerial ability, he realized, is a rare combination of competence and efficiency, and therefore commands a large return. San Bernardino lists four necessary qualifications for the successful entrepreneur: efficiency or diligence (*industria*), responsibility (*solicitudo*), labour (*labores*), and assumption of risks (*pericula*). Efficiency for Bernardino meant being well-informed about prices, costs, and qualities of the product, and being 'subtle' in assessing risks and profit opportunities, which, Bernardino shrewdly observed, 'indeed very few are capable of doing'. Responsibility meant being attentive to detail and also keeping good accounts, a necessary item in business. Trouble, toil, and even personal hardships are also often essential. For all these reasons, and for the risk incurred, the businessman properly earns enough on successful investments to keep him in business and compensate him for all his hardships.

On determination of value, San Bernardino continued in the mainstream scholastic tradition, with value and the just price being determined by the common estimation of the market. Price will fluctuate in accordance with supply, rising if supply is scarce and falling if abundant. Bernardino also has a penetrating discussion of the influence of cost. Cost of labour, skill and risk do not affect price directly, but will affect the supply of a commodity, and *ceteris paribus* (other things being equal – a phrase used by San Bernardino) things requiring greater effort or ingenuity to produce will be more expensive and command a higher price. This insight prefigures the Jevons/Austrian analysis of supply and cost over five centuries later.

As in the case of other scholastics, the common estimation of the market was held to be the common market price (but *not* a price set by individual free bargaining). The government was considered able to fix a common market price by compulsory regulation, but this possibility, as in the case of most other scholastics, was dismissed quickly.

As we have seen, San Bernardino took over word for word the remarkable subjective utility theory of value published (and previously neglected) by the

Franciscan Pierre de Jean Olivi. Bernardino's significant contribution to the theory of the just-as-market price was to apply it to the 'just wage'. Wages are the price of labour services, Bernardino pointed out, and therefore the just, or market wage will be determined by the demand for labour and the available supply of labour on the market. Wage inequality is a function of differences of skill, ability and training. An architect is paid more than a ditch-digger, Bernardino explained, because the former's job requires more intelligence, ability and training, so that fewer men will qualify for the task. Skilled workers are scarcer than unskilled, so that the former will command a higher wage.

In a sophisticated discussion of foreign exchange, Bernardino put his *imprimatur* on transactions that were the dominant way in which hidden interest was charged for a credit transaction. Here, Bernardino followed the latitudinarian view of his master Alexander Lombard. Generally, exchange transactions were conversions of currencies and not loans. Furthermore, usury was only a certain and riskless interest on a loan; foreign exchange rates fluctuated and were therefore unpredictable. This was technically true, but generally lenders received interest on exchange transactions, since the money market was structured to favour the lender in this way. Bernardino also pointed out that conversion of currencies was necessary because of the great diversity of currencies, and because the coinage of one country was not acceptable elsewhere. The money-exchangers, therefore, performed a useful function by enabling foreign trade, 'which is essential to the support of human life', and by transferring funds from one country to another without requiring the actual shipping of specie.

San Bernardino of Siena was a fascinating and paradoxical combination of brilliant, knowledgeable, and appreciative analyst of the capitalist market of his day, and an emaciated ascetic saint fulminating against worldly evils and business practices. Bernardino was born in 1380 to a high official of Siena; his father, Albertollo degli Albizzeschi, was governor of the town of Massa for the Republic of Siena. Bernardino's mother also belonged to a prominent local family. Joining the strictly ascetic order of the Observant Franciscans, Bernardino soon became noted as a persuasive and highly popular travelling orator, preaching throughout northern and central Italy. In the 1430s, Bernardino was appointed vicar general of the Observant Franciscans. Three times in his lifetime, San Bernardino was offered bishoprics (in Siena, Urbino and Ferrara), and each time he refused this honour, since he would have had to give up his preaching.

Some of Bernardino's anti-worldly preaching dwelt on problems of personal morality; thus, he deplored the practice of travelling merchants staying away from home for long periods, and then defiling themselves by living in carnal sin or even sodomy, which the saint habitually referred to as 'filth'.

Indeed, in his youth, Bernardino punched a man who had made homosexual overtures.

But Bernardino's main contradiction between sophisticated analyst of business and denouncer of business practice lay in his fulmination against usury. Surrounded by the home of usury in Tuscany, San Bernardino, in common with so many scholastics, found that realism stopped short at the usury door. On the usury question, the saint's brilliant analysis and benign view of the free market failed him, and he fulminated almost in a frenzy: usury was a vile infection, permeating business and social life. Whereas other scholastics had taken seriously the objection that Church and society depended upon usury, Bernardino did not care. No: it could not be. All those holding that usury was economically necessary were committing the sin of blasphemy, since they would therefore be saying that God had bound them to an impossible course of action. Abolish the charge of interest, Bernardino opined, and people would then lend freely and gratuitously; and besides far too much is being borrowed now, for frivolous and vicious purposes. Usury, the saint thundered, destroys charity; it is a contagious disease; it stains the souls of all in society; it concentrates all the money of the city into a few hands or drives it out of the country; and what is more, it justly brings the wrath of God upon the city, and invites the Four Horsemen of the Apocalypse.

One can only stand in awe at the fury of unreason in which this truly great thinker indulged himself on the usury issue. Ranting about the usurer daring to 'sell time', Bernardino went further than his predecessors in insisting that only Jesus Christ 'knows the time and the hour. If therefore it is not ours to know the time, much less is it ours to sell it'. Is keeping watches and clocks therefore a mortal sin? Bernardino winds up in a fit of almost hysterical frenzy at the hapless usurer:

> Accordingly, all the saints and all the angels of paradise cry then against him [the usurer], saying 'To hell, to hell, to hell.' Also the heavens with their stars cry out, saying, 'To the fire, to the fire, to the fire.' The planets also clamor, 'To the depths, to the depths, to the depths.'

And yet, despite all this, San Bernardino added his great weight to the concept that would eventually scuttle the usury prohibition: *lucrum cessans*. Following Hostiensis and a minority of fourteenth century scholastics, Bernardino admits *lucrum cessans*: it was all right to charge interest on a loan which would be the return sacrificed – the opportunity foregone – for a legitimate investment. It is true that Bernardino, like his predecessors, limited *lucrum cessans* strictly to a charitable loan, and refused to apply it to professional money-lenders. But he made an important analytic advance by explaining that *lucrum cessans* is legitimate because in that situation money is not simply barren money but 'capital'. As Bernardino put it, when a businessman lends from balances which would have gone into commercial investment, he 'gives not money in its simple character, but he also gives his capital'. More fully, he writes that money then 'has not only the character of mere money or a mere thing, but also beyond this, a certain seminal character of something profitable, which we commonly call capital. Therefore, not only must its simple value be returned, but a super-added value as well'.

In short, when money functions as capital, it is no longer barren or sterile; as capital it deserves to command a profit.

There is something more. In the course of lengthy arguing against hidden usury in various forms of contracts, the brilliant mind of San Bernardino stumbles, for one of the first times in history, upon what later would be called 'time-preference': that people prefer present goods to future goods (i.e. the present prospect of goods in the future). But he failed to recognize its importance, and dismissed the point. It was left to the late eighteenth century Frenchman Turgot and then to the great Austrian economist Eugen von Böhm-Bawerk to discover the principle in the 1880s and hence finally solve the age-old problem of explaining and justifying the existence and height of the rate of interest.

3.7 The disciple: Sant'Antonino of Florence

San Bernardino's major disciple was the highly influential and slightly younger Sant'Antonino of Florence (1389–1459). Much of Antonino's influence came from his prolific writings, especially his enormous Thomistic *Summa Moralis Theologiae* (1449), the first treatise in the new science of moral theology. In moral theology, or casuistry, the theologian takes the abstract principles of theology and ethics and applies them to the detailed empirical data of daily life: in short, theology and morality were brought from the abstractions of the study and applied to the details of everyday life.

Sant'Antonino's pioneering *Summa* of moral theology proved to be extraordinarily influential. It was frequently consulted for the next 150 years, and went through 24 printings in that period. His shorter *Confessionals* (1440), a guidebook for confessors, was reprinted 30 times in the same century and a half.

There are striking parallels in the lives and personalities of Antonino and his master Bernardino. Sant'Antonino was born the son of a minor official, the notary of Florence, Ser Niccolo de Pierozzo dei Forciglioni. The son's first name was Antonio, but he was universally called by the diminutive Antonino because of his short stature, and the nickname is listed in the official Church calendar of saints. Although in frail health, Antonino early joined the strict, Observant branch of the Dominican Order. His administrative talents were unusual and spotted quickly, and he soon became prior of the Dominican friary of Cortona, and was then transferred to similar posts in Naples and Rome. After that, Antonino was appointed vicar-general of the Dominican friaries of Lombardy in 1433, and four years later, also of all central and southern Italy. In addition to his vicarate, Antonino continued as prior of San Marco in Florence.

In 1445, Pope Eugene IV appointed Sant'Antonino to the archbishopric of Florence, possibly on the advice of the great Renaissance painter, Fra Angelico. A humble man, Antonino followed Bernardino in stubbornly refusing to accept the post. The pope issued stern commands for Antonino to accept, and the story of a contemporary asserts that he only took the office under penalty of excommunication. In any event, Sant'Antonino refused for the rest of his life to wear episcopal robes and continued to wear the white habit and black cloak of a simple Dominican friar. Ironically, upon his death in 1459, Antonino was buried in full pomp and ceremony.

Despite his reluctance, Antonino became a distinguished administrator and judge, daily making countless economic decisions. In Florence he became steeped in knowledge of the financial and economic practices of the most advanced capitalist centre of his day.

Sant'Antonino is habitually bracketed with Bernardino as two great scholastic thinkers and economists. But Antonino was merely a popularizer and casuist; in his analysis he simply repeated the views of the truly great and creative thinker, San Bernardino. Both men were thoroughly familiar with the economic practices of their day, and Antonino came from Florence, the great banking centre of Europe. Yet both men were humble ascetics, and the same tension and contradiction of worldly asceticism appeared in their works and lives.

Generally, Antonino simply repeated Bernardino's analysis. In his discussion of value theory, however, Antonino further stressed Aquinas's crucial point that any exchange on the market is for the mutual benefit of both parties, since each is better off than he was before. A voluntary sale is a just one. And yet, Antonino seems more sympathetic than his mentor to government price regulation which, where it exists, must be morally binding. Any black market price over a legal maximum is a sin.

On the just wage, Antonino echoes Bernardino and adds material based on his extensive knowledge of the great Florentine woollen industry. The wage of a labourer is properly determined by common market estimation, and any attempt to form a union of workers would be harmful interference. This view implicitly endorsed the Florentine practice of outlawing wool-worker unions as unlawful 'conspiracies'. The monopolistic Wool Guild of clothiers, however, was legal; not surprisingly, since it controlled the government of Florence. The word 'guild' does not appear in Antonino's work on labour conditions; perhaps he felt it more prudent to ignore this controversial issue.

Despite the discipleship, there were definite though subtle differences between the two worldly saints. Even though Antonino was more knowledgeable of the business world, he was, paradoxically, considerably more moralistic. Thus, one of Antonino's numerous works was a pamphlet, *On Women's Fashions* (*De ornate mulierum*), in which he fulminated at great length against women's use of rouge, false hair, fancy hairdos, and other fripperies. His talent for moralism was of course reinforced by his pioneering work in casuistry. Likewise he sounded off on artists, condemning all except religious art, especially exempting the work of his friend, Fra Angelico. Antonino was particularly upset because paintings of non-religious subjects gave artists the opportunity to depict nude women, 'not for the sake of beauty but to arouse libidinous feelings'. (Antonino *did* make the intelligent observation, however, that the price of paintings is determined by the artist's skill rather than by the amount of labour involved.) Antonino's censorious views also reached into music, where he called for going back to the austere Gregorian chant and eliminating the sinful introduction of counterpoint and popular and even lewd ballads.

In more strictly economic concerns, Antonino's heightened moralism was also evident. In contrast to his master, Antonino largely fulminated against foreign exchange transactions as implicit usury. As Raymond de Roover wonderingly remarks: 'This advice, if followed, would have abolished banking altogether, a rather strange attitude on the part of the archbishop of the leading banking center in Western Europe. Most of the theologians were more lenient, although less consistent...'[5]

Antonino's ranting against usury was fully as exuberant as Bernardino's, and was heightened by the fact that he served as the Apostolic commissary for the repression of usury in Tuscany. Antonino is the all-out denouncer of usury, drawing together all possible arguments with their most severe interpretation. As Professor Noonan states,

> ...by being more systematic, Antonino is more severe than many of his predecessors...Antonino draws together all the strict rules of the early usury teaching into a tight set of rules. No later writer of note will be as severe, as uncompromising, as true to the logic of the earlier conceptions as he.[6]

Furthermore, Antonino took no back seat to Bernardino in his hysterical ranting against usury. Usury is 'diabolic'; it is the great harlot of Apocalypse 17, 'who sitteth upon many waters, with whom the kings of the earth have committed fornication'. Not only direct usurers but all who cooperate in usury are 'worthy of eternal death'. Usury, to Antonino, is a worse sin than adultery or murder because it continues on and on, whereas the former sins are only intermittent. The usurer is in a state of 'perpetual sin'. Not only that: usury damns the heirs of the sinner, since the sin is not wiped out until the usurer or his estate makes restitution by giving back the interest charge. Usury, to Antonino, is everywhere, all-pervasive.

And yet Antonino, too, admits *lucrum cessans* as a legitimate source of an interest charge. He is so worried about hint of usury, however, that he declares that in practice *lucrum cessans* must never be advised.

Tragically, the subjective theory of utility, developed by Pierre de Jean Olivi in the thirteenth century, rediscovered by San Bernardino two centuries later, and spread far and wide by his disciple Sant'Antonino, died with the worldly Florentine saint. With minor exceptions, even the late Spanish scholastics of the sixteenth century, so much in the Thomist and utility tradition, did not regain these heights. It was left to the Austrian School of the late nineteenth century to independently replicate and go beyond the subjective theory of value of Olivi, and it was left to the 1950s for this line of scholastic thought to be rediscovered.

3.8   The Swabian liberals and the assault on the prohibition of usury

At about the same time that San Bernardino was developing his great work, a relatively obscure German Dominican was independently setting forth a similar analysis. Johannes Nider (1380–1438) was a Swabian who taught theology at the University of Vienna, and led a reform of the Dominican Order in southern Germany. Nider's brief treatise, *On the Contracts of Merchants* (*De Contractibus Mercantorum*) was written about 1430, and published posthumously in Cologne about 1468; it was reprinted frequently for the rest of the fifteenth century.

Nider begins by justifying the profits of merchants. Recognizing the entrepreneurial role of the merchant, Nider stressed that trade requires market knowledge, and securing that knowledge requires industry, diligence and luck. Business incomes are justified by expenses, care and risks. In analysing market price, Nider emphasizes subjective utility as the determinant. Nider, like Olivi and Bernardino, distinguished between the objective utility inherent in a good, and subjective utility, the status of that good 'in the estimation of men'. Nider was clear that only the latter decisively determined the just market price. Anticipating Jevons four centuries later, Nider suggests that a change in supply will alter price by changing the utility assigned to it. That common market price determines the just price is clear in Nider: 'The proper value of a thing depends upon the ways buyers or sellers may think about prices'. Yet, where there is no common market, Nider joins previous scholastics in stating that sellers may adopt a cost-plus approach to find out the just price that they may ask for.

While only subjective utility is treated in determination of price, there are disquieting signs in Nider of Langensteinian 'status' arguments in justifying business income. For businessmen's incomes, in addition to being determined by the economic factors mentioned above, must also be decided 'in proportion to the nobility' of the effort – a prelude to Nider's making clear that the work of the soldier is nobler than that of the merchant and therefore deserves a higher reward. This is a throwback not just to Langenstein but to ancient Greek veneration of the martial as against the productive arts.

In discussing money, Nider is firm in justifying the activities of money-changers. There is no nonsense about usury here. Nider points out that the exchange of currency is a 'kind of selling and buying', and demonstrates even more cogently that the value of money, like the value of other commodities, also varies in the common estimation of the market. While, following Aquinas, the value of money usually changes less radically than the value of a particular good, change it does nevertheless, merchants incurring legitimate profits or losses from such variation.

Nider writes trenchantly of 'the conversion, or exchange of money or of other things, which is, as it were a kind of selling and buying of one currency for another, and presents, so to speak, the same moral problems as does commerce in goods...'

Far more significant than Nider was the great fifteenth century scholastic and fellow Swabian Gabriel Biel (1430–95), professor of theology at the new University of Tübingen, in Southwest Germany. Biel was a distinguished nominalist and Ockhamite – in fact, the German Ockhamites of the fifteenth century were known as *Gabrielistae*. And yet, recent research has discovered that Biel was essentially a Thomist in his belief in a rational and objective natural law ethic. Indeed, he echoed the belief of his fellow 'Ockhamite' of the previous century, Gregory of Rimini, in the highly rationalistic belief that the natural law was eternal and would exist even if God did not. Furthermore, man by his unaided reason can discern this natural law and reach the right conclusions on his proper conduct.

One of Biel's contributions was to deliver a crystal-clear statement of the scholastic insight that each party to an exchange engaged in the action for mutual subjective benefit. Following Jean Buridan, his fellow nominalist of the previous century, Biel's analysis was cogent and concise: 'For the buyer who desires a good would not buy, unless he hoped for greater satisfaction from the good than from the money he paid over; nor would the seller sell, unless he hoped for a profit from the price'. There had been no clearer demonstration before Biel that every exchange involves an expected mutual benefit by each party to that transaction, and that the satisfaction of the buyer, at least, is purely subjective, though the seller's may be translated into a monetary profit. There would be no real improvement upon Biel until the advent of the Austrian School in the late nineteenth century.

A follower of his fellow Ockhamites Jean Buridan and Nicole Oresme, Biel, in his *Treatise on the Power and Utility of Moneys*, repeated their metallist insights about the value of money and their attack on governmental debasement. Biel also insists, with Buridan, that a sound money must be composed of material with a use independent of its service as money. Biel regards debasement by a king as equivalent to theft: 'if a prince should reject valid money, in order that he may buy it up more cheaply and melt it, and then issue another coinage of less value, attaching the value of the former currency to it, he would be guilty of stealing money and is required to make restitution'.

Furthermore, Biel provided a more sophisticated explanation and justification than previously available of the workings of the foreign exchange market. In his commentary on the *Sentences* (1484), Biel noted that a bank that accepts a bill of exchange permits the drawer of the bill to obtain cash in another city, and thereby provides the important service of 'virtual transportation' of the money. The drawer of the bill is relieved of the cost and the risk of moving the money himself. It is therefore licit for the banker, as lender, to profit on purchasing a foreign bill of exchange. In this way, Biel greatly widened the legitimacy of exchange transactions, for lender as well as borrower, thus strengthening the theoretical insight that the value of money varies as do particular goods.

But the great significance of Gabriel Biel in the history of economic thought was that he began the smashing of the usury prohibition that had held economic thought in thrall since the early centuries of the Christian era. In addition to completing the liberation of the foreign exchange market from the taint of usury, Biel launched the justification of insurance contracts. For if it was sinful and usurious to own property or a right without bearing risk (such as the grantor of a pure loan) then what of a man who had purchased an insurance contract, and therefore was able to transfer risk to the insurer? The defence of insurance Biel takes over from Angelus Carletus de Clavasio, vicar-general of the Observant Franciscans, who had defended riskless insurance contracts in his *Summa Angelica* at the same time that Biel was writing his treatise.

Biel's main contribution in weakening the usury prohibition was his justification of the *census* contract – the purchase of an annuity – and justifying it in its widest possible form. Thus, purchase of an annuity was considered licit as a right to fruitful money as was an insured or guaranteed annuity. Also the buyer was allowed to redeem the annuity, a concession very close to permitting a lender to reclaim the principal of his loan after he has received a return in instalments.

Thus Biel came very close to justifying credit transactions charging interest. Explaining the fact that the seller of an annuity will often be willing to pay a high annual charge in order to get ready cash (i.e. pay interest on a loan) Biel points out with great cogency that both parties to this as any other transaction expect to benefit: 'For a buyer desiring merchandise, unless he hoped for more advantage from the merchandise than from the money he gave, would not buy; nor would a seller sell, unless he hoped for profit from the price'.

But the most comprehensive and systematic assault on the usury prohibition came from Gabriel Biel's most distinguished student and his successor in the theology chair at the University of Tübingen, Conrad Summenhart (1465–1511), who had also been a student at the University of Paris. The critique came in Summenhart's massive *Treatise on Contracts* (*Tractatus de Contractibus*) (1499).

Summenhart's contribution was twofold: first, in enormously widening all the possible exceptions to the usury prohibition, e.g. the *census* and *lucrum cessans*; and second, in launching a blistering direct assault on all the time-honoured arguments against whatever usury contracts remained. On the first, Summenhart developed the argument for insured or guaranteed partnerships far more subtly and extensively than before. He also widened the *lucrum cessans* exception far more than anyone had ever done. Money *is* fruitful, Summenhart declared boldly, it is the merchant's tool, which he can make fruitful by the use of his labour. Consequently, the merchant should be compensated for loss of the use of his money just as a farmer should be recompensed for the loss of his fields. Unfortunately, however, Summenhart's widening of *lucrum cessans* was still limited, as among the earlier scholastics, to loans made out of charity.

The boldest loosening of the usury bonds by Summenhart was in his radical defence of the widest possible interpretation of *census* contracts. Here Summenhart justified many of the credit transactions then used in Germany. Coupled with his development of the idea of the changeable value of money, this meant 'the emptying of the usury prohibition of all practical significance'.[7] Money, declared Summenhart, may licitly be trafficked in for profit. Furthermore, he asserted that a *census* is not a (sinful) loan because the *right* to money is a good of another kind than the money exchanged. But in that case, Summenhart asks himself, couldn't a usurer say the same thing, and simply state that the right to money he was demanding in exchange was a good of a different kind than the money loaned? Astonishingly, Summenhart replied, this was all right, provided that the lender did not *intend* this to be usury, and was himself really convinced that he was buying the right to money which was a different good than the money itself. But if usury was only subjective intention and *not* the objective fact of a loan charging interest, then there was no objective way of identifying or enforcing the prohibition against usury! In this way alone, Summenhart effectively destroyed the prohibition against usury.

But this was not all. For Summenhart explicitly declared that the purchase by someone of a discounted debt is not a usurious loan because it is only the purchase of a right to money. The purchase of a debt was licit in the same way as a *census*. Furthermore, the 'purchase of a debt' could be that of a newly constituted debt, and not simply the purchase of a previous debt. This, too, effectively ended the usury prohibition.

Moreover, in approving 'debt purchase' contracts, Summenhart came close to understanding the primordial fact of time-preference, the preference of present over future money. When someone pays $100 for the right to $110 at a future date, both parties estimate present money more highly than money payable at a future date. The 'buyer' (lender), furthermore, doesn't really profit usuriously from the loan because he values the future $110 as worth $100 at the present time, so that 'the price and the merchandise are equal in fact and in the estimation of the buyer'.

Then, tackling the arguments for usury directly, Summenhart presents 23 standard natural law arguments against usury, and demolishes them all, leaving only two shaky formal arguments; while he also puts forth strong objections of his own against the usury ban. As Professor Noonan concludes, Summenhart's 'examination ends in a rejection of the past. Usury is left assailed in name alone. The early scholastic theory of usury is abandoned'.[8] Summenhart's argument for usury is comprehensive. Contrary to St Thomas, the usurer is charging not for the borrower's use of his money, but for his *own* lack of use. If it is replied that the borrower's restoring of the principal restores to the lender the power of use, Summenhart cogently replies, again sensing time-preference: 'But he does not restore to him [the lender] the use of the intervening time, so that he will be able to use it [the money] for that intervening time…'. Thus interest on a loan becomes a legitimate charge for the foregone use of money during the time period of a loan. It is clear, at least implicitly, that Conrad Summenhart has magnificently demonstrated the justice of 'usury', of interest on a loan.

On the fixed value of money as an argument against usury, Summenhart repeats and develops the argument of earlier critics that the value of money varies over time. Furthermore, on the charge of risklessness of a money loan, Summenhart originates an argument potentially fatal to the usury ban. He points out correctly that the lender is never without risk; he always bears the risk of the borrower going bankrupt. The borrower also has the opportunity of earning more profits from the loan than the interest he has to pay the lender. Furthermore, Summenhart neatly smashed the Aristotelian argument that money by its nature was 'meant' to be used only as a medium of exchange and not to command interest. Summenhart boldly declares that the argument is simply absurd. Does one then commit sin by using wine to put out a fire, or by storing money in a shoe? There is nothing in the natural law that demonstrates that a material good must always be used for one particular purpose rather than for another.

We are left, after Summenhart, with only two very weak arguments against usury: the mere fact that Aristotle said it was unnatural (an 'argument' which

Summenhart could only have meant sardonically), and the divine prohibition. But since usury is really natural, Summenhart, as we have seen, is willing to construe the divine prohibition so narrowly that it virtually disappears; after Summenhart, the usury ban is finished.

Unfortunately for the credibility of scholastic economics, however, the sixteenth century scholastics, superb as they were in many areas of economics, did not accept the bold challenge of Conrad Summenhart to scrap the usury ban completely.

In some cases, particularly in his justification of the guaranteed partnership contract, Summenhart held back from full approval, counselling prudentially against contracts, though licit, which might scandalize the community. It was left to Summenhart's eminent student, Johann Eck, to carry the Summenhartian revolution through to its completion. Eck, professor of theology at the University of Ingolstadt near the financial centre of Augsburg in Bavaria, was soon to find his greatest fame in arguing the Catholic case against Martin Luther. Augsburg was then the leading financial centre of Germany and the home of the great bankers the Fuggers, who had captured the lucrative papal banking business from the city of Florence. In 1514, the 28-year-old Eck, a friend of the Fuggers, criticized his cautious fellow theologians for concealing the truth that the guaranteed partnership contract was fully licit, scandal or no scandal. Arguing his case before a favourable audience of canonists at the University of Bologna, Eck pointed out that merchants generally solicit the guaranteed investment contract and therefore profit by it. Furthermore, this contract had been in general use for 40 years, so that it should be assumed that the guaranteed contract is licit unless proven otherwise. Also, Eck added the modern sophisticated note that, after all, most capitalist investors in this contract are widows and orphans.

It should be noted that the eminent Scottish nominalist theologian, John Major (1478–1548), dean of the faculty of theology at the University of Paris, clearly assented to the controversial Eck–Summenhart defence of the guaranteed investment contract.

3.9 Nominalists and active natural rights

The Dominicans, as we have seen, triumphed over the Franciscans on the property rights question with Pope John XXII's great bull, *Quia vir reprobus* (1329). Individual property rights were now officially established as natural, stemming from God's granting man dominion over the earth. Despite William of Ockham's attempt to refute John XXII, his nominalist followers took the lead in developing this active natural property rights theory. Pierre d'Ailly (1350–1420), and particularly his student and successor as chancellor of the University of Paris, Jean Gerson (1363–1429), developed the theory. Thus, as Gerson put it trenchantly in his *De Vita Spirituali Animae* (1402):

There is a natural dominion as a gift from God, by which every creature has a *ius* (right) directly from God to take inferior things into its own use for its own preservation. Each has this *ius* as a result of a fair and irrevocable justice, maintained in its original purity, or a natural integrity. In this way Adam had dominion over the fowls of the air and the fish in the sea... To this dominion the dominion of liberty can also be assimilated, which is an unrestrained faculty given by God...[9]

It is odd that this nominalist and mystic, after setting forth the view of human rights as a dominion, should also hold, among a minority of scholastics, that any mercantile profit over and above costs and risk is immoral, and that the government should fix all prices to assure a just price.

The active rights theory was championed by the Gersonian Conrad Summenhart, and then advanced further by the nominalist John Major. In his commentary on the *Sentences* of Peter Lombard (1509), Major, a century after Gerson, drew the logical conclusion that not only man's right and dominion were natural but so too was *private* property. Major's student Jacques Almain put it clearly (*Aurea opuscula*, c.1525): 'Natural dominion is thus the dispositional power or faculty of using things which people can employ in their use of external objects, following the precepts of the law of nature – by which everyone can look after their own bodies and preserve themselves.'

Throughout the fifteenth century, and into the sixteenth the active theory of natural rights seemed to reign unchallenged.

3.10   Notes

1. The population decline was roughly uniform throughout western Europe, with the Italian population falling from 10 to 7.5 million, France and the Netherlands from 19 to 12 million, Germany and Scandinavia from 11.5 to 7.5 million, and Spain from 9 to 7 million. The largest percentage drop was in Great Britain, where the number of inhabitants fell from 5 to 3 million in this period.
2. Lionel Rothkrug, *Opposition to Louis XIV: The Political and Social Origins of the French Enlightenment* (Princeton, NJ: Princeton University Press, 1965), p. 14.
3. On Buridan and modern indifference analysis, see Joseph A. Schumpeter, *History of Economic Analysis* (New York: Oxford University Press, 1954), pp. 94n, 1064. For a critique, see Murray N. Rothbard, *Man, Economy and State* (1962, Los Angeles: Nash Publishing Co. 1970), I, pp. 267–8.
4. And more fully:

   Oftentimes have we reflected on a similar abuse
   In the choice of men for office, and of coins for common use;
   For your old and standard pieces, valued and approved and tried,
   Here among the Grecian nations, and in all the world beside,
   Recognized in every realm for trusty stamp and pure assay,
   And rejected and abandoned for the trash of yesterday;
   For a vile, adulterate issue, drossy, counterfeit and base,
   Which the traffic of the city passes current in their place.

   Aristophanes, *The Frogs*

Quoted in J. Laurence Laughlin, *The Principles of Money* (New York: Charles Scribner's Sons, 1903), p. 420.

5. Raymond de Roover, *San Bernardino of Siena and Sant'Antonino of Florence* (Boston: Baker Library, 1967), p. 37.

6. John T. Noonan, Jr, *The Scholastic Analysis of Usury* (Cambridge, Mass.: Harvard University Press, 1957), p. 77.

7. Ibid., p. 233.

8. Ibid., p. 340.

9. Richard Tuck, *Natural Rights Theories* (Cambridge: Cambridge University Press, 1979), p. 27.

4 The late Spanish scholastics

4.1 The commercial expansion of the sixteenth century

The great secular depression of the fourteenth and first half of the fifteenth century began to give way to economic recovery in the second half of the fifteenth. The overland trade from the Mediterranean to northern Europe, cut off by the French king's depredations against the fairs of Champagne, was increasingly replaced by sea trade off the Atlantic coast. Vessels now went through the Straits of Gibraltar and up the coast, increasingly sailing to Antwerp and making that city the big trading centre in northern Europe during the sixteenth century. Commerce moved away from the restrictions and high taxation of Flemish Bruges, and shifted to and expanded in free market Antwerp, where business and trade could flourish free of hampering legislation, privileges, and high taxes. In addition, Atlantic ships headed south and west, and the famous explorations and discoveries of the late fifteenth century changed the face of world history by making European countries world powers, and began to integrate Africa and the New World into the European economy. Spain and Portugal, the leading explorers of the new continents, became the dominant nation-states and empires of the sixteenth century. Slowly but surely, the Italian city-states which had been in the forefront of economic advance and the spearhead of Renaissance culture, began to be left behind in the advance of economic and political power.

Along with commercial expansion came inflation, fuelled by the immense increase of gold and silver brought to Europe by the Spaniards from the newly found mines of the western hemisphere. An approximate tripling of the stock of specie in Europe resulted in a century of inflation, with prices tripling during the sixteenth century. The new money flowed first into the main Spanish port of Seville, then into the rest of Spain, and finally into other countries of Europe, and the geography of price rises followed accordingly.

As Atlantic powers, England and France grew in strength along with the other Atlantic nations of western Europe. They were greatly aided by the end of the destructive Hundred Years' War between the two nations in 1453. The doctrines of the absolute state, previously limited largely to theorists and rulers of the Italian city-states, now spread to all the nation-states of Europe. Absolutism eventually triumphed throughout Europe by the early seventeenth century. The victory was fuelled, as we shall see below, by the rise of Protestantism and a bit later of secularism, beginning in the sixteenth century.

4.2 Cardinal Cajetan: liberal Thomist

Late scholasticism was the product of the sixteenth century, the century that ushered in the Protestant Reformation and the Catholic Counter-Reformation. If the thirteenth century was well described as the golden age of scholastic philosophy, then the sixteenth century was its silver age, the era of a shining renaissance of scholastic thought before the shades of night closed in for good. As we have seen, the fourteenth and fifteenth centuries saw the emergence of nominalism and at least the weakening of the idea of a rational, objective natural law – including a natural law ethics – discoverable by man's reason. The sixteenth century witnessed a renascent Thomism, spearheaded by one of the greatest churchmen of his age, Thomas De Vio, Cardinal Cajetan (1468–1534).

Cardinal Cajetan was not only the pre-eminent Thomist philosopher and theologian of his day; he was also an Italian Dominican who became general of the Dominican Order in 1508. A cardinal of the Church, he was the pope's favourite upholder of the faith in debates with the great founder of Protestantism, Martin Luther. In his *Commentary* on Aquinas's *Summa*, Cajetan of course endorsed the standard scholastic view that the just price is the common market price, reflecting the estimation of the buyers, and held that that price will fluctuate upon changing conditions of demand and supply. In attempting to purge scholastic economics of any trace of Langensteinian 'station in life' theory, however, Cajetan went further to criticize Aquinas for denouncing accumulation of wealth beyond one's status as suffering from the sin of avarice. On the contrary, declared Cajetan, it is legitimate for highly able persons to move up the social ladder in a way that matches their attainments. This candid endorsement of upward mobility in a free market was the broadest attempt yet to rid scholasticism of all traces of the ancient contempt for trade and economic gain.

In his comprehensive treatise on foreign exchange, *De Cambiis* (1499), the great Cajetan set forth the fullest and most unqualified defence yet penned of the foreign exchange market. Sweeping aside the dithering indecisiveness of his fellow Dominican, Fra Santi Rucellai (1437–97), himself a former exchange banker and the son of a banker, the cardinal was firm and hard-hitting. Since the role of the merchant has long since been established as legitimate, then so should that of the exchange banker, who is simply engaging in a kind of commodity transaction. Besides, modern trade could not function without the foreign exchange market, and cities could not exist without trade. Hence it is needful and right that the exchange market exist. As in other markets, the customary market price is the just price.

In the course of his defence of the exchange market in *De Cambiis*, Cajetan proceeded to advance the state of the art in monetary theory. He showed trenchantly that money is a commodity, particularly when moving from one city to another, and is therefore subject to the demand and supply laws governing the prices of commodities. At this point, Cajetan made a great advance in monetary theory, indeed in economic theory generally. He pointed out that the value of money depends not only on *existing* demand and supply conditions, but also on present *expectations* of the future state of the market. Expectations of wars and famines, and of future changes in the supply of money, will affect its current value. Thus, Cardinal Cajetan, a sixteenth century prince of the Church, can be considered the founder of expectations theory in economics.

Furthermore, Cajetan distinguished between the two kinds of 'value of money': its purchasing power in terms of goods, so that gold or silver are 'equated' with goods being bought and sold; and the value of one coin or currency in terms of another on the foreign exchange market. Here, each kind of coin tends to move to that region where its value is highest, and away from wherever its value is lowest.

On the vexed usury question, though Cajetan was not as radical as his German contemporary Summenhart in virtually eradicating the usury prohibition, he did join Summenhart on the doctrine of implicit intention, and was even more radical in the one area where Summenhart had hung back: *lucrum cessans*. Implicit intention meant that if someone really believed his contract not to be a loan, then it was not usurious, even though it might be a loan in practice. This of course paved the way for the practical elimination of the ban on usury. In addition, Cajetan also joined his fellow liberals in endorsing the guaranteed investment contract.

But Cardinal Cajetan's great breakthrough on the usury front was his vindication of *lucrum cessans*. Wielding the mighty authority of being the greatest Thomist since Aquinas himself, Cajetan offered a point-by-point critique of his master's rejection of this exception to the usury ban. He then vindicates, not indeed all of *lucrum cessans*, but any loan to businessmen. Thus a lender may charge interest on any loan as payment for profit foregone on other investments, provided that loan be to a businessman. This untenable split between loans to businessmen and to consumers was made for the first time – as a means of justifying all business loans. The rationale was that money retained its high profit-foregone value in the hands of business, but not of consumer borrowers. Thus for the very first time in the Christian era, Cardinal Cajetan justified the *business* of money lending, provided they were loans to business. Before him, all writers, even the most liberal, even Conrad Summenhart, had justified interest charges on *lucrum cessans* only for *ad hoc* charitable loans; now the great Cajetan was justifying the business of money-lending at interest.

4.3 The School of Salamanca: the first generation
If the newly burgeoning liberal Thomism began with Cardinal Cajetan in Italy, the torch was soon passed to a set of sixteenth century theologians who revived Thomism and scholasticism and kept them alive for over a century: the School of Salamanca in Spain.

It is no more than fitting that Spain should be the centre of scholastic learning in the sixteenth century. That century was pre-eminently the century of Spain. Spain, the leader in the explorations and conquests in the New World; Spain, the nation that brought the treasures of gold and silver across the Atlantic to Europe; Spain, along with Italy and Portugal, the nation in Europe that remained resoundingly Catholic and proved immune to the spread of Protestantism.

The acknowledged founder of the School of Salamanca was the great legal theorist and pioneer in the discipline of international law, Francisco de Vitoria (c.1485–1546). A Basque raised in Burgos in northern Spain and born into a prosperous family, Vitoria became a Dominican and went to study and then teach in Paris. There, in one of the ironies of the history of thought, he became a disciple of a Fleming who had been a pupil of one of the last of the Ockhamites, John Major. This man, Pierre Crockaert (c.1450–1514), had become a student and then teacher of theology late in life. Turning away from his teacher Major, Crockaert abandoned nominalism and moved to Thomism, entering the Dominican Order and coming to teach at the Dominican College of Saint-Jacques in Paris. After spending over 17 years imbibing and then teaching Thomism in Paris, Vitoria returned to Spain to lecture in theology at Valladolid, finally coming to Salamanca – then the queen of Spanish universities – as prime professor of theology in 1526.

A brilliant and highly influential teacher and lecturer, Vitoria set the framework for the Salamanca School for the rest of the century. Even though he did not publish any writings, his lectures have come down to us as transcribed by his students – much as in the case of Aristotle. Much of the glory of the University of Salamanca was the result of reforms instituted by Vitoria himself. Consequently, the university soon had no less than 70 professorial chairs filled by the best scholars of the day, providing instruction not only in the traditional medieval curriculum, but also in such new-fangled disciplines as navigational science and the Chaldean language.

Vitoria's lectures were largely commentaries on Aquinas's moral theory. In the course of the lectures, Vitoria founded the great Spanish scholastic tradition of denouncing the conquest and particularly the enslavement by the Spanish of the Indians in the New World. In an age when thinkers in France and Italy were preaching secular absolutism and the power of the state, Vitoria and his followers revived the idea that natural law is morally superior to the mere might of the state.

Vitoria did not expound much on economic topics, but he was interested in commercial morality, and his views followed the mainstream scholastic tradition: the just price was the common market price, even though if there were a legally fixed price it would also be considered just. In short, legal price edicts are to be obeyed. However, for those goods without a common market – say with only one or two sellers – Vitoria advanced beyond his forbears. Instead of having cost of production determinate, Vitoria, while stating that cost could well be considered, returned to the old, nearly forgotten *laissez-faire* Roman law tradition of free individual bargaining as providing the just price. For in this situation, Vitoria maintained, the price had to be settled by the exchanging parties themselves. Vitoria, however, then added a curious distinction between luxury and non-luxury goods. Luxuries could be sold for a 'fancy price', since the buyer pays the high price voluntarily and out of his free will. Why this 'free will' should disappear with non-luxury items Vitoria unfortunately does not explain.

Vitoria's most eminent student and fellow theologian at Salamanca was the Dominican Domingo de Soto (1494–1560). Born in Segovia of comfortable but not wealthy parents, de Soto studied at the University of Alcalá near Madrid and then went to Paris, where he studied under Vitoria, and later became a professor. Returning to Spain, de Soto became professor of metaphysics at Alcalá, and then entered the Dominican Order, joining his mentor as a theology professor at Salamanca in 1532. Though a shy personality, de Soto was repeatedly involved in university administration, and was several times prior of the college of Estabán in the University. De Soto's work in physics is also considered outstanding.

In 1545 the Emperor Charles V honoured de Soto by naming him as his representative at the great council of Trent, the mighty council of the Catholic Counter-Reformation. Soon de Soto became confessor to the emperor, but gave it up in a few years to return to his professorship at Salamanca. De Soto's fame rested on his treatise *De justitia et jure*, published in 1553 and based on lectures given originally at Salamanca in 1540–41. *De Justitia et jure* was reprinted no less than 27 times before the end of the century, and was read and quoted by jurists and moralists until the mid-eighteenth century.

Unfortunately, on economics de Soto was a reactionary thinker, and set back some of the liberal gains of the previous scholastics. Thus, while de Soto conceded that 'the price of goods is not determined by their nature but by the measure in which they serve the needs of mankind', this utility analysis was weakened by vague concessions to the 'labour, trouble, and risk' involved in a sale. Worse than that, de Soto was not content to concede the propriety of government fixing the price of goods and letting it go at that. Instead, he declared flatly that a fixed price is always superior to the market price, and that ideally all prices should be fixed by the state. And even lacking such control, prices, for de Soto, should be set 'by the opinion of prudent and fair-minded men' (whoever they might be!) who have nothing to do with any transactions. They should not be determined by the free bargaining of the buyers and sellers involved. Thus de Soto, more than any other scholastic thinker, called for statism rather than market determination of price.

On foreign exchange, de Soto's influence was confusing, cutting both for and against that market. In its favour, he contributed perhaps the first cogent explanation of the movements of currencies and exchange rates on the foreign exchange market – what would later be called the 'purchasing-power parity theory' of exchange rates.

The economy of the sixteenth century was marked by an inflation which first hit Spain, in response to gold and silver discoveries in the New World and the consequent importation of specie into Spain. Inflation first struck in Spain, and then spread to the rest of Europe, as the Spaniards spent the increased supply of money. The result was the first large-scale secular inflation in history, price in Europe doubling over the first half of the sixteenth century.

De Soto was concerned to explain the curious fact that more abundant specie in Spain caused it to have an unfavourable balance of payment, with money flowing out of Spain and into the rest of Europe. As he put it:

> the more plentiful money is in Medina the more unfavourable are the terms of exchange, and the higher the price that must be paid by whoever wishes to send money from Spain to Flanders, since the demand for money is smaller in Spain than in Flanders. And the scarcer money is in Medina the less he need pay there, because more people want money in Medina than are sending it to Flanders.

In short, more abundant money in one place causes money to flow out, and lowers the exchange rate relation to other currencies. A more abundant money supply means that money is 'less wanted' there – a primitive way of pointing to the supply increasing along a given falling demand curve for money, so that each unit or coin is less valued. Here is also a rudimentary purchasing-power parity analysis of exchange rates.

But despite this subtle advance in analysing the workings of the market, de Soto backslid on usury to such an extent that he advocated banning the foreign exchange market as usurious. In fact, de Soto managed to influence the court in 1552 to outlaw all internal currency exchange at anything other than the legal par.

As can be seen, de Soto exercised a reactionary influence on the usury ban, and managed to block any general acceptance of the revolutionary contributions of Summenhart and Cajetan on the usury issue. Attempting to turn back the tide, de Soto went so far as to declare the standard guaranteed or insured investment contract as sinful and usurious, on the old discredited medieval ground that risk and ownership must never be separated. He tried to roll back *lucrum cessans*, and in general was more rigorously anti-usury than almost any of the medieval scholastics, insisting anachronistically that money is sterile and bears no fruit, and therefore cannot lawfully command interest.

Ironically, however, while anxious to reverse the tide of liberalization of usury, de Soto himself contributed to the long-run demise of the usury ban. We remember that Pope Urban III, in his decretal *Consuluit* in the late twelfth century, had suddenly pulled a forgotten quotation from Luke (6:35) out of the hat: 'lend freely, hoping nothing thereby', and used this vague counsel to charity as a stick with which to prohibit all interest on loans. More remarkably, all later scholastics had followed this dubious divine ban on interest-taking; even the radical Summenhart had conceded the divine injunction against interest and simply narrowed it down to virtually nothing. It paradoxically now fell to the conservative de Soto to cast the first stone. The Luke statement, he declared contemptuously, has no relevance to lending at interest, and Christ most definitely did not declare usury to be sinful. Therefore, he concluded, if usury is not against the natural law, it is perfectly licit. *Theologically*, there is no problem with usury.

4.4 The School of Salamanca: Azpilcueta and Medina

Fortunately, de Soto's reactionary and statist influence was at least partially offset by another of Vitoria's distinguished students, Martin de Azpilcueta Navarrus (1493–1586). Renowned for his saintly life and vast learning, the gaunt, hook-nosed Dominican Azpilcueta was regarded as the most eminent canon lawyer of his day. After teaching canon law in Cahors and Toulouse in France, Azpilcueta returned to take up a chair at Salamanca, where his overflowing lectures featured a new method of teaching civil law by combining it with canon law. In 1538, Azpilcueta was sent by Emperor Charles V to be rector of the new University of Coimbra, in western Portugal. There he developed the principles of international law originally set forth by his master, Vitoria. Azpilcueta spent his last years in Rome, a trusted adviser to three popes, dying at the advanced age of 93.

Azpilcueta used his great influence to advance economic liberalism farther than it had ever gone before, among the scholastics or anywhere else. In sharp contrast to de Soto's admiration for comprehensive price control, Azpilcueta was the first economic thinker to state clearly and boldly that government price-fixing was imprudent and unwise. When goods are abundant, he sensibly pointed out, there is no need for maximum price control, and when goods are scarce, controls would do the community more harm than good.

But Azpilcueta's outstanding contribution to economics was his theory of money, published in his *Comentario resolutoio de usuras* (1556) as an appendix to a manual on moral theology. The manual and the commentaries in the appendix were translated into Latin and Italian, and proved to be influential for Catholic writers for many years. Azpilcueta built on the analysis of Cardinal Cajetan to present the first clear and unambiguous presentation of the 'quantity theory of money'. Or rather, he breaks firmly with the tradition that money can in any sense be a fixed measure of value of other goods. In contrast to older emphasis on foreign exchange, or money in terms of other monies, Azpilcueta clearly identified the value of money as its purchasing power in terms of goods. Once Azpilcueta grasped these two points firmly, then the 'quantity theory' followed directly. For then, like other goods, the value of money varied inversely with its supply, or quantity available. As Azpilcueta put it: 'all merchandise becomes dearer when it is in great demand and short supply, and that money, in so far as it may be sold, bartered, or exchanged by some other form of contract, is merchandise, and therefore also becomes dearer when it is in great demand and short supply'.

It should be noted that this splendid and concise analysis of the determinants of the purchasing power of money does not make the mistake of later 'quantity theorists' in stressing the quantity or supply of money while ignoring the demand. On the contrary, demand and supply analysis was applied correctly to the monetary sphere.

Gold and silver flooded into Spain and then the rest of Europe in the sixteenth century, driving up prices first in Spain and then in the other countries. Prices doubled by the middle of the century. Historians of economic thought have held the first quantity theorist, the first thinker to attribute the price rise to the influx of specie, to be the French absolutist political theorist Jean Bodin. But Bodin's famous *Reply to the Paradoxes of M. Malestroit* (1568) was anticipated by 12 years by Azpilcueta's work, and since the erudite Bodin probably had read the Spanish Dominican, his announced claim to originality seems in unusually bad taste. And since Spain was the first recipient of the flow of specie from the New World, it is certainly not surprising that a Spaniard should be the first person to decipher the new phenomenon. Thus, Azpilcueta wrote:

> ...other things being equal, in countries where there is a great scarcity of money all other saleable goods, and even the hands and labor of men, are given for less money than where it is abundant. Thus we see by experience that in France, where money is scarcer than in Spain, bread, wine, cloth and labor are worth much less. And even in Spain, in times when money was scarcer, saleable goods and labor were given for very much less than after the discovery of the Indies, which flooded the country with gold and silver. The reason for this is that money is worth more where and when it is scarce than where and when it is abundant.

Martin de Azpilcueta, in this case influenced by his colleague de Soto, also developed the latter's purchasing-power parity theory of exchange rates, at the same time that he worked out the 'quantity theory', supply and demand analysis of the value of money. The two of course, go hand in hand.

One of Azpilcueta's most important contributions was to revive the vital concept of time-preference, perhaps under the influence of the works of its discoverer, San Bernardino of Siena. Azpilcueta pointed out, more clearly than Bernardino, that a present good, such as money, will naturally be worth more on the market than future goods, that is, goods that are now claims to money in the future. As Azpilcueta put it: 'a claim on something is worth less than the thing itself, and ... it is plain that that which is not usable for a year is less valuable than something of the same quality which is usable at once'.

But if a future good is naturally less valuable than a present good on the market, then this insight should automatically justify 'usury' as the charging of interest not on 'time' but on the exchange of present goods (money) for a future claim on that money (an IOU). And yet, this seemingly simple deduction (simple to us who come after) was not made by Azpilcueta Navarrus.

On the foreign exchange market, Azpilcueta struck a blow for economic liberalism by reviving the Cajetan line, and repudiating the statist fulminations of his colleague de Soto, who had called for the prohibition of all foreign exchange transactions as usurious. In addition to repeating Cajetanian arguments, the Spanish Dominican and trusted advisor to three popes injected practical considerations. Azpilcueta pointed out that 'an infinite number of decent Christian' merchants, aristocrats, widows, and even churchmen commonly invest in foreign exchange. Azpilcueta insisted that he refuses to 'damn the whole world' by imposing overly rigorous standards. Furthermore, he warned, to abolish foreign exchange markets 'would be to plunge the realm into poverty', a step he was clearly not willing to take.

On most other aspects of the usury question, however, Azpilcueta Navarrus was surprisingly conservative, and a big step backward from the advanced freemarket position of Conrad Summenhart. On the *census*, or annuity contract, Azpilcueta Navarrus was far harsher than de Soto, who was liberal on this particular aspect of 'usury'. Instead, Azpilcueta was the main influence on Pope Pius V's issue in 1569 of the bull *Cum onus*, in which all *census* is declared illegal except on a 'fruitful, immobile good', for which status money, of course, cannot qualify. The pope had been goaded into issuing the bull by Cardinal San Carlo Borromeo, who as newly appointed archbishop of Milan, professed to find usury everywhere in that sinful city. Borromeo was one of the leaders of the Catholic Counter-Reformation, and his prodding led to *Cum onus*.

But it was too late; the *census* contract was too ingrained in European practice, and too many theologians had adopted the liberal approach. The majority of Catholic theologians rejected this new attempt and simply stated that the pope's arguments were matters of positive rather than natural law, and therefore that the papal bull had to be accepted by the government or be the common practice of a particular country for it to carry the force of law in that country. Interestingly enough, not a single country in Europe accepted *Cum onus*: not Spain, not France, nor Germany, not southern Italy, nor even Rome itself!

The contempt with which *Cum onus* was received throughout Europe is strikingly revealed in its treatment by the recently founded Jesuit Order. The Society of Jesus was founded in 1537 by an invalided Spanish ex-army officer, Ignatius Loyola, born in the Basque country. The rapidly expanding society was installed on rigorous discipline along consciously military lines (Loyola's original title for the society was 'the Company of Jesus'). Under vow of absolute obedience to the pope and to the general of the order, the Jesuits became the 'shock troops' of the Catholic Counter-Reformation. Despite their vow to the pope, the Jesuit general congregation of 1573, only four years after *Cum onus*, validated the mutually redeemable *census* contract. And in 1581, the Jesuit congregation went the whole way and validated every type of census contract. When some German Jesuits became restive at this liberality, the general of the Jesuit Order, Claude Aquaviva, in 1589 ordered that the validity of the *census* contract be upheld by German Jesuits with no further dissent. So much for the pope's *census* prohibition.

In the following century, the *census* loophole was widely used to camouflage interest on loan contracts, particularly in Germany. As Noonan points out, it is certainly significant that the German word for interest on a loan is *zins*, derived from the Latin *census*.

The Summenhart–Cajetan doctrine of implicit intention – that if someone did not *intend* a contract to be a loan, then it was licit – was carried even further by the remarkable Jesuit congregation of 1581. The congregation justified virtually every contract. As Noonan concludes: 'In practice, it meant that only loans to aged or infirm persons without property or loans bearing a rate of interest beyond that obtainable in "a guaranteed investment contract or *census*" were to be regarded as true usurious loans'.

If Azpilcueta Navarrus was conservative on most aspects of usury, he did however became the first writer to justify interest charged on *lucrum cessans* (investment profit foregone) for *all* loans, not just *ad hoc* loans made out of charity (previous writers) or even only for loans to business (Cajetan). Now any profit foregone could be charged as interest, even by professional moneylenders. The only restriction remaining – a feeble one in practice – is that the lender would actually have used his money to make the foregone investment.

Of this first generation of late Spanish scholastics – approximately those who were born in the 1480s and 1490s – the final noteworthy writer was Juan de Medina (1490–1546). Medina, a Franciscan, did not, however, teach theology at Salamanca but at the Collegium at Alcalá. Medina's distinction comes from being the first writer in history to advance the view clearly that charging interest on a loan is legitimate if in compensation to the lender for risk of non-payment. Medina's reasoning was impeccable: exposing one's property 'to the risk of being lost, is sellable, and purchasable at a price, nor is it among those things which are to be done gratuitously'. Furthermore,

Medina pointed out, theologians now admit that someone who guarantees a debtor's loan can licitly charge for that service; but in that case, if the borrower cannot find a guarantor, why cannot the lender charge the borrower for assuming the risk of non-repayment? Isn't *his* charge similar to the charge of the guarantor?

The argument was sound, but the shock to the scholastics was severe, no less so because Medina weakened his risk justification by banning interest on riskless loans and restricting the charge to cases where the borrower could not find a guarantor. Domingo de Soto, in horror, correctly pointed out that to admit a charge for risk of non-payment would destroy the entire usury prohibition, since a charge could be made for a loan above the principal. The usually more liberal Azpilcueta gave Medina even shorter shrift, objecting correctly if insufficiently, that every theologian, canon lawyer, and natural lawyer disagreed with Medina's innovation. And that was supposed to be the end of the matter.

Medina's discussion of value theory, however, was not nearly so cogent. In discussing the just market price, Medina throws in higgledy-piggledy a host of factors: costs, labour, industry, and risk for suppliers; need or utility for buyers; and scarcity or abundance of the good. Clearly, there was much less of a coherent analysis of supply than in the hands of San Bernardino of Siena. On the other hand, whereas the scholastic tradition held that the legal price would have to take precedence over the market price, Medina cited two cases where the market price should be followed: where the market price is lower, and where the authorities were too slow in adjusting the legal edict to a higher market price.

4.5   The School of Salamanca: the middle years

The institution and the structure of thought of the School of Salamanca was established, then, in the first half of the sixteenth century by three great Dominicans: Francisco de Vitoria, and his followers, Domingo de Soto and Martin de Azpilcueta Navarrus. The latter two theologians were the founders of the economic aspect of the systematic theology and philosophy of the Salamanca School.

The middle generation of Salamancans were those men born in the first decades of the sixteenth century, and writing near and after mid-century. The oldest of these second-generation members was the eminent Diego de Covarrubias y Leiva (1512–77) whose handsome and distinguished features grace a stunning portrait by the great Spanish painter El Greco, now hanging in the Greco Museum in Toledo. Acknowledged as the greatest jurist since Vitoria, Covarrubias was the most prominent student of Azpilcueta. After ten years as professor of canon law at the University of Salamanca, Covarrubias was made auditor of the chancellor of Castile by the emperor, after which he became bishop of Ciudad Rodrigo and bishop of Segovia. In 1572, Covarrubias became president of the council of Castile. As did so many other scholastics of the time, Covarrubias' writings ranged over theology, history, numismatics, and other disciplines of human action as well as the law.

The theory of value had lain in the doldrums ever since San Bernardino and Johannes Nider in the fifteenth century, and now, a century later, it was revived by Covarrubias. In his *Variarum* (1554), Covarrubias gets value theory back on the right track: the value of goods on the market is determined by utility, and by the scarcity of the product. The value of goods, then, depends not on matters intrinsic to the good or to its production, but on the estimations of consumers. Thus Covarrubias: 'The value of an article does not depend on its essential nature but on the estimation of men, even if that estimation is foolish. Thus, in the Indies wheat is dearer than in Spain because men esteem it more highly, though the nature of the wheat is the same in both places'. In considering the just price of a good, Covarrubias added, we must consider not its original cost, nor its cost in labour, but only its common market value. Prices fall when buyers are few and goods are abundant, and vice versa.

It should be noted, as will be mentioned further below, that Covarrubias, considered one of the greatest experts on Roman law in his day, exerted considerable influence on the great seventeenth century Dutch Protestant jurist Hugo Grotius. Covarrubias' economic writings were particularly influential in Italy, where they continued to be cited down through the work of the eminent Abbé Ferdinando Galiani, in 1750.

Another important contribution to utility theory was made by a lesser contemporary of Covarrubias, Luís Saravia de la Calle Veroñese. Saravia was one of several influential writers of handbooks on moral theology, which took the teachings of the great theologians and boiled them down for confessors and their penitents. In his *Instrucción de mercades* (Medina del Campo, 1554), Saravia lashed out at all manner of cost-of-production theories of value, insisting that utility and market demand alone, interacting with scarcity of supply, determine the common market price and hence the just price. Saravia's attack on cost of production notions was trenchant and hard-hitting:

> the just price arises from the abundance or scarcity of goods, merchants, and money, as has been said, and not from costs, labor and risk. If we had to consider labor and risk in order to assess the just price, no merchant would ever suffer loss, nor would abundance or scarcity of goods and money enter into the question.

Saravia's work, in addition to being cited many times by later Spanish writers, was also influential in Italy, where it was translated in 1561. The Italian A.M. Venusti became a disciple of Saravia and published a similar treatise.

The next important Salamancan economist was the colourful Dominican Tomás de Mercado (d. 1585). Mercado's was the next important handbook on moral theology after Saravia: *Tratos y contratos de mercaderes* (Salamanca, 1569). Born in Seville, Mercado was raised in Mexico, where he entered the Dominican Order, from which he returned to Salamanca and Seville. Mercado's handbook drew on his extensive knowledge of business practice picked up on his travels, and it was written in a concise and even sardonic style.

Mercado was a perceptive, if sometimes confused, monetary theorist. Applying utility analysis to money, Mercado went right up to the edge of marginal analysis by pointing out that the purchasing power is the highest where money is most scarce and therefore highly 'esteemed.' In short, Mercado dimly realized that the demand for money is a schedule, falling as the supply of money increases, and that the value, or purchasing power, of money is determined by the interaction of its supply and demand. Thus Mercado:

> ...money is esteemed much less in the Indies [where it is mined] than in Spain...After the Indies, the place where money is least esteemed is Seville, the city that gathers unto herself all the good things from the New World, and, after Seville, the other parts of Spain. Money is highly esteemed in Flanders, Rome, Germany and England. This estimation and appreciation are brought about, in the first place, by the abundance or scarcity of these metals; since they are found and mined in America, they are there held in little esteem.

It is not surprising that Mercado, in contrast to de Soto, opposed the outlawing of internal currency exchange in Spain. On the other hand, he was confused enough, in contrast to his keen analysis of the value of money, to favour the outlawing of the export of metals. But wouldn't the 'esteem' for the remaining metals be higher, and wouldn't this check and offset the outward flow of metals?

During the 1570s, a satellite group of theologian–economists arose at Valencia, grounding themselves on their studies at Salamanca. The most important was Francisco Garcia who, in his *Tratado utilismo* (Valencia, 1583) expanded and developed the subjective utility theory of value. In a notable advance in discussions of utility, Garcia pointed out that the utility or value of a thing may vary because: one good may have many uses and serve more purposes than another, may serve a more important service than another, and/ or may perform a given service more efficiently than another.

In addition to utility determining value and price, Garcia noted also its relative abundance or scarcity. And here, Garcia too, came just to the edge – although not over – of discovering the final, missing marginal element in utility theory:

For example, we have said that bread is more valuable than meat because it is more necessary for the preservation of human life. But there may come a time when bread is so abundant and meat so scarce that bread is cheaper than meat.

Garcia went on to detail other determinants of value including the number of buyers and sellers; and the eagerness to buy and sell (i.e. intensity of demand in buying or holding on to a product): 'whether vendors are eager to sell their goods, and buyers much sought after and importuned'. He then went on to integrate monetary into value theory, another determinant of prices being 'whether money is scarce or plentiful'.

In monetary theory, Garcia continued and developed the Azpilcueta–Covarrubias–Mercado line. In the Indies, where gold and silver are plentiful, specie is 'not as highly esteemed' as in Spain, where there is less gold and silver. He similarly pointed out in his comprehensive discussion, that when money is abundant in any given country, its esteem or value will be low, whereas when money is scarce it is far more highly valued. In other words, as Garcia pointed out, these differences in degrees of esteem, or demand, may occur either over place or over time.

This comparative analysis of changes in the value of money over time or place was an important advance in monetary theory. But not only that; Garcia, for the first time, rested his 'macro' analysis on a 'micro' insight: that a very rich man, a man with an abundant personal supply of money, will tend to evaluate each unit of currency less than when he was poor, or than another poor man. Here Garcia actually grasped, though sketchily, the concept of the diminishing marginal utility of money. Marginalism, in this area at least, was actually reached rather than simply approached.

Finally, Garcia arrived at the most integrated utility theory of the value of money to date: the value of money on the market is determined by the supply of money available, the intensity of the demand for money, and the safety of the money itself (called by later economists the 'quality' of the money in the minds of people in the market).

4.6   The late Salamancans

The School of Salamanca, begun by Francisco Vitoria in the 1520s, reached its final flowering at the end of the sixteenth century. One of the leading lights of that era was the Dominican Domingo de Bañez de Mondragon (1527–1604), professor of theology at the University of Salamanca, and friend and confessor of the famous mystic St Theresa of Avila. De Bañez was renowned for the great controversy with his eminent Jesuit colleague Luís de Molina, on the crucial question of determinism versus free will. De Bañez took the Dominican position, which leaned toward the 'Calvinist' – determinist stand that salvation is solely a product of God's grace, ordered from the beginning of time for God's own inscrutable reasons. Molina championed the Jesuit view, which upheld the freedom of will of each individual in achieving salvation. In the latter view, the free will choice of the individual is necessary to effectuate God's grace which is there for him to accept. A historian sums up Molina's view of free will with these inspiring words: 'Liberty is ours, so indisputably ours, that, with the help of God's gifts, it lies in our power to avoid all mortal sin and to attain eternal life. Freedom belongs to the sons of God'.[1]

In a systematic discussion of money, its value, and foreign exchange, De Bañez (in *De Justitia et Jure*, 1594), provided a cogent discussion of the purchasing-power parity theory of exchanges, a theory which had formed the scholastic main line since De Soto and Azpilcueta.

The last notable Salamancan economic thinker was the great theologian Luís de Molina (1535–1601). The ascendancy of Molina in Spanish scholastic thought was a fitting embodiment of the passing of the theological and the natural law torch from the Dominicans to the aggressive new Jesuit Order. By the late sixteenth century, the influence of the Order permeated all of Spain.

Though a Salamancan through and through, Molina only briefly studied and never actually taught at that university. Born in Cuenca of a noble family, Molina went briefly to Salamanca, and then to the University of Alcalá. Entering the new Jesuit Order, Molina was sent to the University of Coimbra in Portugal, since the Jesuit Order was not yet fully organized in Castile. Molina was to remain 29 years as a student and teacher in Portugal. After Coimbra, the habitually shabbily dressed Molina taught theology and civil law for 20 years at the University of Évora. In retirement back in Cuenca, the learned and worldly Molina published his massive six-volume *magnum opus*, *De Justitia et Jure*. The first three volumes were published in 1593, 1597 and 1600, and the other volumes followed posthumously.

Luís de Molina was a solid economic liberal, and he provided a comprehensive analysis, in the Salamancan vein, of supply and demand and their determination of price. The just price is, of course, the common market price. One important addition that Molina made to his forerunners was to point out that goods supplied at retail in small quantities will sell at a higher unit price than at bulk sales before the goods get to the retailer. This argument also served as an added justification for the existence of the much-abused retailer.

But Molina in economics was primarily a monetary theorist. Here, he endorsed and carried forward the purchasing-power parity theory of exchange rates and the Salamancan analysis of the value of money, even explicitly endorsing the work of his theological opponent, Domingo de Bañez. Molina's analysis of the determination of the value of money and its changes was the most subtle to date, using explicit 'other things being equal' (*ceteris paribus*) clauses, and developing the analysis of the determinants of the demand for money.

Thus, on the causes of changes in price and particularly of the Spanish inflation of the sixteenth century, Molina wrote:

> Just as an abundance of goods causes prices to fall (the quantity of money and number of merchants being equal), so does an abundance of money cause them to rise (the quantity of goods and number of merchants being equal). The reason is that the money by itself becomes less valuable for the purpose of buying and comparing goods. Thus we see that in Spain the purchasing-power of money is far lower, on account of its abundance, than it was eighty years ago. A thing that could be bought for two ducats at that time is nowadays worth five, six, or even more. Wages have risen in the same proportion, and so have dowries, the price of estates, the income from benefices, and other things.

After going through the standard Spanish scholastic analysis of how abundance of money causes a fall in its value, first and foremost in the New World, then in Seville and Spain, Molina noted the importance of the demand for money: 'Wherever the demand for money is greatest, whether for buying or carrying goods, conducting other business, waging war, holding the royal court, or for any other reason, there will its value be highest'.

It is not surprising that the economic liberal Molina strongly attacked any government fixing of exchange rates. The value of one currency in terms of another is always changing in response to supply and demand forces, and therefore it is meet and just that exchange rates fluctuate accordingly. Molina then pointed out that fixed exchange rates would create a shortage of money. He did not, however, go into detail.

Molina also inveighed against most governmental price controls, particularly the imposing of ceiling prices on farm commodities.

On usury, Molina, while still not going as far as the radical acceptance of interest by Conrad Summenhart a century earlier, took important steps in widening the accepted bounds of the charging of interest. He put his immense prestige behind Juan de Medina's entirely new defence of charging payment for the lender's assumption of risk. Indeed, he widened Medina's permitted bounds of using the risk defence. Not only that: Molina greatly widened the scope of *lucrum cessans*, and solidly entrenched that permissible title to interest as a broad principle permeating the market economy. One of the few remaining restrictions is intention: the loan is not permissible if the lender had not intended to invest the loaned funds.

Luís de Molina also played an important role in reviving active natural rights and private-property rights theory, which had fallen into a decline since the early part of the sixteenth century. Humanists and Protestants, as we shall see below, had little use for the concept of natural rights, while Vitoria and the Dominicans slipped into a determinist, passive or attenuated view of rights. Only the University of Louvain, in Belgium, began to serve as a centre of free will thought, along with the idea of absolute natural rights of person and property. The Louvain theologian Johannes Driedo stressed freedom of the will (in *De Concordia*, 1537) and active natural rights (*De Libertate Christiana*, 1548).

By the 1580s, the new Jesuit Order began to launch its assault on the Dominicans, whom they suspected of crypto-Calvinism – a suspicion not allayed by the fact that many Dominicans had converted to Calvinism during the sixteenth century. In the course of his championing free will against de Bañez and the Dominicans, Molina also returned to the active natural rights view which had for long only continued to be upheld at Louvain. Attacking the passive claim theory of rights, Molina put the distinction very clearly:

> When we say...that someone has a *ius* to something, we do not mean that anything is owed to him, but that he has a faculty to it, whose contravention would cause him injury. In this way we say that someone has a *ius* to use his own things, such as consuming his own food – that is, if he is impeded, injury and injustice will be done to him. In the same way that a pauper has the *ius* to beg alms, a merchant has the *ius* to sell his wares, etc.

Note that the astute Molina did *not* say that the pauper had the right to be given alms. For Molina, as for all active property rights theorists, a 'right' was not a claim to someone else's property, but was, on the contrary a clear-cut right to use one's own property without someone else's claim being levied upon it.

It was Molina's achievement to link this active natural rights theory with his libertarian commitment to freedom and the free will of each individual, both theologically and philosophically. Professor Tuck sums up this linkage with these stirring words: Molina's 'was a theory which involved a picture of man as a free and independent being, making his own decisions and being held to them, on matters to do with both his physical and his spiritual welfare'.[2]

The School of Salamanca had begun with the distinguished jurist, de Vitoria, and so it is fitting that the last major Salamancan should be another renowned jurist, and perhaps the most illustrious thinker in the history of the Jesuit Order – Francisco Suarez (1548–1617). The last of the great Thomists, this celebrated theologian was born in Granada into an ancient noble family. Entering the University of Salamanca, Suarez applied to the Jesuit Order in 1564 and was the only applicant among 50 candidates that year to be rejected – as mentally and physically below standard! Admitted finally with an inferior rank, Suarez could hardly keep up with his studies and was known – ironically like St Thomas Aquinas before him – as the 'dumb ox'. Soon, however, the humble and modest Suarez became the star pupil, and it was not long before his theology professors were asking him for advice.

In 1571, Suarez became professor of philosophy at Segovia, then taught theology at Avila and Valladolid. Suarez soon attained to the famous chair of theology at the Jesuit College in Rome. From there, due to ill health, Suarez returned to Spain, teaching at Alcalá, where he was virtually ignored, and then to Salamanca, where, as in Alcalá, he lost academic disputes to inferior rivals. In 1593, the emperor insisted on Suarez's accepting the main chair of theology at Coimbra, where, in 1612, he published his masterwork, *De Legibus ac de Deo Legislatore.*

Francisco Suarez never achieved his due in life. His quiet, plodding lecture style made him lose academic influence to flashier though inferior rivals. Perhaps the crowning indignity heaped upon him is that, in 1597, at the age of 49, this brilliant and learned jurist and theologian, perhaps the greatest mind in the history of the Jesuit Order, was forced to leave the University of Coimbra for a year to obtain a doctorate in theology at Évora. Ph.D-itis in the sixteenth century![3]

While Suarez contributed little on strictly economic matters, he added greatly to the weight of the Louvain–Molina rediscovery of the active natural rights view of private property, and he reinforced the great impact of Molinist freewill theory. In addition, Suarez had a much more restricted view of the just power of the king than did Molina or his other predecessors. To Suarez the power of the ruler is in no sense a divinely created institution since political power by natural and divine law devolves solely on the people as a whole. The community as a whole confers political power on the king or other set of rulers; and while Suarez believed that natural law requires *some* form of state, the sovereign power of any particular state 'must necessarily be bestowed upon him by the consent of the community'.

Suarez's theory, of course, held radical implications indeed. For if the people or the community confer state power on a king or a set of rulers, may they not then take it away? Here, Suarez fumbled; he was certainly not prepared to go all the way to a truly radical or revolutionary position. No, he declared inconsistently, once the sovereign power is conferred by the people on a king, it is his forever; the people cannot take it back. But then Suarez shifts once more, adopting the traditional Thomist doctrine of the right of the people to resist tyrants. If a king lapses into tyranny, then the people may rise up and resist, and even assassinate the king. But Suarez, like his forbears, hedged this powerful right of 'tyrannicide' with a thicket of restrictions; in particular, tyranny must be manifest, and a private person cannot rise up himself and kill the king. The act must in some way be mandated by the people or community acting as a whole.

4.7 The learned extremist: Juan de Mariana

One of the last Spanish scholastics was a Jesuit but not a Salamancan. He was the 'extremist' contemporary of Molina and Suarez, Juan de Mariana (1536–1624). Mariana was born near Toledo, of poor and humble parents. He entered the great University of Alcalá in 1553, shone as a student, and a year later was received into the new Society of Jesus. After completing his studies at Alcalá, Mariana went to the Jesuit College at Rome in 1561 to teach philosophy and theology, and after four years moved to Sicily to set up the theology programme at the Jesuit college there. In 1569, Mariana moved to teach theology at the great University of Paris, at the remarkably young age of 33. After four years, ill health forced him to retire to live in Toledo; ill health, however, often does not necessarily mean a short life, and Mariana lived to the then phenomenally ripe old age of 88.

Fortunately, Mariana's 'retirement' was an active one, and his great learning and erudition drew numerous persons, from private citizens to state and ecclesiastical authorities, to ask for his advice and guidance. He was able to published two great and influential books. One was a history of Spain, written first in Latin and then in Spanish, which went into many volumes and many editions in both languages. The Latin version was eventually published in 11 volumes, and the Spanish in 30. The Spanish edition has long been considered one of the classics of Spanish style, and it went into many editions until the mid-nineteenth century.

The other notable work of Mariana, *De Rege (On Kingship)*, was published in 1599, written at the suggestion of King Philip II of Spain and dedicated to his successor Philip III. But monarchy did not fare well at the hands of the hard-hitting Mariana. A fervent opponent of the rising tide of absolutism in Europe, and of the doctrine of such as King James I of England that kings rule absolutely by divine right, Mariana converted the scholastic doctrine of tyranny from an abstract concept into a weapon with which to smite real monarchs of the past. He denounced such ancient rulers as Cyrus the Great, Alexander the Great, and Julius Caesar as tyrants, who acquired their power by injustice and robbery. Previous scholastics, including Suarez, believed that the people could ratify such unjust usurpation by their consent after the fact, and thereby make their rule legitimate. But Mariana was not so quick to concede the consent of the people. In contrast to other scholastics, who placed the 'ownership' of power in the king, he stressed that the people have a right to reclaim their political power whenever the king should abuse it. Indeed Mariana held that, in transferring their original political power from a state of nature to the king, the people necessarily reserved important rights to themselves; in addition to the right to reclaim sovereignty, they retained such vital powers as taxation, the right to veto laws, and the right to determine succession if the king has no heir. It should already be clear that it was Mariana, rather than Suarez, who might be called the forebear of John Locke's theory of popular consent and the continuing superiority of the people to the government. Furthermore, Mariana also anticipated Locke in holding that men leave the state of nature to form governments in order to preserve their rights of private property. Mariana also went far beyond Suarez in postulating a state of nature, a society, previous to the institution of government.

But the most fascinating feature of the 'extremism' of Mariana's political theory was his creative innovation in the scholastic theory of tyrannicide. That a tyrant might be justly killed by the people had long been standard doctrine; but Mariana broadened it greatly in two significant ways. First, he expanded the definition of tyranny: a tyrant was any ruler who violated the laws of religion, who imposed taxes without the people's consent, or who prevented a meeting of a democratic parliament. All the other scholastics, in contrast, had located the sole power to tax in the ruler. Even more spectacularly, to Mariana *any* individual citizen can justly assassinate a tyrant and may do so by any means necessary. Assassination did not require some sort of collective decision by the entire people. To be sure, Mariana did not think that an individual should engage in assassination lightly. First, he should try to assemble the people to make this crucial decision. But if that is impossible, he should at least consult some 'erudite and grave men', *unless* the cry of the people against the tyrant is so starkly manifest that consultation becomes unnecessary.

Furthermore, Mariana added – in phrases anticipating Locke's and the Declaration of Independence's justification of the right of rebellion – that we need not worry about the public order being greatly disrupted by too many people taking up the practice of tyrannicide. For this is a dangerous enterprise, Mariana sensibly pointed out, and very few are ever ready to risk their lives in that way. On the contrary, *most* tyrants have not died a violent death, and tyrannicides have almost always been greeted by the populace as heroes. In contrast to the common objections to tyrannicide, he concluded, it would be salutary for rulers to fear the people, and to realize that a lapse into tyranny might cause the people to call them to account for their crimes.

Mariana has given us an eloquent description of the typical tyrant at his deadly work:

> He seizes the property of individuals and squanders it, impelled as he is by the unkingly vices of lust, avarice, cruelty, and fraud.... . Tyrants, indeed, try to injure and ruin everybody, but they direct their attack especially against rich and upright men throughout the realm. They consider the good more suspect than the evil; and the virtue which they themselves lack is most formidable to them...They expel the better men from the commonwealth on the principle that whatever is exalted in the kingdom should be laid low... They exhaust all the rest so that they can not

unite by demanding new tributes from them daily, by stirring up quarrels among the citizens, and by joining war to war. They build huge works at the expense and by the suffering of the citizens. Whence the pyramids of Egypt were born... The tyrant necessarily fears that those whom he terrorizes and holds as slaves will attempt to overthrow him... . Thus he forbids the citizens to congregate together, to meet in assemblies, and to discuss the commonwealth altogether, taking from them by secret-police methods the opportunity of free speaking and freely listening so that they are not even allowed to complain freely... .

This 'erudite and grave man', Juan de Mariana, left no doubt what he thought of the most recent famous tyrannicide: that of the French King Henry III. In 1588, Henry III had been prepared to name as his successor Henry of Navarre, a Calvinist who would be ruling over a fiercely Catholic nation. Facing a rebellion by the Catholic nobles, headed by the duc de Guise, and backed by the devoted Catholic citizens of Paris, Henry III called the duke and his brother the cardinal to a peace parley into his camp, and then had the two assassinated. The following year, on the point of conquering the city of Paris, Henry III was assassinated in turn, by a young Dominican friar and member of the Catholic League, Jacques Clément. To Mariana, in this way 'blood was expiated with blood' and the duc de Guise was 'avenged with royal blood'. 'Thus perished Clément', concluded Mariana, 'an eternal ornament of France'. The assassination had similarly been hailed by Pope Sixtus V, and by the fiery Catholic preachers of Paris.

The French authorities were understandably edgy about Mariana's theories and at his book *De Rege*. Finally, in 1610, Henry IV (formerly Henry of Navarre, who had converted from Calvinism to the Catholic faith in order to become king of France), was assassinated by the Catholic resister Ravaillac, who despised the religious centrism and the state absolutism imposed by the king. At that point, France erupted in an orgy of indignation against Mariana, and the *parlement* of Paris had *De Rege* burned publicly by the hangman. Before executing Ravaillac, the assassin was questioned closely as to whether reading Mariana had driven him to murder, but he denied ever having heard of him. While the king of Spain refused to heed French pleas to suppress this subversive work, the general of the Jesuit Order issued a decree to his society, forbidding them to teach that it is lawful to kill tyrants. This truckling, however, did not prevent a successful smear campaign in France against the Jesuit Order, as well as its loss of political and theological influence.

Juan de Mariana possessed one of the most fascinating personalities in the history of political and economic thought. Honest, gutsy and fearless, Mariana was in hot water almost all of his long life, even for his economic writings. Turning his attention to monetary theory and practice, Mariana, in his brief treatise *De Monetae Mutatione* (*On the Alteration of Money*, 1609) denounced his sovereign, Philip III, for robbing the people and crippling commerce through the debasement of copper coinage. He pointed out that this debasement also added to Spain's chronic price inflation by increasing the quantity of money in the country. Philip had wiped out his public debt by debasing his copper coins by two-thirds, thereby tripling the supply of copper money.

Mariana noted that debasement and government tampering with the market value of money could only cause grave economic problems:

> Only a fool would try to separate these values in such a way that the legal price should differ from the natural. Foolish, nay, wicked the ruler who orders that a thing the common people value, let us say, at five should be sold for ten. Men are guided in this matter by common estimation founded on considerations of the quality of things, and of their abundance or scarcity. It would be vain for a Prince to seek to undermine these principles of commerce. 'Tis best to leave them intact instead of assailing them by force to the public detriment.

Mariana begins *De Monetae* with a charming and candid apologia for writing the book reminiscent of the great Swedish economist Knut Wicksell over two and a half centuries later: he knows that his criticism of the king courted great unpopularity, but everyone is now groaning under the hardships resulting from the debasement, and yet no one has had the courage to criticize the king's action publicly. Hence, justice requires that at least one man – Mariana – should move in to express the common grievance publicly. When a combination of fear and bribery conspire to silence critics, there should be at least one man in the country who knows the truth and has the courage to point it out to one and all.

Mariana then proceeds to demonstrate that debasement is a very heavy hidden tax on the private property of his subjects, and that, *pace* his political theory, no king has the right to impose taxes without the consent of the people. Since political power originated with the people, the king has no rights over the private property of his subjects, nor can he appropriate their wealth by his whim and will. Mariana notes the papal bull *Coena Domini*, which had decreed the excommunication of any ruler who imposes new taxes. Mariana reasons that any king who practises debasement should incur the same punishment, as should any legal monopoly imposed by the state without the consent of the people. Under such monopolies, the state itself, or its grantee, can sell a product to the public at a price higher than its market worth, and this is surely nothing but a tax.[4]

Mariana also set forth a history of debasement and its unfortunate effects; and he pointed out that governments are supposed to maintain all standards of weight and measure, not only of money, and that their record in adulterating those standards is most disgraceful. Castile, for example, had changed its measures of oil and wine, in order to levy a hidden tax, and this led to great confusion and popular unrest.

Mariana's book attacking the king's debasement of the currency led the monarch to haul the aged (73-year-old) scholar into prison, charging him with the high crime of *lèse-majesté*. The judges convicted Mariana of this crime against the king, but the pope refused to punish him, and Mariana was finally released from prison after four months on the condition that he would cut out the offensive passages in his work, and that he would be more careful in the future.

King Philip and his minions, however, did not leave the fate of the book to an eventual change of heart on the part of Mariana. Instead, the king ordered his officials to buy up every published copy of *De Monetae Mutatione* they could get their hands on and to destroy them. Not only that; after Mariana's death, the Spanish Inquisition expurgated the remaining copies, deleted many sentences and smeared entire pages with ink. All non-expurgated copies were put on the Spanish *Index*, and these in turn were expurgated during the seventeenth century. As a result of this savage campaign of censorship, the existence of the Latin text of this important booklet remained unknown for 250 years, and was only rediscovered because the Spanish text was incorporated into a nineteenth century collection of classical Spanish essays. Hence, few complete copies of the booklet survive, of which the only one in the United States is in the Boston Public Library.

The venerable Mariana was apparently not in enough trouble; after he was jailed by the king, the authorities seized his notes and papers, and found there a manuscript attacking the existing governing powers in the Society of Jesus. An individualist unafraid to think for himself, Mariana clearly took little stock in the Jesuit ideal of the society as a tightly disciplined military-like body. In this booklet, *Discurso de las Enfermedades de la Compañia*, Molina smote the Jesuit Order fore and aft, its administration and its training of novices, and he judged his superiors in the Jesuit Order unfit to rule. Above all, Mariana criticized the military-like hierarchy; the general, he concluded, has too much power, and the provincials and other Jesuits too little. Jesuits, he asserted, should at least have a voice in the selection of their immediate superiors.

When the Jesuit general, Claudius Aquaviva, found that copies of Mariana's work were circulating in a kind of underground *samizdat* both inside and outside the order, he ordered Mariana to apologize for the scandal. The feisty and principled Mariana, however, refused to do so, and Aquaviva did not press the issue. As soon as Mariana died, the legion of enemies of the Jesuit Order published the *Discurso* simultaneously in French, Latin and Italian. As in the case of all bureaucratic organizations, the Jesuits then and since were more concerned about the scandal and not washing dirty linen in public than in fostering freedom of inquiry, self-criticism, or correcting any evils that Mariana might have uncovered.

The Jesuit Order never expelled their eminent member nor did he ever leave. Still he was all his life regarded as a feisty trouble-maker, and as unwilling to bow to orders or peer pressure. Father Antonio Astrain, in his history of the Jesuit Order, notes that 'above all we must bear in mind that his [Mariana's] character was very rough and unmortified'.[5] Personally, in a manner similar to the Italian Franciscan saints San Bernardino and Sant'Antonino of the fifteenth century, Mariana was ascetic and austere. He never attended the theatre and he held that priests and monks should never degrade their sacred character by listening to actors. He also denounced the popular Spanish sport of bull-fighting, which was also not calculated to increase his popularity. Gloomily, Mariana would often stress that life was short, precarious, and full of vexation. Yet, despite his austerity, Father Juan de Mariana possessed a sparkling, almost Menckenesque, wit. Thus his one-liner on marriage: 'Some one cleverly said that the first and the last day of marriage are desirable, but that the rest are terrible'.

But probably his wittiest remark concerned bull-fighting. His attack on that sport met with the objection that some theologians had defended the validity of bull-fighting. Denouncing theologians who palliated crimes by inventing explanations to please the masses, Mariana delivered a line closely anticipating a favourite remark by Ludwig von Mises on economists over three and a half centuries later: 'there is nothing howsoever absurd which is not defended by some theologian'.

4.8   The last Salamancans: Lessius and de Lugo

One of the last great Salamancans was a Jesuit but not a Spaniard. Leonard Lessius (1554–1623) was a Fleming, born at Brecht near the great city of Antwerp. During the sixteenth century, Antwerp had become the outstanding commercial and financial centre of northern Europe, a focus of trade from the Mediterranean. Lessius's parents had originally planned for him to become a merchant, but he entered the University of Louvain, and was received into the Jesuit Order in 1572. He taught philosophy for six years at the English college at Douai, in France, and then went to Rome for two years to study under Francisco Suarez. It was at Rome that Lessius became a Salamancan in spirit, and from then on struck up a friendship with Luís de Molina. Returning to Flanders, Lessius assumed a chair in philosophy and theology at the University of Louvain. In theology, Lessius took up the great Molinist cause of free will against a pro-determinist wing of theologians at Louvain. There he confronted the crypto-Calvinist Dr Michael de Bay, chancellor of the University of Louvain, who had adopted the concept of predestination and salvation of the elect. Lessius also advanced the Suarezian view that original political power was conferred by God on the people, and hence he attacked the growing adherence to the divine right of kings, especially as put forth by King James I of England.

Lessius's most important work was *De Justitia et Jure* (1605), the same title as the works of Molina and de Bañez. The book was enormously influential, being published in nearly 40 separate editions in Antwerp, Louvain, Lyons, Paris and Venice. Not only was Lessius's knowledge of his predecessors encyclopedic, but he was renowned for his knowledge and analysis of contemporary commercial practices and contracts and for his applications of moral principles to such practices. Lessius was consulted frequently on these matters by statesmen and church leaders.

On the theory of price, Lessius, like his scholastic forbears, held the just price to be that determined by the common estimate of the market. A legally fixed price could also be the just price, but in contrast to many of his fellow scholastics, for whom the legal price took precedence, Lessius pointed out several cases in which the market price would have to be chosen over the legal price. Following Juan de Medina, these were: first, when the market price is lower; and second, when, 'in change of circumstances of increasing or diminishing supply and similar factors, the authorities were notably negligent in changing the legal price...'. Even more strongly, even a 'private individual' may request a price above the legal ceiling when the authorities are 'ill informed about the commercial circumstances', which is likely, of course, to happen a good deal of the time.

Attacking the cost of production theory of price, Lessius points to market demand as the determinant of price, regardless of a merchant's expenses:

> But if the merchant's expenses have been greater, that is his hard luck, and the common price may not be increased for that reason, just as it need not be decreased even if he had no expenses at all. This is the merchant's situation; just as he can make a profit if he has small expenses, so he can lose if his expenses are very large or extraordinary.

Leonard Lessius had an insight into how all economic markets are interrelated, and he analysed and defended in turn the workings of foreign exchange, speculation, and the value of money and prices. In particular, Lessius engaged in the most sophisticated analysis yet achieved of the workings of wages and the labour market. Like other scholastics, he saw that wages were governed by the same supply and demand principles, and therefore by the same canons of justice, as any price. In asking what is the 'minimum justifiable wage' for any given occupation, Lessius declared that the existence of other people willing to perform the work at any given wage shows that it is not too low. In short, if a supply exists for the labour at that wage, how can it be unjust?

Lessius also discovered and set forth the concept of psychic income as part of a money wage. A worker can be paid in psychic benefit as well as money: 'if the work brings with it social status and emoluments, the pay can be low because status and associated advantages are, so to say, a part of the salary'. Lessius also advanced the view that workers are hired by the employer because of the benefits gained by the latter, and those benefits will be gauged by the worker's productivity. Here are certainly the rudiments of the marginal productivity theory of the demand for labour and hence of wages, which was set forth by Austrians and other neoclassical economists at the end of the nineteenth century. Indeed, Lessius's sophisticated analysis of wages and the labour market were lost to mainstream economics until they were independently rediscovered in the late nineteenth century.

Lessius also stressed the importance of entrepreneurship in determining income. This quality of entrepreneurial 'industry', of efficiently combining jobs, is rare, and therefore the able entrepreneur can acquire a much higher income than his fellows. Lessius also provides a sophisticated analysis of money, demonstrating that the value of money is dependent on its supply and demand. More abundant money will make it less valuable either for buying goods or foreign exchange, and a greater demand for money will cause the value of the currency to rise: 'For example, if great princes are in urgent need of money for war or other public purposes, or if a large quantity of goods come on to the market; for whenever money is urgently needed for matters of great moment, so is it more highly esteemed in terms of goods.'

In his application of moral principle to trade practice, Lessius had a liberating effect on trade. This was particularly true of usury, where Lessius, while formally continuing the traditional prohibition, was actually a highly influential force in its ongoing destruction. Lessius provided the most sweeping defence so far of the guaranteed investment contract, and he treated benignly even high rates of return on capital. He also removed all the remaining restrictions on *lucrum cessans*. First, he widened the doctrine to apply, not only to specific loans that would otherwise have been invested, but to *any* funds, since they are liquid assets that always might have been invested. Thus the pool of funds can, as a whole, be considered opportunity cost foregone of investment, and therefore interest may be charged on a loan to that extent.

As Lessius puts it:

> Although no particular loan, separately considered, be the cause, all, however, collectively considered, are the cause of the whole *lucrum cessans*: for in order to lend indiscriminately to those coming by, you abstain from business and you undergo the loss of the profit which would come from this. Therefore, since all collectively are the cause, the burden of compensation for this profit can be distributed to single loans, according to the proportion of each.

But this meant that Leonard Lessius justified not only businessmen or investors planning to invest their money, but also *any* people with liquid funds, including professional money-lenders. For the first time among scholastics, *all* loans by money-lenders were now justified. With Leonard Lessius, then, the last of the barriers to interest or usury were smashed, and only the hollow shell of the formal prohibition remained.

Lessius adds that the lender may charge interest, even though a reserve of money is kept out of fear, and even if that fear is irrational. Note that to Lessius the important point was the reality of the lender's subjective fears, not whether the fears are objectively correct.

Furthermore, Lessius takes the Medina–Molina assumption of risk argument for interest, about which they had tended to hedge in practice, and widens it greatly. All loans, he points out, carry risks of non-payment: 'a personal right is almost always joined with some difficulties and dangers'. In a careful analysis of lenders' risk, Lessius pointed out that a greater risk, and a greater charge, would be incurred by lending to someone not known to the lender, or whose credit is doubtful.

But that is not all. For Leonard Lessius contributed his own, new and powerful, weapon against the usury ban: a new 'title' or justification for interest. The new justification – prefigured only by the neglected Summenhart – was *carentia pecuniae*: charging for lack of money. Lessius pointed out quite cogently that the lender suffers the lack of his money, the lack of his liquidity, during the term of the loan, and therefore he is entitled to charge interest for this economic loss. In short, Lessius saw perceptively that everyone derives utility from liquidity, from the possession of money, and that being deprived of this utility is a lack for which the lender may and will demand compensation. Lessius pointed out that unexpected situations can and do arise which could be met far more effectively if one's money were in one's possession and not absent for a period of time. Time, in short, can and should be charged for, for that reason, 'for it can never be obtained that the merchants do not value a long-term concession higher than a short-term one'. And those who are deprived of their money 'value more the lack of their money for five months than the lack of it for four, and the lack of it for four more than three, and this is partly because they lack the opportunity of gaining with that money, partly because their principle is longer in danger...'.

Furthermore, Lessius points out that bills of exchange, or rights to future money, are always at a discount compared to cash. This discount is, of course, the rate of interest. Lessius explains: 'This is a matter of common experience in that money provides the means to a multitude of things which those rights do not provide. Therefore they may be bought at a lower price'. Lessius also notes that merchants and exchangers daily determine the 'price of the lack of money' on the Antwerp Bourse, averaging about 10 per cent; and foreign exchanges, of inestimable value to the economy, would perish if such prices could not be charged.

Thus, for Lessius, the price for a lack of money is established on organized loan markets. But to the extent that a loan market exists, there is no need to justify each merchant's loan on the basis of his *particular* opportunity cost or deprivation of funds. That price, which becomes the just price, is set on the loan market. As Lessius puts it:

> Moreover, any merchant seems able to demand this price… even though there is no gain of his that stops because of his loan. This is the just price for the privation of money among merchants; for the just price of an article or obligation in any community is that which is put upon it by that community in good faith for the sake of the common good in view of all the circumstances…Therefore, even if through the privation of money for a year there is no gain of mine that stops and no risk of capital, because such a price for just causes has been put upon this privation, I may demand it just as the rest do.

With *carentia pecuniae*, therefore, Leonard Lessius delivered the final blow to smash the usury prohibition, while unfortunately still retaining the prohibition in a formal sense. It is no wonder that Professor Noonan, the great scholar of the scholastics on usury, holds Lessius to be 'the theologian whose views on usury most decidedly mark the arrival of a new era. More than any predecessor he would probably have felt completely at ease in the modern financial world.'[6]

The last Salamancan was the Jesuit Cardinal Juan de Lugo (1583–1660). De Lugo takes the Salamancans into the seventeenth century, the century of the decline of Spanish power in Europe. After studying law and theology at Salamanca, de Lugo went to Rome to teach at the great Jesuit College. After teaching theology in Rome for 22 years, de Lugo was made a cardinal and became a member of various influential Church commissions in Rome. A learned and comprehensive theoretician, de Lugo has been called the greatest moral theologian since Aquinas. Author of a book on psychology and another on physics, de Lugo's masterwork in the area of law and economics was *De Justitia et Jure*, published in 1642. This work went through numerous editions during the seventeenth and eighteenth centuries, its last edition having appeared as late as 1893.

In his theory of value, this culminating work of the Salamancan School displayed a subtle and advanced subjective utility explanation. The prices of goods, de Lugo pointed out, fluctuate 'on account of their utility in respect of human need, and then only on account of estimation; for jewels are much less useful than corn in the house, and yet their price is much higher'. Here de Lugo, once again, comes very close to the late nineteenth century marginal utility explanation of value, and to solving the value paradox. Corn is higher than jewellery in use value, but is cheaper in price. The answer to this paradox is that subjective estimates or valuations differ from objective use-value, and these in turn are affected by the relative scarcities of supply. Again, only the marginal concept is needed to complete the explanation.

Subjectivity, de Lugo goes on, means that the 'estimation' or valuation is going to be conducted by 'imprudent' as well as 'prudent' men (no 'rationality' or 'economic man' assumptions here!). In short, the just price is the market price determined by demand and consumer valuations; and, if the consumers are foolish or judge differently than we do, then so be it. The market price is a just price all the same.

In his discussion of merchants' activities, de Lugo adds to the previous opportunity-cost concept of mercantile expenses. For a merchant will only continue to supply a product if the price covers his expenses and the rate of profit he could earn in other activities.

In his theory of money, Cardinal de Lugo follows his confrères: the value or purchasing power of money is determined by the quality of the metal content of coins, the supply of and the demand for money. De Lugo also set forth the idea that money moves from the area of its lower to that of its higher value.

On usury, de Lugo provided a mixed bag. On the one hand, he draws back from the clear implications of Lessius and others that the usury ban should become a hollow shell. For that reason, he refuses to accept Lessius's willingness to have the lender charge for lack of money during the period of the loan. On the other hand, de Lugo widens still further the powerful 'pro-usury' weapons of risk and *lucrum cessans*. He broadens the concept of risk to include explicitly every loan; for, as he puts it with remarkable bluntness: 'Where today is there to be found a debt so placed in safety that in security it equals ready cash?' But that, of course, justifies the charging of interest on every loan. De Lugo also widens *lucrum cessans* still further, for he allows the lender to include not only probable profit foregone from a loan, but also the expectation of *remote* profit foregone. Also, the lender, in charging interest, may calculate the profit he would have made by *re*-investing the lost profit on a loan. In sum, de Lugo asserts sweepingly that *lucrum cessans* is 'the general title for purging usury'.

4.9   The decline of scholasticism

Sixteenth century Spain has well been called the Indian Summer of scholasticism. After that, its decline, not only in Spain but throughout Europe, was rapid. Part of the reason was a stubborn clinging to the *form* of the prohibition of usury. A ban which had made little sense, either by natural or divine law, and which entered Christian thought quite late in the day, was clung to and strengthened in an almost perpetual, irrational frenzy. The systematic weakening of the usury ban by some of the finest minds in Christendom had the beneficial effect of sanctioning the charging of interest, but at the long-run cost of discrediting the scholastic method itself. By clinging to the outer husk of banning usury as a mortal sin, while at the same time finding increasingly sophisticated ways of allowing merchants and finally professional money-lenders to get around the ban, the scholastics opened themselves to unfair charges of evasion and hypocrisy.

The deadly assault on scholasticism came from two contrasting but allied camps. One was the rising groups of Protestants without, and crypto-Calvinists within, the Church who denounced it for its alleged decadence and moral laxity. Protestantism, after all, was in large part a drive to cast off the sophisticated trappings and the refined doctrine of the Church, and to go back to the alleged simplicity and moral purity of early Christianity. Made the very emblem of this hostility was the Jesuit Order, the devoted spearhead of the Counter-Reformation, that order which had taken up from the faltering Dominicans the torch of Thomism and scholasticism.

The second camp of enemies of scholasticism was the rising group of secularists and rationalists, men who might be Catholics or Protestants in their private lives but who mainly wanted to get rid of such alleged excrescences on modern life as the political application of religious principles or the prohibition of usury. Consequently, the crypto-Calvinists attacked the Jesuits for weakening the prohibition of usury, while the secularists attacked them for keeping it.

Neither wing of the opposition was impressed with the brilliance of the scholastic arguments to justify usury, nor with the entire scholastic and Jesuit enterprise of 'casuistry': that is, of applying moral principles, both natural and divine, to concrete problems of daily life. One might think that the task of casuistry should be deemed an important and even noble one; if general moral principles exist, why *shouldn't* they be applied to daily life? But both sets of opponents rapidly succeeded in making the very word 'casuistry' a smear term: for the one, a method of weaselling out of strict moral precepts; for the other, a method of imposing outdated and reactionary dogmas upon the world.

Why, despite the great work of Summenhart and others, did the Catholic Church persist in keeping the formal ban on usury for two centuries thereafter? Probably for the same reason that the Church has always tended to maintain stoutly that it never changes its doctrines while it keeps doing so. Changing content within an unchanging formal shell has long been characteristic, not only of the Catholic Church, but of any long-lived bureaucratic institution, whether it be the Church or the constitutional interpretations of the Supreme Court of the United States.

The two-pronged alliance against scholasticism outside and within the Catholic Church cut far deeper than the quarrel over usury. At the root of Catholicism as a religion is that God can be approached or apprehended through all the faculties of man, not simply through faith but through reason and the senses. Protestantism, and especially Calvinism, sternly put God outside man's faculties, considering, for example, sensate embodiments of man's love for God in painting or sculpture as blasphemous idolatry to be destroyed in order to clear the path for the only proper communication with God: pure faith in revelation. The Thomist stress on reason as a means of apprehending God's natural law and even aspects of divine law was reviled by a sole Protestant emphasis on faith in God's arbitrary will. While some Protestants adopted natural law theories, the basic Protestant thrust was opposition to any natural law attempts to derive ethics or political philosophy from the use of man's reason. For Protestants, man was too inherently sinful and corrupt for his reason or his senses to be anything but an embodiment of corruption; only pure faith in God's arbitrary and revealed commands was permissible as a groundwork for human ethics. But this meant that for Protestants there was also very little natural law groundwork from which to criticize actions of the state. Calvinism and even Lutheranism provided little or no defences against the absolutist state which burgeoned throughout Europe during the sixteenth century and triumphed in the seventeenth century.

If Protestantism opened the way for the absolute state, the secularists of the sixteenth and seventeenth centuries embraced it. Shorn of natural law critiques of the state, new secularists such as the Frenchman Jean Bodin embraced the state's positive law as the only possible criterion for politics. Just as the anti-scholastic Protestants extolled God's arbitrary will as the foundation for ethics, so the new secularists raised the state's arbitrary will to the status of unchallengeable and absolute 'sovereign'.

On the deeper level of the question of how we know what we know, or 'epistemology', Thomism and scholasticism suffered from the contrasting but allied assaults by the champions of 'reason' and 'empiricism'. In Thomist thought, reason and empiricism are not separated but allied and interwoven. Truth is built up by reason on a solid groundwork in empirically known reality. The rational and empirical were integrated into one coherent whole. But in the first part of the seventeenth century, two contrasting philosophers managed between them the fatal sundering of the rational and the empirical that continues to plague the scientific method until the present day. These were the Englishman Francis Bacon (1561–1626) and the Frenchman René Descartes (1596–1650). Descartes was the champion of a dessicated mathematical and absolutely certain 'reason' divorced from empirical reality, while Bacon was the advocate of sifting endlessly and almost mindlessly through the empirical data. Both the distinguished English lawyer who rose to become Lord Chancellor (Lord Verulam), Viscount of the Realm, and corrupt judge, and the shy and wandering French aristocrat, agreed on one crucial and destructive point: the severing of reason and thought from empirical data. Hence, from Bacon there stemmed the English 'empiricist' tradition, steeped mindlessly in incoherent data, and from Descartes the purely deductive and sometimes mathematical tradition of continental 'rationalism'. All this was of course an assault on natural law, which had long integrated the rational and the empirical.

As a corollary to, and intermingled with, this basic and systematic change in European thought in the 'early modern' period (the sixteenth and especially seventeenth centuries) was a radical shift in the locus of intellectual activity away from the universities. The theologians and philosophers who wrote and thought on economics, law, and other disciplines of human action during the medieval and Renaissance periods were university professors. Paris, Bologna, Oxford, Salamanca, Rome, and many other universities were the milieu and arena for intellectual output and combat during these centuries. And even the Protestant universities in the early modern period continued to be centres of natural law teaching.

But the major theorists and writers of the seventeenth and then the eighteenth centuries were almost none of them professors. They were pamphleteers, businessmen, wandering aristocrats such as Descartes, minor public officials such as John Locke, churchmen such as Bishop George Berkeley. This shift of focus was greatly facilitated by the invention of printing, which made the publication of books and writings far less costly and created a much wider market for intellectual output. Printing was invented in the mid-fifteenth century, and by the early sixteenth century it became possible, for the first time, to make a living as an independent writer, selling one's books to a commercial market.

This shift from university professors to private lay citizens meant, at least for that era, a move away from traditional modes of learning and thought towards a more diverse spectrum of idiosyncratic individual views. In a sense, this acceleration of diversity went hand in hand with one of the most important impacts of the Protestant Reformation on social and religious thought. For, in the long run, far more important than such theological disputes as over free will vs predestination and over the significance of communion was the shattering of the unity of Christendom. Luther and even Calvin had no intention of fragmenting Christendom; on the contrary, each set out to reform a unified Christian Church. But the consequences of their revolution was to open Pandora's box. Whereas frictions and heresies had before been either stamped out or accommodated within the Church, now Christianity split apart in literally hundreds of different sects, some quite bizarre, each propounding different theologies, ethics, and prescriptions for social life.

While the variegated strains of social thought stemming from this break within Christianity included rationalists and individualist groups such as the

Levellers as well as absolutists, the value of the resulting diversity must be offset by the unfortunate fading away of scholasticism and Thomism from Western thought.

The severing of the unity of European thought was intensified by the shift during these centuries of written literature from Latin to the vernacular in each country. During the Middle Ages, all intellectuals, jurists and theologians in Europe wrote in Latin, even though of course the spoken language in each country was the vernacular. This meant that for scholars and intellectuals there was only one language, and in a sense one country, so that Englishmen, Frenchmen, Germans, etc. could easily read and be influenced by each others' books and articles. Europe was truly one intellectual community.

In the Middle Ages, only Italian authors wrote, from time to time, in Italian as well as Latin. But the Protestant Reformation gave tremendous impetus toward the abandonment of Latin, since Protestants felt it vital for the Christian masses to read and study the Bible in language they could understand. Martin Luther's famous translation of the Bible into German, in the sixteenth century, inspired a rapid change towards writing in the national language. As a result, since the sixteenth and seventeenth centuries, economic, social, and religious thought began to be isolated in each national language. Later continuing influences of scholastic economic thought became confined to writers in Catholic countries.

4.10   Parting shots: the storm over the Jesuits

While the inspiration for creative and outstanding scholastics was played out, the seventeenth century saw the influence of scholasticism continue in Spain and spread to other countries. The great champion and disseminator of the Salamanca School was of course the Jesuit Order. In Spain and elsewhere the Jesuits produced a huge number of manuals on moral theology for the use of confessors, in which they discussed, among other matters, the application of theological and moral principles to the ethics of business. The most important instance was the pious Father Antonio de Escobar y Mendoza's (1589–1669) *Theologiae Moralis* (1652). This extremely popular work was reprinted in 37 editions in a brief period of time, and was also translated and published in France, Belgium, Germany and Italy. Escobar's work was basically a restatement of two dozen previous books on moral theology, mainly by such Spanish writers as Molina, Suarez and de Lugo. He repeated the Salamancan emphasis on common estimation, scarcity, and the supply of money as determinants of market price.

The Salamanca School was particularly influential in Italy. There the Genoese philosopher and jurist, Sigismundo Scaccia (c.1568–1618), published a *Tractatus de Commerciis et Cambiis* in 1618, which was reprinted often in Italy, France, and Germany down to the middle of the eighteenth century. Scaccia's *Tractatus* repeated the price and foreign exchange theories of the Salamancans, including Covarrubias, Azpilcueta and Lessius.

Other prominent neo-Salamancans in Italy were the Jesuit Cardinal Giambattista de Luca (1613–83), who published his multi-volume *Theatrum Veritatis et Justitiae* in Rome in the 1670s; Martino Bonacina (c.1585–1631); and Antonino Diana (1585–1663).

In France, however, the influential Escobar manual ran into a storm of abuse for its sophisticated permissive attitude towards usury. The abuse was led by an influential crypto-Calvinist group within the French Catholic Church that raised a furious row about the alleged moral laxity of the Jesuit Order.

The assault on the Jesuits and on their devotion to reason and the freedom of the will had begun in Belgium, and was accelerated towards the end of the sixteenth century by Dr Michael de Bay, chancellor of the great University of Louvain. Bay, and Baianism, launched a furious intramural warfare within Louvain against Leonard Lessius and the Jesuits on the faculty. Chancellor de Bay managed to convert most of the Louvain faculty to his creed, which adopted the Calvinist creed of predestination of an elect. In France, the absolutist pro-royalists began a bitter campaign against the Jesuit Order, which they linked with the Catholic Leaguers and the assassination of the centrist and pro-Calvinist Henrys. In particular, the attorney Antoine Arnauld, defending royal absolutism to the hilt, petitioned for the expulsion of the Jesuits from France, angrily declaiming that they were the worst enemies of 'the sacred doctrine of the Divine Right of Kings'. Arnauld was originally employed to press the case against the Jesuits by the University of Paris, and its theological faculty of the Sorbonne, which had also been swept by the crypto-Calvinist tide.

In the early seventeenth century, two disciples of Michael de Bay, both former students of the Jesuits, took up the cudgels for his cause. Most important was Cornelius Jansen, founder of the neo-Calvinist Jansenist movement, which became extremely powerful in France. Jansen, like many openly Protestant theologians, demanded to go back to the moral purity of St Augustine and of the Christian doctrines of the fourth and fifth centuries. If Jansen was the theoretician of the movement, his friend the Abbé Saint-Cyran was the brilliant tactician and organizer. With the help of Mère Angelique, superior of the nuns of Port-Royal, Saint-Cyran gained control of these influential nuns. Mère Angelique was the daughter of Antoine Arnauld, and indeed a dozen of the Port-Royal nuns were members of the powerful Arnauld family.

One of the Port-Royal nuns was the sister of the brilliant young philosopher, mathematician, and French stylist Blaise Pascal, and young Pascal took up the Jansenist cause with a witty and blistering attack on the Jesuits, particularly Escobar, for his alleged moral failure in being soft on usury. Pascal even coined a popular new term, *escobarderie*, with which he denounced the important discipline of casuistry as being evasive quibbling. Another victim of Pascal's poison pen was the austere French Jesuit Étienne Bauny. In his *Somme des Pechez* (1639), Bauny extended the weakening of the usury ban by going so far as to justify interest charges higher than the maximum rate permitted by royal decree for, after all 'the debtors entered into them willingly'. Moreover, Bauny's trenchant voluntaryism defended the usury contract on another incisive ground: since it is licit for a lender to hope for a borrower to give him a free gift, it should also be licit for the lender and the borrower to make such a definite pact beforehand. How can making a contract for something be evil if hoping for the result is permissible? Once permit such justifications by voluntary choice, and then of course all assaults on usury and other free market activities must go by the board.

Although the Jansenists were eventually condemned by the pope, Pascal's scurrilous rampage against the Jesuits had considerable effect in helping to end the reign of scholastic thought, at least in France.

4.11 Notes

1. Frank Bartholomew Costello, S.J., *The Political Philosophy of Luis de Molina, S.J.* (Spokane: Gonzaga University Press, 1974), p. 231.
2. Richard Tuck, *Natural Rights Theories* (Cambridge: Cambridge University Press, 1979), p. 54.
3. The great Molina had also had difficulties in not having a theology doctorate, which was finally conferred upon him by the Jesuit Order with considerable reluctance.
4. The form of Philip's debasement, as Mariana pointed out, was either to double the face value of recoined copper while keeping the same weight, so that the increased value went as profit to the royal treasury; or to keep the face value of silver/copper coins, take out the silver and reduce the copper weight, which gave the treasury a two-thirds profit.
5. Quoted by John Laures, S.J., *The Political Economy of Juan de Mariana* (New York: Fordham University Press, 1928), p. 18.
6. John T. Noonan, Jr, *The Scholastic Analysis of Usury* (Cambridge, Mass.: Harvard University Press, 1957), p. 222.

5   Protestants and Catholics

5.1 Luther, Calvin, and state absolutism

We have seen that the Counter-Reformation of the sixteenth century had to carry on a two-front intellectual war on behalf of scholasticism and natural law: against Protestants and crypto-Protestants, and also against secularist apologists for an absolute state. These latter two seemingly contrasting groups were closer than merely having the same enemy. In many ways, they were twins and not simply fortuitous allies.

Despite their many differences, Martin Luther (1483–1546), son of a German miner, and John Calvin (born Jean Cauvin, of which Calvin is the Latinized name) (1509–64), son of a French attorney and leading town official, whose new religious sects between them swept northern Europe, agreed on some crucial fundamentals. In particular, their social philosophy and theology rested on the basic proposition that man is totally depraved, steeped in sin. If this is so, man could scarcely achieve salvation even partially through his own efforts; therefore, salvation comes, not from man's non-existent free will, but as an arbitrary and unintelligible gift of unearned grace from God, a gift which He for His own reasons hands out only to a predestined elect. All of the non-elect are damned. Furthermore, as man is totally depraved and a slave of Satan, his reason – let alone his sense of enjoyment – can never be trusted. Neither reason nor the senses can in any way be trusted to form a social ethics; that can only come from the divine will through Biblical revelation.

To this day, fundamentalist Calvinists are taught to sum up their creed in the acronym TULIP, perhaps also recalling the Dutch fastnesses of Calvinism:

T – Total damnation
U – Unconditional election
L – Limited atonement
I – Irresistible grace
P – Perseverance of the saints

In short, man is damned totally, his atonement can only be limited and insufficient; the only thing that can and does unconditionally save an elect among men is God's irresistible grace.

If reason cannot be used to frame an ethic, this means that Luther and Calvin had to, in essence, throw out natural law, and in doing so, they jettisoned the basic criteria developed over the centuries by which to criticize the despotic actions of the state. Indeed, Luther and Calvin, relying on isolated Biblical passages rather than on an integrated philosophic tradition, opined that the powers that be are ordained of God, and that therefore the king, no matter how tyrannical, is divinely appointed and must always be obeyed.

This doctrine, of course, played into the hands of the rising absolute monarchs and their theoreticians. Whether Catholic or Protestant, these secularists pushed their religion to the background of life; socially and politically they held, as we shall see below, that the state and its ruler are absolute, that the ruler must seek to preserve and expand his power, and that his dictates must be obeyed. It is therefore the early Jesuits of the Counter-Reformation who saw and analysed the crucial link between the Protestant leaders and such amoralist secularists as Niccolo Machiavelli. As Professor Skinner writes:

> The early Jesuit theorists clearly recognized the pivotal point at which the political theories of Luther and Machiavelli may be said to converge: both of them were equally concerned, for their own very different reasons, to reject the idea of the law of nature as an appropriate moral basis for political life. It is in consequence in the works of the early Jesuits that we first encounter the familiar coupling of Luther and Machiavelli as the two founding fathers of the impious modern State.[1]

Moreover, Luther had to rely for the spread of his religion on the German and other European monarchs; his preaching of all-out obedience to the ruler was reinforced by this practical concern. In addition, the secular princes themselves had a juicy economic motive for becoming Protestant: the confiscation of the often wealthy monasteries and other Church property. Underlying at least part of the motives of the monarchy and nobility of the new Protestant states was the lure of greed-and-grab. Thus, when Gustav Vasa, king of Sweden, became a Lutheran in 1524, he immediately transferred the Church tithes into taxes going to the Crown, and three years later he confiscated the entire property of the Catholic Church. Similarly, in Denmark the newly Lutheran kings seized the monastic lands, and confiscated the lands and temporal powers of the Catholic bishops. In Germany Albert of Hohenzollern accompanied his Lutheran conversion by seizing the lands of the Catholic Teutonic knights, while Philip of Hesse grabbed all the monastic lands in his state, much of the proceeds going into his own personal coffers.

In addition to grabbing the lands and revenues, the monarchs in each of the lands seized control of the Church itself, and converted the Lutheran Church into a state-run Church, to the plaudits of Martin Luther and his disciples, who championed the idea of a state-dominated Church. In the city of Geneva, John Calvin and his disciples imposed a totalitarian theocracy for a time, but this Church-run state proved to be an aberration in mainstream Calvinism, which triumphed in Scotland, Holland and Switzerland, and had considerable influence in France and England.

An outstanding example of a state-run Church as a motive for Reformation was the establishment of the Anglican Church in England. The defection from Catholicism of Henry VIII was accompanied by the confiscation of the monasteries, and the parcelling out of these lands – either by gift or by sale at low cost – to favoured groups of nobles and gentry. About two thousand monks and nuns throughout England, as well as about eight thousand labourers in the monasteries, were thus dispossessed, for the benefit of a new class of large landholders beholden to the Crown and not likely to permit any return to a Roman Catholic monarchy in Britain.

5.2 Luther's economics

As a man fundamentally opposed to later scholastic refinements or even to the kind of integral, systematic thought of scholasticism, as a man hankering after what he believed to be Augustinian purity, Martin Luther cannot be expected to have looked very kindly upon commerce or upon the later scholastic justifications for usury. And indeed he did not. A confused, contradictory, and unsystematic thinker at best, Luther was unsurprisingly least consistent in an area of secular affairs – economics – in which he had little interest.

Thus, on a crucial question which had vexed scholastics for centuries: whether private property is natural or conventional, i.e. merely the product of positive law, Luther was characteristically anti-intellectual. He was not interested in such questions; therefore they were trivial: 'it is vain to mention these things; they cannot be acquired by thought, ...'. As Dr Gary North has commented, 'So much for 1500 years of debate'.[2] All in all, Richard Tawney's assessment of Luther on these matters is perhaps not an overstatement;

> Confronted with the complexities of foreign trade and financial organization, or with the subtleties of economic analysis, he [Luther] is like a savage introduced to a dynamo or a steam engine. He is too frightened and angry even to feel curiosity. Attempts to explain the mechanism merely enrage him; he can only repeat that there is a devil in it, and that good Christians will not meddle with the mystery of iniquity.[3]

The rest is confusion. Upholding the commandment prohibiting theft meant that Luther had to be, at least in some sense, an advocate of the rights of private property. But to Luther, 'stealing' meant not only what everyone defines to be theft, but also 'taking advantage of others at market, warehouses, wine and beer cellars, workshops...'. In different writings, sometimes even within the same one, Luther was capable of denouncing a person who 'makes use of the market in his own wilful way, proud and defiant, as though he had a good right to sell at as high a price as he chose, and none could interfere', while *also* writing: 'Anyone may sell what he has for the highest price he can get, so long as he cheats no one', and then defining such cheating as simply using false weights and measures.

On the just price, Luther tends to revert to the minority medieval view that a just price is not the market price but a cost of production plus expenses and profit for labour and risk of the merchant. On usury in particular, Luther tended to revert to the drastic prohibition that the Catholic Church had long left behind. The *census* contract he would ban, as he would *lucrum cessans*; money was sterile; there should be no increase in price for time as against cash payments for goods, etc. All the old nonsense, which the scholastics had spent centuries burying or transforming, was back intact. It is certainly fitting that, as we have seen, one of Luther's great theological opponents in Germany was his former friend, Johann Eck, a Catholic theologian and friend of the great Fugger banking family, who was even ahead of his time in arguing in thoroughgoing fashion in favour of usury.

Yet, despite his opposition to usury, Luther advised the young ruler of Saxony not to abolish interest or to relieve debtors of the burden of paying it. Interest is, after all, a 'common plague that all have taken upon themselves. We must put up with it, therefore, and hold debtors to it'.

Some of these contradictions can be reconciled in the light of Luther's deeply pessimistic view of man and therefore of human institutions. In the wicked secular world, he believed, we cannot expect people or institutions to act in accordance with the Christian gospel. Therefore, in contrast to the Catholic attempt through the art of casuistry to apply moral principles to social and political life, Luther tended to privatize Christian morality and to leave the secular world and its rulers to operate in a pragmatic and, in practice, an unchecked manner.

5.3   The economics of Calvin and Calvinism

John Calvin's social and economic views closely parallel Luther's, and there is no point in repeating them here. There are only two main areas of difference: their views on usury, and on the concept of the 'calling', although the latter difference is more marked for the later Calvinist Puritans of the seventeenth century.

Calvin's main contribution to the usury question was in having the courage to dump the prohibition altogether. This son of an important town official had only contempt for the Aristotelian argument that money is sterile. A child, he pointed out, knows that money is only sterile when locked away somewhere; but who in their right mind borrows to keep money idle? Merchants borrow in order to make profits on their purchases, and hence money is then fruitful. As for the Bible, Luke's famous injunction only orders generosity towards the poor, while Hebraic law in the Old Testament is not binding in modern society. To Calvin, then, usury is perfectly licit, provided that it is not charged in loans to the poor, who would be hurt by such payment. Also, any legal maximum of course must be obeyed. And finally, Calvin maintained that no one should function as a professional money-lender.

The odd result was that hedging his explicit pro-usury doctrine with qualification, Calvin *in practice* converged on the views of such scholastics as Biel, Summenhart, Cajetan and Eck. Calvin began with a sweeping theoretical defence of interest-taking and then hedged it about with qualifications; the liberal scholastics began with a prohibition of usury and then qualified it away. But while in practice the two groups converged and the scholastics, in discovering and elaborating upon exceptions to the usury ban, were theoretically more sophisticated and fruitful, Calvin's bold break with the formal ban was a liberating breakthrough in Western thought and practice. It also threw the responsibility for applying teachings on usury from the Church or state to the individual's conscience. As Tawney puts it, 'The significant feature in his [Calvin's] discussion of the subject is that he assumes credit to be a normal and inevitable incident in the life of a society.'[4]

A more subtle difference, but in the long run perhaps having more influence on the development of economic thought, was the Calvinist concept of the 'calling'. This new concept was embryonic in Calvin and was developed further by later Calvinists, and especially Puritans, in the late seventeenth century. Older economic historians, such as Max Weber, made far too much of the Calvinist as against Lutheran and Catholic conceptions of the 'calling'. All these religious groups emphasized the merit of being productive in one's labour or occupation, one's 'calling' in life. But there is, especially in the later Puritans, the idea of success in one's calling as a visible sign of being a member of the elect. The success is striven for, of course, not to *prove* that one is a member of the elect destined to be saved but, assuming that one is in the elect by virtue of one's Calvinist faith, to strive to labour and succeed for the glory of God. A Calvinist emphasis on postponement of earthly gratification led to a particular stress on saving. Labour or 'industry' and thrift, almost for their own sake, or rather for God's sake, were emphasized in Calvinism much more than in the other segments of Christianity.[5]

The focus, then, both in Catholic countries and in scholastic thought, became very different from that of Calvinism. The scholastic focus was on consumption, the consumer, as the goal of labour and production. Labour was not so much a good in itself as a means toward consumption on the market. The Aristotelian balance, or golden mean, was considered a requisite of the good life, a life leading to happiness in keeping with the nature of man. And that balanced life emphasized the joys of consumption, as well as of leisure, in addition to the importance of productive effort. In contrast, a rather grim emphasis on work and on saving began to be stressed in Calvinist culture. This de-emphasis on leisure of course fitted with the iconoclasm that reached its height in Calvinism – the condemnation of the enjoyment of the senses as a means of expressing religious devotion. One of the expressions of this conflict came over religious holidays, which Catholic countries enjoyed in abundance. To the Puritans, this was idolatry; even Christmas was not supposed to be an occasion for sensate enjoyment.

There has been considerable dispute over the 'Weber thesis', propounded by the early twentieth century German economic historian and sociologist, Max Weber, which attributed the rise of capitalism and the Industrial Revolution to the late Calvinist concept of the calling and the resulting 'capitalist spirit'. For all its fruitful insights, the Weber thesis must be rejected on many levels. First, modern capitalism, in any meaningful sense, begins not with the Industrial Revolution of eighteenth and nineteenth centuries but, as we have seen, in the Middle Ages and particularly in the Italian city-states. Such examples of capitalist rationality as double-entry bookkeeping and various financial techniques begin in these Italian city-states as well. All were Catholic. Indeed, it is in a Florentine account book of 1253 that there is first found the classic pro-capitalist formula: 'In the name of God and of profit'. No city was more of a financial and commercial centre than Antwerp in the sixteenth century, a Catholic centre. No man shone as much as financier and banker as Jacob Fugger, a good Catholic from southern Germany. Not only that: Fugger worked all his life, refused to retire, and announced that 'he would make money as long as he could'. A prime example of the Weberian 'Protestant ethic' from a solid Catholic! And we have seen how the scholastic theologians moved to understand and accommodate the market and market forces.

On the other hand, while it is true that Calvinist areas in England, France, Holland and the north American colonies prospered, the solidly Calvinist Scotland remained a backward and undeveloped area, even to this day.[6]

But even if the focus on calling and labour did not bring about the Industrial Revolution, it might well have led to another outstanding difference between Calvinist and Catholic countries – a crucial difference in the development of *economic thought*. Professor Emil Kauder's brilliant speculation to this effect will inform the remainder of this work. Thus Kauder:

> Calvin and his disciples placed work at the center of their social theology... All work in this society is invested with divine approval. Any social philosopher or economist exposed to Calvinism will be tempted to give labor an exalted position in his social or economic treatise, and no better way of extolling labor can be found than by combining work with value theory, traditionally the very basis of an economic system. Thus value becomes labor value, which is not merely a scientific device for measuring exchange rates but also the spiritual tie combining Divine Will with economic everyday life.[7]

In their extolling of work, the Calvinists concentrated on systematic, continuing industriousness, on a settled course of labour. Thus the English Puritan divine Samuel Hieron opined that 'He that hath no honest business about which ordinarily to be employed, no settled course to which he may betake himself, cannot please God'. Particularly influential was the early seventeenth century Cambridge University academic, the Rev. William Perkins, who did much to translate Calvinist theology into English practice. Perkins denounced four groups of men who had 'no particular calling to walk in': beggars and vagabonds; monks and friars; gentlemen who 'spend their days in eating and drinking'; and servants, who allegedly spent their time waiting. All these were dangerous because unsettled and undisciplined. Particularly dangerous were wanderers, who 'avoided the authority of all'. Furthermore, believed Perkins, the 'lazy multitude was always inclined ... to popish opinions, always more ready to play than to work; its members would not find their way to heaven'.[8]

In contrast to the Calvinist glorification of labour, the Aristotelian–Thomist tradition was quite different:

> Instead of work, moderate pleasure-seeking and happiness form the center of economic actions, according to Aristotelian and Thomistic philosophy. A certain balanced hedonism is an integrated part of the Aristotelian theory of the good life. If pleasure in a moderate form is the purpose of economics, then following the Aristotelian concept of the final cause, all principles of economics including valuation must be derived from this goal. In this pattern of Aristotelian and Thomistic thinking, valuation has the function of showing how much pleasure can be derived from economic goods.[9]

Hence, Great Britain, heavily influenced by Calvinist thought and culture, and its glorification of the mere exertion of labour, came to develop a labour theory of value, while France and Italy, still influenced by Aristotelian and Thomist concepts, continued the scholastic emphasis on the consumer and his subjective valuation as the source of economic value. While there is no way to prove this hypothesis conclusively, the Kauder insight has great value in explaining the comparative development of economic thought in Britain and in the Catholic countries of Europe after the sixteenth century.

5.4   Calvinists on usury

Perhaps because he was considered the greatest French jurist of the mid-sixteenth century, the merit of the contributions of Charles Du Moulin (latinized name, Carolus Molinaeus) (1500–66), has been highly inflated, in his and in later times. A Catholic who later converted to Calvinism and was then forced to leave for Germany, Du Moulin had nothing but contempt for scholasticism, which he attacked vehemently in his highly publicized work, *The Treatise on Contracts and Usury* (Paris, 1546). Whereas Molinaeus officially denounced the prohibition of usury, in actuality his views were little different from those of the contemporary scholastics or indeed of Calvin. While clearly denouncing the view that money is sterile and demonstrating that it is as productive as the goods bought with it, he hedges his defence of usury sufficiently so that his views are little different from many others. He does maintain that the charge of interest on a loan *per se* is unjust, but ingeniously points out that a lender charges for the utility of the money rather than for the money itself. But Molinaeus attacks the 'cruel usuries' permitted by *lucrum cessans*, and maintains with Calvin that interest may not be charged for loans to the poor. (One wonders that if such a rule were enforced, who in the world would ever lend to the poor, and would the poor then be better off by being deprived of all credit?)

Indeed, it seems that Molinaeus' main contribution was to blacken unjustly the name of poor Conrad Summenhart, a cruel injustice that would last for four centuries. In an act obviously motivated by malice toward scholasticism, Molinaeus took the great Summenhart's arguments against the usury ban and twisted them to make the German theologian a particularly doltish *advocate* of the prohibition. He took Summenhart's initial arguments *for* the prohibition, which he had stated in order to knock down, claimed that they were Summenhart's own, and then plagiarized Summenhart's critique of these arguments without acknowledgment. As a result of this shabby mendacity, as Professor Noonan points out, since 'Du Moulin's writings have alone become famous, Conrad [Summenhart] has appeared to posterity only as Du Moulin caricatures him', i.e., 'as a particularly obstinate and strangely stupid defender of the usury prohibition'.[10]

The honour of putting the final boot to the usury prohibition belongs to the seventeenth century classicist and Dutch Calvinist, Claude Saumaise (latinized name, Claudius Salmasius) (1588–1653). In several works published in Leyden, beginning with *De usuris liber* in 1630 and continuing to 1645, Salmasius finished off this embarrassing remnant of the mountainous errors of the past. His *forte* was not so much in coining new theoretical arguments as in finally willing to be consistent. In short, Salmasius trenchantly pointed out that money-lending was a business like any other, and like other businesses was entitled to charge a market price. He did make the important theoretical point, however, that, as in any other part of the market, if the number of usurers multiplies, the price of money or interest will be driven down by the competition. So that if one doesn't like high interest rates, the more usurers the better!

Salmasius also had the courage to point out that there were no valid arguments against usury, either by divine or natural law. The Jews only prohibited usury against other Jews, and this was a political and tribal act rather than an expression of a moral theory about an economic transaction. As for Jesus, he taught nothing at all about civil polity or economic transactions. This leaves the only ecclesiastical law against usury that of the pope, and why should a Calvinist obey the pope? Salmasius also took some de-

served whacks at the evasions permeating the various scholastic justifications, or 'extrinsic titles', justifying interest. Let's face it, Salmasius in effect
asserted: what the canonists and scholastics 'took away with one hand, they
restored with the other'. The *census* is really usury, foreign exchange is really
usury, *lucrum cessans* is really usury. Usury all, and let them all be licit.
Furthermore, usury is always charged as compensation for something, in
essence the lack of use of money and the risk of loss in a loan.

Salmasius also had the courage to take the hardest case: professional
money-lending to the poor, and to justify that. Selling the use of money is a
business like any other. If it is licit to make money with things bought with
money, why not from money itself? As Noonan paraphrases Salmasius, 'The
seller of bread is not required to ask if he sells it to a poor man or a rich man.
Why should the moneylender have to make a distinction?' And: 'there is no
fraud or theft in charging the highest market price for other goods; why is it
wrong for the usurer to charge the heaviest usuries he can collect?'[11]

Empirically, Salmasius also analysed the case of public usurers in Amsterdam (the great commercial and financial centre of the seventeenth century,
replacing Antwerp of the previous century), showing that the usual 16 per
cent charge on small loans to the poor is accounted for by: the costs of the
usurers borrowing their own money, of holding some money idle, of renting a
large house, of absorbing some losses on loans, of paying licence fees, hiring
employees, and paying an auctioneer. Deducting all these expenses, the average net interest rate of the money-lenders is only 8 per cent, barely enough to
keep them in business.

In concluding that usury is a business like any other, Salmasius, in his
typical witty and sparkling style, declared, 'I would rather be called a usurer,
than be a tailor'. Our examples of his style already demonstrate the aptness
of the great Austrian economist Böhm-Bawerk's conclusion about Salmasius:
that his works

> are extremely effective pieces of writing, veritable gems of sparkling polemic.
> The materials for them, it must be confessed, had in great part been provided by
> his predecessors...But the happy manner in which Salmasius employs these mate-
> rials, and the many pithy sallies with which he enriches them, places his polemic
> far above anything that had gone before.[12]

As a result, Salmasius' essays had wide influence throughout the Netherlands and the rest of Europe. As Böhm-Bawerk declared, Salmasius' views
on usury were the high-water mark of interest theory, to remain so for over
100 years.

5.5   Communist zealots: the Anabaptists

Sometimes Martin Luther must have felt that he had loosed the whirlwind,
even opened the gates of Hell. Shortly after Luther launched the Reformation, various Anabaptist sects appeared and spread throughout Germany. The
Anabaptists believed in predestination of the elect, but they also believed, in
contrast to Luther, that they *knew* infallibly who the elect were: i.e. themselves. The sign of that election was in an emotional, mystical conversion
process, that of being 'born again', baptized in the Holy Spirit. Such baptism
must be adult and not among infants; more to the point, it meant that only the
elect are to be sect members who obey the multifarious rules and creeds of
the Church. The idea of the sect, in contrast to Catholicism, Lutheranism or
Calvinism, was not comprehensive Church membership in the society. The
sect was to be distinctly separate, for the elect only.

Given that creed, there were two ways that Anabaptism could and did go.
Most Anabaptists, like the Mennonites or Amish, became virtual anarchists.
They tried to separate themselves as much as possible from a necessarily
sinful state and society, and engaged in non-violent resistance to the state's
decrees.

The other route, taken by another wing of Anabaptists, was to try to seize
power in the state and to shape up the majority by extreme coercion: in short,
ultra-theocracy. As Monsignor Knox incisively points out, even when Calvin
established a theocracy in Geneva, it had to pale beside one which might be
established by a prophet enjoying continuous, new, mystical revelation.

As Knox points out, in his usual scintillating style:

> ...in Calvin's Geneva...and in the Puritan colonies of America, the left wing of
> the Reformation signalized its ascendancy by enforcing the rigorism of its morals
> with every available machinery of discipline; by excommunication, or, if that
> failed, by secular punishment. Under such discipline sin became a crime, to be
> punished by the elect with an intolerable self-righteousness...
>
> I have called this rigorist attitude a pale shadow of the theocratic principle,
> because a full-blooded theocracy demands the presence of a divinely inspired
> leader or leaders, to whom government belongs by right of mystical illumination.
> The great Reformers were not, it must be insisted, men of this calibre; they were
> pundits, men of the new learning...[13]

And so one of the crucial differences between the Anabaptists and the
more conservative reformers was that the former claimed continuing mystical revelation to themselves, forcing men such as Luther and Calvin to fall
back on the Bible alone as the first as well as the last revelation.

The first leader of the ultra-theocrat wing of the Anabaptists was Thomas
Müntzer (c.1489–1525). Born into comfort in Stolberg in Thuringia, Müntzer
studied at the Universities of Leipzig and Frankfurt, and became highly
learned in the scriptures, the classics, theology, and in the writings of the

German mystics. Becoming a follower almost as soon as Luther launched the Reformation in 1520, Müntzer was recommended by Luther for the pastorate in the city of Zwickau. Zwickau was near the Bohemian border, and there the restless Müntzer was converted by the weaver and adept Niklas Storch, who had been in Bohemia, to the old Taborite doctrine that had flourished in Bohemia a century earlier. This doctrine consisted essentially of a continuing mystical revelation and the necessity for the elect to seize power and impose a society of theocratic communism by brutal force of arms. Furthermore, marriage was to be prohibited, and each man was to be able to have any woman at his will.

The passive wing of Anabaptists were voluntary anarcho-communists, who wished to live peacefully by themselves; but Müntzer adopted the Storch vision of blood and coercion. Defecting very rapidly from Lutheranism, Müntzer felt himself to be the coming prophet, and his teachings now began to emphasize a war of blood and extermination to be waged by the elect against the sinners. Müntzer claimed that the 'living Christ' had permanently entered his own soul; endowed thereby with perfect insight into the divine will, Müntzer asserted himself to be uniquely qualified to fulfil the divine mission. He even spoke of himself as 'becoming God'. Abandoning the world of learning, Müntzer was now ready for action.

In 1521, only a year after his arrival, the town council of Zwickau took fright at these increasingly popular ravings and ordered Müntzer's expulsion from the city. In protest, a large number of the populace, in particular the weavers, led by Niklas Storch, rose in revolt, but the rising was put down. At that point, Müntzer hied himself to Prague, searching for Taborite remnants in the capital of Bohemia. Speaking in peasant metaphors, he declared that harvest-time is here, 'so God himself has hired me for his harvest. I have sharpened my scythe, for my thoughts are most strongly fixed on the truth, and my lips, hands, skin, hair, soul, body, life curse the unbelievers'. Müntzer, however, found no Taborite remnants; it did not help the prophet's popularity that he knew no Czech, and had to preach with the aid of an interpreter. And so he was duly expelled from Prague.

After wandering around central Germany in poverty for several years, signing himself 'Christ's messenger', Müntzer in 1523 gained a ministerial position in the small Thuringian town of Allstedt. There he established a wide reputation as a preacher employing the vernacular, and began to attract a large following of uneducated miners, whom he formed into a revolutionary organization called 'The League of the Elect'.

A turning point in Müntzer's stormy career came a year later, when Duke John, a prince of Saxony and a Lutheran, hearing alarming rumours about him, came to little Allstedt and asked Müntzer to preach him a sermon. This was Müntzer's opportunity, and he seized it. He laid it on the line: he called

upon the Saxon princes to make their choice and take their stand, either as servants of God or of the Devil. If the Saxon princes are to take their stand with God, then they 'must lay on with the sword'. 'Don't let them live any longer,' counselled our prophet, 'the evil-doers who turn us away from God. For a godless man has no right to live if he hinders the godly'. Müntzer's definition of the 'godless', of course, was all-inclusive. 'The sword is necessary to exterminate' priests, monks and godless rulers. But, Müntzer warned, if the princes of Saxony fail in this task, if they falter, 'the sword shall be taken from them…If they resist, let them be slaughtered without mercy…'.
Müntzer then returned to his favourite harvest-time analogy: 'At the harvest-time, one must pluck the weeds out of God's vineyard…For the ungodly have no right to live, save what the Elect chooses to allow them….' In this way the millennium, the thousand-year Kingdom of God on earth, would be ushered in. But one key requisite is necessary for the princes to perform that task successfully; they must have at their elbow a priest/prophet (guess who!) to inspire and guide their efforts.

Oddly enough for an era when no First Amendment restrained rulers from dealing sternly with heresy, Duke John seemed not to care about Müntzer's frenetic ultimatum. Even after Müntzer proceeded to preach a sermon proclaiming the imminent overthrow of all tyrants and the beginning of the messianic kingdom, the duke did nothing. Finally, under the insistent prodding of Luther that Müntzer was becoming dangerous, Duke John told the prophet to refrain from any provocative preaching until his case was decided by his brother, the elector.

This mild reaction by the Saxon princes, however, was enough to set Thomas Müntzer on his final revolutionary road. The princes had proved themselves untrustworthy; the mass of the poor were now to make the revolution. The poor were the elect, and would establish a rule of compulsory egalitarian communism, a world where all things would be owned in common by all, where everyone would be equal in everything and each person would receive according to his need. But not yet. For even the poor must first be broken of worldly desires and frivolous enjoyments, and must recognize the leadership of a new 'servant of God' who 'must stand forth in the spirit of Elijah…and set things in motion'. (Again, guess who!)

Seeing Saxony as inhospitable, Müntzer climbed over the town wall of Allstedt and moved in 1524 to the Thuringian city of Muhlhausen. An expert in fishing in troubled waters, Müntzer found a friendly home in Muhlhausen, which had been in a state of political turmoil for over a year. Preaching the impending extermination of the ungodly, Müntzer paraded around the town at the head of an armed band, carrying in front of him a red crucifix and a naked sword. Expelled from Muhlhausen after a revolt by his allies was suppressed, Müntzer went to Nuremberg, which in turn expelled him after he published some revolutionary pamphlets. After wandering through south-western Germany, Müntzer was invited back to Muhlhausen in February 1525, where a revolutionary group had taken over.

Thomas Müntzer and his allies proceeded to impose a communist regime on the city of Muhlhausen. The monasteries were seized, and all property was decreed to be in common, and the consequence, as a contemporary observer noted, was that 'he so affected the folk that no one wanted to work'. The result was that the theory of communism and love quickly became in practice an alibi for systemic theft:

> ...when anyone needed food or clothing he went to a rich man and demanded it of him in Christ's name, for Christ had commanded that all should share with the needy. And what was not given freely was taken by force. Many acted thus...Thomas [Müntzer] instituted this brigandage and multiplied it every day.[14]

At that point, the great Peasants' War erupted throughout Germany, a rebellion launched by the peasantry in favour of their local autonomy and in opposition to the new centralizing, high-tax, absolutist rule of the German princes. Throughout Germany, the princes crushed the feebly armed peasantry with great brutality, massacring about 100 000 peasants in the process. In Thuringia, the army of the princes confronted the peasants on 15 May with a great deal of artillery and 2 000 cavalry, luxuries denied to the peasantry. The landgrave of Hesse, commander of the princes' army, offered amnesty to the peasants if they would hand over Müntzer and his immediate followers. The peasants were strongly tempted, but Müntzer, holding aloft his naked sword, gave his last flaming speech, declaring that God had personally promised him victory; that he would catch all the enemy cannon-balls in the sleeves of his cloak; that God would protect them all. Just at the strategic moment of Müntzer's speech, a rainbow appeared in the heavens, and Müntzer had previously adopted the rainbow as the symbol of his movement. To the credulous and confused peasantry, this seemed a veritable sign from Heaven. Unfortunately, the sign didn't work, and the princes' army crushed the peasants, killing 5 000 while losing only half a dozen men. Müntzer himself fled and hid, but was captured a few days later, tortured into confession, and then executed.

Thomas Müntzer and his signs may have been defeated, and his body may have mouldered in the grave, but his soul kept marching on. Not only was his spirit kept alive by followers in his own day, but also by Marxist historians from Engels to the present day, who saw in this deluded mystic an epitome of social revolution and the class struggle, and a forerunner of the chiliastic prophesies of the 'communist stage' of the supposedly inevitable Marxian future.

The Müntzerian cause was soon picked up by a former disciple, the book-binder Hans Hut. Hut claimed to be a prophet sent by God to announce that at Whitsuntide, 1528, Christ would return to earth and give the power to enforce justice to Hut and his following of rebaptized saints. The saints would then 'take up double-edged swords' and wreak God's vengeance on priests, pastors, kings and nobles. Hut and his followers would then 'establish the rule of Hans Hut on earth', with Muhlhausen as the favoured capital. Christ was then to establish a millennium marked by communism and free love. Hut was captured in 1527 (before Jesus had had a chance to return), imprisoned at Augsburg, and killed trying to escape. For a year or two, Huttian followers kept emerging, at Augsburg, Nuremberg, and Esslingen, in southern Germany, threatening to set up their communist Kingdom of God by force of arms. But by 1530 they were smashed and suppressed by the alarmed authorities. Müntzerian-type Anabaptism was now to move to north-western Germany.

5.6   Totalitarian communism in Münster

North-western Germany in that era was dotted by a number of small ecclesiastical states, each run by a prince–bishop. The state was run by aristocratic clerics, who elected one of their own as bishop. Generally, these bishops were secular lords who were not ordained. By bargaining over taxes, the capital city of each of these states had usually wrested for itself a degree of autonomy. The clergy, which constituted the ruling élite of the state, exempted themselves from taxation while imposing very heavy taxes on the rest of the populace. Generally, the capital cities came to be run by their own power élite, an oligarchy of guilds, which used government power to cartellize their various professions and occupations.

The largest of these ecclesiastical states in north-west Germany was the bishopric of Münster, and its capital city of Münster, a town of some 10 000 people, was run by the town guilds. The Münster guilds were particularly exercised by the economic competition of the monks, who were not forced to obey guild restrictions and regulations.

During the Peasants' War, the capital cities of several of these states, including Münster, took the opportunity to rise in revolt, and the bishop of Münster was forced to make numerous concessions. With the crushing of the rebellion, however, the bishop took back the concessions, and re-established the old regime. By 1532, however, the guilds, supported by the people, were able to fight back and take over the town, soon forcing the bishop to recognize Münster officially as a Lutheran city.

It was not destined to remain so for long, however. From all over the north-west, hordes of Anabaptist enthusiasts flooded into Münster, seeking the onset of the New Jerusalem. From the northern Netherlands came hundreds of Melchiorites, followers of the itinerant visionary Melchior Hoffmann. Hoffmann, an uneducated furrier's apprentice from Swabia in southern Germany, had for years wandered through Europe preaching the imminence of the Second Coming, which he had concluded from his researches would occur in 1533, the fifteenth centenary of the death of Jesus. Melchiorism had flourished in the northern Netherlands, and many adepts now poured into Münster, rapidly converting the poorer classes of the town.

Meanwhile, the Anabaptist cause in Münster received a shot in the arm, when the eloquent and popular young minister Bernt Rothmann, a highly educated son of a town blacksmith, converted to Anabaptism. Originally a Catholic priest, Rothmann had become a friend of Luther and the head of the Lutheran movement in Münster. Converted to Anabaptism, Rothmann lent his eloquent preaching to the cause of communism as it had supposedly existed in the primitive Christian Church, holding everything in common with no Mine and Thine and giving to each according to his 'need'. In response to Rothmann's reputation, thousands flocked to Münster, hundreds of the poor, the rootless, those hopelessly in debt, and 'people who, having run through the fortunes of their parents, were earning nothing by their own industry...'. People, in general, who were attracted by the idea of 'plundering and robbing the clergy and the richer burghers'. The horrified burghers tried to drive out Rothmann and the Anabaptist preachers, but to no avail.

In 1533, Melchior Hoffmann, sure that the Second Coming would happen any day, returned to Strasbourg, where he had had great success, calling himself the Prophet Elias. He was promptly clapped into jail, and remained there until his death a decade later.

Hoffmann, for all the similarities with the others, was a peaceful man who counselled non-violence to his followers; after all, if Jesus were imminently due to return, why commit against unbelievers? Hoffmann's imprisonment, and of course the fact that 1533 came and went without a Second Coming, discredited Melchior, and so his Münster followers turned to far more violent, post-millennialist prophets who believed that they would have to establish the Kingdom by fire and sword.

The new leader of the coercive Anabaptists was a Dutch baker from Haarlem, one Jan Matthys (Matthyszoon). Reviving the spirit of Thomas Müntzer, Matthys sent out missionaries or 'apostles' from Haarlem to rebaptize everyone they could, and to appoint 'bishops' with the power to baptize. When the new apostles reached Münster in early 1534, they were greeted, as we might expect, with enormous enthusiasm. Caught up in the frenzy, even Rothmann was rebaptized once again, followed by many ex-nuns and a large part of the population. Within a week the apostles had rebaptized 1 400 people.

Another apostle soon arrived, a young man of 25 who had been converted and baptized by Matthys only a couple of months earlier. This was Jan

Bockelson (Bockelszoon, Beukelsz), who was soon to become known in song and story as Johann of Leyden. Though handsome and eloquent, Bockelson was a troubled soul, having been born the illegitimate son of the mayor of a Dutch village by a woman serf from Westphalia. Bockelson began life as an apprentice tailor, married a rich widow, but then went bankrupt when he set himself up as a self-employed merchant.

In February 1534, Bockelson won the support of the wealthy cloth merchant Bernt Knipperdollinck, the powerful leader of the Münster guilds, and shrewdly married Knipperdollinck's daughter. On 8 February, son-in-law and father-in-law ran wildly through the streets together, calling upon everyone to repent. After much frenzy, mass writhing on the ground, and the seeing of apocalyptic visions, the Anabaptists rose up and seized the town hall, winning legal recognition for their movement.

In response to this successful uprising, many wealthy Lutherans left town, and the Anabaptists, feeling exuberant, sent messengers to surrounding areas summoning everyone to come to Münster. The rest of the world, they proclaimed, would be destroyed in a month or two; only Münster would be saved, to become the New Jerusalem. Thousands poured in from as far away as Flanders and Frisia in the northern Netherlands. As a result, the Anabaptists soon won a majority on the town council, and this success was followed three days later, on 24 February, by an orgy of looting of books, statues and paintings from the churches and throughout the town. Soon Jan Matthys himself arrived, a tall, gaunt man with a long black beard. Matthys, aided by Bockelson, quickly became the virtual dictator of the town. The coercive Anabaptists had at last seized a city. The Great Communist Experiment could now begin.

The first mighty programme of this rigid theocracy was, of course, to purge the New Jerusalem of the unclean and the ungodly, as a prelude to their ultimate extermination throughout the world. Matthys called therefore for the execution of all remaining Catholics and Lutherans, but Knipperdollinck's cooler head prevailed, since he warned Matthys that slaughtering all other Christians than themselves might cause the rest of the world to become edgy, and they might all come and crush the New Jerusalem in its cradle. It was therefore decided to do the next best thing, and on 27 February the Catholic and Lutherans were driven out of the city, in the midst of a horrendous snowstorm. In a deed prefiguring communist Cambodia, all non-Anabaptists, including old people, invalids, babies and pregnant women were driven into the snowstorm, and all were forced to leave behind all their money, property, food and clothing. The remaining Lutherans and Catholics were compulsorily rebaptized, and all refusing this ministration were put to death.

The expulsion of all Lutherans and Catholics was enough for the bishop, who began a long military siege of the town the next day, on 28 February.

With every person drafted for siege work, Jan Matthys launched his totalitarian communist social revolution.

The first step was to confiscate the property of the expelled. All their worldly goods were placed in central depots, and the poor were encouraged to take 'according to their needs', the 'needs' to be interpreted by seven appointed 'deacons' chosen by Matthys. When a blacksmith protested at these measures imposed by Dutch foreigners, Matthys arrested the courageous smithy. Summoning the entire population of the town, Matthys personally stabbed, shot, and killed the 'godless' blacksmith, as well as throwing into prison several eminent citizens who had protested against his treatment. The crowd was warned to profit by this public execution, and they obediently sang a hymn in honour of the killing.

A key part of the Anabaptist reign of terror in Münster was now unveiled. Unerringly, just as in the case of the Cambodian communists four-and-a-half centuries later, the new ruling élite realized that the abolition of the private ownership of money would reduce the population to total slavish dependence on the men of power. And so Matthys, Rothmann and others launched a propaganda campaign that it was unchristian to own money privately; that all money should be held in 'common', which in practice meant that all money whatsoever must be handed over to Matthys and his ruling clique. Several Anabaptists who kept or hid their money were arrested and then terrorized into crawling to Matthys on their knees, begging forgiveness and beseeching him to intercede with God on their behalf. Matthys then graciously 'forgave' the sinners.

After two months of severe and unrelenting pressure, a combination of propaganda about the Christianity of abolishing private money, and threats and terror against those who failed to surrender, the private ownership of money was effectively abolished in Münster. The government seized all the money and used it to buy or hire goods from the outside world. Wages were doled out in kind by the only remaining employer: the theocratic Anabaptist state.

Food was confiscated from private homes, and rationed according to the will of the government deacons. Also, to accommodate the immigrants, all private homes were effectively communized, with everyone permitted to quarter themselves anywhere; it was now illegal to close, let alone lock, doors. Communal dining-halls were established, where people ate together to readings from the Old Testament.

This compulsory communism and reign of terror was carried out in the name of community and Christian 'love'. All this communization was considered the first giant steps toward total egalitarian communism, where, as Rothmann put it, 'all things were to be in common, there was to be no private property and nobody was to do any more work, but simply trust in God'. The workless part, of course, somehow never arrived.

A pamphlet sent in October 1534 to other Anabaptist communities hailed the new order of Christian love through terror:

> For not only have we put all our belongings into a common pool under the care of deacons, and live from it according to our need; we praise God through Christ with one heart and mind and are eager to help one another with every kind of service.
> And accordingly, everything which has served the purposes of selfseeking and private property, such as buying and selling, working for money, taking interest and practising usury…or eating and drinking the sweat of the poor…and indeed everything which offends against love – all such things are abolished amongst us by the power of love and community.

With high consistency, the Anabaptists of Münster made no pretence about preserving intellectual freedom while communizing all material property. For the Anabaptists boasted of their lack of education, and claimed that it was the unlearned and the unwashed who would be the elect of the world. The Anabaptist mob took particular delight in burning all the books and manuscripts in the cathedral library, and finally, in mid-March 1534, Matthys outlawed all books except the Good Book – the Bible. To symbolize a total break with the sinful past, all privately and publicly owned books were thrown upon a great communal bonfire. All this ensured, of course, that the only theology or interpretation of the scriptures open to the Münsterites was that of Matthys and the other Anabaptist preachers.

At the end of March, however, Matthys's swollen *hubris* laid him low. Convinced at Eastertime that God had ordered him and a few of the faithful to lift the bishop's siege and liberate the town, Matthys and a few others rushed out of the gates at the besieging army, and were literally hacked to pieces. In an age when the idea of full religious liberty was virtually unknown, one can imagine that any Anabaptists whom the more orthodox Christians might get hold of would not earn a very kindly reward.

The death of Matthys left Münster in the hands of young Bockelson. And if Matthys had chastised the people of Münster with whips, Bockelson would chastise them with scorpions. Bockelson wasted little time in mourning his mentor. He preached to the faithful: 'God will give you another Prophet who will be more powerful'. How could this young enthusiast top his master? Early in May, Bockelson caught the attention of the town by running naked through the streets in a frenzy, falling then into a silent three-day ecstasy. When he rose again, he announced to the entire populace a new dispensation that God had revealed to him. With God at his elbow, Bockelson abolished the old functioning town offices of council and burgomasters, and installed a new ruling council of 12 elders, with himself, of course, as the eldest of the elders. The elders were now given total authority over the life and death, the property and the spirit, of every inhabitant of Münster. A strict system of forced labour was imposed, with all artisans not drafted into the military now public employees, working for the community for no monetary reward. This meant, of course, that the guilds were now abolished.

The totalitarianism in Münster was now complete. Death was now the punishment for virtually every independent act, good or bad. Capital punishment was decreed for the high crimes of: murder, theft, lying, avarice, and quarrelling(!). Also death was decreed for every conceivable kind of insubordination: the young against their parents, wives against their husbands and, of course, anyone at all against the chosen representatives of God on earth, the totalitarian government of Münster. Bernt Knipperdollinck was appointed high executioner to enforce the decrees.

The only aspect of life previously left untouched was sex, and this now came under the hammer of Bockelson's total despotism. The only sexual relation permitted was marriage between two Anabaptists. Sex in any other form, including marriage with one of the 'godless', was a capital crime. But soon Bockelson went beyond this rather old-fashioned credo, and decided to establish compulsory polygamy in Münster. Since many of the expellees had left their wives and daughters behind, Münster now had three times as many marriageable women as men, so that polygamy had become technologically feasible. Bockelson converted the other rather startled preachers by citing polygamy among the patriarchs of Israel, as well as by threatening dissenters with death.

Compulsory polygamy was a bit too much for many of the Münsterites, who launched a rebellion in protest. The rebellion, however, was quickly crushed and most of the rebels put to death. Execution was also the fate of any further dissenters. And so by August 1534, polygamy was coercively established in Münster. As one might expect, young Bockelson took an instant liking to the new regime, and before long he had a harem of 15 wives, including Divara, the beautiful young widow of Jan Matthys. The rest of the male population also began to take to the new decree as ducks to water. Many of the women did not take as kindly to the new dispensation, and so the elders passed a law ordering compulsory marriage for every women under (and presumably also over) a certain age, which usually meant being a compulsory third or fourth wife.

Moreover, since marriage among the godless was not only invalid but also illegal, the wives of the expellees now became fair game, and were forced to 'marry' good Anabaptists. Refusal to comply with the new law was punishable, of course, by death, and a number of women were actually executed as a result. Those 'old' wives who resented the new wives coming into their household were also suppressed, and their quarrelling was made a capital crime. Many women were executed for quarrelling.

But the long arm of the state could reach only just so far and, in their first internal setback, Bockelson and his men had to relent, and permit divorce. Indeed, the ceremony of marriage was now outlawed totally, and divorce made very easy. As a result, Münster now fell under a regime of what amounted to compulsory free love. And so, within the space of only a few months, a rigid puritanism had been transmuted into a regime of compulsory promiscuity.

Meanwhile, Bockelson proved to be an excellent organizer of a besieged city. Compulsory labour, military and civilian, was strictly enforced. The bishop's army consisted of poorly and irregularly paid mercenaries, and Bockelson was able to induce many of them to desert by offering them regular pay (pay for *money*, that is, in contrast to Bockelson's rigid internal moneyless communism). Drunken ex-mercenaries were, however, shot immediately. When the bishop fired pamphlets into the town offering a general amnesty in return for surrender, Bockelson made reading such pamphlets a crime punishable by – of course – death.

At the end of August 1534, the bishop's armies were in disarray and the siege temporarily lifted. Jan Bockelson seized this opportunity to carry his 'egalitarian' communist revolution one step further: he had himself named king and Messiah of the Last Days.

Proclaiming himself king might have appeared tacky and perhaps even illegitimate. And so Bockelson had one Dusentschur, a goldsmith from a nearby town and a self-proclaimed prophet, do the job for him. At the beginning of September, Dusentschur announced to one and all a new revelation: Jan Bockelson was to be king of the whole world, the heir of King David, to keep that Throne until God himself reclaimed his Kingdom. Unsurprisingly, Bockelson confirmed that he himself had had the very same revelation. Dusentschur then presented a sword of justice to Bockelson, anointed him, and proclaimed him king of the world. Bockelson, of course, was momentarily modest; he prostrated himself and asked guidance from God. But he made sure to get that guidance swiftly. And it turned out, *mirabile dictu*, that Dusentschur was right. Bockelson proclaimed to the crowd that God had now given him 'power over all nations of the earth'; anyone who might dare to resist the will of God 'shall without delay be put to death with the sword'.

And so, despite a few mumbled protests, Jan Bockelson was declared king of the world and Messiah, and the Anabaptist preachers of Münster explained to their bemused flock that Bockelson was indeed the Messiah as foretold in the Old Testament. Bockelson was rightfully ruler of the entire world, both temporal and spiritual.

It often happens with 'egalitarians' that a hole, a special escape hatch from the drab uniformity of life, is created – for themselves. And so it was with King Bockelson. It was, after all, important to emphasize in every way the importance of the Messiah's advent. And so Bockelson wore the finest robes, metals and jewellery; he appointed courtiers and gentlemen-at-arms, who also appeared in splendid finery. King Bockelson's chief wife, Divara, was proclaimed queen of the world, and she too was dressed in great finery and had a suite of courtiers and followers. This luxurious court of some two hundred people was housed in fine mansions requisitioned for the occasion. A throne draped with a cloth of gold was established in the public square, and King Bockelson would hold court there, wearing a crown and carrying a sceptre. A royal bodyguard protected the entire procession. All Bockelson's loyal aides were suitably rewarded with high status and finery: Knipperdollinck was the chief minister, and Rothmann royal orator.

If communism is the perfect society, *somebody* must be able to enjoy its fruits; and who better but the Messiah and his courtiers? Though private property in money was abolished, the confiscated gold and silver was now minted into ornamental coins for the glory of the new king. All horses were confiscated to build up the king's armed squadron. Also, names in Münster were transformed; all the streets were renamed; Sundays and feastdays were abolished; and all new-born children were named personally by the king in accordance with a special pattern.

In a starving slave society such as communist Münster, not all citizens could live in the luxury enjoyed by the king and his court; indeed, the new ruling class was now imposing a rigid class oligarchy seldom seen before. So that the king and his nobles might live in high luxury, rigorous austerity was imposed on everyone else in Münster. The subject population had already been robbed of their houses and much of their food; now all superfluous luxury among the masses was outlawed. Clothing and bedding were severely rationed, and all 'surplus' turned over to King Bockelson under pain of death. Every house was searched thoroughly and 83 wagonloads of 'surplus' clothing collected.

It is not surprising that the deluded masses of Münster began to grumble at being forced to live in abject poverty while the king and his courtiers lived in extreme luxury on the proceeds of their confiscated belongings. And so Bockelson had to beam them some propaganda to explain the new system. The explanation was this: it was all right for Bockelson to live in pomp and luxury because he was already completely dead to the world and the flesh. Since he was dead to the world, in a deep sense his luxury didn't count. In the style of every guru who has ever lived in luxury among his credulous followers, he explained that for him material objects had no value. How such 'logic' can ever fool anyone passes understanding. More important, Bockelson assured his subjects that he and his court were only the advance guard of the new order; soon, *they too* would be living in the same millennial luxury. Under their new order, the people of Münster would forge outward, armed with God's will, and conquer the entire world, exterminating the unrighteous, after which Jesus would return and they would all live in luxury and perfection. Equal communism with great luxury for all would then be achieved.

Greater dissent meant, of course, greater terror, and King Bockelson's reign of 'love' intensified its intimidation and slaughter. As soon as he proclaimed the monarchy, the prophet Dusentschur announced a new divine revelation: all who persisted in disagreeing with or disobeying King Bockelson would be put to death, and their very memory blotted out. They would be extirpated forever. Some of the main victims to be executed were women: women who were killed for denying their husbands their marital rights, for insulting a preacher, or for daring to practise bigamy – polygamy, of course, being solely a male privilege.

Despite his continual preaching about marching forth to conquer the world, King Bockelson was not crazy enough to attempt that feat, especially since the bishop's army was again besieging the town. Instead, he shrewdly used much of the expropriated gold and silver to send out apostles and pamphlets to surrounding areas of Europe, attempting to rouse the masses for Anabaptist revolution. The propaganda had considerable effect, and serious mass risings occurred throughout Holland and north-western Germany during January 1535. A thousand armed Anabaptists gathered under the leadership of someone who called himself Christ, son of God; and serious Anabaptist rebellions took place in west Frisia, in the town of Minden, and even in the great city of Amsterdam, where the rebels managed to capture the town hall. All these risings were eventually suppressed, with the considerable help of betrayal to the various authorities of the names of the rebels and of the location of their munition dumps.

The princes of north-western Europe by this time had had enough; and all the states of the Holy Roman Empire agreed to supply troops to crush the monstrous and hellish regime at Münster. For the first time, in January 1535, Münster was totally and successfully blockaded and cut off from the outside world. The Establishment then proceeded to starve the population of Münster into submission. Food shortages appeared immediately, and the crisis was met with characteristic vigour: all remaining food was confiscated, and all horses killed, for the benefit of feeding the king, his royal court and his armed guards. At all times the king and his court ate and drank well, while famine and devastation raged throughout the town of Münster, and the masses ate literally everything, even inedible, they could lay their hands on.

King Bockelson kept his rule by beaming continual propaganda and promises to the starving masses. God would definitely save them by Easter, or else he would have himself burnt in the public square. When Easter came and went, Bockelson craftily explained that he had meant only 'spiritual' salvation. He promised that God would change cobblestones to bread, and of course that did not come to pass either. Finally, Bockelson, long fascinated with the theatre, ordered his starving subjects to engage in three days of dancing and athletics. Dramatic performances were held, as well as a Black Mass. Starvation, however, was now becoming all-pervasive.

The poor hapless people of Münster were now doomed totally. The bishop kept firing leaflets into the town promising a general amnesty if the people would only revolt and depose King Bockelson and his court and hand them over. To guard against such a threat, Bockelson stepped up his reign of terror still further. In early May, he divided the town into 12 sections, and placed a 'duke' over each one with an armed force of 24 men. The dukes were foreigners like himself; as Dutch immigrants they were likely to be loyal to Bockelson. Each duke was strictly forbidden to leave his section, and the dukes, in turn, prohibited any meetings whatsoever of even a few people. No one was allowed to leave town, and any caught plotting to leave, helping anyone else to leave, or criticizing the king, was instantly beheaded, usually by King Bockelson himself. By mid-June such deeds were occurring daily, with the body often quartered and nailed up as a warning to the masses.

Bockelson would undoubtedly have let the entire population starve to death rather than surrender; but two escapees betrayed weak spots in the town's defence, and on the night of 24 June 1535, the nightmare New Jerusalem at last came to a bloody end. The last several hundred Anabaptist fighters surrendered under an amnesty and were promptly massacred, and Queen Divara was beheaded. As for ex-King Bockelson, he was led about on a chain, and the following January, along with Knipperdollinck, was publicly tortured to death, and their bodies suspended in cages from a church tower.

The old Establishment of Münster was duly restored and the city became Catholic once more. The stars were once again in their courses, and the events of 1534–35 understandably led to an abiding distrust of mysticism and enthusiast movements throughout Protestant Europe.

5.7   The roots of messianic communism

Anabaptist communism did not spring out of thin air at the advent of the Reformation. Its roots can be traced back to an extraordinarily influential late twelfth century Italian mystic, Joachim of Fiore (1145–1202). Joachim was an abbot and hermit in Calabria, in southern Italy. It was Joachim who launched the idea that hidden in the Bible for those who had the wit to see were prophecies foretelling world history. Concentrating on the murky Book of Revelation, Joachim decreed that history was destined to move through three successive ages, each of them ruled by one of the members of the Holy Trinity. The first age, the age of the Old Testament, was the era of the Father or the Law, the age of fear and servitude; the second age, the era of the Son, was the age of the New Testament, the era of faith and submission. Mystics generally think in threes; and Joachim was moved to herald the coming of the third and final age, the age of the Holy Spirit, the era of perfect joy, love and freedom, and the end of human history. It would be the age of the end of property, because everyone would live in voluntary poverty; and everyone could easily do so, because there would be no work, since people would be totally liberated from their physical bodies. Possessing only spiritual bodies, there would be no need to eat food or do much else either. The world would be, in the paraphrase of Norman Cohn, 'one vast monastery, in which all men would be contemplative monks rapt continuously in mystical ecstasy until the day of the Last Judgment'. Joachim's vision already resonates with the later Marxian dialectic of the three allegedly inevitable stages of history: primitive communism, class society, and then finally the realm of perfect freedom, total communism and the withering away of the division of labour, and the end of human history.

As with so many chiliasts, Joachim was sure of the date of the advent of the final age and, typically, it was coming soon – in his view, sometime in the first half of the next, the thirteenth century.

The Joachite *bizarreries* quickly exerted enormous influence, particularly in Italy, in Germany, and in the rigourist wing of the new Franciscan Order.

A new ingredient to this witches' brew was added a little later by a learned professor of theology at the great University of Paris at the end of the twelfth century. Once a great favourite of the French royal court, Amalric's odd doctrines were condemned by the pope and, after a forced public recantation, Amalric died shortly thereafter, in 1206 or 1207. His doctrines were then picked up by a small, secret group of erudite clerical disciples, the Amaurians, most of whom had been students in theology at Paris. Centred at the important commercial cloth-making town of Troyes, in Champagne, the Amaurian missionaries influenced many people and distributed popular works of theology in the vernacular. Their leader was the priest William Aurifex, who was either a goldsmith or an alchemist attempting to transform base metals into gold. Subjected to espionage by the bishop of Paris, the 14 Amaurians were all rounded up and either imprisoned for life or burnt at the stake, depending on whether they re-canted their heresies. Most of them refused to recant.

The Amaurians, like Joachim, propounded the three ages of human history, but they added some spice to it; each age apparently enjoyed its own incarna-tion. For the Old Testament, it was Abraham and perhaps some other patri-archs; for the New Testament, the incarnation was of course Jesus; and now, for the dawning age of the Holy Spirit, the incarnation would now emerge in human beings themselves. As might be expected, the Amaurians considered themselves the new incarnation; in other words, they proclaimed themselves as living gods, the embodiment of the Holy Spirit. Not that they would always remain a divine élite among men; on the contrary, they were destined to lead mankind to its universal incarnation.

The congeries of groups throughout northern Europe in the fourteenth century known as the Brethren of the Free Spirit added another important ingredient to the stew; the dialectic of 'reabsorption into God' derived from the third century Platonist philosopher, Plotinus. Plotinus had had his own three stages: the original unity with God, the human-history stage of degradation and separation or alienation from God, and the final 'return' or 'reabsorption' as all human beings are submerged into the One and history is finished. The Brethren of the Free Spirit added a new élitist twist: while the reabsorption of every man must await the end of history, and the 'crude in spirit' must meanwhile meet their individual deaths, there was a glorious minority, the 'subtle in spirit', who could and did become reabsorbed and therefore living gods during their lifetime. This minority, of course, were the Brethren themselves who, by virtue of years of training, self-torture and visions had become perfect gods, more perfect and more godlike than even Christ himself. Once this stage of mystical union was reached, furthermore, it was permanent and eternal. These new gods often proclaimed themselves greater than God himself. Thus a group of female Free Spirits at Schweidnitz claimed to be able to dominate the Holy Trinity such that they could 'ride it as in a saddle'; and one of these women declared that 'when God created all things I created all things with him...I am more than God'. Man himself, therefore, or at least a gifted minority of men, could lift themselves up to divine status by their own efforts far earlier than their fellows.

Being living gods on earth brought many good things in its wake. In the first place, it led directly to an extreme form of the antinomian heresy: if people are gods, then it is impossible for them to sin. Whatever they do is necessarily moral and perfect. That means that any act ordinarily considered as sin, from adultery to murder, becomes perfectly legitimate when performed by the living gods. Indeed, the Free Spirits, like other antinomians, were tempted to demonstrate and flaunt their freedom from sin by performing all manner of sins imaginable.

But there was also a catch. Among the Free Spirit cultists, only a minority of leading adepts were 'living gods'; for the rank-and-file cultists, striving to become gods, there was one sin alone which they must not commit: disobedience to their master. Each disciple was bound by an oath of absolute obedience to a particular living god. Take for example Nicholas of Basle, a leading Free Spirit guru whose cult stretched most of the length of the Rhine. Claiming to be the new Christ, Nicholas held that everyone's sole path to salvation is making an act of absolute and total submission to Nicholas himself. In return for this total fealty, Nicholas granted his followers freedom from all sin.

As for the rest of mankind outside the cults, they were simply unredeemed and unregenerate beings who existed only to be used and exploited by the elect. This attitude of total rule went hand in hand with the social doctrine many Free Spirit cults adopted in the fourteenth century: a communistic assault on the institution of private property. In essence, however, that philosophic communism was a thinly camouflaged cover for *their* – the Free Spirits' – self-proclaimed right to commit theft at will. The Free Spirit adept, in short, regarded all property of the non-elect as rightfully his own. As the bishop of Strasbourg summed it up in 1317: 'They believe that all things are common, whence they conclude that theft is lawful for them'. Or as the Free Spirit adept from Erfurt, Johann Hartmann, put it: 'The truly free man is king and lord of all creatures. All things belong to him, and he has the right to use whatever pleases him. If anyone tries to prevent him, the free man may kill him and take his goods'. As one of the favourite sayings of the Brethren of the Free Spirit put it: 'Whatever the eye sees and covets, let the hand grasp it'.

The final ingredient for the revolutionary communist Müntzer–Münster stew came with the extreme Taborites of the early fifteenth century. All Taborites constituted the radical wing of the Hussite movement, a pre-Protestant revolutionary movement that blended struggles of religion (anti-Catholic), nationality (Czech vs upper-class and upper-clergy German), and class (artisans cartellized in guilds trying to take political power from the patricians).

The new ingredient added by the extreme wing of the Taborites was the duty to exterminate. For the Last Days are coming, and the elect must go out and stamp out sin by exterminating all sinners, which means – at the very least – all non-Taborites. For all sinners are enemies of Christ, and 'accursed be the man who withholds his sword from shedding the blood of the enemies of Christ. Every believer must wash his hands in that blood'. Having that mind-set, the extreme Taborites were not going to stop at intellectual destruction. When sacking churches and monasteries, the Taborites took particular delight in destroying libraries and burning books. For 'all belongings must be taken away from God's enemies and burned or otherwise destroyed'. Besides, the elect have no need for books. When the Kingdom of God on earth arrived, there would no longer be 'need for anyone to teach another. There would be no need for books or scriptures, and all worldly wisdom will perish'. And all people too, one suspects.

Moreover, elaborating anew the theme of a 'return' to a lost golden age, the ultra-Taborites proposed to return to the allegedly early Czech condition of communism: a society with no private property. In order to achieve this classless society, the cities in particular, those centres of luxury and avarice, and especially the merchants and the landlords, must be exterminated. After the elect have established their communist Kingdom of God in Bohemia by revolutionary violence, their task would be to forge and impose such communism on the rest of the world.

In addition to material property, the bodies of the faithful would have to be communized as well. The Taborite *ultras* were nothing if not logical. Their preachers taught: 'Everything will be common, including wives; there will be free sons and daughters of God and there will be no marriage as union of two – husband and wife'.

The Hussite revolution broke out in 1419, and in that same year, the Taborites gathered in the town of Usti, in northern Bohemia near the German border. They renamed Usti, Tabor, i.e. the Mount of Olives where Jesus had foretold his Second Coming, had ascended to heaven, and where he was expected to reappear. The Taborites engaged in a communist experiment at Tabor, owning everything in common, and dedicated to the proposition that 'whoever owns private property commits a mortal sin'. True to their doctrines, all women were owned in common, while if husband and wife were ever seen together, they were beaten to death or otherwise executed. Unfortunately but characteristically, the Taborites were so caught up in their unlimited right to consume from the common store that they felt themselves exempt from the need to work. The common store soon disappeared, and then what? Then, of course, the radical Taborites claimed that their need entitled them to claim the property of the non-elect, and they proceeded to rob others at will. As a synod of the moderate Taborites complained, 'many communities never think of earning their own living by the work of their hands but are only willing to live on other people's property and to undertake unjust campaigns for the sole purpose of robbing'. And the Taborite peasantry who did not join the communes found the radical regime reimposing feudal dues and bonds only six months after they had abolished them.

Discredited among themselves, their more moderate allies, and their own peasantry, the communist regime of the radicals at Usti/Tabor soon collapsed. The torch of frenetic mystical communism was soon picked up, however, by a sect known as Bohemian Adamites. Like the Free Spirits of the previous century, the Adamites held themselves to be living gods, superior to Christ, since Christ had died whereas they still lived. (Impeccable logic, if a bit short-sighted.) Yet, in a curious contradiction, the founder of the Adamites, the former priest Peter Kanisch, had already been captured and burnt by the Hussite military commander, John Zizka. The Adamites dubbed the dead Kanisch Jesus, and then selected as their leader a peasant whom they called Adam–Moses.

For the Adamites, not only were all goods strictly owned in common, but marriage was considered a heinous sin. In short, promiscuity was compulsory, since the chaste were unworthy to enter the messianic kingdom. Any man could choose any woman at will, and that will would have to be obeyed. The Adamites also went around naked most of the time, imitating the original state of Adam and Eve. On the other hand, promiscuity was at one and the same time compulsory and restricted, because sex could only take place with the permission of the leader Adam–Moses.

Like the other radical Taborites, the Adamites regarded it as their sacred mission to exterminate all the unbelievers in the world, wielding the sword until blood floods the world to the height of a horse's bridle. They were God's scythe, sent to cut down and eradicate the unrighteous.

The Adamites took refuge from the Zizka forces on an island in the River Nezarka, from which they went forth in commando raids to try their best, despite their small number, to fulfil their twin pledge of compulsory communism and extermination of the non-elect. At night, they sallied forth in raids, which they called a 'holy war', to steal everything they could lay their hands on and then to exterminate their victims. True to their creed, they murdered every man, woman and child they could discover.

Finally, Zizka sent a force of 400 trained soldiers who besieged the Adamites' island, and finally, in October 1421, overwhelmed the commune and massacred every single person. One more hellish kingdom of God on earth had been put to the sword.

The Taborite army was crushed by the moderate Hussites at the Battle of Lipan, in 1434, and from then on, Taborism declined and went underground. But it continued to emerge here and there, not only among the Czechs, but in Bavaria and other German lands bordering Bohemia. The stage was set for the Müntzer–Münster phenomenon of the following century.

5.8   Non-scholastic Catholics

Turning from the Protestants and the Anabaptist extremists, there were some Catholics during the sixteenth century who were not scholastics, and who did not participate in the Reformation struggles, but who contributed significantly to the development of economic thought.

One of these was a universal genius whose new way of viewing the world has stamped itself on world history: the Pole Nicholas Copernicus (1473–1543). Copernicus was born in Thorn (Torun), part of Royal Prussia, then a subject state of the kingdom of Poland. He came from a well-to-do and even distinguished family, his father being a wholesale merchant and his uncle and mentor the bishop of Ermeland. Copernicus proved an inveterate student and theorist in many areas: studying mathematics at the University of Cracow, becoming a skilled painter, studying canon law and astronomy at the famous University of Bologna. Becoming a cleric, Copernicus was named canon of the cathedral at Frauenburg at the age of 24, but then took leave to lecture at Rome and to study in several fields. He then earned a doctor's degree in canon law at the University of Ferrara in 1503 and a medical degree at the University of Padua two years later. He became physician to his uncle, the bishop, and later served full-time as canon of the cathedral.

Meanwhile, as an avocation in the course of his busy life, this remarkable theorist elaborated the new system of astronomy that the earth and other planets rotated around the sun rather than vice versa.

Copernicus turned his attention to monetary affairs when King Sigismund I of Poland asked him to offer proposals for reform of the tangled currency of the area. Since the 1460s, Prussian Poland, where Copernicus lived, was the home of three different currencies: that of Royal Prussia, the Polish kingdom itself, and that of Prussia of the Teutonic Order. None of the governments maintained a single standard of weight. The Teutonic Order, in particular, kept debasing and circulating cheaper money. Copernicus finished his paper in 1517, and it was delivered to the Royal Prussian Assembly in 1522, and published four years later.

Copernicus' proposals were not adopted, but the resulting booklet, *Monetae cudendae ratio* (1526) made important contributions to monetary thought. In the first place, Copernicus strengthened the exposition of 'Gresham's law' first set forth by Nicole Oresme a century and a half earlier. Like Oresme he began with the insight that money is a measure of common market value. He then proceeded to show that, if its value is fixed by the state, money fixed artificially cheaply will tend to drive out the dearer. Thus Copernicus declared that it is impossible for good full-weighted coin and base and degraded coin to circulate together; that all the good coin is hoarded, melted down or exported; and the degraded coin alone remains in circulation. He also pointed out that in theory the government could keep adjusting the legal values of two moneys in accordance with fluctuating market values, but that in practice, the government would find this too complex a task.

In the course of his discussion, Copernicus also became the first person to set forth clearly the 'quantity theory of money', the theory that prices vary directly with the supply of money in the society. He did so 30 years before Azpilcueta Navarrus, and without the stimulus of an inflationary influx of specie from the New World to stimulate his thinking on the subject. Copernicus was still being a theorist *par excellence*. The causal chain began with debasement, which raised the quantity of the money supply, which in turn raised prices. The supply of money, he pointed out, is the major determinant of prices. 'We in our sluggishness', he maintained, 'do not realize that the dearness of everything is the result of the cheapness of money. For prices increase and decrease according to the condition of the money.' 'An excessive quantity of money', he opined, 'should be avoided.'

Another non-scholastic Catholic who contributed to economic thought in the sixteenth century was a fascinating Italian character named Gian Francesco

Lottini da Volterra (fl. 1548), who began the Italian emphasis on analysis of value and utility. In a sense, Lottini was an archetypal 'Renaissance man': learned Aristotelian scholar; secretary to Cosimo I, de Medici, Duke of Florence; unscrupulous politician; and leader of a Venetian murder ring. At the end of his life in 1548, Lottini published his *Avvedimenti civili*, in the Italian tradition (see further in chapter 6) of writing a handbook of advice to princes. The *Avvedimenti* was the work of an elder statesman dedicated to Francesco, the Medici Grand Duke of Tuscany.

Lottini investigated consumer demand, and pointed out that the valuation of consumers was rooted in the pleasure they could derive from the various goods. In a new hedonistic emphasis, he pointed out that pleasure comes from satisfying man's needs. While counselling the use of moderation (an Aristotelian theme) regulated by reason in satisfying desires, Lottini lamented that some people's wants and demands seem to be infinite: 'I have known many whose demand could not be satisfied'. As in the case of several predecessors, Lottini saw the fact of *time-preference*: people evaluate present goods higher than future goods, i.e. than present expectations of attaining these goods in the future. Unfortunately, Lottini gave to this perfectly reasonable and ineluctable fact of nature a moralistic twist: somehow this was an improper *over*estimation of present and *under*estimation of future goods. This unwarranted moralistic critique was to plague economic thought in the future. As Lottini phrased it: '...the present, which is before our eyes and which can, so to speak, be grasped with our hands, has forced, more often than not, even wise men to pay more attention to the nearest satisfaction than to hope for the far future'. The reasons for this universal fact of time-preference are that people pay more attention to things they can perceive with their senses than things they can learn of by reason, and that 'only a few people follow a long-lasting and risky project stubbornly to its end'. In the first reason, Lottini begs the question: the problem is not senses vs reason, but something evident to the senses *now* versus what is only *expected* to be evident at some time in the future. His second reason is more on the mark: the emphasis on the 'long-lasting' touches on the crucial problem of length of waiting-time, and the word 'risky' brings another and critical factor into play: the degree of risk that the object will never become evident to the senses *at all*.

Lottini's work went into several editions shortly after his death, and a copy has been found belonging to the great English poet and theologian John Donne (1573–1631), whose marginal notes reveal the Aristotelian influence upon Donne.

Successor to Lottini was Bernardo Davanzati (1529–1606), a Florentine merchant, erudite classicist and renowned translator of Tacitus, and an arch-Catholic historian of the Reformation in England. At the age of 17, young Davanzati became a member of the Florentine Academy. In two works, written in lively Italian style, in 1582 and especially in his *Lezione delle Moneta* (1588), Davanzati applied the scholastic type of utility analysis to the theory of money. Thus Davanzati approached, and solved – with the exception of the marginal element – the paradox of value, comparing demand and scarcity. Davanzati also followed Buridan in developing what would later be the excellent analysis by Carl Menger, father of the Austrian School in the late nineteenth century, of the origin of money. Men, wrote Davanzati, need many things for the maintenance of life; but climates and people's skills differ, hence there arises a division of labour in society. All goods are therefore produced, distributed, and enjoyed by means of exchange. Barter was soon found to be inconvenient, and so locations for exchange developed, such as fairs and markets. After that, people agreed – but here Davanzati was cloudy on *how* this 'agreement' took place – to use a certain commodity as money, i.e. as a medium for all exchanges. First, gold and silver were used in lump pieces; then they were weighed, and then stamped to show weight and fineness in the form of coins. Unfortunately, in his later historical sketch of the theory of money, Menger was ungracious enough to dismiss Davanzati brusquely as simply someone who 'traces the origin of money back to the authority of the state'.[15]

5.9   Radical Huguenots

Calvin began his own Reformation after Luther, but it rapidly swept through western Europe, triumphing not only in Switzerland but more importantly in the Dutch Netherlands, the main commercial and financial centre of Europe in the seventeenth century, and coming within a hair's breadth of dominating Great Britain and France. In Britain, Scotland was conquered by Calvinism in the form of the Presbyterian Church, and Calvinist Puritanism heavily influenced the Anglican Church and almost conquered England in the mid-seventeenth century. France was rent by religious–political wars during the last four decades of the sixteenth century, and the Calvinists, known as Huguenots, were not far from triumphing there. Though converting no more than 5 per cent of the population, the Huguenots were extremely influential in the nobility, and in pockets in northern and south-western France.

John Calvin, fully as much as Luther, preached the doctrine of absolute obedience and non-resistance to duly constituted government, regardless of how evil that government may be. But Calvin's embattled followers, enjoying rising aspirations against non-Calvinist rulers, developed justifications for resistance to evil rulers. These were first set forth in the 1550s by the English 'Marian exiles' in Switzerland and Germany during the reign of the last Catholic monarch in England, Queen Mary. This radical tradition, including the people's right to tyrannicide, was carried on by the Huguenots in the following decades.

Stimulated by the horror of the massacre of St Bartholomew's Day in 1572, the Huguenots promptly developed libertarian theories of radical resistance against the tyranny of the Crown. Some of the most notable writings are the jurist, François Hotman's (1524–90) *Francogallia*, written in the late 1560s but first published in 1573; the anonymous *Political Discourses* (1574); and the culminating work, at the end of the 1570s, by Philippe Du Plessis Mornay (1549–1623), the *Defense of Liberty against Tyrants (Vindiciae Contra Tyrannos)* (1579). Defending tyrannicide in particular was the *Political Discourses*, which bitterly attacked the 'so-called theologians and preachers' who asserted that no one may ever lawfully kill a tyrant 'without a special revelation from God'. The other Huguenot writers, however, were far more cautious on this touchy issue.

Furthermore, three decades before the radical Spanish scholastic Juan de Mariana, the Huguenots advanced a pre-Lockean theory of popular sovereignty. In particular, Hotman warned that a people's transference of their right to rule to the king can in no way be permanent or irrevocable. On the contrary, the people and their representative bodies have the right of continual surveillance of the king, as well as of taking away his power at any time. Not only that, but the states-general is supposed to have continuing day-to-day power to rule. Hotman won general Huguenot acceptance of this new creed by cloaking it in terms of Jean Calvin's original, quite contrasting political doctrine.

But Hotman's argument for original popular rule was strictly historical, and the counter-attacks of the royalist writers soon riddled the historical account with gross distortions. It was necessary for the Huguenots to abandon the original Calvinist counsel of total civil obedience and construct a natural law theory of the original sovereignty of the people, preceding the consensual transfer to kingly rule. In short, the Huguenots had to rediscover and reappropriate the scholastic tradition of their hated Catholic opponents. Thus, in contrast to the preaching style and emphasis on divine will of the Marian exiles, Mornay and other Huguenots wrote in a logical, scholastic style, and explicitly referred to Aquinas and to codifiers of the Roman law.

In short, as Professor Skinner writes, there was no 'Calvinist theory of revolution' in the sixteenth century. Paradoxically, the French Calvinists pioneered the development of a revolutionary theory of popular rule by grounding themselves in the natural law tradition of their Catholic adversaries.[16]

Furthermore, Ockhamite scholastics at Paris, e.g. Jean Gerson in the early fifteenth century and the Englishman John Major in the early sixteenth, pioneered specifically the concept of sovereignty which always inheres in the people and which they can therefore take back from the king at any time.

One of the pernicious effects on scholarship of Max Weber's Protestant (actually Calvinist) ethic as the creator of capitalism has already been seen:

the neglect of the actual rise of capitalism in Catholic Italy, as well as in Antwerp and southern Germany. Another associated Weberian fallacy is the popular idea of Calvinism as 'modern' and revolutionary, as the creator of radical and democratic political thought. But we have seen that Calvinist and Protestant political thought was originally statist and absolutist. Calvinism only became revolutionary and anti-tyrannical under the pressure of opposing Catholic regimes, which drove the Calvinists back to natural law and popular sovereignty *motifs* in Catholic scholastic thought.

An important strand of popular sovereignty was worked out by Theodore Beza (1519–1605), Calvin's leading disciple and successor at Geneva. The great Beza, influenced by Hotman, published *The Right of Magistrates* in 1574. Beza insisted that natural law revealed that the people logically and temporally preceded their rulers, so that political power originated in the body of the people. It is 'self-evident', Beza declared, that 'peoples do not come from rulers', and are not created by them. Hence the people originally decided to transfer governing powers to the rulers. An influential radical Huguenot pamphlet, *The Awakener (Le Reveille Matin)* (1574) repeated Beza's argument. (*The Awakener* was probably written by the eminent French jurist, Hugues Doneau.) Man could not be naturally in subjection, *The Awakener* pointed out, for 'assemblies and groups of men existed everywhere before the creation of kings', and 'even today it is possible to find a people without a magistrate but never a magistrate without a people'. If man is not to be naturally free but naturally enslaved, then we must absurdly conclude that 'the people must have been created by their magistrates' when it is obvious, to the contrary, that 'magistrates are always created by the people'.

As usual Philippe Du Plessis Mornay summed up the position with trenchant clarity. 'No one', he observed, 'is a king by nature', and, furthermore, and with particular point, 'a king cannot rule without a people, while a people can rule itself without a king'. Hence, it is evident that the people must have preceded the existence of kings or positive laws, and then later submitted themselves to their dominion. Hence, man's natural condition must be liberty, and we must possess freedom as a natural right, a right that can never be justifiably removed. As Mornay put it, we are all 'free by nature, born to hate servitude, and desirous of commanding rather than yielding obedience'. Further, continuing this proto-Lockean analysis, the people must have submitted themselves to governmental rule to promote their well-being.

Following John Major, Mornay was clear that the *kind* of well-being the people advanced in setting up government was to protect their individual natural rights. To Mornay as to Major, a 'right' over something was being free to hold and dispose of it, i.e. a right in the object as property. The people retain such rights when they establish polities, which they willingly create in order to ensure greater security for their property. These rights of property include the natural right of everyone in their own persons and their liberties. Governments are supposed to maintain those rights, but often become the main transgressors. Mornay was careful to point out that the people, in establishing governments, cannot alienate their sovereignty. Instead they always 'remain in the position of the owner' of their sovereignty, which they merely delegate to the ruler. The 'whole' people therefore continues to be 'greater than the king and is above him'.

On the other hand, Mornay and the other Huguenots were constrained to temper their revolutionary radicalism. First, they made it clear, in a manner wholly consistent with their view that the whole people retain their sovereignty, that the 'people' are not really the people as a whole but their 'representatives' in the magistrates and the states-general. The people have necessarily 'given their sword' to these institutions, and therefore 'when we speak of the people collectively, we mean those who receive authority from the people, that is, the magistrates below the king...[and] the assembly of the Estates'. Moreover, in practice, these alleged representatives keep the enforcement of the king's promises in their hands, since that power of enforcement is a property of 'the authorities that have the power of the people in them'.

Furthermore, according to the Huguenots, the sovereign right is only in the people as a whole and not in any individual, so that tyrannicide by one subject is never permissible. The people as a whole are above the king, but the king is above any single individual. More concretely, since sovereignty rests in the institutions of duly constituted assemblies or magistrates, only these institutions embodying the sovereign power of the people can properly resist the tyranny of the king.

In a few short years, the rebellion of the Dutch against Spanish rule reached a climax in 1580–81. An anonymous Calvinist pamphlet, *A True Warning*, appeared in Antwerp in 1581 which asserted that 'God has created men free', and that the only power over men is whatever they themselves have granted. If the king breaks the conditions of his rule, then the people's representatives have the right and the duty to depose him and to 'resume their original rights'. The leader of the Dutch rebellion, William the Silent, Prince of Orange, adopted the same view in these same years, both in his own *Apology* presented to the states-general at the end of 1580, and in the official *Edict of the States General* issued the following July. (It should be noted that the *Apology* was largely written by Mornay and other Huguenot advisors.) The *Edict* declared that the king of Spain had 'forfeited his sovereignty', and that the United Netherlands had at last been obliged, 'in conformity with the law of nature', to exercise their unquestioned right to resist tyranny, and 'to pursue such means' as necessary to secure their 'rights, privileges and liberties'.

5.10 George Buchanan: radical Calvinist

The most fascinating as well as the most radical of the Calvinist theorists of the late sixteenth century was not a French Huguenot but a Scot who spent most of his time in France. George Buchanan (1506–82) was a distinguished humanist historian and poet, who taught Latin at the College de Guyenne in Bordeaux. Buchanan was trained in scholastic philosophy at the University of St Andrews in the mid-1520s, where he studied under the great John Major. An early convert to Calvinism, Buchanan became a friend of Beza and of Mornay, and served as a member of the general assembly of the Church of Scotland.

British Calvinist thinkers of the 1550s, refugees from the Catholic rule of Queen Mary, had worked out in exile a justification for rebellion against tyranny in terms of the godly against idolatry. It remained to restate revolutionary theory in secular, natural rights, terms rather than in the strictly religious concepts of godliness and heresy. This feat was accomplished by the Scot George Buchanan, in the midst of a struggle of the Calvinist majority of Scotland against their Catholic queen. A revolution in 1560 had conquered the Scottish parliament for Calvinism in a now overwhelmingly Calvinist country, and seven years later the Calvinists deposed the Catholic queen, Mary Stuart.

In the course of this struggle, Buchanan, in 1567, began to draft his great work, *The Right of the Kingdom in Scotland*, which he published in 1579. Parts of Buchanan's argument appeared in speeches delivered by the new Scottish Regent James Stewart, Earl of Moray in 1568, and then in discussions between the Scottish and English governments three years later.

Buchanan began, like the Huguenots, with the state of nature and a social contract by the people with their rulers, a contract in which they retained their sovereignty and their rights. But there were two major differences. In the first place, Beza and Mornay had talked of *two* such contracts: a political social contract, and a religious covenant to act as a godly people. With Buchanan, the religious covenant drops out totally, and we are left with the political contract alone. Some historians have interpreted Buchanan's radical step as secularizing politics into an independent 'political science'. More accurately, Buchanan emancipated political theory from the directly divine or theological concerns of the Protestant founders, and returned it to its earlier base in natural law and in human rights.

More radically, Buchanan swept away the entire inconsistent Huguenot baggage of the people virtually alienating their sovereignty to intermediate 'representatives'. On the contrary, for Buchanan the people consent to and contract with a ruler, and retain their sovereign rights, with no mention of intermediate assemblies. But this puts far more revolutionary implications on natural rights and popular sovereignty. For then, when a king becomes tyrannical and violates his task to safeguard individual rights, this means 'that the whole body of the people, and even individual citizens, may be said to have the authority to resist and kill a legitimate ruler in defence of their rights'. Thus, over two decades before the Spanish Jesuit de Mariana, George Buchanan had arrived, for the first time, at a truly individualist theory of natural rights and sovereignty and therefore a justification for individual acts of tyrannicide. Thus, in what Professor Skinner calls 'a highly individualist and even anarchic view of political resistance', Buchanan stressed that:

> Since the people as a body create their ruler, it is...possible at any time 'for the people to shake off whatever *Imperium*' they may have imposed on themselves, the reason being that 'anything which is done by a given power can be undone by a like power'. Furthermore, Buchanan adds that, since each individual must be pictured as agreeing to the formation of the commonwealth for his own greater security and benefit, it follows that the right to kill or remove a tyrant must be lodged at all times 'not only with the whole body of the people' but 'even with every individual citizen'. So he willingly endorses the almost anarchic conclusion that even when, as frequently happens, someone 'from amongst the lowest and meanest of men' decides 'to revenge the pride and insolence of a tyrant' by simply taking upon himself the right to kill him, such action are often 'judged to have been done quite rightly,...'.[17]

We have seen that the Spanish Jesuit, Juan de Mariana, developed a similar theory of Lockean popular sovereignty and of individual tyrannicide two decades later. As a scholastic, he too had a natural law contract and not any religious covenant at the base of his theory. Skinner ably concludes that

> The Jesuit Mariana may thus be said to link hands with the Protestant Buchanan in stating a theory of popular sovereignty which, while scholastic in its origins and Calvinist in its later development, was in essence independent of either religious creed, and was thus available to be used by all parties in the coming constitutional struggles of the seventeenth century.

More typical, however, of the dominant strand of radical Calvinism emerging from the sixteenth century was the distinguished Dutch jurist, Johannes Althusius (1557–1638). His *magnum opus* was his treatise of 1603, *Politics Methodically Set Forth*. Althusius built upon and was similar to Mornay and the Huguenot theorists. With them, he retained the pre-Lockean popular sovereignty with consensual revocable delegation to the king, and also with them he mediated that sovereignty through representative assemblies and associations. In addition, the justification of individual tyrannicide disappears. However, one innovation of Buchanan's was retained in Althusius' massive treatise: the dropping of any religious covenant. Indeed, Althusius is more explicit, attacking theologians for infusing their political writings with 'teachings on Christian piety and charity', and failing to realize that these matters are 'improper and alien to political doctrine'.

5.11   Leaguers and *politiques*

While the Huguenot monarchomachs have been far more extensively studied than their Catholic counterparts of the late sixteenth century, the latter are an interesting and neglected group. After the accession of King Henry III in 1574, it began to be clear that the Huguenots were no longer in danger of annihilation, and that, on the contrary, it seemed that Henry was soft on Protestants. This softness became an acute problem for the Catholics of France in 1584, when the death of the heir to the throne, the Duc d'Alençon, brought into the first line of succession Henry of Navarre, a committed Calvinist. This threat brought into being the Catholic League, especially in Paris, then the heartland of French Catholicism. The League, headed throughout France by the Duc de Guise, rebelled against Henry and drove him out of Paris. As we have seen, Henry's treacherous assassination of Guise and his brother the cardinal during a peace parley led to a mighty act of tyrannicide, in which the young Dominican priest, Jacques Clément, on 1 August 1589, avenged the Guises by assassinating Henry III.

Paris under the Catholic League was run by a council of 16, supported by the middle classes, professionals and businessmen, and backed fervently by virtually all the priests and curés in the city. The most radical of the Leaguer thinkers, who flourished during the 1580s and 1590s, was a leading attorney, François LeBreton, who, in his *Remonstrance to the Third Estate* (1586), bitterly attacked the king as a hypocrite, advocated a French republic, and called for revolution and civil war to attain it. LeBreton was promptly executed by the Parlement, the leading judicial organ in France.

The rebellion of the Catholic League, which culminated in the revolt of Paris and other parts of France, was not only motivated by concern over the possible imposition of a minority Huguenot faith upon the Catholic French. Leaguer grievances were political and economic as well as religious. Henry III, the last Valois king, had imposed upon his country a huge amount of pillage, a very high tax burden, and large amounts of expense, offices and subsidies. Huge taxes were particularly levied upon the city of Paris.

But Father Clement's act, however heroic, proved in the end to be counter productive. For the first Bourbon, Henry of Navarre, assumed the throne as Henry IV. Realizing that he could scarcely remain a Huguenot and still govern France, Henry, after four years of war, converted to Catholicism, supposedly explaining, in a probably apocryphal phrase, that 'Paris is worth a mass'. Henry IV had won. With the advent of the new Bourbon king came the rule of the centrist or 'moderate' Catholics, the *politiques* – 'the politicals'.

Whether one might call Henry IV and the *politiques* 'moderates' depends on one's perspective. As secularists and men of feeble faith, it is true that the *politiques* were not interested in slaughtering Huguenots, and were anxious to end the religious conflict as soon as possible. Henry did so in his toleration decree, the Edict of Nantes in 1598. In that sense, the *politiques* were 'middle-of-the-roaders' in between the two religious extremes: the Huguenots and the Catholic Leaguers. And that is the light that most historians have shed upon them. But in another important sense the *politiques* were not 'moderate' at all. For they were truly extreme in desiring to give all power to the absolute state and to its embodiment in the king of France. In triumphing over both 'extremes', Henry IV and the *politiques* rode roughshod over the only two groups who had called for resistance against royal tyranny. The victory of Henry also meant the end of French resistance to royal absolutism. Unchecked despotic rule by the Bourbons was now to be France's lot for two centuries, until it was brought to a violent end by the French Revolution. It was a high price indeed to pay for religious concord, especially since Louis XIV, the 'Sun King', the embodiment of French royal despotism, revoked the Edict of Nantes in 1685 and thereby drove many Huguenots out of France. In the long run, the religious 'peace' of absolutist 'moderation' turned out to be the peace of the grave for many Huguenots.

5.12   Notes

1. Quentin Skinner, *The Foundations of Modern Political Thought: Vol. II, The Age of Reformation* (Cambridge: Cambridge University Press, 1978), p. 143. In particular, two late sixteenth century works launched this critique: the Italian Jesuit Antonio Possevino (1534–1611), *A Judgment on the Writings of Jean Bodin, Philippe Mornay and Niccolo Machiavelli* (Lyons, 1594); and the Spanish Jesuit Pedro de Ribadeneyra (1527–1611), *Religion and the Virtues of the Christian Prince against Machiavelli* (Madrid, 1595, trans. and ed. by George A. Moore, Maryland, 1949).
2. Gary North, 'The Economic Thought of Luther and Calvin', *The Journal of Christian Reconstruction*, II (Summer, 1975), p. 77.
3. Richard H. Tawney, *Religion and the Rise of Capitalism* (1927, New York: New American Library, 1954), p. 80.
4. Ibid., p. 95.
5. In contrast to the Catholics, to Luther, and probably to Calvin (who, however, was ambivalent on the subject), the Puritans were 'post-millennialist', i.e. they believed that human beings would have to establish the Kingdom of God on earth for a thousand years before Christ would return. The others were either 'pre-millennialist' (Christ would return to earth and *then* set up a thousand years of the Kingdom of God on earth), or, like the Catholics, amillennialist (Christ would return period, and then the world would end). Post-millennialism, of course, tended to induce in its believers eagerness and even haste to get on with their own establishment of the Kingdom of God on earth so that Jesus could eventually return.
6. The fact that only late Calvinism developed this version of the calling indicates that Weber might have had his causal theory reversed: that the growth of capitalism might have led to a more accommodating Calvinism rather than the other way round. Weber's approach holds up better in analysing those societies, such as China, where religious attitudes seem to have crippled capitalist economic development. Thus, see the analysis of

religion and economic development in China and Japan by the Weberian Norman Jacobs, *The Origin of Modern Capitalism and Eastern Asia* (Hong Kong: Hong Kong University Press, 1958).

7. Emil Kauder, *A History of Marginal Utility Theory* (Princeton, NJ: Princeton University Press, 1965), p.5.

8. Michael Walzer, *The Revolution of the Saints: A Study in the Origins of Radical Politics* (Cambridge, Mass.: Harvard University Press, 1965), p. 216; see also pp. 206–26.

9. Kauder, op. cit., note 7, p. 9.

10. John T. Noonan, Jr, *The Scholastic Analysis of Usury* (Cambridge, Mass.: Harvard University Press, 1957), p. 344*n*.

11. Ibid., p. 371.

12. Eugen von Böhm-Bawerk, *Capital and Interest, Vol. I: History and Critique of Interest Theories* (1921, South Holland, Ill.: Libertarian Press, 1959), p. 24.

13. Ronald A. Knox, *Enthusiasm: A Chapter in the History of Religion* (1950, New York: Oxford University Press, 1961), p. 133.

14. Quoted in Igor Shafarevich, *The Socialist Phenomenon* (New York: Harper & Row, 1980), p. 57.

15. Carl Menger, *Principles of Economics* (New York: New York University Press, 1981), pp. 317–18.

16. Skinner, op. cit., note 1, p. 321.

17. Ibid., pp. 343–4.

18. Ibid., p. 347.

6 Absolutist thought in Italy and France

6.1 The emergence of absolutist thought in Italy

By the twelfth century, the Italian city-states had evolved a new form of government, new at least since ancient Greece. Instead of the usual hereditary monarch as feudal overlord, basing his rule on a network of feudal dominion over land areas, the Italian city-states became republics. The commercial oligarchs who constituted the ruling élite of the city-state would elect as ruler a salaried bureaucratic official or *podesta*, whose term of office was short, and who therefore ruled at the pleasure of the oligarchy. This city-republican form of government began at Pisa in 1085, and had swept northern Italy by the end of the twelfth century.

Since the age of Charlemagne in the ninth century, the German – or 'Holy Roman' – emperors were legally supposed to be rulers of northern Italy. For several centuries, however, this rule was merely *pro forma*, and the city-states were *de facto* independent. By the mid-twelfth century, the Italian city-states were the most prosperous countries in Europe. Prosperity meant the standing temptation of wealth to loot, and so the German emperors, beginning with Frederick Barbarossa in 1154, began a two-centuries-long series of attempts to conquer the northern Italian cities. The incursions came to an end with the resounding defeat of Emperor Henry VII's expedition of 1310–13, followed by the abject withdrawal and dissolution of the imperial army of Louis of Bavaria in 1327.

In the course of this chronic struggle, legal and political theorists arose in Italy to give voice to an eventually successful Italian determination to resist the encroachment of the German monarchs. They evolved the idea of the right of nations to resist imperial attempts at conquest by other states – what would later be called the right of national independence, or 'self-government' or 'national self-determination'.

During the two centuries of conflict, the major ally of the Italian city-states against the German empire was the pope, who in that era was able to put papal armies into the field. As the papal armies helped the cities roll back the emperor's forces during the thirteenth century, the city-states found to their growing chagrin that the pope was beginning to assert temporal power over northern Italy. And those claims could be backed up by the papal armies occupying large sections of the Italian peninsula.

For a while, some theorists toyed with the idea of reversing Italian policy and submitting to the German emperor in order to rid themselves of the papal threat. Prominent among this group was the great Florentine poet Dante Alighieri, who advanced his pro-imperial and anti-papal views in his *Monarchy*, written at the height of the imperial hopes for the 1310 expedition of Henry VII. The end of the imperial threat soon afterwards, however, made this turn to the emperor impractical, as well as unpalatable to the majority of Italians. And so a new political theory was needed by the oligarchs of the

Italian city-states. Such a theory would assert the claims of the secular state – whether republic or monarchy made little difference – to rule at will, unchecked by the age-old moral and often concrete authority of the Catholic Church to limit state invasions of natural law and human rights. In short, the Italian oligarchs needed a theory of state absolutism, of secular power untrammelled. The Church was to be impatiently relegated to the purely theological and 'religious' area while secular affairs would be in the entirely separate hands of the state and its temporal power. This amounted to the *politique* doctrine, as it would come to prevail in late sixteenth century France.

As we have seen above, the Italian oligarchs found their new theory in the writings of the political theorist and university professor, Marsiglio of Padua. Marsiglio can therefore be considered the first absolutist in the modern western world, and his *Defensor Pacis* (1324) the first main expression of absolutism.

While Marsiglio was the founding theorist of absolutism in the West, the specific form of his own cherished polity quickly became obsolete – at least in Padua. For Marsiglio was an adherent of oligarchical republicanism, but this form of government proved short-lived, and disappeared in Padua soon after the publication of his treatise. During the latter half of the thirteenth century, the Italian city-states became riven between the old oligarchs – the *magnati* – striving to retain their power, and the newly wealthy but disenfranchised *popolani*, who kept attempting to gain power. The upshot was that throughout northern Italy during the last half of the thirteenth century – beginning with Ferrara in 1264 – power was seized by one man, one *signor*, one despot who imposed the hereditary rule of himself and his family. In effect, hereditary monarchy had been established once again. They were not called 'kings', since that would have been an absurdly grandiose title for the territory of one city; and so they gave themselves other names: 'permanent lord'; 'captain general'; 'duke', etc. Florence was one of the few cities able to resist the new tide of one-man rule.

In 1328, four years after the publication of *Defensor Pacis*, the della Scala family finally managed to impose their control over the city of Padua. The della Scalas had taken over Verona in the 1260s, and now, after many years of conflict, Cangrande della Scala was able to seize power in Padua as well. Quick to inaugurate a new tradition of fawning adulation of tyranny was the prominent Paduan literary figure Ferreto de Ferreti (c.1296–1337), who abandoned his previous republicanism to compose a long Latin poem on *The Rise of the della Scala*.

The hero Cangrande had come, according to Ferreti, and brought peace and stability at last to 'turbulent' and torn Padua. Ferreti concluded his panegyric by expressing the fervent hope that the descendants of Cangrande della Scala would 'continue to hold their sceptres for long years to come'.

6.2 Italian humanism: the republicans

The defenders of the old oligarchic republics countered the rise of the *signori* with a pro-republican absolutism of their own. This development began in the teaching of rhetoric. By the early twelfth century, the University of Bologna, and other Italian centres for training lawyers, had developed courses in rhetoric, originally the art and style of writing letters, to which was later added the art of public speaking. By the first half of the thirteenth century, the professors of rhetoric were including direct political commentary in their lessons and handbooks. One popular form was a propagandistic history of their particular cities, glorifying the city and its rulers, and expressly devoted to inculcating the ideology of support for the ruling élite of the city. The most prominent early master of this genre was the Bolognese rhetorician Boncampagno da Signa (c.1165–1240), whose most popular work was *The Siege of Ancona* (1201–2). Another prominent form, developed by Italian rhetoricians in the second half of the thirteenth century, was advice-books for rulers and city magistrates, in which political advice was directed to the rulers. The most important early advice-book was John of Viterbo's *The Government of Cities*, which he wrote in the 1240s after serving as a judge under the elected ruler, or *podesta* of Florence. John of Viterbo, however, was not a full absolutist, since his determinedly moral approach counselled the ruler always to pursue virtue and justice and to avoid vice and crime.

Whereas the Italian teaching of rhetoric at Bologna and elsewhere was narrowly practical, the French professors of rhetoric in the thirteenth century upheld the classical Greek and Roman writers as models of style. The French method was taught at the University of Paris and particularly at Orleans. By the second half of the thirteenth century, Italian rhetoricians who had studied in France brought the new approach to Italy, and the broader, more humanistic approach quickly swept the field, dominating even the University of Bologna. Soon these early humanists began to study the ideas as well as the style of the classical poets, historians and orators, and began to enliven their political theory with classical references and models.

The most important of these early humanist rhetoricians was the Florentine Brunetto Latini (c.1220–94). Exiled from his native Florence, Latini went to France at the age of 40 and imbibed the works of Cicero and the French rhetorical approach. During his exile, Latini composed his leading work, *The Books of Treasure*, which introduced Cicero and other classical writers into the traditional works of Italian rhetoric. On his return to Florence in 1266, Latini also translated and published some of Cicero's major works.

Particularly important in the new learning was the University of Padua, beginning with the great judge Lovato Lovati (1241–1309), whom no less a poet than Petrarch (mid-fourteenth century) called the greatest Italian poet up to that time. The most important of Lovati's disciples was the fascinating

character Alberto Mussato (1261–1329). Lawyer, politician, historian, dramatist and poet, Mussato was the leader of the republican faction in Padua, the
main opposition to the lengthy campaign by the della Scala family to seize
power in that city. (Ironically enough, Ferreto de Ferreti, the panegyrist of the
della Scala victory, had been a fellow disciple in the Lovati circle.) Mussato
wrote two histories of Italy; his most prominent literary effort was the notable Latin verse play *Ecerinis* (1313–14), the first secular drama written since
the classical era. Here Mussato employed the new rhetoric as politician and
propagandist. He explains in the introduction to the play that his chief purpose was to 'inveigh with lamentations against tyranny', specifically of course
the tyranny of the della Scalas. The political propaganda value of *Ecerinis*
was quickly recognized by the Paduan oligarchy, which crowned Mussato
with a laurel wreath in 1315, and issued a decree ordering the play to be read
aloud each year before the assembled populace of the city.

The new study of the classics also gave rise to sophisticated city chroni-
cles, such as the *Chronicle* of Florence written in the early fourteenth century
by Dino Compagni (c.1255–1324), a prominent lawyer and politician of the
city. Indeed, Compagni was himself one of the rulers of the Florentine oligarchy. Another important example of republican rhetorical humanism was
Bonvesin della Riva's book, *The Glories of the City of Milan* (1288). Bonvesin
was a leading professor of rhetoric in Milan.

All these writers – Latini, Mussato, Compagni, and others – were concerned to work out a political theory in defence of oligarchical republican
rule. They concluded that there are two basic reasons for the rise of the hated
signori: the emergence of factions within the city, and love of greed and
luxury. Both sets of ills were of course an implicit attack on the rise of the
nouveau riche popolani and the challenge of the *popolani* against the old
republican magnates. Without the new wealth of the *popolani* or the rise of
their factions, the old oligarchy would have gone on their way undisturbed in
the quiet exercise of power. Compagni put it baldly: Florence was disrupted
because 'the minds of the false popolani' had been 'corrupted to do wrong
for the sake of gain'. Latini sees the source of evil in 'those who covet
riches', and Mussato attributes the death of the Paduan republic to 'the lust
for money' which undermined civic responsibility. Note the emphasis on the
'lust' or 'coveting' of money, that is, by *new* wealth; *old* and therefore 'good'
wealth – that of the magnates – does not require lust or coveting since it is
already in the possession of the oligarchy.

The way to end factions, according to the humanists, was for the people to
put aside personal interests for unity on behalf of the 'public' or civic 'interest', of the 'common good'. Latini set the tone by bringing in Plato and
Aristotle, Plato for instructing us that 'we ought to consider the common
profit above everything else', and Aristotle for stressing that 'if each man

follows his own individual will, the government of men's lives is destroyed and totally dissolved'.

Blather about the 'public interest' and the 'common good' may be all very well, until the time comes to interpret in practice what these cloudy concepts are supposed to mean and in particular *who* is supposed to interpret their meaning. To the humanists the answer is clear: the virtuous ruler. Select virtuous rulers, trust in their virtue, and the problem is solved.

How are the people supposed to go about selecting virtuous rulers? That was not the sort of embarrassing question posed or considered by the Italian humanists. For that would have led ineluctably to considering *institutional mechanisms* which might promote the selection of virtuous rulers, or worse yet, prevent the selection of the vicious. Any such tampering with institutions would have led to checks on the absolute power of rulers, and that was not the mind-set of these humanist apologists for the sovereign power of oligarchy.

The humanists were clear, however, that virtue inheres in the individuals and not in noble families *per se*. While it was surely sensible of them to avoid centring virtue in hereditary noble families, it also meant that the virtuous ruler could personally reign unchecked by any traditional family ties or commitments.

The only check offered to ensure the virtue of rulers, the only real criterion for such virtue, was if the rulers followed the advice of these humanists, as elaborated in their advice-books. Happily, while Latini and his humanist followers established all the preconditions for absolute rule, they did not proceed to endorse absolutism itself. For, like John of Viterbo before them, they insisted that the ruler must be truly virtuous, including cleaving to honesty and the pursuit of justice. Like John of Viterbo and others in what has been called the 'mirror-of-princes' literature, Latini and his followers insisted that the ruler must avoid all temptations to fraud and dishonesty, and that he serve as a model of integrity. To Latini and the others, true virtue and the self-interest of the ruler were one and the same. Honesty was not only morally correct, it was also, in a later phrase, 'the best policy'. Justice, probity, being loved by his subjects rather than being feared – all would also serve to maintain the ruler in power. *Seeming* to be just and honest, Latini made clear, was not enough; the ruler, both for the sake of virtue and for keeping his power, 'must actually be as he wishes to seem', for he will be 'grossly deceived' if 'he tries to gain glory by false methods...' There was, in short, no conflict between morality and utility for the ruler; the ethical turned out, harmoniously, to be the useful.

The next great burst of Italian humanism came in the city of Florence, nearly a century later. The independence of Florence, the stronghold of oligarchic republicanism, was threatened, for three-quarters of a century, from the 1380s to the 1450s, by the Visconti family of Milan. Giangeleazzo Visconti, *signor* and duke of Milan, set out in the 1380s to reduce all northern Italy to his subjection. By 1402, Visconti had conquered all northern Italy except Florence, and that city was saved by the sudden death of the duke. Soon, however, Giangeleazzo's son, Duke Filippo Maria Visconti, launched the war of conquest again. All-out war between Florence and imperial Milan continued from 1423 until 1454, when Florence induced Milan to recognize the independence of the Florentine republic.

The embattled status of the Florentine republic led to a revival of republican humanism. While these early fifteenth century Florentine humanists were more philosophically oriented and more optimistic then their early fourteenth century Paduan and other Italian predecessors, their political theory was very much the same. All these leading Florentine humanists (much better known to later historians than the earlier Paduans) had similar biographies: they were trained as lawyers and rhetoricians, and they became either professors of rhetoric and/or top bureaucrats in Florence, in other cities, or at the papal court at the Vatican. Thus the *doyen* of the Florentine humanists was Coluccio Salutati (1331–1406), who studied rhetoric at Bologna and became chancellor at various Italian cities, in the last three decades of his life at Florence. Of Salutati's main disciples, Leonardo Bruni (1369–1444) studied law and rhetoric in Florence, became secretary at the papal curia, and then became a top bureaucrat and finally chancellor of Florence from 1427 until his death. Pier Paolo Vergerio (1370–1444) began training in law in Florence and then rose to secretary at the papal curia; and similarly Poggio Bracciolini (1380–1459) studied civil law at Bologna and Florence and then became a professor of rhetoric at the papal curia.

The second generation of the Salutati circle also followed similar careers and had kindred views. Here should be mentioned the distinguished architect Leon Battista degli Alberti (1404–72) of the great banking family, who earned a doctorate in canon law at Bologna and then became a papal secretary; Giannozzo Manetti (1396–1459) was educated in law and humanistic studies in Florence, and then served for two decades in the Florentine bureaucracy, later becoming secretary at the papal curia and finally secretary to the king of Naples; and Matteo Palmieri (1406–75) became a top bureaucrat for five decades in Florence, including eight different ambassadorships.

6.3   Italian humanism: the monarchists
The political and economic decline of the Italian city-states after the turn to the Atlantic in the late fifteenth and sixteenth centuries, was marked in foreign affairs by the repeated invasions of Italy by armies of the burgeoning nation-states of Europe. The French kings invaded and conquered Italy repeatedly from the 1490s on, and from the early 1520s to the 1550s the armies

of France and the Holy Roman Empire fought over Italy as a battleground for conquest.

While Florence and the remainder of northern Italy were being invaded from without, republicanism throughout Italy finally gave way to despotic one-man rule of the various *signori*. Whereas republican forces, headed by the Colonna family, had managed to deprive the popes of their temporal power during the mid-fifteenth century, by the end of that century the popes, led by Alexander VI (1492–1503) and Julius II (1503–13) managed to reassert themselves as unchallenged temporal monarchs over Rome and the papal states. In Florence, the powerful de Medici family of bankers and politicians began slowly but surely to build up their political power until they could become hereditary monarchs, *signori*. The process began as early as the 1430s with the great Cosimo de Medici, and culminated in the seizure of power in 1480 by Cosimo's grandson Lorenzo 'the Magnificent'. Lorenzo ensured his one-man rule by setting up a 'council of seventy' with complete control over the republic, all comprising his own supporters.

The republican forces fought back, however, and the struggle lasted another half-century. In 1494, the republican oligarchs forced Lorenzo's son Piero into exile after he had surrendered Florence to the French. Republican rule collapsed in 1512, when the Medici took command with the aid of Spanish troops. Medici power then reigned until 1527, when another republican revolution drove them out; but two years later the Medici pope, Clement VII, induced the Habsburg Holy Roman Emperor Charles V to invade and conquer Florence on the Medici's behalf. Charles did so in 1530, and the Florentine republic was no more. Clement VII, left in charge of Florence by the emperor, appointed Alessandro de Medici ruler of the city for life, and Alessandro and all his heirs were also named lords of the city in perpetuity. The government of Florence dissolved into the Medici Grand Duchy of Tuscany, and the Medicis ran Tuscany as monarchs for two more centuries.

The final triumph of the *signori* put an end to the optimism of the early fifteenth century republican humanists, whose successors began to grow cynical about politics and to advocate lives of quiet contemplation.

Other humanists, however, seeing on which side their bread was buttered, executed a quick shift from praising republican oligarchy to lauding one-man monarchy. We have already seen Ferreto Ferreti's swiftness in composing a panegyric to the della Scala tyranny in Padua. Similarly, around 1400, the peripatetic and usually republican P.P. Vergerio, during his stay in monarchical Padua, composed a work *On Monarchy*, in which he hailed that system as 'the best form of government'. Monarchy, after all, ended tumult and the ceaseless conflict of factions and parties; it brought peace, 'safety, security and the defence of innocence'. Also, with the victory of Visconti absolutism in Milan, the Milanese humanists quickly fell into line, composing panegyrics to the glory of princely, and especially of Visconti, rule. Thus Uberto Decembrio (c.1350–1427) dedicated four books on local government to Filippo Maria Visconti in the 1420s, while his son Pier Candido Decembrio (1392–1477), keeping up the family tradition, wrote a *Eulogy in Praise of the City of Milan* in 1436.

With the triumph of the rule of the *signori* throughout Italy in the late fifteenth and early sixteenth centuries, pro-princely humanism reached a peak of enthusiasm. The humanists proved to be nothing if not flexible in adjusting their theories to adapt from republican to princely rule. The humanists started turning out two kinds of advice-books: to the prince, and to the courtier, on how he should conduct himself toward that prince.

By far the most celebrated advice-book for courtiers was *The Book of the Courtier* (*Il libro del Cortegiano*), by Baldassare Castiglione (1478–1529). Born in a village near Mantua, Castiglione was educated at Milan and entered the service of the duke of that city. In 1504, he became attached to the court of the duke of Urbino, which he served faithfully as diplomat and military commander for two decades. Then, in 1524, Castiglione was passed over to the Emperor Charles V in Spain, and for his services, Charles made him bishop of Avila. Castiglione composed the *Book of the Courtier* as a series of dialogues between 1513 and 1518, and the book was first published in 1528 in Venice. The work became one of the most widely read books in the sixteenth century (known to Italians as *Il libro d'oro*), clearly touching a nerve in the culture of that epoch in its description and celebration of the qualities of the perfect courtier and gentleman.

The Florentine humanists of the early fifteenth century had been optimistic for man, for his quest for *virtus* (or *virtú*) or excellence, and for the 'honour, praise, and glory' which more traditional Christians had thought due only to God. It was therefore easy for the later, sixteenth century humanists to transfer that quest for excellence and glory from individual man to being the sole function of the prince. Thus Castiglione declares that the courtier's chief goal, 'the end to which he is directed', must be to advise his prince so that the latter may attain 'the pinnacle of glory' and make himself 'famous and illustrious in the world'.

The earlier republican humanists had nurtured the ideal of 'liberty', by which they meant, not the modern concept of individual rights, but republican, generally oligarchial, 'self-government'. Castiglione expressly condemns such old notions, on behalf of the monarchical virtues of peace, absence of discord, and total obedience to the absolute prince. In *The Book of the Courtier*, one of the characters in the dialogue protests that princes 'hold their subjects in the closest bondage' so that liberty is gone. Castiglione shrewdly counters, in age-old terms used in numerous apologia for despotism, that such liberty is only a plea that we be allowed to 'live as we like' rather than 'according to good laws'. Since liberty is only licence, then, a monarch is needed to 'establish his people in such laws and ordinances that they may live in ease and peace'.

A leading writer of advice-books to both the prince and the courtier, and a man who bears the dubious distinction of being perhaps the first mercantilist, was the Neapolitan duke, Diomede Carafa (1407–87). Carafa wrote *The Perfect Courtier* while serving at the court of Ferdinand, king of Naples, in the 1480s, as well as *The Office of a Good Prince* during the same period. In *The Perfect Courtier*, Carafa set the tone for Castiglione's enormously influential work a generation later. In his *Office of a Good Prince*, Carafa set the model for the form of economic advice presented by consultant administrators. As in many later works, the book begins with principles of general policy and defence, then goes on to administration of justice, to public finance, and finally economic policy proper.

In detailed policies, Carafa's advice is relatively sensible, and not nearly as totally power-oriented or as statist as later mercantilists advising fully fledged nation-states. The budget should be balanced, since forced loans are comparable to robbery and theft, and taxes should be equitable and moderate in order not to oppress labour or drive capital from the country. Business should be left alone but, on the other hand, Carafa called for subsidies of industry, agriculture, and commerce by the state, as well as substantial welfare expenditures. In contrast to the later mercantilists, foreign merchants, declared Carafa, should be made welcome because their activities are highly useful to the country.

But there is no hint in Carafa, in contrast to the scholastics, of any desire to understand or analyse market processes. The only important question was how the ruler can manipulate them. As Schumpeter wrote of Carafa: 'The normal processes of economic life harbored no problem for Carafa. The only problem was how to manage and improve them'.

Schumpeter also attributes to Carafa the first conception of a national economy, of the entire country as one large business unit managed by the prince. Carafa was,

> so far as I know, the first to deal comprehensively with the economic problems of the nascent modern state....the fundamental idea that Carafa clothed in his conception of the Good Prince...of a National Economy...[which] is not simply the sum total of the individual households and firms or of the groups and classes within the borders of a state. It is conceived as a sort of sublimated business unit, something that has a distinct existence and distinct interests of its own and needs to be managed like a big farm.[1]

Perhaps the leading work among the new *genre* of advice-books to princes was that of Francesco Patrizi (1412–94), in his *The Kingdom and the Educa-*

tion of the King, written in the 1470s and dedicated to the first activist pope, Sixtus IV, engaged in restoring the temporal power of the papacy in Rome and the papal states. A Sienese humanist, Patrizi was made bishop of Gaeta.

As in the other humanist advice-books, Patrizi sees the locus of *virtus* in the prince. But it should be noted that, along with his fellow pro-prince humanists as well as the earlier republicans, Patrizi's virtuous prince is very much the model of Christian virtue. The prince must be a staunch Christian, and must always seek and cleave to justice. In particular, the prince must always be scrupulously honest and honourable. He 'is never to engage in deceit, never to tell a lie, and never to permit others to tell lies'. Alone with his fellow later humanists, however, Patrizi speaks of the prince as having a different set of virtues from his more passive subjects. As the maker of history and the seeker after glory, for example, the prince is not supposed to be humble. On the contrary, he is supposed to be generous, lavish in spending and altogether 'magnificent'.

The triumph of the *signori* led to many advice-books entitled, simply *The Prince (Il Principe)*. One was written by Bartolomeo Sacchi (1421–81) in 1471 in honour of the duke of Mantua, and an important one by Giovanni Pontano (1426–1503) who introduced himself to King Ferdinand of Naples by writing *The Prince* in his honour in 1468. In return, King Ferdinand made Pontano his secretary for more than 20 years. Pontano continued to extol his patron, in two separate treatises praising the twin princely virtues in Ferdinand of generosity and lavish splendour. In *On Liberality*, Pontano declares that 'nothing is more undignified in a prince' than lack of generosity. And in *On Magnificence*, Pontano insists that creating 'noble building, splendid Churches and theatres' is a crucial attribute of princely glory, and lauds King Ferdinand for 'the magnificence and majesty' of the public building he had constructed.

6.4   'Old Nick': preacher of evil or first value-free political scientist?

The Italian humanists had propounded the doctrine of absolute political rule, first by republican oligarchs and next by the glorified despot, the monarch or prince. But one crucial point remained to free the ruler of all moral shackles and to allow and even glorify the unchecked and untrammelled rule of royal whim. For while the humanists would hear of no institutional check on state rule, one critical stumbling block still remained: Christian virtue. The ruler, the humanists all admonished, must be Christian, must cleave always to justice, and must be honest and honourable.

What was needed, then, to complete the development of absolutist theory, was a theoretician to fearlessly break the ethical chains that still bound the ruler to the claims of moral principle. That man was the Florentine bureaucrat Niccolò Machiavelli (1469–1527) in one of the most influential works of political philosophy ever written, *The Prince*.

Niccolò Machiavelli was born in Florence, to a moderately well-off Tuscan noble family. His personal preference was clearly for the old oligarchic republic rather than for the *signori*, and in 1494, when the republicans kicked the Medicis out of Florence, young Niccolò entered the city bureaucracy. Rising rapidly in the government, Machiavelli became secretary of the Council of Ten, which managed the foreign policy and the wars of Florence. He held this important post until the Medicis reconquered Florence in 1512, serving in a series of diplomatic and military missions.

Machiavelli was nothing if not 'flexible', and this philosopher *extraordinaire* of opportunism greeted the return of the hated Medicis by attempting to ingratiate himself in their eyes. During the year 1513 he wrote *The Prince*, superficially yet another in the traditional series of advice-books and panegyrics to princes. Hoping to induce the Medicis to read it so that he might be restored to a top bureaucratic post, Machiavelli had the lack of shame needed to dedicate the book 'to the magnificent Lorenzo de Medici'. The Medicis, however, did not take the bait, and the only thing left for Machiavelli was to embark on a literary career, and to drift back into republican conspiracies. Machiavelli took part in conspiratorial republican meetings at the Oricellari Gardens on the outskirts of Florence, owned by the aristocrat Cosimo Rucellai. It was at the Oricellari Gardens that Machiavelli discussed the drafts of his second most important book, the *Discourses on the First Ten Books of Titus Livy*, written from 1514 to 1519.

Niccolò Machiavelli was reviled throughout Europe during the sixteenth century and on into the next two centuries. He was considered to be someone unique in the history of the West, a conscious preacher of evil, a diabolic figure who had unleashed the demons in the world of politics. The English used his given name as a synonym for the Devil, 'Old Nick'. As Macaulay put it: 'Out of his surname they have coined an epithet for a knave, and out of his Christian name a synonym for the Devil.'

In modern times, Machiavelli's reputation as a preacher of evil has been replaced by the admiration of political scientists as the founder of their discipline. For Machiavelli had cast off outdated moralism to look at power coolly and hard-headedly. A tough-minded realist, he was the pioneer developer of modern, positive, value-free political science. As the mercantilist, power-oriented, founder of modern 'scientific' method, Sir Francis Bacon, was to write early in the seventeenth century: 'We are much beholden to Machiavel and others, that write what men do, and not what they ought to do.'

Well, which was Machiavelli, a teacher of evil or a value-free political scientist? Let us see. At first glance, *The Prince* was very much like other mirror-of-princes advice-books of the late fifteenth century humanists. The prince was supposed to seek *virtù*, or excellence, and was supposed to pursue honour, glory and fame in the development of such excellence. But within this traditional form, Machiavelli wrought a radical and drastic transformation, creating in this way a new paradigm for political theory. For what Machiavelli did was to redefine the critical concept of *virtù*. For the humanists, as for Christians and classical theorists alike, *virtù*, excellence, was the fulfilment of the traditional classical and Christian virtues: honesty, justice, benevolence, etc. For Old Nick, on the contrary, *virtù* in the ruler or prince – and for the late humanists, after all, it was only the prince who counted – was, simply and terribly, as Professor Skinner puts it, 'any quality that helps a prince 'to keep his state'.[2] In short, the overriding, if not the only goal for the prince was to maintain and extend his power, his rule over the state. Keeping and expanding his power *is* the prince's goal, his virtue, and therefore any means necessary to achieve that goal becomes justified.

In his illuminating discussion of Machiavelli, Professor Skinner tries to defend him against the charge of being a 'preacher of evil'. Machiavelli did not praise evil *per se*, Skinner tells us; indeed, other things being equal, he probably preferred the orthodox Christian virtues. It is simply that when those virtues became inconvenient, that is, when they ran up against the overriding goal of keeping state power, the Christian virtues had to be set aside. The more naive humanists also favoured the prince's keeping his state and achieving greatness and glory. They believed, however, that this could only be done by always maintaining and cleaving to the Christian virtues. In contrast, Machiavelli realized that cleaving to justice, honesty and other Christian virtues might sometimes, or even most of the time, conflict with the goal of maintaining and expanding state power. For Machiavelli, orthodox virtues would then have to go by the board. Skinner sums up Machiavelli as follows:

> Machiavelli's final sense of what it is to be a man of *virtù* and his final words of advice to the prince, can thus be summarised by saying that he tells the prince to ensure above all that he becomes a man of 'flexible disposition': he must be capable of varying his conduct from good to evil and back again 'as fortune and circumstances dictate'.[3]

Professor Skinner, however, has a curious view of what 'preaching evil' might really be. Who in the history of the world, after all, and outside a Dr Fu Manchu novel, has actually lauded evil *per se* and counselled evil and vice at every step of life's way? Preaching evil is to counsel precisely as Machiavelli has done: be good so long as goodness doesn't get in the way of something you want, in the case of the ruler that something being the maintenance and expansion of power. What *else* but such 'flexibility' can the preaching of evil be all about?

Following straightaway from power as the overriding goal, and from his realism about power and standard morality being often in conflict, is Machiavelli's famous defence of deception and mendacity on the part of the prince. For then the prince is advised always to *appear* to be moral and virtuous in the Christian manner, since that enhances his popularity; but to practise the opposite if necessary to maintain power. Thus Machiavelli stressed the value of appearances, of what Christians and other moralists call 'hypocrisy'. The prince, he writes, must be willing to become 'a great liar and deceiver', taking advantage of all the credulous: for 'men are so simple' that 'the deceiver will always find someone ready to be deceived'. Or, in the immortal words of P.T. Barnum centuries later, 'There's a sucker born every minute'. And again, in praising fraud and deceit, Machiavelli writes that 'contemporary experience shows that princes who have achieved great things have been those who have given their word lightly, who have known how to trick men with their cunning, and who, in the end, have overcome those abiding by honest principles'. Or, in the words of another astute American social critic: 'nice guys finish last'.

There is, of course, an inner contradiction in a preacher of deceit candidly(!) broadcasting such views to one and all. For, as rulers begin to adopt a 'pragmatic' philosophy which is their natural inclination in any case, the deluded public may begin to awaken to the true state of affairs ('the suckers may wise up'), and then continuing deceit by the ruling class might well prove counterproductive. The 'great liars and deceivers' might no longer find so many subjects so 'ready to be deceived'.

Niccolò Machiavelli, therefore, was unquestionably a new phenomenon in the western world: a conscious preacher of evil to the ruling class. What of his alleged contributions in founding a hard-nosed, realistic, value-free political science?

First, one of his main contributions has been claimed to be the overwhelming use of power, of force and violence, by the rulers of state. Machiavelli was scarcely the first political philosopher who understood that force and violence are at the heart of state power. Previous theorists, however, were anxious to have that power curbed by ancient or Christian virtues. But there is a certain refreshing realism in Machiavelli's total casting off the cloak of virtue in politics and in his seeing the state plainly as unadorned brutal force in the service of sheer power.

There is a profound sense, too, in which Machiavelli was the founder of modern political science. For the modern 'policy scientist' – political scientist, economist, sociologist, or whatever – is a person who has put himself quite comfortably in the role of adviser to the prince or, more broadly, to the ruling class. As a pure technician, then, this counsellor realistically advises the ruling class on how to achieve their goals, which, as Machiavelli sees, boils down to achieving greatness and glory by maintaining and expanding their power. The modern policy scientists eschew moral principles as being 'unscientific' and therefore outside their sphere of interest.

In all this, modern social science is a faithful follower of the wily Florentine opportunist. But in one important sense the two differ. For Niccolò Machiavelli never had the presumption – or the cunning – to claim to be a true scientist because he is 'value-free'. There is no pretend value-freedom in Old Nick. He has simply replaced the goals of Christian virtue by *another* contrasting set of moral principles: that of maintaining and expanding the power of the prince. As Skinner writes:

> it is often claimed that the originality of Machiavelli's argument...lies in the fact that he divorces politics from morality, and in consequence emphasises the 'autonomy of politics'...[but] the difference between Machiavelli and his contemporaries cannot adequately be characterized as a difference between a moral view of politics and a view of politics as divorced from morality. The essential contrast is rather between two different moralities – two rival and incompatible accounts of what ought ultimately to be done.[4]

Modern social scientists, in contrast, pride themselves on being realistic and value-free. But in this, ironically, they are far *less* realistic or perhaps less candid than their Florentine mentor. For, as Machiavelli knew full well, in taking on their role of adviser to the rulers of state, the 'value-free scientist' is willy-nilly, committing himself to the end, and therefore to the overriding morality, of strengthening the power of those rulers. In advocating public policy, if nowhere else, value-freedom is a snare and a delusion; Old Nick was either too honest or too much of a realist even to consider thinking otherwise.

Niccolò Machiavelli, therefore, was *both* the founder of modern political science *and* a notable preacher of evil. In casting out Christian or natural law morality, however, he did not presume to claim to be 'value-free' as do his modern followers; he knew full well that he was advocating the new morality of subordinating all other considerations to power and to the reasons of state. Machiavelli was the philosopher and apologist *par excellence* for the untrammelled, unchecked power of the absolute state.

Some historians like to contrast the 'bad' Machiavelli of *The Prince* with the 'good' Machiavelli of his later though less influential *Discourses*. Failing to convince the Medicis of his change of heart, Machiavelli reverted, in the *Discourses*, to his republican leanings. But the Old Nick of the *Discourses* is in no sense transformed by goodness; he is simply adapting his doctrine to a republican as against a monarchical polity.

Obviously, as a republican Machiavelli can no longer stress the *virtù* and the greatness of the prince, and so he shifts ground to a kind of collective *virtù* by the community as a whole. Except that in the case of the community, of course, *virtù* can no longer be doing great deeds and maintaining one man's power. It now becomes acting always in the 'public good' or the 'common good', and always subordinating an individual's or a group's private, 'selfish' interests to an alleged greater good.

In contrast, Machiavelli condemns the pursuit of private interest as 'corruption'. In short, Machiavelli is *still* holding the maintenance and expansion of state power to be the highest good, except that now the state is oligarchic and republican. What he is really preaching is similar to the creed of earlier republican humanists: each individual and group subordinates itself and obeys without question the decrees of the oligarchic ruling class of the republican city-state.

Niccolò Machiavelli is the same preacher of evil in the *Discourses* as he had been in *The Prince*. One of the first atheist writers, Machiavelli's attitude toward religion in the *Discourses* is typically cynical and manipulative. Religion is helpful, he opined, in keeping subjects united and obedient to the state, and thus 'those princes and those Republics which desire to remain free from corruption should above all else maintain incorrupt the ceremonies of their religion'. Religion could also make a positive contribution if it glorified strength and other warlike qualities, but unfortunately Christianity has sapped men's strength by preaching humility and contemplation. In a tirade anticipating Nietzsche, Machiavelli charged that Christian morality has 'glorified humble and contemplative men' and that this peaceful spirit has led to existing corruption.

Machiavelli thundered that citizens can only achieve *virtù* if their highest goal is maintaining and expanding the state, and that therefore they must subordinate Christian ethics to that end. Specifically, they must be prepared to abandon the restraints of Christian ethics and be willing 'to enter on the path of wrongdoing' in order to maintain the state. The state must always take precedence. Therefore, any attempt to judge politics or government on a scale of Christian ethics must be abandoned. As Machievelli puts it with crystal clarity and great solemnity at the end of his final *Discourse*, 'when the safety of one's country depends upon the decision to be taken, no considerations of justice or injustice, humanity or cruelty, nor of glory or shame, should be allowed to prevail'.

Machiavelli's views, and the essential unity with his outlook in *The Prince*, are shown in his discussion in *The Discourses* of Romulus, the legendary founder of the city of Rome. The fact that Romulus murdered his brother and others is justified by Machiavelli's view that only one man should impose the founding constitution of a republic. Machiavelli's wily conflation of the 'public good' with the private interests of the ruler is shown in the following mendacious passage: 'A sagacious legislator of a republic, therefore, whose object is to promote the public good, and not his private interests [sic]...should concentrate all authority in himself'. In such concentration, the end of establishing the state excuses any necessary means: 'a wise mind will never censure any one for taking any action, however extraordinary, which may be of service in the organizing of a kingdom or the constituting of a republic'. Machiavelli concludes with what he calls the 'sound maxim' that 'reprehensible actions may be excused by their effects, and that when the effect is good, as it was in the case of Romulus, it always excuses the action'.

Throughout the *Discourses*, Machiavelli preaches the virtue of deceit for the ruler. He insists, also, in contrast to previous humanists, that it is better for a ruler to be feared than to be loved, and that punishment is far better than clemency in dealing with his subjects. Furthermore, when a ruler finds that a whole city is rebelling against his rule, by far the best course of action is to 'wipe them out' altogether.

Thus, Professor Skinner is perceptive and correct when he concludes, *in re The Prince* and the *Discourses*, that

> the underlying political morality of the two books is thus the same. The only change in Machiavelli's basic stance arises out of the changing focus of his political advice. Whereas he was mainly concerned in *The Prince* with shaping the conduct of individual princes, he is more concerned in the *Discourses* with offering his counsel to the whole body of the citizens. The assumptions underlying his advice, however, remain the same as before.

Machiavelli is still at one and the same time a preacher of evil and a founder of modern political and policy science.

6.5 The spread of humanism in Europe

The newly fashionable Italian humanism, marked by its philological and literary devotion to the classical texts, its absolutist political thought, and its contempt for the systematic thinking and natural law doctrines of the scholastics, spread like wildfire to the north – to France, England, Germany, and the Netherlands – during the fifteenth century. This conquest of northern scholarship and northern universities by the sixteenth century was nearly as influential as the upsurge of the Protestant Reformation in putting an end to scholastic thought, and in paving the way for the dominance of the absolute state. There was one important difference, however, in the political thought taken over by the northern humanists: in countries such as France, Germany and England, where the king was acquiring ever more centralized and dominant power, all discussion of the virtues of oligarchic republicanism seemed like bizarre and irrelevant blather. For the northern humanists, in contrast, were solidly committed to the 'prince' – although of course, to the virtuous pre-Machiavellian prince – and to themselves as sage counsellors to power.

The first Italian humanist to teach in France, and to cause a sensation in so doing, was the Neapolitan Gregorio da Tiferna (c.1415–66), who arrived at the University of Paris in 1458 to become its first professor of Greek. Other Italian humanists soon came to storm successfully that venerable redoubt of medieval and early renaissance scholasticism. Filippo Beroaldo (c.1440–1504) came in 1476 to lecture on poetry, philosophy and humanist studies. Particularly influential at the University of Paris was Fausto Andrelini (c.1460–1518), who taught at the University of Paris for 30 years, beginning in 1489, winning great fame for his classical scholarship on the Latin poets and essayists.

Humanism penetrated England beginning with Pietro del Monte (d.1457) who, from 1435 to 1440, was a collector of papal revenues in England, and more importantly, was a literary adviser to Duke Humphrey of Gloucester, brother to King Henry V, who became the first English patron of humanism. Gloucester brought an Italian rhetorician into his household, and he collected a remarkable library, including all the major humanist texts, many of which he later presented to Oxford University. Oxford and Cambridge also served as the home for Italian humanist scholars in the later fifteenth century. The Milanese scholar Stefano Surigone (fl. 1430–80), taught grammar and rhetoric at Oxford between 1454 and 1471, and Cornelio Vitelli (c.1450–1500) became the first professor of Greek at an English university, coming to teach at New College, Oxford in the 1470s. The Italian humanist Lorenzo da Savona taught at Cambridge in the 1470s, and published a handbook on rhetoric in 1478, which went into two printings by the end of the century. And Caio Auberino (fl. 1450–1500) became official professor of rhetoric at Cambridge, and taught Latin literature there in the 1480s.

Humanism also came to northern Europe because many young scholars, often inspired by Italian professors in their country, travelled to Italy to learn the new humanism at its source. Thus, Robert Gaguin (1435–1501), after being converted to humanism by the lectures of Gregorio da Tiferna, paid two extended visits to Italy in the late 1460s, and returned to become a distinguished French humanist at the Sorbonne in 1473, where he lectured on rhetoric and Latin literature, translated Livy, and published a treatise on Latin verse and the first history of France to be written in full rhetorical style. From England came William Grocyn (c.1449–1519), a student of Vitelli at Oxford, who studied humanism in Florence in the late 1480s. Grocyn returned to Oxford to become its first professor of Greek in 1491. William Latimer (c.1460–1545), another young Oxford student, accompanied his friend Grocyn on his trip to Italy, and then went to the University of Padua to perfect his Greek studies. Soon after Grocyn's initial Oxford post, Latimer was appointed teacher at Magdalen College, Oxford, inaugurating Magdalen as a centre of humanist studies.

The most eminent of the Oxford travellers to Italy was John Colet (c.1467–1519), a student of Grocyn at Oxford, who spent the years 1493 to 1496 in Italy. On his return from Italy, Colet, too, was appointed a professor at Oxford, and he delivered before the entire university a famous series of lectures on the Epistles of St Paul from 1498 to 1499.

6.6   Botero and the spread of Machiavellianism

The northern humanists, along with the Italians, were staunch believers in the necessity for the prince to practise the Christian virtues of honesty and justice. At about the same time that Machiavelli was writing his defence of the new pragmatic morality in *The Prince*, the greatest humanist of the age was penning a famous advice-book to princes, sternly reiterating the Christian virtues. Desiderius Erasmus (c.1466–1536), a Dutch Augustinian canon persuaded to study theology by John Colet, dedicated his account of *The Education of a Christian Prince* to the future Emperor Charles V in 1516. While Old Nick was proclaiming that no consideration must stand in the way of maintaining the ruler in state power, Erasmus warned the prince that he must never do anything, regardless of his motives, which may harm the cause of justice.

Machiavelli's *Prince* was not printed until 1532, and after that, as we have noted, a storm of attack on 'Machiavel' proceeded throughout Europe. In England the favourite term for Machiavelli was 'the politic atheist'. Thus, one James Hull wrote a book on Machiavelli in 1602, entitled *The Unmasking of the Politic Atheist*. The northern humanists generally took the same position, defending the focus of traditional political philosophy on justice and honesty and attacking the overriding concern of the new theorists with what one Machiavellian aptly termed the 'reason of state' (*ragione di stato*). Thus, Cardinal Reginald Pole (1500–58), one of the champions of English Catholicism as against the Henrician Reformation, and a distinguished humanist, attacked Machiavelli's political theory in 1539, in his *Apology to Charles V*, as destroying all the virtues. Roger Ascham (1515–68), another leading humanist and a long-time tutor to Queen Elizabeth in Greek and Latin, commented in horror in his *Report and Discourse of the Affairs and State of Germany* that Machiavelli taught that one may 'think, say and do whatever may serve best for profit and pleasure'.

Machiavelli also proved to be grist for the Huguenots' mill during the French religious war of the 1570s. The Huguenots attributed the St Bartholomew's Day Massacre of 1572 to the wicked designs of the Queen Mother, Catherine de Medici, daughter of the selfsame Lorenzo the Magnificent to whom Machiavelli had dedicated *The Prince*. The Huguenots attributed the massacre to the philosophical outlook of Machiavelli. Thus *The Awakener* continually denounced the 'pernicious heresy' of Machiavelli, and asserted that the king 'was actually persuaded by the doctrines of Machiavelli' to try to eradicate the Huguenots. Another tract, *The Alarm Bell* (1577), maintained that Catherine had deliberately trained her son in the doctrines of 'the atheist Machiavelli', thereby instructing the young king 'in the precepts most suitable for a tyrant'. To other Huguenots Machiavelli was a preceptor in the 'science of cheating', a 'science' imported by Italians such as Catherine into France.

The outstanding example of the genre of anti-Machiavellian tracts was the *Anti-Machiavel* of Innocent Gentillet (c.1535–1595), published in 1576. Gentillet was a French Huguenot who fled to Geneva after the massacre of St Bartholomew. Machiavelli, he pointed out, was essentially a satanic writer of handbooks on 'how to become a complete tyrant'.

But still the seductive nature of the new morality, of the justifying of evil means by the allegedly overriding end of maintaining and advancing state power, began to take hold among various writers. In Italy, a group of Machiavellians appeared during the sixteenth century, headed by Giovanni Botero (1540–1617), and his treatise of 1589, *The Reason of State*.

Botero was a leading humanist from Piedmont who joined the Jesuit Order. It is indicative of the decay of scholasticism in Italy in this period that this proponent of 'reason of state' and hence opponent of natural law ethics in political life should have been a member of the great Jesuit Order. Since Machiavelli was scarcely popular in Europe, especially in Catholic circles, Botero took care to attack Machiavelli explicitly and *pro-forma*. But that was merely a ritualistic cover for Botero's adoption of the essence of Machiavellian thought. While beginning by paying lip service to the importance of the prince's cleaving to justice, Botero quickly goes on to justify political prudence as crucial to all government, then defines the essence of prudence that 'in the decisions made by princes, interest will always override every other argument'; all other considerations, such as friendship, treaties or other commitments must go by the board. The overall view of Botero is that a prince must be guided primarily by 'reason of state', and that actions so guided 'cannot be considered in the light of ordinary reason'. The morality and justification for actions of the prince is diametrically opposed to the principles that must guide the ordinary citizen.

Botero's work touched off a raft of similar works in Italy over the next 40 years, all of which had the same title, *The Reason of State*.

In addition to being a leading theorist of political pragmatism and reason of state, Giovanni Botero has the notable but dubious distinction of being the first 'Malthusian', the first bitter complainer about the alleged evils of population growth. In his *On the Cause of the Greatness of Cities* (1588), translated into English in 1606, Botero laid out almost the entire thesis of Malthus's famous essay on population two centuries later. The analysis was, therefore, highly mechanistic: human population tends to increase without limit, or rather the only limit is the maximum possible degree of human fertility. The means of subsistence, on the contrary, can only be increased slowly. Therefore, the growth of population always – to use Malthus's famous words – tends to 'press on the means of subsistence', with the result being ever-present poverty and starvation. Population growth, then, can only be checked in two ways. One is the dying of large numbers of people through starvation, plague, or wars over scarce resources (Malthus's 'positive' check). Second is the only element of free will or active human response permitted by Botero's theory: that starvation and poverty may induce some people to abstain from marriage and procreation (Malthus's 'preventive' or 'negative' check).

In an epoch marked by rising population *and* rising living standards and economic growth, Botero's gloom-and-doom about population growth was hardly likely to fall on friendly ears. Indeed, as we shall see further below, those seventeenth and eighteenth century theorists who foresaw unlimited population growth *favoured* the idea as a spur to prosperity and economic growth.[5]

In any case, whether one draws pessimistic, neutral or optimistic conclusions from the thesis of unlimited population growth, its basic flaw is assuming that people will not react if they see their living standards declining from bearing large families. Botero (and Malthus after him) indeed gave the case away by even mentioning 'preventive' checks. For if people will lower the number of children when faced with absolute destitution, why may they not lower it long before that? And if so, no such mechanistic tendency can be postulated.

Historically, indeed, the facts totally contradict the gloomy Malthusian forecasts. Population only tends to rise *in response to* greater economic growth and prosperity and the consequent rise in living standards, so that population and standards of living tend to move together, rather than in diametric opposition. This rise in population generally comes in response to falling death rates caused by the better nutrition, sanitation, and medical care attendant on higher living standards. The dramatic declines in death rates lead to accelerated population growth (roughly measured by birth rate minus death rate). After a few generations, the birth rate usually falls, as people act to preserve their higher living standards, so that population growth then levels off.

The main defect of the Botero–Malthus doctrine of population is that it assumes that two entities – population and the means of subsistence (or production, or living standards) – operate under laws that are totally independent of each other. And yet, as we have seen, population growth may be highly responsive to changes in production. Similarly, the reverse can be true. Increases in population may well encourage the growth of investment and production, by providing a greater market for more products as well as more labour to work on these processes.[6] Schumpeter puts the overall point well in his critique of Malthus: '...there is of course no point whatever in trying to formulate independent "laws" for the behavior of two interdependent quantities.'[7]

In England, a leading humanist and colleague of Cardinal Pole in defending the Catholic Church as against the Anglican reform was Stephen Gardiner (c.1483–1555), bishop of Winchester. Gardiner, in contrast to Pole, was the first northern humanist to take a pro-Machiavellian line. Written appropriately enough when he was Lord Chancellor under the despotic Queen Mary Tudor in the early 1550s, Gardiner's *Discourse on the Coming of the English and Normans to Britain* was dedicated to King Philip II of Spain. Written as an advice-book to King Philip on the eve of his marriage to Queen Mary, the book counselled the king on how to govern England. Gardiner openly endorsed Machiavelli's view that it was far more important for a prince to *appear* virtuous than actually to be so. It is useful, opines Gardiner, for the prince to appear 'merciful, generous and observant of faith', but any ruler who really feels bound to actually observe such qualities would come to more harm than good.

An ardent if implicit disciple of Machiavellism was the prominent late sixteenth century Belgian classical scholar and humanist Justus Lipsius (1547–1606). Lipsius had moved from Antwerp to Leyden, in Holland, to avoid the rigours of the war against Spanish rule. In 1589, in Leyden, Lipsius published his *Six Books of Politics*. The prince, wrote Lipsius, must learn how to engage in 'profitable deceit', and judiciously be able to 'intermingle that which is profitable with that which is honest'. Reason of state was again triumphant.

6.7   Humanism and absolutism in France

Before humanism made its mark in France, political thought was medieval rather than absolutist. Thus, near the end of his life, the prominent royal bureaucrat, jurist, and churchman, Claude de Seyssel (c.1450–1520), published a treatise on monarchy summing up the post-medievalist perspective in politics. He wrote *The Monarchy of France* on the death of King Louis XII in 1515, and presented it to the new king, Francis I. The book was published four years later under the more presumptuous title, *The Grand Monarchy of France*, and was reissued often thereafter.

De Seyssel was born in Savoy, trained as a jurist, and served King Charles VIII and King Louis XII, the latter as member of the Grand Council and on numerous occasions as ambassador. But despite his long service in the bureaucracy and his great admiration for Louis XII, de Seyssel was a constitutionalist rather than an absolutist. The king, he averred, is indeed absolute within his own sphere, but that sphere is severely delimited by a network of rights held by others in accordance with customary, natural, and divine law.

In contrast, the lengthy reign of Francis I (1515–47) saw the beginning of the triumph of absolutism in French political thought. This new trend was launched by the leading humanist in France, Guillaume Budé (1467–1540). A highly erudite classical and legal scholar, Budé travelled in Italy in the early 1500s, imbibed humanism there, and returned to write a bitter attack on scholastic jurisprudence in his *Annotations on the Pandects* in 1508. The advent of Francis I in 1515 had characteristically contrasting effects on the veteran de Seyssel and on the younger Budé. De Seyssel wrote his *magnum opus* to instruct the young king on the greatness of what he believed to be the old king's constitutionalist regime. Budé was inspired by the advent of the new prince to write *The Institution of a Prince* in 1519, celebrating the king's potentially absolute greatness and power.

In this French form of advice-book to the king, Budé developed the idea, then new in France, of the prince as totally and absolutely sovereign, whose power and every whim must never be limited or questioned. The prince, intoned Budé, was a quasi-divine person, a man necessarily superior to all others. Laws that bind the prince's subjects do not bind or apply to him; for laws apply only to the average and the equal, not to the prince who closely approaches the perfect ideal of mankind. The prince, in short, was a god among men and a law unto himself. The monarch, therefore, was super-human, himself the source and the criterion of all justice.

For Budé, the king's actions are always right because 'the heart of the king moves by instinct and by impulsion of God, who controls and attracts it according to his pleasure, to undertake enterprises that are praiseworthy and honest and useful to his people and himself...'. Ruling by divine right and inspired directly by God, the king needs only the advice of philosophers – and it did not take much imagination to see *who* the great Budé had in mind as philosophic counsellor to Francis I.

Budé's work was carried on and developed by succeeding decades of humanists and particularly legists. The French kings were delighted at these dominant theories of their age, and proceeded happily to put them into practice. In this they were greatly aided by the absolutist jurists being themselves top bureaucrats in the service of the king. Two of the leading jurists wrote in the reign of Francis I: Barthélemy de Chasseneux (1480–1541), whose *Catalogue of the Glory of the World* was published in 1529, and Charles de Grassaille, whose *Regale of France* was written in 1538. Grassaille declared that the king of France was God in the flesh, that all his actions were inspired and brought about by God operating through the person of the king. The king was therefore God's vicar on earth and a living law. In a sense, then, Charles de Grassaille said it all: the king is God on earth.

The sixteenth century French legalists also systematically tore down the legal rights of all corporations or organizations which, in the Middle Ages, had stood between the individual and the state. There were no longer any intermediary or feudal authorities. The king is absolute over these intermediaries, and makes or breaks them at will. Thus, as one historian sums up Chasseneux's view:

> All jurisdiction, said Chasseneux, pertains to the supreme authority of the prince; no man may have jurisdiction except through the ruler's concession and permission. The authority to create magistrates thus belongs to the prince alone; all offices and dignities flow and are derived from him as from a fountain.[8]

The most important contribution to the tearing down of the intermediary structures hampering the monarch's absolute rule over his subjects was that of the greatest jurist of his age, Charles du Moulin. We have already seen du Moulin's (Molinaeus') critique of the prohibition of usury, in his *Treatise on Contracts and Usury* (1546). Far more important was his *magnum opus*, *Commentaries on the Customs of Paris* (1539), a compilation and commentary on customary law in France. This book dealt a lethal blow to the medieval rights and privileges of intermediary orders, and placed virtually all authority into the hands of the monarch and his state.

6.8   The sceptic as absolutist: Michel de Montaigne

It is a favourite conceit of modern, twentieth century liberals that scepticism, the attitude that nothing can really be known as the truth, is the best groundwork for individual liberty. The fanatic, convinced of the certainty of his views, will trample on the rights of others; the sceptic, convinced of nothing, will not. But the truth is precisely the opposite: the sceptic has no ground on which to stand to defend his or others' liberty against assault. Since there will always be men willing to aggress against others for the sake of power or pelf, the triumph of scepticism means that the victims of aggression will be rendered defenceless against assault. Furthermore, the sceptic being unable to find any principle for rights or for any social organization, will probably cave in, albeit with a resigned sigh, to any existing regime of tyranny. *Faute de mieux*, he has little else to say or do.

An excellent case in point is one of the great sceptics of the modern world, the widely read and celebrated sixteenth century French essayist, Michel Eyquem de Montaigne (1533–92).[9] Montaigne was born to a noble family in the Périgord region of south-western France, near the city of Bordeaux. He became a judge in the Bordeaux *parlement* in 1557, at the age of 24, as his father had been before him. He also joined at the *parlement* an uncle (his father's brother), a first cousin of his mother, and a brother-in-law. Remaining in the *parlement* for 13 years, and then denied promotion to the upper chamber of that body, Montaigne retired to his rural chateau in 1570 to write his famous *Essays*. There he remained, except for a four-year stint as mayor of Bordeaux in the early 1580s. A leading humanist, Montaigne virtually created the essay form in France. He started writing these brief essays in the early 1570s, and published the first two volumes in 1580. The third book of essays was published in 1588, and all three volumes were posthumously published seven years later.

Though a practising Catholic, Montaigne was a thoroughgoing sceptic. Man can know nothing, his reason being insufficient to arrive either at a natural law ethics or a firm theology. As Montaigne put it: 'reason does nothing but go astray in everything, and especially when it meddles with divine things'. And for a while, Montaigne adopted as his official motto the query, 'What do I know?'

If Montaigne knew nothing, he could scarcely know enough to advocate setting one's face against the burgeoning abolutist tyranny of his day. On the contrary, stoic resignation, a submission to the prevailing winds, became the required way of confronting the public world. Skinner sums up Montaigne's political counsel, as holding 'that everyone has a duty to submit himself to the existing order of things, never resisting the prevailing government and where necessary enduring it with fortitude'.[10]

In particular, Montaigne, though sceptical about religion itself, cynically stressed the social importance of everyone outwardly observing the same religious forms. Above all, France must 'submit completely to the authority of our [Catholic] ecclesiastical government'.

Submission to constituted authority was, indeed, the key to Montaigne's political thought. Everyone must remain obedient to the king at all times no matter how he discharges his obligation to rule. Unable to use reason as a guide, Montaigne had to fall back on the *status quo*, on custom and on tradition. He warned gravely and repeatedly that everyone must 'wholly follow the accepted fashion and forms', for 'it is the rule of rules, and the universal law of laws, that each man should observe those of the place he is in'. Montaigne hailed Plato for wanting to prohibit any citizen from looking 'even into the reason of the civil laws', for those laws must 'be respected as divine ordinances'. Although we may wish for different rulers, we 'must nevertheless obey those that are here'. The finest achievement of the Christian religion, according to Montaigne, was its insistence on 'obedience to the magistrates and maintenance of the government'.

Considering Montaigne's fundamental outlook, it is no wonder that he warmly embraced the Machiavellian concept of 'reason of state'. (May we say that he held the reason of *man* to be worthless, but the reason of *state* to be overriding?) Characteristically, while Montaigne writes that he personally likes to keep out of politics and diplomacy because he prefers to avoid lying and deceit, he also asserts the necessity of 'lawful vice' in the operations of government. Deceit in a ruler may be necessary, and furthermore, such vices are positively needed 'for sewing our society together, as [are] poisons for the preservation of our health'. Montaigne then goes on to integrate his defence of deceit in a prince with his seemingly paradoxical defence of reason of state while having no use for human reason at all. For in following reason of state, the prince has simply 'abandoned his own reason for a more universal and powerful reason', and this mystical super-reason has shown him that an ordinarily evil action needed to be done.

Michel de Montaigne made a notable and highly influential contribution to mercantilism – the strictly economic aspect of state absolutism – as well. Although he claimed that he knew nothing, on one thing he certainly asserted truth, his much vaunted scepticism suddenly vanishing: in what Ludwig von Mises was later to call the 'Montaigne fallacy', he insisted, as in the title of his famous Essay Number 22, that 'The Plight of One Man is the Benefit of Another'. There is the essence of mercantilist theory, in so far as mercantilism has a theory at all; in contrast to the fundamental truth well known to the scholastics that both parties benefit from an exchange, Montaigne opined that in a trade, one man can only benefit at the expense of another. By analogy, in international trade, one nation must benefit at the expense of another. The implication is that the market is a ravening jungle, so why should not a Frenchman urge the French state to grab as much from others as it can?

Montaigne developed his theme in Essay 22 in a characteristically worldly-wise and cynical manner. He notes that an Athenian once condemned a funeral director

on the charge that he demanded unreasonable profit, and this profit could not accrue to him but by the death of a great number of people. This judgment appears to be ill-grounded, inasmuch as no profit can possibly be made but at the expense of another, and because by the same rule every kind of gain would have to be condemned.

All work is done at the expense of others, and Montaigne correctly notes that the physician could be condemned in the same way. The same charge could be levied at the farmer or retailer for 'gaining because of people's hunger', the tailor for 'profiting because of someone's need for clothing', and so forth. He concluded broadly that the benefit of any one entity is necessarily 'the dissolution and corruption of some other thing'. Unfortunately, of course, he could not see also that these producers did not *create* such needs, but instead were fulfilling them and thereby removing the want and pain of their customers and adding to their happiness and standard of living. If he had gone that far, he would have realized the nonsense of his dog-eat-dog, or what would now be called his 'zero-sum game', view of the marketplace.

6.9   Jean Bodin: apex of absolutist thought in France

While Montaigne paved the way for the dominance of absolutist thought in France, surely the founder, or at least the *locus classicus* of sixteenth century French absolutism was Jean Bodin (1530–96). Born in Angers, Bodin studied law at the University of Toulouse, where he taught for 12 years. Bodin later went to Paris to become a jurist, and soon became one of the leading servitors of King Henry III, and one of the leaders of the statist *politique* party, which upheld the power of the king as against the principled militants among the Huguenots on one side, and the Catholic League on the other.

Bodin's most important work was *The Six Books of a Commonwealth* (*Les Six livres de la republique*) (1576). Perhaps the most massive work on political philosophy ever written, the *Six Books* was certainly the most influential book on political philosophy in the sixteenth century. In addition to this work, Bodin published books on money, law, the historical method, natural science, religion and the occult. Central to Bodin's theory of absolutism, written in the face of the challenge of Huguenot rebellion, was the notion of sovereignty: the unchallengeable power of command in the monarch ruling over the rest of society. Characteristically, Bodin defined sovereignty as 'the most high, absolute, and perpetual power over the citizens and subjects in a commonwealth'. Central to sovereignty in Bodin was the sovereign's function as law-giver to society, and 'the essence of lawmaking was command – in exercise of will with binding force'.[11]

Since the sovereign is the maker or creator of the law, he must therefore be above that law, which applies only to his subjects and not to himself. The sovereign, then, is a person whose will creates order out of formlessness and chaos.

The sovereign, furthermore, must be unitary and indivisible, the locus of command in society. Bodin explains that 'we see the principal point of sovereign majesty and absolute power to consist in giving laws to subjects in general, without their consent'. The sovereign must be above the law that he creates as well as any customary law or institutions. Bodin urged the sovereign prince to follow God's law in framing his edicts, but the important point was that no human action or institution could be employed to see that the prince follows the divine path or to call him to account.

Bodin, however, called upon the prince to rely for advice or counsel on a small number of wise advisers, men who, allegedly lacking motives of self-interest, would be able to aid the king in legislating for the public good of the entire nation. In short, a shall élite of wise men would share in the sovereign power behind the scenes, while publicly, the sovereign would hand down decrees as if solely the product of his own will. As Keohane writes, in Bodin's system 'the monarch's dependence on his counsellors is hidden by the impressive and satisfying fiction that the law is handed down by one benevolent, absolute, superhuman will...'.[12]

It is hardly far-fetched to conclude that Bodin, court politician and jurist, saw himself as one of the sages running government from behind the scenes. Plato's ideal of combined philosopher–king had now been transformed into the more realistic and, for Bodin, more self-serving goal of philosopher guiding the king. And all this cloaked in the illusory assumption that such a court philosopher has no self-interest in money or power in his own right.

Bodin also envisaged a broad role for various groups to participate in the government of the commonwealth, as well as a wide scope for bureaucrats and administrators. The crucial point is that all be subordinated to the power of the king.

It is often true that political analysts are at their most acute in revealing the flaws in systems with which they disagree. Accordingly, one of Bodin's keenest insights was his examination of the popular democracies of the past. Bodin points out that 'if we rip up all the popular states that ever were', and closely examine their real condition, then we shall find that the alleged rule of the people was always rule by a small oligarchy. Anticipating such perceptive late nineteenth century theorists of the power élite or ruling class as Robert Michels, Gaetano Mosca and Vilfredo Pareto, Bodin pointed out that in reality rule is always exercised by an oligarchy, for whom 'the people serves but for a mask'.

There is a curious *lacuna*, however, in the agenda of absolutist power proclaimed by Jean Bodin. That *lacuna* lies in an area always crucial to the practical exercise of state power: taxation. We have seen that before the fourteenth century, French monarchs were expected to live off their own seigneurial rents and tolls, and that tax levies were only granted begrudgingly and in emergencies. And while a regular and oppressive system of taxation was in place in France by the early sixteenth century, even the royal and absolutist theorists hesitated to grant the monarch the unlimited right to tax. In the late sixteenth century, both the Huguenots and the Catholic Leaguers bitterly condemned the arbitrary power of the king to tax as a crime against society. As a result Bodin and his fellow establishment *politiques* were reluctant to play into the hands of the king's enemies. Like the French writers before him, then, Bodin inconsistently upheld the rights of private property, as well as the invalidity of the king's taxing his subjects without their consent: 'It is not in the power of any prince in the world, at his pleasure to raise taxes upon the people, no more than to take another man's goods upon him...' Bodin's notion of 'consent', however, was scarcely a thoroughgoing or radical one; instead, he was content with the existing formal agreement to taxation by the states-general.

Bodin's own actions as a deputy from the Vermandois at the states-general meeting at Blois (1576–77) emphatically stressed the limited taxes aspect of his consistent attitude toward sovereignty. The king had proposed to substitute a graduated income tax on all commoners with no exemptions (what might now be called 'a flat tax with bumps') for the myriad of different taxes they then were forced to pay. Curiously enough, this scheme was almost precisely the one which Bodin himself had publicly advocated a short while before. But Bodin's opposition to the king's proposal displayed his shrewdly realistic attitude toward government. He noted 'that the king could not be trusted when he said this tax would be substituted for the tailles, aides, and gabelles. Rather, it was much more likely that the king was plotting to make this an additional tax'.[13] Bodin also engaged in a perceptive interest-analysis of the reason that the Parisian deputies had taken the lead in support of the new, higher tax. For he showed that the Parisians had not been paid any interest on their government bonds for a long while, and were hoping that the higher taxes would allow the king to resume his payments.

Jean Bodin, anxious to prevent the king from launching an all-out war against the Huguenots, led the estates in blocking not only the single-tax plan, but also other emergency grants to the king. Bodin pointed out that 'temporary' grants often became permanent. He also warned the king and his countrymen that 'one cannot find more frequent upsets, seditions, and ruins of commonwealths than because of excessive tax burdens and imposts'.

Among the absolutist writers following Bodin, the seventeenth century servitors of the absolute state, all hesitance or piety to the medieval legacy of strictly limited taxation was destined to disappear. State power, unlimited, was to be glorified.

In the more narrowly economic sphere of the theory of money, Bodin, as we have seen above, has long been credited by historians with pioneering the quantity theory of money (more strictly, the direct influence of the supply of money on prices) in his *Response to the Paradoxes of M. de Malestroit* (1568). Malestroit had attributed the unusual and chronic price increases in France to debasement, but Bodin pinpointed the cause as the increased supply of specie from the New World. We have seen, however, that the quantity theory had been known since the time of the fourteenth century scholastic Jean Buridan and of Nicolas Copernicus in the early sixteenth century. The increased specie from the New World was spotted as the cause of price rises a dozen years earlier than Bodin by the eminent Spanish scholastic Martin de Azpilcueta Navarrus. As a highly learned scholar, Bodin would certainly have read Navarrus's treatise, especially since Navarrus had taught at the University of Toulouse a generation before Bodin came there to study. Bodin's claim of originality in this analysis should therefore be taken with many grains of salt.[14]

Jean Bodin was also one of the first theorists to point out the influence of social leaders on demand for goods, and therefore on their price. People, he points out, 'esteem and raise in price everything that the great lords like, though the things in themselves are nor worth that valuation'. Then, a snob effect takes over, after 'the great lords see that their subjects have an abundance of things that they themselves like'. The lords then 'begin to despise' these products, and their prices then fall.

Despite his numerous keen economic and political insights, however, Bodin was ultra-orthodox in his view of usury, ignoring the work of his near-contemporary Du Moulin as well as the Spanish scholastics. Interest-taking was prohibited by God, according to Bodin, and that was that.

6.10   After Bodin

Jean Bodin's exaltation of sovereignty struck French political thought like a thunderclap; here at last was a way to justify and expand the ever-increasing powers of the Crown. In particular, the new view was adopted and subtly transformed by writers who were far more absolutist, *in practice*, than was Bodin himself. The one element that Bodin's veneration of sovereignty lacked was the Protestant notion of divine sanction; for to Bodin absolute sovereignty was simply a fact of nature. Other *politiques*, however, soon added the missing ingredient, since they had long been accustomed to think of rule as by divine right. The idea of the king's rule being commanded by God was a familiar one in the sixteenth century; none, however, had extended kingly rule to the notion of absolute sovereignty created by Bodin.

The most important immediate follower of Bodin was Pierre Grégoire, in his *De republica* (1578). The king, for Grégoire, was God's appointed vicar in the temporal sphere, and his rule was under the constant influence of God's will. The king's command was therefore equivalent to God's, and was equally owed absolute obedience by his subjects. 'The prince is the image of God, in power and in authority', wrote Grégoire.

Bodin and others had still retained the idea that true justice was a concept separate and apart from the king's edicts, so that the king's actions could well be unjust; no one, however, was allowed to obstruct or disobey such actions. But in the doctrine of the gallicized Scot Adam Blackwood, the two concepts become almost totally conflated (*Adversus Georgii Buchanani*, 1581). The will of the prince, for Blackwood, becomes just virtually by definition. The king was necessarily just and virtually superhuman, a living law unto himself. Indeed, Blackwood carried the glorification of divinely constituted monarchy to its apogee, asserting that the very *person* of the king, and not simply the authority of his office, was divine, and that he was in a literal sense a god on earth.

As its title indicates, Blackwood's work was written as an attack on his fellow gallicized Scot, the radical Calvinist George Buchanan. Buchanan's libertarian and pro-tyrannicide doctrine had rested, unsurprisingly, on the concept of natural law. And so Blackwood denounced natural law as a source of anarchistic liberty, prompting in its believers an aversion to law and to political authority. Against natural law, Blackwood upheld the *jus gentium*, the positive law of nations, as the explanation and justification of political authority.

It is not surprising that the consensual limit on taxation, still active in Bodin's thought, should drop out immediately upon the fusion of absolute sovereignty and divine right. The leader of that fusion, Pierre Grégoire, introduced erasing the tax limit as well. Whereas even Bodin had conceded that natural law established a right to private property, with Grégoire natural law only ratifies the unchecked power of the king. For Grégoire, the king had the unlimited prerogative to levy taxes, since the good of the state is higher than the property rights of the individual. Indeed, the king possessed by divine grant an absolute authority over all the persons and properties of his subjects. To avoid confusion, therefore, or any implication of consent to taxation, the states-general should be abolished altogether.

It was, indeed, Adam Blackwood who uniquely and radically reached the clarity of consistency on the ruler's right to tax. For if property rights are important, and the king has the absolute right to tax or otherwise seize private property at will, then this must mean that 'All lands were originally held by the king and were granted by him to others...And the granting of fiefs by the king was but a partial transfer; all lands owed tribute to him and remained subject to his authority'.[15] In short, in an odd version of the state of nature, only the king had original or continuing property rights; all other seeming property rights are simply allowances by the king, temporary possessions that are regulatable by the king and revocable by him at any time.

Whereas Adam Blackwood had been a lone extremist in absolutism in the early 1580s, a host of royalist pamphleteers were soon adopting his views. From approximately 1585 to Henry IV's conversion to Catholicism eight years later, the royal power was beleaguered and subordinate to the strength of the militant Catholic League. The royalist writers therefore felt obliged to push the divine sanction of the sovereign to the maximum, in order to eliminate any power of the pope in France, and to counsel absolute obedience to any legitimate sovereign, regardless of his religion. The king had absolute authority over the Catholic Church in France as well as all other institutions. Thus, François Le Jay (*On the Dignity of Kings*, 1589) asserted that kings were established for the honour and service of God, and that subjects should obey their rulers as they would a god on earth. Louis Servin, in his *Vindiciae* (1590), trumpeted of Henry IV, then still a Huguenot, that 'God is our king; by Him he lives and flourishes, and by His spirit is he animated'. Probably the most extreme version of this doctrine was expressed in a speech of Jacques de La Guesle, procurator general of France, asking the *parlement* to condemn a priest who had upheld the supreme temporal authority of the pope:

> Sirs, the authority of the king is sacrosanct, ordained by God, the principal work of His Providence, the masterpeice of His hands, the image of His sublime Majesty and proportionate to His immense grandeur, so as to bear comparison of the creature with the Creator...For, just as God is by nature the first King and Prince, so is the King, by creation and imitation, God of all on earth...[16]

The subjects, according to these Henrician absolutists, owed this quasi-divine figure absolute obedience. These writers developed the Blackwoodian theme that the king's decrees were *ipso facto* and necessarily just. Jacques Hurault, in his *On the Offices of State* (1588), developed this doctrine most clearly. Hurault explained that the prince was guided by the hand of God and therefore could do no wrong. The ruler was not simply a man but justice itself, which he dispensed according to the will of God. The constitution of the state was subordinated, in Hurault, to two simple points: the prince's necessarily just commands, and the obedience of his subjects. The ruler commands and the subjects obey. Period. Furthermore, in reaction to the Leaguer emphasis on the people, the royalists counselled the king not to allow naturally restless subjects much liberty.

Since the *politiques* and Henry IV triumphed shortly thereafter, these ultra-absolutist views of the embattled Henrician pamphleteers inspired and were followed fairly completely by the dominant theoreticians of the great age of absolutism: seventeenth century France.

6.11 Notes

1. Joseph A. Schumpeter, *History of Economic Analysis* (New York: Oxford University Press, 1954), pp. 163–4.
2. Quentin Skinner, *The Foundations of Modern Political Thought: Vol. I, The Renaissance* (Cambridge: Cambridge University Press, 1978), p. 138n.
3. Ibid., p. 138.
4. Ibid., pp. 134–5.
5. We shall see in a later volume that the renowned left Keynesian Alvin Henry Hansen, in his famous 'stagnation' thesis of the late 1930s, forecast permanent stagnation for the American economy partially because of the recent *decline* in population growth. We shall see further that Hansen developed this doctrine as the logical outcome of a rigid Walrasian framework. This of course is in stark contrast to the pro-'zero population growth' hysteria of the left liberals of the 1970s.
6. Thus, for the world of the twentieth century, P.T. Bauer notes: 'Indeed, over large parts of the Third World the extreme sparseness of the population presents obstacles to the economic advance of enterprising people, obstacles which are more effective than those supposedly presented by population pressure. A sparse population precludes the construction of transport facilities and communications, and thus retards the spread of new ideas and methods. In this way, it circumscribes the scope for enterprise.' P.T. Bauer, *Equality, the Third World and Economic Delusion* (Cambridge, Mass.: Harvard University Press, 1981), p. 45.
7. Schumpeter, op. cit., note 1, p. 579.

8. William Farr Church, *Constitutional Thought in Sixteenth-Century France: A Study in the Evolution of Ideas* (1941, New York: Octagon Books, 1969), p. 53.

9. Pronounced Mon–TAN–ye rather than the usual Mon–TAYN, for he came from an area of south-western France where *langue d'oc* (Occitan) was spoken rather than the northern (essentially the area around Paris) *langue d'oeil* or *d'oui* (French). The southern regions had only been conquered by France in the course of a savage extirpation of their religion (Albigensian) and culture during the thirteenth century. The area around Bordeaux, furthermore, had been acquired by England and governed by the English for three centuries, from the mid-twelfth to the mid-fifteenth. When the French captured Bordeaux and the surrounding region in the 1450s, they proceeded to extirpate the Gascon (which includes Périgord) wing of Occitan as a written language, a language that the English had left alone. Thus, in 1539, a few years after Montaigne's birth, the French outlawed the use of Occitan as an administrative, written language, in the Edict of Villers–Cotterêts. People like Montaigne were thus induced to write in the official French language, and while he was always loyal to the French Crown, Montaigne still considered himself far more of a Gascon than a Frenchman.

10. Skinner, op. cit., note 2, p. 279.

11. Nannerl O. Keohane, *Philosophy and the State in France: the Renaissance to the Enlightenment* (Princeton, NJ: Princeton University Press, 1980), p. 70.

12. Ibid., p. 75.

13. Martin Wolfe, *The Fiscal System of Renaissance France* (New Haven: Yale University Press, 1972), p. 162.

14. In 1907, a descendant of Bodin asserted that the first writer to explain the influence of specie from the New World on prices in Europe was the Frenchman Noël du Fail, in 1548.

15. William Farr Church, *Constitutional Thought in Sixteenth Century France: A Study in the Evolution of Ideas* (1941, New York: Octagon Books, 1969), p. 259.

16. My translation from the French. See ibid., pp. 266n–67n.

7 Mercantilism: serving the absolute state

7.1   Mercantilism as the economic aspect of absolutism

By the beginning of the seventeenth century, royal absolutism had emerged victorious all over Europe. But a king (or, in the case of the Italian city-states, some lesser prince or ruler) cannot rule all by himself. He must rule through a hierarchical bureaucracy. And so the rule of absolutism was created through a series of alliances between the king, his nobles (who were mainly large feudal or post-feudal landlords), and various segments of large-scale merchants or traders. 'Mercantilism' is the name given by late nineteenth century historians to the politico-economic system of the absolute state from approximately the sixteenth to the eighteenth centuries. Mercantilism has been called by various historians or observers a 'system of Power or State-building' (Eli Heckscher), a system of systematic state privilege, particularly in restricting imports or subsidizing exports (Adam Smith), or a faulty set of economic theories, including protectionism and the alleged necessity for piling up bullion in a country. In fact, mercantilism was all of these things; it was a comprehensive system of state-building, state privilege, and what might be called 'state monopoly capitalism'.

As the economic aspect of state absolutism, mercantilism was of necessity a system of state-building, of Big Government, of heavy royal expenditure, of high taxes, of (especially after the late seventeenth century) inflation and deficit finance, of war, imperialism, and the aggrandizing of the nation-state. In short, a politico-economic system very like that of the present day, with the unimportant exception that now large-scale industry rather than mercantile commerce is the main focus of the economy. But state absolutism means that the state must purchase and maintain allies among powerful groups in the economy, and it also provides a cockpit for lobbying for special privilege among such groups.

Jacob Viner put the case well:

> The laws and proclamations were not all, as some modern admirers of the virtues of mercantilism would have us believe, the outcome of a noble zeal for a strong and glorious nation, directed against the selfishness of the profit-seeking merchant, but were the product of conflicting interests of varying degrees of respectability. Each group, economic, social, or religious, pressed constantly for legislation in conformity with its special interest. The fiscal needs of the crown were always an important and generally a determining influence on the course of trade legislation. Diplomatic considerations also played their part in influencing legislation, as did the desire of the crown to award special privileges, *con amore*, to its favorites, or to sell them, or to be bribed into giving them, to the highest bidders.[1]

In the area of state absolutism, grants of special privilege included the creation by grant or sale of privileged 'monopolies', i.e. the exclusive right granted by the Crown to produce or sell a given product or trade in a certain area. These 'patents of monopoly' were either sold or granted to allies of the Crown, or to those groups of merchants who would assist the king in the collection of taxes. The grants were either for trade in a certain region, such as the various East India companies, which acquired the monopoly right in each country to trade with the Far East, or were internal – such as the grant of a monopoly to one person to manufacture playing cards in England. The result was to privilege one set of businessmen at the expense of their potential competitors and of the mass of English consumers. Or, the state would cartellize craft production and industry and cement alliances by compelling all producers to join and obey the orders of privileged urban guilds.

It should be noted that the most prominent aspects of mercantilist policy – taxing or prohibiting imports or subsidizing exports – were part and parcel of this system of state monopoly privilege. Imports were subject to prohibition or protective tariff in order to confer privilege on domestic merchants or craftsmen; exports were subsidized for similar reasons. The focus in examining mercantilist thinkers and writers should not be the fallacies of their alleged economic 'theories'. Theory was the last consideration in their minds. They were, as Schumpeter called them, 'consultant administrators and pamphleteers' – to which should be added lobbyists. Their 'theories' were any propaganda arguments, however faulty or contradictory, that could win them a slice of boodle from the state apparatus.

As Viner wrote:

> The mercantilist literature...consisted in the main of writings by or on behalf of 'merchants' or businessmen, who had the usual capacity for identifying their own with the national welfare...The great bulk of the mercantilist literature consisted of tracts which were partly or wholly, frankly or disguisedly, special pleas for special economic interests. Freedom for themselves, restrictions for others, such was the essence of the usual program of legislation of the mercantilist tracts of merchant authorship.[2]

7.2   Mercantilism in Spain

The seeming prosperity and glittering power of Spain in the sixteenth century proved a sham and an illusion in the long run. For it was fuelled almost completely by the influx of silver and gold from the Spanish colonies in the New World. In the short run, the influx of bullion provided a means by which the Spanish could purchase and enjoy the products of the rest of Europe and Asia; but in the long run price inflation wiped out this temporary advantage. The result was that when the influx of specie dried up, in the seventeenth century, little or nothing remained. Not only that: the bullion prosperity induced people and resources to move to southern Spain, particularly the port of Seville, where the new specie entered Europe. The result was malinvestment in Seville and the south of Spain, offset by the crippling of potential economic growth in the north.

But that was not all. At the end of the fifteenth century, the Spanish Crown cartellized the developing and promising Castilian textile industry by passing over 100 laws designed to freeze the industry at the current level of development. This freeze crippled the protected Castilian cloth industry and destroyed its efficiency in the long run, so that it could not become competitive in European markets.

Furthermore, royal action also managed to destroy the flourishing Spanish silk industry, which centred in southern Spain at Granada. Unfortunately, Granada was still a centre of Muslim or Moorish population, and so a series of vindictive acts by the Spanish Crown brought the silk industry to its virtual demise. First, several edicts drastically limited the domestic use and consumption of silk. Second, silks in the 1550s were prohibited from being exported, and a tremendous increase in taxes on the silk industry of Granada after 1561 finished the job.

Spanish agriculture in the sixteenth century was also crippled and laid waste by government intervention. The Castilian Crown had long made an alliance with the Mesta, the guild of sheep farmers, who received special privileges in return for heavy tax contributions to the monarchy. In the 1480s and 1490s, enclosures that had been made in previous years for grain farming were all disallowed, and sheepwalks (*cañadas*) were greatly expanded by government decree at the expense of the lands of grain farmers. The grain farmers were also hobbled by special legislation passed on behalf of the carters' guild – roads being in all countries special favourites for military purposes. Carters were specially allowed free passage on all local roads, and heavy taxes were levied on grain farmers to build and maintain the roads benefiting the carters.

Grain prices rose throughout Europe beginning in the early sixteenth century. The Spanish Crown, worried that the rising prices might induce a shift of land from sheep to grain, levied maximum price control on grain, while landlords were allowed unilaterally to rescind leases and charge higher rates to grain farmers. The result of the consequent cost–price squeeze was massive farm bankruptcies, rural depopulation, and the shift of farmers to the towns or the military. The bizarre result was that, by the end of the sixteenth century, Castile suffered from periodic famines because imported Baltic grain could not easily be moved to the interior of Spain, while at the same time one-third of Castilian farm land had become uncultivated waste.

Meanwhile, shepherding, so heavily privileged by the Spanish Crown, flourished for the first half of the sixteenth century, but soon fell victim to financial and market dislocations. As a result, Spanish shepherding fell into a sharp decline.

Heavy royal expenditures and taxes on the middle classes also crippled the Spanish economy as a whole, and huge deficits misallocated capital. Three massive defaults by the Spanish king, Philip II – in 1557, 1575 and 1596 – destroyed capital and led to large-scale bankruptcies and credit stringencies in France and in Antwerp. The resultant failure to pay Spanish imperial troops in the Netherlands in 1575 led to a thoroughgoing sack of Antwerp by mutinying troops the following year in an orgy of looting and rapine known as the 'Spanish Fury'. The name stuck even though these were largely German mercenaries.

The once free and enormously prosperous city of Antwerp was brought to its knees by a series of statist measures during the late sixteenth century. In addition to the defaults, the major problem was a massive attempt by the Spanish king, Philip II, to hold on to the Netherlands and to stamp out the Protestant and Anabaptist heresies. In 1562, the Spanish king forcibly closed Antwerp to its chief import – English woollen broadcloths. And, when the notorious duke of Alva assumed the governorship of the Netherlands in 1567, he instituted repression in the form of a 'Council of Blood', which had the power to torture, kill, and confiscate the property of heretics. Alva also levied a heavy value-added tax of 10 per cent, the *alcabala*, which served to cripple the sophisticated and interrelated Netherlands economy. Many skilled woollen craftsmen fled to a hospitable home in England.

Finally, the breakaway of the Dutch from Spain in the 1580s, and another Spanish royal default in 1607, led to a treaty with the Dutch two years later which finished Antwerp by cutting off its access to the sea and to the mouth of the River Scheldt, which was confirmed to be in Dutch hands. From then on, for the remainder of the seventeenth century, decentralized and free market Holland, and in particular the city of Amsterdam, replaced Flanders and Antwerp as the main commercial and financial centre in Europe.

7.3   Mercantilism and Colbertism in France

In France, which was to become in the seventeenth century the home *par excellence* of the despotic nation-state, the promising cloth trade and other commerce and industry in Lyons and the Languedoc region in the south were crippled by the devastating religious wars in the last four decades of the sixteenth century. In addition to the devastation and the killing and emigration of skilled Huguenot craftsmen to England, high taxes to finance the war served to cripple French economic growth. Then, the *politique* party, riding to power on the promise of ending religious strife, ushered in the unchecked reign of royal absolutism.

Crippling regulation of French industry had begun in the late fifteenth century, when the king issued scores of guild charters, conferring the power to control and to set standards of quality in the different occupations upon urban guilds and their officials. The Crown conferred cartellizing privileges on the guilds while levying taxes upon them in exchange. A major reason why Lyons had flourished during the sixteenth century was that it was granted a special exemption from guild rule and guild restrictions.

By the end of the sixteenth century and the religious wars, the old regulations were still in place, ready to be enforced. The new absolute monarchy was ready to enforce them and carry them further. Thus, in 1581, King Henry III ordered all the artisans of France to join and group themselves into guilds, whose orders were to be enforced. All except Parisian and Lyonnaise craftsmen were forced to confine their activity to their current towns; in that way, mobility in French industry was brought to an end. In 1597, Henry IV re-enacted and strengthened these laws, and proceeded to enforce them thoroughly.

The result of this network of restriction was the total crippling of economic and industrial growth in France. The typical ploy of preserving 'standards of quality' meant that competition was hobbled, production and imports limited, and prices kept high. It meant, in short, that consumers were not allowed the option of paying less money for lower-quality products. State-privileged monopolies grew as well, with similar effects; and upon the guilds and the monopolies the state levied increasing and stifling taxes. Growing inspection fees for quality also exacted a great burden on the French economy. Furthermore, luxury production was particularly subsidized, and the profits of expanding industries diverted to subsidize the weak. Capital accumulation was thereby slowed and the growth of promising and strong industries crippled. The subsidizing and privileging of luxury industries meant a shift of resources away from cost-cutting innovations in new mass-production industries, and towards such areas of high-cost craftsmanship as glass and tapestries.

The increasingly powerful French monarchy and aristocracy were large consumers of luxury goods and were therefore particularly interested in fostering them and maintaining their quality. Price was no great object since the monarchy and nobility lived off compulsory levies in any case. Thus, in May 1665, the king established monopoly privileges for a group of French lace manufacturers, using the transparently canting argument that this was done to prevent 'the export of money and to give employment to the people'. Actually, the point was to prohibit anyone other than the privileged licensees from making lace, in return for hefty fees paid to the Crown. Domestic cartels are worthless if the consumer is allowed to buy cheaper substitutes from abroad, and so protective tariffs were levied on imported lace. But apparently smuggling abounded, and so in 1667, the government made enforcement easier by prohibiting all foreign lace whatsoever. In addition, to prevent unlicensed competition, it was necessary for the French Crown to prohibit any lace work at home, and to force all lace work to occur at fixed, visible points of manufacture. Thus, as the finance and commerce minister and general economic czar Jean-Baptiste Colbert wrote to a government lace supervisor: 'I beg you to note with care that no girl must be allowed to work at the home of her parents and that you must oblige them all to go to the house of the manufactures...'

Perhaps the most important of the numerous mercantile restrictions on the French economy imposed in the seventeenth century was the enforcing of 'quality' standards on production and trade. This tended to mean a freezing of the French economy at the level of the early or mid-seventeenth century. That coerced freeze effectively hobbled or even prevented the innovation – new products, new technologies, new methods of handling production and exchange – so necessary to economic and industrial development. One example was the loom, invented in the early seventeenth century, at first used principally for the production of the luxury item, silk stockings. When looms began to be applied to relatively mass-consumption woollen and linen goods, the handknitters balked at the efficient competition, and persuaded Colbert, in 1680, to outlaw the use of the loom on any article except silk. Fortunately, in the case of the loom, the excluded woollen and linen manufacturers were politically powerful enough to get the prohibition repealed four years later, and to get themselves included in the protectionist/cartellist system of advantage.

All these tendencies of French mercantilism reached a climax in the era of Jean-Baptiste Colbert (1619–83), so much so that he gave the name Colbertisme to the most hypertrophied embodiment of mercantilism. The son of a merchant born at Reims, Colbert early in life joined the French central bureaucracy. By 1651, he had become a leading bureaucrat in the service of the Crown, and from 1661 to his death 22 year later, Colbert was the virtual economic czar – absorbing such offices as superintendent of finance, of commerce, and secretary of state – under the great Sun King, that epitome of absolutist despotism, Louis XIV.

Colbert engaged in a virtual orgy of grants of monopoly, subsidies of luxury, and cartellizing privilege, and built up a mighty system of central bureaucracy, of officials known as *intendants*, to enforce the network of controls and regulations. He also created a formidable system of inspections, marks and measurements to be able to identify all those straying from the detailed list of state regulations. The *intendants* employed a network of spies and informers to ferret out all violations of the cartel restrictions and regulations. In the classic mode of spies everywhere, they also spied on each other, including the *intendants* themselves. Penalties for violations ranged from confiscation and destruction of the 'inferior' production, to heavy fines, public mockery, and deprivation of one's licence to stay in business. As the major historian of mercantilism summed up French enforcement: 'No measure of control was considered too severe where it served to secure the greatest possible respect for the regulations.'[3]

Two of the most extreme examples of the suppression of innovation in France occurred shortly after the death of Colbert during the lengthy reign of

Louis XIV. Button-making in France had been controlled by various guilds, depending on the material used, the most important part belonging to the cord- and button-makers' guild, who made cord buttons by hand. By the 1690s, tailors and dealers launched the innovation of weaving buttons from the material used in the garment. The outrage of the inefficient hand-button-makers brought the state leaping to their defence. In the late 1690s, fines were imposed on the production, sale, and even the wearing of the new buttons, and the fines were continually increased. The local guild wardens even obtained the right to search people's houses and to arrest anyone in the street who wore the evil and illegal buttons. In a few years, however, the state and the hand-button-makers had to give up the fight, since everyone in France was using the new buttons.

More important in stunting France's industrial growth was the disastrous prohibition of the popular new cloth, printed calicoes. Cotton textiles were not yet of supreme importance in this era, but cottons were to be the spark of the Industrial Revolution in eighteenth century England. France's strictly enforced policy made sure that cottons would not be flourishing there.

The new cloth, printed calicoes, began to be imported from India in the 1660s, and became highly popular, useful for an inexpensive mass market, as well as for high fashion. As a result, calico printing was launched in France. By the 1680s, the indignant woollen, cloth, silk and linen industries all complained to the state of 'unfair competition' by the highly popular upstart. The printed colours were readily outcompeting the older cloths. And so the French state responded in 1686 by total prohibition of printed calicoes: their import or their domestic production. In 1700, the French government went all the way: an absolute ban on every aspect of calicoes including their use in consumption. Government spies had a hysterical field day: 'peering into coaches and private houses and reporting that the governess of the Marquis de Cormoy had been seen at her window clothed in calico of a white back-ground with big red flowers, almost new, or that the wife of a lemonade-seller had been seen in her shop in a casquin of calico'.[4] Literally thousands of Frenchmen died in the calico struggles, either being executed for wearing calicoes or in armed raids against calico-users.

Calicoes were so popular, however, especially among French ladies, that the fight was eventually lost, even though the prohibition stayed on the books until the late eighteenth century. The smuggling of calicoes simply could not be stopped. But it was of course easier to enforce the prohibition against domestic calico manufacture than against the entire French consuming population, and so the result of the near-century of prohibition was to put a total stop to any domestic calico-printing industry in France. The calico entrepreneurs and skilled craftsmen, many of them Huguenots oppressed by the French state, emigrated to Holland and England, strengthening the calico industry in those countries.

Furthermore, pervasive maximum wage controls discouraged workers from moving or, in particular, entering industry, and tended to keep workers on the farm. Apprenticeship requirements of three or four years greatly restricted labour mobility and prevented entrance into crafts. Each master was limited to one or two apprentices, thereby preventing the growth of any single firm.

Before Colbert, most French revenue came from taxation, but grants of monopoly proliferated so much during the Colbert regime to try to pay for swelling expenditures, that monopoly grant revenue came to more than one-half of all state income.

Most onerous and strictly enforced was the government's salt monopoly. Salt producers were required to sell all salt produced to certain royal store-houses at fixed prices. The consumers were then forced to purchase salt and, to expand state income and deprive smugglers of revenue, to purchase a fixed amount at four times the free market price and divide it among the inhabitants.

Despite the enormous increase in monopoly grant revenue, taxes rose greatly in France as well. The land tax, or *taille réelle*, was the single largest source of revenue for the state, and in the early part of his regime, Colbert tried to expand the burden of the *taille* still further. But the *taille* was hampered by a network of exemptions, especially including all the nobility. Colbert tried his best to spy on the exempt, to ferret out 'false' nobles, and to stop the network of bribes of the tax-collectors. An attempt to lower the *taille* slightly and greatly to increase the *aides* – indirect internal taxes at wholesale and retail, particularly on beverages – came a cropper on the bribery and corruption of the tax farmers. And then there was the *gabelle* (tax on salt), revenue from which rose tenfold in real terms between the early sixteenth and mid-seventeenth centuries. During the Colbert era, *gabelle* revenues rose not so much from an increase in tax rates as from the tightening of enforcement of the existing steep taxes.

The land and consumption taxes fell heavily upon the poor and upon the middle class, gravely crippling saving and investment, especially, as we have seen, in the mass-production industries. The parlous state of the French economy may be seen by the fact that, in 1640, just as King Charles I of England was facing a successful revolution largely brought about by his imposition of high taxes, the French Crown was collecting three to four times as much taxes per capita as did King Charles.

As a result of all these factors, even though the population of France was six times that of England during the sixteenth century, and its early industrial development had seemed promising, French absolutism and strictly enforced mercantilism managed to put that country out of the running as a leading nation in industrial or economic growth.

7.4   Mercantilism in England: textiles and monopolies

It was in the sixteenth century that England began its meteoric rise to the top of the economic and industrial heap. The English Crown in effect tried its best to hobble this development by mercantilist laws and regulations, but was thwarted because for various reasons the interventionist edicts proved unenforceable.

Raw wool had for several centuries been England's most important product, and hence its most important export. Wool was shipped largely to Flanders and to Florence to be made into fine cloth. By the early fourteenth century, the flourishing wool trade had reached a height of an average annual export of 35 000 sacks. The state naturally then entered the picture, taxing, regulating and restricting. The principal fiscal weapon to build the nation-state in England was the 'poundage', a tax on the export of wool and a tariff on the import of woollen cloth. The poundage kept increasing to pay for continuing wars. In the 1340s King Edward III granted the monopoly of wool exporting to small groups of merchants, in return for their agreeing to collect the wool taxes on the king's behalf. This monopoly grant served to put out of business Italian and other foreign merchants who had predominated in the wool export trade.

By the 1350s, however, these monopoly merchants had gone bankrupt, and King Edward finally resolved the issue by widening the monopoly privilege and extending it to a group of several hundred called the 'Merchants of the Staple'. All wool exported had to go through a fixed town under the auspices of the company of the Staple, and be exported to a fixed point on the Continent, by the end of the fourteenth century at Calais, then under English control. The monopoly of the Staple did not apply to Italy, but it did apply to Flanders, the major place of import for English wool.

The Merchants of the Staple soon proceeded to use their privileged monopoly in the time-honoured manner of all monopolists: to force lower prices upon English wool growers, and higher prices upon Calais and Flemish importers. In the short run, this system was quite pleasant for the Staplers, who were able to more than recoup their payments to the king, but in the long run the great English wool trade was crippled beyond repair. The artificial gap between domestic and foreign wool prices discouraged the production of English wool, while it also injured the demand for wool abroad. By the mid-fifteenth century, average annual exports of wool had fallen greatly to only 8 000 sacks.

The only benefit to Englishmen from this disastrous policy (apart from the joint short-term gains to King Edward and to the Staplers) was to give an unintended boost to the English production of woollen cloth. English clothmakers could now benefit from their artificially lower prices of wool in England, coupled with the artificially high prices of wool abroad. Once

again, the market managed to get a leg-up in its unending, zig-zag struggle
with power. By the mid-fifteenth century fine, expensive, broadcloth 'woollens' were being produced abundantly in England, centring in the West
Country, where swift rivers made water plentiful for fulling the woven cloth,
and where Bristol could serve as the major port of export and entry.

During the mid-sixteenth century, a new form of woollen cloth manufacture sprang up in England, soon to become dominant in the textile industry.
This was the 'new draperies', or worsteds, cheaper and lighter-weight cloth
that could be exported to warmer climates and far more suitable for dyeing
and decoration, since each individual strand of yarn was now visible in the
cloth. Since the worsted was not fulled, the draperies did not need to be
situated near running water, and so new textile manufacturers and workshops
sprang up in the countryside – and in new towns such as Norwich and Rye –
all round London. London was the largest market for the cloths, so transportation costs were now cheaper, and furthermore, the south-east was a centre
for sheep bearing the coarse, long stapled wool particularly suitable for
worsted production. The new rural firms around London were also able to
hire skilled Protestant textile artisans who had fled the religious persecution
in France and the Netherlands. Most important, going to the countryside or to
new towns meant that the expanding and innovating textile industry could
escape from the stifling guild restrictions and frozen technology of the old
towns.

Now that over 100 000 cloths were exported annually compared to a few
thousand two centuries earlier, sophisticated production and marketing innovations took place. Establishing a 'putting-out' system, merchants paid artisans by the piece to work on cloth owned by the former. In addition, marketing middlemen sprang up, yarn brokers serving as middlemen between spin-
ners and weavers, and drapers specializing in selling the cloth at the end of
the production chain.

Seeing the rise of effective new competition, the older urban and broadcloth artisans and manufacturers turned to the state apparatus to try to shackle
the efficient upstarts.

As Professor Miskimin puts it: 'As often happens during an evolutionary
period, the older, vested interests turned to the state for protection against the
innovative elements within the industry and sought regulation that would
preserve their traditional monopoly.'[5]

In response, the English government passed the Weavers' Act in 1555,
which drastically limited the number of looms per establishment outside the
towns to only one or two. Numerous exemptions, however, vitiated the effect
of the act, and other statutes placing maximum controls on wages, restricting
competition in order to preserve the old broadcloth industry came to naught
from systemic lack of enforcement. The English government then turned to

the alternative of propping up and tightening the urban guild structure to exclude competition. These measures succeeded, however, only in isolating and hastening the decay of the old urban broadcloth firms. For the new rural firms, especially the new draperies, were beyond guild jurisdiction. Queen Elizabeth then went national, with the Statute of Artificers in 1563, which placed the nation-state squarely behind guild power. The number of apprentices each master could employ was severely limited, a measure calculated to stifle the growth of any one firm, and to decisively cartellize the wool industry and cripple competition. The number of years of apprenticeship, before the apprentice could rise to become a master, was universally extended by the statute to seven years, and maximum wage rates for apprenticeships were imposed throughout England. Beneficiaries of the Statute of Artificers were not only the old, inefficient urban broadcloth guilds, but also the large landlords, who had been losing rural workers to the new, high-paying clothing industry. One announced aim of the Statute of Artificers was compulsory full employment, with labour directed to work according to a system of 'priorities'; top priority was accorded to the state, which attempted to force workers to remain in rural and farm work and not leave the farm for glittering opportunities elsewhere. To enter commercial or professional fields, on the other hand, required a graded series of qualifications such that the occupations were happy in having entry restricted by this cartellizing statute, while the landlords were delighted to have workers forced to remain on the farm at lower wages than they could achieve elsewhere.

If the Statute of Artificers had been strictly enforced, industrial growth might have been permanently arrested in England. But fortunately, England was far more anarchic than France, and the statute was not well enforced, particularly where it counted, in the new and fast-growing worsted industry.

Not only was the countryside beyond the grasp of the urban guilds and their nation-state ally, but so too was fast-growing London, where custom decreed that any guild member could engage in any sort of trade, and no guild could exercise restrictive control over any line of production.

London as the great export centre for the new draperies – largely to Antwerp – partially accounted for the enormous growth of this city during the sixteenth century. London's population grew at three times the rate of England as a whole over the century, specifically from 30–40 000 at the beginning of the sixteenth century to a quarter of a million early in the next.

The London merchants were not, however, content with free market development, and power began to move in on the market. Specifically, the London merchants began to reach for export monopoly. In 1486 the City of London created the Fellowship of the Merchant Adventurers of London, which claimed exclusive rights to the export of woollens to its members. For provincial merchants (outside of London) to join required a stiff fee. Eleven years later the king and parliament decreed that any merchant exporting to the Netherlands had to pay a fee to the Merchant Adventurers and obey its restrictionist regulations.

The state tightened the monopoly of the Merchant Adventurers in the mid-sixteenth century. First in 1552, the Hanseatic merchants were deprived of their ancient rights to export cloth to the Netherlands. Five years later, customs duties were raised on the import of cloth, thereby conferring more special privileges on the domestic cloth trade and increasing the financial ties of the Crown to the cloth merchants. And finally, in 1564, in Queen Elizabeth's reign, the Merchant Adventurers were reconstituted under tighter and more oligarchic control.

In the late sixteenth century, however, the mighty Merchant Adventurers began to decline. The English war with Spain and the Spanish Netherlands lost the Adventurers the city of Antwerp, and at the turn of the seventeenth century, they were formally expelled from Germany. The English monopoly of woollen exports to the Netherlands and the German coast was finally abolished after the revolution of 1688.

It is instructive to note what happened to printed calico in England as compared to the supression of the industry in France. The powerful woollen industry managed to get the importation of calicoes banned from England in 1700, a decade or so after France, but in this case domestic manufacture was still permitted. As a result, domestic manufactures of calico spurted ahead, and when the woollen interests managed to get a prohibition of calico consumption act passed in 1720 (The Calico Act), the domestic calico industry was already powerful and could continue to export its wares. In the meanwhile, calico smuggling continued, as did domestic use – all stimulated by the fact that prohibition was not enforced nearly as strictly in England as in France. Then, in 1735, the English cotton industry won an exemption for the domestic printing and use of 'fustians', a mixed cotton and linen cloth, which were the most popular form of calico in England in any case. As a result, the domestic cotton textile industry was able to grow and flourish in England throughout the eighteenth century.

Prominent in English mercantilism was the pervasive creation by the Crown of grants of monopoly privilege: exclusive power to produce and sell in domestic and in foreign trade. The creation of monopolies reached its climax in the reign of Queen Elizabeth (1558–1603), in the latter half of the sixteenth century. In the words of historian, Professor S.T. Bindoff: '…the restrictive principle had, like some giant squid, fastened its embracing tentacles round many branches of domestic trade and manufacture', and 'in the last decade of Elizabeth's reign scarcely an article in common use – coal, soap, starch, iron, leather, books, wine, fruit – was unaffected by patents of monopoly'.[6]

In sparkling prose, Bindoff writes how lobbyists, using the lure of monetary gain, obtained royal courtiers to sponsor their petitions for grants of monopoly: 'their sponsorship was usually a mere episode in the great game of place-and-fortune-hunting which swayed and swirled incessantly around the steps of the throne'. Once granted their privileges, the monopolists got themselves armed by the state with powers of search-and-seizure to root out all instances of now illegal competition. As Bindoff writes:

> The 'saltpetre men of the gunpowder contract dug in every man's house' for the nitrate-laden soil which was their raw material. The minions of the playing-card monopoly invaded shops in search of cards lacking its seal and browbeat their owners, under threat of summons to a distant court, into compounding for their offences. The search-warrant was, indeed, indispensable to the monopolist if he were to eliminate competition and leave himself free to fix the price of his wares.[7]

The result of this expulsion of competition, as we might expect, was the lowering of quality and the raising of price, sometimes by as much as 400 per cent.

England was pre-eminently the home of foreign trade companies receiving grants of monopoly for trade with portions of the globe. The granddaddy of the English foreign trade companies was the Muscovy Company, chartered in 1553, and granted a monopoly of all English trade with Russia and Asia through the White Sea port of Archangel. In the late 1570s and early 1580s, Queen Elizabeth granted trading privileges to a spate of new monopoly companies including the Barbary, Eastland, and Levant Companies. A small group of politically powerful men, centred originally in the Muscovy Company, was at the core of every one of these monopoly companies. The Muscovy Company, for a while, held a monopoly on all exploration and trade with North America. Further, when in the 1580s the Muscovy Company's trade with Russia was severely injured by the Cossacks' disruption of the Volga trade route from Asia, Muscovy Company leaders formed both the Turkey Company and the Venice Company in 1581 for trading with India. The two companies merged in 1592 into the Levant Company, which enjoyed a monopoly grant trade with India through the Levant and Persia.

Running like a powerful thread through all these interlocking monopoly companies was the person and the family of Sir Thomas Smith (1558–1625). Smith's grandfather, Andrew Judd, was a principal founder of the Muscovy Company. His father, Sir Thomas Smith, Sr (1514–77), attorney, had been an architect of the Tudor system of royal absolutism, high taxation, and economic restriction. By the 1590s, the junior Smith was the governor – the head – of literally every single monopoly company concerned with foreign trade and colonization. These included the Muscovy Company, which held the monopoly charter for the colonization of Virginia. But the climax of Smith's career came when, to all his other posts, was added governor of the mighty East India Company, chartered in 1600 with a monopoly of all trading to the East Indies.

7.5   Enserfdom in eastern Europe

What happened in eastern Europe was even worse than mercantilism. There, absolutism by the kings and the feudal nobility was so rampant and un-checked that they decided to crush nascent capitalism. Former serfs, now free, had been moving from the rural lands to the towns and cities, there to work for higher wages and better opportunities in emerging capitalist produc-tion and industry. By the beginning of the fifteenth century, eastern Europe, specifically Prussia, Poland and Lithuania, had a freed peasantry. Towns and monetary exchange flourished, and clothmaking and manufacturing grew and prospered. In the sixteenth century, however, the state and the nobility of eastern Europe reasserted themselves and re-enserfed the peasantry. In par-ticular, a rise in the price of grain (mainly rye) in Europe in the early sixteenth century made grain farming more profitable, spurring the socializ-ing of cheap labour in service of the noble landlords. The peasants were forced back on to the land, and compelled to remain there, and were also coerced into *corvées* (periodic forced labour for the nobility). The peasants were forced into large manorial estates owned by the nobles, since large estates meant cheaper costs of supervising and coercing peasant labour on the part of the nobility. In addition, in Poland, the nobles induced the state to pass further laws, severely restricting the activities of urban merchants. Polish merchants now had to pay higher tolls for shipping produce on the Vistula River than did landlords, and Polish merchants were prohibited from export-ing domestic products. Moreover, the repression of the formerly free peas-antry greatly lowered their money income for purchasing goods. These poli-cies combined to destroy the Polish towns, the urban economy, and the internal market for Polish goods. As Professor Miskimin writes, 'Out of self-interest the nobles successfully contrived to crush Polish economic develop-ment in order to reserve for themselves the rich grain trade and to assure adequate supplies of agricultural labor for the maximum exploitation of their estates'.[8]

In Hungary, a similar process of re-enserfment occurred, but in the service of cattle-raising and wine-growing rather than rye production. In the later Middle Ages, rents by the peasantry had been converted from payments in kind to monetary payments. Now, in the sixteenth century, the nobles mark-edly increased the rents and reconverted them into payments in kind. Taxes on peasants were raised substantially and the burden of forced *corvée* labour was increased greatly in one area ninefold from seven days per year to 60. The lords got themselves granted a tight monopoly of wine sales, as well as exemptions from heavy export taxes on cattle payable by merchants. In that way, the landlords gained themselves privileged monopolies of buying and selling for the vital wine and cattle trades.

7.6   Mercantilism and inflation

The post-medieval state acquired most of its eagerly sought revenues by taxation. But the state has always been attracted by the idea of creating its own money in addition to plundering directly the wealth of its subjects. Before the invention of paper money, however, the state was limited in money creation to occasional debasements of the coinage, of which it had long managed to secure a compulsory monopoly. For debasement was a one-shot process, and could not be used, as the state would always like, to create money continually and feed it into state coffers for use in building palaces, pyramids, and other consumption goods for the state apparatus and its power élite.

The highly inflationary instrument of government paper money was first discovered in the Western world in French Quebec in 1685. Monsieur Meules, the governing *intendant* of Quebec, pressed as usual for funds, decided to augment them by dividing some playing cards into quarters, marking them with various denominations of French currency, and then using them to pay for wages and materials. This card money, later redeemed in actual specie, soon became repeatedly issued paper tickets.

The first more familiar form of government paper began five years later, in 1690, in the British colony of Massachusetts. Massachusetts had sent soldiers on one of their customary plunder expeditions against prosperous French Quebec, but this time had been beaten back. The disgruntled Massachusetts soldiery was even more irritated by the fact that their pay had always come out of their individual shares of French booty sold at auction, but that now there was no money for them to collect. The Massachusetts government, beset by demands for payment of their salary by a mutinous soldiery, was not able to borrow the money from Boston merchants, who shrewdly considered its credit rating unworthy. Finally, Massachusetts hit upon the expedient of issuing 7 000 pounds in paper notes, supposed to be redeemable in specie in a few years. Inevitably, the few years began to stretch out on the horizon, and the government, delighted with this new-found way of acquiring seemingly costless revenue, poured on the printing presses, and quickly issued 40 000 more paper pounds. Fatefully, paper money had been born.

It was to be two decades before the French government, under the influence of the fanatically inflationist Scottish theoretician John Law, turned on the taps of paper money inflation at home. The English government turned instead to a more subtle device for accomplishing the same objective: the creation of a new institution in history: a central bank.

The key to English history in the seventeenth and eighteenth centuries is the perpetual wars in which the English state was continually engaged. Wars meant gigantic financial requirements for the Crown. Before the advent of the central bank and government paper, any government not willing to tax the country for the full cost of war relied on an ever more extensive public debt. But if the public debt continues to rise, and taxes are not increased, something has to give, and the piper must be paid.

Before the seventeenth century, loans were generally made by banks, and 'banks' were institutions in which capitalists lent out funds that they had saved. There was no deposit banking; merchants who wanted a safe place to keep their surplus gold deposited them in the King's Mint in the Tower of London – an institution accustomed to storing gold. This habit, however, proved highly costly, for King Charles I, needing money shortly before the outbreak of the civil war in 1638, simply confiscated the huge sum of 200 000 pounds in gold stored at the Mint – announcing it to be a 'loan' from the depositors. Understandably shaken by their experience, merchants began depositing their gold in the coffers of private goldsmiths, who were also accustomed to the storing and safe keeping of precious metals. Soon, goldsmiths' notes began to function as private bank notes, the product of deposit banking.

The Restoration government soon needed to raise a great deal of money for wars with the Dutch. Taxes were greatly increased, and the Crown borrowed extensively from the goldsmiths. In late 1671, King Charles II asked the bankers for further large loans to finance a new fleet. Upon the goldsmiths' refusal, the king proclaimed, on 5 January 1672, a 'stop of the Exchequer', that is, a wilful refusal to pay any interest or principal on much of the outstanding public debt. Some of the 'stopped' debt was owed by the government to suppliers and pensioners, but the vast bulk was held by the victimized goldsmiths. Indeed, of the total stopped debt of 1.21 million pounds, 1.17 million was owned by the goldsmiths.

Five years later, in 1677, the Crown grudgingly began paying interest on the stopped debt. But by the time of the eviction of James II in 1688, only a little over six years of interest had been paid out of the 12 years' debt. Furthermore, the interest was paid at the arbitrary rate of 6 per cent, even though the king had originally contracted to pay interest at rates ranging from 8 to 10 per cent.

The goldsmiths were even more intensively thwarted by the new government of William and Mary, ushered in by the Glorious Revolution of 1688. The new regime simply refused to pay any interest or principal on the stopped debt. The hapless creditors took the case to court, but while the judges agreed in principle with the creditors' case, their decision was overruled by the Lord Keeper, who candidly argued that the government's financial problems must take precedence over justice and property right.

The upshot of the 'stop' was that the House of Commons settled the affair in 1701, decreeing that half of the capital sum of the debt be simply wiped out; and that interest on the other half begin to be paid at the end of 1705, at the remarkable rate of 3 per cent. Even that low rate was later cut to two-and-a-half.

The consequences of this declaration of bankruptcy by the king were as could be predicted: public credit was severely impaired, and financial disaster struck for the goldsmiths, whose notes were no longer acceptable to the public, and for their depositors. Most of the leading goldsmith–creditors went bankrupt by the 1680s, and many ended their lives in debtors' prison. Private deposit banking had received a crippling blow, a blow which would only be overcome by the creation of a central bank.

The stop of the Exchequer, then, coming only two decades after the confiscation of the gold at the Mint, managed virtually to destroy at one blow private deposit banking and the government's credit. But endless wars with France were now looming, and where would government get the money to finance them?[9]

Salvation came in the form of a group of promoters, headed by the Scot, William Paterson. Paterson approached a special committee of the House of Commons formed in early 1693 to study the problem of raising funds, and proposed a remarkable new scheme. In return for a set of important special privileges from the state, Paterson and his group would form the Bank of England, which would issue new notes, most of which would be used to finance the government's deficit. In short, since there were not enough private savers willing to finance the deficit, Paterson and company were graciously willing to buy interest-bearing government bonds, to be paid for by newly created bank notes, carrying a raft of special privileges with them. As soon as Parliament duly chartered the Bank of England in 1694, King William himself and various MPs rushed to become shareholders of this new money-creating bonanza.

William Paterson urged the English government to grant Bank of England notes legal tender power, but this was going too far, even for the British Crown. But Parliament did give the bank the advantage of holding deposits of all government funds.

The new institution of government-privileged central banking soon demonstrated its inflationary power. The Bank of England quickly issued the enormous sum of 760 000 pounds, most of which were used to buy government debt. This issue had an immediate and substantial inflationary impact, and in two short years, the Bank of England was insolvent after a bank run, an insolvency gleefully abetted by its competitors, the private goldsmiths, who were happy to return to it the swollen Bank of England notes for redemption of specie.

At this point, the English government made a fateful decision: in May 1696, it simply allowed the bank to 'suspend specie payment'. In short, it allowed the bank to refuse indefinitely to pay its contractual obligations to redeem its notes in gold, while at the same time continuing blithely in operation, issuing notes and enforcing payments upon its *own* debtors. The bank resumed specie payments two years later, but this act set a precedent for British and American banking from that point on. Whenever the bank inflated itself into financial trouble, the government stood ready to allow it to suspend specie payments. During the last wars with France, in the late eighteenth and early nineteenth century, the bank was allowed to suspend payments for two decades.

The same year, 1696, the Bank of England had another scare: the spectre of competition. A Tory financial group tried to establish a national land bank, to compete with the Whig-dominated central bank. The attempt failed, but the Bank of England moved quickly to induce Parliament, in 1697, to pass a law prohibiting any new corporate bank from being established in England. Any new bank would have to be either proprietary or owned by a partnership, thereby severely limiting the extent of competition with the bank. Furthermore, counterfeiting of Bank of England notes was now made punishable by death. In 1708, Parliament followed up this set of privileges by another crucial one: it now became unlawful for any corporate bank other than the Bank of England, and for any bank partnership over six persons, to issue notes. And, moreover, incorporated banks and partnerships over six were also prohibited from making any short-term loans. The Bank of England now only had to compete with tiny banks.

Thus, by the end of the seventeenth century, the states of western Europe, particularly England and France, had discovered a grand new route towards the aggrandizement of state power: revenue through inflationary creation of paper money, either by government or, more subtly, by a privileged, monopolistic, central bank. In England, private banks of deposit were inspired to proliferate (especially checking accounts) under this umbrella, and the government was at last able to expand the public debt to fight its endless wars; during the French war of 1702–13, for example it was able to finance 31 per cent of its budget via public debt.

7.7 Notes

1. Jacob Viner, *Studies in the Theory of International Trade* (New York: Harper & Bros, 1937), pp. 58–9.
2. Ibid., p. 59.
3. Eli F. Heckscher, *Mercantilism* (1935, 2nd ed., New York: Macmillan, 1955) vol. I, p. 162.
4. Charles Woolsey Cole, *French Mercantilism, 1683–1700* (New York: Columbia University Press, 1943), p. 176.
5. Harry A. Miskimin, *The Economy of Later Renaissance Europe: 1460–1600* (Cambridge: Cambridge University Press, 1977), p. 92.

6.   S.T. Bindoff, *Tudor England* (Baltimore: Penguin Books, 1950), p. 228.

7.   Ibid., p. 291.

8.   Harry A. Miskimin, *The Economy of Later Renaissance Europe: 1460–1600* (Cambridge: Cambridge University Press, 1977), p. 60.

9.   Of the 66 years from 1688 to 1756, fully 34, or more than half, were spent in wars with France. Later wars, such as 1756–63, 1777–83, and 1794–1814, were even more spectacular, so that of the 124 years from 1688 to 1814, no less than 67 were spent by England in wars with the 'French threat'.

8 French mercantilist thought in the seventeenth century

8.1   Building the ruling élite

The system of mercantilism needed no high-flown 'theory' to get launched. It came naturally to the ruling castes of the burgeoning nation-states. The king, seconded by the nobility, favoured high government expenditures, military conquests, and high taxes to build up their common and individual power and wealth. The king naturally favoured alliances with nobles and with cartellizing and monopoly guilds and companies, for these built up his political power through alliances and his revenue through sales and fees from the beneficiaries. Neither did the cartellizing companies need much of a theory to come out in favour of themselves acquiring monopoly privilege. Subsidy to export, keeping out of imports, needed no theory either: nor did increasing the supply of money and credit to the kings, nobles or favoured business groups. Neither did the famous urge of mercantilists to build up the supply of bullion in the country: that supply in effect meant increased bullion flowing into the coffers of kings, nobles and monopoly export companies. And who does not want the supply of money in their pockets to rise?

Theory came later; theory came either to sell to the deluded masses the necessity and benevolence of the new system, or to sell to the king the particular scheme being promoted by the pamphleteer or his confrères. Mercantilist 'theory' was a set of rationales designed to uphold or expand particular vested economic interests.

Many twentieth century historians have lauded the mercantilists for their proto-Keynesian concern for 'full employment', thus showing allegedly surprising modern tendencies. It should be stressed, however, that the mercantilist concern for full employment was scarcely humanitarian. On the contrary, their desire was to stamp out idleness, and to force the idle, the vagrant, and the 'sturdy beggars' to work. In short, for the mercantilists, 'full employment' frankly implied its logical corollary: forced labour. Thus, in 1545, the 'sturdy beggars' of Paris were forced to work for long hours, and two years later, 'to take away all opportunity for idleness from the healthy', all women able but unwilling to work were whipped and driven out of Paris, while all men in the same category were sent to the galleys as slave labour.

The class basis of this mercantilist horror of idleness should be instantly noted. The nobility and the clergy, for example, were scarcely concerned with *their own* idleness; it was only that of the lower classes that must be ended by any means necessary. The same is true of the privileged merchants of the third estate. The thinly veiled excuse was the necessity of increasing 'the productivity of the nation', but these classes *constituted* the ruling élite, and such forced ending of idleness, whether on public works or in private production, was a boon to the rulers. It not only increased production for the latter's benefit; it also lowered wage rates by adding to the supply of labour by coercion.

Thus, at the meeting of the states general, the parliamentary body of France, in 1576, all three estates united in their call for forced labour. The clergy urged that 'no idle person...be allowed or tolerated'. The third estate wanted 'sturdy beggars' to be put to work, whipped or exiled. The nobles urged that 'sturdy beggars and idlers' be forced to work and whipped if they refused to comply.

The same states-general made their special pleading all too painfully clear in the matter of protective tariffs. The estates called for the prohibition of imports of all manufactured goods and the export of all raw materials. The purpose of both measures was to throw a wall of monopoly protection around domestic manufactures and to force producers of raw materials to sell their goods to those domestic businesses at an artificially low price. The excuse that such measures were necessary to 'keep bullion' or money 'at home' would seem patently absurd to any objective person. For if French consumers are to be prevented from buying imports in order to safeguard 'their bullion', what might happen otherwise? Was there really any danger of Frenchmen sending all their bullion abroad and keeping none for themselves? Clearly, such an event would be absurd, but *even* if it happened – the worst-case scenario – there is an evident hard maximum limit to any outflow of bullion from home. For where are the consumers bent on further importation going to get more bullion? Clearly, only by exporting other products abroad.

Consequently, the 'keeping money at home' argument is patently fraudulent, whether in seventeenth century France or in the twentieth century United States. The states-general were interested in protecting certain French industries, period.

The 'keeping money at home' argument was also a convenient stick to beat foreign businessmen or financiers who could outcompete natives. Thus the prospect of German bankers and Italian financiers flourishing in France gave rise to paroxysms of fury at the 'ill-gotten gains' of foreigners, taking money out of the country, fury that was of course fed by the typically mercantilist egregious 'Montaigne fallacy' that one man's (or one nation's) gain on the market was *ipso facto* another man's (or nation's loss). These disgruntled Frenchmen often suggested that foreign financiers be expelled from the country, but the kings were typically too bogged down in debt to afford such counsel.

8.2   The first major French mercantilist: Barthélemy de Laffemas

The first French mercantilist of note was Barthélemy de Laffemas (1545–1612), an uneducated son of a very poor Protestant family in Dauphiné. All his life he was the servitor of Henry of Navarre, the Protestant pretender, rising in 1582 to the exalted post of honorary tailor and valet to his master. When Henry of Navarre became King Henry IV, Laffemas's fortune was made, and he became in 1601 controller-general of commerce and head of the Commission of Commerce, to remain so until the king's death. Like a devoted dog who dies shortly after his master, Laffemas, now broken in power, died a year after Henry was assassinated in 1610. Laffemas comes to our attention because of the literally dozens of execrably written pamphlets he produced during his decades in power, on behalf of the mercantile system which he was helping to put into place in France.

Laffemas's focal point, his criterion for numerous economic policies, was whether or not they brought bullion into the kingdom. But note that these views need not necessarily be interpreted as dim-witted reliance on money-as-wealth; for when Laffemas wrote that gold and silver were 'the sinews and support of kingdoms and monarchies...the true matter and substance which maintains the state against...enemies', he was of course quite right. The more money kings can amass from their subjects, the wealthier and more powerful they would become. There is nothing odd or fallacious about *that*. The fallacy existed – should the argument be taken seriously – for anyone who identified the king's interest with that of all of French society.

The one spark of economic intelligence here came with the fact that Laffemas was one of the first mercantilists to shrewdly advise the king not to directly prohibit the export of bullion. Far better, he believed, to allow bullion to flow in and out of the country freely, and then strictly regulate commerce and industry in such a way that bullion would flow into the country.

Apart from that, Laffemas's economic advice was a dreary litany: prohibit all manufactured imports, prohibit fairs which drained money out of the kingdom and into the hands of foreigners, force merchants to buy only raw materials abroad and not manufactures, prohibit the export of raw materials. Guilds must be revived and used to regulate all urban work and to keep up the quality of products; committees of masters should supervise guilds; a bureau of manufactures should supervise them, and so on up to the royal court.

Promoting the usual mercantilist cant, Laffemas assured agriculture that it would benefit, not suffer, from the establishment of protected manufactures, since these would supply a home market for farm products. That this would be a highly inefficient and costly home market Laffemas did not bother to add.

Everyone who opposed his views, according to Laffemas, was selfish, ignorant, and/or a traitor, and should be dealt with accordingly. All who disobeyed the regulations and prohibitions should suffer confiscation of their goods as well as death.

Like most of his mercantilist confrères, Barthélemy de Laffemas was enamoured of the idea of full employment and the eradication of idleness.

Full employment, of course, meant coerced employment, and Laffemas called for an end to idleness by putting the idle to work, the reluctant to be forced into it by 'chains and prisons'. Taverns and cabarets were to be severely restricted, and confirmed drunkards arrested and put into the pillory.

Protectionism begins by trying to ensure national self-sufficiency in goods that can be made at home, and then continues by expanding the definition of what can indeed be made. For when profitability on the market is abandoned as a criterion, virtually every good in creation can be made – at *some* cost – at home. If Americans wanted to, they could undoubtedly grow all their bananas in hothouses in Maine or Montana at astronomical cost. But what would be the point, apart from subsidies to a few privileged hothouse growers?

One of Barthélemy de Laffemas's daftest projects, which as controller-general he did his best to put into effect, was to make France self-sufficient in one of her favourite luxury imports: silks. Many of his pamphlets and practical efforts were devoted to force-feeding an enormous expansion of the French silk industry, hitherto small and confined to the south of France.

Laffemas insisted that the climate of France was ideal for raising silk-worms; any belief to the contrary, any subversive talk that France was largely too cold and stormy for silk growing, was merely propaganda spread by the 'evil designs of certain French merchants, retailers of foreign silks'. Laffemas pointed to his own successful silk-growing, to King Henry's planting of mulberry trees (on which silkworms were fed). He advocated a law compelling all property owners, including the clergy and monasteries, to plant two or three mulberry trees per acre. He painted a beautiful picture of vast profits that were sure to flow from mulberry trees and silk culture. Laffemas also claimed magical medicinal properties for mulberries: they would cure tooth-ache and stomach trouble, relieve burns, chase away vermin, and be an antidote to poisons.

Even though Laffemas persuaded the king to pour hundreds of thousands of *livres* into fostering the growth of mulberry trees and silk culture, and the king duly ordered each diocese in France to establish a nursery of 50 000 mulberries, the great silk experiment proved an abject failure. The climate of most of France indeed proved inhospitable, a product of hard reality rather than misinformation spread by selfish and traitorous importers. The mass of the French clergy understandably dragged their feet at suddenly being forced to become silk producers. France continued to be a heavy net importer of silks.

Laffemas's main if not only disciple was his son Isaac. At the tender age of 19, young Isaac de Laffemas (1587–1657), keen to become the heir of his powerful father in every sense, published a *History of Commerce in France* (1606). The *History* was scarcely a memorable work, distinguished mainly for the fawning praise which he lavished upon his father and on King Henry, and on the slavish repetition of his father's pet notions and nostrums. The tone of this work may be gauged from the fact that Isaac lauded Henry IV as the source of all that is good in France. Addressing his Majesty, young Isaac wrote that heaven 'has favored my father in having let him live during your reign'.

With the fall of his father from grace and his subsequent death, Isaac's career as a political economist came to an untimely end, and he ended his days as a minor but faithful lieutenant of the chief minister, Cardinal Richelieu.

8.3   The first 'Colbert': the duc de Sully

What Jean-Baptiste Colbert would be in the last half of the seventeenth century to Louis XIV, Maximilien de Béthune, Baron de Rosny, the duc de Sully (1560–1641) was to Henry IV. The young Béthune was born a Huguenot aristocrat, Baron de Rosny. Naturally, he too gravitated to the court of Henry of Navarre, and fought and was wounded during the religious wars. It is characteristic of Rosny that he urged Henry IV to turn Catholic in order to save his throne, although he himself refused to do so.

The arrogant and ruthless Rosny quickly became Henry IV's leading minister as superintendent of finance, and for his services was made by his master the duc de Sully. Sully's own views stem from his *Memoirs* (1638), written in old age as a glowing apologia for his own term in office, for Sully had been forcibly retired to private life after the assassination of his royal patron. In his *Memoirs*, Sully claims to have opposed the more crackpot schemes of his fellow top bureaucrat Laffemas. Thus, he writes at length of his opposition to Laffemas's silk fiasco. Silk could not readily grow in the French climate, he had warned, and also it would lead Frenchmen into undue luxury.

It is not, of course, that Sully was not a mercantilist. It is just that, instead of proceeding with the folly of force-feeding domestic luxury industries, such as silk, he would have passed laws directly against luxurious consumption. He was eager to ban the export of gold and silver directly, paying fees to himself and others for ferreting out evaders of the law. Some of his specific views, of course, such as on the silk scheme, might be a rewriting of history to make himself look good to contemporaries; after all, neither Laffemas nor King Henry were then alive to verify his recollections. Others might be simply the product of bureaucratic infighting with his fellow economic czar.

A dedicated absolutist, who indeed did much to entrench centralized absolutism in France, the Duc de Sully was basically as much a protectionist as his colleague Laffemas, despite the claim of some historians that Sully (and his monarch) was some sort of 'free-trader'. The one significant case where Sully opposed a Laffemas protection scheme was the latter's proposal to ban all imports of textiles. But here the basic reason was his loyalty to the city of

Lyons, the leading Protestant stronghold in south-eastern France, which would have suffered greatly from the prohibition of such trade. Throughout his career, Sully fought to uphold the fortunes and privileges of Lyons.

8.4   The eccentric poet: Antoine de Montchrétien

One of the most bizarre characters in the history of economic thought was the poet and dramatist Antoine de Montchrétien (c.1575–1621). Born in Falaise, in Normandy, Montchrétian grew up in a middle-class household, his father probably having been an apothecary. He went to a fashionable school at Caen, and at the age of 20 began to write poetry and tragic plays, some of which, including *Hector* and *L'Écossaise*, are still considered classics of French literature. At 30 Montchrétien became involved in a scandalous duel, and fled to England. After travelling in Holland, he returned to France around 1610 and married a rich Norman widow, who financed his start in the hardware business. He thereupon set up a factory at Ousonne-sur-Loire, where he produced knives and scythes.

In 1615, at the age of 40, Antoine de Montchrétien published his one and only work on economics, the *Traicté de l'Oeconomie Politique* (*Treatise on Political Economy*). The only distinction of this book was its title, for it was the first time in history that the phrase 'political economy' had ever appeared. The *Treatise* is a rambling, disorganized account of the economic resources of the country, and a plea to the twin rulers of France (the young King Louis XIII and his Regent and Queen Mother, Marie de Medici) to impose order, rule with an iron hand, and advance the greatness of their nation-state, France. As Charles Cole puts it, the book 'is based in large part on the tacit assumption that control and direction of the economic life of the country is one of the chief functions of government, and it is a plea for greater activity in economic matters on the part of the rulers'.[1] One sentence from the work will convey its essential spirit: 'Your Majesties possess a great state, agreeable in geographic situation, abounding in wealth, flourishing in peoples, powerful in good and strong cities, invincible in arms, triumphant in glory'. All France needs, Montchrétien opined, is 'order': 'Order is the entelechy of states'.

The alleged need for a state-imposed order was linked neatly with Montchrétien's conscious echoing of the Montaigne fallacy: 'It is said that no one ever loses without another gaining. This is true and is borne out in the realm of commerce more than anywhere else'.

For Montchrétien, the French Crown in particular was supposed to regulate and foster production and trade, and especially manufactures, so that France could become self-sufficient. Foreign goods and foreign manufacturers should be driven out of France. Thus Dutch linen manufacturers were at the time allowed to operate in France; that must be ended. English textiles should be banned. France must be made self-sufficient in silk, Montchrétien asserted, and he claimed that the fiasco of silk subsidy in the reign of Henry IV had come about only because of faithlessness on the part of the monarch's aides. Furthermore, since 'whatever is foreign corrupts us', foreign books should be prohibited, since they 'poison our spirits' and 'corrupt our manners'.

Nor did Montchrétien neglect his own scythe business. It was a national tragedy, he warned, that German scythes were outcompeting French products, even though French scythes were superior. One wonders, then, why French consumers were perverse enough to prefer the German product – unless, of course, its price was lower.

Idleness, according to Montchrétien, was evil and had to be stamped out, by force if necessary. Man, to Montchrétien, is born to live in continual labour; the policy of the state should therefore be to make sure that no part of the population ever remains idle. Idle hands are the devil's hands; idleness corrupts the strength of men and the chastity of women. Idleness, in short, is the mother of all sins. The criminals and the unruly should, therefore, be made to work. As for so many other mercantilists, full employment for Montchrétien meant at bottom coerced employment.

The most pervasive motif in Montchrétien's work was his deep and abiding hatred and revulsion towards foreigners, towards their imported products and towards their persons. Foreigners, he fulminated, 'are leeches who attach themselves to this great [French] body, suck out its best blood, and gorge themselves with it, then leave the skin and detach themselves'. All in all, France, 'once so pure, so clean', had been turned into 'a bilge, a sewer, a cesspool for other countries'.

It is impossible to know if Montchrétien was hoping for great things from the French monarch, but in any case nothing happened, and so he began to ordain himself into the nobility, by simply calling himself the 'sieur de Vateville'. And even though he implied in several spots in his *Treatise* that he was Catholic, and declared his adoration for the absolute monarchy often enough, yet he took part in a Huguenot uprising in Normandy in 1621, and was killed in battle. Four days later, a judicial tribunal condemned the dead man posthumously, dragged, broke and burned his body, and then scattered his ashes to the winds. Such was the punishment handed out to Antoine de Montchrétien by his much vaunted absolute rulers.

8.5   The grandiose failure of François du Noyer

François du Noyer, sieur de Saint-Martin, had a dream. It was a grandiose vision of the future. All around him, in the early seventeenth century, and in all major nations of the West, the state was creating monopoly companies. Then why not, du Noyer reasoned, go all the way? If monopoly companies for specific products or specific areas of trade were good, why not go one better? Why not one big company, one gigantic monopoly for virtually everything?

King Henry IV listened to du Noyer's schemes with interest. They were, after all, only logical conclusions of doctrines and notions that were every-where in the air. But it was not until 1613 that du Noyer worked out his plan in detail, and set it before the council of state. It was to be an enor-mous, virtually all-inclusive company, to be called the French Royal Com-pany of the Holy Sepulchre of Jerusalem. The company, to be headed of course by du Noyer himself, was to have either a privileged monopoly, or the right to regulate all other firms, in virtually every trade. Thus, the Royal Company was to make cloth, and regulate all other manufacture and prepa-ration of all types of cloth; control all aspects of wine making, and all merchants and hotels buying wine would have to invest certain sums in the company, at a low fixed return; hold four privileged fairs a year in Paris; have a monopoly of all public coaches; control all mines in France; obtain gratis various unoccupied Crown lands and abandoned quarries; dig canals, erect mills; have a monopoly on sale of playing cards; make munitions; borrow and lend money; and numerous other activities. Furthermore, du Noyer would have the Royal Company obtain extraordinary powers from the Crown:

- it would have the right to seize beggars and vagabonds and take them to the French colonies, which it would presumably run;
- all convicted criminals would be sentenced to forced labor for the company in the colonies;
- all bankrupts who had managed to save some money from their wreck-age would be forced to invest that amount in the company;
- all people exiled from France could be let back into the country by serving or paying money to the company;
- all who conducted trade higher than their rank or privileges would be forced to join the company;
- all business documents whatsoever would have to use stamped paper sold to them by the company.

The council of state was impressed by du Noyer's vision and ordered an investigation of the project. The following year, 1614, the Royal Company plan was approved by the states-general of France, and various generals, admirals, and other high-level officials joined in the praise. Du Noyer reached the peak of his influence, being given the old Laffemas post of controller-general of commerce. It seemed as if the grandiloquent Royal Company plan was actually going to be adopted. Du Noyer elaborated on his plan in a pamphlet which he presented to the king in 1615.

The king, or rather the regent, Marie de Medici, was impressed, and in 1616 recreated the old Commission of Commerce, formerly headed by

Laffemas, with instructions to study the du Noyer project in detail. The commission met, and the following year approved the plan of the Royal Company, and urged that all persons carrying on trade be forced to invest their money exclusively in it. In short, the Royal Company would be the monopoly company to end all companies. The delighted du Noyer, in the meanwhile, seeing his cherished scheme close to fruition, published a longer pamphlet on the plan, urging his one big company upon France. Like the king himself, the Royal Company would be unique and universal, and its capital would come from both private and royal sources.

The Royal Company project seemed to keep barrelling along, the council of state granting its approval in 1618, and again in 1620, when King Louis XIII himself gave it his warm endorsement. In early 1621, public criers throughout Paris announced the glad tidings that the Royal Company had been formed, and was open to receive funds for investment.

The problem, however, was money. No one seemed to want to provide actual cash or even pledges to the new enterprise, however grandiloquent and privileged it appeared to be. The king urged every city in France to join, but the cities kept hanging back, pleading that they had no funds. In desperation, controller-general of commerce du Noyer scaled down the Royal Company to concentrate only on commerce and trade with the Indies and other overseas areas. Finally, du Noyer narrowed the scope of his beloved company's capital still further to just Paris and Brittany. But even the Bretons proved not to be interested.

The coming to power as prime minister of Cardinal Richelieu in 1624 put the du Noyer scheme into abeyance. But four years later, the project had its final fling. The king urged the commission of Commerce to act, and in the spring of 1629, it again approved the plan, this time adding to its original grandiose powers the right to make treaties with foreign countries, and to establish colonial islands for entrepôt trade.

After nearly three decades of planning and lobbying, du Noyer now needed only the simple signature of King Louis to put his hypertrophied vision into effect. But for some reason, the royal signature never came. No one knows quite why. Perhaps the powerful Richelieu didn't want a rival's scheme to be approved. Or perhaps the king was getting weary of the aging monomaniac and his untiring enthusiasm. Repeated entreaties and importuning, however, fell only on deaf ears. The Royal Company was at last dead, stillborn, and old du Noyer's loss was the French public's gain.

8.6 Under the rule of the cardinals, 1624–61

The 1620s to the 1650s were decades of rule in France by two very secular cardinals. The first was the stern, implacable, cunning, and charismatic Armand Jean du Plessis, Cardinal de Richelieu (1585–1642). A scion of an old family of lesser nobility in Poitou, Richelieu's father, François, had been a particular favourite of Henry III and Henry IV. As a result, young Armand was made bishop of Luçon by Henry IV in 1606. Eight years later, Richelieu attracted the attention of the Queen Mother, Marie de Medici, and became chief adviser in her exile. He was made a cardinal in 1622, and became prime minister in 1624, to remain so until his death 20 years later.

Richelieu's main interest was his participation in the Thirty Years' War (1618–48), which devastated Germany for decades to come. This war symbolized a fundamental shift in European wars from the strictly religious conflicts of the previous century to the political nation-state ambitions of the seventeenth century. Thus Richelieu, the at least nominally Catholic (albeit *politique*) cardinal of a Catholic country, found himself heading a largely Protestant European coalition against the Catholic Habsburgs of Austria and Spain.

The cardinal's theoretical views were set forth in two books written near the end of his life, his *Memoirs on the Reign of Louis XIII* and his *Political Testament*. While his major practical interest had not been domestic or economic affairs, he had helped build up the absolutism of the French state. In his works, he repeated the usual absolutist mercantilist views of the France of his era. France should be self-sufficient in all things, the navy and merchant marine built up, monopolies granted, the idle put to work or locked up in institutions, and luxurious consumption prohibited.

An interesting new variant was Richelieu's candid attitude towards the mass of Frenchmen as simply animals to be prodded or coerced in ways that were optimal for the French state. Thus taxes should not be so high that commerce and industry are discouraged, but neither should they be so low as to leave the public too well off. For if the people were too comfortable and complacent, it would be impossible to 'contain them in the rules of their duty'. Richelieu added the revealing comment that 'It is necessary to compare them [the people] to mules, who, being accustomed to burdens, are spoiled by a long rest more than by work'.

It is clear that in the course of promoting the interests of the nation-state and of his monarch, Richelieu did not neglect his own concerns. A receiver of a modest annual income of 25 000 *livres* upon his entry into the post of prime minister, by the end of his career in office Cardinal Richelieu was earning some 3 million *livres* per annum. Apparently, the cardinal had no problem in serving the enrichment of his sovereign and of himself at the same time.

Richelieu's successor was a fascinating character, a Sicilian whose father was a high official attached to the powerful Colonna family. Jules Mazarin (1602–61) was educated in Rome by the Jesuits, and then became a Church official at the University of Alcalá in Spain. Returning to Rome to earn his doctorate in law, Mazarin was a captain of infantry, and then a papal diplomat of note. He was made a church canon without ever having been a priest. While serving as papal nuncio to France, he gained the favour of the great Richelieu, who offered Mazarin a high official post if he should become a naturalized French citizen.

It is not many men who emigrate, become a citizen of another land (as Mazarin did in 1639), and then become prime minister of that country only three years later. Mazarin, however, achieved that feat, becoming cardinal (still without being a priest) in 1641, and succeeding Richelieu when the latter died a year later. Mazarin was shrewd enough to court the favour of the queen, so that when Louis XIII died the next year, and the queen became regent, Mazarin could continue in his powerful post. Except for a year or two's hiatus, Mazarin continued as prime minister until his death in 1661.

Mazarin had far less interest in economic affairs than his predecessor, and was no theoretician, devoting himself largely to diplomacy and war. He didn't need much theoretical insight, however, to amass a fortune in high office that put even his predecessor to shame. By the end of his rule, he had accumulated an immense personal fortune of approximately 50 million *livres*.

One noteworthy work written during Mazarin's term was by a Carmelite monk, Jean Éon, whose religious name was Mathias de Saint-Jean (c.1600–81). Éon was born in Saint-Malo, in Brittany, and became a friend and adviser of the governor of Brittany, a relative of Richelieu's, Marshal de la Meilleraye. Éon eventually became Carmelite provincial in Touraine, and refused the opportunity to become attorney-general of that province.

During Éon's life in Brittany, the Breton merchants became interested in founding a privileged commercial company, and in 1641 a group of merchants, consulting with de la Meilleraye, worked out plans for a large company, centred at Nantes, to be called the Société de la Bourse Commune de Nantes. The company was approved by the council of state in 1646, but it provoked an anonymous pamphlet in opposition. Éon was hired by the city of Nantes, and encouraged by la Meilleraye to write a book in defence of the company. The result was the lengthy *Honourable Commerce or Political Considerations* (*Le Commerce honorable ou considérations politiques*) (Nantes, 1647). The book was dedicated to Éon's friend and patron la Meilleraye, whom he extolled as inheriting the mantle of economic leadership of the nation from Richelieu.

Éon's book was a compilation of standard mercantilist doctrines and need not be examined in detail here. He almost rivalled Montchrétien in his hatred for foreigners, and in his wish to drastically curtail their activities in or selling to France. Two of his personal and original contributions were his paean to the sea, shipping, and the seafaring life, and his eulogy to the city of Nantes, its glory and its unique suitability for locating a privileged company.

8.7   Colbert and Louis XIV

Jean-Baptiste Colbert (1619–83) was no scholar or theorist, but he knew with firm conviction what ideas he liked, and these were the mercantilist notions that had filled the air in France and the rest of Europe for generations. Colbert's accomplishment, while functioning as the Sun King's economic czar, was to put this compendium of mercantilist ideas into effect on a grand scale. Colbert was convinced that the ideas were good, just and correct, and he fervently believed that any opponent was completely wrong, either ignorant or biased by personal motives and special pleading. His opponents, such as businessmen who preferred competition or free exchange, were narrow, short-sighted, and selfish; only he, Jean-Baptiste Colbert, had the long-run interests of the nation and the nation-state at heart. Merchants, he repeatedly declared, were little men with only 'little private interests'. For example, they often preferred liberty to compete with each other, whereas it is in the 'public interest' and the 'good of the state' to see to it that all products are uniform in make-up and quality. Colbert was speaking here, of course, of the joint interests of the state, its rulers and bureaucracy, and of cartellists, all of whose private interests were in fact at stake. But although the myth of the 'public' was, as usual, a mask for particular individuals and groups, their interests were indeed far grander than those of 'little' individual merchants.

The mercantilist ideas of Colbert were familiar: encouraging and keeping bullion in the country so that it can flow into the coffers of the state; prohibiting the export of bullion; cartellizing through compulsory high standards of quality; subsidizing of exports; and restriction on imports until France became self-sufficient. Colbert's ideas on taxation were those of almost every minister of finance everywhere, except they were more clearly and far more candidly expressed: 'The art of taxation', he said, 'consists in so plucking the goose as to obtain the largest amount of feathers with the least amount of hissing'. There is no more dramatic encapsulation of the inherently conflicting interests of the people *vs* the state. From the point of view of the state and its rulers, the people are but a giant goose to be plucked as efficaciously as possible.

Furthermore, that swelling the coffers of the king and the state was the simple reason for the otherwise silly 'bullionist' doctrines of the mercantilists can be seen in this revealing statement of Colbert's to the king: 'The universal rule of finances should be always to watch, and use every care, and all the authority of Your Majesty, to attract money into the kingdom, to spread it out into all the provinces so as to pay their taxes'.

Like other mercantilists, Colbert warmly embraced the 'Montaigne fallacy' about trade. Trade was war and conflict. The total amount of trade in the world, the total number of ships, the total production of manufacturing, was fixed. One nation could only improve its trade, or shipping or manufactures, by depriving some other country of this fixed quantum. One nation's gain must be another's loss. Colbert gloried in the fact that French trade was growing, allegedly at the expense of misery inflicted on other nations. As Colbert wrote to King Louis XIV in 1669, 'This state is flourishing not only in itself, but also by the want which it has inflicted upon all the neighbouring states'.

In reality, trade and conquest are not akin, but are diametric opposites. Each party to every exchange benefits, whether the exchange is between nationals of the same country or of different countries. Political boundaries have nothing to do with the economic gain from trade and markets. In exchange, one man's gain is only accomplished by contributing to the gain of someone else; just as both 'nation' (i.e. people living in certain countries or any other geographical area) mutually benefit from trade between them. Colbert's theories, however, fitted in with deep hostility toward all foreigners, particularly such prosperous nations as England and Holland.

Like other mercantilists, Colbert detested the idleness of others, and sought to force them into working for the nation and state. All vagabonds must be driven out of the country or put to forced labour as galley-slaves. Holidays should be reduced, so that people would work harder.

Colbert was unusual among mercantilists in giving especial care to bringing the intellectual and artistic life of the nation under state control. The object was to make sure that art and intellect served to glorify the king and his works. An enormous amount of money was poured into palaces and *chateaux* for the king, the mightiest of which was approximately 40 million *livres* on the great, isolated palace at Versailles. During Colbert's term, some 80 million *livres* were spent on royal edifices. Moreover, Colbert mobilized artists and intellectuals into academies, and supported them by grants and government projects. The French Academy, created shortly before as an uninfluential semi-private group, was nationalized by Colbert and put in charge of the French language. The Academy of Painting and Sculpture, founded under Mazarin and given a legal monopoly of art instruction, was reinforced by Colbert, who imposed strict regulations on these artists so that their work would be proper and orderly and always in service to the king. Colbert founded an academy of architecture to work on royal buildings and to inculcate the proper architectural principles.

Neither were music nor the theatre safe from the all-encompassing rule of Colbert. Colbert preferred the Italian opera form to the French ballet, and so doomed the latter to the benefit of the Italian import. In 1659, the Abbé Perrin produced the first French opera, and so a decade later, Colbert conferred upon the abbé a monopoly of all rights to present musical performances. Perrin, however, was a poor manager, and he went bankrupt. While in a debtor's prison, Perrin sold his monopoly right to Jean Batiste Lulli, an Italian musician and composer. Lulli was given the right to form the Royal Academy of Music, and Lulli's permission was necessary for any further musical performance with more than two instruments.

Similarly, Colbert created a theatrical monopoly. In 1673, he forced two existing theatres to unite: when a third troupe was later forced to join them, the *Comédie française* was thereby formed in 1680. The *Comédie française* was given a monopoly of all dramatic performances in Paris, was subjected to tight state regulation and control, and aided by state funds.

With regulation and monopoly came subsidy and subvention. Pensions, grants, no-show appointments as valets of the king, lucrative appointments as artists to the king, exemptions from taxes or from the wrath of creditors, all poured out into the arts. Similarly, for the theatre, writers, scientists, historians, philosophers, mathematicians and essayists. All manner of largesse poured out to them from the state trough. It was subvention that put to shame any contemporary national endowment for the humanities or national science foundation. The outpouring truly subverted any sort of spirit of independence that French intellectuals might have attained. The mind of a whole nation had been corrupted into the service of the state.

What manner of man was this, then, this grand bureaucrat who scorned the interests of mere individuals and merchants as petty and narrow, who presumed always to speak and act for the 'national' and even 'public' interest? Jean-Baptiste Colbert was born in Reims, into a merchant family. His father, Nicolas, purchased a minor government office in Paris; his more influential uncle, Odart Colbert, was a successful merchant-banker. Jean-Baptiste was an uneducated young man, but his uncle knew a banker for Cardinal Mazarin. More importantly, one of Odart's sons married the sister of an important government official, Michel Le Tellier. Uncle Odart got young Colbert a job working for Le Tellier, who had just been appointed to the post of secretary of state for military affairs. Jean-Baptiste's lifelong service in the top French bureaucracy had begun. After seven years in this post, Colbert married Marie Charon, after obtaining for her father, a wealthy financial official, an important tax exemption.

Soon Colbert became a counsellor of state, and then one of the top aides of Cardinal Mazarin. Soon after Mazarin's death, Colbert rose to become virtual economic czar of Louis XIV, keeping this status until his death.

Cold, humourless, hard and implacable, 'a man of marble' as he was called by a contemporary, Jean-Baptiste Colbert yet had the wit to engage in boundless flattery and demeaning personal service to his royal patron. Thus Colbert wrote to Louis on the occasion of a military victory: 'One must, Sire, remain in silent wonder, and thank God every day for having caused us to be born in the reign of a king like Your Majesty'. And no service to the Sun King was too demeaning. Colbert searched for the king's missing swans, supplied

Louis with his favourite oranges, arranged for the birth of the king's illegitimate children, and bought jewels for mistresses on the king's behalf. Colbert's
personal philosophy was best summed up in his advice to his beloved son,
Seignelay, on how to get ahead in the world. He told his son that 'the chief
end that he should set himself is to make himself agreeable to the king, he
should work with great industry, during his whole life to know well what
might be agreeable to His Majesty'.

Colbert was well rewarded for his life of hard work and abject sycophancy
in the service of the king. Apparently only the interests of individual merchants and citizens were narrow and 'petty'. Colbert had little difficulty in
identifying the lucrative feathering of his own nest with the 'public interest',
national glory, and the common weal. A stream of offices, benefices, pensions and grants streamed into his coffers from the ever grateful king. In
addition, Colbert received special bonuses or 'gratifications' from the king;
thus, in one order, in February 1679, Colbert received a gratification of no
less than 400 000 *livres*. The overall sum poured into Colbert's coffers was
immense, including lands, and bribes for subsidies and exemptions from
grateful lobbyists and economic interests. All in all, he amassed at least 10
million *livres*, notable to be sure, but not the enormous extent of Cardinal
Mazarin's boodle as prime minister.

Colbert also did extremely well by his extensive family. Brothers, cousins,
sons and daughters of Colbert were showered with favours, and became
bishops, ambassadors, military commanders, *intendants*, and abbesses of
leading convents. The Colbert family certainly did well by doing 'good' on
behalf of the sovereign and the 'public interest' of France.

After Colbert's death in 1683, his successors under Louis XIV developed
and strengthened the policy of *Colbertisme*. Protective tariffs were greatly
increased, imports of various goods limited to specific ports, quality regulations strengthened, and innovations hobbled for the protection of the industrial and occupational status quo. *Colbertisme* was frozen into the French
political economy.

8.8 Louis XIV: apogee of absolutism (1638–1714)

For his part, Louis XIV had no trouble fitting the absolutist role. Even more
than Colbert, he totally identified his own private interest as monarch with
the interests of the state and with the 'public good'. Whether or not Louis
uttered the famous words often attributed to him, 'I am the state', he certainly
believed and acted upon them, as did his father Louis XIII before him, who
had said, 'It is not I who speak, it is my state'. Statism logically implies that
the state owns all the property in the land, and that all who live on or use such
property do so only by the sufferance of the 'true' owner. And Louis certainly
believed that he was the true owner of all property in France. Hence justice

was '*my* justice', and hence he claimed the inherent right to tax all his subjects at will. And why not indeed, if they were all truly existing in his realm only at his, the owner's pleasure?

Furthermore, virtually everyone, even the king's opponents, believed that he ruled by divine grace and divine right. Previously, Cardinal Richelieu had called kings the images of God. Early in the Sun King's reign, court propagandist Daniel de Priézac, in his *Political Discourses* (1652, 1666), called monarchical sovereignty a 'great light that never sets'. Furthermore, that light is a great divine Mystery hidden from mere mortals. As de Priézac put it:

> the source of the majesty of kings is so high, its essence so hidden and its force so divine that it should not seem strange that it should make men reverent without their being permitted to understand it, just as is true with celestial things.[2]

In contrast to the adulatory worshippers at the shrine of the king's quasi-divinity were the Montaigne-type sceptics and pessimists about human nature who fed the stream of panegyrics to Louis XIV in their own way. In a set of three *Sceptical Discourses* (1664), the cynical Samuel Sorbière, admirer and translator of Thomas Hobbes, decried the tendencies of bestial and corrupt modern man in grabbing from the public trough and having no sense of the common good. But there is, opined Sorbière, a way out: absolute submission to the commands of the (presumably superhuman) king, so that order is established out of perpetual conflict. In that total submission, the people will find their way back to the instinctual child-like simplicity of the state of nature preceding their entry into civil society. As Professor Keohane writes of Sorbière: 'as the subjects of an absolute despot, they would live much the same way, he argues, in serene simplicity, totally dependent on the sovereign for their lives and fortunes, protected against the encroachments of their fellows, happy in their slavery'[3]

King Louis XIV was able to combine both strands into a worshipful blend of absolutist thought. On the one hand, as he makes clear in his private *Memoirs*, written for the instruction of his son, his view of human nature (at least of the nature of ordinary mortals) was pessimistic and Machiavellian. Individuals are by nature limited, striving always for their own personal ends, and heedless of the reasons why they should be subordinated to the commands of others. The king, on the other hand, is superhuman, a man who is above all and sees all and is the only one working for the 'public' good, which is identical with his own. And the Sun King also took unto himself quasi-divine status; for he, Louis XIV, is like the sun,

> the noblest of all…which, by virtue of its uniqueness, by the brilliance that surrounds it, by the light it imparts to the other heavenly bodies that seem to pay it

court, by its equal and just distribution of this same light to all the various parts of the world, by the good that it does everywhere, constantly producing life, joy, and activity everywhere, by its perpetual yet always imperceptible movement, by never departing or deviating from its steady and invariable course, assuredly makes a most vivid and a most beautiful image for a great monarch.

Professor Keohane justly comments that Louis XIV 'is not content to compare himself to God; he compares in such a manner that it is clear that it is God who is the copy'.[4]

The acme of absolutist thought was provided by Jacques-Bénigne Bossuet (1627–1704), bishop of Meaux, court theologian and political theorist under Louis XIV. The whole state, opined the bishop, 'is in the person of the prince...In him is the will of the whole people'. The kings identify with the public good, because 'God has raised them to a condition where they no longer have anything to desire for themselves'. Absolutism is necessary, asserted Bossuet, because any constitutional limits on the prince raise the dread spectre of 'anarchy', than which nothing can be worse. The only limits on the power of the sovereign should be those he imposes on himself in his own interest, which must be identical to the public interest whenever the prince 'regards the state as his possession, to be cultivated and passed on to his descendants'.

Finally, Bossuet conflates the king and God as follows:

Majesty is the image of the grandeur of God in the prince. God is infinite, God is all. The prince, as prince, is not to be considered an individual man: he is the public person, the whole state is included in him...Just as all perfection and all virtue are united in God, so all the power of the individuals is brought together in the person of the prince. What grandeur, that a single man can contain so much.[5]

Catholic political thought had come a long way from the Spanish scholastics.

8.9 Notes

1. Charles Woolsey Cole, *Colbert and a Century of French Mercantilism* (1939, Hamden, Conn.: Archon Books, 1964), vol. I, p. 85.
2. Quoted in Nannerl O. Keohane, *Philosophy and the State in France: The Renaissance to the Enlightenment* (Princeton, NJ: Princeton University Press, 1980), p. 241.
3. Ibid., p. 244.
4. Passage from the *Memoirs* quoted in Keohane, op. cit., note 2, p. 251.
5. Quoted in Keohane, op. cit., note 2, p. 252.

9 The liberal reaction against mercantilism in seventeenth century France

9.1   The *croquants'* rebellion

The kings and their minions did not impose an accelerating burden of absolutism without provoking grave, deep and continuing opposition. Indeed, there were repeated rebellions by groups of peasants and nobles in France from the 1630s to the 1670s. Generally, the focus of discontent and uprising was rising taxes, as well as the losses of rights and privileges. There were also similar rebellions in Spain, in mid-century, and in autocratic Russia, throughout the seventeenth century.

Consider, for example, the remonstrances of the peasants in the first great French rebellion of the seventeenth century, the *croquants'* (literally, 'crunchers') revolt in 1636 in south-western France. The *croquants'* rebellion was precipitated by a sudden near-doubling of direct taxes upon the peasantry to raise funds for the war against Spain. The *intendant* La Force, sent to investigate the disturbances, reported on the peasants' grievances and demands. The peasants focused on the eternal and acclerating increases of taxation. They pointed out that in the reign of Henry IV more taxes had been collected than in all previous reigns of the monarchy taken together; and that in but two years of the reign of Louis XIII they had paid more than in all the years of Henry IV. The peasants also protested that the royal tax-collectors carried off their cattle, clothes and tools, merely to cover the costs of enforcement, so that the principal of the tax debt could never be reduced. The result was ruin. Deprived of their means of labour, the peasants had been forced to leave their fields untilled, and even to leave their ancient lands and beg for bread. In a letter to his superior, La Force feels compelled to endorse their complaints: 'It is not, Monseigneur, that I am not, by natural feeling, touched with very great compassion when I see the extraordinary poverty in which these people live'.

The peasants protested that they were not subversives; they were willing to pay the old customary taxes, provided the recent increases were repealed. New taxes should only be imposed in extreme emergencies, and then only by the states-general (which hadn't met since 1615, and was not to meet again until the eve of the French Revolution). Like deluded subjects at all times and places, the peasants placed the blame for their ills not on the king himself but on his evil and tyrannical ministers, who had led the sovereign astray. The peasants insisted that they had had to revolt in order that 'their cries may reach the ears of the King himself and no longer just those of his Ministers, who advise him so badly'. Whether a ruler be king or president, it is convenient for him to preserve his popularity by deflecting protest and hostility to advisers or prime ministers who surround him.

But despite this unfortunate limitation, the *croquants* had the insight and the wit to zero in on the 'public interest' myth propounded by the royal ministers. The 'needs of the state', the peasants declared, were only a 'pretext for enriching a few private persons' – the hated tax farmers, who had bought the privilege from the Crown of collecting taxes which then went into their pockets; and the 'creatures of the man who rules the state', i.e. Richelieu and his entourage. The peasants called for the abolition of courtiers' pensions, as well as the salaries of all the newly created officials.

The following year, 1637, the *croquants* of the neighbouring region of Périgord rose in rebellion. Addressing King Louis XIII, the commune of Périgord set forth its reasons for the revolt: 'Sire..., we have taken an unusual step in the way we have expressed our grievances, but this is so that we may be listened to by Your Majesty....' Their overriding grievance was against the tax farmers and tax officials, who 'have sent among us a thousand thieves who eat up the flesh of the poor husbandmen to the very bones, and it is they who have forced them to take up arms, changing their ploughshares for swords, in order to ask Your Majesty for justice or else to die like men'.

Shaken by the rebellion, the Crown organized its faithful servitors. The royal printer, F. Mettayer, published a statement by the 'inhabitants of the town of Poitiers', denouncing the 'seditious' commune of Périgord. The Poitiers men declared that 'We know, as Christians and loyal Frenchmen, that the glory of Kings is to command, while the glory of subjects, whoever they may be, is to obey in all humility and willing submission...following God's express commandment'. All the people of France know that the king is the life and soul of the state. The king is directly guided by the Holy Spirit, and further, 'by the superhuman decisions of your royal mind and the miracles accomplished in your happy reign, we perceive plainly that God holds your heart in his hand'. There is therefore only one explanation for the rebellion, concluded the Poitiers loyalists: the rebels must be tools of Satan.

Not all the Catholics agreed, nor even the Catholic clergy of France. In 1639, an armed rebellion broke out in Normandy, resting on two demands: an opposition to oppressive taxation, and a call for Norman autonomy as against the centralized Parisian regime. It was a multi-class movement of the relatively poor, grouped together in an 'army of suffering', and calling themselves the *Nu-Pieds* – the barefoot ones – after the salt-makers in the southwestern Norman region of Avranches, who walked barefoot on the sand. The general of the army was a mythical figure named Jean Nu-Pieds; the actual directorate of the army consisted of four priests from the Avranches area, of whom the leader was Father Jean Morel, parish priest of Saint-Gervais. Morel called himself 'Colonel Sandhills', but he was a poet–propagandist as well as army commander. In his 'manifesto of the High Unconquerable Captain Jean Nu-Pieds, General of the Army of Suffering', directed against the 'men made rich by their taxes', Father Morel wrote:

> And I, shall I leave a people languishing

> Beneath the heel of tyranny, and allow a *crowd of outsiders* [non-Normans]
> To oppress this people daily with their tax-farms?

The reference to 'outsiders' shows the continuing strength of particularist, or separatist national movements in France, in this case Normandy. The Norman and *croquants* movements were rising against centralizing Parisian imperialism imposed only recently on independent or autonomous nations as much as against the high taxes themselves.

9.2   Claude Joly and the *fronde*

The most prominent rebellions in the mid-seventeenth century France were those of the nobles and the judges and known as the *fronde*. The leading theoretician of the parliamentary (judges') *fronde* was Claude Joly, whose *Receuil de maximes veritables* was published in 1653. Joly's treatise was a collection of constitutionalist maxims, remnants of a pre-absolutist age, and included trenchant attacks on two contributions of Cardinals Richelieu and Mazarin to political thought and practice in France. One was the new notion that the king is rightly the master – in effect the owner – of the persons and property of all inhabitants of France. The other was the Machiavellian view that successful public policy requires the systematic use of immoral means.

The king's power, warned Joly, is limited and not automatically sanctioned by divine law. Frenchmen possess just title to their lives and properties, and are not the slaves of a despot or tyrant. The king's original divine power is mediated through the French people, Joly added, and the king cannot rightfully tax the French without the consent of the states-general. The fact that Joly was reviled by the king and his party as a rebel and a traitor, he declared, shows that the old constitution has been overcome by new views holding the king to have unlimited authority above all law. For Joly, this new view was 'pure usurpation', bred in the monstrous cauldron of 'Machiavel'.

9.3   A single tax

In the late sixteenth century, Jean Bodin and others had raised the question of removing many or all of the crippling network of taxation, and substituting a single universal direct tax proportionate to property or income. With taxes far higher and more oppressive by the mid-seventeenth century, the call for a simpler, single direct tax was heard once again. Not only the people, but even the Crown, would benefit by eliminating a legion of unproductive and parasitic tax farmers and other tax officials.

One of the earliest of these tax reformers was Isaac Loppin, who published *Les mines gallicanes* in 1638. The tract went through four editions, including one during the *fronde* era in 1648, and directly influenced later tax reformers. Loppin explained how all members of society, from the poorest to the king, suffered from the depredations of the tax officials: 'without excepting even the sacred person of His Majesty, there is not a single inhabitant of his Kingdom who, from the top of his head to the soles of his feet, does not carry some vestment or eat some food which is not burdened by the said subsidies and imposts'. Loppin urged the abolition of all existing taxes, and their replacement by a small fixed tax per year on the wealthiest 10 per cent of the population.

Loppin's pamphlet greatly influenced a one-time assistant to the secretary of state for foreign affairs, the Sieur de Bresson. Bresson addressed a tract to King Louis XIV in 1675, entitled *Propositions au Roi*. He realistically denounced the tax 'officials and exacters' as having 'no other goal than their private interests'. He then pointed out that the king himself was at the mercy of the tax collectors, and repeated the above quotation from Loppin word for word. Bresson divided up the wealthiest 10 per cent or so of the non-privileged into 19 income classes, and suggested a single direct tax upon them, graduated by class.

In the meanwhile, in 1668, Geraud de Cordemoy urged his own single tax plan upon the government. In his *Letter Concerning the Reform of State*, Cordemoy urged a single head tax, payable by everyone. He set forth the plan in the form of a dream recounting an ideal state in a distant land, a land enjoying such a single head tax (or capitation) paid 'by each person' for the 'charges and necessities of state'. Furthermore, in an unusual twist, Cordemoy declared that such a head tax would be 'voluntary', since everyone would know that he was much better off then he had been in the current, existing system.

An immensely popular work, written about the same time, was Paul Hay, Marquis du Chastelet's *Traité de la politique de la France*. The *Traité* was written in 1667, with copies circulating throughout France until its publication two years later. Attacking the oppressive burden of taxation, Chastelet called for a tax on property extending to the previously exempt estates of the nobility, and the transformation of the onerous salt tax into a universal direct tax on income. He also urged relief of the tax burden on the peasantry by accepting payment in kind as a legal substitute for specie.

A more radical plan, originating in the late 1650s, was conceived by a marshall of France, and governor of the principality of Sedan, Abraham de Fabert. Fabert died in 1662, but in 1679, an unknown author presented the Fabert plan to the chancellor of France. Fabert had called for transformation of the salt tax into a graduated direct tax upon the non-privileged members of society. This plan was not designed as a single tax, but 'all new taxes' could be abolished, and other taxes could be brought down to their original rates. Reminiscent of Bresson, Fabert's plan was to divide the non-privileged Frenchmen into 30 income classes, the tax graduated by class. Collection costs for enforcing the tax would be reduced to a minimum, and the king would be liberated from 100 000 'blood-sucking' tax officials. In 1684, a second edition of the Fabert-based pamphlet added a substantial amount of statistical backing to the plan.

9.4   Rising opposition to collectivism by merchants and nobles

The imposition of Colbert's regime of statism, monopoly and prohibitive tariffs, combined with Louis XIV's high taxation and centralization, gave rise, by the late 1660s, to a growing tide of opposition by merchants and nobility alike. An important compendium of criticisms was the anonymous treatise, *Mémoires pour servir à l'histoire*, published in 1668. The *Mémoires* comprise the first extended published polemic against Colbert and Colbertism. Politically, the author denounced Colbert for substituting centralizing innovations for the old constitution. Attacking Colbert's policies across the board, especially tariffs and monopolies, the book pointed out that the French refusal to purchase from the Dutch had induced the Dutch to cease purchasing from France. On trade, the *Mémoires* made the important point that the Colbertian ideal of national self-sufficiency was contrary to natural law, since providence had created a great diversity of natural resources throughout the world, in order that mankind be united by the bonds of mutual interdependence through international trade.

After an upsurge of denunciations of Colbert in the late 1660s, the controller-general reacted by cracking down on all dissent. In consequence, when Colbert died on 6 September 1683, there was intense joy throughout France, and especially in Paris. In fact, only protection by the soldiery prevented the populace from demonstrating their attitude by dragging Colbert's body through the streets of Paris. Many oppressed Frenchman exulted that a new dawn had arrived: 'Taxes would cease and the Golden Age would return'.

Such was not to be, however, and absolutism and consequent economic distress became even worse. But the death of Colbert allowed a raft of dissent to arise once more. A torrent of hatred poured out against Colbert's son, nephew, and other of his hand-picked successors.[1] The outpouring of opposition, encouraged by official inquiries and investigations of the Colbertian past, was not merely personal, however. It was also in opposition to the mercantilism stifling the economy. In May 1684, a nobleman accused Colbert of being responsible for the 'ruin of finance and trade'. The establishment of subsidized and privileged manufactures 'has deprived commerce of liberty…and denied merchants the means to attract money from abroad'. The high protective tariffs, the unknown nobleman pointed out, crippled foreign demand for French farm products, and thereby reduced the French farmers to penury.

This line of attack on Colbertism was developed in the following year by Gatien de Courtilz de Sanras, Sieur du Verger, who published a book on *The*

New Interests of the Princes of Europe. Trying to bolster domestic producers, the French government had only succeeded in wrecking them by crippling their export markets. This popular work had gone into four editions by 1689. In the same year, the famous collection of tracts, published in Amsterdam, *Les soupirs de la France esclave* (*The Sighs of an Enslaved France*) also inveighed against protective tariffs as leading to misery and the crushing of commerce.

Particularly eloquent in the *Soupirs* collection was the attack on Colbertism by the merchant Michel le Vassor, who wrote:

> the king by the frightful and excessive taxes which he levies on all goods has drawn to himself all the money, and commerce has dried up. There are no rigors and cruelties which have not been employed upon the merchants by the farmers of the customs, a thousand trickeries to find grounds for making confiscations... Besides this, certain merchants, through the favor of the Court, put commerce into monopoly and get privileges given to them to exclude all the others...And finally the prohibition of foreign goods, far from turning out well for commerce, is, on the contrary, what has ruined it...And all through this the despotic and sovereign power which prides itself on every whim, on reordering everything and reforming all things by an absolute power.[2]

During this depressed period, the directors of Colbert's French East India Company denied, in 1685, that they had caused the hard times by exporting specie in order to import goods from the Indies. Arguing for 'freedom of trade' in their *Responses aux mémoires*, when they really only valued *their own* freedom to import from their privileged monopoly position, the directors yet tapped an important vein of free trade thought:

> Experience has shown that trade cannot be conducted without a total liberty and with a mutual correspondence with foreign countries. The moment we...violated [trade]...the foreigners withdrew. They attracted French workers and established our manufactures in their country...and have dispensed with ours.

The directors also defended vigorously their practice of exporting specie in exchange for Asian imports. They escalated their reply by pointing out that in Holland (always a country whose prosperity and trade was admired and envied during the seventeenth century)

> the ports are always open for the entry and exit of specie with every possible liberty...moreover, in Holland the same liberty is accorded for the export of money in the coin of the country. It is this great freedom which attracts abundance to the point where it is and renders them [the Dutch] masters of all trade.

During the intense merchant agitation for freedom of trade and enterprise during the 1680s, Louis XIV's *intendant* at Rouen reported on advice given him by two leading merchants of the city. On 5 October 1685, René de Marillac wrote to the controller-general that the two merchants had declared:

> The greatest secret is to leave trade entirely free; men are sufficiently attracted to it by their own interests...Never have manufactures been so depressed, and trade also, since we have taken it into our heads to increase them by way of authority.

One of these two merchants, Thomas Le Gendre, was supposed to have been the first, during a slightly earlier period, to have coined the famous phrase, *laissez-faire*. The great late eighteenth century *laissez-faire* thinker and states-man, Anne Robert Jacques Turgot, reports as a family tradition that Le Gendre had told Colbert: '*Laissez-nous faire*' (leave us alone). Turgot's afflu-ent grandparents were close friends of the immensely wealthy Le Gendre and his family, and they also had mutual business dealings.

Thomas Le Gendre (1638–1706), coiner of the phrase *laissez-faire* as applied to policies and the economy, was the most eminent of a long line of merchant-bankers traced back to the early sixteenth century. A multi-million-aire, Le Gendre owned vast interests in Africa and the New World, was the leading importer of alum from the Levant, and was frequently called upon to arbitrate disputes between merchants at home and abroad.

Despite his wealth, multi-national commercial connections, and public honours, Thomas Le Gendre had what seemed to be only a negative rather than positive influence upon the French government. Time and again the Crown refused to allow him permission to send vessels abroad or to load merchandise on to foreign ships. This treatment only changed in the 1690s, when the government, engaged in war with Protestant England and Holland, made use of Le Gendre and other ex-Protestants to trade with their contacts in those countries while the war was going on.

Not only the merchants, but also some *intendants*, were joining the *laissez-faire* camp during the 1680s. On 29 August 1686 the *intendant* in Flanders, Dugué de Bagnols, wrote a bitter protest against a decree of the previous year levying a 20 per cent tariff on imports from the Levant, except for goods carried on French ships from the Middle East that had entered the ports of Marseille or Rouen. Dugué pointed out that textile firms in northern France should not have to pay more for their imported thread by being forced to buy it from inefficient French ships. And all to subsidize Marseille merchants and shippers who could not compete suc-cessfully with the English and Dutch in the Levant! Dugué generalized this insight into a *laissez-faire* position:

> Trade can flourish and subsist only when merchants are free to procure the merchandise they need in the places where they are [sold] at the lowest price, and every time we wish to compel them to buy in one place at the exclusion of all

others, merchandise will become more expensive and trade will consequently fall into ruin.[3]

9.5   The merchants and the council of commerce

In June 1700, King Louis XIV, seeking advice from the nation's leading merchants, established a council of commerce, in which merchants of ten leading towns elected ten deputies who would serve as a kind of advisory economic parliament. The king soon came to regret this step, for the merchants' representatives seized the occasion to unleash a torrent of attack against the mercantilist polices developed by the Sun King.[4]

In particular, the enraged merchants zeroed in on the grants of monopoly privilege bestowed by the government on chartered companies. Pointing out that such monopolies restrict trade and raise prices, a number of merchants declared: 'It is a most certain maxim that nothing but competition and liberty in trade can render commerce beneficial to the State; and that all monopolies or traffic appropriated to companies exclusive of others are infinitely burdensome and pernicious'.

The most consistent and most radical of the merchants' voices was the deputy from the western port city of Nantes, Joachim Descazeaux du Hallay, a wealthy shipper and merchant and former associate of Thomas Le Gendre. Arguing vehemently against privileged monopolies that restrict trade, Descazeaux widened his argument into a general plea for freedom and free competition. Free competition, Descazeaux pointed out, benefits the public by supplying abundant goods at low prices. Even business losses, he declared perceptively, benefit the public, since they reflect plentiful production at low prices. Furthermore, liberty causes innovations and fuels the spirit of enterprise:

> Liberty is the soul and element of commerce; she excites the genius and application of merchants who never cease to meditate on new methods to make discoveries and found enterprises. [Liberty] kindles a perpetual movement which produces abundance everywhere. The moment we limit the genius of merchants by restrictions, we destroy trade.

9.6   Marshal Vauban: royal engineer and single taxer

The bluff, hearty, patriotic Maréchal Sebastian Le Prestre, Seigneur de Vauban (1633–1707), was scarcely a fervent or militant oppositionist to royal or Colbertist policies. The leading military engineer in France, the man who constructed the mighty military fortifications guarding the French state, ennobled by Louis XIV for his services, was scarcely an opponent of the Crown. Although a loyal monarchist and absolutist, Vauban, after revocation of the Edict of Nantes in 1685, grew deeply troubled at the policies of Louis XIV, especially the crippling system of taxation as well as the oppression of the Huguenots. Upon the revocation, the naive Vauban, convinced that the good king was surrounded by evil or purblind advisers, wrote a *Mémoire* for the recall of the Huguenots' addressed to the king. Vauban pointed out that the revocation had disrupted trade and commerce, and was causing opposition to the monarchy itself.

The heedlessness of the king did not daunt Vauban, who continued to write similar pleas to King Louis. Finally, at the end of his life, in 1707, this man who had risen from birth in poverty in St Leger to become the land's greatest military engineer, a marshal and a nobleman, published his comprehensive treatise, *Projet de dixme royale* (*Project for a royal tithe*). Vauban proposed the abolition of most of the oppressive network of taxation, and its replacement by a single tax, a proportional tenth of the income of each subject. The reasoning was that the state provided the people with the service of security, and that those who receive such service should pay accordingly. One wonders, however, how anyone can demonstrate that those who receive such a service are enjoying the service in proportion to their income. Furthermore, *every other* service on the market is paid for, not in proportion to the buyer's income, but in a uniform single price, paid by one and all. The purchasers of bread, or automobiles, or stereo sets, pay a single price for each product, and not in proportion to their income or wealth. Why then do so for the alleged service of security?

At any rate, Vauban was highly effective in pointing out that the impoverished producers of the country were shouldering a large part of the burden of taxation, and was eloquent in urging their relief.

Vauban refused to publish the *Dixme royale* widely in 1707, and only circulated a small number of copies among friends. This did not save the aged marshal from Louis XIV's wrath, however. The king's censors and police condemned the book, and the publishers were hunted down and punished. Marshal Vauban died on the day the king's order was executed.

9.7   Fleury, Fénélon, and the Burgundy circle

During the early 1670s, the devout Abbé Claude Fleury (1640–1723), a young theologian, moralist, and man of letters, launched an influential opposition to the absolutism and mercantilism of Louis XIV. In a small pamphlet, *Pensées politiques*, Fleury upheld the agrarian ideal and opposed the mercantilist forced subsidization of industry. Furthermore, in a companion work, *Reflections on the works of Machiavelli*, Fleury attacked Montaigne-type scepticism, which resulted in endorsing an unrestrained exercise of power over depraved men who were virtually devoid of reason. He also denounced Machiavelli's view that politics should be divorced from ethics. Combining the latter themes, Fleury contended that man can use reason to take the path of justice and virtue, while Machiavelli's prince was a godless tyrant who had no desire to lead his subjects to happiness. In contrast to Machiavelli's view that 'men are bad', Fleury countered sensibly that 'they are for the most part neither very bad nor very good', and that the ruler had the duty to improve their virtue and happiness.

The outstanding clerical opponent of absolutism and mercantilism in late seventeenth century France, however, was not so much Fleury as his friend and student, François de Salignac de la Mothe, Archbishop Fénélon of Cambrai (1651–1715). Fénélon led a powerful cabal at court who were deeply opposed to the absolutist and mercantilist policies of the king and determined to reform them in the direction of free trade, limited government and *laissez-faire*. By means of his post as religious instructor to the king's mistress, Madame de Maintenon,[5] Fénélon got himself appointed in 1689 as preceptor to the royal children, in particular the young Duke of Burgundy, grandson of Louis XIV, who seemed destined one day to be king. Assisted by Fleury, Fénélon made the duke into a disciple, surrounding him with ardent oppositionists to the policies of the Sun King.

In 1693, Fénélon, incensed at the continuing wars against the English and Dutch, wrote the king an impassioned and hard-hitting though anonymous letter, which he probably sent only to Madame de Maintenon. Blaming the king's evil ministers, he declared:

> Sire...for the past thirty years your...ministers have violated and overturned all the ancient maxims of state in order to raise your power, which was theirs because it was in their hands, to the highest possible point. We no longer heard of the State nor of its rules; they only spoke of the King and his pleasure. They have increased your revenues and your expenditures to the infinite. They have elevated you to the heavens...and impoverished all of France so as to introduce and maintain an incurable and monstrous luxury at Court. They wanted to raise you on the ruins of all classes in the State, as if you could become great by oppressing your subjects...

The king's ministers, Fénélon continued, only wish to crush all who resist. They have made the king's name 'odious', have wanted 'only slaves', and have 'caused bloody wars'. The wars and their attendant taxes have crushed trade and the poor, driving the people to desperation 'by exacting from them for your wars, the bread which they have endeavored to earn with the sweat from their brows'.[6]

Fénélon's *magnum opus* was his political novel, *Télémaque*, written for the edification of the young Duke of Burgundy, on whom he and his confrères pinned all the hopes for the radical liberalization of France. *Télémaque* was written during 1695 and 1696, and published without his permission in 1699. Télémaque was a mythical young prince, who travelled through the world of antiquity seeking instruction on the wisest forms of government. What

Télémaque learned were the lessons of pure *laissez-faire*. For example, young Télémaque asked Mentor, a wise man among the Phoenicians, how that people was able to flourish so remarkably in world commerce. Mentor answered, *laissez-faire*:

> Above all never do anything to interfere with trade in order to turn it to your views. The Prince must not concern himself [with trade] for fear of hindering it. He must leave all profits to his subjects who earned them, otherwise they will become discouraged...Trade is like certain springs; if you turn them from their course they will dry up. Profit and convenience can alone attract foreigners to your shores; if you make trade difficult and less useful for them they will gradually withdraw and not return...[7]

Similarly, in the land of Salente, 'the liberty of commerce was entire', by which Fénélon explicitly meant the absence of state interference in domestic as well as foreign trade. Every good entered and left the country with complete freedom; trade 'was similar to the ebb and flow of the tide'.

In his *Treatise on the Existence of God*, Fénélon attacked mercantilist nationalism by stressing the unity of all peoples dispersed over the earth. Moreover, he stressed that human reason is 'independent and above man, [and] is the same in all countries'. And just as God unites all peoples through a common and universal reason, so the sea and the earth unite mankind by providing communication and resources which can be exchanged for one another. Fénélon waxed eloquent on natural specialization and free trade uniting all peoples:

> It is the effect of a wise overruling Providence that no land yields all that is useful to human life. For want invites men to commerce, in order to supply one another's necessities. Want therefore is the natural tie of society between nations; otherwise all peoples would be reduced to one sort of food and clothing, and nothing would invite them to know and visit one another.

Following his mentor Fleury, Fénélon stressed the importance and productivity of agriculture, and attacked rulers for impoverishing the countryside through crippling taxation, and for diverting resources from agriculture to luxury products.

Fénélon was eloquent in his attack on tyranny and absolutism. Absolute monarchs, he thundered:

> take all and ruin everything. They are sole possessors of the entire state, but the whole realm languishes. The countryside is uncultivated and almost deserted, towns diminish every day, trade stagnates...The King's absolute power creates as many slaves as he has subjects...This monstrous power swollen to its most violent excess cannot endure; it has no support in the heart of the people...At the first blow the idol will fall, crack and be crushed underfoot. Contempt, hate, vengeance, defiance, in a word all passions will unite against so odious a rule.

To Fénélon, 'war is the greatest of evils', and France's pernicious policy of constant wars was the result of her nationalist and mercantilist economic policies. Cursed be those rulers, declared Fénélon, who augment their power at the expense of other nations and who seek a 'monstrous glory' in the blood of their fellow men.

To educate the young duke of Burgundy on the evils of war, Fénélon engaged a man who was called 'one of the cleverest men of the century'. François Le Blanc had published a massive treatise on money and coinage in 1690 (*An Historical Treatise on the Moneys of France from the beginning of the Monarchy until the Present*). There Le Blanc had condemned kings for engaging in debasement for their monetary profit. Fénélon commissioned Le Blanc to write a tome for the young duke on all the treaties between the nations of Europe, and the causes and consequences of all the wars that ensued, as well as the ways they might have been avoided. Unfortunately, Le Blanc died before he could finish this monumental task.

One of the key figures in the Burgundy circle was Charles de Sainte-Maure, the duc de Montausier. Montausier was governor of the royal dauphin, and Le Blanc (before taking on the book) and Abbé Fleury were both employees in the service of Montausier. Le Blanc's place in teaching the duke had been preceded by Pierre Daniel Huet, bishop of Avranches. Huet, a friend of Le Blanc, denounced French mercantilist and protectionist policies in 1694, and praised the free trade that had brought prosperity to the Dutch.

In 1711, the Grand Dauphin, son of Louis XIV, died, and the Burgundy circle was overjoyed, since the duke was now in line for the throne to succeed the aged Sun King. But tragedy struck the following year, when the duke, his wife and his eldest son were all struck dead of measles. All the hopes, all the plans, were cruelly destroyed and, Fénélon wrote to a friend in despair, 'Men work by their education to form a subject full of courage and ornamented by knowledge; then God comes along to destroy this house of cards...'.

The tragic end of the Burgundy circle illuminates a crucial strategic flaw in the plans, not only of the Burgundy circle, but also of the physiocrats, Turgot, and other *laissez-faire* thinkers of the later eighteenth century. For their hopes and their strategic vision were invariably to work within the matrix of the monarchy and its virtually absolute rule. The idea, in short, was to get into court, influence the corridors of power, and induce the king to adopt libertarian ideas and impose a *laissez-faire* revolution, so to speak, from the top. If the king could not be persuaded directly, then a new king's ideas and values would be formed from childhood by liberal preceptors and tutors.

Reliance on the good will of the king, however, suffered from several inherent defects. One, as in the case of the Duke of Burgundy, was reliance on the existence and good health of one person. A second is a more systemic flaw: Even if one can convince the king that the interests of his subjects require liberty and *laissez-faire*, the standard argument that *his own* revenue will increase proportionately to their prosperity is a shaky one. For the king's revenue might well be maximized, certainly in the short run and even in the long run, by tyrannically sweating his subjects to attain the maximum possible revenue. And relying on the altruism of the monarch is a shaky reed at best. For all these reasons, appealing to a monarch to impose *laissez-faire* from above can only be a losing strategy. A far better strategy would have been to organize a mass opposition from below among the ruled and exploited masses, an opposition that would have given *laissez-faire* a far more solid groundwork in adherence by the bulk of the population. In the long run, of course, mass opposition, even revolution, was precisely what happened to France, a revolution from below that was partially if not largely inspired by *laissez-faire* ideals. The erudite and sophisticated *laissez-faire* thinkers of the seventeenth and eighteenth centuries, however, would have rebuffed such a suggested strategy as certainly inconvenient and probably lunatic, especially in the light of the failure of the various inchoate peasant and other *fronde* rebellions of the mid-seventeenth century. Not least of all, men of influential and privileged status themselves are rarely inclined to toss all their privileges aside to engage in the lonely and dangerous task of working outside the inherited political system.

9.8 The *laissez-faire* utilitarian: the Seigneur de Belesbat

One of the influential anti-mercantilist and pro-*laissez-faire* thinkers of the last decades of Louis XIV was Charles Paul Hurault de l'Hopital, Seigneur de Belesbat (d. 1706). The great-grandson of a chancellor of France, Belesbat was an influential member, during the 1690s, of an oppositional political salon in the Luxembourg palace in the Luxembourg gardens district of Paris. The salon met weekly at the home of Belesbat's first cousin, François Thimoleon, the abbé de Choisy.

In the autumn of 1692, Belesbat presented six memoirs to Louis XIV, copies and extracts of which were reproduced throughout France. Belesbat, too, focused on the wars with the Dutch as being the key to the economic problems of France. States became wealthy, advised Belesbat, not by seizing or destroying the commerce of other nations, but by encouraging trade that conformed to the natural interest of the nation. Instead of the French government trying artificially to capture Dutch commerce, it should allow its own agriculture to flourish.

Belesbat, too, emphasized that God had woven all peoples into an interdependent network of reciprocal advantage by means of trade and specialization: 'There is nothing that one [country] lacks which the others do not produce. ...God...having created men for society, has so well divided them that they cannot do without one another'. Restrictions on trade by government only crippled this natural interdependence; therefore, merchants should be free to pursue 'the commerce of their choice'. The direction of economic activities in each country is usually determined by the natural resources and the type of capital investment in that area.

It is not the case, concluded Belesbat, that trade in one country benefits one party at the expense of others. Instead, the reverse is true. Moreover, freedom for merchants in domestic trade was as important as in foreign trade. The network of trade and exchange is internal as well as external. Furthermore, in a prefigurement of the Hayekian argument for the free market, Belesbat noted, as Professor Rothkrug points out, that

> Every transaction, either domestic or foreign, required complete freedom because it was carried out in special circumstances by merchants whose fortunes depended partially upon the secret and unique procedures by which each conducted his business.[8]

State regulation, then, far from protecting the market, would cripple the liberty necessary to any prosperous trade. Natural resources, Belesbat explained, are worthless without people to cultivate them and to engage in trade and commerce. Belesbat then engaged in a sophisticated analysis of the elements necessary for successful market activity:

> We call commerce an exchange between men of the things they mutually need...In both [domestic and foreign trade] the principles for success are the same. And despite the fact that there is an infinite number of ways in which to practice trade, all different, they are founded on a great liberty, large capital investment, a lot of good faith, much application, and a great secrecy. Each merchant, having his particular views, in such a way that he who profits from a sale of his products, does not prevent the one who buys them from profiting considerably by disposing of them...Thus the entire success of commerce, consisting as it does in liberty, large capital investment, application, and secrecy, prevents princes from ever intervening without destroying the principles.

Thus Belesbat, in addition to a sensitive appreciation of the role of individual entrepreneurship and energy by the merchant, and of the mutual profitability of exchange, sees, if only vaguely, that the great variety of individual trade can yet be analysed correctly in a small number of formal laws, laws or truths which apply to all entrepreneurship and exchange.

In one vital area, Belesbat advanced significantly beyond the *laissez-faire* views of Fénélon and others, who were so opposed to the luxury of the absolutist court and the *nouveau riche* bureaucracy that they wished the government to restrict luxury production and trade. Belesbat swept away such inconsistent exceptions to *laissez-faire*. The natural laws of trade, which for him encompassed considerations of utility, applied to luxury as well as to all other branches of production and trade.

Belesbat eloquently concluded from his analysis that 'It must be taken as a principle that liberty is the soul of commerce, without which...good harbors, great rivers, and...fertile [lands] are of no use. When liberty is absent nothing is of any avail'.[9] In short, the government should 'let commerce go where it wishes' (*laissant faire le commerce que l'on voudra*).

The Seigneur de Belesbat made it clear that he grounded his hope of applying libertarianism in an extreme form of early utilitarianism, a utilitarianism that he expected would be applied by the king. The king was urged to channel people's self-interest into free and harmonious activities by seeing to it that virtue is rewarded and evil (theft and other interference with trade) is punished. In that way, men would become accustomed to pursue virtue. Belesbat went very far in utilitarianism by maintaining that 'justice' was always and only utility or self-interest. A fatal weakness in his theory was the confident view that the self-interest of the king, who was supposed to put all this into effect, was always identical to the harmonious self-interest of his subjects.

Belesbat also anticipated the later view that Montaigne-type scepticism about reason, rather than providing support for going along with state absolutism, teaches men humility so that they will accept liberty and the free market. Reason, however, is not the sole, and not even the main, motive for the drive for the exercise of power: acquisition of wealth and privilege would seem to be motive enough. And since there will always be people and groups who will seek to seize and aggrandize state power for their own purposes, scepticism towards reason and a rational political philosophy seems more likely to subvert any determined opposition to statism than to hinder any statist drive for power.

9.9 Boisguilbert and *laissez-faire*

The best known of the late seventeenth century French advocates of *laissez-faire* is Pierre le Pesant, Sieur de Boisguilbert (1646–1714). Born in Rouen into a high-born Norman family of judicial officers, and a cousin of the poet–dramatist Corneille brothers, Boisguilbert was educated by the Jesuits, and eventually purchased two judicial offices at Rouen. He served there as lieutenant-general of the court from 1690 until his death. Boisguilbert was also a large landowner, businessman, *litterateur*, translator, attorney and historian.

Boisguilbert was a combination of genius and crank. His first and most important work, *Le Détail de la France* (*A Detailed Account of France*), published in 1695, was revealingly subtitled *La France ruinée sous le règne de Louis XIV* (*France Ruined Under the Rule of Louis XIV*).[10] Boisguilbert penned innumerable letters to successive controllers-general of France on the virtues of free trade and *laissez-faire*, and on the evils of government intervention. After 1699, Boisguilbert kept hammering away at controller-general

Michel Chamillart for years, but to no effect. Chamillart kept refusing him permission to print his tomes, but Boisguilbert published them anyway, finally printing his collected works under the title *Le Détail de la France* in 1707. In that year, the same year that Vauban's *Dixme Royale* was censored, Boisguilbert's work was also outlawed, and its author sent into brief exile. He returned under promise of silence, but promptly reprinted his book four times between 1708 and 1712.

Arguing for *laissez-faire*, Boisguilbert denounced the mercantilist preoccupation with amassing specie, pointing out that the essence of wealth is in goods not coin. Money, Boisguilbert explained, is just a convenience. Thus the influx of bullion from the New World in the sixteenth century only served to raise prices. If nature were left to herself, all men would enjoy plenty and the government's attempts to improve upon nature only caused havoc. The simple remedy for the manifold evils under which France was suffering was, as Professor Keohane puts it: 'for the government to stop interfering with natural patterns of trade and commerce, and *laissez faire la nature*. No superhuman effort for reform was needed, only the cessation of ill-considered effort'.[11]

Collective or social harmony, Boisguilbert wrote, arises from the efforts of innumerable individuals to advance their self-interest and their happiness. If the government removed all artificial restrictions upon trade, all participants would have incentive to produce and exchange, and self-interest would then be free to do its constructive work. Only the use of coercion or state privilege pits one self-interest against another, whereas submission to the wise natural order would ensure harmony between individual greed and universal benefit. As Keohane summarizes Boisguilbert, 'So long as we do not interfere with her [Nature's] workings, our attempts to get as much as we can for ourselves will maximize everybody's happiness in the long run'.[12] It is not, then, that individuals *aim* at the general good while pursuing their own self-interest. On the contrary, it is the glory of the natural order that, while individuals aim at their own 'private utility', they will also promote the interests of all. Although individuals may try to subvert the laws and gain at the expense of their neighbours, the natural order of liberty and *laissez-faire* will maintain peace, harmony, and universal benefit. As Boisguilbert declares, 'But nature alone can introduce that order and maintain the peace. Any other authority spoils everything by trying to interfere, no matter how well-intentioned it may be'. In the free market established by the natural order, 'the pure desire for profit will be the soul of every market for buyer and seller alike; and it is with the aid of that equilibrium or balance that each partner to the transaction is equally required to listen to reason, and submit to it'.

The natural order of the free market prevents any exploitation from taking place. Thus: 'Nature or Providence [had]...so ordered the business of life that, provided it is left alone (*on le laisse faire*) it is not within the power of the most powerful in buying goods from some poor wretch to prevent the sale from providing the subsistence of the latter'. Everything works out all right 'provided that nature is left alone (*on laisse faire la nature*)...[i.e.] provided that it is left free and that no one meddles with this business save to grant protection in it to all and to prevent violence'.[13]

Boisguilbert also specifically demonstrated the counterproductive results of government intervention. Thus, when the French government tried to alleviate hunger by lowering grain prices and controlling trade, all it accomplished was to diminish the cultivation and production of grain, and hence to intensify the very hunger that the government was trying to relieve. Such intervention, in the summary of Professor Keohane,

> would make sense only if grain, like manna or mushrooms, sprang up without human effort, since it ignores the effects of low prices on the habits of cultivators. If government simply ceased tampering, the French economy, like a city from which a siege is lifted, would regain its health. Free to set their own price for grain, and to import grain freely throughout the land, Frenchmen would be plentifully supplied with bread.[14]

In illustrating the nature and advantages of specialization and trade, Boisguilbert is one of the first economists to begin with the simplest hypothetical exchange: two workers, one producing wheat and the other wool, and then to extend the analysis to a small town, and finally to the entire world. This method of 'successive approximation', of beginning with the simplest, and then extending the analysis step by step, would eventually prove to be the most fruitful way of developing an economic theory to analyse the economic world.

Graphically illustrating the respective workings of power and market, Boisguilbert supposes a tyrant who tortures his subjects by tying them up within sight of each other, each surrounded by an abundance of the particular good that he produces: food, clothing, liquor, water, etc. They would be made instantly happy if the tyrant were to remove their chains and allow them to exchange their surplus goods for those of one another. But if the tyrant says, no he can only remove the chains of his people when some war or other is settled, or at some future time, he is only adding ridicule and mockery to their grievous torture. Here, Boisguilbert was bitterly mocking the reply that Louis XIV and his ministers habitually made to the pleas of reformers and oppositionists: 'We must wait for the peace'. Again, like the other oppositionists, war was exposed as the standard excuse for maintaining the crippling interventions of government.

Like Belesbat, Boisguilbert had no patience with inconsistent reformers who tried to make an exception to *laissez-faire* in luxury products. To

Boisguilbert, natural wealth was not just biological necessities; rather 'true wealth consists of a full enjoyment, not only of the necessaries of life, but even of all the superfluities and all that which can give pleasure to the senses'.

In addition, Boisguilbert was perhaps the first to integrate discussion of fiscal policy with his general economic doctrines. Adopting Vauban's proposal for the elimination of all taxes and their substitution by a single direct tax of 10 per cent on all incomes, Boisguilbert analysed and bitterly denounced the effects of indirect taxes on agriculture. Heavy taxes on grain, he pointed out, have raised costs and crippled grain production and trade. For four decades, he argued, the French government had virtually declared war on consumption and trade by its monstrous taxation, resulting in severe depression in every area of the economy.

On the free market, in contrast, everyone benefits, for 'trade is nothing but reciprocal utility; and all parties, buyers and sellers, must have an equal interest or necessity to buy or to sell'.

Hence, with Belesbat and Boisguilbert, the focus of the classical liberal attack on statism shifted from moralistic denunciation of luxury or pernicious Machiavellism to meeting mercantilist doctrine on its own utilitarian grounds. Even setting aside classical morality, then, utility and general happiness require the private property and *laissez-faire* of the natural order. In a sense, old-fashioned natural law had been extended to the economic sphere and to the meshing of individual utility and self-interest through the working of the free market. In contrast to devout mystics like Fénélon, Belesbat and Boisguilbert were in harmony with the new mechanistic cosmologies of Isaac Newton and others of the late seventeenth century. God had created a set of natural laws of the world and of society; it was the task of man's reason, a reason universal to all, regardless of nation or custom, to understand those laws and to achieve their self-interest and happiness within them. In the economy, free trade and free markets, through the harmony of reciprocal benefits, advanced the interest and happiness of all by each seeking his own personal utility and self-interest. The Golden Rule, and absence of violence, was the natural moral law that uncovered the key to social harmony and economic prosperity. While such analysis was not in itself anti-Christian, it certainly replaced the ascetic aspects of Christianity with an optimistic, more man-centred, creed; and also it was consistent with the rising religion of deism, in which God was the creator, or clock-winder, who created the mechanism of the universe and its self-subsistent natural laws, and then retired from the scene.

As Professor Spengler has pointed out:

> the eighteenth century conceptualized the economic (or social) universe. It made the hidden processes of the social order visible even as the seventeenth had

become aware of those of the physical order and made them visible; it generalized to the realm of man the notion of the 'frame' hidden behind 'the most common Phenomena' and the 'Invisible Hand' by which 'Nature works' in 'all things'.

As for Boisguilbert, his contribution was to be

> among the first, if not the first, to conceive, albeit imperfectly, of the system of relations that underlies the economic order...His contribution consisted in his sequestering (however imperfectly) the economic order from the total societal system, in becoming aware of the comparatively autonomous character of this order, in discovering the essentially mechanical and psychological connections binding men together in an economic order and in drawing attention to the manner in which the economic order was subject to disturbances by impulses originating in the political order.[15]

It should also be mentioned that it surely seemed easier to convince the king and his ruling élite of the general utility of private property and the free market, than to convince them that they were behaving as the heads of an immoral and criminal system of organized theft. So that the basic strategy of trying to convert the king led inexorably to at least a broadly utilitarian approach to the problems of freedom and government intervention.

9.10   Optimistic handbook at the turn of the century

The rapid spread and even social dominance of these new ideas of *laissez-faire*, crypto-deism, and the morality of utility and the Golden Rule, may be seen in the *Dialogues*, a virtual handbook of fashionable manners and ideas for the social climber, published in 1701 by the young *littérateur*, Nicholas Baudot de Juilly. In *Dialogues*, Baudot, son of a tax farmer in Vendôme, after lauding the manners taught in fashionable salons, proceeds to the ruling ideas of the day, where he vulgarizes the *laissez-faire* doctrine into one grounded in a frank and candid hedonism. The desire for pleasure and for the avoidance of pain was grounded in the natural drive for self-preservation. Furthermore, the God of Christianity, in the hands of Baudot, became a quasi-deistic god who has provided 'all nature' as a 'great feast where in His inexhaustible goodness God has convened us'. The Garden of Eden had been a realm of enjoyment and sensate pleasure; the purpose of Jesus's arrival on earth was to recall mankind to that original enjoyment. Asceticism, furthermore, causes economic misery. Specialization, trade, and the pursuit of wealth in the marketplace were the truest, and therefore the God-given, forms of charity.

As Baudot put it: God had 'purposely permitted us to multiply our needs in order to cause money to circulate among all men, passing from the purses of the rich to those of the poor'.

Trade, then, is the genuine charity:

All this [regional specialization and communication] has been so admirably accomplished in order to bind men to one another, who in effect should form only one single family so that the need they would have for one another would accomplish among them what charity alone ought to do. It is for this reason that men…, however different in mores, language, and Religion … are becoming united from one end of the world to another by reciprocal trade. It is also for this reason that they exchange equally things which are agreeable and those that which are necessary, so that they can not only sustain life as in a pasture like beasts, but also to render it sweeter, more humane and more polished by pleasures.

9.11 Notes

1. In his 'Justification of M. Colbert', his nephew, Nicolas Desmaretz, whom Colbert had wanted to succeed him, wrote angrily that: 'The memory of Monsieur Colbert was attacked with great animosity after his death. At that time all authority was in the hands of his enemies, and they had the pleasure of exercising their hatred by violent persecution against all those whom he employed…' Quoted by Lionel Rothkrug, *Opposition to Louis XIV: The Political and Social Origins of the French Enlightenment* (Princeton, NJ: Princeton University Press, 1965), p. 223.
2. Quoted in Charles Woolsey Cole, *French Mercantilism, 1683–1700* (1943, New York: Octagon Books, 1965), p. 248.
3. Rothkrug, op. cit., note 1, pp. 231–2.
4. In addition to the ten elected deputies, the king appointed two merchants 'representatives' from Paris. Unsurprisingly, they proved far tamer in their attitudes toward the Crown.
5. Madame Françoise d'Aubigne, Marquise de Maintenon (1635–1719).
6. Rothkrug, op. cit., note 1, pp. 267–9.
7. Rothkrug, op. cit., note 1, p. 270.
8. Rothkrug, op. cit., note 1, p. 333.
9. See Rothkrug, op. cit., note 1, pp. 333–4.
10. Under the circumstances, the title of the English translation two years later, *The Desolation of France*, does not seem inaccurate.
11. N.O. Keohane, *Philosophy and the State in France: The Renaissance to the Enlightenment* (Princeton, NJ: Princeton University Press, 1980), p. 352.
12. Ibid., p. 353.
13. Quoted in Cole, op. cit., note 2, p. 266. Or, in another place: 'il est seulement nécessaire de laisser agir la nature'. (It is only necessary to let nature act.) See Joseph J. Spengler, 'Boisguilbert's Economic Views Vis-à-vis those of Contemporary *Réformateurs*', *History of Political Economy*, 16 (Spring 1984), p. 81n.
14. Keohane, op. cit., note 11, pp. 354–5.
15. Spengler, op. cit., note 13, pp. 73–4. Spengler adds that the term 'invisible hand' was first used by the English writer Joseph Glanville, in his *The Vanity of Dogmatizing* (1661), a century before Adam Smith used the concept similarly. In his philosophical essays, Smith treated philosophy as 'representing the invisible chains which bind together' seemingly unconnected phenomena. Ibid., p. 73n.

10 Mercantilism and freedom in England from the Tudors to the Civil War

10.1 Tudor and Stuart absolutism

Dominant in English political thought from the early sixteenth to the early seventeenth century was a form of simplistic and militant absolutist thought that has been called the 'correspondence theory' or the 'political theory of order'. This royalist doctrine was fashioned for the Tudor–Stuart age in which the king struggled to establish his absolute power as against the international influence of the old religion, Catholicism, and over the Calvinist Puritans, who had definite republican and populist tendencies. In contrast, God was now supposed to be speaking through the English king and therefore through the head of the Anglican Church.

The basic philosophic groundwork was the 'natural order' – the 'great chain of being' – which, since the Middle Ages, had been seen as strictly hierarchical, with God at the head and man as the highest of his material creatures. But then came the fundamental methodology: flimsy analogy, or 'argument by correspondence'. Just as God was sovereign, and superior to various ranks of angels and finally to man and then other inferior earthly creatures in the 'macrocosm', so in the individual 'microcosm', within each person, the head must be sovereign over the body, and reason and will dominant over the appetites. Similarly, the father is sovereign over his family. More specifically and pointedly in the political realm, the king, the father of his people, must be sovereign over the body politic.

This flimsy organicist analogy was pushed to great lengths. The head in the human body 'was' the king in the body politic; health in the former constituted social well-being in the latter; the circulation of the blood was the same as circulation of money; rule of the rational soul was royal sovereignty, and so on. The only 'argument' was correspondence: that the 'governmental' and social ranking alleged to exist in the heavenly sphere must be duplicated in earthly government and in social life.

One problem with the argument from correspondence is that freedom of the human will enters into politics and social life but does not do so elsewhere. It is rare for the liver to 'rebel' against the head, and yet an important conclusion of this royalist political philosophy was that political rebellion is as evil and anti-natural as such 'rebellion' by the liver. Similarly, individual subjects *must* obey the divinely appointed monarch, else the divine order collapses into anarchy and disorder, and corruption and decay then rule in human life.

While the liver has not often rebelled against the head, the royal absolutists *did*, of course, have an analogy to fall back on in heavenly government: Satan's wicked rebellion against the sovereignty of God. Similarly, the great fact of human history was Adam's Fall, brought on by rebelliousness against divine authority and by overweening self-pride.

God and the king; Satan, Adam, and rebellious subjects; these were the analogies and correspondences that the royal absolutists tried to drive home.

Thus, Anglican Church homilies on obedience, in 1547 and 1570, called obedience to the sovereign 'the very root of all virtues', while 'a wicked boldness' is the source of all sin and misery. As the homilies stated: all 'sins possible to be committed against God or man be contained in rebellion', which 'turn(s) all good order upside down...'. It is the absolute duty of all inferiors 'always and only to obey', just as the body obeys the soul, and as the universe obeys God.

In stark contrast to the scholastics, as well as to Calvinist or Leaguer monarchomach thinkers, the Anglican preachers of order stressed time and again that the subjects must obey the king in any and all circumstances, whether or not the king or his actions were good or evil. There must be no resistance whatever, even to evil princes. The king is the divinely mandated representative of God on earth by hereditary right. To question, much less to disobey the king, therefore, was not only treason but blasphemy. Disobeying the king is disobeying God. As the influential *Mirror for Magistrates*, which went through many editions from 1559 to 1587, maintained: 'God ordains all magistrates'. Therefore, God ordains 'good when he favoureth the people; and evil when he will punish them'. In short, good kings are a blessing sent to the people by God; wicked kings are a punishment equally sent by the divinity. In either case the duty of the subject is absolute obedience to God's/the king's commands. 'And therefore whosoever rebelleth against any ruler either good or bad, rebelleth against GOD, and shall be sure of a wretched end...'

To the royalist thinkers, the rising claims of individual freedom and the natural rights of each individual only led to mischief and destruction of God's rational order. Thus Richard Hooker (c.1554–1600), the leading Anglican theologian of the sixteenth century, in his famous *Laws of Ecclesiastical Polity* (1594–97), lashed out at any notion of individualism. Though himself a moderate on royal absolutism, Hooker wrote that the idea of every man 'his own commander' 'shaketh universally the fabric of government, tendeth to anarchy and mere confusion, dissolveth families, dissipateth colleges, corporations, armies, overthroweth kingdoms, churches and whatsoever is now through the providence of God by authority and power upheld'.

One of the most extreme royal absolutists in the Tudor–Stuart era was Edward Forset (c.1553–1630), a playwright, owner of the manor of Tyburn, a justice of the peace and MP. Forset's *magnum opus* was *A Comparative Discourse of the Bodies Natural and Politic* (1606), whose very title reeks of the argument by correspondence and the political philosophy of order. At some points, Forset came close to saying that a monarch could *never* harm his people: in other words, however evil his deeds may *seem*, they must *really* be good, virtually by definition. Indeed, at one point, Forset came close to the justification of a king's acts by mystery and power as in the Book of Job. Thus, as Professor Greenleaf puts it in his discussion of Forset's doctrine: 'the seemingly evil acts of a ruler were only an appearance the real nature of which was misconstrued by the fallible minds of the citizens'.[1] The strong implication, of course, is that the mind of the monarch, in contrast to that of the lowly citizen, is *in*fallible.

Probably the most intelligent and surely the most influential of the absolutist order-theorists in seventeenth century England was Sir Robert Filmer (1588– 1653). Towards the end of his life, this obscure Kentish nobleman published a series of royal absolutist essays in the late 1640s and early 1650s. Then, three decades later, a Filmer revival took place, his collected essays being published in 1679 and his most famous work, *Patriarcha or the Natural Power of Kings*, written in the late 1630s or early 1640s, was printed for the first time the following year. Filmer immediately and posthumously became the leading defender of royal absolutism from the older perspective of order theory.

Filmer angrily rejected the idea that 'by law of nature all men are born free' as 'heathen' doctrine. Linking individualism and self-direction to sinful rebellion against God, Filmer warned against the 'very desire for freedom which caused Adam's fall from grace.'[2]

Most notable in Filmer was his searching critique of the rising contractarian doctrine, which laid the foundation of, and therefore justified, the state in some original social contract. Thomas Hobbes (1588–1679) had spent all his life in service as a tutor, companion, and intellectual guide to the Cavendishes, who were related to the royal Stuart family. Hobbes had worked out a contractarian justification for royal absolutism during the 1640s.

Filmer spotted crucial flaws in Hobbes's social contract theory which were to apply just as fully to John Locke's libertarian version four decades later:

> Filmer asked how likely it was,...that all men would agree to a contract, as was necessary before it could become universally binding; he wanted to know how and why a contract should bind all subsequent generations; he suggested it was unreasonable to invoke the specious notion of tacit consent...[3]

Filmer also trenchantly criticized the growing classical liberal idea of grounding government in the consent of the governed. Governments, he pointed out, could not then be stable, for governments could sometimes find that consent to be withdrawn. Once concede the power of the people to consent as well as the natural law of 'equal freedom from subjection', and the logical consequence must be anarchism. For then

> every petty company hath a right to make a kingdom by itself; and not only every city, but every village, and every family, nay, every particular man, a liberty to choose himself to be his own King if he please; and he were a madman that being by nature free, would choose any man but himself to be his own governor. Thus to avoid the having but of one King of the whole world, we shall run into a liberty of

having as many Kings as there be men in the world, which upon the matter, is to have no king at all, but to leave all men to their natural liberty.[4]

It should be noted that Filmer and other absolutists of the era found great inspiration in the French theorist Jean Bodin, who has been called the political writer most favourably and most often cited in England during the first half of the seventeenth century.

10.2   Sir Thomas Smith: mercantilist for sound money

The honour – if that be the proper term – of being the first English mercantilist writer should have gone, for four centuries, to Sir Thomas Smith the Elder (1513–77). Instead, his remarkable work, *A Discourse on the Commonwealth of this Realm of England*, written in 1549 and published anonymously in 1581, was at first unidentified, and since its 1893 reprint has been incorrectly attributed to another Tudor official, John Hales (d. 1571).

Thomas Smith was born into a poor family of small shepherds in the county of Essex. Impoverished but brilliant, Smith managed to enter Cambridge, where his scholarly abilities were soon recognized. There he rose to become Regius professor of civil law, and then vice-chancellor of the university. Smith was a notable orator and a learned and brilliant polymath, who wrote books on Greek pronunciation and English spelling, and was deeply interested in mathematics, chemistry, linguistics and history.

Smith embarked on a career as politician and bureaucrat by becoming a secretary under the protectorate of Lord Somerset, from 1547 to 1549. Though an Anglican, Smith was a moderate who cared little for religious matters, so he was able to serve as Privy Councillor under Catholic Queen Mary, on the recommendation of his old Cambridge colleague, the Catholic Bishop Stephen Gardiner. Under Queen Elizabeth, his influence continued through the powerful position at court of his old Cambridge student, Sir William Cecil, later Lord Burghley. Smith, however, was often out of power, a fate helped by his arrogant, boorish and feisty personality.

Thomas Smith was a bitter critic of debasement, and he therefore became a vocal opponent of his mentor, Lord Somerset's, policy of repeated debasement in order to acquire increased revenue for the Crown. Sent into exile from the court in 1549, Smith brooded and then did what was characteristic of him: marshalled and wrote down his thoughts in the form of a treatise. This penetrating, lively work was written in the form of a dialogue among several characters, with The Doctor being the spokesman for the author's own views. Later Smith was to repeat the dialogue form in his book, *Dialogue on the Queen's Marriage* (1561). The former work was not meant for publication, Smith noting in the tract that 'it is dangerous to meddle in the king's matters', as indeed it was.

The basic thrust of the *Discourse on the Commonwealth* was an attack on debasement, and its consequences in high prices, inflation and social unrest. Debasement, and not the arbitrary decision of farmers or merchants, is responsible for higher prices. The principal losers from this policy are people on fixed incomes. The *Discourse* was published after Sir Thomas's death by his nephew William; included are later passages, interpolated by Thomas during the 1570s, attributing the Elizabethan inflation of the later sixteenth century to another factor: the influx of newly mined specie from the western hemisphere. It is not known whether Smith was familiar with the similar Navarrus analysis of 1556, or the Bodin analysis of French inflation 12 years later, or whether this was Smith's independent discovery as price inflation moved from Spain northwards into Europe.

In 1562, Smith returned to the debasement theme, in a lengthy work, still unpublished, 'The Wages of a Roman Footsoldier, or A Treatise on the Money of the Romans'. This treatise on Roman money and coinage was written in answer to a question posed to him by his friend and colleague Cecil, at this point Queen Elizabeth's principal secretary. Again, Smith returns to his attack on debasement as evidence of 'the decay of the state', and as a cause of 'excessive prices'.

In both the *Discourse* and the 'Treatise' Smith took the convenient if fallacious position that the king himself is the greatest loser from the high prices caused by debasement. Since debasement adds to the king's revenue immediately and before prices have had a chance to rise, the king, on the contrary, is the prime beneficiary of debasement and other measures of monetary inflation.

Smith's *Discourse* is strikingly modern in frankly grounding its social analysis in the individual's drive for his own self-interest. Self-interest, Smith declared, is 'a natural fact of human life to be channelled by constructive policy rather than thwarted by repressive legislation'. Not that Smith abandons nascent mercantilism for any sort of liberal or *laissez-faire* outlook. Self-interest is not to be left alone within a property rights framework. It is to be channelled and directed by government to a 'common goal' set by the state. But at least Smith was wise enough to point out that it is better for men to be 'provoked with lucre' towards proper goals than to have governments 'take this reward from them'. In short, government should work in tandem with the powerful incentive provided by individual self-interest.

Smith sees that economic incentives are always at work in the market to move economic resources out of less profitable, and into more profitable, uses. And governments should work with such incentives, rather than against them.

Smith, however, was assuredly a mercantilist, as seen by his desire to foster the manufacture of woollen cloth within England, and his desire to prohibit the export of raw wool to be manufactured abroad.

John Hales came from a prominent Kentish family, and was a friend and fellow Tudor official of Smith. Yet his economic and social philosophy was very different. In 1549, for example, the year that Smith's *Discourse* was written (and which included an attack on new taxes on manufactured cloth) Hales was the very person responsible for instituting the tax. Hales also disliked two favourite themes of the *Discourse*: love for the civil law, and admiration for sheep farming. Hales, furthermore, far from being indifferent to religion, was a deacon and a dedicated organizer of Bible readings.

Most important in any contrast between Hales and the author of the *Discourse*, Hales attributed the high prices, not to debasement, but to three very different supply-side factors: scarcity of cattle and poultry; speculation; and excessively high taxes. None of these factors in truth can account for any general price increase.

Finally, Hales took the old-fashioned moral position of attributing all ills, including high prices, to man's all-pervasive greed. (Why greed should have *increased* rapidly in recent years to account for high prices was of course a problem that was not even addressed.) Greed and the desire for profit were the great social evils. The only cure for all this, opined Hales, was to purge man of self-love: 'To remove the self love that is in many men, to take away the inordinate desire of riches wherewith many be cumbered, to expel and quench the insatiable thirst of ungodly greediness, wherewith they be diseased...' and to replace this 'diseased' self-love by a twin other-love of Church-and-state: 'to make us know and remember that we all...be but members of one body mystical of our Saviour Christ and of the body of the realm'.

Again, in his *Defence*, written the same year as the *Discourse*, John Hales expressly denies that self-love can be in any sense the foundation of the public good: 'It may not be lawful for everyman to use his own as he listeth, but everyman must use that he hath to the most benefit of his country. There must be something devised to quench the insatiable thirst of greediness of men, covetousness must be weeded out by the roots, for it is the destruction of all good things'.

Sir Thomas Smith was responsible, rather than his associate Sir Thomas Gresham (c.1519–79), for the first expression of 'Gresham's law' in England. Until recently, it had been thought that the well-known and anonymous *Memorandum for the Understanding of the Exchange* had been submitted by Gresham to Queen Elizabeth early in her reign in 1559. It now turns out, however, that the *Memorandum* was written by Smith early in Queen Mary's reign, in 1554. The *Memorandum* was certainly not a free market tract, advocating as it did various state controls over the foreign exchange market. It did, however, not only denounce debasement and call for a high-valued currency, but it also enunciated 'Gresham's law' that the cause of a shortage of gold coin in England was the legal undervaluation of gold.

Gresham, fiscal agent of the Crown in Antwerp, himself adhered to 'Gresham's law', which was set forth by the royal commission of 1560 that he heavily influenced. Gresham was also a full-fledged statist and architect of Tudor monopoly privilege. A member of the monopoly wool cloth export company, the Merchant Adventurers, Gresham was the chief architect of England's tightening of that monopoly during the 1550s and 1560s: banning Hanseatic merchants from exporting English cloth, increasing tariffs on foreign cloth and, finally, making the Adventurers far more oligarchic and tightly controlled from the top.

Influenced greatly by the *Memorandum*, and echoing its Gresham's law position, was the younger Sir Richard Martin (1534–1617), goldsmith, warden and master of the Mint during all of Queen Elizabeth's reign. Trained as a goldsmith from youth, Martin also served as prime warden of the Worshipful Company of Goldsmiths, alderman of London for many years and was twice Lord Mayor. In the royal commission of 1576 on currency and the exchanges, whose members were hand-picked by Sir Thomas Smith, then principal secretary to the queen, Gresham and Martin, as well as Cecil, were all included. The commission did not include Smith himself, who had fallen ill. Their backing of Gresham's law was echoed a generation later by the royal commission of 1600, on which Martin served, and prepared the principal memoranda.

10.3 The 'economic liberalism' of Sir Edward Coke

It used to be held that the famous 'anti-monopoly' common law decisions of Chief Justice Sir Edward Coke (1552–1634), the eminent early seventeenth century jurist, were an expression of the alleged commitment of a rising class of puritan merchants to economic liberalism and *laissez-faire*. A particularly prominent advocate of this thesis is the prolific English Marxist historian, Christopher Hill, who needs this view to fit into the Marxian schema of the English Civil War.

It turns out, however, that there are many grave flaws in this thesis. Coke himself was a moderate Anglican, and not particularly concerned with religious issues. He was also not in any sense a merchant or a spokesman for merchants; he was a country gentleman from Norfolk who successively married two heiresses, and spent most of his career as a government lawyer, successively attorney-general and chief justice. Also, Coke showed no interest whatever in the new juristic concerns of merchants: such new branches of the law as joint-stock ownership, insurance bankruptcy, negotiable instruments and commercial contracts.

More important, Coke never displayed any sympathy for *laissez-faire*. As an MP, Coke supported many mercantilist measures. Furthermore, he had imbibed from his close associate, William Cecil, Lord Burghley, an admiration for the elaborate Tudor structure of state controls. His approach to foreign trade was profoundly mercantilist. Thus, in the 1621 session of Parliament, after he had broken with the Crown, Coke deplored the economic effects of the alleged scarcity of coin. He attacked the unfavourable balance of trade, deplored the fact that the East India Company was allowed to export bullion, and attacked the import trade with France as introducing into England immoral luxury items, such as 'wines and lace, and such like trifles'. Coke also called for outlawing the importation of tobacco from Spain.

Coke also tried his best to cripple the new practice of exporting unfinished cloth to the Continent and then re-importing the finished cloth. He consistently advocated prohibiting the importation of foreign cloths, as well as the export of unfinished cloth, and also tried to outlaw the export of raw wool to be used by foreign manufactures.

In general, Sir Edward Coke had no quarrel with government regulation and control of trade, or with the creation of monopolies; what he objected to was the *king* doing the regulating or monopolizing, rather than Parliament. Coke favoured the detailed regulation and cartellization of industry, the wage controls, and compulsory employment, imposed by the Statute of Artificers of 1563. He supported the laws against 'forestalling and engrossing' which, under the guise of attacks on monopoly and high prices, were actually price-raising and cartellizing devices prohibiting speculation in food products and prohibiting sales outside officially designated local 'markets'. Laws against forestalling were lobbied for by privileged owners of local markets trying to exclude competitors and to raise their own prices.

Most important, Coke's well-known opposition to government-granted monopolies was merely an opposition to grants by the king rather than to grants by parliament. Thus, in the famous Statute of Monopolies, passed in 1623 and drafted largely by Coke, Parliament abolished royal grants of monopoly privilege, but explicitly reserved to itself the right to grant such privileges, which it soon proceeded to do. The statute also specifically exempted from abolition large categories of royal monopoly, including such industries as printing, gunpowder and saltpetre, the rights of 'corporations' such as London to prevent non-Londoners from engaging in trade within the city limits, or monopoly corporations engaged in foreign trade. Furthermore, Coke personally favoured the monopoly Russia, Virginia, and East India Companies.

Coke's legal–economic philosophy might be summed up in a phrase he used in Parliament, in 1621: 'That no Commodity can be banished, but by Act of Parliament'.[5]

10.4   The 'bullionist' attack on foreign exchange, and on the East India trade

Having survived the assaults of ignorant moralists before the Reformation, the foreign exchange market was subjected, during the far more secular age of the late sixteenth century onwards, to the assaults of regulators on behalf of the nation-state. Writers who have been misnamed 'bullionists' adopted the ignorant view that an outflow of gold or silver bullion abroad was iniquitous, and that this calamity was brought about by the machinations of evil foreign exchange dealers, who deliberately sought gain by depreciating he value of the nation's currency. Nowhere was there any insight that the outflow of bullion might have been performing an economic function, or was the result of underlying supply and demand forces. Despite their insights into Gresham's law and debasement, Thomas Smith and Gresham would have to be placed in the 'bullionist' category. The policy conclusion of the bullionists was all too simple: the state should outlaw the export of bullion and should severely regulate or even nationalize the foreign exchange market.

The exchange dealers battled back, with sensible and powerful arguments. Thus in 1576 they argued, in a 'Protest against the State Control of Exchange Business', that state intervention would cause a drying up of commerce. On the low value of the English pound, they replied that 'we can say nothing but that our exchanges are made with a mutual consent between merchant and merchant, and that abundance of the deliveries or of the takers make the exchange rise and fall'.

One prominent bullionist of the early seventeenth century was Thomas Milles (c.1550–c.1627). In a series of tracts from 1601 to 1611, Milles advances the old bullionist position. Foreign exchange transactions, Milles opined, were evil; they were institutions with which private merchants and bankers, 'covetous persons (whose end is private gain)', rule in the place of kings. Something new, however, had been added. For the powerful East India Company had been chartered in 1600, to monopolize all trade with the Far East and the Indies. The East India trade was unique in that Europeans purchased a great deal of valuable muslins and spices, but the Indies in turn bought very little from Europe except gold and silver. European nations, therefore, had an 'unfavourable balance of trade' with the Far East, and the India trade therefore quickly became a favourite target for mercantilist writers. Not only were goods being imported from the East as against few exports, but specie, bullion, seemed to flow eternally eastwards. Milles therefore took up the bullionist cudgels by calling for restriction or prohibition of the Indies trade, and attacking the activities of the East India Company.

Milles was also eager to intensify regulations against the Merchant Adventurers, the governmentally privileged monopoly for the export of woollen cloth to the Netherlands. Instead, he craved a return to the old privileged raw wool export monopoly of the Merchant Staple. In fact, Milles went so far as to call the old regulated Staple trade the 'first step towards heaven'.

It is certainly likely that Milles's eagerness to regulate and prohibit foreign trade and bullion flows was connected with his own occupation as customs official. The more regulation, the more work and power for Thomas Milles.

Stung to the quick, the secretary of the Merchant Adventurers, John Wheeler (c.1553–1611) replied to Milles's charges in his *Treatise of Commerce*, in 1601. Wheeler upheld the 'orderly competition' of the 3500 merchant members joined together in the privileged monopoly, as against the unorganized, dispersed, 'straggling and promiscuous trade' of free competition. He also engaged in semantic trickery by asserting that monopoly by definition means only 'single seller'; hundreds of merchants linked together into a privileged export company were able, after all, to act virtually as one privileged firm. In Wheeler's own words, these merchants were 'united and held together by their good government and by their politic and merchantilike orders' – backed up, we must not forget, by the armed might of the state. Sneering at the idea of free competition, Wheeler smugly opined that any merchant who loses a little liberty will be better off 'being restrained...in that estate, than if he were left to his own greedy appetite'. When John Kayll, over a decade later in *The Trades Increase* (1615), protested that the monopoly of the Merchant Adventurers would 'unjustly keep others out forever', his pamphlet was suppressed by the archbishop of Canterbury and he earned a stint in jail for his pains.[6]

Later, in the 1650s, Thomas Violet had a Milles-type motive for special pleading in his call for prohibition of the export of bullion. Violet had been a professional 'searcher' and government informer seeking out violations of the law prohibiting the export of bullion. Now, in *A True discoverie to the commons of England* (1651), he sought to reinstate that good old law, and he accompanied his call for reinstatement of bullion prohibition with a request that he himself be employed once again to seek out violators. To the embarrassing fact that he, Violet, had himself been convicted and punished for violating these very provisions, he countered with a ready quip, 'an old deerstealer is the best keeper of a park'.

The most distinguished bullionist of the early seventeenth century was Gerard de Malynes (d.1641). Malynes was a Fleming born in Antwerp to the prominent van Mechelen family, probably changing his name to Malynes when he emigrated to London in the 1580s (perhaps in response to the Spanish persecution of Protestants in the Netherlands in that era). Malynes was listed as an alien in the records of that period, and as a member of the 'Dutch' Protestant Church. He is also depicted in the records as a 'merchant stranger', that is, as a merchant from abroad.

Malynes turned out be a speculator and an unscrupulous, even crooked, businessman, embezzling money from his Dutch business associates. He was often on the verge of bankruptcy, and his partner and father-in-law, the Antwerp-born Willem Vermuyden, died in debtors' prison. Malynes, nonetheless, was a linguist, and highly educated scholar, deeply interested in literature, the Latin language, mathematics and classical Greek philosophy. He was also well versed in scholastic doctrine.

A member of a royal commission of 1600 to study economic problems, Malynes began his bullionist writings in 1601, in particular *A Treatise on the Canker of England's Commonwealth*, and published many tracts on into the 1620s. Like Gresham and the sixteenth century bullionists, Malynes fulminated against the foreign exchange dealers, asserting superficially and incorrectly that exchange rates were set by wilful conspiracies of exchange dealers. Malynes was more rigorous than previous bullionists; instead of institutions to control exchange dealings, he advocated a government 'bank' which would enjoy a monopoly on all foreign exchange transactions.

Intertwined with his star-crossed business career was Malynes's service in government, becoming at various times a top bureaucrat at the Royal Mint and a financial adviser to the Crown. Malynes also had a personal stake in the revival of rigorous exchange control, for he himself eagerly anticipated filling the resurrected post of royal exchanger. To Malynes, there was a 'just' exchange rate at the legal par, and the government's task was to enforce it.

In an earlier tract in 1601, *Saint George for England Allegorically Described*, Malynes, harking back to an old theme, denounced foreign exchange dealings as 'usury', and expressed the hope that by tight control this usury could die a gradual death.

To advocate rigorous exchange control, Malynes of course had to deny that the foreign exchange market could in any way equilibrate or regulate itself, or that exchange rates were set by supply and demand forces. To Malynes goes the dubious credit for the emergence of the spurious and pernicious 'terms-of-trade' fallacy. This doctrine argues that a balance of trade deficit and export of bullion will not regulate itself. For higher foreign exchange rates and cheaper domestic currency, will *not*, as one might believe, spur exports and retard imports. Instead, the 'unfavourable' terms of trade of, say, the pound in terms of foreign currency will lead to even more imports and fewer exports, thus driving more bullion out of the country. Even if a cheaper pound will bring in less foreign exchange revenue (a highly unlikely event seen more often in armchair speculation than in practice), one wonders *where* the English would continue to find either foreign currency or specie to pay for the higher-priced foreign products. Surely the specie would eventually run out, and for that reason alone, *some* market mechanism would have to come into play to restrict foreign imports or the export of specie.

Thus Malynes managed to take the absurd position that, *whatever* happens in the foreign exchange market, specie will keep flowing out of England. Flowing out if the pound should be expensive, since this will restrict exports and encourage imports (a correct insight), but *also* flowing out if the reverse happens, because of the 'terms-of-trade' argument. The specie outflow was therefore blamed on the metaphysical malevolence of the exchange dealers, and it could only be cured by severe government control, including prohibition of the export of bullion. Malynes also advocated control of the exchange rate at the legal mint par, which would mean in the context of the time a substantial appreciation, or higher value, of the pound sterling. Yet, continuing in the faulty terms-of-trade mode, Malynes saw no problem of specie outflow from such a marked appreciation of the currency. In fact, he hailed the higher domestic prices that would supposedly draw *more* specie into the country.

In a similar bizarre twist, Malynes, correctly noting that the inflationary influx of specie from the New World had hit the other countries of Western Europe before coming into England, yet concluded that this was a terrible event for England. For instead of realizing that lower prices made English goods more competitive abroad, Malynes concluded that these 'unfavourable terms of trade' put England into a poor competitive position and led to a permanent outflow of specie.

In view of his record in propounding tissues of egregious fallacies, it is curious that Malynes has had a good press among historians of economic thought, even among those who disagree with his basic outlook. They seem to laud him for recognizing that prices vary directly with the quantity of money, so that a country losing gold will find its prices falling, whereas a country accumulating gold will see its prices rise. But Malynes, eager to indict the workings of international prices and exchanges rather than explain how they work, was scarcely willing to develop the full implication of his occasional insights. Furthermore, considering that this 'quantity theory' had long been known, and developed and integrated for centuries, by the Spanish scholastics, Bodin, and others, Malynes's achievements seem dubious at best.

10.5 The East India apologists strike back

England suffered a severe recession in the early 1620s, and Gerard Malynes returned to the attack, publishing a series of tracts repeating his well-known views, and calling for stringent measures to curb the Merchant Adventurers and especially the East India Company, as well as any other traders who dared to export bullion from the kingdom. His influence was bolstered by having been a member of the royal commission on the exchanges in 1621.

Taking up the torch in defence of the Merchant Adventurers was one of its members, Edward Misselden (d. 1654). In a tract entitled *Free Trade or the Means to Make Trade Flourish* (1622), following service on a Privy Council committee of inquiry on the depression of trade, Misselden advanced somewhat beyond Malynes's analysis. He acknowledged that bullion was exported from England, not due to the machinations of wicked exchange dealers, but from imports exceeding exports, from what would later be called an 'unfavourable balance of trade'. Misselden, then, was not concerned with regulating the exchanges. But he *did* want the state to force a favourable balance into being by subsidizing exports, restricting or prohibiting imports, and cracking down on the export of bullion. In short, he called for the usual set of mercantilist measures. Misselden was largely concerned to defend his Merchant Adventurers. Like Wheeler a generation earlier, he maintained that his company was not at all a monopolist, but simply the organization of orderly and structured competition. Besides, wrote Misselden, his Merchant Adventurers exported cloth to Europe and therefore fitted in with the interests of England. The truly evil firm was the privileged East India Company, which had a decidedly unfavourable balance of trade of its own with the Indies, and which continually exported bullion abroad.

Misselden now entered into a series of angry pamphlet debates with Malynes, who replied in the same year with *The Maintenance of Free Trade*. (Neither party, of course, had the slightest interest in what would now be called 'free trade'.) In 1623, Misselden accepted a post as deputy governor of the Merchant Adventurers in Holland, perhaps as a reward for his stirring defence of the company in the public prints. But, in addition, the East India Company, seeing in Misselden an effective champion and a troublesome foe, made him a member and one of their commissioners in Holland during the same year. As a result, when his second pamphlet, *The Circle of Commerce*, was published in 1623, Misselden displayed a miraculous change of heart. For the East India Company had been suddenly transformed from villain to hero. Misselden, quite sensibly, now pointed out that while the East India Company did export specie in exchange for products from the Indies, it can and does *re*-export these goods in exchange for specie.

The outstanding defender of the East India Company in the early seventeenth century was one of its prominent directors, Sir Thomas Mun (1571–1641). Mun was early engaged as a merchant in the Mediterranean trade, especially with Italy and the Middle East. In 1615, Mun was elected a director of the East India Company, and after that he 'spent his life in actively promoting its interests'. He entered the lists on behalf of the company in 1621, with his tract, *A Discourse of Trade from England unto the East-Indies*. The following year he and Misselden were both members of the Privy Council committee of inquiry. Mun's second and major work, *England's Treasure by Forraign Trade, or the Balance of Forraign Trade is the Rule of our Treasure*, taking a broader view of the economy, was written about 1630 and published posthumously by Mun's son John in 1664. When published, it carried the stamp of approval of Henry Bennett, secretary of state in the Restoration government, and also an architect of England's mercantilist policy against the Dutch. The pamphlet was highly influential and was reprinted in several editions, the last being published in 1986.

Thomas Mun set forth what would become the standard mercantilist line. He pointed out that there was nothing particularly evil about the East India Company trade. The company imported valuable drugs, spices, dyes and cloth from the Indies, and it re-exported most of these products to other countries. Overall, in fact, the company has actually imported more specie than it has exported. In any case, the focus of English policy should not be on the specific trade of one company or with one country, but on the overall or general balance of trade. There it must make sure that the country exports more than it purchases from abroad, thereby also increasing the wealth of the nation. As Mun succinctly put it at the beginning of *England's Treasure*: 'The ordinary means to increase our wealth and treasure is by foreign trade, wherein we must ever observe this rule: to sell more to strangers yearly than we consume of theirs in value'. To that end, Mun advocated sumptuary laws banning consumption of imported goods, protective tariffs, and subsidies and directives to consume domestic manufactures. Mun, on the other hand, opposed any direct restrictions on the export of bullion, such as conducted by the East India Company.

Mun was wise enough in combating the fallacies of Malynes and Misselden. Against Malynes, he pointed out that the movements of the exchange rate reflect, not the manipulations of bankers and dealers, but the supply and demand of currencies: 'That which causes an under or overvaluing of monies by exchange is the plenty or scarcity thereof'. Misselden had advocated debasement of the currency as a means of increasing the price level. Such increase, Misselden had argued in pre-Keynesian fashion, 'will be abundantly recompensed unto all in the plenty of money, and quickening of trade, in every man's hand'. As a leader of the Merchant Adventurers, Misselden was undoubtedly highly interested in the spur that debasement would give to exports. But Mun denounced debasement, first, as bringing confusion by changing the measure of value, and second by increasing prices all around: 'If the common measure be changed, our lands, leases, wares both foreign and domestic, must alter in proportion'.

Neither did Mun bend his energies towards an export surplus because he was enamoured of the idea of accumulating specie in England. Adhering to the quantity theory of money, Mun realized that such accumulation would simply drive prices up, which would not only be to no avail but would discourage exports. Mun wanted to accumulate specie not for its own sake, nor to drive up prices at home, but to 'drive trade', to increase foreign trade still further. An expansion of foreign trade *per se* seems to be Thomas Mun's main objective. And this overriding goal is not very puzzling from a leader of the great East India Company.

Furthermore, foreign trade, for Thomas Mun fully as much as for Montaigne, increased the national power – as well as the power of English traders – at the expense of other nations. England and her inhabitants only wax great at the expense of foreigners. As Mun put it succinctly, in trade 'one man's necessity becomes another man's opportunity', and 'one man's loss is another man's gain'. In an odd prefigurement of the Keynesian view that national debt held at home is immaterial because 'we only owe it to ourselves', Mun and his fellow mercantilists considered internal trade unimportant because there we only transfer wealth among ourselves. The export balance in foreign trade then becomes of crucial importance, so that the export merchant becomes by far the most productive occupation in the economy.

That Mun was far from being a primitive inflationist is seen by the scorn he properly and contemptuously heaped upon the common plea – and favourite mercantilist complaint – that business and the economy were suffering from a 'scarcity of money'. (The conclusion invariably drawn from such analysis is that the government was duty-bound to do something quickly to augment the money stock.) Mun wittily riposted in his *Discourse of Trade*:

> concerning the evil or want of silver, I think it hath been, and is a general disease of all nations, and so will continue until the end of the world; for poor and rich complain they never have enough; but it seems that the malady is grown mortal here with us, and therefore it cries out for remedy. Well, I hope it is but imagination maketh us sick, when all our parts be sound and strong...

Thomas Mun may have been the most prominent and sophisticated of the early seventeenth century mercantilists in England. Yet, as Schumpeter points out, these were all pamphleteers not particularly interested in analysis of the economy, special pleaders rather than aspiring scientists.[7]

Perhaps the best economic analyst of all in this period was Rice Vaughn, whose *A Discourse of Coin and Coinage*, though published in 1675, was written in the mid-1620s. Vaughn, in the first place, held that the disappearance of silver during this period was the effect of what we now call 'Gresham's law': the bimetallic undervaluation by the English government of silver as against gold. Since silver, rather than gold, was the money for most transactions, this undervaluation had a certain deflationary effect. In the course of his tract, Vaughn pointed out that an export surplus will not have the desired effect of bringing precious metals into the kingdom, if the value of the gold or silver pound in England is low in terms of purchasing power; for then goods will be imported instead of the monetary metals, and the export surplus will disappear.[8] Vaughn was also astute enough to recognize that prices do not all move together when the value of money changes: for example, that domestic prices usually lag behind the debasement or devaluation of money standards.

Most importantly, Rice Vaughn, remarkably, harked back to the scholastic continental subjective utility and scarcity tradition in the determination of the values and prices of goods. Vaughn concisely pointed out that the value of a good is dependent on its subjective utility and hence demand by consumers ('Use and delight, or the opinion of them, are the true causes why all things have a Value and Price set upon them'), while the actual price is determined by the interaction of this subjective utility with the relative scarcity of the good ('the proportion of that value and price is wholly governed by rarity and abundance').[9]

10.6   Prophet of 'empiricism': Sir Francis Bacon

The status and reputation of Sir Francis Bacon (1561–1626) is one of the great puzzles in the history of social thought. On the one hand, Bacon was universally hailed as the greatest man of his age. Over a century later, in the great manifesto of the French Enlightenment, the *Encyclopédie*, Bacon was hailed extravagantly as 'the greatest, the most universal, and the most eloquent of philosophers'. Yet what had he actually accomplished to warrant all the accolades?

This prolific statesman and writer, with great fanfare and self-advertisement, in a series of books from the 1600s to the 1620s, set forth a series of injunctions about *the* proper method of scientific inquiry into the world, including social as well as natural sciences. Essentially, Bacon wrote numerous exhortations to everyone else to engage in detailed factual investigation into all life, all the world, all human history. Francis Bacon was the prophet of primitive and naive empiricism, the guru of fact-grubbing. Look at 'the facts', all 'the facts', long enough, he opined, and knowledge, including theoretical knowledge, will rise phoenix-like, self-supporting and self-sustained, out of the mountainous heap of data.

Although he talked impressively about surveying in detail all the facts of human knowledge, Bacon himself never came close to fulfilling this monstrous task. Essentially, he was the meta-empiricist, the head coach and cheerleader of fact-grubbing, exhorting *other* people to gather all the facts and castigating any alternative method of knowledge. He claimed to have invented a new logic, the only correct form of material knowledge – 'induction' – by which enormous masses of details could somehow form themselves into general truths.

This sort of 'accomplishment' is dubious at best. Not only was it a prolegomenon to knowledge rather than knowledge itself; it was completely wrong about how science has ever done its work. No scientific truths are ever discovered by inchoate fact-digging. The scientist must first have framed hypotheses; in short, the scientist, before gathering and collating facts, must have a pretty good idea of what to look for, and why. Once in a while, social scientists get misled by Baconian notions into *thinking* that their knowledge is 'purely factual', without presuppositions and therefore 'scientific', when what this really means is that their presuppositions and assumptions remain hidden from view.

The mystery, then, is why Sir Francis Bacon's dubious achievement garnered so much praise. One reason is that he succeeded in capturing the *Zeitgeist*: he was the right man for his notions at the right time. For Bacon came after two centuries of sniping at scholasticism, which was now ripe for an open and all-out assault. Echoing many other thinkers of past generations but putting it squarely and bluntly, Bacon divided all knowledge into two parts, divine and natural. Man's knowledge of supernatural and spiritual matters came from divine revelation, and that was that. On the other hand, knowledge of material affairs, man and the world around him, was wholly empirical, inductive, arrived at through the senses. In neither case was there any room for human reason, that great conduit of knowledge lauded by classical philosophy from the Greeks to the scholastics. Knowledge of spiritual and divine matters was purely fideistic, the product of faith in divine revelation. Earthly knowledge was purely sensate and empirical; there was no room for reason there either.

In ethical and political philosophy, then, Bacon found no room for the classical doctrine that human reason supplies knowledge of ethics through investigation of natural law. Instead, ethical knowledge is purely relative, the tentative accumulation of mounds of unsifted historical data. And if there is no rational knowledge of ethics or natural law, then there are no natural rights limits to be placed on the power and actions of the state. Curiously enough, Bacon had the best of both worlds by proclaiming that endless arrays of facts were not just the only conduit to knowledge, but that they would enable man to arrive at an ethics that would improve his life. The ultimate purpose of engaging in all the fact-grubbing was utilitarian. Yet how he expected valid ethical laws to emerge out of all this busy empiricism was left unexplained.

Recent research, however, has cleared up some of the lacunae in Bacon's methodological position. For it turns out that much of Bacon's vaunted 'empiricism' was not just ordinary science, but the allegedly empirical mystical mumbo-jumbo that various renaissance thinkers had cobbled out of the 'Ancient Wisdom'. Renaissance mysticism was a pseudo-science that combined the occult and magic traditions of the hermetic literature, with that of a Christianized version of the Jewish Cabala. A year after Bacon died, his proposed despotic utopia, the *New Atlantis* (1627) was published. In the renaissance mystic tradition, Bacon proposed a utopia ruled by enlightened despots, in which all men are happy and content. Happiness was achieved because Adam's sin was not, as in the standard Christian tradition, trying to know too much and to become in some sense divine. On the contrary, the mystical hermetic view held that Adam's sin was turning his back on the Ancient Wisdom that could have been revealed to him. In contrast, man will now be made happy because wise rulers, possessed of this divine knowledge, will guide man to perfection and happiness by fulfilling his true God-like nature. In Bacon's utopian novel, the symbols he used heavily – such as the 'rose' or 'rosy' cross – reveal Bacon's closeness to the newly founded and mysterious Rosicrucian Order, which added to the rest of the Ancient Wisdom the pseudo-science of alchemy, in which man becomes as God in helping to create the universe.[10]

The arrogant Baconian claim to be the prophet of the only true scientific method takes on a high irony when we realize that Francis Bacon's vision of science was close to that of the magic-oriented occultists of the Rosicrucian Order. And since renaissance occult 'knowledge' was definitely part of the new spirit of the age, and later even of the allegedly 'rational' Enlightenment as well, Francis Bacon may be considered far closer to the *Zeitgeist* of his day than current Baconians would care to acknowledge.

Francis Bacon was also in tune with the *Zeitgeist* in another way. The simple-minded proclamation of the absolute power and glory of the English king was no longer as tenable as it had appeared to the Anglican theorists of the sixteenth or even to Bacon's absolutist contemporaries of the early seventeenth century. The naive argument by 'correspondence' – the analogies to the lordship of God, the head on a single man's body, and to the king as head of the great body politic – was no longer being accepted as self-evident truth. The new discoveries, and the expansion of the economy and of the nations of Europe into new worlds, made the older view that any change wrought by human beings merely corrupted God's static order of nature increasingly untenable. The idea that every man and group was born into a divinely ordained fixed order and station in life was rebutted by the increasing mobility and social and economic progress of the western world. And so the old admixture of the material and the divine into one heady brew of unquestioned absolutism could no longer command respect. A new fallback position for the state and the monarch was necessary, one more in tune with the new fashion of 'science' and scientific advance.

And so the 'scientific realism' of Sir Francis Bacon was perfectly suited to the new task. The idea that the king was quasi-divine or received an absolute divine imprimatur would no longer do. Sir Francis Bacon in the service of the state was far more the 'realistic political scientist' heralded by Machiavelli. Indeed, Bacon consciously modelled himself on Machiavelli's teachings. Like the neo-pagan Machiavelli, Bacon called upon his prince to do great deeds, to achieve glory. He particularly called upon the king to achieve empire, to expand and to conquer territories overseas. Domestically, Bacon was what might be called a moderate absolutist. The king's prerogative was still dominant, but this should be within the ancient historical constitution, and should follow the law, and there should be at least discussions and debates in the courts and in Parliament about royal decrees.

Bacon went beyond most other apologists of empire by declaring it a high moral duty of the king to expand, as well as preserve, the 'bonds of empire'. The duty to conquer went even beyond Machiavelli, who worried about undue speed in achieving conquest. To stand ready to serve the high duty of expanding empire, the British nation had to be trained in the study of arms and particularly in naval prowess, and had to display the virtue of fortitude, to be 'stout and warlike'.

This brings us to the last and not the least of the reasons for Bacon's enormous influence beyond the merits of his achievements. For Sir Francis Bacon, Baron Verulam, Viscount St Albans, was one of the leading politicians and members of the power élite in Great Britain. He was, first, the youngest son of Sir Nicholas Bacon (1509–79), a close friend and brother-in-law of Sir William Cecil, Lord Burghley, a leading aide to Queen Elizabeth. As a result, Nicholas Bacon became Privy Councillor, Lord Chancellor, and the Lord Keeper of the Great Seal.

Francis Bacon was, therefore, born with a silver spoon. As a young attorney, Bacon became an MP and, in 1591, a confidential adviser to the earl of Essex, favourite of the queen. As Essex began to lose favour with the queen, the ever alert Bacon sensed the shift in the wind and turned against his old patron, taking the lead in the condemnation that led to Essex's execution. To explain this sordid affair, Bacon was assigned by the queen to write what became the official public denunciation of Essex. Later, to quiet a festering canker of criticism, Bacon was moved to write an *Apology* for his own treacherous role in the Essex affair.

Despite Bacon's apologia, the queen, for obvious reasons, continued not to trust him very much, and political preferment eluded the highly placed courtier. Under the new king James I, however, Bacon came into his own, his career propelled by his cousin Thomas Cecil, the second Lord Burghley. In 1608, Bacon became the king's solicitor, and then attorney-general. Finally, in 1617, he followed in his father's footsteps as Lord Keeper of the Great Seal, and the following year became Lord Chancellor.

After three years in the nation's highest political post, however, Sir Francis Bacon was laid low. Charges of systematic bribery and corruption against him were proved and he then confessed his guilt, retiring to private life and to pursuing his publishing career. Characteristically, while Bacon admitted to taking bribes, he claimed that they never affected his judgement, and that his 'intentions' had remained forever 'pure'. Judging him by his own empirical method, however, one may be permitted to be sceptical of such 'metaphysical' claims.

In the narrowly economic sphere, Bacon's output was sparse and his opinions unremarkable, except for their scarcely being in the forefront of modern or scientific advance. On the balance of trade, he took the standard broadly mercantilist line. Thus, in his 'Advice to Sir George Villiers', written in 1616 but only first published in 1661, Bacon hailed the export 'trade of merchandise which the English drive in foreign parts'. The crucial point of the trade is 'that the exportation exceed in value the importation; for then the balance of trade must of necessity by returned in coin or bullion'. On the ancient question of usury, Bacon took a surprisingly reactionary and moralistic stand, calling for its prohibition on moral and religious grounds. More interestingly, he also declared that allowing high interest rates restricted beneficial agricultural improvements on behalf of riskier (and presumably less worthy) projects – an indication that some of the clamour to repress usury came from blue-chip investors who balked at the competition of more speculative borrowers willing to pay higher interest. In a similar vein, Bacon also attacked the charging of interest because it drew men from their appointed callings and brought them income they did not really 'earn'.

10.7   The Baconians: Sir William Petty and 'political arithmetic'

Since Bacon's thought fitted well into the spirit of the age, it is not surprising that he developed enthusiastic followers. One little recognized follower was Thomas Hobbes, the philosophic apologist for monarchical absolutism who, on the eve of the Civil War, was searching for a 'modern' defence of monarchical despotism which relied neither on the outworn correspondence theory of order, nor on the Grotian variant of natural law as did his friends in the Tew circle. Grotius's conservative version of consent theory held that the right of sovereignty had indeed originated with the people, but that the people, at some murkily distant point in the past, had surrendered their sovereignty irrevocably to the king. This defence of royal absolutism had been continued in England by the Tew circle, Hobbes's only disagreement being that each individual, in the last analysis, had the 'right of self-preservation' and therefore had the right to disobey any orders from the king that were tantamount to the particular individual's murder.[11] But more importantly, Hobbes's political theory forswore scholastic natural law methodology for a 'modern' mechanistic, scientistic methodology far more in keeping with Francis Bacon. This shift is not surprising, considering that Hobbes served his philosophic apprenticeship as secretary to Bacon himself. Later on, in addition to a life in service to the royalist Cavendish family, Hobbes served as a mathematical tutor to the future King Charles II.

The leading Baconian in political economy, who was also fittingly a pioneer in statistics and in the alleged science of 'political arithmetic', was the fascinating opportunist and adventurer Sir William Petty (1623–87). Petty was the son of a poor rural cloth-worker from the county of Hampshire. He learnt Latin at a country school, and was put to sea as a cabin-boy at 13. When his leg was broken at sea, he was put ashore in France by the captain.

Petty got himself admitted to the Jesuit university at Caen by applying for admission in Latin. There he received an excellent education in languages and mathematics, supporting himself by tutoring and trading in custom jewellery. Soon, Petty was off to Holland to study medicine; there he became friendly with Dr John Pell, professor of mathematics at Amsterdam. Travelling to Paris to study anatomy, Petty was armed with an introduction by Pell to Thomas Hobbes. Soon, Petty became Hobbes's secretary and research assistant, and from Hobbes imbibed Baconian and Hobbesian empiricism, mechanism and absolutism. Through Hobbes, Petty also joined advanced circles, including new scientists plus the philosophic friends of science. We must remember that science did not enjoy the professional specialization of the twentieth century, and new scientific discoveries were often made in an atmosphere of scientists surrounded by dilettantish philosophical cheerleaders. Through Hobbes, Petty participated in the Parisian circle of Father Marin Mersenne, which included scientists such as Fermat and Gassendi as well as philosopher–mathematicians Pascal and Descartes.

After a year in Paris, Petty returned to England in 1646 to continue his medical studies at Oxford. Armed again with an introduction opening crucial doors from Professor Pell, Petty was embraced by the man who has been called 'the master of ceremonies to the new learning', the enthusiastic Baconian, half-English Prussian immigrant from Poland and exile from Catholic rule, Samuel Hartlib (1599–1670). Pell was Hartlib's earliest disciple, and his first job had been schoolmaster at a school run by the wealthy and well-connected Hartlib, whose father had been 'merchant-royal' to the king of Poland. With Hartlib's backing, Petty's career at Oxford now zoomed upward with incredible speed. Petty was welcomed into a circle of mathematicians, scientists and physicians who had gathered at Oxford to escape the Civil War and engage in multi-partisan, trans-religious Baconian science. This group, which called itself the 'invisible college', not only received Petty warmly but they even met periodically at his lodgings which, being at an apothecary's house, was convenient to scientific and alchemical experimentation in drugs. Hardly did Petty become a fellow of Brasenose College in Oxford than he was made vice-principal, and hardly did he become a physician when he was made professor of anatomy. Finally, Hartlib got his friend and protegé Petty made professor of music in 1651 at the Gresham College in London, a new college dedicated to the experimental and mechanical arts. Petty apparently taught the applied mathematics of music. At only 28, William Petty had been vaulted to the top of the academic profession. The rapidity of Petty's climb was undoubtedly aided by the fact that the new republican regime tossed out previously openly royalist incumbents, and the 'invisible college' Baconians were able to sail under the colours of value-free, Baconian science.

Hartlib also wrote voluminously inductive histories of trade, especially agriculture, helping to further the Baconian programme. Hartlib himself was a friend and disciple of his fellow-Baconian, the mystical millennialist Czech theologian and educationist Johann Amos Comenius (1592–1670). Comenius, a bishop in the pietist Hussite Moravian church and an exile from Catholic rule, was employed by the Swedish government to organize its school system. He went beyond Bacon to invent a new hermetic religious system, pansophism, which promised to combine all the sciences in a mystical road to all knowledge. Hartlib subscribed to these gnostic tenets, and he also followed Bacon in outlining his own new utopia, which he called *Macaria* (1641).

Hartlib and Comenius were the favourite philosophers and theoreticians of the puritan country gentry, the party of the Pyms and the Cromwells. Indeed, in the summer of 1641, when the country Puritans thought that they had successfully achieved lasting rule under the king, Parliament eagerly brought Comenius to England, and it was during the Autumn that Hartlib published his *Macaria*, a welfare state utopia he expected to institute in England. Arrived in England, Comenius drew up his own plans for a pansophical 'reform', or transformation of the English educational system, led by a 'pansophical college'. Comenius proclaimed 'that the last age of the world is drawing near, in which Christ and his Church shall triumph,... an age of Enlightenment, in which the earth shall be filled with the knowledge of God, as the waters cover the sea.'[12]

The renewed outbreak of the Civil War put an end to plans for quiet social and educational reconstruction, and so Comenius returned to the continent of Europe the following year, 1642. But Hartlib and the others remained, and continued under munificent puritan patronage; during Cromwell's Protectorate, these Baconians flourished, and Pell and other Hartlib disciples were used by Cromwell as envoys to various Protestant countries in Europe.

One of Hartlib's favourite continuing projects was to try to found new colleges and institutions to promote the new science. One prospective donee was the wealthy, aristocratic, and much younger friend, the distinguished physicist Robert Boyle (1627–91). At one point, Hartlib tried to get Boyle to finance William Petty in compiling a 'history of [all] trades'; at another point Petty, in his first published work at the age of 25, urged Hartlib to finance a new college to advance 'real learning', which would be a '*gymnasium medicum* or a college of tradesmen'. This college, wrote Petty, would provide 'the best and most effectual opportunities and means for writing a history of trades in perfection and exactness...'[13] Neither of these particular projects was to pan out.

No sooner had William Petty reached the apex of academia in 1651, however, and before giving his first lecture, than he left the university world for good. He was out to make a fortune, and he saw his opportunity in the midst of Cromwell's devastating conquest and decimation of Ireland. A fellow Oxford 'invisible', Jonathan Goddard, had gone off to become physician-in-chief of Cromwell's army in Ireland, and had returned two years later to the prestigious post of warden of Merton College; taking a two-year leave from Oxford, Petty went to Ireland as Goddard's replacement. When Petty got to Ireland, he found a golden opportunity to make his fortune. Cromwell had despoiled Irish lands, and decided to pay his soldiers and the financial supporters of his military campaign by handing out conquered and confiscated Irish land. But to parcel out the land, it first had to be surveyed, and this task was being conducted by a surveyor-general, a friend of Petty and Hartlib, Dr Benjamin Worsley, a fellow-physician who had published influential pamphlets that led to the Navigation Act of 1652, a mercantilist measure for the subsidizing and privileging of English shipping. Petty, however, did not let friendship stand in his way. Reaching Ireland in the autumn of 1652 and sizing up the situation, Petty launched a propaganda campaign denouncing the alleged slowness of Worsley's survey, and promising to perform the task himself in a mere 13 months. Getting the job in February 1653, despite the ferocious opposition of Worsley, Petty indeed completed the task on time.

With the huge sum of cash earned from this job, Petty set about accumulating ownership of the confiscated Irish lands: some lands he acquired in lieu of cash payment; others he got by buying land claims from needy English soldiers. By 1660, William Petty had accumulated Irish landed estates totalling 100 000 acres, making him one of the largest landowners in Ireland. In fact, his eventual accumulation of Irish land was still greater, for by the time of his death in 1687 Petty owned 270 000 acres in south Kerry alone. By the late 1650s, Petty was back in London, serving for a time in Parliament and renewing his friendships in scientific circles.

Back in England, Petty joined a Baconian–Hartlibian circle headed by another German emigré, Theodore Haak, the organizing secretary of Comenius's English disciples. Other members included Dr Jonathan Goddard, now Protector Cromwell's personal physician; and the famed architect Christopher Wren, whose first architectural work was a transparent three-storey beehive-like structure built for Hartlib. The group met largely in the Oxford home of Cromwell's brother-in-law, John Wilkins, whom the protector had made ruler of Oxford University.

The Baconians, it must be understood, though flourishing under Cromwell, were never truly committed to any particular form of government. Like Bacon himself, they could flourish under an absolute monarchy. Monarchy, republic, Parliament, Crown, Church – all these forms of government made no particular difference to these 'scientific', 'value-free' would-be rulers of the nation. So long as the regime was sufficiently statist, and at least nominally Protestant, the polity could afford ample scope for the dreams of power and 'science' held by these Baconian philosophers and men of affairs.

Hence Petty and his colleagues, always seekers of the main chance whatever the government, were well placed when the Stuart monarchy was restored in 1660.[14] Petty himself was well received at the court of Charles II, who granted him a knighthood, and in 1662 Petty's and his colleagues' Baconian dreams culminated when Petty became a founding member of the newly chartered Royal Society of London for the Improving of Natural Knowledge. The Royal Society was specifically dedicated to the Baconian project of empirical observation and experiment, first to the study of the natural world and technology, and then to the study of society.[15] Throughout his life, Petty remained an active member of the Royal Society, especially contributing to its studies of the history of trades and technology. Petty's own contribution, 'political arithmetic', or statistics, he saw as the application of the empiricist Baconian programme to the social world.

True to Petty's goal of 'empirical' science, each of his studies was designed to promote his own economic or political advancement. His major publication, a *Treatise of Taxes and Contributions*, was published in 1662, and went into three further editions in his lifetime. Petty, however, was disappointed, since the tract did not lead to his hoped-for public office or political influence. Petty's later tracts were written, but not published, in his lifetime, the others being published in 1690 or later, after his death. This was because, in the words of a generally admiring historian, they were written 'not for publication but for circulation in the corridors of power or with a view to acquiring influence and jobs – which he never managed to obtain.[16] And even though Petty's daughter, from a marriage a few years later, was to give rise to the aristocratic Shelburne and Landsdowne families, Petty derived little enjoyment from his vast ill-gotten lands in Ireland, since he had to spend half his days in that country, defending his claims from lawsuits from royalist claimants, or his lands from 'bandits' who believed that he had despoiled their land.

As befitted a presumed experimental scientist, Petty claimed several important inventions, only one of which, however – the double-hulled ship – ever came to fruition. He spent a great deal of money building several versions of this ship, but they all suffered from the same problem: even though very fast, they all 'had an embarrassing tendency to break up in a storm', a defect, we are told, 'in which Charles II took a certain amount of malicious glee'.[17]

What then was there about Sir William Petty that, despite his gifts, his seizure of the main chance, and his powerful friends, brought him up sharply against a 'glass ceiling', that limited his political influence and his power at court, and that led even the king of England to treat his discomfiture with 'malicious glee'? Apart from his sabotage of Benjamin Worsley, the problem was that Petty could not resist the impolitic dig, whether he was wickedly mimicking the aristocracy at a party, or was reproving His Majesty's policies in the very pamphlet he was writing to court the king's favour. Not being a gentleman by birth, Sir William could ill afford to act less than a gentleman to his betters.

While publishing his *Treatise of Taxes*, Petty delivered several papers to the Royal Society on the histories of the dyeing of cloth, and shipping, advancing the Baconian history of trades programme. His major work, the *Political Arithmetic*, was written in the 1670s and published posthumously in 1690. The goal was to show that England, far from suffering from a decline as commonly believed, was actually wealthier than ever before. In the *Political Arithmetic*, Petty claimed to eschew mere 'words' and 'intellectual arguments', and state only 'arguments of sense' – that is, derived from sensate facts of nature, which could all be boiled down to 'number, weight, and measure' – a slogan which he enjoyed repeating on many occasions. Thus, at the end of an essay on algebra, Petty grandiloquently maintained that he had at last applied algebra 'to other than purely mathematical matters, viz: to policy, by the name of Political Arithmetic, by reducing many terms of matter to terms of number, weight, and measure, in order to be handled mathematically'.[18]

In fact, there is virtually no mathematics in Petty; what there is are statistics, loosely gathered, and arbitrarily asserted, employing many hidden assumptions, to arrive at preordained ideological conclusions.

As William Letwin writes, in his rewarding study of Petty:

> Petty's way with numbers, here as always, was utterly cavalier. The facts, whatever they were, always had a congenial way of upholding Petty's conclusions. Or rather, Petty's factual assertions did; for he was not averse to citing authorities mysterious, unknown, and even non-existent, when he needed their help.

Letwin then cites the conclusion of Major Greenwood, a modern historian of statistics: 'It is not I believe too cynical to say that any calculation Petty made would have produced war losses around 600,000'.[19] At one point, Petty actually submits the justification for his arbitrary figures and assumptions that they make no difference anyway since the figures are not totally false, and therefore can illustrate the method of arriving at knowledge. But fake illustrations, of course, are scarcely an advertisement for the method of political arithmetic. Thus Petty tried to come to conclusions pleasing to the king – that England was gaining not declining in wealth – by borrowing the spurious precision of numbers and the prestige of science. Sometimes his conclusions were so wildly optimistic as to abandon all sense: as when he claimed that it was 'a very feasible matter, for the King of England's subjects, to gain the universal trade of the whole commercial world'.[20]

In the course of his discussions, Petty delivered himself of some economic theories – *qualitative* not quantitative theories we might add – in violation of his stated programme. They were either not very remarkable – urging the king not to levy taxes that are so high that they will lead to severe declines in output or employment – or incorrect, such as attributing the value of goods not to the demand for them but to their costs of production.

Indeed, the quality of Petty's economic reasoning was generally that of a jejune mercantilist. Like all early modern writers, with the exception of Botero, Petty was a naive expansionist on population: the more people, the more 'income' and output will increase. Like mercantilists generally, Petty counselled and identified with the aristocratic power élite rather than with the labourers. His yen for increased or 'full' employment stemmed from a wish to increase the national output at the command of the state and employed by the élite. So little was Petty, like most mercantilists, concerned for the labouring classes that he denounced them for becoming more idle and drunken whenever their real wages rose. Petty, in fact, was more imaginative than his mercantilist confrères in proposing a governmental price-support scheme for keeping up the price of corn – specifically in order to prevent real wage rates from ever rising and thereby keeping the workers' noses to the grindstone and preventing them from enjoying more idleness (or leisure). Petty, indeed, denounced these labourers as 'the vile and brutish part of mankind'. Sometimes Petty's imagination ran away with him, his zeal for increasing the labouring population of England leading him to recommend, in the *Political Arithmetic*, forcibly moving the bulk of the population of Scotland and Ireland to England, allegedly in 'their own interests', so as to increase English productivity and to raise rents in England.[21]

The seventeenth century enthusiasm for the sciences, building upon the quasi-underground age-old numerological mysticism of the hermetic and cabala tradition, led to an arrogant frenzy of enthusiasm for quantitative and mathematical study of social life as well, among the scientists and especially their cheering sections. The eminent Harvard sociologist Pitirim Sorokin has perceptively referred to this frenzy, from that day to the present, as 'quantophrenia' and 'metromania'. Thus, writes Sorokin:

> The mathematical study of psychosocial phenomena was especially cultivated in the seventeenth and the eighteenth centuries. Spinoza, Descartes, Leibnitz, Newton... and others, began to build a universal quantitative science, *Pantometrika* or *Mathesis universae*, with its branches of *Psychometrika*, *Ethicometrika*, and *Sociometrika* designed for investigating psychosocial phenomena along the lines of geometry and physical mechanics. 'All truths are discovered only through measurement', and 'without mathematics human beings would live as animals and beasts', were the mottoes of the Social Physicists of these centuries.[22]

William Letwin writes perceptively of this metrophrenic phenomenon among the Baconians of England during the Stuart Restoration period. The 'scientific revolution' of this period, writes Letwin, 'owed much of its vigor to faith...the simple belief that many things in nature, as yet mysterious, could and should be measured precisely'. Unfortunately, 'Hand in hand with this revolutionary ideal went a devout but misplaced notion that to measure and to understand were one and the same. Restoration scientists believed that to cast a mathematical mantle over a problem was tantamount to solving it'. As a result, Letwin goes on,

> The scientists united themselves in the Royal Society and set off on an absolute orgy of measurement....the virtuosi continued, endlessly and pointlessly, to record, catalogue and count. The best minds of England squandered their talents in minutely recording temperature, wind and the look of the skies hour by hour, in various corners of the land. Their efforts produced nothing more than the unusable records.

This impassioned energy was turned also to the measurement of economic and social dimensions of various sorts. The search for number, weight and measure was conducted in the happy belief that good numbers would inevitably make for good policy.[23]

Unfortunately, this quantophrenia and metrophrenia seems to have taken over the modern economics profession. Fortunately for the development of economic thought, however, the quantophrenic enthusiasm in the social sciences dribbled away after the effusion of some Baconian writers in the 1690s. It would be nice to think that this decline was speeded up by the brilliant and devastating satires directed against the Baconians in the 1720s by the great Tory libertarian Anglo-Irish satirist Jonathan Swift (1667–1745). In his classic *Gulliver's Travels*, Swift effectively lampooned the crazed scientists of Laputa and elsewhere who were putting into effect what would now be called the Baconian 'research programme'. Finally, in 1729, Swift followed up this satire with his famous *Modest Proposal*, what Letwin justly calls 'the last word on political arithmetic as an instrument of social policy'. For Swift went after Petty, taking as his text Petty's claim that the more people the better, and in particular, Petty's serious proposal, in his *Treatise of Taxes*, to cure Ireland's alleged cause of poverty, underpopulation, by urging government subsidies for births among unmarried Irish women. The subsidies were to be financed by a tax on all Irish, especially on Irish men. The subsidies were only to be allowed if the woman kept records registering each father's time of cohabitation, and signed agreements by the father on the disposal of the children.

Swift's *Modest Proposal* satirized every aspect of Petty's style, from the solemnly avowed absurd policy proposals, to the fake precision of the numerological style. Thus, the *Modest Proposal* doggedly stated:

> The number of souls in this Kingdom being usually reckoned one million and a half, of these I calculate there may be about two hundred thousand couples whose wives are breeders; from which number I subtract thirty thousand couples who are able to maintain their own children...this being granted, there will remain a hundred and seventy thousand breeders.

After making due deductions for miscarriage, or for children who die each year, Swift is left with 'a hundred and twenty thousand children of poor parents annually born'. After demonstrating that there is no way by which these poor children can be reared or employed, Swift concludes with his famous 'modest' proposal, not 'liable to the least objection'. Being assured by a knowledgeable American in London that a young healthy well-nursed child of one year old is 'a most delicious, nourishing and wholesome food, whether stewed, roasted, baked or boiled', Swift then goes on to demonstrate, in the best value-free, numerological, empiricist Pettyite manner, the economic advantages of selling 100 000 children per annum to be eaten.

Most of the special pleading economic writers of the day ended their tracts professing no personal gain and their devotion to the public weal. And so Swift ends his *Modest Proposal* accordingly!

> I profess, in the sincerity of my heart, that I have not the least personal interest in endeavouring to promote this necessary work, having no other motive than the public good of my country, by advancing our trade, providing for infants, relieving the poor, and giving some pleasure to the rich. I have no children by which I can propose to get a single penny, the youngest being nine years old, and my wife past child-bearing.[24]

10.8 Notes

1. W.H. Greenleaf, *Order, Empiricism and Politics: Two Traditions of English Political Thought* (London: Oxford University Press, 1964), p. 52.
2. In the paraphrase of Professor Greenleaf, op. cit., note 1, p. 92.
3. Greenleaf, op. cit., note 1, p. 93.
4. In Peter Laslett (ed.), *Patriarcha and Other Political Works of Sir Robert Filmer* (Oxford: Basil Blackwell, 1949), p. 286. Quoted in Carl Watner, '"Oh, Ye are for Anarchy!"': Consent Theory in the Radical Libertarian Tradition', *Journal of Libertarian Studies*, VIII (Winter 1986), p. 119.
5. Coke did not fully break with the king and adopt the Parliament-over-all position until 1621. In 1616, he was ousted from his post in the Privy Council, but immediately won his way back into King James's favour by marrying his daughter to Sir John Villiers, the older brother of the duke of Buckingham. He was still a privy councillor in 1621, and was expected to remain in the Court Party, but the king's by-passing him for promotion to Lord Chancellor led to Coke's final break with the Crown.
6. See Joyce Oldham Appleby, *Economic Thought and Ideology in Seventeenth-Century England* (Princeton, NJ: Princeton University Press, 1978), p. 106.
7. As Schumpeter puts it, these men were 'special pleaders for or against some individual interest, such as the Company of Merchant Adventurers or the East India Company; advocates or foes of a particular measure or policy.... All of them flourished...owing to the rapid increase of the opportunities for printing and publishing. Newspapers also, rare

ventures in the sixteenth century, became plentiful in the seventeenth...' J.A. Schumpeter, *History of Economic Analysis* (New York: Oxford University Press, 1954), pp. 160–61.

8. Barry E. Supple, *Commercial Crisis and Change in England, 1600–1642* (Cambridge: Cambridge University Press, 1964), pp. 219–20.

9. Appleby, op. cit., note 6, pp. 49, 179; also see Terence W. Hutchison, *Before Adam Smith: The Emergence of Political Economy, 1662–1776* (Oxford: Basil Blackwell, 1988), p. 386.

10. For a fascinating discussion of Bacon's important role in immanentizing the sacral in the form of the pseudo-science of the Ancient Wisdom, see Stephen A. McKnight, *Sacralizing the Secular: the Renaissance Origins of Modernity* (Baton Rouge, LA: L.S.U. Press, 1989), pp. 92–7. Also see Frances Yates, 'Francis Bacon, 'Under the Shadow of Jehova's Wings', in *The Rosicrucian Enlightenment* (London, Routledge and Kegan Paul, 1972). Paolo Rossi, *Francis Bacon: From Magic to Science* (Chicago: University of Chicago, 1968).

11. On Hobbes and the Tew circle, see the illuminating work by Richard Tuck, *Natural Rights Theories* (Cambridge: Cambridge University Press, 1979).

12. See the fascinating article by H.R. Trevor-Roper, 'Three Foreigners and the Philosophy of the English Revolution', *Encounter*, 14 (Feb. 1960), pp. 3–20, esp. p. 15, and on Comenius and his neo-Rosicrucian group, Yates, op. cit., note 1, pp. 156–92. Also see the illuminating discussion in William Letwin, *The Origins of Scientific Economics* (Garden City, NY: Doubleday, 1965), pp. 125–6, 134–5.

13. In Petty's *The Advice of W.P. to Mr. Samuel Hartlib, for the advancement of some particular parts of learning...*See Letwin, op. cit., note 12, pp. 136–7.

14. The exception was poor Hartlib, who lost his Cromwellian pension and died in 1670 after fleeing his creditors to Holland.

15. The Royal Society was headed by Dr John Wilkins, head of Oxford University and later bishop of Chester. In addition to being Cromwell's brother-in-law, Wilkins, author of the book *Mathematical Magick* (1648), was a leading adept of the hermetic and magic-steeped Rosicrucian movement as well as of the leading Elizabethan *magus*, Dr John Dee and his hermetic alchemist disciple, Robert Fludd. See Yates, op. cit., note 10, pp. 182ff.

16. Hutchison, op. cit., note 9, p. 29.

17. Letwin, op. cit., note 12, p. 131.

18. Letwin, op. cit., note 12, p. 140.

19. Letwin, op. cit., note 12, pp. 144–5.

20. Hutchison, op. cit., note 9, p. 39.

21. Hutchison, op. cit., note 9, pp. 38–9. Also see in particular Edgar S. Furniss, *The Position of the Laborer in a System of Nationalism: A Study of the Labor Theories of the Later English Mercantilists* (1920, NY: Kelley & Millman, 1957), pp. 128, 134.

22. Pitirim A. Sorokin, *Fads and Foibles in Modern Sociology* (Chicago: Henry Regnery, 1956), p. 103, p. 110 and passim.

23. Letwin, op. cit., note 12, pp. 106–7.

24. Letwin, op. cit., note 12, pp. 149–51. On the libertarian impact of Swift's writings, see Caroline Robbins, *The Eighteenth-Century Commonwealthman* (Cambridge, Mass.: Harvard University Press, 1959), pp. 152–3; and James A. Preu, *The Dean and the Anarchist* (Tallahassee, Fl: Florida State University Press, 1959). On the *Modest Proposal*, see Louis A. Landa, 'A Modest Proposal and Populousness', in *Essays in Eighteenth-Century English Literature* (1942, Princeton, NJ: Princeton University Press, 1980), pp. 39–48.

11 Mercantilism and freedom in England from the Civil War to 1750

11.1   The Pettyites: Davenant, King and 'the law of demand'

Jonathan Swift's *A Modest Proposal* should have provided the last word on political arithmetic, except that an epilogue has been furnished by the quantophrenic and metromanic folly of modern historians of economic thought, who have resurrected a Baconian or Pettyite 'quantitative law' expounded in the 1690s as if it were a veritable marvel of anticipation of modern econometrics.

Charles Davenant (1656–1714), son of a poet laureate and dramatist, was an attorney who spent his life scrambling for the main chance. To supplement his meagre income from law practice, he managed to obtain the appointment of commissioner of excise in 1678. By the mid-1680s, Davenant was making a handsome salary as commissioner and was also an MP. His comfortable and placid existence, however, was grievously disrupted by the Revolution of 1688, which lost Davenant his high post; moreover, substantial loans of his to the Crown of Charles II remained unrepaid.

A Tory confronting a Whig regime, Davenant now began to turn his attention to writing economic tracts on the problems of the day. All his publications centred around special pleading for his own political interests, a quest for subsidy or for resuming his high post in the government. Davenant's first tract, *An Essay upon the Ways and Means of supplying the War* was published in 1694, after five years of war with the Dutch, and after the same number of years of Davenant's trying unsuccessfully to get back his old post as commissioner of excise. The burden of the tract was denouncing the government for financing any part of the war by public debt, and urging instead that it rely almost totally on the excise, coincidentally Davenant's own area of expertise. After again denouncing the government that stubbornly refused to see his own virtues, Davenant turned to another area of self-interest.

Davenant has been termed inconsistent and confused on the free trade issue, sometimes appearing to favour free trade and other times favouring protection. But these inconsistencies magically clear up if we realize that Davenant, in an attempt to get on the East India Company bandwagon, revived the by now grand seventeenth century tradition of arguing about the rights and wrongs of the East India trade. Davenant unsurprisingly took the standard Munian line of supporting an overall, or general, 'favourable' balance of trade, but pointed out the absurdity of trying to balance trade with each country, and defending the East India Company's deficit with the Far East. Davenant's pro-East India trade position was expressed in his 1696 tract, *Essay on the East India Trade*. The following year, Davenant urged the East India Company to send him to India; failing that, Davenant continued to curry favour with the company by publishing two *Discourses on the Publick Revenues and on the Trade of England* (1697–98), and another *Essay upon...the Balance of Trade* in 1699, continuing his Munian foreign trade analysis.

By 1698, indeed Charles Davenant's fortune had changed; he was now a Tory MP and the East India Company agreed to send him to India. From then on, Davenant's writings were mainly strictly political, and in 1703 he finally achieved his objective of regaining a high government post, inspector-general of exports and imports. Davenant was in and out of trouble, however, his writings changing radically from 'moderation' to 'extremism' and back with each change of the political winds, or from Tory to Whig, until he ended his career generally scorned and trusted by none, in financial difficulties and living on the largesse of his old friend James Brydges, the Duke of Chandos. All in all, his biographer Professor Waddell does not seem too severe when he concludes that:

> Davenant's career was thus not much of a success. He lacked the force of personality and obvious integrity necessary for the role...he...tried to play – that of a partisan pamphleteer who was yet a man of independent judgment and not a mere hack. He was on the losing side in nearly every controversy he joined.... He proved incapable of managing his own affairs and became a burden on his friends.... He was neither an original thinker, nor a practical man of affairs, but merely a competent publicist. The relationship between his writings and his personal circumstances suggests that his enemies had some excuse for regarding him as a purely self-seeking and mercenary time-server.[1]

It is intriguing that Davenant, as a devoted follower of political arithmetic, would try to justify his self-seeking wavering by employing political arithmetic as a kind of cost–benefit analysis, in which the statesman, possessing 'a computing head', arrives at a balance of advantages, 'by summing up the difficulties on either side, and by computing upon the whole. In that way, he shall be able to form a sound judgment and to give right advice; and this is what we mean by Political Arithmetic'.[2]

Davenant would be a forgotten and no-account minor mercantilist writer, except for the extravagant praise lavished by modern quantophrenic historians of thought upon a previously unknown and alleged 'economic law' discovered by Davenant and by his quiet political arithmetical and political ally, the accountant Gregory King (1648–1712). This 'law of demand' is now hailed as the origin of econometrics, predating Bernoulli's alleged law of the diminishing utility of money of 1738 (see below). Embarrassing adulation has been heaped upon this absurd 'law' by modern economists zealously trying to find prefigurements of econometric 'science'. There has been much confusion on the precise credit for authorship of this alleged law, how attribution should be shared between King and Davenant, and even, solemnly, whether it should be called the 'Davenant–King' or the 'King–Davenant' law, as valueless a piece of scholarly disputation as has appeared in many a moon. The law first appeared in Davenant's *Essay upon...the Balance of Trade* of 1699, citing an unpublished manuscript by King, the *Natural and Political Observations*...written in 1696.[3] The 'law' states baldly, and without evidence, that the following will happen when the supply of the harvest of corn (wheat) is reduced below the usual amount: not simply, as has been known since the scholastics, that a lower supply of a product will tend to raise the price, but that the effect will be a definite quantitative relation, as follows:

Reduction of corn harvest	Increase in corn price
1/10	3/10
2/10	8/10
3/10	16/10
4/10	28/10
5/10	45/10

Modern economists have generally, *pace* Alfred Marshall, grievously misinterpreted this quantitative statement as a 'demand schedule', or tabular basis for a demand curve, and as a pioneering attempt to 'measure' the elasticity of such a curve. But the grave fallacy here is that this quantitative relation has nothing whatever to do with the consumer demand schedule that plays such a deservedly important part in modern economics. The genuine demand schedule is hypothetical, subjective, and instantaneous: all it says is that at a given moment, at price *x*, consumers would purchase a certain quantity *y* of the product. And the point of this schedule is precisely that we don't know and *can't* know this subjective relation, that there is no way to find out, and that the only point of the demand schedule is to show that, at any given time, the demand curve is 'falling', that is, as the price falls the quantity demanded increases, and vice versa. Properly, the law is qualitative and never quantitative, and there is never any way to establish such quantities.

What the pro-Davenant 'law' economists fail to realize, then, is that even if this Davenant table were based on historical fact, all it would establish is *not* a demand schedule or curve, but only the factual 'equilibrium' points each year, that is, each year's price and quantity produced. These points have nothing to do with any genuine demand schedule or 'law of demand', which is strictly qualitative and subjective to the minds of consumers.

Second, even if these historical data were correct, they would *only* establish a relation for the particular years and particular markets in question; they would in no sense establish any sort of 'law' for the same continuing quantitative relationship between supply and price in any other year or place.

But finally, there is no evidence that this table is based on any factual evidence *at all*! Thus, despite the solemn repetition of this table from the late nineteenth century onwards, and despite its alleged pioneering of econometric science, this Davenant–King table has no value whatever either as factual data, as statistics, as econometrics, or as economic theory. It is testimony only to the quantophrenic folly of modern economics.[4]

And yet economists, striving desperately to maintain that the Davenant–King 'law' *must* have clothes, have taken one of two contradictory directions in presuming the importance of the law, and sometimes have taken both stances at once. Thus Jevons (1871), without any evidence at all, simply assumed that the Davenant–King table was 'accurate' and pronounced it a scandal that economists and statisticians hadn't yet matched these numbers in accuracy. On the other hand, William Whewell, an odd combination of expert Cambridge mathematician and arch-empiricist in the philosophy of science and economics had, two decades earlier (1850), sensed that the Davenant table was really the mere working out of a mathematical formula, and yet he still assumed that it must have been based on empirical observations. Similarly, in his recent careful study, Professor Creedy has convincingly shown that the King–Davenant numbers were the working out of the mathematical formula of 'factoral expansion of a polynomial', a method first discovered by the English mathematician James Gregory and then used by Isaac Newton for his great work in physics. But, after usefully pointing out how King could have rapidly discovered and used the new Gregory–Newton method Creedy, instead of concluding sensibly that the statistical or econometric soundness of the Davenant–King 'law' lies in ruins, blithely proceeds to save the theory by simply asserting that it 'was quite possible' that the polynomial formula 'was fitted to actual observations'. 'Quite possible', but there is no evidence whatever, and, since this 'law' was never replicated, and was even changed by King, it is far more likely that, enchanted with the new maths as Creedy himself concedes, 'hypothetical values of coefficients were used with an arbitrarily chosen polynomial in order to generate the basic "data"'; in other words, that King and/or Davenant made it all up, as part of their 'new science'.[5]

11.2   Liberty and property: the Levellers and Locke
The turmoil of the English Civil War in the 1640s and 1650s generated political and institutional upheaval, and stimulated radical thinking about politics. Since the Civil War was fought over religion and politics, much of the new thinking was grounded in, or inspired by, religious principles and visions. Thus, as we shall see further in the chapter on 'The roots of Marxism' (Chapter 9 in Volume II), millennial communist sects popped up again, for the first time since the Anabaptist frenzy of the early sixteenth century in

Germany and Holland. Particularly prominent in the frenzy of the Civil War Left were the Diggers, the Ranters, and the Fifth Monarchists.[6]

At the opposite pole of new thought generated by the Civil War was the prominence, in the midst of the forces of the mainstream republican Left, of the world's first self-consciously libertarian mass movement: the Levellers. In a series of notable debates within the Republican Army – notably between the Cromwellians and the Levellers – the Levellers, led by John Lilburne, Richard Overton and William Walwyn, worked out a remarkably consistent libertarian doctrine, upholding the rights of 'self-ownership', private property, religious freedom for the individual, and minimal government interference in society. The rights of each individual to his person and property, furthermore, were 'natural', that is, they were derived from the nature of man and the universe, and therefore were not dependent on, nor could they be abrogated by, government. And while the economy was scarcely a primary focus of the Levellers, their adherence to a free market economy was a simple derivation from their stress on liberty and the rights of private property.

For a while it seemed that the Levellers would triumph in the Civil War, but Cromwell decided to resolve the army debates by the use of force, and he established his coercive dictatorship and radical puritan theocracy by placing the Leveller leadership in jail. The victory of Cromwell and his Puritans over the Levellers proved fateful for the course of English history. For it meant that 'republicanism', in the eyes of the English, would be forever associated with the bloody rule of Cromwell's saints, the reign of religious fanaticism, and the sacking of the great English cathedrals. Hence the death of Cromwell led swiftly to the restoration of the Stuarts, and the permanent discrediting of the republican cause. It is likely, on the contrary, that a Leveller rule of freedom, religious toleration and minimal government might have proved roughly acceptable to the English people, and might have ensured a far more libertarian English polity than actually evolved after the Restoration and the Whig Settlement.[7]

Historiographical discussion of the great libertarian political theorist John Locke (1632–1704), who emerged to prominence after the Civil War, and particularly in the 1680s, has been mired in a welter of conflicting interpretations. Was Locke a radically individualistic political thinker or a conservative Protestant scholastic? An individualist or a majoritarian? A pure philosopher or a revolutionary intriguer? A radical harbinger of modernity or one who harked back to the medieval or to classical virtue?

Most of these interpretations are, oddly enough, not really contradictory. By this point, we should realize that the scholastics may have dominated medieval and post-medieval traditions, but that despite this fact, they were pioneers and elaborators of the natural law *and* natural rights traditions. The pitting of 'tradition' vs 'modernity' is largely an artificial antithesis. 'Moderns' like Locke or perhaps even Hobbes may have been individualists and 'right-thinkers', but they were also steeped in scholasticism and natural law. Locke may have been and indeed was an ardent Protestant, but he was also a Protestant scholastic, heavily influenced by the founder of Protestant scholasticism, the Dutchman Hugo Grotius, who in turn was heavily influenced by the late Spanish Catholic scholastics. As we have already seen, such great late sixteenth century Spanish Jesuit scholastics as Suarez and Mariana were contractual natural rights thinkers, with Mariana being positively 'pre-Lockean' in his insistence on the right of the people to resume the rights of sovereignty they had previously delegated to the king. While Locke developed libertarian natural rights thought more fully than his predecessors, it was still squarely embedded in the scholastic natural law tradition.[8]

Neither are John Pocock and his followers convincing in trying to posit an artificial distinction and clash between the libertarian concerns of Locke or his later followers on the one hand, and devotion to 'classical virtue' on the other. In this view eighteenth century Lockean libertarians from 'Cato' to Jefferson become magically transmuted from radical individualists and free marketeers into nostalgic reactionaries harking back to ancient or renaissance 'classical virtue'. Followers of such virtue somehow become old-fashioned communitarians rather than modern individualists. And yet, why can't libertarians and opposers of government intervention *also* oppose government 'corruption' and extravagance? Indeed, the two generally go together. As soon as we realize that, generally, and certainly until Bentham, devotees of liberty, property and free markets have generally been moralists as well as adherents of a free market economy, the Pocockian antitheses begin to fall apart. To seventeenth and eighteenth century libertarians, indeed to libertarians in most times and places, attacks on government intervention and on government moral corruption go happily hand in hand.[9]

There are still anomalies in John Locke's career and thought, but they can be cleared up by the explicit discussion and implications of the impressive work by Richard Ashcraft.[10] Essentially Ashcraft demonstrates that Locke's career can be divided into two parts. Locke's father, a country lawyer and son of minor puritan country gentry, fought in Cromwell's army and was able to use the political pull of his mentor Colonel Alexander Popham, MP, to get John into the prominent Westminster School. At Westminster, and then at Christ Church, Oxford, Locke obtained a BA and then an MA in 1658, then become a lecturer at the college in Greek and rhetoric in 1662, and became a medical student and then a physician in order to stay at Oxford without having to take holy orders.

Despite or perhaps because of Locke's puritan background and patronage, he clearly came under the influence of the Baconian scientists at Oxford, notably including Robert Boyle, and hence he tended to adopt the 'scientific', empiricist, low-key absolutist viewpoint of his friends and mentors. While at Oxford, Locke and his colleagues enthusiastically welcomed the restoration of Charles II, and indeed the king himself ordered Oxford University to keep Locke as medical student without having to take holy orders. While at Oxford, Locke adopted the empiricist methodology and sensate philosophy of the Baconians, leading to his later *Essay Concerning Human Understanding*. Moreover, in 1661, Locke, this later champion of religious toleration, wrote two tracts denouncing religious tolerance, and favouring the absolute state enforcing religious orthodoxy. In 1668, Locke was elected to the Royal Society, joining his fellow Baconian scientists.

Something happened to John Locke in the year 1666, however, when he became a physician and in the following year when he became personal secretary, advisor, writer, theoretician, and close friend of the great Lord Ashley (Anthony Ashley Cooper), who in 1672 was named the first Earl Shaftesbury. It was due to Shaftesbury that Locke, from then on, was to plunge into political and economic philosophy, and into public service as well as revolutionary intrigue. Locke adopted from Shaftesbury the entire classical liberal Whig outlook, and it was Shaftesbury who converted Locke into a firm and lifelong champion of religious toleration and into a libertarian exponent of self-ownership, property rights, and a free market economy. It was Shaftesbury who made Locke into a libertarian and who stimulated the development of Locke's libertarian system.

John Locke, in short, quickly became a Shaftesburyite, and thereby a classical liberal and libertarian. All his life and even after Shaftesbury's death in 1683, Locke only had words of adulation for his friend and mentor. Locke's epitaph for Shaftesbury declared that the latter was 'a vigorous and indefatigable champion of civil and ecclesiastical liberty'. The editor of the definitive edition of Locke's *Two Treatises of Government* justly writes that 'Without Shaftesbury, Locke would not have been Locke at all'. This truth has been hidden all too often by historians who have had an absurdly monastic horror of how political theory and philosophy often develop: in the heat of political and ideological battle. Instead, many felt they had to hide this relationship in order to construct an idealized image of Locke the pure and detached philosopher, separate from the grubby and mundane political concerns of the real world.[11]

Professor Ashcraft also shows how Locke and Shaftesbury began to build up, even consciously, a neo-Leveller movement, elaborating doctrines very similar to those of the Levellers. Locke's entire structure of thought in his *Two Treatises of Government*, written in 1681–82 as a schema for justifying the forthcoming Whig revolution against the Stuarts, was an elaboration and creative development of Leveller doctrine: the beginnings in self-ownership or self-propriety, the deduced right to property and free exchange, the justification of government as a device to protect such rights, and the right of overturning a government that violates, or becomes destructive of, those ends. One of the former Leveller leaders, Major John Wildman, was even close to the Locke–Shaftesbury set during the 1680s.

The deep affinity between Locke and scholastic thought has been obscured by the undeniable fact that to Locke, Shaftesbury and the Whigs, the real enemy of civil and religious liberty, the great advocate of monarchical absolutism, during the late seventeenth century and into the eighteenth century, was the Catholic Church. For by the mid-seventeenth century, Catholicism, or 'popery', was identified not with the natural rights and the checks on royal despotism as of yore, but with the absolutism of Louis XIV of France, the leading absolutist state in Europe, and earlier with absolutist Spain. For the Reformation, after a century, had succeeded in taking the wraps off monarchical tyranny in the Catholic as well as Protestant countries. Ever since the turn of the seventeenth century, indeed, the Catholic Church in France, Jansenist and royalist in spirit, had been more a creature of royal absolutism than a check on its excesses. In fact, by the seventeenth century, the case could be made that the most prosperous country in Europe which was also the freest – in economics, in civil liberties, in a decentralized polity and in abstinence from imperial adventures – was Protestant Holland.[12]

Thus it was easy for the English Whigs and classical liberals to identify the absolutism, the arbitrary taxes, the controls, and the incessant wars of the Stuarts with the Catholicism towards which the Stuarts were not so secretly moving, as well as with the spectre of Louis XIV, towards whom the Stuarts were moving as well. As a result, the English and American colonial tradition, even the libertarian tradition, became imbued with a fanatical anti-Catholicism; the idea of including evil Catholics in the rubric of religious toleration was rarely entertained.

One common confusion about Locke's systematic theory of property needs to be cleared up: Locke's theory of labour. Locke grounded his theory of natural property rights in each individual's right of self-ownership, of a 'propriety' in his own person. What then establishes anyone's original right of material, or landed or natural resource property, apart from his own person? In Locke's brilliant and very sensible theory, property is brought out of the commons, or out of non-property, into one's private ownership, in the same way that a man brings non-used property into use: that is, by 'mixing his self-owned labour', his personal energy, with a previously unused and unowned natural resource, thereby bringing that resource into productive use and hence into his private property. Private property of a material resource is established by first use. These two axioms: self-ownership of each person, and the first use, or 'homesteading', of natural resources, establishes the 'naturalness', the morality, and the property rights underlying the entire free market economy. For if a man justly owns material property he has settled in and worked on, he has the deduced right to exchange those property titles for the property someone else has settled in and worked on with *his* labour. For if someone owns property, he has a right to exchange it for someone else's property, or to give that property away to a willing recipient. This chain of deduction establishes the right of free exchange and free contract, and the right of bequest, and hence the entire property rights structure of the market economy.

Many historians, especially Marxists, have taken glee in claiming that John Locke is thereby the founder of the Marxian 'labour theory of value' (which Marx in turn acquired from Smith and especially Ricardo). But Locke's is a labour theory of *property*, that is, how material property justly comes into ownership by means of labour exertion or 'mixing'. This theory has absolutely nothing to do with what determines the *value* or price of goods or services on the market, and therefore has nothing to do with the later 'labour theory of value'.

11.3   Child, Locke, the rate of interest, and the coinage

One of the most prominent economic writers of the latter half of the seventeenth century in England was the eminent Sir Josiah Child (1630–99). He was a wealthy merchant who was usually affiliated with the powerful East India Company and indeed rose to be its governor, and the central concern in his economic writings was the by now traditional apologetics for the East India interests. That is: no one need worry about balance of trade from one specific country to another; a broader look at a nation's balance should be taken; and therefore the East India Company's notorious gold and silver exports to, or deficits with, the Far East are justified if we consider the company's re-exports to, and hence surpluses with, other countries. Because of this broader emphasis on the overall balance of trade, later economists often associated Child with a free trade, *laissez-faire* approach.

Unwary historians were also entrapped by many of Child's fulminations against monopolies and monopolistic privileges granted by the state to cities, guilds or trading companies. Again, they assume that Child was an advocate of *laissez-faire*; what they overlooked was that Child was always careful to defend, as a special exception, the monopoly granted to the East India Company.[13]

Child never attained the genuine *laissez-faire* view that even the overall balance of trade was unimportant; on the contrary, he insisted that gold and silver bullion could only be exported freely if the overall effect of such export would be a net import of specie, in other words, an overall favourable balance of trade.[14]

Unfortunately, Child's work was interpreted as solid *laissez-faire* doctrine in the eighteenth century, and particularly by the mid-eighteenth century devotee of *laissez-faire*, Viscount de Gournay, who translated Child into French as part of his programme of spreading *laissez-faire* doctrine in France. As a result, Child's work achieved undeserving fame in the following century.

One of Josiah Child's main deviations from free market and *laissez-faire* doctrine was to agitate for one of the favourite programmes of the mercantilists: to push the legal maximum rate of interest ever lower. Formerly discredited 'usury laws' were making a comeback on faulty economic rather than natural law or theological grounds.

From the early decades of the seventeenth century, English mercantilists were bitter at the superior prosperity and economic growth enjoyed by the Dutch. Observing that the rate of interest was lower in Holland than in England, they chose to leap to the causal analysis that the *cause* of the superior Dutch prosperity was Holland's low rate of interest, and that therefore it was the task of the English government to force the maximum rate of interest down until the interest rate was lower than in Holland. The first prominent mercantilist tract calling for lowering the interest rate was that of the country gentleman Sir Thomas Culpeper, in his brief *Tract Against the High Rate of Usury* (1621). Culpeper declared that Dutch prosperity was caused by their low rate of interest; that the English high interest rate crippled trade; and therefore that the government should force maximum interest rates down to outcompete the Dutch. Culpeper's pamphlet played a role in Parliament's lowering the maximum usury rate from 10 to 8 per cent. Culpeper's tract was reprinted several times, and Parliament duly pushed the maximum rate in later years down to 8 and then 6 per cent.

Each time, however, resistance increased, especially as government intervention forced down the maximum rate repeatedly. Finally, in 1668, the mercantilists tried for their most important conquest: a lowering of the maximum interest rate from 6 to 4 per cent, which would presumably result in rates below the Dutch. As a propaganda accompaniment to this bill, Culpeper's son, Sir Thomas Culpeper, in 1668 reprinted his father's tract, along with one of his own, whose title says it all: *A Discourse showing the many Advantages which will accrue to this Kingdom by the Abatement of Usury together with the Absolute Necessity of Reducing Interest of Money to the lowest Rate it bears in other Countreys.*

Culpeper Senior's pamphlet was published along with the influential contribution by the already eminent merchant and man of affairs, Josiah Child, in his first pamphlet, *Brief Observations concerning trade, and interest of money.* Child was a prominent member of the king's council of trade, established in 1668 to advise him on economic matters. Child treated lowering the maximum rate of interest to 4 per cent as virtually a panacea for all economic ills. A lower rate of interest would vivify trade, and raise the price of land; it would even cure drunkenness.

Josiah Child's pamphlet and his testimony before Parliament were centrepieces of the debate swirling around the proposal. Child's critics pointed out effectively that low interest in a country is the *effect* of plentiful savings and of prosperity, and not their cause. Thus, Edward Waller, during the House of Commons debate, pointed out that 'it is with money as it is with other commodities, when they are most plentiful then they are cheapest, so make money [savings] plentiful and the interest will be low'. Colonel Silius Titus pressed on to demonstrate that, since low interest is the consequence and not the cause of wealth, any maximum usury law would be counterproductive: for by outlawing currently legal loans, 'its effect would be to make usurers call in their loans. Traders would be ruined, and mortgages foreclosed; gentlemen who needed to borrow would be forced to break the law....'[15]

Child feebly replied to his critics that usurers would never not lend their money, that they were forced to take the legal maximum or lump it. On the idea that low interest was an effect not a cause, Child merely recited the previous times that English government had forced interest lower, from 10 to 8 to 6 per cent. Why not then a step further? Child, of course, did not deign to take the scenario further and ask why the state did not have the power to force the interest rate down to zero.

Child's critics raised another telling point: how is it that the Dutch were able to get their interest rates low purely by economic means; how come the Dutch did not *need* a usury statute? Child's absurd rejoinder was that the Dutch *would have* pushed their interest rate down by statute if their market rate had not fallen low by itself.

It should be noted that this low interest deviation from *laissez-faire* accorded with Josiah Child's personal economic interest. As a leading East India merchant, Child and his colleagues were great borrowers not lenders, and so were interested in cheap credit. Even more revealing was Child's reply to the charge of the author of *Interest of Money Mistaken* that Child was trying to 'engross all trade into the hands of a few rich merchants who have money enough of their own to trade with, to the excluding of all young men that want it'. Child replied to that shrewd thrust that, on the contrary, his East India Company was not in need of a low rate since it could borrow as much money as it pleased at 4 per cent. But that of course is precisely the point. Sir Josiah Child and his ilk were eager to push down the rate of interest below the free market level in order to create a shortage of credit, and thereby to ration credit to the prime borrowers – to large firms who could afford to pay 4 per cent or less and *away* from more speculative borrowers. It was precisely because Child knew full well that a forced lowering of interest rates would indeed 'engross all trade into the hands of a few rich merchants' that Child and his colleagues were so eager to put this mercantilist measure into effect.[16]

When the House of Lords' committee held hearings on the interest-lowering bill during 1668–69, it decided to hold testimony from members of the king's council of trade, of whom Josiah Child was a central figure. But another important figure was a very different member of the council of trade, and also a member of the Lords' committee, the great Lord Ashley, John Locke's new and powerful patron. As a classical liberal, Ashley opposed the bill, and at his behest, Locke wrote his first work on economic matters, the influential though as yet unpublished manuscript, 'Some of the Consequences that are like to follow upon Lessening of Interest to Four Percent' (1668). Locke made clear in this early work his profound insight, as well as thoroughgoing commitment, to a free market economy, as well as to his later structure of property rights theory.

Locke displayed straightaway his skill at polemics; the essay was basically a critique of Child's influential work. First, Locke cut through the holistic rhetoric; of course, he pointed out, the borrowing merchant will be happy to pay only 4 per cent interest; but this gain to the borrower is not a gain for the national or general good, since the lender loses by the same amount. Not only would a forced lowering of interest be at best redistributive, but, Locke added, the measure would restrict the supply of savings and credit, thereby making the economy worse off. It would be better, he concluded, if the legal rate of interest were set at the 'natural rate', that is the free market rate 'which the present scarcity [of funds] makes it naturally at...'. In short, the best interest rate is the free market, or the 'natural' interest rate, set by the workings of free man under natural law, i.e. the rate determined by the supply of and demand for money loans at any given time.

Whether or not Locke or Ashley proved decisive, the House of Lords finally killed the 4 per cent bill in 1669. Three years later, Ashley became chancellor of the Exchequer as Earl Shaftesbury, and the following year Locke became secretary to the council for trade and plantations, which replaced the old council of trade. At the end of 1674, however, Shaftesbury was fired, the council of trade and plantations was disbanded, and Locke followed his mentor into political opposition, revolutionary intrigues, and exile in Holland.

John Locke finally returned to London with the overthrow of the Stuarts and the Revolution of 1688, returning in triumph on the same ship as Queen Mary. Locke returned to England to find the old East India crowd up to their old tricks. England was in dire financial straits, Charles II having ruined public credit with his Stop of the Exchequer, and the East India people had once again introduced a bill in 1690 for the compulsory lowering of interest to 4 per cent. At the same time, Sir Josiah Child was brought back to expand his pamphlet into a *Discourse About Trade* (1690), an anonymous book reprinted three years later as *A New Discourse of Trade*, with Child's name blazoned on the title page. It was the *New Discourse* that was to make such an excessive impression on eighteenth century thinkers. In addition to the renewed arguments for lower interest, the *Discourse* and the *New Discourse* added more apologetics for the East India line on trade and on monopolies.

In response, John Locke's new political patron, now that Shaftesbury had died, Sir John Somers, MP, apparently asked Locke to expand *his* 1668 paper to refute Child's and other proponents of the 4 per cent bill. Locke responded the following year with his expanded book, *Some Considerations of the Consequences of the Lowering of Interest and Raising the Value of Money* (1692) which brought Locke's previously unpublished arguments into public debate. Locke's work may have been influential in the 4 per cent bill once again being killed in the House of Lords.

The latter part of Locke's *Considerations* was devoted to the great recoinage controversy, into which England had been plunged since 1690. In that year, England's basic money stock of silver coins had deteriorated so far, due to erosion and coin-clipping, and the contrast of these inferior 'hammered' coins to the newer, uneroded and unclipped 'milled' coins was so great, that Gresham's law began to operate intensely. People either circulated the over-valued eroded coins and hoarded the better ones, or else passed the poor coins at their lower weight rather than at their face value. By 1690 the older hammered coins had lost approximately one-third of their worth compared to their face value.

It was increasingly clear that the Mint had to offer recoinage into the new superior coins. But at what rate? Mercantilists, who tended to be inflationist, clamoured for debasement, that is, recoinage at the lighter weight, devaluating silver coin and increasing the supply of money. In the meanwhile, the monetary problem was aggravated by a burst of bank credit inflation created by the new Bank of England, founded in 1694 to inflate the money supply and finance the government's deficit. As the coinage problem came to a head in that same year, William Lowndes (1652–1724), secretary of the treasury and the government's main monetary expert, issued a 'Report on the Amendment of Silver Coin' in 1695 calling for accepting the extant debasement, and for officially debasing the coinage by 25 per cent, lightening the currency name by a 25 per cent lower weight of silver. In his *Considerations*, Locke had denounced debasement as deceitful and illusionist: what determined the real value of a coin, he declared, was the amount of silver in the coin, and not the name granted to it by the authorities. Debasement, Locke warned in his magnificently hard-money discussion, is illusory and inflationist: if coins, for example, are devalued by one-twentieth, 'when men go to market to buy any other commodities with their new, but lighter money, they will find 20s of their new money will buy no more than 19 would before'. Debasement merely dilutes the real value, the purchasing power, of each currency unit.

Threatened by the Lowndes report, Locke's patron John Somers, who had been made Lord Keeper of the Great Seal in a new Whig ministry in 1694, asked Locke to rebut Lowndes's position before the Privy Council. Locke published his rebuttal later in the year 1695, *Further Considerations Concerning Raising the Value of Money*. This publication was so well received that it went into three editions within a year. Locke superbly put his finger on the supposed function of the Mint: to maintain the currency as purely a definition, or standard of weight of silver; any debasement, any change of standards, would be as arbitrary, fraudulent, and unjust as the government's changing the definition of a foot or a yard. Locke put it dramatically: 'one may as rationally hope to lengthen a foot by dividing it into fifteen parts instead of twelve, and calling them inches…'.

Furthermore, government, the supported guarantor of contracts, thereby leads in contract-breaking:

> The reason why it should not be changed is this: because the public authority is guarantee for the performance of all legal contracts. But men are absolved from the performance of their legal contracts, if the quantity of silver under settled and legal denominations be altered…the landlord here and creditor are each defrauded of twenty percent of what they contracted for and is their due…[17]

One of Locke's opponents both on coinage and on interest was the prominent builder, fire insurance magnate and land bank projector, Nicholas Barbon (1637–98). Barbon, son of the fanatic London Anabaptist preacher and leather merchant and MP Praisegod Barbon,[18] studied medicine and became an MD in Holland, moving to London and going into business in the early 1660s. In the same year as Child's *Discourse About Trade*, Barbon, who had just been elected to Parliament, published the similarly titled *Discourse of Trade* (1690), again timed to push for the 4 per cent interest bill in Parliament. An inveterate debtor and projector, Barbon of course would have liked to push down his interest costs.

In 1696, Barbon returned to the lists in a bitter attack on Locke's *Further Considerations* on the coinage. Arguing against Locke's market commodity, or 'metallist', view of money, Barbon, urging devaluation of silver, countered with the nominalist and statist view that money is not the market commodity but whatever government says it is. Wrote Barbon: 'Money is the instrument and measure of commerce and not silver. It is the instrument of commerce from the authority of that government where it is coined…'[19]

Fortunately, Locke's view triumphed, and the recoinage was decided and carried out in 1696 on Lockean lines: the integrity of the weight of the silver denomination of currency was preserved. In the same year, Locke became the dominant commissioner of the newly constituted board of trade. Locke was appointed by his champion Sir John Somers who had become chief minister from 1697 to 1700. When the Somers regime fell in 1700, Locke was ousted from the board of trade, to retire until his death four years later. The Lockean recoinage was assisted by Locke's old friend, the great physicist Sir Isaac Newton (1642–1727) who, while still a professor of mathematics at Cambridge from 1669 on, also became warden of the Mint in 1696, and rose to master of the Mint three years later, continuing in that post until his death in 1727. Newton agreed with Locke's hard-money views of recoinage.

Barbon and Locke set the trend for two contrasting strands in eighteenth century monetary thought: Locke, the Protestant scholastic, was essentially in the hard-money, metallist, anti-inflationist tradition of the scholastics; Barbon, on the other hand, helped set the tone for the inflationist schemers and projectors of the next century.[20]

11.4   The North brothers, deductions from axioms, and Tory *laissez-faire*

Weighing in on the side of John Locke, not only on interest rates but also in a general and comprehensive vision of economic *laissez-faire* that even surpassed Locke, were two brothers, Dudley and Roger North, who came from a distinguished Tory family. Here was a fascinating convergence of views of a radical Whig, and high Tories and zealous subjects of Charles and James II. This juncture presaged a later meeting of minds of 'extreme Left' and 'extreme Right' during the eighteenth century, when the imperialist–Whig–mercantilist one-party Establishment, from 1715 to the 1750s, was opposed on the Left by radical libertarian Commonwealthmen and on the Right by the anti-imperialist, Catholic or proto-Catholic opposition, all agreeing on denunciations of the mercantilistic, high tax, high public debt, central banking state.[21]

Dudley and Roger North were sons of the fourth Baron North. Showing little aptitude for schooling, Dudley (1641–91), went to Turkey and became a prominent trader, as well as a director of both the Levant Company, which had been granted a monopoly of English trade with the Middle East, and the African Company, which enjoyed a monopoly of trade with that continent. Dudley North returned to London from Turkey in 1681, just in time to aid King Charles and his elder brother, Francis, Lord Guilford (1637–85), in the patriotic cause of trying to indict John Locke's patron, Lord Shaftesbury, on the charge of treason. Francis, a distinguished jurist, had risen swiftly from solicitor-general to attorney-general, to Lord Chief Justice of the Common Pleas, and finally, in 1682 at the age of 45, to Lord Keeper of the Great Seal, the highest law office in England. Indictments for treason had to be handed down by grand juries appointed by sheriffs of London, and so Dudley North, in a famous and irregular election, ran for and was elected sheriff, after which he and his juries became scourges of the Whig party.

At the end of the year, Dudley North was knighted by the king for his services, and soon rose in appointive office, becoming commissioner of the customs, MP and manager for King James II of all revenue matters in Parliament.

Toward the end of his brief but distinguished term in government service, Sir Dudley was inspired to think deeply about the two main monetary and financial questions agitating Parliament: the 1690 law to push down the rate of interest, and the recoinage question. Dudley wrote two *Discourses upon Trade* in 1691, one on interest and one on coinage, along with a postscript, that was scheduled for publication as a pamphlet when Dudley North died unexpectedly on December 31. His younger brother Roger (1653–1734), who was helping Dudley edit the booklet, then revised the draft, added a preface, and published it anonymously in early 1692. Despite the booklet's brilliance, and its systematic devotion to *laissez-faire* and hard-money views, the tract sank without a trace, and was not at all influential in the development of eighteenth century economic thought or in monetary or financial policy.

Roger North was not only the youngest of the brothers, he outlived them all by decades. Himself a queen's attorney-general, he spent much of his life defending his brothers' reputations. He wrote voluminously in his lifetime on music, accounting, law, the English constitution, and on numerous philosophic and scientific subjects, but natural reticence led him to keep all these writings unpublished. A decade after Roger's death, his biographies, or *Lives*, of three of his eminent brothers were published, in two volumes, in 1742 and 1744.[22]

Even the publication of these two well-written volumes, however, made no dent in the history of economic thought until resurrected and praised by James Mill and by John Ramsay McCulloch in the early nineteenth century.[23]

Roger North, who in his preface explained the groundwork and methodology of his brother and made his conclusions more consistent, pointed out the innovation in Dudley's method of economic analysis. For Dudley pioneered, at least in the history of English thought, the method which would later be adopted by Cantillon and Say and Senior, and which Ludwig von Mises would, in the twentieth century, call 'praxeology'. Praxeology is economic theory resting on a few broad, self-evident axioms grounded in apprehension of reality, then logically deducing the implications of these emphatically true axioms. But if *A* implies *B*, *C*, etc., and *A* is definitely true, the deductions can be accepted as truths as well.

Roger wrote of Dudley's method in his preface: 'I find trade here treated at another rate than usually has been; I mean philosophically; for...he begins at the quick, *from principles indisputably true*....'[24] The older method of reasoning, Roger North added, 'dealt in abstracts more than truths', in 'forming hypotheses to fit abundance of precarious and insensible principles'. In contrast, the new method, which North attributed to Descartes, builds knowledge 'upon clear and evident truths'.

In addressing trade and its problems, Dudley North began in his first discourse by setting forth the clear and simple general axiom or principle: 'Trade is nothing else but a commutation of superfluities'. In other words, as Buridan and the scholastics had emphasized but the world had forgotten: men only 'commute' or exchange goods or services because each benefits more from the good he receives than from the good he gives up in exchange (his 'superfluity'). Trade, therefore, whether intranational or international, benefits both parties; trade is not a Montaigne–mercantilist form of warfare where one party or nation exploits, or benefits at the expense of the other trader. Wealth and riches, then, are the goods that people are able to produce and accumulate, and not the money, the gold or silver, that enables them to buy those goods. Dudley North concludes that 'he who is most diligent, and raises most fruits or makes most of manufactory, will abound most in what others make or raise, and consequently be free from want and enjoy most conveniences, which is truly to be rich, although there were no such thing as gold, silver or the like…'.

There is no magic, then, to gold or silver; they are simply commodities selected by the market for their special qualities to be monies; as Dudley North says, gold and silver, in contrast to other market metals, are 'by nature very fine, and more scarce than others', and 'imperishable, as well as convenient for easy storage…'.

Proceeding from there, North rediscovers the scholastic analysis of money. If gold and silver are commodities, their value is determined, as are all other commodities on the market, by supply and demand.

Having laid the groundwork in systematic and general analysis, Dudley North proceeds to the vexed question of the rate of interest. In the market, North points out, some people, in consequence of hard work and judgement, are able to accumulate property. If the property is accumulated in the form of land, the landowners will rent out some of the land to those who wish to cultivate it. Similarly, those who accumulate property in terms of money will 'rent out' their money, charging a rate of interest. And just as the rental price of land on the market will be determined by the supply and demand of land, so the interest rate – the price of loans – will be determined by the supply and demand for credit.

Since interest is a market price, government control will have consequences as injurious as the control of any price. Interest is low because the supply of capital is high; low interest itself does not create abundance of capital. As Letwin paraphrases North: 'Nothing can lower interest rates except an increased supply of capital and as no law can by fiat increase the community's supply of capital, the proposed law is futile and injurious'.[25] Furthermore, North pointed out: usury laws will reduce the supply of savings and capital and thereby *raise* instead of lower the market rate of interest; and the quantity of trade will diminish. Moreover, intervention to reduce interest rates is unjust, because all prices should be treated alike, and be equally free.

In his discourse on coinage, North did not really deal with the recoinage question, but he anticipated Smith, Ricardo and the classical economists in his keen and principled hard-money analysis. Everyone cries about a 'shortage of money', North noted, but what they really *want* is more goods, or, in the case of merchants, what they really mean is that the prices for their goods are not satisfactory. Analysing the components of the demand for money and its supply, North traced transactions and emergency demands, as well the different aspects of money supply. Unfortunately, he faltered when discussing how much money a nation really *needed*, failing to realize that *any* supply on the market is optimal; he believed that an increase in trade required an increase in the supply of money, not understanding that an increased demand for money could simply raise the market value of money (i.e. lowering prices), thereby increasing the value of each unit of currency.

Despite this failure, however, North ended up in the right *laissez-faire* place, for he pioneered breaking down the supply of money into coin and bullion. He demonstrated that coin, being more suitable for exchange, would tend to command a market premium over bullion. However, the coin premium is regulated by the respective supplies and demands for coin and bullion. Thus, if there is an increase in the stock of coin, the premium over bullion would fall, and coin would tend to be melted down into bullion. If, on the other hand, there is a shortage of coin, the coin premium would rise, and more people would mint bullion into coin. In this way, coin and bullion would tend to be kept in equilibrium. North likened the process to two 'buckets': 'Thus the buckets work alternately; when money is scarce, bullion is coined; when bullion is scarce money is melted'.

So although Dudley North never reached the point of saying that the supply of *money*, compared to trade, is always optimal, he arrived at a similar *laissez-faire*, or market-equilibrating, conclusion by saying that no one has to worry about the supply of *coin*, which will always be kept optimal on the market.

As a result of his systematic, praxeological analysis, Dudley North arrived at firm, principled *laissez-faire* conclusions across the board. He opposed any usury laws: 'It will be found best for the nation to leave the borrower and the lender to make their own bargains'. He opposed any sumptuary laws; he denounced laws trying to keep gold and silver inside a country as doomed to failure. Government laws and decrees could only diminish, and never promote human energy, thrift and ingenuity.

But it was Dudley's brother Roger who took the final step, not only in explaining his brother's methodology, but also in expounding consistent *laissez-faire* conclusions. Attacking government intervention across the board, Roger North declared:

> There can be no trade unprofitable to the public, for if it prove so, men leave off; and wherever the trades thrive, the public, of which they are part, thrives also. No law can set prices in trade, the rates of which must and will make themselves. But when such laws do happen to lay any hold, it is so much impediment to trade... All favour to one trade or interest against another is an abuse...

Therefore, concluded Roger, 'Laws to hamper trade, whether foreign or domestic, relating to money or other merchandises, are not the ingredients to make a people rich...'

What *can* government do for a prosperous economy? 'If peace be procured, easy justice maintained, the navigation not clogged, the industrious encouraged...' in short, wrote North: 'It is peace, industry and freedom that brings trade and wealth, and nothing else'.[26]

11.5 The inflationists

It is not surprising that mercantilists, with their concentration on greater revenues and power to the state, should fasten on inflationist schemes of creating bank paper and credit, as well as government paper money. Such proposals and schemes, however, had to wait for the discovery of printing in the fifteenth century, for the development of bank paper and fractional reserves in sixteenth century Italy, and finally, for the invention of government paper money and central banking, both dubious innovations of Britain in the 1690s.

The first English inflationist was William Potter, whose most famous tract was *The Key of Wealth* (1650). It was Potter whose theories and proposed schemes set the stage for more famous inflationist followers, such as the Scotsman John Law. Potter, who worked in the government land office, began with the generally agreed axiom that a greater amount of money is beneficial to society. But with impeccable logic, Potter asked: if more money is good, why shouldn't a perpetual and greater increase of money be even better? Why indeed? Why not an increasing supply of money leading to infinity?

Potter offered a plethora of money-creating schemes, in which paper money would be secured, not by specie, which is inconveniently scarce, but by the 'nation's land'. More relevantly, of course, paper notes can actually be redeemed in physical gold or silver coin, whereas redemption of notes 'in land' would prove a chimera. How are you supposed to carry around a few acres of land with you to make exchanges? But that of course is the idea of a 'land bank': money seemingly and in the eyes of the deluded public backed by the land of the nation, but actually not backed at all.

William Potter saw other wonders emerging from a land bank. Thus, increasing the money supply would increase land values, and thereby increase the 'value of the backing' of the money: a sort of magical perpetual motion machine! Actually, of course, the increased land values simply reflect the increasing prices and values caused by the manufacture of more money.

Since Potter was anxious to inflate money and land values, he was almost frantically opposed to 'hoarding', since he realized that if the new money were 'hoarded', that is piled up in cash balances and not spent, the supposed benefits of inflation would not accrue. Indeed, one reason Potter greatly preferred paper money to specie is that paper is far less likely to be 'hoarded'; this means, of course, that paper money is far more likely to depreciate sharply in value as people try to get rid of it rather than add to their cash holdings.

William Potter, however, was cagey about prices rising as a result of his proposed monetary inflation. He believed, instead, that the increased money supply would greatly expand the 'volume of trade' and therefore the amount of production of goods, and that wealth would therefore accumulate. Potter preferred to believe that all the increased money supply would be absorbed in increased production, so that prices would not rise at all; but even if prices rose, everyone would be better off. Rising prices, of course, is the Achilles heel of inflationists' schemes, so that all of them deprecate the extent of subsequent price inflation and currency depreciation. They did not recognize, of course, that the 'volume of trade' may increase in money terms, but that this gain, like the alleged rise in land values, would simply reflect the increase in all monetary terms and values as more money supply is created and spreads throughout the system.

The argument of the alleged increase of trade and production largely rested on a flimsy analogy to the physical sciences. The Englishman William Harvey had only recently, in 1628, discovered the circulation of the blood within the human body. And Potter launched the very popular analogy between blood in the human body and money in the body economic. Just as people depend on the circulation of their blood, so the economy needs the circulation of money. But the inflationist notion of the more money the better can scarcely be supported by this feeble analogy; after all, who advocates the more blood the better in the human body, or the faster the circulation the better?[27]

In his bold moments, William Potter actually maintained that monetary inflation would cause prices to fall(!). Trade would be vivified and production would increase so greatly that supply would rise, and prices would fall.

William Potter, however, proved to be only preparation for the *locus classicus* of inflationism, the prince of proto-Keynesian money cranks, both theorist and activist, John Law of Lauriston (1671–1729). Son of James Law, a wealthy Scottish goldsmith and banker, John was born and grew up in Edinburgh, proceeding to squander his father's substantial inheritance on gambling and fast living. Convicted of killing a love rival in a duel in London in 1694, Law bribed his way out of prison and escaped to the Continent. After a decade in Europe pondering monetary problems, Law returned in 1703 to Scotland, where he was not subject to arrest. There, Law concentrated on developing and publishing his monetary theory *cum* scheme, which he presented to the Scottish Parliament in 1705, publishing the memorandum the same year in his famous or infamous tract, *Money and Trade Considered, with a Proposal for Supplying the Nation with Money* (Edinburgh, 1705). The Scottish Parliament considered but turned down his scheme; the following year, the advent of the union of Scotland with England forced Law to flee to the Continent once more, since he was still wanted by English law under the old murder charge.

Karl Marx, in a sense, should have been proud of the way John Law 'unified theory and practice' in his proposal. On the one hand, Law was the theorist, arguing for a central land bank to issue inconvertible paper money, or rather, paper money 'backed' mystically by the land of the nation. As a crucial part of his proposal, the grateful nation – in this case Scotland – was supposed to appoint Law himself, the expert and theoretician, in charge of putting this inflationist central bank scheme into effect.

John Law, as his subtitle states, proposed to 'supply the nation' with a sufficiency of money. The increased money was supposed to vivify trade, increase employment and production – the 'employment' motif providing a nice proto-Keynesian touch. Law stressed, in opposition to the scholastic hard-money tradition, that money is a mere government creation, that it has no intrinsic value as a metal. Its only function is to be a medium of exchange, and not any store of value for the future.

Even more than William Potter, John Law assured the nation that the increased money supply and bank credit would not raise prices, especially under Law's own wise *aegis*. On the contrary, Law anticipated Irving Fisher and the monetarists by assuring that his paper money inflation would lead to 'stability of value', presumably stability of the price of labour, or the purchasing power of money.

Law also anticipated Adam Smith in the latter part of the eighteenth century in his fallacious justification for fractional-reserve banking that it would provide a costless 'highway in the air' – furnishing a money supply without spending resources on the mining of gold or silver. In the same way, of course, *any* expenditure of resource can be considered a 'waste' if we supply our own assumptions that are not held by people on the free market. Thus, as Professor Walter Block has pointed out, *if there were no crime*, all expenditure on locks, fences, guards, alarm systems, etc. could be denounced as 'wasted resources' by external observers criticizing these expenditures. Similarly, if there were no such thing as governmental inflation, market expenditure on gold or silver could be considered 'wasteful' by observers.

If domestic price rises constitute the Achilles heel of monetary inflation, another worry has been the outflow of gold and silver from the country, in short, an 'unfavourable balance of trade' or of 'payment'. But John Law dismissed this problem too. On the contrary, he declared that an increase in the money supply would expand employment and output and 'therefore' increase exports, thus causing a *favourable* balance of payment, with gold and silver flowing into the country. Note that there is no analysis of *why* an increase in the money supply should increase output or employment, let alone drag exports along with it in this seemingly universal expansion.

Interestingly enough, one of Law's talking points about the need for more money was, as in the case of low interest, based on a striking misinterpretation of the reasons for the prosperity of the Dutch, whom all other nations envied in the seventeenth century. We have seen that everyone saw that the Dutch had low interest rates, leading English mercantilists to put the cart before the horse and attribute Dutch prosperity to low interest rates, instead of realizing that high savings and higher standards of living had brought about these low interest rates. Hence the mercantilists suggested that England force the maximum usury rate still lower.

Similarly, John Law saw that prosperous Holland enjoyed a plenty of metallic money; he attributed the prosperity to the abundance of money, and proposed to supply paper money instead. Again, he overlooked the point that it was Dutch property and high production and export that brought a plenitude of coin into the country. The export surplus and abundant coin was a reflection of Dutch prosperity, not its cause.[28]

Not that John Law neglected the low interest argument for Dutch prosperity. But instead of direct usury laws, Law proposed to arrive at low interest rates in what would become the standard inflationist manner: expanding bank credit and bank money and thereby pushing down the rate of interest. Indeed, Law worked out a proto-Keynesian mechanism: increasing the quantity of money would lower interest rates, thereby expanding investment and capital accumulation and assuring general prosperity.

To Law, as to Potter before him and Keynes after him, the main enemy of his scheme was the menace of 'hoarding', a practice which would defeat the purpose of greater spending; instead, lower spending would diminish trade and create unemployment. As in the case of the late nineteenth century German money crank Silvio Gesell, Law proposed a statute that would prohibit the hoarding of money.[29]

It took John Law another decade to find a ruler of a country gullible enough to fall for his scheme. Law found his 'mark' in the regent of France, a country that had been thrown into confusion and turmoil upon the death of its seemingly eternal ruler, Louis XIV, in 1715. The regent, the duke of Orleans, set Law up as head of the Banque Générale in 1716, a central bank with a grant of the monopoly of the issue of bank notes in France. Soon the banque became the Banque Royale. Originally, banque notes were receivable in French taxes and were redeemable in silver; soon, however, silver redeemability was ended. Quickly, by 1717, John Law had all monetary and financial power in the realm placed into his hands. To his old scheme he added the financing of the massive government debt. He was made the head of the new Mississippi Company, as well as director-general of French finances; the notes of the Mississippi Company were allegedly 'backed' by the vast, undeveloped land which the French government owned in the Louisiana territory in North America. Law's bank created the notorious hyperinflationary 'Mississippi bubble'; notes, bank credit, prices and monetary values skyrocketed from 1717 to 1720. One aristocratic observer in Paris noted that for the first time the world 'millionaire' had become prevalent, as suddenly many people seemed to possess millions. Finally, in 1720, the bubble collapsed, Law ended a pauper heavily in debt, and he was forced once again to flee the country. As before, he roamed Europe, making a precarious living as a gambler, and trying to find another country that would adopt his scheme. He died in 1729, in Naples, trying to persuade the Neapolitan government to make him its inflationary central banker.[30]

The cataclysm of John Law's experiment and his Mississippi bubble provided a warning lesson to all reflective writers and theorists on money throughout the eighteenth century. As we shall see below, hard-money doctrines prevailed easily throughout the century, from Law's former partner and outwitter Richard Cantillon down to the founding fathers of the American Republic. But there were some who refused to learn any lessons from the Law failure, and whose outlook was heavily influenced by John Law.[31]

Perhaps the most prominent of the post-Law inflationists in the eighteenth century was the eminent Anglo-Irish idealist philosopher, Bishop George Berkeley (1685–1753). Berkeley studied at Trinity College, Dublin, the intellectual centre of the Anglo-Irish Establishment, and his great philosophical works were all written in his 20s, while he was a fellow at Trinity. Berkeley then spent several years in the late 1720s vainly trying to establish a Christian college in Newport, Rhode Island. After that, Berkeley was appointed dean of Derry and then bishop of Cloyne.

Berkeley's major pronouncements on economic questions came in his pamphlet, *The Querist* (1735–37), published in three instalments. *The Querist* was highly influential, ten editions being published in Berkeley's lifetime. It was written solely as a series of 900 loaded questions, by which Berkeley hoped to influence public opinion through sheer rhetoric without having to engage in reasoning. Berkeley's monetary views were heavily influenced by John Law. A typical example of one of Berkeley's loaded queries is 'whether the public is not more benefited by a shilling that circulates than a pound that lies dead?' Money, for Berkeley, was a mere ticket, and the centrepiece of *The Querist* was the advocation of a Law-type central bank that would expand money and credit, lower interest rates (as Berkeley put it, 'put an end to usury'), and expand employment and prosperity.

Berkeley was shrewd enough to recognize that he had to answer objections based on John Law's egregious flop, and so he hastened to put some distance between his own schemes and the 'madness of France'. Like Law before him, Berkeley promised that *his* proposed bank notes would only be injected into the economy 'by slow degrees', and that he or his surrogates would take pains to keep the expansion of bank credit 'proportional' to the 'multiplication of trade and business'. In that way, prices would supposedly not rise. But of course Berkeley embodied the usual inflationist failure to see that 'the multiplication of trade and business' *in money terms* would precisely be the result of the monetary inflation and the consequent inflation of all prices and monetary values. (Berkeley's manipulative query on this theme is: 'Whether therefore bank bills should at any time be multiplied, but as trade and business were also multiplied?')

11.6 The hard-money response

The bulk of the eighteenth century response to the doctrines and failures of John Law, however, was understandably to return to and redouble devotion to the original continental tradition of hard money, a tradition now challenged by the new institutions of central banking and fractional-reserve banking. One of the earliest and most brilliant responses, which cannot be limited to the term 'hard money', was that of Law's former partner and sceptic in the Mississippi bubble, Richard Cantillon, who virtually founded modern economics in his remarkable *Essay* written about 1730. (On Cantillon, see Chapter 12.)

The most immediate hard-money reaction to Law in England was also one of the most remarkable. Isaac Gervaise (d. 1739) was born in Paris of a French Protestant father who owned a firm manufacturing and trading in silk. Gervaise senior moved to London, where his son Isaac was employed in the family firm. In 1720, Gervaise published a brief but extraordinary pamphlet of less than 30 pages, *The System or Theory of the Trade of the World*.[32] In the course of attacking Law's doctrine of bank credit and monetary expansion, Gervaise arrived, before Cantillon and Hume, at the process towards international monetary equilibrium, or the specie-flow-price 'mechanism'. Without artificial bank credit expansion, Gervaise pointed out, the supply of money in each country would tend to be proportionate to its production or volume of trade. Each nation's consumption and production, and its imports and exports, would tend to be in balance. If this equilibrium should be disturbed, and, for example, 'excessive' gold or silver flow into a particular country, then this excess would be spent on imports, the balance of trade would tilt and imports exceed exports, and this excess would have to be paid for by an outflow of specie. This outflow, in turn, would reduce the excess of money and return the country to a monetary and foreign trade balance.

But, Gervaise charged, schemes such as John Law's upset this balance: bank credit, serving as substitute money, artificially and unnaturally increases the money supply, expanding consumption including imports, raising domestic prices and lowering exports, so that the increased bank credit will cause an outflow of specie. The artificial credit can bring no lasting gain. There is also a strong hint in Gervaise that the credit expansion will only manage to divert investment and production from those 'natural' fields serving consumers efficiently into those areas that will prove to be wasteful and uneconomic.[33]

Gervaise's analysis of the effects of monetary expansion was also significant in being more akin to Cantillon, by stressing the expansion of money inducing people to spend more, than to Hume, who confined his analysis to the increased money supply causing rising prices – neglecting the outflow of specie caused by greater monetary spending, on imports as well as on domestic products.[34]

From his analysis of natural law, trade, self-equilibration on the market and their disruptions by government, Isaac Gervaise proceeded to a strong recommendation of all-out free trade, free of any distortions or restrictions by government. Gervaise's uncompromising free trade conclusion was all the more remarkable because his own firm enjoyed monopoly privileges conferred on it by the English Parliament. But Gervaise courageously concluded that 'trade is never in a better condition, than when it's natural and free; and forcing it either by laws, or taxes being always dangerous; because though the intended benefit or advantage be perceived, it is difficult to perceive its contrecoup; which ever is at least in full proportion to the benefit'. Here Gervaise anticipated the keen insights of the nineteenth century French *laissez-faire* economist Frédéric Bastiat, who stressed that government intervention stemmed from the fact that the benefits of subsidies or privileges are often direct and immediate, whereas the greater unfortunate consequences are more remote and indirect. The former are 'seen' whereas the latter are 'unseen', and therefore the seeming benefits get all the attention. Gervaise concluded with a plea for freedom and natural law that would anticipate Turgot and other French *laissez-faire* thinkers of his century: 'Man naturally seeks, and finds, the most easy and natural means of attaining his ends, and cannot be diverted from those means, but by force, and against his will'.[35]

Isaac Gervaise wrote no more on economic questions, but he did become a distinguished Anglican clergyman, which makes it all the more puzzling that his exceptional and innovating pamphlet exerted no influence whatever on English opinion. It was lost to the world until resurrected by historians in the twentieth century.

Another hard-money advocate who developed a theory of international monetary equilibrium was a timber merchant of Dutch extraction, Jacob Vanderlint (d. 1740), in his tract, *Money Answers All Things* (1734). Despite the title, Vanderlint's theme was that money is distributed properly and optimally on the free market. There is a tendency on the market for all nations' prices to be equal, and if one country should acquire more money, its higher price level would soon draw the money out of the country until prices are back in equilibrium. It doesn't matter, then, how much specie a nation may have, since prices would adjust. Thus, if a nation had little specie, its prices would be low and it would outcompete other nations, with gold and silver consequently flowing into the country. Indeed, so concerned was Vanderlint to keep prices low and competitive with other nations that he unknowingly replicated Cantillon's advice for rulers or other worthies to hoard their gold and silver so as to keep national prices low.[36]

Vanderlint consistently carried over his hard-money analysis to the problem of expanding bank credit. Bank credit, Vanderlint pointed out, expands the money supply, and so, 'as the Price of things will hence be rais'd, it must and will make us the Market, to receive the Commodities of every Country whose Prices of Things are cheaper than ours ...[and hence] turn the Balance of Trade against us...'.[37]

Vanderlint, like Gervaise, was thus a severe critic of inflation and fractional-reserve banking, as well as an analyst of the international harmonies of money, prices and the balance of trade on the free market. Like Gervaise, Vanderlint was also an advocate of unrestricted free trade, concluding 'In general, there should never be any restraints of any kind on trade, nor any greater taxes than are unavoidable'. Attempts to fix the price of gold and silver or to prohibit the export of coin are also futile: 'it's no less absurd for the government to fix the price they will give for gold and silver brought to be coined, than it would be to make a law to fix and ascertain the prices of every other commodity'. Vanderlint also deplored the rise, during the eighteenth century, of the war-making state, and of the high taxes and public debts which war brings in its wake. Indeed, for Vanderlint, free trade and free markets, and international peace, go hand in hand, while war is the enemy of freedom. War, warned Vanderlint, is 'one of the greatest calamities to which mankind can be subjected; the end of which none can well foresee, and the burdens of which (i.e. public debts and taxes) are seldom discharged in one generation...'. Eloquently, Vanderlint concluded that 'it's monstrous to imagine, the author of this world hath constituted things so as to make it any ways necessary for mankind to murder and destroy each other'.[38]

The culminating hard-money theorist in eighteenth century England was Joseph Harris (1702–64), who published a massive two-volume *Essays Upon Money and Coins* (1757–58). Harris began life as a country blacksmith, but then went to London, where he became a prominent writer on navigation, mathematics and astronomy. He was an employee at the Mint, and was made assay master of the Mint in 1748.

Harris was a hard-money critic of debasement or fractional-reserve banking and bank credit expansion. He was an explicit follower of Cantillon's analysis of money flows. Thus he saw, with Cantillon, that international monetary matters tended towards an equilibrium, but he also saw, with Cantillon, that inflows or increases of the money supply did not simply raise prices; they also necessarily affected the distribution of money, benefiting some people at the expense of others. Hence the flows of money, though self-adjusting, would cause economic harm, especially during the adjustment process. As Hutchison sums up Harris's view: 'Inflows of money enrich some at the expense of others, and such processes may for a time cause distress'. Sudden fluctuations of money, therefore, whether flowing in or out, 'would be pernicious while it lasted and for some time afterwards'.[39]

As a result of his analysis, Harris was determinedly opposed to any alteration whatever of the monometallic monetary standard of a country (Harris favoured silver over gold as being more stable). As Harris emphatically warned: 'The established standard of money should not be violated or altered, under any pretence whatsoever'.[40]

11.7 *Laissez-faire* by mid-century: Tucker and Townshend

If a hard-money stance had been pretty well established in English thought by the middle of the eighteenth century, so too had a corresponding if not fully consistent commitment to free markets and freedom of international trade. The Vanderlint-Cantillon–Harris analysis of international trade and money flows lent powerful arguments in the direction of freedom of trade. And, as we shall see in later chapters, the Scottish views of Carmichael, Hutchison and Hume were leading in the same direction in the northern part of Great Britain.

Josiah Tucker (1713–99), Anglican clergyman and dean of Gloucester from 1758 on,[41] was a celebrated eighteenth century writer on religion, politics and economics who was extravagantly hailed in his day as a free trader by such men as the great *laissez-faire* statesman and economist A.R.J. Turgot, who translated two of Tucker's works into French.[42] But Tucker's devotion to freedom of trade was only moderate, and marred by inconsistencies and contradictions. Thus Tucker favoured absolute prohibition on the export of raw materials, tariffs on manufactures, protective tariffs for infant industries, government compulsion – under severe penalties – of landlords to set aside 20 out of every 400 acres for timber, and heavy taxes on consumption of sports, recreation and luxuries. In general, even though he anticipated Adam Smith in praising the consequences of self-interest and 'self-love', he also believed in the importance of government directing and guiding the activities based on self-interest. He was also a characteristic mercantilist in urging the government to encourage ever greater population. It is true, however, that Tucker attacked the restrictionism of the navigation acts and the usury laws, both areas in which he was closer to a free trade position than that of the chronically over-praised Adam Smith.

On one free market point, moreover, Tucker was consistent and determined: opposition to war and conquest. In a letter to Lord Kames, during the Seven Years' War with France, Tucker wrote: 'War, conquests and colonies are our present system and mine is just the opposite'. Interestingly enough, however, Tucker was not at all moved by sympathy for the American cause. On the contrary, he believed that Britain had the full right to tax the colonies. But Tucker's opposition to war triumphed, including a war to keep the colonies; to Tucker America 'ever was a millstone hanging about the neck of this country, to weigh it down; and as we ourselves had not the wisdom to cut the rope and to let the burden off, the Americans have kindly done it for us'.[43]

Actually, Josiah Tucker's main historical contribution was to highlight the views of a far sounder *laissez-faire* economist who has been shamefully neglected by virtually all historians of economic thought. Charles, the third Viscount Townshend (1700–64), has been virtually unknown, and often confused with his son of the same name who was infamously responsible for the fateful Townshend taxes on tea and other imports into the American colonies.

Our Lord Townshend was a scion of one of the great agricultural estates in England, son of the well-known diplomat and scientific farmer 'Turnip' Townshend, and husband of the glamorous socialite Audrey. Lord Townshend's first published pamphlet cut against his own personal economic interest by denouncing the policy of large subsidies on the export of corn. The pamphlet, *National Thoughts* (1751), was signed 'By a Landowner" to emphasize this point of arguing against his own subsidy.[44]

Dean Tucker struck up a correspondence with Townshend, in defence of the export bounty on corn. But soon Tucker was converted on the issue. Thus Townshend pointed out the folly of the British government subsidizing foreigners by allowing them to buy cheaper corn than the British themselves had to pay. Tucker was especially admiring of Townshend's uniqueness in arguing particular cases from general principles instead of the other way round, and specifically the general interest in favouring free competition as against grants of monopoly by government. Thus, Tucker writes to Townshend that

I am mightily pleased with your Lordship's...manner of accounting for People's frequent and gross Mistakes in the Affairs of Commerce...by arguing from Particulars to Generals; whereas in this case a Man should form to himself a General Plan drawn from the Properties of Commerce, and then descend to Particulars and Individuals, and observe whether they are cooperating with the general Interest: Unless he doth this, he studies Trade only as a Monopolist, and doth more Hurt than Good to the Community.[45]

Tucker declared himself convinced that 'bounties cannot be of any national service to a manufacture which is passed its infancy'.

A bit later in this correspondence, Lord Townshend demonstrated his adherence to free market principles by criticizing the inconsistencies of Sir Matthew Decker, a director of the East India Company. Decker (1679–1749), a Dutch immigrant, had also attacked the corn bounty, but Townshend was sharply critical because 'Notwithstanding this sound Doctrine he [Decker] proposes to form [monopoly] Companies and to erect [governmental] Magazines of Corn in every County.... A most surprising absurdity and inconsistency'.[46] Of course, the inconsistency is not so surprising if we realize that Decker was a director of the greatest monopoly company of them all. Townshend then goes on to point out that if, as he advocates, 'Trade and Industry and all our Ports were thrown open and all Duties, Prohibitions, Bounties, and Monopolies of every kind whatever were taken off and destroyed', then 'private Traders here would erect Warehouses for Corn as they have done for other manufactures and we should then have them on a regular and natural footing and this Island would then be, as Holland has been, the great market of Europe for Corn. But as long as the Bounty remains this cannot be...'.

In *National Thoughts* Lord Townshend was worried about the poor, and paternalistically advocated removing the enforceability in court of small amounts of debt in order to help their condition. In later letters, however, Townshend introduced a bill in Parliament which would, instead, increase the mobility of the labouring poor by removing 'certain Disabilities and Restraints' upon them. Professor Rashid speculates that the change in stance came about because, 'having accepted the validity of laissez-faire, Townshend came to believe that the poor could not be helped more than by making them free to help themselves'.[47]

So eager was Lord Townshend to spread the principles of free markets and free trade that in 1756 he sponsored prizes at Cambridge for essays on economic topics. Essay contests after the first year were discontinued because Townshend and the university could not agree on essay questions. Thus Cambridge turned down Townshend's suggested topic: 'What influence has Trade on the Morals of a Nation?' Lord Townshend was indignant at Cambridge University's implicit denial of any connection between trade and morality, and he replied indignantly and with keen perception: 'There is not any moral Duty which is not of a Commercial nature. Freedom of Trade is nothing more than a freedom to be moral Agents'. This latter sentence expresses the crucial libertarian insight of the unity between free moral agency and freedom to act, produce, and exchange property.

Other questions suggested by Lord Townshend also put the libertarian rhetorical case very well:

- 'Has a free trade or a free Government the greater effect in promoting the wealth and strength of a Nation?'
- 'Can any restraints be laid on trade or industry without lessening the advantages of them? And if there can, what are they?'
- 'Is there any method of raising taxes without prejudice to Trade? And if there is what is it?'[48]

Despite his neglect by historians, Lord Townshend's views seem to have had substantial influence in his day. The prominent *Monthly Review* guessed the identity of 'the Landowner' author of *National Thoughts* immediately upon publication, and the pamphlet was quoted in another tract on the corn bounty the following year. Lord Townshend had a prominent connection with the important periodical, *The Gazetteer*. And in 1768, four years after Lord Townshend's death, an anonymous pamphlet on *Considerations on the Utility and Equity of the East India Trade* argued, once again, for breaking the East India Company monopoly, and lamented the death of Lord Townshend, so sound and knowledgeable on commercial questions.

Clearly, Lord Townshend was far more influential in mid-eighteenth century England than later historians would know. Moreover, he was both an example and an embodiment of a rising tide of *laissez-faire* sentiment in the Britain of that era.

11.8   Notes

1. D.A.G. Waddell, 'Charles Davenant (1656–1714) – A Biographical Sketch', *Economic History Review*, ser. 2, 11 (1958), p. 288.
2. W. Letwin, *The Origins of Scientific Economics* (Garden City, NY: Doubleday, 1965), p. 122. Also see T.W. Hutchison, *Before Adam Smith: The Emergence of Political Economy, 1662–1776* (Oxford: Basil Blackwell, 1988), p. 51. Professor Hutchison, however, takes Davenant's scientific posturing all too seriously.
3. King's manuscript remained unpublished for over a century, when it was published in 1802, by George Chalmers. King was an antiquarian clerk and accountant who wrote several unpublished tracts on statistics and political arithmetic. *The Natural and Political Observations* was published, along with another previously unpublished tract by King, in George E. Barnett (ed.), *Two Tracts by Gregory King* (Baltimore: Johns Hopkins University Press, 1936).
4. The shakiness of both the factual data and the 'law' can be seen by the fact that, in a slightly later tract, King presented a totally different quantitative 'law', amounting to:

Reduction in supply	Price increase
2/10	30/10
3/4	40/10

Hutchison, op. cit., note 2, p. 387.

5. John Creedy, 'On the King–Davenant Law of Demand', *Scottish Journal of Political Economy*, 33 (August 1986), pp. 208–10, and ibid., pp. 193–212. Also see the presentation in John Creedy, *Demand and Exchange in Economic Analysis* (Aldershot, Hants: Edward Elgar, 1992), pp. 7–23, a similar account with slightly different wording.

6. There was a direct filtration of ideas from Thomas Müntzer and the communist Anabaptists into England. One of Müntzer's collaborators, Henry Niclaes, survived the smashing of Anabaptism to found familism, a pantheistic creed claiming that man *is* God, and calling for the establishment of the Kingdom of (man) God on earth, as the only place such a kingdom could ever exist. Familist ideas were carried to England by a disciple of Niclaes, Christopher Vittels, a Dutch joiner, and familism spread in England during the late sixteenth century. A centre of familism in early seventeenth century England was in Grindleton, in Yorkshire. There, in the decade after 1615, 'the Grindletonians' were led by Grindleton's Anglican curate, the Rev. Roger Brearly. Part of the attraction of familism was its antinomianism, the view that truly godly persons, such as themselves, could never commit a sin, by definition, and therefore antinomians usually flaunted behaviour generally considered sinful in order to demonstrate to one and all their godly and 'sin-free' status.

7. The Levellers have acquired a left-wing colouration because of their label, and because they have been admired by Marxist historians, enthusiastic about their radicalism, and as the most consistent figures in the 'bourgeois revolution' of the seventeenth and later centuries. The Levellers, however, were in no sense egalitarians, except in the *laissez-faire* libertarian sense that they were opposed to special privileges granted by the state. On the Levellers, see especially Don M. Wolfe (ed), *Leveller Manifestoes of the Puritan Revolution* (1944, New York: Humanities Press, 1967), including the editor's lengthy introduction; and the latest collection of Leveller tracts in A.L. Morton (ed), *Freedom in Arms: A Selection of Leveller Writings* (London: Lawrence & Wishart, 1975). Also see the classic H.N. Brailsford, *The Levellers and the English Revolution* (Stanford, Calif.: Stanford University Press, 1961).
    One of the best brief summaries of Leveller doctrine is in C.B. Macpherson, *The Political Theory of Possessive Individualism: Hobbes to Locke* (Oxford: Clarendon Press, 1962), pp. 137–59.

8. Much mischief has been wrought by the interpretation of Leo Strauss and his followers that Locke was a natural rights-er who (following Hobbes) broke with the wise ancient tradition of natural law. Actually, Locke the natural rights-er developed the scholastic natural law tradition, and was the opposite of Hobbes's right-wing Grotian apologia for state absolutism. On Hobbes, Locke, and the Tew circle, see Richard Tuck, *Natural Rights: Their Origin and Development* (Cambridge: Cambridge University Press, 1979). Leo Strauss's interpretation is in his *Natural Right and History* (Chicago: University of Chicago Press, 1953). For a critique of Strauss, and insistence that Locke was not a Hobbesian but in the natural law tradition, see Raghuveer Singh, 'John Locke and the Theory of Natural Law', *Political Studies*, 9 (June 1961), pp. 105–18.

9. The *locus classicus* of the Pocockian thesis is J.G.A. Pocock, *The Machiavellian Movement* (Princeton, NJ: Princeton University Press, 1975). In addition to the contrasting works of Isaac Kramnick and Joyce Appleby, see in particular the scintillating refutation of Pocock's central example: the alleged 'classical virtue' emphasis of the radically Lockean *Cato's Letters*, which provided the greatest single libertarian influence on the American revolutionaries. Ronald Hamowy, '*Cato's Letters*: John Locke and the Republican Paradigm', *History of Political Thought*, 11 (1990), pp. 273–94.

10. Richard Ashcraft, *Revolutionary Politics and Locke's Two Treatises on Government* (Princeton, NJ: Princeton University Press, 1986).

11. Ibid., pp. 75–82, 370–71.

12. A more detailed analysis of seventeenth century Dutch politics would show, however, that the free market, decentralized, pro-peace party was the republicans or Arminians, followers of the Protestant theologian Jacobus Arminius, who was theologically closer to Catholics in believing in free will for salvation. On the other hand, the 'Calvinist' party in Holland favoured the Orange monarchy, statism, controlled markets, and a warlike foreign policy.

13. As Letwin states, '[Child] urged that foreign trade – except that with the East Indies – be opened to anyone who chose to engage in it; and the argument is studded with catchwords suggestive of *laissez-faire*.... No doubt Child opposed certain mercantilist restrictions, as many other mercantilists did, but he did not oppose them in principle. He objected to those restrictions which embarrassed the branches of industry that concerned him and consistently advocated restrictions which fostered those branches. His position was exactly analogous with that of a textile manufacturer, for instance, who opposes import restrictions or protective duties on the fibers he buys while insisting that heavy duties be placed on foreign finished goods that compete with those he sells...' Letwin, op. cit., note 2, pp. 46–7.

14. Schumpeter's favourable assessment of Child rests on his assumption that Child was the author of the tract by 'Philopatris' that took the *laissez-faire* view that money was simply another commodity and that therefore it didn't matter whether it was imported or exported. But for a convincing demonstration that Child was not 'Philopatris', see Letwin, op. cit., note 2, pp. 50, 253–5.

15. Letwin, op. cit., note 2, p. 8. Also see the critical pamphlets of Thomas Manley, *Usury at Six Per Cent Examined* (1669), and the anonymous tract with the fully revealing title: *Interest of Money Mistaken, Or, A Treatise proving that the abatement of interest is the effect and not the cause of the riches of a nation....* (1668).

16. See Henry W. Spiegel, *The Growth of Economic Thought* (3rd ed., Durham, NC: Duke University Press, 1991), pp. 154–5.

17. In Hutchison, op. cit., note 2, p. 67. See in particular, the discussions in Letwin, op. cit., note 2, pp. 69–81, 182–4, 260–70.

18. Actually, Praisegod's real Christian name was highly unwieldy, even if more pious. He was named 'Unless-Jesus-Christ-Had-Died-For-Thee-Thou-Hadst-Been-Damned' Barbon.

19. In Barbon's *A Discourse Concerning Coining the New Money Lighter, In Answer to Mr. Lock's Considerations...*(1696). See Letwin, op. cit., note 2, pp. 78–9.

20. Despite the hostility to Locke's point of view among modern inflationist and Keynesian historians, it is clear from Letwin's account, op. cit., note 2, pp. 69–77, 260–70, that the calamitous price contraction that inflationists would have expected from the monetary contraction of the Lockean recoinage did not take place.

    On Locke's clearly scholastic-influenced view of the just price as the market price, as expressed in his book *Venditio* (1695), see Karen I. Vaughn, *John Locke: Economist and Social Scientist* (Chicago: University of Chicago Press, 1980), pp. 123–31.

21. A complicating point is that the Whig Establishment was run at the top by Robert Walpole and the Pelham family, who were really *laissez-faire*, pro-peace liberals trying to run a Whig Party of totally contrasting principles. Walpole managed this feat in the 1720s through the 1740s, and the Pelhams continued for some years after, largely by brilliant political manipulation and by tactical management of what both Left and Right denounced as 'corruption'. The main device by which Walpole managed to placate the Whig magnates temporarily was to pass the mercantilist measures in Parliament (e.g. restricting American colonial trade and production) and then simply failing to enforce them. See Murray N. Rothbard, *Conceived in Liberty, Vol. II: 'Salutary Neglect'* (New Rochelle, NY: Arlington House, 1975), Part III.

22. The 1742 *Life* was of Francis, Baron Guilford, and the 1744 *Lives* were biographies of Dudley, and of Dudley's younger brother, John (1645–83), who in his brief life became professor of Greek and master of Trinity College, Cambridge. The first and eldest brother, Charles North (1630–90), lived a retired life and little is known of him.

23. For an excellent discussion of the contributions of Dudley and Roger North, see Letwin, op. cit., note 2, pp. 196–220, 271–94.

24. Letwin, op. cit., note 2, p. 204. Italics added by Letwin.

25. Letwin, op. cit., note 2, p. 209.

26. Letwin, op. cit., note 2, pp. 215–16.

27. The following year, in his famed *Leviathan* (1651), the authoritarian political philosopher Thomas Hobbes also used the money–blood analogy; after writing on how money 'goes round about, nourishing (as it passeth) every part thereof [of the commonwealth],' Hobbes adds that 'natural blood is in like manner made of the fruits of the earth; and circulating nourisheth by the way, every member of the body of man'. See Jacob Viner, *Studies in the Theory of International Trade* (New York: Harper & Bros, 1937), p. 37n.

28. Charles Rist justly criticized Law that: 'To infer from the abundance of metallic money in a prosperous country that it is enough to "create" paper money...in a poor country in order to develop industry or natural resources in which it is lacking, is an idea that affronts common sense...Scotland, a country of shepherds and fisherman, mountainous and poor in raw materials...could have increased its currency, but it would have given the country neither industry, nor trade, nor agriculture, nor a prosperous shipping industry. That could be attained only by the labour and frugality of its inhabitants'. Charles Rist, *History of Monetary and Credit Theory from John Law to the Present Day* (1940, New York: A.M. Kelley, 1966), pp. 47–8.

29. See Joseph T. Salerno, 'Two Traditions in Modern Monetary Theory: John Law and A.R.J. Turgot', *Journal des Économistes et des Études Humaines*, 2, note 2–3 (June–Sept 1991), pp. 340–41.

30. For the relations between Law and Cantillon in this dramatic period, see Chapter 12 on Cantillon. On the interrelationships of Law, Cantillon, and the contemporaneous Mississippi and South Sea bubbles, see Antoin E. Murphy, *Richard Cantillon: Entrepreneur and Economist* (Oxford: The Clarendon Press, 1986); on the evolution of Law's doctrines, see Antoin E. Murphy, 'The Evolution of John Law's Theories and Policies, 1707–1715', *European Economic Review*, 34 (July 1991), pp. 1109–25. For an analysis of Law's doctrines and his unheralded influence upon modern economics, see Salerno, op. cit., note 29, pp. 337–79. For Law's influence on Adam Smith, see also Roy Green, *Classical Theories of Money, Output and Inflation* (New York: St Martin's Press, 1992), pp. 110–27.

31. For example, Sir Humphrey Mackworth 'plagiarized' Law and his inflationist arguments in his tract, *A Proposal for Payment of the Publick Debts* (2nd ed., 1720). See Viner, op. cit., note 27, pp. 44–5.

32. The full title of the Gervaise pamphlet reveals its grounding in the denunciation of Law-like monetary and credit expansion: *The System or Theory of the Trade of the World, Treating of the Different Kinds of Value, of the Balances of Trade, of Exchange, of Manufactures, of Companies, and Shewing the Pernicious Consequences of Credit, and That it Destroys the Purpose of National Trade.*

33. Gervaise wrote: 'All the profit a nation gains by unnaturally swelling its denominator [its supply of money], consists only in the inhabitants living for a time in proportion to that swelling so as to make a greater figure than the rest of the world, but always at the cost of their coin, or of their store of real and exportable labour... [N]o thing in the world is of any solid or durable worth, but what is the produce of labour; and whatever else bears a denomination of value, is only a shadow without substance, which must either be wrought for, or vanish to its primitive nothing...' See Hutchison, op. cit., note 2, pp. 127–8.

34. Sekine is right in calling this Gervaise–Cantillon analysis 'the cash-balance effect' rather than a Keynesian 'income effect'. Thomas T. Sekine, 'The Discovery of International Monetary Equilibrium by Vanderlint, Cantillon, Gervaise, and Hume', *Economia Internazionale*, 26 no. 2 (May 1973), pp. 270–74.

35. Hutchison, op. cit., note 2, p. 128.

36. By hoarding specie, Vanderlint counselled, 'by thus keeping so much of those Metals out of Trade...it will...prevent our Markets from rising so high, as to hinder the Exportation of our Commodities, or give too great Encouragement to the Importation of Foreign Goods'. See Chi-Yuen Wu, *An Outline of International Price Theories* (London: George Routledge & Sons, 1939), p. 64.

37. Ibid., pp. 64–5.

38. Hutchison, op. cit., note 2, p. 132–3.
39. The latter quote is from Harris. See Hutchison, op. cit., note 2, p. 244.
40. For David Hume's similar, 100 per cent reserve banking analysis at about the same time in Scotland, see Chapter 15 on the Scottish Enlightenment.
41. Tucker was the son of a Welsh farmer and salt officer who went to Oxford and, after graduation, became an Anglican clergyman. His admirers like to repeat the story, apparently true, that Tucker walked back and forth from Wales to Oxford at the beginning and end of each term, leaving his father to use the sole family horse. No doubt admirable for Josiah, although the story does not improve his economic performance.
42. Tucker's first work on economics was his *Essay on Trade* (1749), which was something of a best-seller, going into four editions by 1764. He then planned to write a comprehensive treatise on economics, but only two fragmentary parts were written, both printed privately for friends and not published: *The Elements of Commerce and Theory of Taxes* (1755) and *Instruction for Travellers* (1757).

    In our time, Hutchison suffers from excessive admiration of Tucker. His intemperate remark that Jacob Viner's calling Tucker a 'mercantilist' is a 'kind of *reductio ad absurdum* of that problematic term' is uncalled-for; Viner's treatment of Tucker is judicious and well-balanced. Hutchison, op. cit., note 2, p. 238; Viner, op. cit., note 27, p. 64, 71–2, 87, 98–100.
43. Tucker's view found an echo in other exasperated British Tories. Thus the great John Wesley, founder of Methodism, stated, 'I say, as Dean Tucker, "Let them drop" ...Four-and-thirty millions they have cost us to support them since Queen Anne died. [1715] Let them cost us no more.' The celebrated Dr Johnson, in his *Taxation No Tyranny* (1775) observed that 'The Dean of Gloucester has proposed, and seems to propose it seriously, that we should at once release our claims, declare them masters of themselves, and whistle them down the wind...It is however a little hard, that having so lately fought and conquered for their safety, we should govern them no longer'. Johnson countered with a 'wild proposal' of his own: 'Let us restore to the French what we have taken from them. We shall [then] see our colonists at our feet...' Tucker, however, would undoubtedly have seriously agreed to Johnson's attempted *reductio ad absurdum*. See George Shelton, *Dean Tucker and Eighteenth-Century Economic and Political Thought* (New York: St Martin's Press, 1981), pp. 214–5.
44. The full title was: *National Thoughts, Recommended to the Serious Attention of the Public. With an Appendix, Shewing the Damages Arising from a Bounty on Corn.* In Salim Rashid, 'Lord Townshend and the Influence of Moral Philosophy on *Laissez Faire*', *The Journal of Libertarian Studies*, 8, no. 1 (Winter 1986), pp. 69–74. Rashid is virtually the only historian to resurrect Townshend and demonstrate his importance. But see Shelton, op. cit., note 43, pp. 79, 88.

    Rashid points out that several leading scholarly libraries have erroneously attributed authorship of this pamphlet to Townshend's son. Rashid, op. cit., p. 73.
45. Tucker to Townshend, 22 April 1752. Rashid, op. cit., note 44, p. 73.
46. It is amusing to contrast Townshend's critical attitude toward Decker with the laudatory appraisal of T.W. Hutchison, who virtually finds Decker a free trade hero, calling for 'the abolition of all duties', and opposing the Navigation Act as well as retaliatory tariffs. Rashid, op. cit., note 44, p. 71; Hutchison, op. cit., note 2, pp. 393–4.
47. The Townshend bill was introduced in 1753, but no action was taken on it. Rashid, op. cit., note 44, pp. 71, 73.
48. Rashid, op. cit., note 44, p. 72. The libertarian answers, presumably to be elicited by Lord Townshend's questions, are, respectively: free trade, no, and no.

12 The founding father of modern economics: Richard Cantillon

Most people, economists and laymen alike, think that economics sprang full-blown, so to speak, from the head of Adam Smith in the late eighteenth century. What has become known as the first, or 'classical' period of modern economic thought then developed, out of Smith, through David Ricardo, including an aggregative approach, and a cost-of-production, or even a labour, theory of value. We now know, however, that this account is flatly incorrect. For modern economic thought, i.e., analysis centring on explaining the market economy, developed a half-century before Smith's *Wealth of Nations*, not in Britain but in France. More significantly, the French writers, despite their diversity, must be set down not as pre-Ricardian but as proto-'Austrian', that is, as forerunners of the individualistic, micro, deductive, and subjective value approach that originated in Vienna in the 1870s.

12.1 Cantillon the man

The honour of being called the 'father of modern economics' belongs, then, not to its usual recipient, Adam Smith, but to a gallicized Irish merchant, banker, and adventurer who wrote the first treatise on economics more than four decades before the publication of the *Wealth of Nations*. Richard Cantillon (c. early 1680s–1734) is one of the most fascinating characters in the history of social or economic thought. Little is known about Cantillon's life despite the fact that he died a multimillionaire, but the best modern researches show that he was born in Ireland in County Kerry of a family of Irish landed gentry, who had been dispossessed by the depredations of the English puritan invader Oliver Cromwell. Cantillon's first cousin once removed, also named Richard, emigrated to Paris to become a successful banker, thereby perpetuating the tradition, born in the sixteenth century, of religio-political exiles from Britain emigrating to France.[1] The Cantillons were part of the Catholic emigration, centring, by the end of the seventeenth century, around the Stuart pretender to the throne of Great Britain.

Richard Cantillon joined the emigration to Paris in 1714, quickly becoming the chief assistant to his cousin at the latter's bank. Moreover, Richard's mother's uncle, Sir Daniel Arthur, was a prominent banker in London and Paris, and Arthur had named Richard's cousin as the Paris correspondent of his London-based bank.[2] In two years, Cantillon was in a position to buy his cousin's ownership of the bank.

Richard Cantillon was now in the important position of banker for the Stuart court in exile, as well as for the bulk of the British and Irish emigrés in Paris. But his most important *coup* came from his association with the Scottish adventurer and arch-inflationist John Law (1571–1729), who had captured the imagination and the greed of the regent of France. The death of the aged Louis XIV in 1715 had inaugurated a looser and more optimistic regime, control of which had been seized by the regent, the duke of Orleans.

John Law persuaded the regent that France could find permanent prosperity and need have no further worries about the public debt. The French government need only finance heavy deficits by a massive infusion of the relatively new device of government paper money. Becoming the leading financier of the French government, and even controller-general of the finances of France, Law set loose a rampant inflation that generated the wildly speculative Mississippi bubble (1717–20). The bubble created instant millionaires before it collapsed, leaving John Law in poverty and disgrace. Indeed, the very word 'millionaire' was coined during the heady years of the Mississippi bubble.[3]

But when the dust had settled, the shrewd Richard Cantillon emerged, after being a top partner in John Law's Mississippi speculations, as a multimillionaire. Legend has it that, at the beginning of his meteoric career running French finances, John Law had come to Cantillon and warned him that 'If we were in England we would have to strike a deal and settle matters, but as we are in France, I can send you this evening to the Bastille, if you do not give me your word to leave the kingdom within twenty-four hours'. To which Cantillon is supposed to have replied: 'Hold on, I will not go and I will make your system succeed'. In any case, we know that Law, Cantillon, and the English speculator, Joseph Edward ('Beau') Gage, formed a private company in November 1718. Gage was so wealthy from paper speculation in Law's government-sponsored paper-issue bank, the Mississippi Company, that he seriously attempted, in this period, to purchase the kingdom of Poland from its king, Augustus.

As the Mississippi bubble careened onward, Cantillon, an astute analyst of monetary affairs, saw deeply that the bubble was bound to burst soon, and he took steps to make millions out of the foolishness of his partners and clients. Lending money to Gage and others with which to buy inflated Mississippi Company shares, Cantillon quietly sold all of his own shares as well as the inflated shares that his borrowers had left him as collateral, locked all his papers in a strongbox, took his accumulated millions and left town for Italy, there to await in safety 'the financial storm that he could see developing'. After Gage and the other Cantillon clients went broke in the 1720 crash, Cantillon pursued them to repay his loans, for which they had been happy to pay a rate of interest up to 55 per cent, which had incorporated a huge inflation premium.

Richard Cantillon returned to Paris a multimillionaire, albeit unpopular with his former associates and debtors. Soon he married Mary Anne, daughter of the late Count Daniel O'Mahony, an Irish general. His mother-in-law, Charlotte Bulkeley, was the sister-in-law of James Fitzjames, the duke of Berwick, marshal of France and the natural son of the English King James II; he was, therefore, the Stuart pretender, James III. Cantillon thus married into an Irish military family closely connected with the Stuarts and with the French court.

At some time during the early 1730s, probably around 1730, this success-ful banker and speculator wrote his great work, in French, the *Essai sur la nature du commerce en général*. In the fashion of the day, the result of the censorship of that era, this treatise was not published, but circulated widely in manuscript, in literary and intellectual circles, until it was finally published two decades later, in 1755.

Richard Cantillon's exit from this life was as mysterious and adventurous as his overall career. In May 1734, while living in London, in one of his many houses in the leading cities of Europe, Cantillon died in a fire that burned his house to the ground. It was subsequently found that he was murdered inside the house, the fire being presumably set to cover the murder. Three of his servants were tried for his murder and found not guilty, while his French cook, who had been dismissed three weeks earlier, fled overseas with a considerable amount of valuables. The runaway cook was never found. Earl Egmont, whose brother lived next door to Cantillon, wrote in his diary that Cantillon 'was a debauched man, and his servants of bad reputation'. And so ended, under highly mysterious circumstances, the only leading economist in history who lost his life as a victim of murder.[4]

12.2 Methodology

Richard Cantillon's *Essai* has been justly called by W. Stanley Jevons 'the first treatise on economics', and the historian of economic thought Charles Gide referred to it as the first systematic treatment of political economy. The best overall assessment is that of F.A. Hayek, the Austrian economist who has done important work in the history of thought: 'this gifted independent observer, enjoying an unsurpassed vantage point in the midst of the action, coordinated what he saw with the eyes of the born theoretician and was the first person who succeeded in penetrating and presenting to us almost the entire field which we now call economics.[5]

The scholastics had written general treatises on almost all of human knowl-edge, in which discussions of economics or the market played a subordinate part; and in the mercantilist era the mercantilists and their critics delivered at best intelligent *aperçus* on particular economic – usually economic policy – topics. But Richard Cantillon was the first theorist to demarcate an independ-ent area of investigation – economics – and to write a general treatise on all its aspects.

One reason that Cantillon was the 'first of the moderns' is that he emanci-pated economic analysis from its previous intertwining with ethical and political concerns. The mercantilists, dominant in economic thought for the preceding century or two, were special pleaders whose titbits of analysis were pressed into the service of political ends, either in subsidizing particular interests or in building up the power of the state. The medieval and renaissance scholastics, while incomparably more thoughtful and systematic, had imbedded their economic analysis in a moral and theological framework. To break out of the mercantilist morass, it was necessary to step aside, to focus on the economic features of human action and to analyse them, abstracting them from other concerns, however important. Separating out economic analysis from ethics, politics, or even concrete economic data did not mean that these matters were unimportant or should never be brought back in. For it was impossible to decide the ethics of economic life, or what government should or should not do, without finding out how the market worked, or what the effect of interventions might be. Cantillon presumably, at least dimly, saw the need for this at least temporary emancipation of economic analysis.

Furthermore, Cantillon was one of the first to use such unique tools of economic abstraction as what Ludwig von Mises would later identify as the indispensable method of economic reasoning: the Gedanken-experiment (or thought-experiment). Human life is not a laboratory, where all variables can be kept fixed by the experimenter, who can then vary one in order to determine its effects. In human life, all factors, including human action, are variable, and nothing remains constant. But the theorist can analyse cause-and-effect relations by substituting mental abstractions for laboratory experiment. He can hold variables fixed mentally (the method of assuming 'all other things equal') and then reason out the effects of allowing one variable to change. By starting with simple 'models' and introducing successive complications as the simpler ones are analysed, the economist can at last discover the nature and operations of the market economy in the real world. Thus the economist can validly conclude from his analysis that 'All other things equal (*ceteris paribus*), an increase in demand will raise price'.

In the 1690s, as we have seen (Chapter 9), a leader of the emergent classical liberal opposition to the statism and mercantilism of Louis XIV, the provincial judge the Sieur de Boisguilbert, had introduced into economics the method of abstraction and successive approximations, beginning with the simplest model and proceeding in increasing complexity. In illustrating the nature and advantages of specialization and trade, Boisguilbert had begun with the simplest hypothetical exchange: two workers, one producing wool, the other wheat, and then extended his analysis to a small town, and finally to the entire world.

Richard Cantillon greatly developed this systematic method of abstractions and successive approximations. He liberally used the *ceteris paribus* method. Through this analytic method he uncovered 'natural' cause-and-effect relations in the market economy. The France of Cantillon's day was a country of great landed feudal estates, the result of the conquests of previous centuries. And so Cantillon brilliantly began the economic analysis in his *Essai* with the assumption that the whole world consists of one giant estate.

In that admittedly 'unrealistic' but illuminating construct, all production is dependent on the wishes, the desires, of the monopoly owner, who simply tells everyone what to do. Put another way, production depends on demand, except that here there is in effect one demander, the monopoly landowner.

Cantillon then makes one simple realistic change in his model. The landowner has farmed out the land to various producers of all kinds. But as soon as that happens, the economy cannot continue with one man giving orders. For its continued operation, the individual producers must exchange their products, and a free market economy comes into being, with its attendant competition, trade and price system. Furthermore, money arises out of this exchange as a commodity serving as a much-needed medium of exchange and 'measure' of values.

12.3 Value and price

Cantillon engaged in the first sophisticated modern analysis of market pricing, showing in detail how demand interacts with existing stock to form prices. In contrast to the later Smith–Ricardo classicists, and foreshadowing the Austrians, Cantillon was largely interested in price formation in the real world, i.e. actual market prices, rather than in the chimera of long-run 'normal' pricing. In an important recent interchange on Cantillon, Professor Vincent Tarascio interprets him as a classicist or neoclassicist, at least in so far as holding that market prices tend in the long run to approach the 'intrinsic value' of a good, that is, the cost of production, in terms of land and labour inputs, of the product. This was the Smith–Ricardo theory of 'equilibrium' pricing, which has been basically expanded into Walrasian 'general equilibrium' theory.

But while there are passages in Cantillon justifying this approach, and the term 'intrinsic value' is certainly an unfortunate one, Professor David O'Mahony, in a perceptive comment on the Tarascio article, points out that Cantillon's approach was, in reality, pre-Austrian. First, O'Mahony shows that Cantillon's market price analysis was the Austrian one of a given existing *stock* of a good evaluated and demanded by consumers.

Quoting from Cantillon: 'It is clear that the quantity of product or of merchandise offered for sale, in proportion to the demand or number of Buyers, is the basis on which is fixed or always supposed to be fixed the actual market prices...'. Demand, in turn, is subjective, dependent on 'humours, fancies, mode of living', etc. These subjective valuations are what impart value to the products offered for sale. It is the 'consent of mankind', says Cantillon, which gives value to 'lace, linen, fine cloths, copper and other metals'. For Cantillon, actual market prices are determined by demand: 'It often happens that many things which actually have this intrinsic value are not sold in the market at that value: That will depend on the humors and fancies of men and on their consumption'. Thus the value of products is imparted by consumer valuation: a crucial proto-Austrian insight derived from medieval and late Spanish scholastics. For centuries, in fact, the scholastic and post-scholastic position had been that the value of goods is determined by 'utility' and 'scarcity', by subjective valuation of a given supply. The more utility the higher the value, and the more abundant the supply the lower the value and price of any good on the market. Cantillon's is a sophisticated and elaborated development of the scholastic approach.

While Cantillon considers the 'intrinsic value of a thing' 'the measure of the Land and Labour which enter into its Production', he concedes immediately that subjective valuation by consumers rather than 'intrinsic value' determines price.[6]

Going into detail on intrinsic value, Cantillon refers to the hypothetical case of an American who travels to Europe to sell beaver skins for hats, but is then 'rightly astonished to learn that woollen hats are as serviceable as those made of beaver, and that all the difference, which causes so long a sea journey, is in the fancy of those who think beaver hats lighter and more agreeable to the eye and the touch'. In short: the entire cost of production, all the labour and effort that went into the production and transport of beaver skins, means nothing unless the product satisfies the consumer enough to pay for the costs, and to enable the product to compete with another commodity made more cheaply at home. It is consumer demand that determines sales as well as price.

O'Mahony goes on to point out that Cantillon's monopoly estate model clearly shows that demand (in this case that of the world monopoly landowner) and not cost of production determines price. Cantillon, then, did *not* foreshadow the classical equilibrium theory that cost of production constituted the long-run, and presumably therefore the most important, determinant of market price. On the contrary, for Cantillon, cost of production had a very different function: deciding whether a business could make profits or else have to suffer losses and go out of business. If consumer value and therefore the selling price of a product is high enough to more than cover costs, the firm makes a profit; if not high enough, it suffers losses and eventually has to go out of business. This is an important part of the Austrian view of the role of costs. Thus Cantillon discusses costs and prices in the manufacture of Brussels lace:

> If the price which the Ladies pay for the Lace does not cover all the costs and profits there will be no encouragement for this Manufacture, and the undertaker will cease to carry it on or become bankrupt; but as we have supposed this Manufacture is continued, it is necessary that all costs be covered by the prices paid by the Ladies of Paris....

Hence the movement toward long-run equilibrium is *not* a process of adjusting market prices to intrinsic long-run costs of production, but one of labourers and entrepreneurs moving in and out of various lines of production until costs of production and selling prices are equal. As O'Mahony well puts it:

> For Cantillon then it is not so much that intrinsic values exist automatically and spontaneously and that market prices are drawn towards them, as that the prices offered in the market determine whether or not it is worth producing things. In other words, it is the prices offered that determine what production costs can be incurred not that production costs determine what the prices must be.

Of course, there is a big gap, both in Cantillon's approach and that of the later Smith–Ricardo classicists, as well as of the modern Ricardian neoclassicists: Where do the 'costs of production' come from? In contrast to the Cantillon and classical approach, they are neither intrinsic nor mandated from some mysterious force outside the economic system. Costs of production, as it took the Austrians to finally point out, are themselves determined by the expected consumer demand for goods and services.

12.4   Uncertainty and the entrepreneur

One of Cantillon's remarkable contributions to economic thought is that he was the first to stress and analyse the entrepreneur.[7] To this real-world merchant, banker and speculator, it would have been inconceivable to fall into the Ricardian, Walrasian and neoclassical trap of assuming that the market is characterized by perfect knowledge and a static world of certainty. The real-world marketplace is permeated by uncertainty, and it is the function of the businessman, the 'undertaker', the entrepreneur, to meet and bear that uncertainty by investing, paying expenses and then hoping for a profitable return. Profits, then, are a reward for successful forecasting, for successful uncertainty-bearing, in the process of production. The crucial Smithian–Ricardian and Walrasian (classical and neoclassical) assumption that the economy is perpetually in a state of long-run equilibrium fatally rules out the real world of uncertainty. Instead, it focuses on a never-never land of no change, and hence of perfect certainty and perfect knowledge of present and future.

Thus Cantillon divides producers in the market economy into two classes: 'hired people' who receive fixed wages, or fixed land rents, and entrepreneurs with non-fixed, uncertain returns. The farmer–entrepreneur bears the risk of fixed costs of production and of uncertain selling prices, while the merchant or manufacturer pays similar fixed costs and relies on an uncertain return. Except for those who only sell 'their own labour', business entrepreneurs must lay out monies which, after they have done so, are 'fixed' or given from their point of view. Since sales and selling prices are uncertain and not fixed, their business income becomes an uncertain residual.

Cantillon also sees that the pervasive uncertainty borne by the entrepreneurs is partly the consequence of a decentralized market. In a world of one monopoly owner, the owner himself decides upon prices and production, and there is little entrepreneurial uncertainty. But in the real world, the decentralized entrepreneurs face a great deal of uncertainty and must bear its risks. For Cantillon, competition and entrepreneurship go hand in hand.

As in the case of Frank Knight and the modern Austrians, Cantillon's theory of entrepreneurship focuses on his function, his role as uncertainty-bearer in the market, rather than, as in the case of Joseph Schumpeter, on facets of his personality.

Cantillon's concept also anticipates von Mises and the modern Austrians in another respect: his entrepreneur performs not a disruptive (as in Schumpeter) but an *equilibrating* function, that is, by successfully forecasting and investing resources in the future, the entrepreneur helps adjust and balance supply and demand in the various markets.

Professor Tarascio points out that Cantillon's pioneering insight into the pervasive uncertainty of the market was largely forgotten, and before long dropped out of economic thought until independently resurrected in the twentieth century by Knight and by such modern Austrians as Ludwig von Mises and F.A. Hayek. But, as Professor O'Mahony wryly comments: 'To acknowledge his [Cantillon's} recognition of uncertainty when we look at him as Professor Tarascio does from a current perspective is thus more of a reflection on many modern economists whose capacity to ignore uncertainty is nothing short of bizarre than a tribute to Cantillon's prescience'.

Bizarre it may well be, but there is a method to the madness. For, as Professor O'Mahony himself understands full well, modern economics is a set of formal models and equations purporting to fully determine human behaviour, at least in the economic realm. And there is no way that uncertainty can be compressed into determinate mathematical models. As O'Mahony puts it, one might 'ask if entrepreneurial activity can in the nature of things be made the subject of formal representations or models at all. If they could, would there be any room for uncertainty, in the true sense of the term, and, therefore, any room for entrepreneurship itself?' Economic theory, in short, must choose between formally elegant but false and distorting mathematical models, and the 'literary' analysis of real human life itself.

12.5 Population theory

Richard Cantillon's theory of wages is dependent on population in a way that was copied almost word for word by Adam Smith in the *Wealth of Nations*, which in turn inspired Malthus's famous anti-populationist hysteria. Cantillon's long-run wage theory depends on the supply of labour, which in turn depends on levels and growth of population. In contrast to the later Malthus, however,

Cantillon engaged in a sophisticated analysis of the determinants of population growth. Natural resources, cultural factors, and the state of technology he diagnosed as particularly important. He saw prophetically that the colonization of North America would not be a simple displacement of one people by another, but that new agricultural technology would support a far larger population per acre of land. Hence the extent to which existing resources, land and labour, can be utilized depends on the existing state of technology. Thus pre-colonial North America was not 'overpopulated' by Indians, as some had believed; instead, the Indian population level had adjusted to the given resources and technology available. In short, Cantillon foreshadowed the modern theory of 'optimum' population, in which the size of population tends to adjust to the most productive level given the resources and technology available.

While Cantillon described a pre-Malthusian alleged tendency of human beings to multiply like 'rats in a barn', without limit, he also recognized that religious and cultural values can modify such tendencies. An increase in the demand for agricultural products that are land-intensive would tend to reduce the demand for agricultural labour and eventually cause a fall in the supply of such labour and hence of the population as a whole. (Cantillon, it must be remembered, was writing in an age when the overwhelming bulk of the population was engaged in agriculture.) An increase in the demand for labour-intensive farm products, on the other hand, would bring about an increase in the demand for labour and hence of the population. Living, once again, in a country and an era of large feudal landed estates, Cantillon observed that it was the tastes of the proprietary classes that determined the consumer tastes and values of society, and hence the demand for products.

It should be noted that in an unusually sophisticated way, Cantillon pointed out that it was outside the scope of economic analysis to decide whether it is better to have a large population of poorer people or a smaller population of people who enjoy a higher standard of living: that must be for the values of the citizenry to decide.

Professor Tarascio points out that Cantillon's population analysis was far more subtle and modern than that of Smith, Ricardo, or Malthus. Rather than worry about a future unchecked population explosion, Cantillon's theoretical framework accounted for the current cultural change to smaller families in industrialized countries, as well as the likelihood that population will adjust itself downward to any future depletion of resources. Cantillon pointed out, for example, that as ancient civilizations declined, their population size declined along with them. The number of inhabitants of the Roman state in Italy, for example, declined from 25 million to about 6 million over a period of 17 centuries.

12.6   Spatial economics

Richard Cantillon was also the founder of spatial economies, of the analysis of economic activity in relation to geographic space. In a sense, of course, mercantilists, by advocating a favourable balance of geographical trade, analysed (even if badly) economic activities to the extent that they crossed national borders. Spatial analysis, as Professor Hebert has pointed out, deals with *distance* (transportation cost, and its relation to prices as well as to the location of economic activities), and *area* (the geographical development and boundaries of markets). Cantillon not only developed location theory but integrated it into his general microeconomic analysis. In particular, he saw that the prices of produce, even when money and monetary prices were in equilibrium, would always be higher in the cities than in their place of production by an amount needed to cover the costs and risks of transport. In consequence, products that are bulky and/or perishable would be too costly or impossible to transport to the cities, and hence would be far cheaper at their places of production. Such products, then, would generally be grown in border areas around the cities, where the transport costs to the urban markets are not prohibitive. In manufacturing, furthermore, Cantillon saw that in cases where plants have to use bulky, low value-per-unit-weight raw materials, they would tend to locate near the output of such materials. For in that case it would be less costly to transport the less bulky, more valuable finished products to urban markets than to ship the raw materials.

On the location of areas of urban markets, Cantillon was highly suggestive, pointing out that it is far less costly for buyers and sellers to gather at one spot than to travel around the periphery seeking each other out and finding out the various prices that buyers were willing to pay or sellers were willing to accept. In modern terms, Cantillon might say that central markets develop naturally because they enormously lower the transaction, transport, information and other costs of trade.

While Cantillon, therefore, saw how markets and the location of economic activity were able to regulate themselves harmoniously, he was not a consistent free trader internally just as he was not in the foreign trade area. Internally, he held inconsistently that manufacturers needed 'much encouragement and capital' to find and invest in the optimum locations.

12.7   Money and process analysis

A highlight of Cantillon's theory of money is his treatment of the value of money as a special case of the value of market commodities in general. As in the case of any product, the alleged 'intrinsic value' of gold is the cost of its production. The value of gold and silver, like other commodities, is set by the values and hence the demands of users in the market – by the 'consent of mankind'. As in the case of other commodities, too, Cantillon has no cost of production theory of the value of gold and silver; he simply holds, as elsewhere, that these products can only be produced if costs can be covered by the value of the product.

The process of aligning costs and values in gold, however, takes a relatively long time since its annual output is a small proportion of the total stock in existence. If the nominal value of gold falls below its cost of production, it will cease being mined; and if costs fall sharply, production of gold will be stepped up, thus tending to align costs and normal values. Cantillon recognized that government paper and bank money virtually *have no* costs of production, and therefore no 'intrinsic value' in his terminology, but he pointed out that market forces keep the value of such fiduciary money at par with the value of the gold or silver in which that paper can be redeemed. As a consequence, an increase in the supply 'of fictitious or imaginary money has the same effect as increase in the circulation of real money'. But, Cantillon noted, let confidence in the money be damaged, and monetary disorder ensues and the fictitious money collapses. He pointed out, too, that government is particularly subject to the temptation to print fictitious money – a lesson he had undoubtedly learned from or at least seen embodied in, the John Law experiment. Cantillon also provided a sound analysis of how the market determines the ratio of the values of gold and silver.

One of the superb features of Cantillon's *Essai* is that he was the first, in a pre-Austrian analysis, to understand that money enters the economy as a step-by-step process and hence does not simply increase or raise prices in a homogeneous aggregate.[8] Hence he criticized John Locke's naive quantity theory of money – a theory still basically followed by monetarist and neoclassical economists alike – which holds that a change in the total supply of money causes only a uniform proportionate change in all prices. In short, an increased money supply is not supposed to cause changes in the relative prices of the various goods.

Thus Cantillon, asking 'in what way and in what proportion the increase of money raises prices?', answers in an excellent process analysis:

in general an increase of actual money causes in a State a corresponding increase of consumption which gradually brings about increased prices. If the increase of actual money comes from Mines of gold and silver in the State the Owner of these Mines, the Adventurers, the Smelters, the Refiners, and all the other workers will increase their expenses in proportion to their gains. They will consume…more… commodities. They will consequently give employment to several Mechanicks who had not so much to do before and who for the same reason will increase their expenses. All this increase of expense in Meat, Wine, Wool, etc. diminishes the share of the other inhabitants of the State who do not participate at first in the wealth of the Mines in question. The alteration of the Market, or the demand for Meat, Wine, Wool, etc., being more intense than usual, will not fail to raise their prices. These high prices will determine the Farmers to employ more land to produce them in another year; these same Farmers will profit by this rise of prices and will increase the expenditure of their Families like the others. Those then who will suffer from this dearness and increased consumption will be first of all the Landowners, during the term of their Leases, then their Domestic Servants and all the Workmen or fixed Wage-earners who support the families on their wages. All these must diminish their expenditure in proportion to the new consumption...it is thus, approximately, that a considerable increase of Money from the Mines increases consumption....

In short, the early receivers of the new money will increase spending according to their preferences, raising prices in these goods, at the expense of a lower standard of living among the late receivers of the new money, or among those on fixed incomes who don't receive the new money at all. Furthermore, relative prices will be changed in the course of the general price rise, since the increased spending is 'directed more or less to certain kinds of products or merchandise according to the idea of those who acquire the money, [and] market prices will rise more for certain things than for others...'. Moreover, the overall price rise will not necessarily be proportionate to the increase in the supply of money. Specifically, since those who receive new money will scarcely do so in the same proportion as their previous cash balances, their demands, and hence prices, will not all rise to the same degree. Thus, 'in England the price of Meat might be tripled while the price of Corn rises no more than a fourth'. Cantillon summed up his insight splendidly, while hinting at the important truth that economic laws are qualitative but not quantitative:

An increase of money circulating in a State always causes there an increase of consumption and a higher standard of expenses. But the dearness caused by this money does not affect equally all the kinds of products and merchandise proportionably to the quantity of money, unless what is added continues in the same circulation as the money before, that is to say unless those who offered in the Market one ounce of silver be the same and only ones who now offer two ounces when the amount of money in circulation is doubled in quantity, and that is hardly ever the case. I conceive that when a large surplus of money is brought into a State the new money gives a new turn to consumption and even a new speed to circulation. But it is not possible to say exactly to what extent.[9]

Not only that, but as Professor Hebert has pointed out, Cantillon also provided a remarkable proto-Austrian analysis of the different effects of the money going into consumption or investment. If the new funds are spent on consumer goods, then goods will be purchased 'according to the inclination of those who acquire the money', so that the prices of those goods will be driven up and relative prices necessarily changed. If, in contrast, the increased money comes first into the hands of lenders, they will increase the supply of credit and temporarily lower the rate of interest, thereby increasing investment. Repudiating the common superficial view, brought back to economics in the twentieth century by John Maynard Keynes, that interest is purely a monetary phenomenon, Cantillon held that the rate of interest is determined by the number and interactions of lenders and borrowers, just as the prices of particular goods are determined by the interaction of buyers and sellers. Thus, Cantillon pointed out that

> If the abundance of money in a State comes into the hands of money-lenders it will doubtless bring down the current rate of interest by increasing the number of money-lenders: but if it comes into the hands of those who spend it will have quite the opposite effect and will raise the rate of interest by increasing the number of entrepreneurs who will find activity by this increased spending and who will need to borrow in order to extend their enterprise to every class of customers.

An increased supply of money, therefore, can either lower or raise interest rates temporarily, depending on who receives the new money – lenders, or people who will be inspired by their new-found wealth to borrow for new enterprises. In his analysis of expanding credit lowering the rate of interest, furthermore, Cantillon provides the first hints of the later Austrian theory of the business cycle.

In addition, Cantillon presented the first sophisticated analysis of how the demand for money, or rather its inverse, the speed or velocity of circulation, affects the impact of money and hence the movement of prices. As he put it, 'an acceleration or greater rapidity in circulation of money in exchange, is equivalent to an increase of actual money up to a point'. One of the reasons why prices do not change in exact proportion to a change in the quantity of money is alterations in velocity: 'A river which runs and winds about in its bed will not flow with double the speed when the amount of water is doubled'. Cantillon also saw that the demand for cash balances will depend on the frequency of payments made in the society. As Monroe sums up Cantillon's position: 'the longer the interval between payments, the larger are the sums which have to accumulate in the payers' hands, and the more money is required in the country'.[10] If people save large sums, furthermore, they may have to 'keep money locked up for considerable periods'. On the other hand, the development of more efficient clearing systems for debts, as well as of paper money, will economize on cash: 'The rapidity of circulation is increased by the practice of offsetting accounts between merchants, and by the use of bankers' and goldsmiths' notes, for these men do not keep an equivalent amount of money on hand'. Cantillon summed up his analysis of the interaction of quantity and velocity: 'According to the principles we have established the quantity of money circulating in exchange fixes and determines the price of everything in a State taking into account the rapidity or sluggishness of circulation'.

Cantillon also provided a masterful discussion of the relations between gold and silver, and advocated freely fluctuating exchange rates between gold and silver, attacking any attempts, certainly any long-lived attempts, to fix the exchange rate between them. For such a rate is soon bound to vary from the market rate. Thus Cantillon saw the problem in trying to maintain a bimetallic standard with fixed parities between two precious metals.

All in all we can understand Hayek's enthusiasm when he concludes that Cantillon's monetary theory 'constitutes, without doubt, the supreme achievement of a man who was the greatest pre-classical figure in at least this field and whom the classical writers themselves in many instances not only failed to surpass but even failed to equal'.[11]

12.8   International monetary relations

One of the most notable features – and certainly the one drawing the most attention from historians – of Cantillon's extensive monetary theory was his pioneering analysis of the tendency towards international monetary equilibrium, or the specie-flow-price mechanism that has been generally attributed to the later writings of David Hume.

Cantillon applied his 'micro-analysis' of changes of the money supply *within* a country to changes in the distribution of money between countries. For over two centuries, mercantilist writers and statesmen in Europe had advocated an increased supply of specie in a country as a means of building up state power, and they were increasingly clear that, short of having gold or silver mines a nation could only increase its stock of money by having a favourable balance of trade. It was clear to the mercantilists that this was not a policy every nation could successfully pursue, for the 'favourable' balances of trade of some nations would necessarily have to be offset by the 'unfavourable' balances of others. In this disequilibrium situation, it was every nation for itself, as each attempted to benefit at the expense of other nations by restrictionist and warlike policies. But there was a further problem in the background; since most writers were at least roughly familiar with the 'quantity theory', or supply–demand analysis of the value of money, an inner contradiction loomed. For if nation *A* managed to acquire a favourable balance of trade and to accumulate specie, the increase of specie would raise prices in nation *A*, make the country's products uncompetitive in the world markets, and bring the favourable balance to an end.

No one was more lucid about the problem of money and international payments than Cantillon. He pointed out that specie can either be acquired within a country by mining ore, or through subsidies, warfare, 'invisible' payments, borrowing, or a favourable balance of trade with other countries. But then, in the Cantillon process analysis, either the mine owners or the exporters would spend or lend the money. Part of the expenditure of the new money would surely be spent abroad, and furthermore the increased stock of money would raise prices at home, making domestic goods less competitive. Exports would fall and imports of cheaper foreign products would increase, and gold would flow out of the country, reversing the favourable balance of trade.

In this way, Cantillon worked out an international monetary theory integrated with his domestic analysis, and was one of the first to work out a theory of international monetary equilibrium. For the world market managed to frustrate, at least in the long run, governmental attempts to intervene and secure favourable balances of trade. It should be noted, further, that Cantillon's analysis contained the basis of both major parts of the equilibrating specie-flow-price mechanism: the expenditure of new monetary cash balances increasing imports; and the increase of domestic prices caused by a higher money supply, the price effect lowering exports and adding to imports.

Richard Cantillon understood the grave inner contradiction of mercantilism: increased specie raising prices and thereby destroying the favourable balance of payments that brought the specie. His unsatisfactory way out was to advise the king to hoard much of the increased stock so as not to drive up prices; unsatisfactory because money is meant to be spent eventually, and once spent the dreaded price increase would willy-nilly take place.

Professor Salerno, however, has introduced a cautionary note in the encomiums to Cantillon, pointing out that he has been called only a 'semi-equilibrium' theorist because he did not portray a satisfactory picture of what the equilibrium state would be like, and he did not think of the world economy as tending firmly towards equilibrium. As a result, Cantillon did not present a theory of the international distribution of gold and silver in equilibrium.[12] He thought of the economy instead as engaging in endless cycles of disequilibrium rather than as tending towards equilibrium.

12.9 The self-regulation of the market

There is no point wasting time in fruitless speculation on whether or not Richard Cantillon was a 'mercantilist'. Eighteenth century writers did not group themselves into such categories. While he inconsistently suggested, in accordance with state-building notions of the age, that the king should amass treasure from a favourable balance of trade, the entire thrust of Cantillon's work was in a free trade, *laissez-faire* direction. For it was clear that mercantilist measures would ultimately be self-defeating. More important, Cantillon was the first to show in detail that all parts of the market economy fit together in a 'natural', self-regulative, equilibrating pattern, with existing supply and demand determining prices and wages, and ultimately the pattern of production. Consumer values, furthermore, determined demand, with population adjusting to cultural and economic factors. The equilibrators of the economy were the entrepreneurs, who adjust to and cope with the all-pervasive uncertainty of the market. And if the market economy, despite the 'chaos' it might seem to superficial observers, is really harmoniously self-regulating, then government intervention as such is either counterproductive or unnecessary.

Particularly instructive is Cantillon's attitude towards usury laws, that vexed question which had at last brought unwarranted discredit on the entire economic analysis of the medieval renaissance Catholic scholastics. This shrewd merchant and banker saw that particular interest rates, on the market, are proportionate to the risks of default faced by the creditor. High interest is the result of high risk, not of exploitation or oppression. As Cantillon wrote: 'All the Merchants in a State are in the habit of lending merchandise or produce for a time to Retailers, and proportion the rate of their profit or interest to that of their risk'. High rates of interest bring about only a small profit, because of the high proportion of default on risky loans. Cantillon observed too that the later Catholic scholastics had eventually if reluctantly agreed to allow high rates of interest for risky loans. Furthermore, there should be no imposed maximum on interest, since only the lenders and borrowers can determine their own fears and needs: 'for they would be hard put to find any certain limit since the business depends in reality on the fears of the Lenders and the needs of the Borrowers'.

Finally, Cantillon saw that usury laws could only restrict credit and thereby drive up interest rates even further on the inevitable black markets. Hence, usury laws would not lower interest rates but rather raise them: 'because the Contracting parties, obedient to the force of competition or the current price settled by the proportion of Lender or Borrowers, will make secret bargains, and this legal constraint will only embarrass trade and raise the rate of interest instead of settling it'.

12.10 Influence

Richard Cantillon's pioneering *Essai* was widely read and highly influential throughout the eighteenth century. It was widely read as was the custom of the day, in 'underground' manuscript form, by literary, scientific and intellectual people interested in the advance of thought and in the practical problems of the day. The wide reliance on such manuscripts resulted from the severe French censorship of that period.

The *Essai*, then, was widely read from its writing in the early 1730s, and still more so after its publication in 1755. It was read eagerly and thoroughly by the first school of economists, the physiocrats, and by their great associate, or fellow-traveller, A.R.J. Turgot. In that cosmopolitan eighteenth century society where British and French intellectuals intermingled, the *Essai* was certainly read and echoed by the eminent Scottish philosopher, David Hume. And it has the honour of being one of the very few books cited by

Hume's close friend Adam Smith – a man whose hyperdeveloped sense of his own originality prevented him from citing or recognizing many predecessors. Cantillon was thus highly influential among Continental and British economists until the publication of the *Wealth of Nations* in 1776. After the publication of that work, however, the knowledge and influence of Cantillon fell prey to the general post-Smithian custom of ignoring any and every economist preceding Adam Smith. The general nineteenth century habit of obliterating knowledge of economists before Adam Smith committed grave injustice against earlier economists and gave rise to the erroneous – and still widely held – illusion that economic science sprang full-blown out of the head of one Great Man, much as Athena was supposed to have sprung, fully grown and fully armed, from the brow of Zeus. But the most malignant aspect of this Smith-worship is that the lost economists were in many respects far sounder than Adam Smith, and in forgetting them, much of sound economics was lost for at least a century. In many ways, as we shall see, Adam Smith deflected economics, the economics of the Continental tradition beginning with the medieval and later scholastics and continuing through French and Italian writers of the eighteenth century, from a correct path, and on to a very different and fallacious one. Smithian 'classical economics', as we have come to call it, was mired in aggregative analysis, cost-of-production theory of value, static equilibrium states, artificial division into 'micro' and 'macro', and an entire baggage of holistic and static analysis.

The unfortunate erasure of pre-Smithian economics enabled Smithian classical economics to take hold and dominate economic thought for 100 years. The 'marginal revolution' of the 1870s, especially the Austrian theory beginning in that decade, in many ways returned economics to the proper individualistic, micro and subjective value pre-Smithian path on the European continent. It is no accident that Cantillon himself was rediscovered in 1881 by the quasi-'Austrian' English marginal revolutionist W. Stanley Jevons, who was commendably eager to rediscover lost economists buried by the dominant Smith–Ricardo orthodoxy.

But economics has unfortunately far from rid itself of the Smith–Ricardo baggage. The current revival of Austrian theory, and the increasing search for a way out of contemporary orthodoxy by many mainstream economists, is an attempt to complete the promise of the badly named 'marginal revolution' (really an individualist–subjectivist revolution), and to complete the casting out of the classical British paradigm.

12.11 Notes

1. Considerable confusion has been sown in Cantillon studies by the fact that Richard's cousin, father, great-grandfather, and great-great-grandfather were all named Richard.
2. To add to the genealogical confusion, Richard's mother, Bridget, was also a Cantillon, from County Limerick. Richard's father and his bride Bridget were distant cousins in the

Cantillon family. Richard's grandfather and Bridget's great-grandfather were both sons of Sir Richard Cantillon I.

3. At the height of the bubble, the duchess of Orleans wrote, in wonder: 'It is inconceivable what wealth there is in France now. Everybody speaks in millions. I don't understand it at all, but I see clearly that the god Mammon reigns an absolute monarch in Paris'. Quoted in John Carswell, *The South Sea Bubble* (Stanford: Stanford University Press, 1960), p. 101.

4. The Egmont quote is in Antoin E. Murphy, 'Richard Cantillon–Banker and Economist', *Journal of Libertarian Studies* 7 (Autumn 1985), p. 185.

5. F.A. von Hayek, 'Introduction to a German translation of Cantillon's *Essai*' (Jena: Gustav Fischer, 1931); from translation of Hayek's Introduction by Mícheál Ó'Súilleábháin, *Journal of Libertarian Studies*, 7 (Autumn 1985), p. 227.

6. In an Aristotelian flourish, Cantillon declared that land 'is the source or matter from which Wealth is extracted', while 'human labour is the form which produces it', while wealth, however, is not intrinsic in the goods but is 'in itself no other than the sustenance, the conveniences, and the comforts of life'.

7. In the *Essai*, a work of only 165 pages, Cantillon makes no less than 110 separate references to the entrepreneur.

8. Vickers aptly writes that 'In Cantillon, as opposed to other writers of the first half of the [eighteenth] century, the move in theory and in explanation toward a dynamic as opposed to a definitional and static description of monetary affairs took on a microscopic, microeconomic form. His economic analysis always started from individual economic magnitude and quantities'. And again: 'Market prices, money prices, and levels of activity and employment were not to be regarded as homogeneous variables. The *Essai* is interested in the *structure* of market prices, the structure of market supply conditions, and the structure of activity in the economy'. Douglas Vickers, *Studies in the Theory of Money 1690–1776* (Philadelphia: Chilton Co., 1959), pp. 187–8.

9. See the citations and discussion in Chi-Yuen Wu, *An Outline of International Price Theories* (London: George Routledge & Sons, 1939), pp. 66–7.

10. Arthur Eli Monroe, *Monetary Theory before Adam Smith* (1923, repr. Gloucester, Mass.: Peter Smith, 1965), pp. 255–6.

11. von Hayek, op. cit., note 5, p. 226.

12. Salerno points out that at least in this respect Cantillon's treatment was inferior to the neglected pamphlet by an unknown English author, Isaac Gervaise, *The System or Theory of the Trade of the World* (1720). Gervaise worked out the process of equilibration and, believing as he did in a firm trend toward an equilibrium position, he was the first to point out that in such equilibrium, the precious metals would be distributed in accordance with the international demand for them. That demand would be embodied in the productive activities of each particular nation. Gervaise's pamphlet remained unread until resurrected by Professor Jacob Viner in the mid-twentieth century. Isaac Gervaise, *The System or Theory of the Trade of the World*, ed. J.M. Letiche (Baltimore: Johns Hopkins University Press, 1954).

Gervaise, however, was inferior to Cantillon, presenting an aggregative, macroeconomic approach instead of the latter's pioneering microeconomic process analysis.

13 Physiocracy in mid-eighteenth century France

13.1 The sect

The first self-conscious school of economic thought developed in France shortly after the publication of Cantillon's *Essai*. They called themselves 'the economists', but later came to be called the 'physiocrats', after their prime politico-economical principle: *physio-cracy* (the rule of nature). The physiocrats had an authentic leader – the creator of the physiocratic paradigm – a leading propagandist, and several highly placed disciples and editors of journals. The physiocrats promoted each other, reviewed each others' prolific works in glowing terms, met frequently and periodically in *salons* to deliver papers and discuss each other's essays, and generally behaved as a self-conscious movement. They had a cadre of hard-core physiocrats, and a penumbra of influential fellow-travellers and sympathizers. Unfortunately, the physiocrats soon took on the dimensions of a cult as well as a school, heaping lavish and uncritical praise upon their leader, who thus became a guru as well as the creator of an important paradigm in economic thought.

The founder, leader, and guru of physiocracy was Dr François Quesnay (1694–1774), a restless, charismatic and intellectually curious soul who was typical of Enlightenment intellectuals of the eighteenth century. Smitten with the physical sciences, as so many intellectuals were in the shadow of the great Isaac Newton, Quesnay, son of a well-to-do farmer, read widely in his chosen profession of medicine. Gaining fame as a surgeon and physician, Quesnay wrote medical works and also became expert in agricultural science, writing on its technology. In 1749, at the age of 55, Quesnay became personal physician to King Louis XV's mistress, Madame de Pompadour, and a few years later also became personal physician to the king himself.

It was in the late 1750s, when in his mid-60s, that Dr Quesnay began to dabble in economic topics. The founding of the physiocratic movement may be dated precisely at the moment in July 1757 when the guru met his chief adept and propagandist. For it was then that Dr Quesnay met the restless, flighty, enthusiastic, and slightly crackpot Victor Riqueti, the Marquis de Mirabeau (1715–89). Mirabeau, a disgruntled aristocrat with plenty of leisure time on his hands, had just published the first several parts of a multi-part work, a grandiloquently entitled best-seller *L'Ami des hommes* (*The Friend of Man*). This work had charmed many Frenchmen through its very flamboyance and lack of system, as well as its curious use of an archaic seventeenth-century style. While writing *L'Ami des hommes*, Mirabeau was a quasi-disciple of the later Cantillon, glossing and publishing the *Essai*, but contact with Quesnay soon converted him into the doctor's leading fugleman and propagandist. The ruminations of one seemingly harmless eccentric physician had now become a School of Thought, a force to be reckoned with.

The high placement of the two founding physiocrats served their cause well. Quesnay's crucial place at court, as well as Mirabeau's fame and aristocratic position, gave the movement power and influence. Still, political economy was dangerous in that age of absolutism and censorship, and Quesnay prudently published his work under pseudonyms or through his disciples. Indeed, Mirabeau was imprisoned for a couple of weeks in 1760 for his book, *Théorie de l'impôt* (*Theory of Taxes*) specifically for his blistering attack on oppressive taxation and on the financial system of 'tax farming', in which the king sold the rights to tax to private firms or 'farmers'. He was released, however, by the good offices of Madame de Pompadour.

The physiocrats conducted their operations through a succession of journals, and through periodic salons, some conducted at the home of Dr Quesnay, the most prominent in regular Tuesday evening seminars at the home of the Marquis de Mirabeau. The chief physiocratic figures were: Pierre François Mercier de la Rivière (1720–93), whose *L'Ordre natural et essentiel des sociétés politiques* (*The Natural and Essential Order of Political Societies*) (1767) was the major work on political philosophy of the school; the Abbé Nicolas Baudeau (1730–92), the editor and journalist of the physiocrats; Guillaume François Le Trosne (1728–80), jurist and economist; and the youngest member of the group, the secretary, editor, and government official Pierre Samuel Du Pont de Nemours (1739–1817), who would later emigrate to the United States to found the famous gunpowder manufacturing family.

In no way did the cult aspect of the physiocratic group show itself more starkly than in the adjectives used about their master. His followers claimed that Quesnay looked like Socrates, and they habitually referred to him as the 'Confucius of Europe'. Indeed, despite the fact that Adam Smith and others spoke of his great 'modesty', Dr Quesnay identified himself with the alleged wisdom and glory of the Chinese sage. Mirabeau went so far as to proclaim that the three greatest inventions in the history of mankind were writing, money, and Quesnay's famous diagram, the *Tableau économique*.

The sect lasted for less than two decades, going rapidly downhill after the mid-1770s. Several factors accounted for the precipitate decline. One was the death of Quesnay in 1774, and the fact that in his later years the physician had lost much interest in his cult and had shifted to work on mathematics, where he claimed to have solved the age-old problem of squaring the circle. Furthermore, the fall from grace as finance minister of their fellow-traveller, A.R.J. Turgot, two years later, and the disgrace heaped upon Mirabeau by a public smear campaign launched by his wife and children at about the same time, caused physiocracy to fall from influence. And the advent of Smith's *Wealth of Nations* in the same year soon led to the unfortunate habit of ignoring all pre-Smithian thought, as if the new science of 'political economy' had been created single-handed and *ex nihilo* by Adam Smith.

13.2 *Laissez-faire* and free trade

The main stress of the physiocrats was in two areas: political economy and technical economic analysis, and the difference in the quality of their respective contributions is so great as to be almost stupefying. For in general political economy, they were usually perceptive and made important contributions, whereas in technical economics they introduced egregious and often bizarre fallacies which were to plague economics for a long time to come.

In political economy, the physiocrats were among the first *laissez-faire* thinkers, casting aside contemptuously the entire mercantilist baggage. They called for complete internal and external free enterprise and free trade, unfettered by subsidies, monopoly privileges or restrictions. By removing such restrictions and exactions, commerce, agriculture and the entire economy would flourish. On international trade, while the physiocrats lacked the specie-flow-price mechanism of the brilliant and sophisticated Cantillon, they were far bolder than he in laying down the gauntlet to all mercantilist fallacies and restrictions. It is absurd and self-contradictory, they pointed out, for a nation to attempt to sell a great deal to foreign countries and to buy very little; selling and buying are only two sides of the same coin. Furthermore, the physiocrats anticipated the classical economic insight that money is not crucial, that in the long run, commodities – real goods – exchange for each other, with money simply an intermediary. Therefore, the key goal is not to amass bullion, or to follow the chimera of a permanently favourable balance of trade, but to have a high standard of living in terms of real products. Seeking to amass specie means that people in a nation are giving up real goods in order to acquire mere money; hence, they are losing rather than gaining wealth in real terms. Indeed, the whole point of money is to exchange it for real wealth, and if people insist on piling up an unused hoard of specie they will lose wealth permanently.

When Turgot became finance minister of France in 1774, his first act was to decree freedom of import and export of grain. The preamble of his edict, drawn up by his aide Du Pont de Nemours, summed up the *laissez-faire* policy of the physiocrats – and of Turgot – in a fine and succinct manner: the new free trade policy, it declared, was designed

> to animate and extend the cultivation of the land, whose produce is the most real and certain wealth of a state; to maintain abundance by granaries and the entry of foreign corn, to prevent corn from falling to a price which would discourage the producer; to remove monopoly by shutting out private license in favor of free and full competition, and by maintaining among different countries that communication of exchange of superfluities for necessities which is so comfortable to the order established by Divine Providence.[1]

Although the physiocrats were officially in favour of complete freedom of trade, their besetting passion – and this reflects their often bizarre economics – were repealing all restrictions on free export of grain. It is understandable that they would concentrate on the elimination of a long-standing restriction, but they seemed to show little zeal for the freedom of *importation* of grain or for the freedom of export of manufactures. All this was wrapped up in the physiocrats' unremitting enthusiasm for high agricultural prices, almost as a good in itself. Indeed, the physiocrats frowned on exports of manufactured products as competing with, and lowering the price of, agricultural exports. Dr Quesnay went so far as to write that 'happy the land which has no exports of manufactures because agricultural exports maintain farm prices at too high a level to permit the sterile class to sell its products abroad'. As we shall see below, 'sterile' by definition meant everyone outside agriculture.

13.3   *Laissez-faire* forerunner: the marquis d'Argenson

While the physiocrats were the first economists to stress and develop the case for *laissez-faire*, they had distinguished forerunners among statesmen and merchants in France. As we have seen, the *laissez-faire* concept developed among classical liberal oppositionists to the absolutism of late seventeenth century France. They included merchants such as Thomas Le Gendre and utilitarian officials like Belesbat and Boisguilbert.

Bridging the gap between turn of the eighteenth century *laissez-faire* writers and the physiocrats of the 1760s and 1770s was the eminent statesman, René-Louis de Voyer de Paulmy, Marquis d'Argenson (1694–1757). The heir of a long line of ministers, magistrates, and *intendants*, d'Argenson's ambition was to become prime minister and save France from what he saw as impending revolution by instituting *laissez-faire*. A voracious reader and prolific writer throughout his life, d'Argenson only published in his lifetime a few articles in his *Journal Oeconomique* in the early 1750s, and these were not printed but widely circulated in manuscript form. For a long while, d'Argenson was erroneously credited by historians with originating the phrase '*laissez-faire*' in one of the articles in his *Journal* of 1751.

While d'Argenson did not originate the term, *laissez-faire* was his repeated cry to the French authorities, a cry he continued to stress even though his ideas were dismissed as eccentric by all his governmental colleagues. As *intendant* in his early years on the Flemish border, d'Argenson was struck with what he saw to be the economic and social superiority of free people and free markets across the border in Flanders. He then became greatly influenced by the writings of Fénélon, Belesbat, and Boisguilbert.

D'Argenson saw self-love and self-interest as the mainspring of human action, as bringing about energy and productivity in the pursuit of each man's happiness. Human social life, to d'Argenson, has the 'natural tendency to inherent harmony when artificial constraints and artificial harmony and artificial stimuli are removed'. Looking to an enlightened monarch to remove these artificial subsidies and restrictions, d'Argenson pointed out that in the ideal society, the sovereign would have very little to do. 'One spoils everything by meddling too much... The best government is that which governs least'. Thereby the marquis anticipated the famous phrase attributed to Thomas Jefferson.

D'Argenson concluded that 'each individual [should] be left alone to labor on his own behalf, instead of suffering constraint and ill-conceived precautions. Then everything will go beautifully...'. Then continuing the proto-Hayekian point made by Belesbat:

> It is precisely this perfection of liberty that makes a science of commerce impossible, in the sense that our speculative thinkers understand it. They want to direct commerce by their orders and regulations; but to do this one would need to be thoroughly acquainted with the interests involved in commerce...from one individual to another. In the absence of such knowledge, it [a science of commerce] can only be...much worse than ignorance in its bad effects...Therefore, *laissez-faire*! (*Eh, qu'on laisse-faire!*')

13.4 Natural law and property rights

Not only were the physiocrats generally consistent advocates of *laissez-faire*, but they also supported the operation of a free market and the natural rights of person and property. John Locke and the Levellers in England had transformed the rather vague and holistic notions of natural law into the clear-cut, firmly individualistic concepts of the natural rights of every individual human being. But the physiocrats were the first to apply natural rights and property rights concepts fully to the free market economy. In a sense, they completed the work of Locke and brought full Lockeanism to economics. Quesnay and the others were also inspired by the typically eighteenth century Enlightenment version of natural law: where the individual's rights of person and property were deeply embedded in a set of natural laws that had been worked out by the creator and were clearly discoverable in the light of human reason. In a profound sense, then, eighteenth century natural rights theory was a refined variant of medieval and post-medieval scholastic natural law. The rights were now clearly individualistic and not societal or pertaining to the state; and the set of natural laws was discoverable by human reason. The seventeenth century Dutch Protestant, and in essence Protestant scholastic, Hugo Grotius, deeply influenced by the late Spanish scholastics, developed a natural law theory which he boldly declared was truly independent of the question of whether God had created them. The seeds of this thought were in St Thomas Aquinas and in later Catholic scholastics, but never had it been formulated as clearly and as starkly as by Grotius. Or, to put it in terms that had fascinated political philosophers since Plato: did God love the good because it *was in fact good*, or is something good because God loves it? The former has always been the answer of those who believe in objective truth and objective ethics, that is, that something might be good or bad in accordance with the objective laws of nature and reality. The latter has been the answer of fideists who believe that no objective rights or ethics exist, and that only the purely arbitrary will of God, as expressed in revelation, can make things good or bad for mankind. Grotius's was the definitive statement of the objectivist, rationalist position, since natural laws for him are discoverable by human reason, and the eighteenth century Enlightenment was essentially the spinning out of the Grotian framework. To Grotius the Enlightenment added Newton, and his vision of the world as a set of harmonious, precisely if not mechanically interacting natural laws. And while Grotius and Newton were fervent Christians as was almost everyone in their epoch, the eighteenth century, starting with their premises, easily fell into deism, in which God, the great 'clock-maker', or creator of this universe of natural laws, then disappeared from the scene and allowed his creation to work itself out.

From the standpoint of political philosophy, however, it mattered little whether Quesnay and the others (Du Pont was of Huguenot background) were Catholics or deists: for given their world outlook, their attitude toward natural law and natural rights could be the same in either case.

Mercier de la Rivière pointed out in his *L'Ordre naturel* that the general plan of God's creation had provided natural laws for the government of all things, and that man could surely not be any exception to that rule. Man needed only to know through his reason the conditions that would lead to his greatest happiness and then follow that path. All ills of mankind follow from ignorance or disobedience of such laws. In human nature, the right of self-preservation implies the right to property, and any individual property in man's products from the soil requires property in the land itself. But the right to property would be nothing without the freedom of using it, and so liberty is derived from the right to property. People flourish as social animals, and through trade and exchange of property they maximize the happiness of all. Furthermore, since the faculties of human beings are by nature diverse and unequal, an inequality of condition arises naturally from an equal right to liberty of every man. In this way, property rights and free markets, concluded Mercier, is a social order that is natural, evident, simple, immutable and conducive to the happiness of all.

Or, as Quesnay declared in his *Le Droit naturel* (*Natural Law*): 'Every man has a natural right to the free exercise of his faculties provided he does not employ them to the injury of himself or others. This right to liberty implies as a corollary the right to property', and the only function of the government is to defend that right.[2]

Many rulers of Europe were either entranced or intrigued by this fashionable new doctrine of physiocracy, and endeavoured to find out about it from its major theorists. The dauphin of France once complained to Quesnay of the difficulty of being a king, and the physician replied that it was really quite simple. 'What then', asked the dauphin, 'would you do if you were king?' 'Nothing', was the straightforward, stark, and magnificently libertarian answer of Dr Quesnay. 'But then who would govern?' sputtered the dauphin. 'The law', that is, the natural law, was Quesnay's accurate but no doubt unsatisfying reply.

A similar reply was certainly unsatisfactory to Catherine the Great, czarina of all the Russias, who sent for Mercier de la Rivière, jurist and at one time *intendant* (governor) of Martinique, to instruct her on how to govern. Pressed as to what the 'law' should be grounded on, Mercier answered the empress: 'On one [thing] alone, madame, the nature of things and of man'. 'But how then, can a king know what laws to give to a people?' the czarina continued. To which Mercier replied sharply: 'To give or make laws, Madame, is a task which God has left to no one. Ah! What is man, to think himself capable of dictating laws to beings whom he knows not...? The science of government, Mercier added, is to study and recognize the 'laws which God has so evidently engraven in the very organization of man, when He gave him existence'. Mercier added the pertinent warning: 'To seek to go beyond this would be a great misfortune and a destructive undertaking'.

The czarina was polite, but was definitely not amused. 'Monsieur', she replied curtly, 'I am very pleased to have heard you. I wish you good day'.

13.5   The single tax on land
Natural rights, *laissez-faire* libertarians always confront several problems or *lacunae* in their theory. One is taxation. If every individual is to have inviolable property rights, and those rights are to be guaranteed by the government, taxation, itself an infringement of property rights, presents an immediate problem to *laissez-faire* theorists. For *how high* should taxes be, and *who* should pay them?

Classical liberalism, however inchoate, had been born in France as an opposition to the statist absolutism of King Louis XIV in the latter decades of the seventeenth, and the early years of the eighteenth, century. A favourite programme of these liberals, as set forth by Marshal Vauban and by the Sieur de Boisguilbert, among others, was a single tax, a proportional tax on all income or property. The idea was that this simple, direct, universal tax would replace the monstrous and crippling network of taxation that had grown up in seventeenth century France.

To solve the problem of taxation, Dr Quesnay and the physiocrats came up with their own original single tax (*l'impôt unique*) – a single tax on land. The idea was that tax would be low, and that it would be proportional and confined only to a tax on land and on landlords.

The rationale of the *impôt unique* stems from the singular physiocratic view that only land is productive. Land *produces* because it creates matter; whereas all other activities, such as trade, commerce, manufacturing, services, etc. are 'sterile', although admittedly useful, because they only shuffle around or transform matter without creating it. Since only land is productive, and all other activities are sterile, it follows, according to the physiocrats, that any other taxes will wind up being shifted on to land, through the price system. Therefore, the choice is to tax the land indirectly and remotely, while crippling and distorting economic activities, or taxing the land openly and uniformly through the single tax, thereby freeing economic activity from a fearsome tax burden.

From the standpoint of economic theory, the famous physiocratic tenet that only land is productive must be considered bizarre and absurd. It is certainly a tremendous loss of insight compared to Cantillon, who identified land *and labour* as original productive factors, and entrepreneurs as the motor of the market economy who adjust resources to the demands of consumers and to the uncertainty of the market. It is surely true that agriculture was the chief occupation of the day, and that most commerce was the transportation and sale of agricultural products, but this scarcely salvages or excuses the absurdity of the land-as-only-productive-factor doctrine.

It is possible that one explanation for this odd doctrine is to apply to the physiocrats the insight of Professor Roger Garrison on the basic world-outlook of Adam Smith. Smith, in a less outlandish version of the physiocratic bias, held that only *material* output – in contrast to intangible services – is 'productive', while immaterial services are unproductive. Garrison points out that the contrast here is not really between material and immaterial goods and services, but between capital goods and consumer goods – which are basically either direct services or a stream of services to be available in the future. Hence, for Smith, 'productive' labour is only effort that goes into capital goods, into building up productive capacity for the future. Labour in direct service to consumers is 'unproductive'. In short, Smith, despite his reputation as an advocate of the free market, refuses to accept free market allocations to the production of consumer *vis-à-vis* capital goods; he would prefer more investment and growth than the market prefers.

In the same way, could it not be true that the physiocrats had a similar outlook? The physiocrats, too, stressed *material* goods, and agriculture was the main material product. The physiocrats were also greatly concerned with economic growth, with increasing investment and national output, and especially with greater capital investments in agriculture. Indeed, the physiocrats were disgruntled with free market choice, and wanted to strengthen consumer demand for agricultural products in particular. High consumption of farm products was beneficial according to the physiocrats, whereas high consumption of manufactured goods would promote 'unproductive' expenses and crowd out desirable purchases of agricultural products.

Some economists have gone so far as to speculate that the physiocrats would have been overjoyed at a policy of farm-price supports. Professor Spiegel believes that if the physiocrats

> had been faced with a choice between laissez faire and intervention on behalf of farm price supports, they would have chosen intervention. The means to resolve the economic problem that was foremost in their minds was the development of domestic agriculture rather than unconditional reliance on private initiative within a framework of competition.[3]

Perhaps the tip-off on applying the Garrison insight is the common attitude of Smith and the physiocrats on usury laws. Despite their generally consistent advocacy of absolute and inviolate property rights, and of the freedom to trade within and without a nation, Quesnay and the physiocrats championed usury laws, denying the freedom to lend and borrow. Adam Smith had a similar aberration. Smith, as we shall see further below (Chapter 16), and as Garrison pointed out, took this position in a conscious effort to divert credit from 'unproductive' high risk and high interest-paying speculators and consumers and toward 'productive' low risk investors. Similarly, Quesnay denounced the restrictions on investment and capital growth resulting from high interest rates and from the competition of unproductive borrowers crowding out credit that would otherwise go into capitalized agriculture. Usury laws were upheld on traditional moralistic grounds of alleged 'sterility' of money. But to the physiocrats, *all* activity except agriculture was 'unproductive', and so the problem was rather the competition such borrowing imposed on the 'productive sector'. As Elizabeth Fox-Genovese puts it: 'Quesnay... argues that the high interest rate constitutes neither more nor less than a tax upon the productive life of the nation – upon those who do not borrow as much as upon those who do'.[4]

It is true that part of the physiocratic attention here was on government debt, and it is certainly true that government debt raises interest rates and diverts capital from productive to unproductive sectors. But there are two flaws in such an approach. First, not all non-agricultural debt is state debt, and therefore not all higher interest is a 'tax' on producers. This returns us to the eccentric view of the physiocrats that only land is productive. Usury laws would cripple not only government debt, but also other forms of borrowing. And second, it seem odd to allow government debt and then to try to offset its unfortunate effects by the meat-axe approach of imposing restraints on usury. Surely it would be simpler, more direct, and less distorting to tackle the problem at its source and call for the elimination of government debt. Usury laws only make things worse, and injure free and productive credit.

And so Quesnay – himself the son of a well-to-do farmer – was far more interested in subsidizing credit to farmers and keeping out competing borrowers than in stopping government debt.

There is another way of explaining the physiocratic attitude towards land as the sole producer. And that is to concentrate on the proposed *impôt unique*. More specifically, the physiocrats held that the productive classes were the farmers, who rented the land from the landlords and actually tilled it. The landlords were only partially productive, the *partially* coming from the capital advances they had made to the farmers. But the physiocrats were sure that the farmers' returns were all bid away by their competition to rent lands, so that in practice all the 'net product' (*produit net*) – the *only* net product in society – is reaped by the nation's landlords. Therefore, the single tax should be a proportionate tax upon the landlords alone.

Professor Norman J. Ware has interpreted physiocracy and its emphasis on the sole productivity of land as merely a rationalization of the interests of the landlord class. This hypothesis has been taken seriously by many historians of economic thought. But let us ask ourselves: what sort of self-serving doctrine says: 'Please: put all the taxes on me'? The beneficiaries of physiocratic policies would surely be every economic class *except* the landlords, including Dr Quesnay's own class of farmers.[5]

13.6 'Objective' value and cost of production

Although the physiocrats had useful insights into political economy and the importance of the free market, their distinctive contributions to technical economics were not only wrong, but in some cases proved to be a disaster for the future of the economic discipline.

Thus for centuries the mainstream of economic thought, generally embedded in scholastic treatises, held that the value, and therefore the prices, of goods were determined on the market by utility and scarcity, that is, by consumer valuations of a given supply of a product. Scholastic and post-scholastic economics had basically solved the age-old 'value paradox' of diamonds and bread, or diamonds and water: how is it that bread, so useful to man, is worth very little on the market, whereas diamonds, a mere frippery, are so expensive? The solution was that if quantities of supply are taken into account, the seeming contradiction between 'use value' and 'exchange value' disappears. For the supply of bread is so abundant that any given loaf will have a negligible value – in use or in exchange – whereas diamonds are so scarce that they will command a high value on the market. 'Value', then, does not pertain in the abstract to a class of goods; it is imparted by consumers to specific, real units, and such value depends inversely on the supply of a good.

The only thing left to complete the explanation was the 'marginal' insight imparted by the Austrians and other neoclassicals in the 1870s. The scholastics saw that the utility of any good diminishes as its stock increases; the only thing lacking was the marginal analysis that real-world purchases and evaluations focus on the next unit (the 'marginal' unit) of the good. Diminishing utility is diminishing *marginal* utility. But while the capstone of utility and subjective value theory was yet missing, enough was already in place to provide a cogent explanation of value and price.

Despite his troubling injection of 'intrinsic value' as a quantity of land and labour in production, Cantillon had continued in this late scholastic, proto-Austrian, tradition and had indeed made many contributions to it, particularly in the study of money and entrepreneurship. It was the physiocrats who broke with centuries of sound economic reasoning and contributed to what would become, in the hands of Smith and Ricardo, a reactionary and obscurantist destruction of the correct analysis of value.

Dr Quesnay begins his value analysis by disregarding centuries of value theory and tragically sundering the concepts of 'use value' and 'exchange value'. Use value reflects the individual needs and desires of consumers, but, according to Quesnay, these use values of different goods have little or no relation to each other or, therefore, to prices. Exchange value, or relative prices, on the other hand, have no relation to man's needs or to agreements among bargainers and contractors. Instead, Quesnay, the would-be 'scientist', rejected subjective value and insisted that the values of goods are 'objective' and mystically embedded in various goods irrespective of consumers' subjective valuations. This objective embodiment, according to Quesnay, is the cost of production, which in some way determines the 'fundamental price' of every good. As was even true for Cantillon, this 'objective' cost of production appears to be somehow determined externally, from outside the system.

13.7   The *Tableau économique*

Not as devastating for the development of economics as his fallacy of the cost of production or 'productive labour', but more irritating nowadays is Dr Quesnay's *Tableau économique*, the very invention that his glorifier Mirabeau called one of the three great human inventions of all time. The *Tableau*, first published in 1758, was an incomprehensible, jargon-filled chart purporting to depict the flow of expenditures from one economic class to another. Generally dismissed as turgid and irrelevant in its day, it has been rediscovered by twentieth century economists, who are fascinated *because* of its very incomprehensibility. All the better to publish journal articles on!

Dr Quesnay's *Tableau économique* has been hailed for anticipating many of the most cherished developments of twentieth century economics: aggregative concepts, input–output analysis, econometrics, depiction of the 'circular flow' of equilibrium, Keynesian stress on expenditure and consumer demand, and the Keynesian 'multiplier'. In recent years tens of thousands of words have been lovingly expended on trying to piece together what the *Tableau* had to say, and to reconcile it with its own figures and with the economy of the real world.

To the extent that Quesnay's *Tableau* anticipates all these developments, so much the worse for both the forerunner and the later product! It is true that the *Tableau* shows that ultimately real goods exchange for real goods, with money as an intermediary, and that everyone is both a consumer and a producer in the market. But these simple facts were known for centuries, and charts, lines (Quesnay's cherished 'zig-zags'), and numbers can only obscure rather than highlight their importance. At best the chart elaborates spending and income patterns to no purpose.[6] Furthermore, the *Tableau* is holistic, aggregative, and macroeconomic, with no solid grounding in the methodological individualism of sound microeconomics.

The *Tableau* not only introduced ungrounded and unsound macro thinking into economics; it also laid up mischief for the future by anticipating Keynesianism. For it glorified expenditures, including consumption, and worried about savings, which it tended to regard as crippling the economy by 'leaking' out of the constant circular flow of spending. This stress on the vital importance of maintaining spending was faulty and superficial in ignoring two fundamental considerations: saving is spent on investment goods, and the key to harmony and equilibrium is *price* – lower spending can always be equilibrated easily on the market by a fall in prices. It can be laid down as a veritable law that any picture or analysis of the economic system that omits prices from consideration can only be crackpot; and the *Tableau économique* was the first – but alas not the last – economic model which did precisely that.

Dr Quesnay of course gave to his circular flow model his own physiocratic twist: it was particularly important to keep up spending on 'productive' agricultural products, and to avoid diversion of spending to 'sterile' and 'unproductive' products, i.e. to anything else. Keynes, of course, was to avoid the physiocratic bias when he resurrected a similar analysis.

While the analytic merits of macro concepts, input–output analysis and econometrics are highly dubious at best, they are surely worse than nothing if the numbers are incorrect. But Quesnay's figures are spurious, for the France of his day or for any other epoch. And the would-be great mathematician made many simple mistakes in arithmetic in the portrayals of his beloved *Tableau*. At best, then, the *Tableau* was elaborate frippery; at worst, false, mischief-making, and deceptive. And in no sense did the *Tableau* do anything but detract and divert attention from genuine economic analysis and insight.

After contemplating this piece of egregious folly, it is a relief to turn to the blistering satirical attack on the *Tableau* by a conservative statist opponent of the physiocrats, the attorney Simon Nicolas Henri Linguet (1736–94). In his *Réponse Aux Docteurs modernes* (*Reply to the Modern Doctors*) (1771), Linguet begins by ridiculing the idea that the physiocrats were not a cult, or sect:

> Evidence shows it: your mysterious words, *physiocratie, produit net;* your mystic jargon, *ordre, science, le maitre* [the master] your titles of honor showered on your patriarchs; your wreaths scattered through the provinces on obscure if excellent persons…Not a sect? You have a rallying cry, banners, a march, a trumpeter [Du Pont], a uniform for your books, and a sign like freemasons. Not a sect? One cannot touch one of you but all rush to his aid. You all laud and glorify each other, and attack and intimidate your opponents in unmeasured terms.

Linguet then turns his scornful attention to the *Tableau*:

> You affect an inspired tone and seriously discuss on what particular day the symbol of your faith, the masterpiece, the *Tableau Economique* was born – a symbol so mysterious that huge volumes cannot explain it. It is like the Koran of Mohamet. You burn to lay down your lives for your principles, and talk of your apostleship. You attack [the Abbé] Galiani and me because we have no reverence for that ridiculous hieroglyphic which is your holy Gospel. Confucius drew up a table, the I-Ching, of sixty-four terms, also connected by lines, to show the evolution of the elements, and your *Tableau Economique* is justly enough compared to it, but it comes three hundred years too late. Both alike are equally unintelligible. The *Tableau* is an insult to common sense, to reason, and philosophy, with its columns of figures of *reproduction nette* terminating always in a zero, striking symbol of the fruit of the researches of any one simple enough to try in vain to understand it.[7]

13.8   Strategy and influence

One problem that any *laissez-faire* liberal thinker must face is: granted that government interference should be minimal, what form should that government take? Who shall govern?

To French liberals of the latter seventeenth or eighteenth century there seemed to be only one answer: government is and always will be rule by an absolute monarch. Oppositionist rebels had been crushed in the early and mid-seventeenth century, and from then on only one answer was thinkable: the king must be converted to the truths and wisdom of *laissez-faire*. Any idea of inspiring or launching a mass opposition movement against the king was simply out of the question; it was not part of any thinkable dialogue.

The physiocrats, like classical liberals earlier in the eighteenth century, were not simply theorists. The nation had gone awry, and they possessed a political alternative they were trying to promote. But if absolute monarchy was the only conceivable form of government for France, the only strategy for liberals was simple, at least on paper; to convert the king. And so the strategy of classical liberals, from the exertions of the Abbé Claude Fleury and his able student, Archbishop Fénélon in the late seventeenth century, to the physiocrats and Turgot in the late eighteenth, was to convert the ruler.

The liberals were well placed to pursue the strategy of what might be called their projected 'revolution from the top'. For they were all highly placed at court. Archbishop Fénélon placed his hopes in the dauphin, rearing the duke of Burgundy as an ardent classical liberal. But we have seen that these carefully laid plans turned to ashes when the duke died of illness in 1711, only four years before the death of Louis himself.

A half-century later, Dr Quesnay, again working through a king's mistress, this time Madame de Pompadour, used his position at court to try to convert the ruler. Success in France was only partial. When Turgot, who agreed with the physiocrats on *laissez-faire*, became finance minister and started putting sweeping liberal reforms into effect, he quickly ran into a wall of entrenched opposition that removed him from office only two years later. His reforms were angrily repealed. The leading physiocrats were exiled by King Louis XVI, their journal was quickly suppressed, and Mirabeau was ordered to cancel his famous Tuesday evening seminars.

The physiocrats' strategy proved a failure, and there was more to the failure than the vagaries of a particular monarch. For even if the monarch could be convinced that liberty conduced to the happiness and prosperity of his subjects, his own interests are often to maximize state exactions and therefore his own power and wealth. Furthermore, the monarch does not rule alone, but as the head of a ruling coalition of bureaucrats, nobles, privileged monopolists and feudal lords. He rules, in short, as the head of a power élite, or 'ruling class'. It is theoretically conceivable but scarcely likely that a king and the rest of the ruling class will rush to embrace a philosophy and a political economy that will end their power and put them, in effect, out of business. It certainly did not happen in France and so, after the failure of the physiocrats and Turgot, came the French Revolution.

In any event, the physiocrats did manage to convert some rulers, though not the monarch of France. Their leading disciple among the rulers of the world – and one of the most enthusiastic and lovable ones – was Carl Friedrich, margrave of the duchy of Baden (1728–1811) in Germany. Converted by the works of Mirabeau, the margrave wrote a précis of physiocracy, and proceeded to try to institute the system in his realm. The margrave proposed free trade in corn to the German Diet, and in 1770, he introduced the *impôt unique* at 20 per cent of the agricultural 'net product' in three villages of Baden. Administering the experiment was the margrave's chief aide, the enthusiastic German physiocrat Johann August Schlettwein (1731–1802), professor of economics at the University of Giessen. The experiment, however, was abandoned in a few years in two villages, although the single tax continued in the village of Dietlingen until 1792. For a few years, the margrave also imported Du Pont de Nemours to be his adviser and tutor to his son.

In one notable meeting, the fervent margrave of Baden asked his master Mirabeau whether or not the physiocratic ideal was making sovereign rulers unnecessary. Perhaps they might all be reformed out of existence. The margrave had divined the anarchistic – or at least the republican – core underlying the *laissez-faire* libertarian and natural rights doctrine. But Mirabeau, dedicated as were all the physiocrats to absolute monarchy, drew back, sternly reminding his younger pupil that while the role of the sovereign would ideally be limited, he would still be the owner of the public domain and the preserver of social order.

Several other rulers of Europe at least dabbled in physiocracy. One of the most eager was Leopold II, grand duke of Tuscany, later emperor of Austria, who ordered his ministers to consult with Mirabeau and carried out some of the physiocratic reforms. A fellow-traveller was Emperor Joseph II of Austria. Another physiocratic enthusiast was Gustavus III, king of Sweden, who conferred upon Mirabeau the grand cross of the newly founded Order of Wasa, in honour of agriculture. Du Pont in turn, was made a Knight of the Order. More practically, when the physiocratic journal was suppressed upon the fall of Turgot, King Gustavus and the margrave of Baden joined in commissioning Du Pont to edit a journal which would be published in their realms.

But the physiocratic appeal to monarchy lost what little effect it had after the onset of the French Revolution. Indeed, after the revolution, physiocracy, with its pro-agricultural bias and devotion to absolute monarchy, was discredited in France and the rest of Europe.

13.9 Daniel Bernoulli and the founding of mathematical economics

We should not leave the *Tableau* without mentioning a French–Swiss contemporary of Cantillon who prefigured the *Tableau* in one and only one sense: he can be said to be the founder, in the broadest sense, of mathematical economics. As such, his work contained some of the typical flaws and fallacies of that method.

Daniel Bernoulli (1700–82) was born into a family of distinguished mathematicians. His uncle, Jacques Bernoulli (1654–1705), was the first to discover the theory of probability (in his Latin work, *Ars conjectandi*, 1713) and his father Jean (1667–1748) was one of the early developers of the calculus, a method that had been discovered in the late seventeenth century. In 1738, Daniel, trying to solve a problem in probability theory and the theory of gambling by use of the calculus, stumbled on the concept of the law of diminishing marginal utility of money. Bernoulli's essay was published in Latin as an article in a scholarly volume.[8]

Bernoulli was presumably not familiar with the arrival at a similar law, albeit in non-mathematical form, by the Spanish Salamancan scholastics Tomás de Mercado and Francisco Garcia nearly two centuries earlier. Certainly he displayed no familiarity whatever with their monetary theories or with any other aspect of economics, for that matter. And being a mathematician, he got even his own particular point wrong, introducing the form of the Law of Diminishing Marginal Utility that would return to plague economic thought in future centuries. For the use of mathematics necessarily leads the economist to distort reality by making the theory convenient for mathematical symbolism and manipulation. Mathematics takes over, and the reality of human action loses out.

One fundamental flaw of Bernoulli's formulation was to put his symbolism into a ratio, or fractional form. If one insists on putting the concept of diminishing marginal utility of money for each individual into symbolic form, one could say that if a man's wealth, or total monetary assets, at any time is x, and utility or satisfaction is designated as u, and if Δ is the universal symbol for change, that

$$\frac{\Delta u}{\Delta x} \quad \text{diminishes as } x \text{ increases.}$$

But even this relatively innocuous formulation would be incorrect, for utility is *not* a thing, it is not a measurable entity, it cannot be divided, and therefore it is illegitimate to put it in ratio form, as the numerator in a non-existent fraction. Utility is neither a measurable entity, nor, even if it were, could it be commensurate with the money unit involved in the denominator.

Suppose that we ignore this fundamental flaw and accept the ratio as a kind of poetic version of the true law. But this is only the beginning of his problem. For then Bernoulli (and mathematical economists from then on) proceeded to multiply mathematical convenience illicitly, by transforming his symbols into the new calculus form. For if these increases of income or utility are reduced to being infinitesimal, one can use both the symbolism and the powerful manipulations of the differential calculus. Infinitely small increases are the first derivatives of the amount at any given point, and the Δs above can become the first derivatives, d. And then, the discrete jumps of human action can become the magically transformed smooth arcs and curves of the familiar geometric portrayals of modern economic theory.

But Bernoulli did not stop there. Fallacious assumption and method are piled upon each other like Pelion on Ossa. The next step towards a dramatic, seemingly precise conclusion is that every man's marginal utility not only diminishes as his wealth increases, but diminishes in fixed inverse proportion to his wealth. So that, if b is a constant and utility is y instead of u (presumably for convenience in putting utility on the *y*-axis and wealth on the *x*-axis), then

$$\frac{dy}{dx} = \frac{b}{x}$$

What evidence does Bernoulli have for this preposterous assumption, for his assertion that an increase in utility will be 'inversely proportionate to the quantity of goods already possessed'? None whatever, for this allegedly precise scientist has only pure assertion to offer.[9] There is no reason, in fact, to assume any such constant proportionality. No such evidence can ever be found, because the entire concept of constant proportion in a non-existent entity is absurd and meaningless. Utility is a subjective evaluation, a ranking by the individual, and there is no measurement, no extension, and therefore no way for it to be proportional to itself.

After coming up with this egregious fallacy, Bernoulli topped it by blithely assuming that *every* individual's marginal utility of money moves in the very same constant proportion, b. Modern economists are familiar with the difficulty, nay the impossibility, of measuring utilities between persons. But they do not give sufficient weight to this impossibility. Since utility is subjective to each individual, it cannot be measured or even compared across persons. But more than that; 'utility' is not a thing or an entity; it is simply the name for a subjective evaluation in the mind of each individual. Therefore it cannot be measured even *within* the mind of each individual, much less calculated or measured from one person to another. Even each individual person can only compare values or utilities ordinally; the idea of his 'measuring' them is absurd and meaningless.

From this multi-illegitimate theory, Bernoulli concluded fallaciously that 'there is no doubt that a gain of one thousand ducats is more significant to a pauper than to a rich man though both gain the same amount'. It depends, of course, on the values and subjective utilities of the particular rich man or pauper, and that dependence can never be measured or even compared by anyone, whether by outside observers or by either of the two people involved.[10]

Bernoulli's dubious contribution won its way into mathematics, having been adopted by the great early nineteenth century French probability theorist Pierre Simon, Marquis de Laplace (1749–1827), in his renowned *Théorie analytique des probabilités* (1812). But it was fortunately completely ignored in economic thought[11] until it was dredged up by Jevons and the mathematically inclined wing of the late nineteenth century marginal utility theorists. Its neglect was undoubtedly aided by its having been written in Latin; no German translation appeared until 1896, nor an English one until 1954.

13.10 Notes

1. Quoted in Henry Higgs, *The Physiocrats* (1897, New York: The Langland Press, 1952, p. 62.
2. See the paraphrase by Higgs, ibid., p. 45.
3. Henry William Spiegel, *The Growth of Economic Thought* (2nd ed., Durham, NC: Duke University Press, 1983), p. 192.
4. Elizabeth Fox-Genovese, *The Origins of Physiocracy* (Ithaca: Cornell University Press, 1976), p. 241.
5. I absorbed this insight from Professor Joseph Dorfman's lectures on the history of economic thought at Columbia University. As far as I know, this view has never seen print.
6. Foley provides the interesting speculation that Dr Quesnay's *Tableau économique* was heavily influenced by his erroneous conception of how blood circulates in the human body. V. Foley, 'The Origin of the Tableau Economique', *History of Political Economy* 5 (Spring 1973), pp. 121–50.
7. In Higgs, op. cit., note 1, pp. 149–50.
8. As 'Specimen Theoriae Novae de Mensura Sortis', in *Commentarii Academiae Scientiarum Imperialis Petropolitanae*, Tomus (1738), pp. 175–92. The article was translated by Louise Sommer as 'Exposition of a New Theory on the Measurement of Risk', *Econometrica*, 22 (Jan. 1954), pp. 23ff.
9. Schumpeter points out that Bernoulli noted that this assumption had been anticipated by a decade by the mathematician Cramer, who, however, had assumed that marginal utility diminished by a constant proportion, not of x but of the square root of x. One wonders how one is supposed to choose between either of these absurd assertions. The lesson is that when genuine science is replaced by arbitrary assumptions, deuces become wild, and any assumption is as good or as bad as any other. J.A. Schumpeter, *History of Economic Analysis* (New York: Oxford University Press, 1954), p. 303.
10. Emil Kauder notes the claim of Oskar Morgenstern that, while 'interindividual comparison of utilities cannot be justified', yet 'we live in making continuously such comparisons...'. Of course we do, but that process has nothing to do with science, and therefore has no place in economic theory, either in literary or mathematical form. Emil Kauder, *A History of Marginal Utility* (Princeton, NJ: Princeton University Press, 1965), p. 34n.
11. With one isolated exception, the important nineteenth century German economist, Friedrich Benedikt Wilhelm von Herrmann (1795–1868), *Staatswirtschaftliche Untersuchungen* (1832).

14 The brilliance of Turgot

14.1   The man

There is a custom in chess tournaments to award 'brilliancy' prizes for particularly resplendent victories. 'Brilliancy' games are brief, lucid and devastating, in which the master innovatively finds ways to new truths and new combinations in the discipline. If we were to award a prize for 'brilliancy' in the history of economic thought, it would surely go to Anne Robert Jacques Turgot, the baron de l'Aulne (1727–81). His career in economics was brief but brilliant and in every way remarkable. In the first place, he died rather young, and second, the time and energy he devoted to economics was comparatively little. He was a busy man of affairs, born in Paris to a distinguished Norman family which had long served as important royal officials. They were royal 'masters of requests', magistrates, *intendants* (governors). Turgot's father, Michel-Étienne, was a councillor of state, president of the Grand Council – an appeals tribunal of the *parlement* of Paris – a master of requests, and top administrator of the city of Paris. His mother was the intellectual and aristocratic Dame Magdelaine-Françoise Martineau.

Turgot had a sparkling career as a student, earning honours at the Seminary of Saint-Sulpice, and then at the great theological faculty of the University of Paris, the Sorbonne. As a younger son of a distinguished but not wealthy family, Turgot was expected to enter the Church, the preferred path of advancement for someone in that position in eighteenth century France. But although he became an Abbé, Turgot decided instead to follow family tradition and join the royal bureaucracy. There he became magistrate, master of requests, *intendant*, and, finally, as we have seen, a short-lived and controversial minister of finance (or 'controller-general') in a heroic but ill-fated attempt to sweep away statist restrictions on the market economy in a virtual revolution from above.

Not only was Turgot a busy administrator, but his intellectual interests were wide-ranging, and most of his spare time was spent in reading and writing, not in economics, but in history, literature, philology and the natural sciences. His contributions to economics were brief, scattered and hastily written, 12 pieces totalling only 188 pages. His longest and most famous work, 'Reflections on the Formation and Distribution of Wealth' (1766), comprised only 53 pages. This brevity only highlights the great contributions to economics made by this remarkable man.

Historians are wont to lump Turgot with the physiocrats, and to treat him as merely a physiocratic disciple in government, although he is treated also as a mere fellow-traveller of physiocracy out of an aesthetic desire to avoid being trapped in sectarian ways. None of this does justice to Turgot. He was a fellow-traveller largely because he shared with the physiocrats a devotion to free trade and *laissez-faire*. He was not a sectarian because he was a unique genius, and the physiocrats were scarcely that. His grasp of economic theory was immeasurably greater than theirs, and his treatment of such matters as capital and interest has scarcely been surpassed to this day.

In the history of thought the style is often the man, and Turgot's clarity and lucidity mirrors the virtues of his thought, and contrasts refreshingly with the prolix and turgid prose of the physiocrat school.

14.2   *Laissez-faire* and free trade

Turgot's mentor in economics and in administration was his great friend Jacques Claude Marie Vincent, Marquis de Gournay (1712–59). Gournay was a successful merchant who then became royal inspector of manufactures and minister of commerce. Although he wrote little, Gournay was a great *teacher* of economics in the best sense, through numberless conversations not only with Turgot but with the physiocrats and others. It was Gournay who spread the word in France about Cantillon's achievement. In addition, Gournay translated English economists such as Sir Josiah Child into French, and his extensive notes on these translations were widely circulated in manuscript in French intellectual circles. It was from Gournay that Turgot absorbed his devotion to *laissez-faire*, and indeed the origin of the phrase 'laissez-faire, laissez-passer' has often been incorrectly attributed to him.

It is fitting, then, that Turgot developed his *laissez-faire* views most fully in one of his early works, the 'Elegy to Gournay' (1759) a tribute offered when the Marquis died young after a long illness.[1]

Turgot made it clear that, for Gournay, the network of detailed mercantilist regulation of industry was not simply intellectual error, but a veritable system of coerced cartelization and special privilege conferred by the state. Turgot spoke of

> innumerable statutes, dictated by the spirit of monopoly, the whole purpose of which were [sic] to discourage industry, to concentrate trade within the hands of few people by multiplying formalities and charges, by subjecting industry to apprenticeships and journeymanships of ten years in some trades which can be learned in ten days, by excluding those who were not sons of masters, or those born outside a certain class, and by prohibiting the employment of women in the manufacture of cloth...

For Turgot, freedom of domestic and foreign trade followed equally from the enormous mutual benefits of free exchange. All the restrictions 'forget that no commercial transactions can be anything other than reciprocal', and that it is absurd to try to sell everything to foreigners while buying nothing from them in return. Turgot then goes on, in his 'Elegy', to make a vital pre-Hayekian point about the uses of indispensable particular knowledge by individual actors and entrepreneurs in the free market. These committed, on-the-spot participants in the market process know far more about their situations than intellectuals aloof from the fray.

> There is no need to prove that each individual is the only competent judge of the most advantageous use of his lands and of his labour. He alone has the particular knowledge without which the most enlightened man could only argue blindly. He learns by repeated trials, by his successes, by his losses, and he acquires a feeling for it which is much more ingenious than the theoretical knowledge of the indifferent observer because it is stimulated by want.

In proceeding to more detailed analysis of the market process, Turgot points out that self-interest is the prime mover of that process, and that, as Gournay had noted, individual interest in the free market must *always* coincide with the general interest. The buyer will select the seller who will give him the best price for the most suitable product, and the seller will sell his best merchandise at the lowest competitive price. Governmental restrictions and special privileges, on the other hand, compel consumers to buy poorer products at high prices. Turgot concludes that 'the general freedom of buying and selling is therefore... the only means of assuring, on the one hand, the seller of a price sufficient to encourage production, and, on the other hand, the consumer of the best merchandise at the lowest price'. Turgot concluded that government should be strictly limited to protecting individuals against 'great injustice' and the nation against invasion. 'The government should always protect the natural liberty of the buyer to buy, and the seller to sell'.

It is possible, Turgot conceded, that there will sometimes, on the free market, be a 'cheating merchant and a duped consumer'. But then, the market will supply its own remedies: 'the cheated consumer will learn by experience and will cease to frequent the cheating merchant, who will fall into discredit and thus will be punished for his fraudulence'.

Turgot, in fact, ridiculed attempts by government to insure against fraud or harm to consumers. In a prophetic rebuttal to the Ralph Naders of all ages, Turgot highlighted in a notable passage the numerous fallacies of alleged state protection:

> To expect the government to prevent such fraud from ever occurring would be like wanting it to provide cushions for all the children who might fall. To assume it to be possible to prevent successfully, by regulation, all possible malpractices of this kind is to sacrifice to a chimerical perfection the whole progress of industry; it is to restrict the imagination of artificers to all narrow limits of the familiar; it is to forbid them all new experiments...
>
> It means forgetting that the execution of these regulations is always entrusted to men who may have all the more interest in fraud or in conniving at fraud since the fraud which they might commit would be covered in some way by the seal of public authority and by the confidence which this seal inspires in the consumers.

Turgot added that all such regulations and inspections 'always involve expenses, and that these expenses are always a tax on the merchandise, and as a result overcharge the domestic consumer and discourage the foreign buyer'.

Turgot concludes with a splendid flourish:

> Thus, with obvious injustice, commerce, and consequently the nation, are charged with a heavy burden to save a few idle people the trouble of instructing themselves or of making inquiries to avoid being cheated. To suppose all consumers to be dupes, and all merchants and manufacturers to be cheats, has the effect of authorizing them to be so, and of degrading all the working members of the community.

Turgot goes on once more to the 'Hayekian' theme of greater knowledge by the particular actors in the market. The entire *laissez-faire* doctrine of Gournay, he points out, is grounded on the 'complete impossibility of directing, by invariant rules and continuous inspection a multitude of transactions which by their immensity alone could not be fully known, and which, moreover, are continually dependent on a multitude of ever changing circumstances which cannot be managed or even foreseen'.

Turgot concludes his elegy to his friend and teacher by noting Gournay's belief that most people were 'well disposed toward the sweet principles of commercial freedom', but prejudice and a search for special privilege often bar the way. Every person, Turgot pointed out, wants to make an exception to the general principle of freedom, and 'this exception is generally based on their personal interest'.

One interesting aspect of the elegy is Turgot's noting of the Dutch influence on the *laissez-faire* views of Gournay. Gournay had had extensive commercial experience in Holland, and the Dutch model of relative free trade and free markets in the seventeenth and eighteenth century, especially under the republic, served as an inspiration throughout Europe. In addition, Turgot notes that one of the books that most influenced Gournay was the *Political Maxims* of Johan de Witt (1623–72), the great martyred leader of the classical liberal republican party in Holland. Indeed, in an article on 'Fairs and Markets', written two years earlier for the great *Encyclopédie*, Turgot had quoted Gournay as praising the free internal markets of Holland. Whereas other nations had confined trade to fairs in limited times and places, 'In Holland there are no fairs at all, but the whole extent of the State and the whole year are, as it were, a continuous fair, because commerce in that country is always and everywhere equally flourishing'.

Turgot's final writings on economics were as *intendant* at Limoges, in the years just before becoming controller-general in 1774. They reflect his embroilment in a struggle for free trade within the royal bureaucracy. In his last work, the 'Letter to the Abbé Terray [the controller-general] on the Duty on

Iron' (1773), Turgot trenchantly lashes out at the system of protective tariffs as a war of all against all using state monopoly privilege as a weapon, at the expense of the consumers:

> I believe, indeed, that iron masters, who know only about their own iron, imagine that they would earn more if they had fewer competitors. There is no merchant who would not like to be the sole seller of his commodity. There is no branch of trade in which those who are engaged in it do not seek to ward off competition, and do not find some sophisms to make people believe that it is in the State's interest to prevent at least the competition from abroad, which they most easily represent as the enemy of the national commerce. If we listen to them, and we have listened to them too often, all branches of commerce will be infected by this kind of monopoly. These fools do not see that this same monopoly which they practice, not, as they would have the government believe, against foreigners but against their own fellow-citizens, consumers of the commodity, is returned to them by these fellow citizens, who are sellers in their turn, in all the other branches of commerce where the first in their turn become buyers.

Turgot indeed, in anticipation of Bastiat three-quarters of a century later, calls this system a 'war of reciprocal oppression, in which the government lends its authority to all against all', in short a 'balance of annoyance and injustice between all kinds of industry' where everyone loses. He concludes that 'Whatever sophisms are collected by the self-interest of a few merchants, the truth is that all branches of commerce ought to be free, equally free, and entirely free...'.[2]

Turgot was close to the physiocrats, not only in advocating freedom of trade, but also in calling for a single tax on the 'net product' of land. Even more than in the case of physiocrats, one gets the impression with Turgot that his real passion was in getting rid of the stifling taxes on all other walks of life, rather than in imposing them on agricultural land. Turgot's views on taxes were most fully, if still briefly, worked out in his 'Plan for a Paper on Taxation in General' (1763), an outline of an unfinished essay he had begun to write as *intendant* at Limoges for the benefit of the controller-general. Turgot claimed that taxes on towns were shifted backwards to agriculture, and showed how taxation crippled commerce and how urban taxes distorted the location of towns and led to the illegal evasion of duties. Privileged monopolies, furthermore, raised prices severely and encouraged smuggling. Taxes on capital destroyed accumulated thrift and hobbled industry. Turgot's eloquence was confined to pillorying bad taxes rather than elaborating on the alleged virtues of the land tax. Turgot's summation of the tax system was trenchant and hard-hitting: 'It seems that Public Finance, like a greedy monster, has been lying in wait for the entire wealth of the people'.

On one aspect of politics Turgot parted apparently from the physiocrats. Evidently, Turgot's strategy was the same as theirs: attempting to convince the king of the virtues of *laissez-faire*. And yet one of Turgot's most incisive epigrams, delivered to a friend, was: 'I am not an *Enclopédiste* because I believe in God; I am not an *économiste* because I would have no king'. However, the latter was clearly not Turgot's publicly stated view; nor did it guide his public actions.

14.3   Value, exchange and price

One of the most remarkable contributions by Turgot was an unpublished and unfinished paper, 'Value and Money', written around 1769.[3] In this paper Turgot, working in a method of successive approximations and abstractions, developed an Austrian-type theory first of Crusoe economics, then of an isolated two-person exchange, which he later expanded to four persons and then to a complete market. By concentrating first on the economics of an isolated Crusoe figure, Turgot was able to work out economic laws that transcend exchange and apply to all individual actions. In short, praxeological theory transcends and is deeper than market exchange; it applies to all action.

First, Turgot examines an isolated man, and works out a sophisticated analysis of his value or utility scale. By valuing and forming preference scales of different objects, Crusoe confers value on various economic goods, and compares and chooses between them on the basis of their relative worth to him. Thus these goods acquire different values. Crusoe chooses not only between various present uses of goods but also between consuming them now and accumulating them for 'future needs'. He also sees clearly that more abundance of a good leads to a lower value, and vice versa. Like his French and other continental precursors, then, Turgot sees that the subjective utility of a good diminishes as its supply to a person increases; and like them, he lacks only the concept of the marginal unit to complete the theory. But he went far beyond his predecessors in the precision and clarity of his analysis. He also sees that the subjective values of goods (their 'esteem-value' to consumers) will change rapidly on the market, and there is at least a hint in his discussion that he realized that this subjective value is strictly ordinal and not subject to measurement (and therefore to most mathematical procedures).

Turgot begins his analysis at the very beginning; one isolated man, one object of valuation:

> Let us consider this man as exerting his abilities on a single object only; he will seek after it, avoid it, or treat it with indifference. In the first case, he would undoubtedly have a motive for seeking after this object; he would judge it to be suitable for his enjoyment, he will find it *good*, and this relative goodness could generally speaking be called *value*, it would not be susceptible to measurement...

Then, Turgot brings in other goods:

If the same man can choose between several objects suitable to his use, he will be able to prefer one to the other, find an orange more agreeable than chestnuts, a fur better for keeping out the cold than a cotton garment; he will regard one as *worth more* than another; he will consequently decide to undertake those things which he prefers, and leave the others.

This 'comparison of *value*', this evaluation of different objects, changes continually: 'These *appraisals* are not permanent, they change continually with the need of the person'. Turgot proceeds not only to diminishing utility, but to a strong anticipation of diminishing *marginal* utility, since he concentrates on the *unit* of the particular goods: 'When the savage is hungry, he values a piece of game more than the best bearskin; but let his appetite be satisfied and let him be cold, and it will be the bearskin that becomes valuable to him'.

After bringing the anticipation of future needs into his discussion, Turgot deals with diminishing utility as a function of abundance. Armed with this tool of analysis, he helps solve the value paradox:

water, in spite of its necessity and the multitude of pleasures which it provides for man, is not regarded as a precious thing in a well-watered country; man does not seek to gain its possession since the abundance of this element allows him to find it all around him.

Turgot then proceeds to a truly noteworthy discussion, anticipating the modern concentration on economics as the allocation of scare resources to a large and far less limited number of alternative ends:

To obtain the satisfaction of these wants, man has only an even more limited quantity of strength and resources. Each particular object of enjoyment costs him trouble, hardship, labour and at the very least, time. It is this use of his resources applied to the quest for each object which provides the offset to his enjoyment, and forms as it were the cost of the thing.

While there is an unfortunate 'real cost' flavour about Turgot's treatment of cost, and he called the cost of a product its 'fundamental value', he comes down generally to a rudimentary version of the later 'Austrian' view that all costs are really 'opportunity costs', sacrifices foregoing a certain amount of resources that would have been produced elsewhere. Thus Turgot's actor (in this case an isolated one) appraises and evaluates objects on the basis of their significance to himself. First Turgot says that this significance, or utility, is the importance of his 'time and toil' expended, but then he treats this concept as equivalent to productive opportunity foregone: as 'the portion of his resources, which he can use to acquire an evaluated object without thereby sacrificing the quest for other objects of equal or greater importance'.

Having analysed the actions of an isolated Crusoe, Turgot brings in Friday, that is, he now assumes two men and sees how an exchange will develop. Here, in a perceptive analysis, he works out the 'Austrian' theory of isolated two-person exchange, virtually as it would be arrived at by Carl Menger a century later. First, he has two savages on a desert island, each with valuable goods in his possession, but the goods being suited to different wants. One man has a surplus of fish, the other of hides, and the result will be that each will exchange part of his surplus for the other's, so that both parties to the exchange will benefit. Commerce, or exchange, has developed. Turgot then changes the conditions of his example, and supposes that the two goods are corn and wood, and that each commodity could therefore be stored for future needs, so that each would not be automatically eager to dispose of his surplus. Each man will then weigh the relative 'esteem' to him of the two products, and weight the possible exchange accordingly. Each will adjust his supplies and demands until the two parties agree on a price at which each man will value what he obtains in exchange more highly than what he gives up. Both sides will then benefit from the exchange. As Turgot lucidly puts it:

> This superiority of the esteem value attributed by the acquirer to the thing he acquires over the thing he gives up is essential to the exchange for it is the sole motive for it. Each would remain as he was, if he did not find an interest, a personal profit, in exchange; if, in his own mind, he did not consider what he receives worth more than what he gives.

Turgot then unfortunately goes off the subjective value track by adding, unnecessarily, that the terms of exchange arrived at through this bargaining process will have 'equal exchange value', since otherwise the person cooler to the exchange 'would force the other to come closer to his price by a better offer'. It is unclear here what Turgot means by saying that 'each gives equal value to receive equal value'; there is perhaps an inchoate notion here that the price arrived at through bargaining will be halfway between the value scales of each.

Turgot, however, is perfectly correct in pointing out that the act of exchange increases the wealth of both parties to the exchange. He then brings in the competition of two sellers for each of the products and shows how the competition affects the value scales of the participants.

As Turgot had pointed out a few years earlier in his most important work, 'The Reflections on the Formation and Distribution of Wealth',[4] the bargaining process, where each party wants to get as much as he can and give up as little as possible in exchange, results in a tendency towards one uniform price of each product in terms of the other. The price of any good will vary in accordance with the urgency of need among the participants. There is no 'true price' to which the market tends, or should tend, to conform.

Finally, in his repeated analysis of human action as the result of *expectations*, rather than in equilibrium or as possessing perfect knowledge, Turgot anticipates the Austrian emphasis on expectations as the key to actions on the market. Turgot's very emphasis on expectations of course implies that they can be and often are disappointed in the market.

14.4   The theory of production and distribution

In one sense Turgot's theory of production followed the physiocrats: the unfortunate view that only agriculture is productive, and that, in consequence, there should be a single tax on land. But the main thrust of his theory of production was quite different from that of physiocracy. Thus, before Adam Smith's famous example of the pin factory and stress on division of labour, Turgot, in his 'Reflections', had worked out a keen analysis of that division:

> If the same man who, on his own land, cultivates these different articles, and uses them to supply his own wants, was also forced to perform all the intermediate operations himself, it is certain that he would succeed very badly. The greater part of these operations require care, attention and a long experience, such as are only to be acquired by working continuously and on a great quantity of materials.

And further, even if a man

> did succeed in tanning a single hide, he only needs one pair of shoes; what will he do with the rest? Shall he kill an ox to make this pair of shoes?...The same thing may be said concerning all the other wants of man, who, if he were reduced to his own field and his own labour, would waste much time and trouble in order to be very badly equipped in every respect, and would also cultivate his land very badly.

Even though only land was supposed to be productive, Turgot readily conceded that natural resources must be transformed by human labour, and that labour must enter into each stage of the production process. Here Turgot had worked out the rudiments of the crucial Austrian theory that production takes *time* and that it passes through various *stages*, each of which takes time, and that therefore the basic classes of factors of production are land, labour and time.

One of Turgot's most remarkable contributions to economics, the significance of which was lost until the twentieth century, was his brilliant and almost off-hand development of the law of diminishing returns, or, as it might be described, the law of variable proportions. This gem arose out of a contest which he had inspired to be held by the Royal Agricultural Society of Limoges, for prize-winning essays on indirect taxation. Unhappiness with the winning physiocratic essay by Guérineau de Saint-Péravy led him to develop his own views in 'Observations on a Paper by Saint-Péravy' (1767). Here Turgot went to the heart of the physiocratic error, in the *Tableau*, of assuming a fixed proportion of the various expenditures of different classes of people. But, Turgot pointed out, these proportions are variable, as are the proportions of physical factors in production. There are no constant proportions of factors in agriculture, for example, since the proportions vary according to the knowledge of the farmers, the value of the soil, the techniques used in production, and the nature of the soil and the climatic conditions.

Developing this theme further, Turgot declared that 'even if applied to the same field it [the product] is not proportional [to advances to the factors], and it can never be assumed that double the advances will yield double the product'. Not only are the proportions of factors to product variable, but also after a point, 'all further expenditures would be useless, and that such increases could even become detrimental. In this case, the advances would be increased without increasing the product. There is therefore a *maximum* point of production which it is impossible to pass...'. Furthermore, after the maximum point is passed, it is 'more than likely that as the advances are increased gradually past this point up to the point where they return nothing, each increase would be less and less productive'. On the other hand, if the farmer reduces the factors from the point of maximum production, the same changes in proportion would be found.

In short, Turgot had worked out, in fully developed form, an analysis of the law of diminishing returns which would not be surpassed, or possibly equalled, until the twentieth century.

(According to Schumpeter, not until a journal article by Edgeworth in 1911!) We have Turgot spelling out in words the familiar diagram in modern economics:

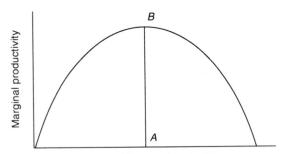

Quantity of factors of production

Increasing the quantity of factors, in short, raises the marginal productivity (the quantity produced by each increase of factors) until a maximum point, *AB*, is reached, after which the marginal productivity falls, eventually to zero, and then becomes negative.

14.5   The theory of capital, entrepreneurship, savings and interest

In the roster of A.R.J. Turgot's outstanding contributions to economic theory, the most remarkable was his theory of capital and interest which, in contrast with such fields as utility, sprang up virtually full-blown without reference to preceding contributions. Not only that: Turgot worked out almost completely the Austrian theory of capital and interest a century before it was set forth in definitive form by Eugen von Böhm-Bawerk.

Turgot's theory of capital proper was echoed in the British classical economists as well as the Austrians. Thus in his great 'Reflections', Turgot pointed out that wealth is accumulated by means of unconsumed and saved annual produce. Savings are accumulated in the form of money, and then invested in various kinds of capital goods. Furthermore, as Turgot pointed out, the 'capitalist–entrepreneur' must first accumulate saved capital in order to 'advance' his payment to labourers while the product is being worked on. In agriculture, the capitalist–entrepreneur must save funds to pay workers, buy cattle, pay for buildings and equipment, etc., until the harvest is reaped and sold and he can recoup his advances. And so it is in every field of production.

Some of this was picked up by Adam Smith and the later British classicists. But they failed to absorb two vital points. One was that Turgot's capitalist was also a capitalist–*entrepreneur*. He not only advanced savings to workers and other factors of production; he also, as Cantillon had first pointed out, bore the risks of uncertainty on the market. Cantillon's theory of the entrepreneur as a pervasive risk-bearer facing uncertainty, thereby equilibrating market conditions, had lacked one key element: an analysis of capital and the realization that the major driving force of the market economy is not just *any* entrepreneur but the *capitalist*–entrepreneur, the man who combines both functions.[5] Yet Turgot's memorable achievement in developing the theory of the capitalist–entrepreneur has, as Professor Hoselitz pointed out, 'been completely ignored' until the twentieth century.[6]

If the British classicists totally neglected the entrepreneur, they also failed to absorb Turgot's proto-Austrian emphasis on the crucial role of *time* in production, and the fact that industries may require many stages of production with lengthy periods of advance payment before production and sale. Turgot perceptively pointed out that it is the owner of capital

who will wait for the sale of the leather to return him not only all his advances, but also a profit sufficient to compensate him for what his money would have been worth to him, had he turned it to the acquisition of an estate, and moreover, the wages due to his labour and care, to his risk, and even to his skill.

In this passage, Turgot anticipated the Austrian concept of opportunity cost, and pointed out that the capitalist will tend to earn his imputed wages and the opportunity that the capitalist sacrificed by not investing his money elsewhere. In short, the capitalist's accounting profits will tend to a long-run equilibrium plus the imputed wages of his own labour and skill. In agriculture, manufacturing, or any other field of production, there are two basic classes of producers in society: the entrepreneurs, owners of capital, 'which they invest profitably as advances for setting men at work'; and the workers or 'simple Artisans, who have no other property than their arms, who advance only their daily labour, and receive no profit but their wages'.

At this point, Turgot incorporated a germ of valuable insight from the physiocratic *Tableau* – that invested capital must continue to return a steady profit through continued circulation of expenditures, else dislocations in production and payments will occur. Integrating his analyses of money and capital, Turgot then pointed out that before the development of gold or silver as money, the scope for entrepreneurship, manufacturing or commerce had been very limited. For to develop the division of labour and stages of production, it is necessary to accumulate large sums of capital, and undertake extensive exchanges, none of which is possible without money.

Seeing that 'advances' of savings to factors of production are a key to investment, and that this process is only developed in a money economy, Turgot then proceeded to a crucial 'Austrian' point: since money and capital advances are indispensable to all enterprises, labourers are therefore willing to *pay* capitalists a discount out of production for the service of having money paid them in advance of future revenue. In short: the interest return on investment (what the Swedish 'Austrian' Knut Wicksell would over a century later call the 'natural rate of interest') is the payment by labourers to the capitalists for the function of advancing them present money so that they do not have to wait for years for their income. As Turgot put it in his 'Reflections':

> Since capitals are the indispensable foundation of all lucrative enterprises,...those who, with their industry and love of labour, have no capitals, or who do not have sufficient for the enterprise they wish to embark on, have no difficulty in deciding to give up to the owners of such capital or money who are willing to trust it to them, a portion of the profits they expect to receive over and above the return of their advances.

The following year, in his scintillating comments on the paper by Saint-Péravy, Turgot expanded his analysis of savings and capital to set forth an excellent anticipation of Say's law. Turgot rebutted pre-Keynesian fears of the physiocrats that money not spent on consumption would 'leak' out of the circular flow and thereby wreck the economy. As a result, the physiocrats tended to oppose savings *per se*. Turgot, however, pointed out that advances of capital are vital in all enterprises, and where might the advances come from, if not out of savings? He also noted that it made no difference if such savings were supplied by landed proprietors or by entrepreneurs. For entrepreneurial savings to be large enough to accumulate capital and expand production, profits have to be higher than the amount required to reproduce current entrepreneurial spending (i.e. replace inventory, capital goods, etc. as they are drawn down or wear out).

Turgot goes on to point out that the physiocrats assume without proof that savings simply leak out of circulation, and lower prices. Instead, money will return to circulation, savings will immediately be used either to buy land; to be invested as advances to workers and other factors; or to be loaned out at interest. All these uses of savings return money to the circular flow. Advances of capital, for example, return to circulation in paying for equipment, buildings, raw material or wages. The purchase of land transfers money to the seller of land, who in turn will either buy something with the money, pay his debts, or relend the amount; in any case, the money returns promptly to circulation.

Turgot then engaged in a similar analysis of spending flows if savings are loaned at interest. If consumers borrow the money, they borrow in order to spend, and so the money expended returns to circulation. If they borrow to pay debts or buy land, the same thing occurs. And if entrepreneurs borrow the money, it will be poured into advances and investment, and the money will once again return to circulation.

Money saved, therefore, is not lost; it returns to circulation. Furthermore, the value of savings invested in capital is far greater than piled up in hoards, so that money will tend to return to circulation quickly. Furthermore, Turgot pointed out, even if increased savings actually withdrew a small amount of money from circulation for a considerable time, the lower price of the produce will be more than offset for the entrepreneur by the increased advances and the consequent greater output and lowering of the cost of production. Here, Turgot had the germ of the much later von Mises–von Hayek analysis of how savings narrows but lengthens the structure of production.

The acme of Turgot's contribution to economic theory was his sophisticated analysis of interest. We have already seen Turgot's remarkable insight in seeing interest return on investment as a price paid by labourers to capitalist–entrepreneurs for advances of savings in the form of present money. Turgot also demonstrated – far ahead of his time – the relationship between this natural rate of interest and the interest on money loans. He showed, for example, that the two must tend to be equal on the market, since the owners of capital will continually balance their expected returns in different channels of use, whether they be money loans or direct investment in production. The lender sells the use of his money now, and the borrower buys that use, and the 'price' of those loans, i.e. the loan rate of interest, will be determined, as in the case of any commodity, by the variations in supply and demand on the market. Increased demand for loans ('many borrowers') will raise interest rates; increased supply of loans ('many lenders') will lower them. People borrow for many reasons, as we have seen: to try to make an entrepreneurial profit, to purchase land, pay debts or consume; while lenders are concerned with just two matters: interest return and the safety of their capital.

While there will be a market tendency to equate loan rates of interest and interest returns on investment, loans tend to be a less risky form of channelling savings. Thus investment in risky enterprises will only be made if entrepreneurs expect that their profit will be greater than the loan rate of interest. Turgot also pointed out that government bonds will tend to be the least risky investment, so that they will earn the lowest interest return. He went on to declare that the 'true evil' of government debt is that it presents advantages to the public creditors but channels their savings into 'sterile' and unproductive uses and maintains a high interest rate in competition with productive uses (or, as we would say nowadays, public debt 'crowds out' productive private uses of savings).

Pressing on to an analysis of the nature and use of lending at interest, Turgot engaged in an incisive and hard-hitting critique of usury laws, which the physiocrats were still trying to defend.

A loan, Turgot pointed out, 'is a reciprocal contract, free between the two parties, which they make only because it is advantageous to them'. But a contracted loan is then *ipso facto* advantageous to *both* the lender and the borrower. Turgot moved in for the clincher: 'Now on what principle can a crime be discovered in a contract advantageous to two parties, with which both parties are satisfied, and which certainly does no injury to anyone else?' There is no exploitation in charging interest just as there is none in the sale of any commodity. To attack a lender for 'taking advantage' of the borrower's need for money by demanding interest 'is as absurd an argument as saying that a baker who demands money for the bread he sells, takes advantage of the buyer's need for bread'.

And, if the money spent on bread might be considered its equivalent, then in the same way 'the money which the borrower receives today is equally an equivalent of the capital and interest he promises to return at the end of a certain time'. In short: a loan contract establishes the present value of a future payment of capital and interest. The borrower gets use of the money during the term of the loan; the lender is deprived of such use; the price of this advantage, or disadvantage, is 'interest'.

It is true, Turgot says to the anti-usury wing of the scholastics, that money as a 'mass of metal' is barren and produces nothing; but money employed successfully in enterprises yields a profit, or invested in land yields revenue. The lender gives up, during the term of the loan, not only possession of the metal, but also the profit he could have obtained by investment: the 'profit or revenue he would have been able to procure by it, and the interest which indemnified him for this loss cannot be looked on as unjust'. Thus Turgot integrates his analysis and justification for interest with a generalized view of opportunity cost, of income foregone from lending money. And then, above all, Turgot declares, there is the property right of the lender, a crucial point that must not be overlooked. A lender has

> the right to require an interest for his loan simply because the money is his property. Since it is property he is free to keep it...; if then he does lend, he may attach such conditions to the loan as he sees fit. In this, he does no injury to the borrower, since the latter agrees to the conditions, and has no right of any kind over the sum lent.

As for the Biblical passage in Luke that had for centuries been used to denounce interest, the passage that urged lending without gain, Turgot pointed out that this advice was simply a precept of charity, a 'laudable action inspired by generosity', and not a requirement of justice. The opponents of usury, Turgot explained, never press on to a consistent position of trying to *force* everyone to lend his savings at zero interest.

In one of his last contributions, the highly influential 'Paper on Lending at Interest' (1770), A.R.J. Turgot elaborated on his critique of usury laws, at the same time amplifying his noteworthy theory of interest.[7] He pointed out that usury laws are not rigorously enforced, leading to widespread black markets in loans. But the stigma of usury remains, along with pervasive dishonesty and disrespect for law. Yet, every once in a while, the usury laws are sporadically and unpredictably enforced, with severe penalties.

Most importantly, Turgot, in the 'Paper on Lending at Interest', focused on the crucial problem of interest: *why* are borrowers willing to pay the interest premium for the use of money? The opponents of usury, he noted, hold that the lender, in requiring more than the principal to be returned, is receiving a value in excess of the value of the loan, and that this excess is somehow deeply immoral. But then Turgot came to the critical point: 'It is true that in repaying the principal, the borrower returns exactly the same weight of the metal which the lender had given him'. But why, he adds, should the weight of the money metal be the crucial consideration, and not the 'value and usefulness it has for the lender and the borrower?' Specifically, arriving at the vital Böhm-Bawerkian–Austrian concept of time-preference, Turgot urges us to compare 'the difference in usefulness which exists at the date of borrowing between a sum currently owned and an equal sum which is to be received at a distant date'. The key is time-preference – the discounting of the future and the concomitant placing of a premium upon the present. Turgot points to the well known motto, 'a bird in the hand is worth two in the bush'. Since a sum of money actually owned now 'is preferable to the assurance of receiving a similar sum in one or several years' time', the same sum of money paid and returned is scarcely an equivalent value, for the lender 'gives the money and receives only an assurance'. But cannot this loss in value 'be compensated by the assurance of an increase in the sum proportioned to the delay?' Turgot concluded that 'this compensation is precisely the rate of interest'. He added that what has to be compared in a loan transaction is *not* the value of money loaned with the sum of money repaid, but the 'value of the *promise* of a sum of money compared to the value of money available now'. For a loan is precisely the transfer of a sum of money in exchange for the current *promise* of a sum of money in the future. Hence a maximum rate of interest imposed by law would deprive virtually all risky enterprises of credit.

In addition to developing the Austrian theory of time preference, Turgot was the first person, in his *Reflections*, to point to the corresponding concept of *capitalization*, that is, the present capital value of land or other capital good on the market tends to equal the sum of its expected annual future rents, or returns, discounted by the market rate of time-preference, or rate of interest.[8]

As if this were not enough to contribute to economics, Turgot also pioneered a sophisticated analysis of the interrelation between the interest rate and the 'quantity theory' of money. There is little connection, he pointed out, between the value of currency in terms of prices, and the interest rate. The supply of money may be plentiful, and hence the value of money low in terms of commodities, but interest may at the same time be very high. Perhaps following David Hume's similar model, Turgot asks what would happen if the quantity of silver money in a country suddenly doubled, *and* that increase were magically distributed in equal proportions to every person. Specifically, Turgot asks us to assume that there are one million ounces of silver money in existence in a country, and 'that there is brought into the State, in some manner or other, a second million ounces of silver, and that this increase is distributed to every purse in the same proportion as the first million, so that he who had two ounces before, now has four'. Turgot then explains that prices will rise, perhaps doubling, and that therefore the value of silver in terms of commodities will fall. But, he adds, it by no means follows that the interest rate will fall, if people's expenditure proportions remain the same, 'if all this money is carried to the market and employed in the current expenses of those who possess it...'[9]. The new money will not be loaned out, since only saved money is loaned and invested.

Indeed, Turgot points out that, depending on how the spending–savings proportions are affected, a rise in the quantity of money could *raise* interest rates. Suppose, he says, that all wealthy people decide to spend their incomes and annual profits on consumption and spend their capital on foolish expenditures. The greater consumption spending will raise the prices of consumer goods, and there being far less money to lend or to spend on investments, interest rates will rise along with prices. In short, spending will accelerate and prices rise, while, at the same time, time-preference rates rise, people spend more and save less, and interest rates will increase. Thus Turgot is over a century ahead of his time in working out the sophisticated Austrian relationship between what von Mises would call the 'money-relation' – the relation between the supply and demand for money, which determines prices or the price level – and the rates of time-preference, which determine the spending–saving proportion and the rate of interest. Here, too, was the beginning of the rudiments of the Austrian theory of the business cycle, of the relationship between expansion of the money supply and the rate of interest.

As for the movements in the rate of time-preference or interest, an increase in the spirit of thrift will lower interest rates and increase the amount of savings and the accumulation of capital; a rise in the spirit of luxury will do the opposite. The spirit of thrift, Turgot notes, has been steadily rising in Europe over several centuries, and hence interest rates have tended to fall. The various interest rates and rates of return on loans, investments, land, etc. will tend to equilibrate throughout the market and tend towards a single rate of return. Capital, Turgot notes, will move out of lower profit industries and regions and into higher profit industries.

14.6 Theory of money

While Turgot did not devote a great deal of attention to the theory of money proper, he had some important contributions to make. In addition to continuing the Hume model and integrating it with his analysis of interest, Turgot was emphatic in his opposition to the now dominant idea that money is purely a conventional token. In his critique of a prize-winning paper by J.J. Graslin (1767), Turgot declares Graslin totally mistaken in 'regarding money purely as a conventional token of wealth'. In contrast, Turgot declares, 'it is not at all by virtue of a convention that money is exchanged for all the other values: it is itself an object of commerce, a form of wealth, because it has a value, and because any value exchanges in trade for an equal value'.

In his unfinished dictionary article on 'Value and Money', Turgot develops his monetary theory further. Drawing on his knowledge of linguistics, he declares that money is a kind of language, bringing forms of various conventional things into a 'common term or standard'. The common term of all currencies is the actual value, or prices, of the objects they try to measure.

These 'measures', however, are hardly perfect, Turgot acknowledges, since the values of gold and silver always vary in relation to commodities as well as each other. All monies are made of the same materials, largely gold and silver, and differ only on the units of currency. And all these units are reducible to each other, as are other measures of length or volume, by expressions of weight in each standard currency. There are two kinds of money, Turgot notes, *real* money – coins, pieces of metal marked by inscriptions – and *fictitious* money, serving as units of account or *numéraires*. When real money units are defined in terms of the units of account, the various units are then linked to each other and to specific weights of gold or silver.

Problems arise, Turgot shows, because the real monies in the world are not just one metal but two – gold and silver. The relative values of gold and silver on the market will then vary in accordance with the abundance and the relative scarcity of gold and silver in the various nations.

14.7 Influence

One of the striking examples of injustice in the historiography of economic thought is the treatment accorded to Turgot's brilliant analysis of capital and interest by the great founder of Austrian capital and interest theory, Eugen von Böhm-Bawerk. In the 1880s, Böhm-Bawerk set out, in the first volume of his *Capital and Interest*, to clear the path for his own theory of interest by studying and demolishing previous, competing theories. Unfortunately, instead of acknowledging Turgot as his forerunner in pioneering Austrian theory, Böhm-Bawerk brusquely dismissed the Frenchman as a mere physiocratic naive land-productivity (or 'fructification') theorist. This unfairness to Turgot is all the more heightened by recent information that Böhm–Bawerk, in his first evaluation of Turgot's theory of interest in a still unpublished seminar paper in 1876, reveals the enormous influence of Turgot's views on his later developed thought. Perhaps we must conclude that, in this case, as in other cases, Böhm-Bawerk's need to claim originality and to demolish all his predecessors took precedence over the requirements of truth and justice.[10]

In the light of Böhm-Bawerk's mistreatment, it is heartwarming to see Schumpeter's appreciative summation of Turgot's great contributions to economics. Concentrating almost exclusively on Turgot's *Reflections*, Schumpeter declares that his theory of price formation is 'almost faultless, and, barring explicit formulation of the marginal principle, within measurable distance of that of Böhm-Bawerk'. The theory of saving, investment and capital is 'the first serious analysis of these matters' and 'proved almost unbelievably hardy. It is doubtful whether Alfred Marshall had advanced beyond it, certain that J.S. Mill had not. Böhm-Bawerk no doubt added a new branch to it, but substantially he subscribed to Turgot's propositions'. Turgot's interest theory is 'not only by far the greatest performance...the eighteenth century produced but it clearly foreshadowed much of the best thought of the last decades of the nineteenth'. All in all,

> It is not too much to say that analytic economics took a century to get where it could have got in twenty years after the publication of Turgot's treatise had its content been properly understood and absorbed by an alert profession.[11]

Turgot's influence on later economic thought was severely limited, probably largely because his writings were unfairly discredited among later generations by his association with physiocracy, and by the pervasive myth that Adam Smith had founded economics. And those nineteenth century economists who did read Turgot failed to grasp the significance of his capital, interest and production theories. Though Adam Smith knew Turgot personally, and read the *Reflections*, the influence on Smith, whose conclusions, apart from a broadly *laissez-faire* approach, were so different, was apparently minimal. Ricardo, typically, was heedless and uncomprehending, simply admiring Turgot for his thankless political role as liberal reformer. James Mill had a similar reaction. Malthus admired Turgot's views on value, but the only substantial Turgotian influence in England was on the great champion of the subjective utility theory of value, Samuel Bailey. Although the influence on Bailey is patent, he unfortunately did not refer to Turgot in his work, so that the utility tradition in Britain could not rediscover its champion.

It is on the French, self-avowed Smithian, J.B. Say, that Turgot had the most influence, especially in the subjective utility theory of value, and to some extent in capital and interest theory. Say was the genuine heir of the French *laissez-faire*, proto-Austrian, eighteenth century tradition. Unfortunately, his citations of Turgot underplayed the influence, and his obeisances to Smith were highly exaggerated, both probably reflecting Say's characteristic post-French Revolutionary reluctance to identify himself closely with the pro-absolute monarchy, pro-agriculture physiocrats, with whom Turgot was unfortunately lumped in the eyes of most knowledgeable Frenchman. Hence the ritualistic turn toward Smith.

14.8 Other French and Italian utility theorists of the eighteenth century

Two other distinguished French writers on economics, both contemporaries of Turgot, must be mentioned as contributing greatly to economic thought. The Abbé Ferdinando Galiani (1728–87) was a fascinating character who, though a Neapolitan, may be counted as largely French. Reared by his uncle, the chief almoner to the king, Galiani early came into contact with the leaders of Neapolitan thought and culture. At the age of 16, Galiani translated some of Locke's writings on money into Italian, and began an eight-year study of money. During the same period, Galiani took religious orders. At the age of 23, he published his remarkable major work, *Della Moneta* (*On Money*) (1751) which set forth a utility–scarcity theory of the value of goods and money. Unfortunately, *Della Moneta* has never been fully translated from the Italian.

In 1759, the Abbé Galiani became secretary and later head of the Neapolitan embassy in Paris, where he stayed for ten years, and where the erratic, witty, erudite, $4^1/2$ foot tall Galiani became the social lion of the Paris salons. After his return to Italy, though he wrote several minor works in linguistics and politics, and held several leading positions in the civil service, he considered himself an exile from his beloved France.

In the late scholastic–French–Italian tradition, Galiani expounded the value of goods as subjective valuation by consumers. Value is not intrinsic, he pointed out, but 'a sort of relationship between the possession of one good and that of another in the human mind'. Man always compares the valuation of one good with another, and exchanges one good for another in order to increase the level of his satisfactions. The quantity demanded of a good is inverse to its price, and the utility of each good is in inverse relation to its supply. Alert to the law of diminishing utility upon increasing supply, Galiani, like his predecessors, stops just short of the marginal concept, but is at any rate able to solve the 'value paradox': the view that use-value is severed from price- or exchange-value because bread or water, goods highly useful to man, are very cheap on the market whereas fripperies like diamonds are highly expensive.

Thus Galiani writes, with great subtlety and perception and with his usual flair:

> It is obvious that air and water, which are very useful for human life, have no value because they are not scarce. On the other hand, a bag of sand from the shores of Japan would be an extremely rare thing – yet, unless it has a certain utility, it is without value.

Galiani then states the alleged value paradox, quoting from the seventeenth century Italian writer, Bernardo Davanzati. Davanzati laments that 'A living calf is nobler than a golden calf, but how much less is its price!' while 'others say: "A pound of bread is more useful than a pound of gold".' Galiani then brilliantly demolishes this doctrine:

> This is a wrong and foolish conclusion. It is based on neglect of the fact that 'useful' and 'less useful' are relative concepts, which depend on the specific circumstances. If somebody is in want of bread and of gold, bread is surely more useful for him. This agrees with the facts of life, because nobody would forego bread, take gold, and die from hunger. People who mine gold never forget to eat

and to sleep. But somebody who has eaten his fill will consider bread the least useful of goods. He will then want to satisfy other needs. This goes to show that the precious metals are companions of luxury, that is, of a status in which the elemental needs are taken care of. Davanzati maintains that a single egg, priced at $^1/_2$ grain of gold, would have had the value of protecting the starving Count Ugolino from death at his tenth day in gaol – a value in excess of that of all the gold in the world. But this confuses awkwardly the price paid by a person un-afraid to die from hunger without the egg, and the needs of Count Ugolino. How can Davanzati be sure that the Count would not have paid 1,000 grains of gold for the egg? Davanzati obviously had made a mistake here, and, although he is not aware of it, his further remarks indicate that the knows better. He says: What an awful thing is a rat. But when Casilino was under siege, prices went up so much that a rat fetched 200 guilders – and this price was not expensive because the seller died from hunger and the buyer could save himself.

Professor Einaudi informed us in 1945 that 'this is the classical section which is always read in Italian seminars when a telling illustration of the principle of diminishing utility is to be given'. In addition to illuminating this crucial principle, the above passage also shows how people, satiated with bread, turn to the consumption or use of other goods foregone.[12]

In addition to taking a subjectivist, 'pre-Austrian' approach to utility and value of goods, Galiani also introduced the same approach towards interest on loans, outlining at least the rudiments of the time-preference theory of interest in passages that influenced Turgot. Thus Galiani wrote:

From this arises the rate of exchange and the rate of interest – brother and sister. The former equalizes the present and the spatially distant money. It operates with the help of an apparent agio, which...equate(s) the real value of the one to that of the other, one being reduced because of lesser convenience or greater risk. Interest equalizes present and future money. Here the effect of time is the same as that of spatial distance in the case of the rate of exchange. The basis of either contract is the equality of the real value.

Galiani defines a loan as 'the surrender of a good, with the proviso that an equivalent good is to be returned, not more'. But, in contrast to the centuries-long tradition of anti-'usury' writers who proceed from the same premise to denounce all interest on loans as illegitimate, Galiani points out what would later be a fundamental insight of the Austrian School: a good, in this case an 'equivalent', is not to be described by its physical properties or similarities, but rather by its subjective value in the minds of individual actors. Thus Galiani writes that those who conventionally define the equivalence of goods as 'weight, or similarity of form', focus on the physical objects in each exchange (such as units of money). But, he adds, those who adopt such definitions 'understand little of human activities'. He reiterates, instead, that value is not an objective characteristic inherent in goods, but rather it is 'the relationship of goods to our needs'. But then, 'Goods are equivalent when they provide equal convenience to the person with reference to whom they are considered as equivalent'.

Another prefigurement of the Austrian approach was Galiani's intimations towards a theory of distribution, which were not taken up until Böhm-Bawerk, probably independently, arrived at a similar but much fuller analysis a century and a half later. For Galiani hinted in his *Della Moneta* that it was not labour costs that determine value, but the opposite: it is value that determines labour costs. Or, more concretely, that the utility of products and the scarcity of various types of labour determine the prices of labour on the market. Though he begins his discussion by stating that labour in the sense of human energy 'is the sole source of value', he quickly goes on to point out that human talents vary greatly, so that the price of labour will vary. Thus:

> I believe that the value of human talents is determined in the very same way as that of inanimate things, and that it is regulated by the same principles of scarcity and utility combined. Men are born endowed by Providence with aptitudes for different trades, but in different degrees of scarcity.... It is not utility alone, therefore, which governs prices: for God causes the men who carry on the trades of greatest utility to be born in large numbers, and so their value cannot be great, these being, so to speak, the bread and wine of men; but scholars and philosophers, who may be called the gems among talents, deservedly bear a very high price.

Galiani was undoubtedly over-optimistic about the 'very high price' to be commanded by scholars and philosophers on the market, having overlooked his own scintillating example of scarce goods, such as 'bags of sand from the shores of Japan', which, though rare, may have little or no utility or value in the minds of consumers.

On the theory of money proper, the Abbé Galiani paved the way for the Austrian Menger–von Mises analysis of the origin of money by demonstrating that money – the medium of exchange – *must* originate on the market as a useful metal, and that it cannot be selected *de novo*, as a convention by some sort of social contract. In a lively assault on money-as-a-convention that could apply to any social contract explanation of the origin of the state, Galiani derided

> those who insist that all men had once come to an agreement, making a contract providing for the use, as money, of the *per se* useless metals, thus attaching value to them. Where did these conventions of all mankind take place, and where were the agreements concluded? In which century? At which place? Who were the deputies with whose help the Spaniards and Chinese, the Goths and the Africans made an agreement so lasting that during the many centuries which have passed the opinion never was changed?

Galiani pointed out that the sort of metal that would be chosen on the market would have to be universally acceptable, and hence would need to be highly valuable as a non-monetary commodity, easily portable, durable, uniform in quality, easily recognizable and calculable, and be difficult to counterfeit. Wiser than Smith and Ricardo after him, Galiani warned that money should not be regarded as ideally an invariable measure of value, for the value of a unit of account necessarily varies as the purchasing power of money changes, and therefore such an invariable standard cannot exist. As Galiani put it with typical pungency: 'Finally, this concept of stable money is a dream, a mania. Every new and richer mine that is discovered immediately changes all measures, without showing an effect on them but changing the price of the goods measured'.

Galiani made clear throughout *Della Moneta* that his entire analysis was embedded in the conceptual framework of the natural law. Natural laws, he explained, have a universal validity in economic affairs as much as in the laws of gravity or of fluids. Like physical laws, economic laws can only be violated at one's peril; any action defying the order of nature will be certain to fail.

The abbé proved his point by citing a hypothetical case: suppose that a Mohammedan country suddenly converts to Christianity. The drinking of wine, previously prohibited, now becomes legal, and its price will rise because of the small quantity available in the country. Merchants will bring wine into the country, and new wine producers will enter the field, until profits in dealing with wine fall back to their normal equilibrium level, 'as when waves are made in a vessel of water, after the confused and irregular movement the water returns to its original level'.

This equilibrating action of the market, which Galiani shows also applies to money, is furthermore propelled, marvellously enough, by self-interest, greed, and the quest for profit:

And this equilibrium wonderfully suits the right abundance of commodities of life and earthly welfare, although it derives not from human prudence or virtue but from the very vile stimulus of sordid profit: Providence having contrived the order of everything for her infinite love of men, that our vile passions are often, in spite of us, ordered to the advantage of the whole.

The economic process, Galiani concluded, was guided by a 'Supreme Hand' (shades of Adam Smith's 'invisible hand' a generation later!).

The institution of money, indeed, enables all people to 'live together', to be interdependent on each other, while still benefiting greatly in pursuing their individual ends. As Galiani eloquently puts it:

I saw, and everyone can now see, that trade, and money which drives it, from the miserable state of nature in which everyone thinks for himself, have brought us to the very happy one of living together, where everyone thinks and works for everybody else: and in this state not for the principle of virtue and piety alone (which are insufficient in dealing with entire nations), but we earn our living for the purpose of our personal interest and welfare.

Galiani's analysis is fuelled by an original and profound comparative analysis of seeing, mentally, what happens in different social systems. Thus he noted that, to avoid the inconveniences of barter, people might try 'living together' literally, in communities, as monasteries and convents do, but this is hardly feasible for entire nations. In a larger society, there might be a system where everyone produces whatever goods he wishes and then deposits them in a public warehouse where everyone could draw on the common store. (Galiani might have phrased it as, 'from each according to his ability, to each according to his needs'). But the system would collapse because lazy people would try to live at the expense of exploiting the hard-working ones, who in turn would work less. The public warehouse could, on the other hand, give producers 'receipts' which would then exchange for other goods at relative prices fixed by the prince; but one problem is that the prince might well inflate by printing an excessive number of such receipts. So that metals are the only viable money.

Galiani's youthful work *On Money* was his great contribution to economics. In his early days an ardent Catholic, abbé and monsignore, in Paris Galiani became a free thinker, roué, and Voltairean wit. In the course of rising in the bureaucracy, he completely changed his economic views, publishing the well-known *Dialogues on the Grain Trade* in 1770, which ridiculed *laissez-faire* and free trade, natural rights and the very idea of economic laws transcending time and place. Thus Galiani was not only an excellent utility theorist, but in his later years a forerunner of the nineteenth century historicists.

In his private letters, Galiani reveals quite frankly the underlying reason for his later conservatism, adherence to the *status quo*, cynical Machiavellianism, and critique of any liberal or *laissez-faire* disruption of the existing state of affairs. Attacking the idea of worrying about anyone's welfare but one's own, Galiani writes: 'The devil take one's neighbor!' and that 'All nonsense and disturbance arise from the fact that everybody is busy pleading somebody else's cause, and nobody his own'. He wrote that he was well satisfied with the existing French government because it was frankly expedient for him to do so; specifically, he did not wish to lose his luxurious income of 15 000 *livres*.

Of course Galiani found it expedient to confine his Machiavellianism to private letters while pretending to moralism in his public writings.[13] Thus in his *Della Moneta*, in both the original edition and in the second edition in

1780, Galiani bitterly denounced the institution of slavery: 'There is nothing that appears to me more monstrous than to see human beings like ourselves, vilified, enslaved and treated like animals'. But his approach was very different in a letter written in 1772:

> I believe that we should continue to buy negroes as long as they are sold, unless we succeed in letting them live in America...The only profitable trade is to exchange the blows one gives for the rupees one collects. It is the trade of the strongest.[14]

In short, anything is right if it succeeds.

Another Italian utility theorist, in his case an analyst of exchange, was the highly influential Neapolitan Abate Antonio Genovesi (1712–69). Genovesi was born near Salerno, and became a priest in 1739. At first a professor of ethics and moral philosophy at the University of Naples, Genovesi shifted his interests and became a professor of economics and commerce, in which he was a notable teacher. In his rather disjointed *Lezione de economia civile* (*Lessons on Civil Economy*) (1765), the learned Genovesi took a moderate free trade stance. More important, he pointed out the essential double inequality of value involved in any exchange. In any exchange, he said each party desires the object he acquires more than he does the object given up. The superfluous is given up for the necessary. Hence the mutual benefit necessarily present in any exchange.

The last gasp of subjective utility theory in the eighteenth century was set forth brilliantly by the French philosopher, Étienne Bonnot de Condillac, abbé de Mureaux (1715–80). Condillac, a leading empiricist–sensationalist philosopher, was the younger brother of the communist writer Gabriel Bonnot de Mably, and son of the Vicomte de Mably, who served as secretary to the parliament of Grenoble. After being educated at a theological seminary in Paris, Condillac left to pursue philosophy, publishing several philosophical works in the 1740s and 1750s.

In 1758, Condillac went to Italy as tutor to the son of Duke Ferdinand of Parma. There his interest was stimulated in economics by acquaintance with the pro-free trade economic policymaker, Tillot, state secretary to the duke. At the same time, Condillac learned of the work of Galiani and other Italian subjective value theorists. After a decade as tutor of the future duke, Condillac published a 16-volume *Course of Studies* he had prepared for his pupil.

When Condillac returned to Paris in the late 1760s, interest in trade, political economy and physiocracy was at its height, and Condillac, always favouring free trade on his own subjectivist grounds very different from the physiocrats, was stimulated to write his last work, *Le commerce et le gouvernement considérés relativement l'un à l'autre (Commerce and Government)*, published in 1776, only a month before *The Wealth of Nations*.

In *Commerce and Government*, unfortunately destined to be swept away by Smith's all-commanding influence, Condillac set forth and defended a sophisticated subjective utility theory of value. The last of the utility–scarcity theorists before the advent of the British classicists, Condillac declared that the source of value of a good is its utility as evaluated by individuals in accordance with their needs and desires. Utility of goods increases with scarcity and decreases with abundance. Exchange arises because the utility and value of the two goods exchanged is different – indeed the reverse – for the two people engaging in the exchange.

As in the case of Genovesi, in exchange the superfluous is exchanged for the object in insufficient supply. But Condillac was careful to point out that exchange does not mean we give up things which are totally useless. An exchange only implies, as a later commentator summed it up, 'that what we acquire is worth more to us than what we part with'.[15]

As Condillac put it: 'It is true that I might sell a thing that I wanted; but as I would not do so except to procure one that I wanted still more, it is evident that I regard the first as useless to me in comparison with the one that I acquire'. The point is *relative*, rather than *absolute*, superabundance. And this set of superfluous-for-scarce exchanges greatly increases the all-round productivity of the market economy. Notes Condillac:

> The superabundance of the cultivators forms the basis of commerce...the cultivators procure the thing which has a value for them, while they give up one which has a value for others. If they could make no exchanges, their superabundance would remain in their hands, and would have no value for them. In fact, the superabundant corn which I keep in my granary, and which I cannot exchange, is no more wealth for me than the corn which I have not yet produced from the earth. Hence next year I shall sow less...

Furthermore, Condillac pressed on and generalized Galiani's utility theory of costs and distribution, declaring that 'a thing does not have value because it costs, as people suppose; it costs because it has a value'.[16] And the value is determined by the subjective opinions of individuals on the market.[17]

Condillac, moreover, refuted the typical classical and preclassical doctrine, dominant since Aristotle, that the fact that one good exchanges for another must mean that the two goods are of 'equal value'. Condillac rebutted this point neatly, a rebuttal which was promptly lost for 100 years: 'It is false that in exchanges one gives equal value for equal value. To the contrary, each of the contractors always surrenders a lesser for a greater value'.

Since consumer utility and demand determines value, people will tend to receive income from production to whatever extent they satisfy consumers in the production process. Hence, as Hutchison summarizes, 'people could expect to receive in income whatever they could expect to receive from the sale of such productive agents as they commanded.... Pay was regulated in markets by sellers and buyers, and depended on productivity and the expected utility of what was produced'.[18] Since greater intelligence and skill is in scarcer supply, it will tend to command a higher price, or wage, on the market.

Condillac's theory of entrepreneurship followed Cantillon, profits of the entrepreneur depending on the way in which he meets uncertainty and is able to forecast future markets. Like Cantillon, too, Condillac denied that money's value is arbitrary or determined by mere convention or government. The value of metallic money depends on the utility of monetary metals and their supply on the market, so that money's value is determined, as is that of other goods, by supply and demand. And Condillac also followed Cantillon in analysing the equilibrating, self-adjusting processes in international money flows and the balance of payments.

It was, then, not a great exaggeration when, nearly a century afterwards, the British economist Henry Dunning Macleod waxed rhapsodic over his rediscovery of the then forgotten Condillac. Macleod noted that Condillac drew from his insights an ardent devotion to complete free trade, and to an attack, far more consistent than that of his contemporary Adam Smith, on all forms of government intervention in the economy. Macleod noted Condillac's discussion of the 'mischievous consequences produced by all violations of, and attacks on' the principle of free markets:

> These are wars, custom-houses, taxes on industry, privileged and exclusive companies, taxes on consumption, tamperings with the currency, government loans, paper money, laws about the export and import of corn, laws about the internal circulation of grain, tricks of monopolists...

Condillac, Macleod went on,

> first proclaimed, as far as we are aware, the doctrine that in commerce *both* sides gain; the old doctrine sanctioned by Montaigne, Bacon, and many others, was that what one side gains, the other loses. This pernicious folly was the cause of many bloody wars. The Physiocrats then maintained that in exchange the values are equal. But Condillac laid down the true doctrine, that in commerce both sides gain. And he shows truly that the whole of commercial dynamics arise from these inequalities of value.

Himself joining in anticipation of the imputation, or marginal productivity theory of wages or other factor pricing, Macleod also underlined the significance of Condillac's insight that costs are determined by a good's value to the consumer rather than the other way round. In that way, Condillac helped inadvertently to refute the entire Smithian labour theory of value apparatus which was coming into being the same year that Condillac published his work. As Macleod puts it:

> Thus, too, he strikes at the root of many of the prevailing theories of value, which are based upon labour; he says that people pay for things because they value them, and they do not value them because they pay for them, as is commonly supposed. This is exactly the doctrine of Dr. [Archbishop Richard] Whately, when he says that people dive for pearls because they fetch a high price, and they do not fetch a high price because people dive for them...that it is not labour that is the cause of value, but value that attracts labour.

Macleod concludes his discussion with a rhetorical flourish. Noting that Condillac and Smith's classic works were published in the same year, he contrasted Smith's 'universal celebrity' with Condillac's neglect, but then notes that the world is rediscovering Condillac and learning of the superiority of his conception of economics to that of Smith. And, besides, Macleod wrote not without justification, 'the beautiful clearness, and simplicity' of Condillac contrasts notably with 'the incredible confusions and contradictions of Adam Smith'. However, 'at length he will receive justice...'.[19] If we contrast, however, the hypertrophy of Smith's bicentennial celebration with the non-existence of Condillac's, we might not be so quick to conclude that history has yet judged correctly.

14.9 Notes

1. The 'Elegy' was prepared by Turgot in a few days as material for Gournay's official eulogist, the writer Jean François Marmontel. Marmontel simply took extracts from Turgot's essay and published them as the official eulogy.
2. In the course of arguing for free trade in iron in this letter, Turgot anticipated the great 'Ricardian' doctrine of comparative advantage, in which each region concentrates on producing that commodity it can make efficiently relative to other regions.
3. Although the incomplete article remained unpublished for decades, it was written for an aborted dictionary of commerce to be edited by Turgot's lifelong friend and fellow Gournay disciple, the Abbé André Morellet (1727–1819). Morellet published a prospectus for the new dictionary in the same year, a prospectus that repeated Turgot's model of isolated exchange very closely. It is known, furthermore, that this prospectus was owned by Adam Smith.
4. The 'Reflections' (1766), remarkably, were 'scribbled' hastily in order to explain to two Chinese students in Paris questions Turgot was preparing to ask them about the Chinese economy. Rarely has a work so important arisen from so trivial a cause!
5. In an illuminating recent work on the history of the theory of the entrepreneur, Professors Hebert and Link examine the problem of whether an entrepreneur is only a capitalist or whether everyone, including workers without capital, is an entrepreneur. Turgot is considered as retreating from Cantillon's wider concept of entrepreneurship. But the important point here is that the capitalist–entrepreneur is the motor force of the market economy, and that by focusing for the first time on this vitally important figure, Turgot made an enormous stride forward. And we can hail this achievement even if it is also true that Turgot neglected the wider, less important areas of entrepreneurship. See Robert F. Hebert and Albert N. Link, *The Entrepreneur: Mainstream Views and Radical Critiques* (New York: Praeger, 1982), pp. 14–29 and passim.
6. Bert F. Hoselitz, 'The Early History of Entrepreneurial Theory', in J. Spengler and W. Allen (eds), *Essays in Economic Thought* (Chicago: Rand McNally and Co., 1960), p. 257.

7. Turgot's paper was applauded in Bentham's notable *Defence of Usury*, and was reprinted along with Bentham's essay in its French and Spanish translations in the late 1820s.

8. As Turgot puts it: 'a capital is the equivalent of a rent equal to a fixed portion of that capital and conversely, an annual rent represents a capital equal to the amount of that rent repeated a certain number of times, according as the interest is at a higher or lower rate'.

9. While the Hume–Turgot model is highly useful in isolating and clarifying distinctions between the price level and interest, and in highlighting the impact of a change in the quantity of money, it is still a retrogression from the sophisticated process analysis of Cantillon.

10. The paper, written for the seminar of Karl Knies in Heidelberg, was presented to the Austrian F.A. von Hayek by Böhm-Bawerk's widow in 1922–23. See P.D. Groenewegen (ed.) *The Economics of A.R.J. Turgot* (The Hague: Martinus Nijhoff, 1977), pp. xxix–xxx. For Böhm's dismissal of Turgot, see Eugen von Böhm-Bawerk, *Capital and Interest* (South Holland, Ill.: Libertarian Press, 1959), I, pp. 39–45. For the American Austrian Frank Fetter's defence of Turgot as against Böhm, see Frank A. Fetter, *Capital, Interest, and Rent: Essays in the Theory of Distribution*, ed. by M. Rothbard (Kansas City: Sheed Andrews and McMeel, 1977), pp. 24–6. For more on the treatment of Turgot's theory of interest by economists, see Groenewegen 'A Reinterpretation of Turgot's Theory of Capital and Interest', *Economic Journal*, 81 (June 1971), pp. 327–8, 333, 339–40. For Schumpeter on Böhm's mistreatment of Turgot, see J.A. Schumpeter, *History of Economic Analysis* (New York, Oxford University Press, 1954), p. 332n. On the Marshall–Wicksell–Cassel controversy over Böhm-Bawerk's treatment of Turgot's theory of interest, see Peter D. Groenewegen, 'Turgot's Place in the History of Economic Thought: A Bicentenary Estimate', *History of Political Economy*, 15 (Winter 1983), pp. 611–15.

11. Schumpeter, op. cit., note 10, pp. 249, 325.

12. 'Einaudi on Galiani', in H.W. Spiegel (ed.), *The Development of Economic Thought* (New York: John Wiley & Sons, 1952), pp. 77–8.

13. Indeed publicly self-professed Machiavellianism or amoralism is almost always self-contradictory, since it will hardly serve Machiavellian ends.

14. See Joseph Rossi, *The Abbé Galiani in France* (New York: Publications of the Institute of French Studies, 1930), pp. 47–8.

15. Oswald St Clair, *A Key to Ricardo* (New York: A.M. Kelley, 1965), p. 293.

16. My translation. See Emil Kauder, 'Genesis of the Marginal Utility theory', *Economic Journal* (Sept. 1953), p. 647.

17. T. Hutchison, *Before Adam Smith: The Emergence of Political Economy, 1662–1776* (Oxford: Basil Blackwell, 1988), p. 326.

18. Hutchison, op. cit., note 17, p. 327.

19. Henry Dunning Macleod, *A Dictionary of Political Economy* (London, 1863), I, pp. 534–5.

15 The Scottish Enlightenment

The temptation is to entitle this chapter: 'The forerunners of Adam Smith', himself a leading product of the Scottish Enlightenment. The problem, however, is that Smith, in most aspects of economics, was a retrogression and deterioration, rather than an advance, from his notable predecessors.

By the later seventeenth and during the eighteenth century, the once mighty Oxford and Cambridge Universities, previously in the forefront of thought and scholarship, had deteriorated to being merely the playground of wealthy young men. Instead, for over a century, the intellectual leadership of Great Britain devolved on the two great universities of Scotland: the University of Glasgow and particularly the University of Edinburgh.

15.1 The founder: Gershom Carmichael

The founder of the tradition of academic economics in Scotland was Gershom Carmichael (c.1672–1729). Carmichael's father was a Presbyterian minister, who was exiled for heresy by the Scottish, Presbyterian-run government. Born in England, Carmichael graduated from Edinburgh University. He then became 'regent' at St Andrews and Glasgow Universities, where courses were taught by 'regents' who were essentially young graduate students. After that, Carmichael was Presbyterian minister at Fife. When the regenting system was abolished in 1727, Carmichael was named the first professor of moral philosophy at Glasgow, where he died two years later.

Economics, or political economy, was taught as a subset of a course in moral philosophy, and thus the analysis of trade and the economy was embedded in a groundwork and treatment of natural law. In many ways, the eighteenth century Scottish professors followed the post-medieval and late Spanish scholastic method of including economic analysis as one segment of an integrated tome covering ethics, natural law, jurisprudence, ontology, and theology as well as economics proper.

The term, 'Protestant scholastic' has been coined for such writers as John Locke, and indeed the phrase is a coherent one, since one does not have to be Catholic to use the rational scholastic method or arrive at scholastic conclusions. A fascinating example of this was perhaps the first Protestant scholastic, the Dutch jurist Hugo Grotius (1583–1645). Grotius, who studied law at the University of Leyden and later became chief magistrate of Rotterdam, was an eminent natural law theorist who brought the concepts of natural law and natural rights to the Protestant countries of northern Europe. In his outstanding work, which made him the founder of international law, *De jure belli ac pacis* (*On the Law of War and Peace*) (1625), Grotius clearly pushed natural law to its logical and rationalist conclusion: even if God did not exist, natural law would still be eternal and absolute; such law is discoverable by unaided human reason; and even God could not negate – even if He wanted to – such natural law insights as 2 + 2 = 4. Natural law required the rights of property to be secure in order to enjoy social cooperation, and under Grotius's influence, the idea of the rights of property became expanded to the economic sphere. In a prefigurement of eighteenth century natural law–natural rights theory, Grotius believed in the harmony of human interaction based on free action and property rights. Grotius had been able to work in the rationalist and natural law tradition because his mentor Jacobus Arminius had previously broken off from orthodox Calvinism to stress the freedom of will of every individual. On these important matters of social philosophy, the Arminians had what might be called a 'neo-Catholic' position. In politics, Grotius was a leader in the classical liberal, free trade, republican party in Holland, then engaged in their century-long struggle with the monarchist orthodox Calvinists.

Particularly influential on northern European theorists was the late sixteenth century Spanish Jesuit scholastic Francisco Suarez. Suarez and his school heavily influenced two men who are generally considered founders of 'modern' philosophy: the early seventeenth century Frenchman, René Descartes: and the late seventeenth century German, Gottfried Leibniz. Suarez's *Disputationes Metaphysicae (Metaphysical Disputations)* was his most influential work, published in Salamanca in 1597. Particularly important was the second edition, published in Mainz, Germany in 1600, which became the leading philosophy textbook in most European universities, both Catholic and Protestant, for over a century. Leibniz, indeed, referred to the *Disputationes* as the *philosophia recepta* (the 'received philosophy').

Suarez's work was heavily influential in Protestant central Europe, Bohemia, Germany and Holland. The university of Leyden, a leading academic centre in Holland during the seventeenth century, was a particular focus of Suarezian dominance. And it was at Leyden that Hugo Grotius pursued his studies.

Though Gershom Carmichael, who inaugurated the teaching of economics in Scotland, launched the tradition of reading and studying Grotius – a tradition that was followed by Adam Smith in the eighteenth century line of Scottish intellectual descent – more directly important for Carmichael was Grotius's best-known follower, Samuel, Baron von Pufendorf (1632–94). Pufendorf was born in Saxony, son of a Lutheran pastor. He first studied theology, and then shifted to mathematics, jurisprudence and natural law. Graduating from the University of Jena, Pufendorf went to Leyden, where he published his first work on jurisprudence in 1661. On the basis of this achievement, Karl Ludwig, the elector palatine, created for the young Pufendorf a chair of natural and international law at the University of Heidelberg. In 1672, while teaching at the University of Lund, in Sweden, Pufendorf published his great work *De jure naturae et gentium*: the following year, he produced the *De officio hominis et civis*, a resumé or abstract of his great *De jure*. It turned out, not surprisingly, that the more concise *De officio* proved more useful as a teaching tool and therefore became the far more directly influential, if inferior product of Pufendorf's pen.

Not only did Professor Gershom Carmichael bring the study of the new natural and international law teachings of Grotius and Pufendorf to British shores, but also he was himself the English translator of *De Officio*. Carmichael published the English translation in 1718, along with extensive notes and a supplementary commentary. This work turned out to be Carmichael's most important achievement, certainly in economics or the social sciences.[1] Six years later, Carmichael published an improved second edition of *De Officio*, and this edition was reprinted in 1769. Carmichael saw to it that his students were steeped in Pufendorf and in his own commentaries.

Carmichael was the first teacher in Scotland to expound Locke, Leibniz and Descartes, as well as Grotius and Pufendorf. A knowledgeable observer has called Gershom Carmichael 'the true founder of the Scottish school of philosophy'. A contemporary noted that he was 'of very great reputation, and was exceedingly valued both at home and abroad'. So much so, in fact, that another observer noted that 'on Mr Carmichael's death, all the English students have left the University and, indeed, it's very thin this winter, and his name and reputation brought many to it'. Thus Carmichael led the way in the emerging custom of bright English students deserting Oxbridge and going up to a Scottish university for intellectual attainment.

On Carmichael's commentary on the *De Officio*, the testimony of Carmichael's most distinguished student, Francis Hutcheson, is telling: '...Pufendorf's smaller work, *De Officio Hominis et Civis*, which that worthy and ingenious man, the late Professor Gershom Carmichael of Glasgow, by far the best commentator on that book, has so supplied and corrected that the notes are of much more value than the text'.

Samuel von Pufendorf, like the eighteenth century French and Spanish scholastics, was a pre-Austrian subjective utility–scarcity theorist. That is, he believed that the value of goods on the market was determined by their common valuation placed on them by the consumers, and that the more abundant the supply the lower the value. Thus, Pufendorf:

> Of common value the foundation is that aptitude of the good or service by which it helps directly or indirectly to meet human needs...Yet there are some things most *useful* for human life upon which no definite value is set...The necessity of the good or its great usefulness are so far from always being the first determinant that we can observe men putting a very low value on what is indispensable to human life. This is because nature...gives us a plentiful supply of such goods. In fact a high value proceeds from *scarcity*....

In his notes to Pufendorf, Carmichael adds some valuable and not so valuable insights. He stresses the subjective nature of utility, pointing out that the usefulness of a good, which is essential to its value, may be either real or imagined. Unfortunately, he also muddied the waters by adding to scarcity as a determinant of value, 'the difficulty of acquiring' goods – an obvious 'real cost' attempt to measure the value of goods by the effort put into their production.

15.2   Francis Hutcheson: teacher of Adam Smith

Carmichael's most prominent student and follower was his successor at the chair of moral philosophy at Glasgow, Francis Hutcheson (1694–1746). Hutcheson, too, was the son of a Presbyterian minister of Ulster Scottish (or 'Scots–Irish') stock, who was born in Ireland. Educated in Glasgow and then Dublin, Hutcheson succeeded to the moral philosophy chair at Glasgow in 1730, upon the demise of Carmichael, where he taught until his death 16 years later. Hutcheson brought to Scottish philosophy a solid belief in natural rights and in the beneficence of nature. Hence Hutcheson brought to Scottish thought the basic classical liberal world-view.

Francis Hutcheson was a stimulating and dynamic lecturer, who introduced the style of pacing up and down in front of his class. The 'never-to-be-forgotten Dr. Hutcheson', as Adam Smith referred to him in a letter half a century later, was the first Glasgow professor to teach in English instead of Latin, and also the first to become friend, guardian, and even banker to his students. His lectures on philosophy, politics, law, ethics and political economy drew students from all over Britain, the most famous of whom was Adam Smith, who studied under him from 1737 to 1740. Hutcheson's major work, the *System of Moral Philosophy* (1755), was published by his son after his death.[2]

Hutcheson's treatment of value in his *System* is virtually identical to that of Pufendorf. Again, utility and scarcity are the determinants of value. Beginning with the statement, 'when there is no *demand*, there is no price', Hutcheson also points out that some highly useful things, such as air and water, have little or no value because of the bountiful supply furnished by nature. An increasingly scarce supply will raise the value or price of a good; a more abundant supply will lower them. Furthermore, Hutcheson perceptively defines 'use' highly subjectively, not simply as a good which naturally yields pleasure, but as '*any* tendency to give any satisfaction, by prevailing custom or fancy'.

Unfortunately, however, Hutcheson also took the Carmichael confusion about real costs and escalated it. For Hutcheson not only brought in the 'difficulty of labour' as a determinant, he also made it even *more* determining 'where the demand for two sorts of goods is equal'.

Foreshadowing Adam Smith's famous analysis, Francis Hutcheson stressed the importance of an advancing division of labour in economic growth.

Liberty on the market involves reciprocal aid through mutually beneficial exchange, a prime example of the beneficence of nature. The division of labour is a key to the preservation of human life, and Hutcheson shows the enormous advantages of specialization, skill, and exchange over the puny productivity of an isolated Crusoe. Extended division of labour also connotes a more extensive communication of knowledge, and permits greater use of machinery in production.

In his analysis of money, Hutcheson set forth an analysis of which commodities are likely to be chosen as money on the market that used to be standard in money and banking texts until governments destroyed the gold standard in the early 1930s. Money, Hutcheson pointed out, is a commodity generally accepted in a particular country, that becomes used as a general medium of exchange, and as a common standard of value and measure for economic calculation. Commodities which are chosen as money on the market are those with the most money-ish qualities: already generally desirable and acceptable in exchange; divisible into small quantities without losing their *pro rata* share of value; durable for long periods of time; and portable, for which quality they must have a high value per unit weight. Generally, he pointed out, silver and gold have been the two commodities that have been chosen as by far the most suitable as money, with coins becoming the most popular form precisely for being divisible and easily carrying a warrant of purity.

Debasement of coins increases their supply proportionately and raises prices of goods in terms of the money unit. As in the case of all other goods, an increase in the supply of gold or silver, Hutcheson pointed out, lowers their value in terms of other goods, i.e., increases their prices in terms of specie.

Hutcheson's most impressive achievement was his sharp rebuttal of the satiric Bernard de Mandeville (1670–1733), whose enormously popular *Fable of the Bees, or, Private Vices, Public Benefits* was published in 1714, and expanded and reprinted in several editions over the next 15 years.[3] In a pre-physiocratic, proto-Keynesian piece of mischief, the *Fable* maintained that the vice of luxury, no matter how deplorable, performs the important economic function of maintaining the prosperity of the economy. Many historians, especially F.A. von Hayek, have held Mandeville to be a forerunner of Smithian *laissez-faire*, since Smith held that individual self-interest is harmonized with the interests of all through the operation of competition and the free market. But the intent and the analysis are very different, for Mandeville stressed the alleged paradox of 'private vice, public benefits', and the 'benefit' was to come through the pre-Keynesian mechanism of consumption spending. Mandeville, furthermore, did not in any sense draw *laissez-faire* conclusions from this analysis; on the contrary, in a *Letter to Dion* (1732) published shortly before his death, Mandeville insisted that not the free market but the 'wisdom' and 'dexterous management of a skilful politician' are needed to transform private vices into public gain.

Mandeville's work, furthermore, was virtually the living embodiment of what the nineteenth century French *laissez-faire* economist Frédéric Bastiat would call the 'broken window fallacy'. Mandeville not only defended the importance of luxury but also of fraud, as providing work for lawyers, and theft, for having the virtue of employing locksmiths. And then there was Mandeville's classically imbecilic defence, in his *Fable of the Bees*, of the Great Fire of London:

> The Fire of London was a great Calamity, but if the Carpenters, Bricklayers, Smiths, and all, not only that are employed in Building but likewise those that made and dealt in the same Manufactures and other Merchandizes that were Burnt, and other Trades again that got by them when they were in full Employed, were to Vote against those who lost by the Fire; the Rejoicings would equal if not exceed the Complaints.[4]

'Keynesianism' gone mad; or rather, carried to its consistent conclusion.

Mandeville's defence of the 'vice' of luxury was enough to outrage both the rational economist and the Presbyterian in Francis Hutcheson. In rebuttal, in a prefiguration of Say's law, he pointed out that 'income not spent in one way will be spent in another and if not wasted in luxury will be devoted to useful prudent purposes'. Luxurious spending, then, is scarcely necessary for economic prosperity. In fact, he went on, it is the thrifty and the industrious who provide prosperity by supplying goods to the public. Declared Hutcheson: the 'good arising to the public is in no way owing to the luxurious, intemperate or proud but to the industrious, who must supply all customers'. Ridiculing Mandeville, the ordinarily sober Hutcheson riposted: 'Who needs to be surprised that luxury or pride are made necessary to public good, when even theft and robbery are supposed by the same author [Mandeville] to be subservient to it, by employing locksmiths?' The money saved by not spending on luxury (or locks) would be profitably employed elsewhere, unless all other wants had been totally saturated, that is, 'unless all men be already so well provided with all sorts of convenient utensils...that nothing can be added...'.

As a general proposition, Hutcheson called for liberty and the natural right of property. As he put it in his *System*:

> each one has a natural right to exert his powers, according to his own judgment and inclination, for those purposes, in all such industry, labour or amusements as are not harmful to others in their persons or goods, while no more public interest necessarily require his labours...This right we call *natural liberty*.

An unexceptionable statement, except for the ominous vagueness in the concept of public interest that 'requires' a man's labour.

Hutcheson's devotion to *laissez-faire*, however, was limited and guarded. Thus, in his *Introduction to Moral Philosophy*, he opines that 'the populace often needs also to be taught, and engaged by laws, into the best methods of managing their own affairs and exercising their mechanic arts...' In international trade, for example, Hutcheson was mired in old-fashioned mercantilism, advocating state regulation to insure a 'favourable balance of trade', and high protective tariffs as well as government subsidies of shipping, to develop industry.

Hutcheson's devotion to natural rights was weakened still further by his being the first to adumbrate the chimerical and disastrous formula of utilitarianism: 'the greatest happiness for the greatest number', possibly after having acquired it or its equivalent from Gershom Carmichael.

The specific influences of Hutcheson on Adam Smith will be detailed further below; suffice it to say here that the order of topics of Hutcheson's lectures, as published in the *System* and as heard by young Smith at the University of Glasgow, is almost the same as the order of chapters in the *Wealth of Nations*.

15.3   The Scottish Enlightenment and Presbyterianism

The Enlightenment was a general movement in European thought in the eighteenth century that stressed the power of human reason to discern truth. Generally, it was dedicated to natural law and natural rights, although in the later years of the century it began to shade off into utilitarianism. While scholasticism was compatible with an emphasis on natural law and natural rights, it was generally discarded and reviled as ignorant 'superstition', along with revealed religion. In religion, therefore, Enlightenment thinkers tended to discard Christianity, attack the Christian Church, and adopt scepticism, deism, or even atheism.

In this atmosphere corrosive of Christian faith and values, it is remarkable that the Scottish Enlightenment was linked very closely with the Presbyterian Church. How did this happen? How did a Scottish kirk which in the sixteenth century under the *aegis* of John Knox, had been fiery and militant, become softened into a church that welcomed the Enlightenment, i.e. natural law, reason, and latitudinarian if not sceptical Christianity?

The answer is that in the two centuries since John Knox the hard-nosed Calvinist faith had weakened in Scotland. In particular, after 1752, a powerful group of moderate Presbyterian clergy was able to take over and dominate the Church of Scotland, the established Church which, since the union of Scotland and England in 1707, had been established by the British Crown even though it was Presbyterian rather than Anglican, as was the Church of England.[5] Bitterly opposed to the moderates were the evangelical party, that is, clergy true to the basic Calvinist faith. The well-connected and highly educated moderates, strong in the lowland areas of Edinburgh and Glasgow, and on the east coast up to Aberdeen, were able to form the dominant power elite in the Church of Scotland after the 1750s, even though they represented a minority of the local kirks.

The moderates, embodying a soft and latitudinarian theological outlook, were intimately connected with the Edinburgh and Glasgow intellectuals who constituted the Scottish Enlightenment. Most of their tactics were planned in meetings in Edinburgh taverns. The dominant figure among the moderates was the Rev. William Robertson (1721–93), an incessant talker and indefatigable organizer who led the moderates since their formation in 1752, and who became the moderator, or head, of the general assembly of the Church of Scotland from 1766 to 1780. In 1762, furthermore, Robertson became the principal of the University of Edinburgh, and it was his leadership and administration that vaulted Edinburgh into the front ranks of European universities. Robertson was also the founder and leading light of various learned societies, which brought together weekly, for papers, discussion, and socializing, the leading figures of the Scottish Enlightenment, including university professors, lawyers, and the major figures of the moderate clergy.

Thus, Robertson founded the Select Society of Edinburgh in 1750. Prominent during the 1750s, the Select Society met weekly and included in its ranks such university figures as Robertson, David Hume, Adam Ferguson and Adam Smith, classical liberal lawyers such as Henry Home (Lord Kames) and Alexander Wedderburn (later Lord Chancellor of Great Britain), and such youthful but prominent moderate clergy as Robertson, Alexander ('Jupiter') Carlyle, Robert Wallace, Hugh Blair, John Home and John Jardine. Carlyle was a charismatic figure as well as a heavy drinker, as many moderate clergymen were in that era; Wallace was in charge of Church of Scotland patronage, as well as being royal chaplain. Wallace, in his private papers, favoured illicit sex almost to the point of promiscuity, quickly warning that the activity would have to be kept hidden. Blair, in addition to his duties in the clergy, was professor of rhetoric at the University of Edinburgh. Jardine was a shrewd politician, whose daughter married the son of Lord Kames who in turn was a cousin of David Hume. John Home was a moderate clergyman and secretary to Lord Bute, close friend of David Hume, and a playwright – an activity which in itself was a matter of deep suspicion to the dour, fundamentalist evangelical clergy. Thus, Home wrote a play, *Douglas*, in 1756, which was put on with many top leaders of the moderate Enlightenment acting in the play, including: the Rev. Robertson, Alexander Carlyle, David Hume, Hugh Blair, and the Rev. Adam Ferguson, professor of moral philosophy at the University of Edinburgh.

The lax views of the moderates were under constant attack from the evangelical forces. Particular targets were Lord Kames and especially the philosopher David Hume, who was almost excommunicated for heresy by the general assembly of the Church of Scotland, but was saved by his powerful moderate friends. Even his moderate university connections, however, could not gain for Hume any post in a Scottish university, so great was the enmity of the Presbyterian evangelicals.

It should be noted that one of the key leaders of the moderate party was none other than Francis Hutcheson. Thus, the Enlightenment intellectuals, philosophers, and economists of eighteenth century Scotland were intimately connected with the fortunes and the institutions of the establishment moderate wing of the Church of Scotland.

Hutcheson, Hume and Smith, then, while scarcely orthodox Calvinists, were dedicated Presbyterians according to their own lights, and hence their rationalism and theological laxity were nevertheless infused from time to time with hard-nosed Presbyterian values.

15.4 David Hume and the theory of money

David Hume (1711–76), the famous Scottish philosopher, was a close friend of Adam Smith, who was named Smith's executor, an acquaintance of Turgot and the French adherents of *laissez-faire*, and member of the moderate élite of the Scottish Enlightenment. Born in Edinburgh the son of a Scottish lord, Hume studied on the Continent, where he published his epochal philosophical work, *A Treatise of Human Nature* (1739–40), at the age of 28. Hume's *Treatise* was pivotal in its corrosive and destructive scepticism, managing unfairly to discredit the philosophy of natural law, to create an artificial split between fact and value, and therefore to cripple the concept of natural rights on behalf of utilitarianism and indeed to undermine the entire classical realist analysis of cause and effect. There is no figure more important in the unfortunate discrediting of the classical philosophical tradition of natural law realism, a tradition that had lasted from Plato and Aristotle at least through Aquinas and the late scholastics. In a sense, Hume completed the corrosive effect of the seventeenth century French philosopher René Descartes's influential view that only the precisely mathematical and analytic could provide certain knowledge. Hume's sceptical and shaky empiricism was the other side of the Cartesian coin.

While highly influential in later decades, Hume's *Treatise* was ignored in his own day, and after writing it he turned to brief essays on political and economic topics, and eventually to his then famous multi-volume *History of England*, which he presented from a Tory point of view.

Barred from academia for his scepticism and alleged irreligion, Hume joined the diplomatic corps, and served as secretary to Lord Hertford, the British ambassador to France. In 1765, Hume became the British chargé d'affaires in Paris, and two years later rose to the post of under-secretary of state. Finally, in 1769, Hume retired to Edinburgh.

Hume's contribution to economics is fragmentary, and consists of approximately 100 pages of essays in his *Political Discourses* (1752). The essays are distinguished for their lucid and even sparkling style, a style that shone in comparison to his learned but plodding contemporaries.

Hume's most important contribution is his elucidation of monetary theory, in particular his clear exposition of the price-specie-flow mechanism that equilibrates national balances of payments and international price levels. In monetary theory proper, Hume vivifies the Lockean quantity theory of money with a marvellous illustration, highlighting the fact that it doesn't matter what the quantity of money may be in any given country: any quantity, smaller or larger, will suffice to do money's work of facilitating exchange. Hume pointed up this important truth by postulating what would happen if every individual, overnight, should find the stock of money in his possession to have doubled miraculously:

> For suppose that, by miracle, every man in Great Britain should have five pounds slipped into his pocket in one night; this would much more than double the whole money that is at present in the kingdom; yet there would not next day, nor for some time, be any more lenders, nor any variation in the interest.

Prices then, following Locke's quantity theory of money, will increase proportionately.

The price-specie-flow mechanism is the quantity theory extrapolated into the case of many countries. The rise in the supply of money in country *A* will cause its prices to rise; but then the goods of country *A* are no longer as competitive compared to other countries. Exports will therefore decline, and imports from other countries with cheaper goods will rise. The balance of trade in country *A* will therefore become unfavourable, and specie will flow out of *A* in order to pay for the deficit. But this outflow of specie will eventually cause a sharp contraction of the supply of money in country *A*, a proportional fall in prices, and an end to, indeed a reversal of, the unfavourable balance. As prices in *A* fall back to previous levels, specie will flow back in until the balance of trade is in balance, and until the price levels in terms of specie are equal in each country. Thus, on the free market, there is a rapidly self-correcting force at work that equilibrates balances of payments and price levels, and prevents an inflation from going very far in any given country.

While Hume's discussion is lucid and engaging, it is a considerable deterioration from that of Richard Cantillon. First, Cantillon did not believe in aggregate proportionality of money and price level changes, instead engaging in a sophisticated micro-process analysis of money going from one person to the next. As a result, money and prices will not rise proportionately even in the eventual new equilibrium state. Second, Cantillon included the 'income effect' of more money in a country, whereas Hume confined himself to the aggregate price effect. In short, if the money supply in country *A* increases, it will equilibrate not only by prices rising in *A*, but also by the fact that monetary assets and incomes are higher in *A*, and therefore more money will be spent on imports. This income or more precisely, the cash balance, effect will generally work faster than the price effect.

There are more problems with Hume's analysis, problems other than the omission of previously discovered truths. For while Hume conceded that it does not matter for production or prosperity what the level of the money supply may be, he *did* lay great importance on *changes* in that supply. Now it is true that changes *do* have important consequences, some of which Cantillon had already analysed. But the crucial point is that all such changes are disruptive, and distort market activity and the allocation of resources. But David Hume, on the contrary, in a pre-Keynesian fashion, hailed the allegedly vivifying effects of increases in the quantity of money upon prosperity, and called upon the government to make sure that the supply of money is always at least moderately increasing. The two contradictory prescriptions of Hume for the supply of money are actually presented in two successive sentences:

> From the whole of this reasoning we may conclude, that it is of no manner of consequence, with regard to the domestic happiness of a state, whether money be in a greater or less quantity. The good policy of the magistrate consists only in keeping it, if possible, still increasing; because, by that means he keeps alive a spirit of industry in the nation...

Hume goes on, in proto-Keynesian fashion, to claim that the invigorating effect of increasing the supply of money occurs because employment of labour and other resources increases long before prices begin to rise. But Hume stops (as Keynes did) just as the problem becomes interesting: for then, it must be asked, why were resources underemployed before, and what *is* there about an increase in the money supply that might add to their employment? As W.H. Hutt was to point out in the 1930s, deeper reflection would show that the only possible reason for unwanted unemployment of resources is if the resource-owner demands too high a price (or wage) for its use. And more money could only reduce such unemployment when selling prices rise before wages or the price of resources, so that workers or other resource-owners are fooled into working for a lower *real* though not lower money wage.

Furthermore, why should idle resources, as Hume implicitly postulates, reappear after the effects of new money have been fully digested in the economy in the form of higher prices? The answer can only be that after the price increases are accomplished and a new equilibrium attained, wages and other resource prices have caught up and the 'money illusion' has evaporated. Real resource prices return to being excessively high for the full employment of resources.[6]

Hume's inner contradictions on the quantity of money and inflation permeate his meagre writings on economics. On the one hand, continuing inflation over the centuries is depicted as bringing about economic growth; on the other, Hume sternly favoured ultra-hard money in relation to the banking system. Thus Hume delivered a hard-hitting attack on the unproductive and inflationary nature of the very existence of fractional-reserve banking. He wrote of

> those institutions of banks, funds, and paper credit, with which we are in the kingdom so much infatuated. These render paper equivalent to money, circulate it throughout the whole state, make it supply the place of gold and silver, raise proportionately the price of labour and commodities, and by that means either banish a great part of those precious metals, or prevent their further increase. What can be more short-sighted than our reasoning on this head? We fancy, because an individual would be much richer, were his stock of money doubled, that the same good effect would follow were the money of every one increased; not considering, that this would raise as much the price of every commodity, and reduce every man, in time, to the same condition as before.

Elsewhere Hume noted that inconveniences result from the increase of genuine money (specie), but at least they are 'compensated by the advantages which we reap from the possession of these precious metals', including bargaining power in negotiations with other nations. But, he added, 'there appears no reason for increasing that inconvenience by a counterfeit money, which foreigners will not accept of in any payment, and which any great disorder in the state will reduce to nothing'. To 'endeavour to increase' paper credit 'artificially', then, merely increases money 'beyond its natural proportion to labour and commodities', thereby increasing their prices.

Hume concluded his penetrating analysis with an ultra-hard money policy proposal – 100 per cent specie-reserve banking: 'it must be allowed, that no bank could be more advantageous, than such alone as locked up all the money it received, and never augmented the circulating coin...' Hume added that this was the practice of the famous 100 per cent specie-reserve Bank of Amsterdam.

Another important flaw in Hume's analysis of money was his propensity, picked up and magnified by Smith, Ricardo and the classical school, for leaping from one long-run equilibrium state to another, without bothering about the dynamic process through time by which the real world actually moves from one state to another. It is this brusque neglect (or 'comparative statics') that leads Hume to omit the Cantillonian analysis of micro-changes in cash balances and income, and that causes him to neglect income effects in the price-specie-flow mechanism of international monetary adjustment.[7] Ironically, by doing so, and thereby neglecting the 'distribution effects' of changing assets and incomes during the process, Hume – as well as countless other economists following him – distorts what happens in equilibrium itself. For they then cannot see that the new equilibrium will be very different from the old. Thus, when the money supply changes, there will not be an equiproportionate increase in all prices across the board.

Professor Salerno puts the point very well:

> ...there is some truth to Keynes' statement that...'Hume began the practice amongst economists of stressing the importance of the equilibrium position as compared with the ever-shifting transition towards it'. For, in reading Hume, one gets an unmistakable whiff, if not the full flavor, of the notion that it is in the states of long-run equilibrium that the economy actually resides most of the time. The transition between these states, Hume conceives as proceeding rapidly and terminating before another change in the economic data can intervene and propel the economy toward a new equilibrium. This notion at times leads Hume to truncate a full step-by-step analysis of a given change in the data, thus slighting or skipping over altogether its short-run effects in order to focus upon a comparative-static analysis of its ultimate consequences.[8]

In reality, as the Austrians have emphasized, the situation is precisely the reverse of the Hume–British classical assumptions. Rather than the long-run equilibrium state being the fundamental reality, it never exists at all. Long-run equilibrium provides the tendency towards which the market is ever moving, but is never reached because the underlying data of supply and demand – and therefore the ultimate equilibrium point – are always changing. Hence a full step-by-step analysis of a given change in the data is precisely what is needed to explain the process of successive short-run states which tend towards but never reach equilibrium. In the real world, the 'long run' is not equilibrium at all, but a series of such short-run states, which will keep changing direction as underlying data are altered.

A final problem with Hume's monetary views is that, in contrast to the French *laissez-faire* school, he believed that money need not be a useful marketable commodity but was a mere convention. Writing to Abbé Andre Morellet (1727–1819), a disciple of Gournay and lifelong friend of Turgot, Hume opines that money functions as such because of the belief that others would accept it. Very true: but this does not mean that money originated as a mere convention. And Hume acknowledges that money should be made of materials 'which have intrinsic value', for 'otherwise it would be multiplied without end, and would sink to nothing'.

Hume's thoughts on interest are illuminating, if only in contrast to the profundity and brilliance of Turgot's exposition 20 years later. Since money's impact is ultimately on prices only, Hume shows that interest can only be a phenomenon of real capital rather than of money. He discusses the relation between interest rates and profit rates (i.e. the fundamental rates of return on investment). Here he points out correctly that 'no man will accept of low profits, where he can have high interest; and no man will accept of low interest where he can have high profits'. In short, interest and profit rates tend to be equal on the market. Very true, but which causes which, or what is the underlying cause of both? Hume characteristically abandons the search for cause, and says that 'both arise from an extensive commerce, and mutually forward each other'. Böhm-Bawerk is surely right when he says that this view is 'somewhat superficial'.[9] But more than that: it is incorrect and reverses cause and effect by stating that 'extensive commerce, by producing large stocks (capital), diminishes both interest and profits'. For there is no reason why larger stocks of capital should lower interest or profit rates; what they *do* lower is the prices of capital goods and consumer goods. The casual chain is the other way round: lower time-preference rates, which usually but not always attend higher standards of living and greater prosperity, will cause both capital to accumulate *and* profit and interest rates to fall. The two, as the Austrian School would later point out, are different sides of the same coin.[10]

Turning to the other areas of economics, it is possible that some of the deep flaws in Adam Smith's value theory were the result of David Hume's influence. For Hume had no systematic theory of value, and had no idea whatever of utility as a determinant of value. If anything, he kept stressing that labour was the source of all value.

On political economy, David Hume may be considered a free trader and opponent of mercantilism. A friend and mentor of Adam Smith from their first meeting in 1752, Hume came to know the French *laissez-fairists* during his years in that country, and Turgot himself translated Hume's *Political Discourses* into French.

15.5 Notes

1. In the same year, 1718, Carmichael published a *System of Natural Theology*, and two years later produced an introduction to logic. In the year of his death he wrote a *Synopsis of Natural Theology*.
2. A more concise but less effective version, an *Introduction to Moral Philosophy*, had been published immediately after his death in 1747.
3. Mandeville was a Dutch physician who spent much of his life in England. The *Fable of the Bees* was itself an expanded version of a satirical essay, *The Grumbling Hive, or Knaves Turned Honest* (1705).
4. *Fable of the Bees* (1924), p. 359. Cited in the excellent article by Salim Rashid, 'Mandeville's *Fable*: Laissez-faire or Libertinism?', *Eighteenth-Century Studies*, 18 (Spring 1985), p. 322.
5. So bitter were the Anglican priests in Scotland at the governmental establishment of Presbyterianism that they, as well as the Roman Catholics, formed the backbone of the Jacobite rebels dedicated to the restoration of the Stuart monarchy in Great Britain.
6. Professor Salerno attempts to justify Hume's curious assumption of a permanent tendency to unemployed resources by applying the Alchian–Allen information cost analysis. But this approach only explains the maintenance of any business inventory, inventory which, as Salerno shows, is not truly 'idle' but performs an important function to the businessman of

dealing with uncertainty. But such inventory hardly explains the unemployment of labour and other resources, which is presumably unwanted (since inflation supposedly eliminates this idleness) and hence involuntary. Of course if, as we would maintain, unemployment results from excessively high asking prices for resources, then this unemployment is brought upon the resource-owners by their own actions, although as an undesired consequence. In a deep sense, then, this unemployment is really 'voluntary'. See Joseph T. Salerno, 'The Doctrinal Antecedents of the Monetary Approach to the Balance of Payments' (doctoral dissertation, Rutgers University, 1980), pp. 160–2, and W.H. Hutt, *The Theory of Idle Resources*, (2nd ed., Indianapolis: Liberty Press, 1977).

7. Unfortunately for the development of the British classical school and of economics itself, Hume failed to heed the criticism of his friend, and Adam Smith's childhood friend, James Oswald of Dunnikier (1715–69). Oswald, an important MP who might have become Chancellor of the Exchequer, and whose advice on economics was sought by Hume and Smith, wrote to Hume that 'the increased quantity of money would not necessarily increase the price of all labour and commoditys; because the increased quantity, not being confined to the home labour and commoditys, might, and certainly would, be sent to purchase both from foreign countries...' Though Hume answered by conceding this cash balance effect in the balance of payments adjusting mechanism, he failed to incorporate it into his fuller presentation of the price-specie-flow process. See Salerno, op. cit., note 6, pp. 252–3.

8. Salerno, op. cit., note 6, pp. 165–6.

9. Eugen von Böhm-Bawerk, *Capital and Interest* (South Holland, Ill.: Libertarian Press, 1959), I, p. 30.

10. Spiegel hails Hume's analysis as presaging 'modern economic theory, with its functional approach' that replaces old-fashioned concern with cause and effect. Hume, he says, foreshadows 'the later concern of economic science with functional rather than casual relationships, which...did not become common before the twentieth century'. So much the worse for both Hume and twentieth century theory! For the functional, non-casual relations of mathematics are scarcely appropriate for an analysis of human action, where human preferences and choices are the *cause*, and have specifically traceable *effects*. Ironically, moreover, the great destroyer of cause and effect did *not* lack a causal theory of interest; instead, he picked the wrong end of the causal chain by claiming that low interest and profits were both caused by the accumulation of capital goods. Cf. Henry W. Spiegel, *The Growth of Economic Thought* (Englewood Cliffs, NJ: Prentice-Hall, 1971), pp. 211–2.

16 The celebrated Adam Smith

16.1   The mystery of Adam Smith

Adam Smith (1723–90) is a mystery in a puzzle wrapped in an enigma. The mystery is the enormous and unprecedented gap between Smith's exalted reputation and the reality of his dubious contribution to economic thought.

Smith's reputation almost blinds the sun. From shortly after his own day until very recently, he was thought to have created the science of economics virtually *de novo*. He was universally hailed as the Founding Father. Books on the history of economic thought, after a few well-deserved sneers at the mercantilists and a nod to the physiocrats, would invariably start with Smith as the creator of the discipline of economics. Any errors he made were understandably excused as the inevitable flaws of any great pioneer. Innumerable words have been written about him. At the bicentennial of his *magnum opus*, *An Inquiry into the Nature and the Causes of the Wealth of Nations* (1776), a veritable flood of books, essays, and memorabilia poured forth about the quiet Scottish professor. His profile sculpted on a medallion by Tassie is known throughout the world. A hagiographic movie was even made about Smith during the bicentennial by a free market foundation, and businessmen and free market advocates have long hailed Adam Smith as their patron saint. 'Adam Smith ties' were worn as a badge of honour in the upper echelons of the Reagan Administration. On the other hand, Marxists, with somewhat more justice, hail Smith as the ultimate inspiration of their own Founding Father, Karl Marx. Indeed, if the average person were asked to name two economists in history whom he has heard of, Smith and Marx would probably be the runaway winners of the poll.

As we have already seen, Smith was scarcely the founder of economic science, a science which existed since the medieval scholastics and, in its modern form, since Richard Cantillon. But what the German economists used to call, in a narrower connection, *Das AdamSmithProblem*,[1] is much more severe than that. For the problem is not simply that Smith was not the founder of economics. The problem is that he originated nothing that was true, and that whatever he originated was wrong; that, even in an age that had fewer citations or footnotes than our own, Adam Smith was a shameless plagiarist, acknowledging little or nothing and stealing large chunks, for example, from Cantillon. Far worse was Smith's complete failure to cite or acknowledge his beloved mentor Francis Hutcheson, from whom he derived most of his ideas as well as the organization of his economic and moral philosophy lectures. Smith indeed wrote in a private letter to the University of Glasgow of the 'never-to-be-forgotten Dr. Hutcheson', but apparently amnesia conveniently struck Adam Smith when it came time to writing the *Wealth of Nations* for the general public.[2]

Even though an inveterate plagiarist, Smith had a Columbus complex, accusing close friends incorrectly of plagiarizing *him*. And even though a plagiarist, he plagiarized badly, adding new fallacies to the truths he lifted. In castigating Adam Smith for errors, therefore, we are not being anachronistic, absurdly punishing past thinkers for not being as wise as we who come later. For Smith not only contributed nothing of value to economic thought; his economics was a grave deterioration from his predecessors: from Cantillon, from Turgot, from his teacher Hutcheson, from the Spanish scholastics, even – oddly enough – from his *own* previous works, such as the *Lectures on Jurisprudence* (unpublished, 1762–63, 1766) and the *Theory of Moral Sentiments* (1759).

The mystery of Adam Smith, then, is the immense gap between a monstrously overinflated reputation and the dismal reality. But the problem is worse than that; for it is not just that Smith's *Wealth of Nations* has had a terribly overblown reputation from his day to ours. The problem is that the *Wealth of Nations* was somehow able to blind all men, economists and laymen alike, to the very knowledge that other economists, let alone better ones, had existed and written before 1776. The *Wealth of Nations* exerted such a colossal impact on the world that all knowledge of previous economists was blotted out, hence Smith's reputation as Founding Father. The historical problem is this: how could this phenomenon have taken place with a book so derivative, so deeply flawed, so much less worthy than its predecessors?

The answer is surely not any lucidity or clarity of style or thought. For the much revered *Wealth of Nations* is a huge, sprawling, inchoate, confused tome, rife with vagueness, ambiguity and deep inner contradictions. There is of course an advantage, in the history of social thought, to a work being huge, sprawling, ambivalent and confused. There is sociological advantage to vagueness and obscurity. The bemused German Smithian, Christian J. Kraus, once referred to the *Wealth of Nations* as the 'Bible' of political economy. In a sense, Professor Kraus spoke wiser than he knew. For, in one way, the *Wealth of Nations* is like the Bible; it is possible to derive varying and contradictory interpretations from various – or even the same – parts of the book. Furthermore, the very vagueness and obscurity of a work can provide a happy hunting ground for intellectuals, students and followers. To make one's way through an obscure and difficult tract, to weave dimly perceived threads of a book into a coherent pattern – these are rewarding tasks in themselves for intellectuals. And such a book also provides a welcome built-in exclusion process, so that only a relatively small number of adepts can bask in their expertise about a work or a system of thought. In that way they increase their relative income and prestige, and leave other admirers behind to form a cheering section for the leading disciples of the Master.

Adam Smith did not found the science of economics, but he did indeed create the paradigm of the British classical school, and it is often useful for the creator of a paradigm to be inchoate and confused, thereby leaving room for disciples who will attempt to clarify and systematize the contributions of the Master. Until the 1950s, economists, at least those in the Anglo-American tradition, revered Smith as the founder, and saw the later development of economics as a movement linearly upward into the light, with Smith succeeded by Ricardo and Mill, and then, after a bit of diversion created by the Austrians in the 1870s, Alfred Marshall establishing neoclassical economics as a neo-Ricardian and hence neo-Smithian discipline. In a sense, John Maynard Keynes, Marshall's student at Cambridge, thought that he was only filling in the gaps in the Ricardian–Marshallian heritage.

Into this complacent miasma of Smith-worship, Joseph A. Schumpeter's *History of Economic Analysis* (1954) came as a veritable blockbuster. Coming from the continental Walrasian and Austrian traditions rather than from British classicism, Schumpeter was able, for virtually the first time, to cast a cold and realistic eye upon the celebrated Scot. Writing with thinly veiled contempt, Schumpeter generally denigrated Smith's contribution, and essentially held that Smith had shunted economics off on a wrong road, a road unfortunately different from that of his continental forbears.[3]

Since Schumpeter, historians of economic thought have largely retreated to a fallback position. Smith, it is conceded, created nothing, but he *was* the great synthesizer and systematizer, the first one to take up all the threads of his predecessors and weave them together into a coherent and systematic framework. But Smith's work was the reverse of coherent and systematic, and Ricardo and Say, his two major disciples, each set themselves the task of forging such a coherent system out of the Smithian muddle. And, furthermore, while it is true that pre-Smithian writings were incisive but sparse (Turgot) or embedded in moral philosophy (Hutcheson), it is also true that there were two general treatises on economics *per se* before the *Wealth of Nations*. One was Cantillon's great *Essai* which, after Smith, fell into grievous neglect, to be rescued a century later by Jevons; the other, and the first book to use political economy in its title, was Sir James Steuart's (1712–80) outdated two-volume work, *Principles of Political Oeconomy* (1767). Steuart, a Jacobite who had been involved in Bonnie Prince Charlie's rebellion, was for much of his life an exile in Germany, where he became imbued with the methodology and ideals of German 'cameralism'. Cameralism was a virulent form of absolutist mercantilism that flourished in Germany in the seventeenth and eighteenth centuries. Cameralists, even more than western European mercantilists, were not economists at all – that is, they did not analyse the processes of the market – but were technical advisers to rulers on how and in what way to build up state power over the economy. Steuart's *Principles* was in that tradition, scarcely economics but rather a call for massive government intervention and totalitarian planning, from detailed regulation of trade to a system of compulsory cartels to inflationary monetary policy. His only 'contribution' was to refine and expand previously fleeting and inchoate notions of a labour theory of value, and to elaborate a proto-Marxian theory of inherent class conflict in society. Furthermore, Steuart had written an ultra-mercantilist tome just at the time when classical liberal and *laissez-faire* thought was rising and becoming dominant at least in Britain and France.

Even though Steuart's *Principles* was out of step with the emerging classical liberal *Zeitgeist*, it was no foregone conclusion that the work would have little or no influence. The book was well received, highly respected, and sold very well, and five years after its publication, in 1772, Steuart won out over Adam Smith in acquiring a post as monetary consultant to the East India Company.

One reason that the Schumpeter view of Smith shocked the economics profession is that historians of economic thought, similar to historians of other disciplines, have habitually treated the development of science as a linear and upward march into the truth. Each scientist patiently formulates, tests and discards hypotheses, and thereby each succeeding one stands on the shoulders of the one who came before. What might be called this 'Whig theory of the history of science' has now been largely discarded for the far more realistic Kuhnian theory of paradigms. For our purposes the important point of the Kuhn theory is that a very few people patiently test anything, particularly the fundamental assumptions, or basic 'paradigm', of their theory: and shifts in paradigms can take place even when the new theory is worse than the old. In short, knowledge can be and is lost as well as gained, and science often proceeds in a zig-zag rather than linear manner. We might add that this would be particularly true in the social or humane sciences. As a result, paradigms and basic truths get lost, and economists (as well as people in other disciplines) can get worse, and not better, over time. The years may well bring retrogression as well as progress. Schumpeter had heaved a bombshell into the temple of the Whig historians of economic thought, specifically of the partisans of the Smith–Ricardo–Marshall tradition.[4]

We have thus posed our own version of the *Das AdamSmithProblem*: how did so badly flawed a work as the *Wealth of Nations* rapidly become so dominant as to blot out all other alternatives? But before considering this question, we must examine the various aspects of Smithian thought in more detail.

16.2   The life of Smith

Adam Smith was born in 1723 in the small town of Kirkcaldy, near Edinburgh. His father, also Adam Smith (1679–1723), who died shortly before he was born, was a distinguished judge advocate for Scotland and later comptroller of customs at Kirkcaldy, who had married into a well-to-do local landowning family. Young Smith was therefore raised by his mother. The town of Kirkcaldy was militantly Presbyterian, and in the Burgh School in the town he met many young Scottish Presbyterians, one of whom, John Drysdale, was to become twice moderator of the general assembly of the Church of Scotland.

Smith, indeed, came from a customs official family. In addition to his father, his cousin Hercules Scott Smith, served as collector of customs at Kirkcaldy, and his guardian, again named Adam Smith, was to become customs collector at Kirkcaldy as well as inspector of customs for the Scottish outports. Finally, still another cousin named Adam Smith later served as customs collector at Alloa.

From 1737 to 1740, Adam Smith studied at Glasgow College, where he fell under the spell of Francis Hutcheson, and imbibed the excitement of the ideas of classical liberalism, natural law and political economy. In 1740, Smith earned an MA with great distinction at the University of Glasgow. His mother had baptized Adam in the Episcopalian faith, and she was eager for her son to become an Episcopalian minister. Smith was sent to Balliol College, Oxford, on a scholarship designed to nurture future Episcopalian clerics, but he was unhappy at the wretched instruction in the Oxford of his day, and returned after six years, at the age of 23, without having taken holy orders. Despite his baptism and his mother's pressure, Smith remained an ardent Presbyterian, and returning to Edinburgh in 1746, he remained unemployed for two years.

Finally, in 1748, Henry Home, Lord Kames, a judge and a leader of the liberal Scottish Enlightenment and a cousin of David Hume, decided to promote a series of public lectures in Edinburgh to educate lawyers. Along with Smith's childhood friend, James Oswald of Dunnikier, Kames got the Philosophical Society of Edinburgh to sponsor Smith in several years of lectures on natural law, literature, liberty and commercial freedom. In 1750, Adam Smith obtained the chair in logic at his *alma mater*, the University of Glasgow, and he found no difficulty in the requisite signing of the Westminster Confession before the Presbytery of Glasgow. Finally, in 1752, Smith had the satisfaction of ascending to his beloved teacher Hutcheson's chair of moral philosophy at Glasgow, where he was to remain for 12 years.

Smith's Edinburgh and Glasgow lectures were very popular, and his major stress was on the 'system of natural liberty', on the system of natural law and *laissez-faire* which he was then advocating with far less qualification than later in his more cautious *Wealth of Nations*. He also managed to covert many of the leading merchants of Glasgow to this exciting new creed. Smith also plunged into the social and educational associations that were beginning to be formed by the moderate Presbyterian clergy, university professors, literati, and attorneys in both Glasgow and Edinburgh. It is likely that David Hume attended Smith's Edinburgh lectures in 1752, for the two became fast friends shortly thereafter.

Smith was a founding member of the Glasgow Literary Society the following year; the society engaged in high-level discussions and debates, and met diligently every Thursday evening from November to May. Hume and Smith were both members, and at one of the first sessions, Smith read an account of some of Hume's recently printed *Political Discourses*. Oddly enough, the two friends, clearly the brightest members of the Society, were extremely diffident, and never said a word in any of the discussions.

Despite his diffidence, Smith was a busy and inveterate clubman, becoming a leading member of the Philosophical Society of Edinburgh and of the Select Society (Edinburgh), which flourished in the 1750s, and met weekly, bringing together the moderate power élite from the clergy, university men, and the legal profession. Smith was also an active member of the Political Economy Club of Glasgow, the Oyster Club (Edinburgh); Simson's Club of Glasgow; and the Poker Club (Edinburgh), founded by his friend Adam Ferguson, professor of moral philosophy at the University of Edinburgh, specifically to promote the 'martial spirit'. As if this were not enough, Adam Smith was one of the leading contributors and editors of the abortive *Edinburgh Review* (1755–56), dedicated largely to the defence of their friends Hume and Kames against the hard-core evangelical Calvinist clergy of Scotland. The *Edinburgh Review* was founded by the brilliant young lawyer, Alexander Wedderburn (1733–1805), who was to become a judge, an MP in England, and finally Lord Chancellor (1793–1801). Wedderburn was so latitudinarian as to favour the licensing of brothels. Other luminaries on the *Edinburgh Review* were top moderate leaders: the politician John Jardine (1715–60), whose daughter married Lord Kames's son; the powerful Rev. William Robertson, and the Rev. Hugh Blair (1718–1800), professor of rhetoric at the University of Edinburgh.

The intensity of Adam Smith's Presbyterianism, even though not fundamentalist, may be seen in his relationship to Hugh Blair. Blair, the minister at the High Kirk, Greyfriars, was in constant hot water with the orthodox Calvinist clergy, who repeatedly denounced him to the Glasgow and Edinburgh Presbyteries. In the *Wealth of Nations*, Adam Smith delivered the following encomium to the Presbyterian clergy: 'There is scarce, perhaps, to be found anywhere in Europe, a more learned, decent, independent, and respectable set of men than the greater part of the Presbyterian clergy of Holland, Geneva, Switzerland, and Scotland'. To which his old friend Blair, though himself a leading if embattled Presbyterian clergyman, commented in a letter to Smith: 'You are, I think, by much too favourable to Presbytery'.

After Smith published his moral philosophy in his *Theory of Moral Sentiments* (1759), his increasing fame won him a highly lucrative position in

1764 as tutor to the young duke of Buccleuch. For three years of tutoring, which he spent with the young duke in France, Smith was awarded a lifetime annual salary of £300, twice his annual salary at Glasgow. In three pleasant years in France, he made the acquaintance of Turgot and the physiocrats. His tutorial task accomplished, Smith returned to his home town of Kirkcaldy, where, secure in his lifetime stipend, he worked for ten years to complete the *Wealth of Nations*, which he had started at the beginning of his stay in France. The fame of the *Wealth of Nations* led his proud erstwhile pupil, the Duke of Buccleuch, to help secure for Smith in 1778 the highly paid post of commissioner of Scottish customs at Edinburgh. With a pay of £600 per annum from his government post, which he kept until the day of his death in 1790, added to his handsome lifetime pension, Adam Smith was making close to a £1 000 a year, a 'princely revenue', as one of his biographers has described it. Even Smith himself wrote in this period that he was 'fully as affluent as I could wish'. He regretted only that he had to attend to his customs post, which took time away from his 'literary pursuits'.

And yet his regrets were scarcely profound. In contrast to most historians, who have treated Smith's customs post embarrassedly as virtually a no-show sinecure in reward for intellectual achievements, recent research has shown that Smith worked full-time at his post, often chairing the daily meetings of the board of customs commissioners. Moreover, Smith sought the appointment and apparently found the position enjoyable and relaxing. It is true that Smith spent little time or energy on scholarship and writing after his appointment; but there were leaves of absence available which Smith showed no interest in pursuing. Furthermore the groundwork for Smith's quest for the appointment was not so much his intellectual attainments as a reward for his advice as consultant on taxes and the budget to the British government since the mid-1760s.[5]

16.3 The division of labour

It is appropriate to begin a discussion of Smith's *Wealth of Nations* with the division of labour, since Smith himself begins there and since for Smith this division had crucial and decisive importance. His teacher Hutcheson had also analysed the importance of the division of labour in the developing economy, as had Hume, Turgot, Mandeville, James Harris and other economists. But for Smith the division of labour took on swollen and gigantic importance, putting into the shade such crucial matters as capital accumulation and the growth of technological knowledge. As Schumpeter has pointed out, never for any economist before or since did the division of labour assume such a position of commanding importance.

But there are more troubles in the Smithian division of labour than his exaggerating its importance. The older and truer perception of the motive power for specialization and exchange was simply that each party to an exchange (which is necessarily two-party and two-commodity) benefits (or at least expects to benefit) from the exchange; otherwise the trade would not take place. But Smith unfortunately shifts the main focus from mutual benefit to an alleged irrational and innate 'propensity to truck, barter and exchange', as if human beings were lemmings determined by forces external to their own chosen purposes. As Edwin Cannan pointed out, Smith took this tack because he rejected the idea of innate differences in natural talents and abilities, which would naturally seek out different specialized occupations. Smith instead took the egalitarian–environmentalist position, still dominant today in neoclassical economics, that all labourers are equal, and therefore that differences between them can only be the *result* rather than a cause of the system of the division of labour.

In addition, Smith failed to apply his analysis of the division of labour to international trade, where it would have provided powerful ammunition for his own free trade policies. It was to be left to James Mill to make such an application in his excellent theory of comparative advantage. Furthermore, domestically, Smith placed far too much importance on the division of labour *within* a factory or industry, while neglecting the more significant division of labour *among* industries.

But if Smith had an undue appreciation of the importance of the division of labour, he paradoxically sowed great problems for the future by introducing the chronic modern sociological complaint about specialization that was picked up quickly by Karl Marx and has been advanced to a high art by socialist gripers about 'alienation'. There is no gainsaying the fact that Smith totally contradicted himself between Book I and Book V of the *Wealth of Nations*. In the former, the division of labour *alone* accounts for the affluence of civilized society, and indeed the division of labour is repeatedly equated with 'civilization' throughout the book. And yet, while in Book I the division of labour is hailed as expanding the alertness and intelligence of the population, in Book V it is condemned as leading to their intellectual as well as moral degeneration, to the loss of their 'intellectual, social and martial virtues'. There is no way that this contradiction can be plausibly reconciled.[6]

Adam Smith, though himself a plagiarist of considerable dimensions, also had a Columbus complex, often accusing other people unfairly of plagiarizing him. In 1755 he actually laid claim to having invented the concept of *laissez-faire*, or the system of natural liberty, asserting that he had taught these principles since his Edinburgh lectures in 1749. That may be: but the claim ignores previous such expressions by his own teachers as well as by Grotius and Pufendorf, to say nothing of Boisguilbert and the other French *laissez-faire* thinkers of the late seventeenth century.

In 1769, the contentious Smith levied a plagiarism charge against Principal William Robertson, upon the occasion of the publication of the latter's *History of the Reign of Charles V*. It is not known what the topic of the literary theft was supposed to be, and it is difficult to guess, considering the remoteness from Smith's work of the theme of the Robertson book.

The most famous plagiarism charge hurled by Smith was against his friend Adam Ferguson on the question of the division of labour. Professor Hamowy has shown that Smith did *not* break with his old friend, as had previously been thought, because of Ferguson's use of the concept of the division of labour in his *Essay on the History of Civil Society* in 1767. In view of all the writers who had employed the concept earlier, this behaviour would have been ludicrous, even for Adam Smith. Hamowy conjectures that the break came in the early 1780s, because of Ferguson's discussion at their club of what would later be published as part of his *Principles of Moral and Political Science* in 1792. For in the *Principles*, Ferguson summed up the pin-factory example that constituted the single most famous passage in the *Wealth of Nations*. Smith had pointed to a small pin-factory where ten workers, each specializing in a different aspect of the work, could produce over 48 000 pins a day, whereas if each of these ten had made the entire pin on his own, they might not have made even one pin a day, and certainly not more than 20. In that way the division of labour enormously multiplied the productivity of each worker. In his *Principles*, Ferguson wrote: 'A fit assortment of persons, of whom each performs but a part in the manufacture of a *pin*, may produce much more in a given time, than perhaps double the number, of which each was to produce the whole, or to perform every part in the construction of that diminutive article'.

When Smith upbraided Ferguson for not acknowledging Smith's precedence in the pin-factory example, Ferguson replied that he had borrowed nothing from Smith, but indeed that *both* had taken the example from a French source 'where Smith had been before him'. There is strong evidence that the 'French source' for both writers was the article on *Epingles* (pins) in the *Encyclopédie* (1755), since that article mentions 18 distinct operations in making a pin, the same number repeated by Smith in the *Wealth of Nations*, although in English pin factories 25 was the more common number of operations.

Thus Adam Smith broke up a long-standing friendship by unjustly accusing Adam Ferguson of plagiarizing an example which, in truth, both men had taken without acknowledgement from the French *Encyclopédie*. The Rev. Carlyle's comment that Smith had 'some little jealousy in his temper' seems a vast understatement, and we are informed by his obituary notice in the 1790 *Monthly Review* that 'Smith lived in such constant apprehension of being robbed of his ideas that, if he saw any of his students take notes of his lectures, he would instantly stop him and say, 'I hate scribblers'.[7] While there is also evidence that Smith allowed students to take notes, the point about his crabbed temper and Columbus complex is well made.

Smith's use of an example of a small French pin-factory rather than a larger British one highlights a curious fact about his celebrated *Wealth of Nations*: the renowned economist seems to have had no inkling of the Industrial Revolution going on all about him. Although he was a friend of Dr John Roebuck, the owner of the Carron iron works, whose opening in 1760 marked the beginning of the Industrial Revolution in Scotland, Smith showed no indication that he knew of its existence. Although he was at least an acquaintance of the great inventor James Watt, Smith displayed no knowledge whatever of some of Watt's leading inventions. He made no mention in his famous book of the canal boom which had begun in the early 1760s, of the very existence of the burgeoning cotton textile industry, or of pottery or of the new methods of making beer. There is no reference to the enormous drop in travel costs that the new turnpikes were bringing about.

In contrast, then, to those historians who praise Smith for his empirical grasp of contemporary economic and industrial affairs, Adam Smith was oblivious to the important economic events around him. Much of his analysis was wrong, and many of the facts he did include in the *Wealth of Nations* were obsolete and gathered from books 30 years old.

16.4   Productive *vs* unproductive labour

One of the physiocrats' more dubious contributions to economic thought was their view that only agriculture was productive, that only agriculture contributed a surplus, a *produit net*, to the economy. Smith, heavily influenced by the physiocrats, retained the unfortunate concept of 'productive' labour, but expanded it from agriculture to material goods in general. For Smith, then, labour on material objects was 'productive'; but labour on, say, consumer services, on immaterial production, was 'unproductive'.

Smith's bias in favour of material objects amounted to a bias in favour of investment in capital goods, since a stock of capital goods by definition has to be embodied in material objects. Consumer goods, on the other hand, either consist of immaterial services, or they get used up – consumed – in the process of consumption. Smith's imprimatur on *material* production, therefore, was an indirect way of advocating investment in an accumulation of capital goods as against the very *goal* of producing capital goods: increased consumption. When discussing exports and imports, Smith realized full well that there was no point to amassing intermediate objects except that they eventually be consumed – that the only goal of production is consumption. But as Professor Roger Garrison has pointed out, and as we shall see further on the question of usury laws, Adam Smith's Presbyterian conscience led him to value the expenditure of labour *per se*, for its own sake, and led him to balk at free market time-preferences between consumption and saving. Clearly, Smith wanted far more investment towards future production and less present consumption than the market was willing to choose. One of the contradictions of this position, of course, is that accumulating more capital goods at the expense of present consumption will eventually result in a higher standard of living – unless Smith prepared to counsel a perpetual and accelerated shift toward more and more never-to-be-consumed means of production.

In Book II of the *Wealth of Nations*, Smith opines that labour on material objects is productive, while other labour is not because it does not 'fix or realize itself in any particular subject...which endures after that labour is past and for which an equal quantity of labour could afterward be purchased'. Included in immaterial and hence unproductive labour are servants, 'churchmen, lawyers, physicians, men of letters of all kinds; players, buffoons, musicians, opera-singers, opera-dancers, etc.' To Smith the important point was that the 'work of all' unproductive labourers 'perishes in the very instant of its production'. Or, as he put it, 'Like the declamation of the actor, the harangue of the orator, or the tune of the musician, the work of all of them perishes in the very instant of its production'. Smith also writes that 'productive' labour 'adds to the value of the subject on which it is bestowed', whereas 'unproductive labour does not' – another way of putting the fact that labour on services is not embodied in 'any particular subject'. 'Productive' labour, moreover, allegedly creates a 'surplus' for profit in manufacturing. Adam Smith's lingering physiocratic bias was also shown in his preposterous assertion that agriculture is a far more productive industry than manufacturing, because in agriculture nature works alongside man and provides extra rent for landlords as well as profit for capitalists. In addition to other fallacies, Smith here failed to realize that nature in the form of ground land collaborates in *all* activities of man, not just agriculture, and that all activities, including manufacturing, will therefore yield ground rent to landowners.

In his thorough and searching critique of Adam Smith, Edwin Cannan speculated that Smith, if pressed, 'would probably have admitted...that the declamation, harangues, and tunes, have a value'. Smith oddly identified the build-up of material capital goods with annual production. On the latter, as Cannan points out, 'the durability of the things produced by labour is in reality of no significance. The declamations, harangues, and tunes are just as much a part of the annual produce as champagne or boots...'. Yet Smith, in Book II, excludes all production of immaterial services from the annual product, which is allegedly produced entirely by the 'productive labourers', who in turn 'maintain' not only themselves but all the unproductive classes of labour as well.

In a witty and charming passage, Cannan then comments:

> People have always been rather apt to imagine that the class which they happen to
> think the most important 'maintains' all the other classes with which it exchanges
> commodities. The landowner, for instance, considers, or used to consider, his
> tenants as his 'dependants'. All consumers easily fall into the idea that they are
> doing a charitable act in maintaining a multitude of shopkeepers. Employers of all
> kinds everywhere believe that the employed ought to be grateful for their wages,
> while the employed firmly hold that the employer is maintained entirely at their
> expense. So the physiocrats alleged that the husbandman maintained himself and
> all other classes; and Adam Smith alleged that the husbandman, the manufacturer,
> and the merchant maintained themselves and all other classes. The physiocrats did
> not see that the husbandman was maintained by the manufacturing industries of
> thrashing, milling, and baking, just as much as the millers or the tailors are
> maintained by the agricultural industries of ploughing and reaping. Adam Smith
> did not see that the manufacturer and merchant are maintained by the menial
> services of cooking and washing just as much as the cooks and laundresses are
> maintained by the manufacturer of bonnets and the import of tea.[8]

It is not just durable objects, however, that Adam Smith was interested in;
it was durable *capital* goods. Durable consumer goods, like houses, were
again, for Smith, 'unproductive', although he grudgingly conceded that a
house 'is no doubt extremely useful' to the person who lives in it. But it is not
'productive', wrote Smith, because 'If it is to be let to a tenant for rent, as the
house itself can produce nothing, the tenant must always pay the rent out of
some other revenue which he derives either from labour, or stock [capital], or
land'. Again, Cannan provides the proper riposte: 'It did not occur to Adam
Smith to reflect that if a plough is let for rent, as a plough itself can produce
nothing the tenant must always pay the rent out of some other revenue'.[9]

Adam Smith's bias against consumption and in favour of saving and investment is summed up in Professor Rima's analysis:

> It is clear from his third chapter in Book II, 'On the Accumulation of Capital or of
> Productive and Unproductive Labour', that he is concerned with the effect of
> using savings to satisfy the desire for luxuries by those who are prodigal instead
> of channelling them into uses that will enhance the supply of fixed or circulating
> capital. He is, in effect, arguing that savings should be used in such a way that
> they will create a flow of income and new equipment, and that failure to use
> savings in this manner is an impediment to economic growth.[10]

Perhaps – but it *also* means that Smith was not content to abide by free
market choices between growth on the one hand, and consumption on the
other.

Professor Edwin West, a modern admirer of Smith who generally portrays
the Scotsman as an advocate of *laissez-faire*, admits Smith's bias: 'Yet Smith,
like a prudent steward of a Scottish aristocrat's estate, could hardly disguise a
strong personal preference for much private frugality, and therefore for "productive labor", in the interests of the nation's future accumulation'. He then

proceeds to concede implicitly Professor Garrison's insight that Smith exhorted us to negative or at least zero time-preference. Citing Smith's *Theory of Moral Sentiments*, West notes that the virtue of frugality 'commands the esteem' of Smith's alter ego, man's innate moral sense, the 'impartial spectator'. Quoting from Smith: 'The spectator does not feel the solicitations of our present appetites. To him the pleasure which we are to enjoy a week hence, or a year hence, is just as interesting as that which we are to enjoy this moment'.[11]

We might note that the lofty refusal to discount future satisfactions in favour of the present, i.e. the rejection of positive time-preference, is all too easy of any 'impartial spectator'. But is the impartial spectator truly human, or is he simply a floating wraith, who does not participate in the human condition and therefore whose insight can be brusquely dismissed?

Adam Smith's Calvinistic scorn of consumption can be seen in his attack on dancing as 'primitive and rude'. As we shall see, in his 'paradox of value' Smith dismissed diamonds in an excessive way as having 'scarce any value in use'. He also puritanically denounced luxury as being biologically harmful, reducing the birth rate of the upper classes: 'Luxury in the fair sex, while it inflames perhaps the passion for enjoyment, seems always to weaken, and frequently to destroy altogether the powers of generation'.

Smith, furthermore, favoured low and criticized high profits, because high profits induce capitalists to engage in excessive consumption. And since large capitalists set an influential example for others in society, it is all the more important for them to keep to the path of thrift and industry. Thus:

> besides all the bad effects to the country in general, which have already been mentioned as necessarily resulting from a high rate of profit; there is one more fatal, perhaps, than all these put together, but which, if we may judge from experience, is inseparably connected with it. The high rate of profit seems everywhere to destroy that parsimony which in other circumstances is natural to the character of the merchant. When profits are high, that sober virtue seems to be superfluous, and expensive luxury to suit better the affluence of his situation.

Because of the influence of the example of the higher orders, Smith adds,

> If his employer is attentive and parsimonious, the workman is very likely to be so too; but if the master is dissolute and disorderly, the servant who shapes his work according to the pattern which his master prescribes to him, will shape his life according to the example which he sets him. Accumulation is thus prevented in the hands of all those who are naturally the most disposed to accumulate.... The capital of the country, instead of increasing, gradually dwindles away....[12]

But if Adam Smith was excessively in favour of capital investment as against consumption, he at least was sound in realizing that capital investment was important in economic development and that saving was the necessary and sufficient condition of such investment. The only way to increase capital, then, is by private savings or thrift. Thus, Smith wrote, 'Whoever saves money, as the phrase is, adds proportionately to the general mass of capital.... The world can augment its capital only in one way, by parsimony'. Savings, and not labour, is the cause of accumulation of capital, and such savings promptly 'puts into motion an additional quantity of industry [labour]'. The saver, then, spends as readily as the spendthrift, except that he does so to increase capital and eventually benefit the consumption of all; hence 'every frugal man is a public benefactor'. All this was a pale shadow of the scintillating and creative work of Turgot, with his emphasis on time, the structure of production, and time-preference. And it was probably cribbed from Turgot to boot. But at least it was sound, and it stamped its imprint indelibly on classical economics. As Schumpeter put it, in discussing what he calls 'the Turgot–Smith theory of saving and investment': 'Turgot, then, must be held responsible for the first serious analysis of these matters, as A. Smith must (at the least) with having it inculcated into the minds of economists'.[13]

Finally, apart from the Marxists, even the abject Smithians of today reject or at least dismiss the Master's productive vs unproductive labour distinction. Characteristically, however, Smith was not even clear and consistent in his fallacies. His presentation in Book I of the *Wealth of Nations* contradicts Book II. In Book I, he properly states that 'Every man is rich or poor according to the degree in which he can afford to enjoy the necessaries, conveniences, and amusements of human life', a phrase almost directly lifted from Cantillon. But in that case, of course, there is no difference in productivity between material objects and immaterial services, all of which contribute to such 'necessaries, conveniences, and amusements', and indeed Smith's discussion of wages proceeds in Book I as if there were no distinction between productive and unproductive work.

16.5 The theory of value

Adam Smith's doctrine on value was an unmitigated disaster, and it deepens the mystery in explaining Smith. For in this case, not only was Smith's theory of value a degeneration from his teacher Hutcheson and indeed from centuries of developed economic thought, but it was also a similar degeneration from Smith's own previous unpublished lectures. In Hutcheson and for centuries, from the late scholastics onward, the value and price of a product were determined first by its subjective utility in the minds of the consumers, and second, by the relative scarcity or abundance of the good being evaluated. The more abundant any given good, the lower its value; the scarcer the good, the higher its value. All that this tradition needed to complete its explanation was the marginal principle of the 1870s, a focus on a given unit of the good, the unit actually chosen or not chosen on the market. But the rest of the explanation was in place.

In his lectures, furthermore, Smith had solved the value paradox neatly, in much the same way as had Hutcheson and other economists for centuries. Why is water so useful and yet so cheap, while a frippery like diamonds is so expensive? The difference, said Smith in his lectures, was their relative scarcity: 'It is only on account of the *plenty* of water that it is so cheap as to be got for the lifting, and on account of the scarcity of diamonds…that they are so dear'. Furthermore, with different supply conditions, the value and price of a product would differ drastically. Thus Smith points out in his lectures that a rich merchant lost in the Arabian desert would value water very highly, and so its price would be very high. Similarly, if the quantity of diamonds could 'by industry…be multiplied', the price of diamonds on the market would fall rapidly.

But in the *Wealth of Nations*, for some bizarre reason, all this drops out and falls away. Suddenly, only ten or a dozen years after the lectures, Smith finds himself unable to solve the value paradox. In a famous passage in Book I, Chapter IV of *Wealth*. Smith sharply and hermetically separates and sunders utility from value and price, and never the twain shall meet:

> The word value…has two different meanings, and sometimes expresses the utility of some particular object, and sometimes the power of purchasing other goods which the possession of that object conveys. The one may be called 'value in use': the other, 'value in exchange'. The things which have the greatest value in use have frequently little or no value in exchange; and on contrary, those which have the greatest value in exchange have frequently little or no value in use. Nothing is more useful than water; but it will purchase scarce any thing; scarce any thing can be had in exchange for it. A diamond, on the contrary, has scarce any value in use; but a very great quantity of other goods may frequently be had in exchange for it.

And that is that. No mention of the solution of the value paradox by stressing relative scarcities. Indeed, 'scarcity'– that concept so fundamental and crucial to economic theory – plays virtually no role in the *Wealth of Nations*. And with scarcity gone as the solution to the value paradox, subjective utility virtually drops out of economics as well as does consumption and consumer demand. Utility can no longer explain value and price, and the two sundered concepts will reappear in later generations as left-wingers and socialists happily prate about the crucial difference between 'production for profit' and 'production for use', the heir of the Smithian emphasis on the alleged gulf between 'value in use' and 'value in exchange'.[14]

And since economic science was reborn after Adam Smith, since all previous economists were cast into limbo by prevailing fashions of thought, the entire tradition of subjective utility – scarcity as determinants of value and price, a tradition dominant since Aristotle and the medieval and Spanish scholastics, a tradition that had continued down through writers in eighteenth century France and Italy – that great tradition gets poured down the Orwellian memory hole by Adam Smith's fateful decision to discard even his own previous concepts. Although Samuel Bailey almost restored it, the great tradition was not to be fully resurrected until its independent rediscovery by the Austrians and other marginalists in the 1870s. Adam Smith has a lot to answer for at the bar of history.

Paul Douglas put it eloquently in a commemorative volume for the Adam Smith sesquicentennial: 'Smith helped to divert the writers of English Classical School into a cul-de-sac from which they did not emerge, in so far as their value theory was concerned, for nearly a century...'.[15] And we can understand the anguish of Professor Emil Kauder when, after lamenting the sinking into oblivion of the great French and Italian economists of the eighteenth century, he wrote:

> Yet it was the tragedy of these writers that they wrote in vain, they were soon forgotten. No scholar appeared to make out of these thoughts the new science of political economy. Instead, the father of our economic science wrote that water has a great utility and a small value. With these few words Adam Smith had made waste and rubbish out of the thinking of 2,000 years. The chance to start in 1776 instead of 1870 with a more correct knowledge of value principles had been missed.[16]

How could Smith have made such a colossal blunder? In effect, he turned away from his almost sole emphasis on explaining market price in the lectures to another concept which for him took on overriding importance: the 'natural price', or what might be called the 'long-run normal' price. This concept, similar to Cantillon's 'intrinsic value' or Hutcheson's 'fundamental value', had appeared in the lectures, but occupied a minor role as it did in the work of these other economists. But suddenly, the 'natural price' and its alleged determinants now became more important, more truly 'real' than the market price of the real world that had always been the prime focus of economists. Value and price theory shifts, because of Adam Smith's unfortunate and drastic change of focus in the *Wealth of Nations*, from prices in the real world to a mystical non-existent price in the never-never land of long-run 'equilibrium'.

But this alleged natural price is neither more real than nor equally real as the current market price. It is, in fact, not real at all. Only the market price is the real price. At best, the long-run price is useful in providing a vital clue to the direction of price and production changes in the real world. But the long-run price is never reached, and never can be reached, for it keeps shifting as underlying supply and demand forces continually change. The long-run normal price is important but only for explaining the directional tendencies and the underlying architectonic structure of this economy, and also for analysis of how uncertainty affects real-world income and economic activity. The virtually exclusive classical and neoclassical absorption in the unreal 'long-run', to the neglect and detriment of analysing real-world prices and economic activity, shunted economic thought on to a long, fallacious and even tragic detour, from which it has not yet fully recovered.

Another terrible loss inflicted on economic thought by Adam Smith was his dropping out of the concept of the entrepreneur, so important to the contributions of Cantillon and Turgot. The entrepreneur disappeared from British classical thought, never to be resurrected until some of the continental thinkers and especially the Austrians. But the point is that there is no room for the entrepreneur, if the focus is to be on the unchanging, certain world of long-run equilibrium.

Before the *Wealth of Nations*, economists had always concentrated on the market price, and had seen readily that it was determined by the forces of supply and demand, and hence of utility and scarcity. Indeed, while David Hume knew nothing of utility and spoke of labour as the source of value, he was far sounder on value theory than his close friend Adam Smith. On receiving a copy of the newly published *Wealth of Nations*, Hume, on his deathbed, was able to write to his friend on one important criticism: 'I cannot think that the rent of farms make any part of the price of produce, but that the price is determined altogether by the quantity and the demand'. In short, compared to Smith, Hume was in the continental tradition and almost proto-Austrian.

But if Smith stressed the long run, what is supposed to determine the non-real concept of a 'natural' or 'long-run normal' price? Following up unfortunate hints of his eighteenth century predecessors, Smith concluded that the natural price is equal to and determined by costs of production, a concept that had only occupied a fitful and subordinate place in economic thought since the medieval scholastics.

Not that the long-run normal price, or as we now call it the 'equilibrium' price, is nonsense. The equilibrium price is the long-run tendency of the market price. As Adam Smith indeed saw, if the market price is higher than the long-run equilibrium, then extra gains will be made and resources will flow into this particular industry, until the market price falls to reach equilibrium. Conversely, if the market price is lower than equilibrium, the resulting losses will drive resources out of the industry until the price rises to reach equilibrium. The equilibrium concept is highly useful in pointing to the direction in which the market will move. But equilibrium will only be *reached* in reality if the 'data' of the market are magically frozen: that is, if the values, resources, and technological knowledge on the market continue to remain precisely the same. In that case, equilibrium would be reached after a certain span of time. But since these data are always changing in the real world, equilibrium is never attained.

'Cost of production' is defined by Adam Smith as total expenses paid to factors of production, that is, wages, profits and rent. More specifically, in what was to become the famous classical triad, Smith reasoned that there were three types of factors of production: labour, land and capital. Labour receives wages, land earns rent, and capital earns 'profits' – actually long-run rather than short-run rates of return, or what might be called the 'natural' rate of interest. In equilibrium, which Smith seems to have believed was more real and hence far more important than the actual market price, the wage rate equals the 'average' or the 'natural' rate: and the other returns similarly equal the 'natural' rent and the long-run average rate of profit.

There is one striking fallacy in his analysis of cost that Adam Smith shared, though in an aggravated fashion, with earlier writers. Whereas market price is changeable and ephemeral, 'cost' is somehow determined objectively and exogenously, i.e. from outside the world of market economic activity. But cost is not intrinsic or given; on the contrary, it itself is determined, as the Austrians were later to point out, by the value foregone in using resources in production. This value, in turn, is determined by the subjective valuations that consumers place on those products. In brief, rather than cost in some 'fundamental' sense determining value, cost at any and all times is *itself* determined by the subjective value, or expected value, that consumers place on the various products. So that, even if we might say that prices will equal cost of production in long-run equilibrium, there is no reason to assume that such costs *determine* long-run price; on the contrary, expected consumer valuation determines what the value of costs will be on the market. Cost is strictly dependent on utility, in the short and long runs, and never the other way around.

Another grave problem with all cost-of-production theory is that it necessarily abandons any attempt to explain the pricing of goods and services that have no cost because they are not produced, goods that are simply *there*, or were produced in the past but are unique and not reproducible, such as art works, jewellery, archaeological discoveries, etc. Similarly, immaterial consumer services such as the prices of entertainment, concerts, physicians, domestic servants, etc., can scarcely be accounted for by costs embodied in a product. In all these cases, only subjective demand can explain the pricing or the fluctuations in those prices.

But this analysis scarcely exhausts Smith's sins in discussing the central concept in economics – the theory of value. For side by side with the standard cost-of-production analysis as equalling wages + rents + profits, another, new, and far more bizarre theory was set forth. In this alternative view, the relevant cost of production that determines equilibrium price is simply the quantity of labour embodied in its production. It was, indeed, Adam Smith who was almost solely responsible for the injection into economics of the labour theory of value.[17] And hence it was Smith who may plausibly be held responsible for the emergence and the momentous consequences of Marxism.

Side by side and unintegrated with Smith's cost-of-production theory of the natural price lay his new quantity-of-labour-pain theory. Thus:

> The real price of every thing, what every thing really costs to the man who wants to acquire it, is the toil and trouble of acquiring it. What every thing is really worth to the man who has acquired it, and who wants to dispose of it or exchange it for something else, is the toil and trouble which it can save to himself, and which it can impose upon other people. What is bought with money or with goods is purchased by labour, as much as what we acquire by the toil of our own body... They contain the value of a certain quantity of labour which we exchange for what is supposed at the time to contain the value of an equal quantity.

Thus goods exchange on the market for equal quantities which they 'contain' of labour hours, at least in their 'real', long-run prices.

Immediately, Smith recognized that he faced a profound difficulty. If labour quantity is the source and measure of all value, how can the mere quantity of labour hours be equated to the quantity of labour pain or labour toil? Surely they are not automatically equal. As Smith himself admitted, in addition to labour time, 'the different degrees of hardship endured or ingenuity exercised must likewise be taken into account'. Yet such equating is 'not easy', for indeed 'there may be more labour in an hour's hard work than in two hours easy business: or in an hour's application to a trade which it cost ten years labour to learn, than in a month's industry at an ordinary and obvious employment'.

How does this crucial equating take place? According to Smith, 'by the higgling and bargaining of the market' bringing them into a 'rough sort of equality'. Yet here Smith fell into an iron trap of circular reasoning. For, like Ricardo and Marx after him, he attempted to explain prices and values by the quantity of labour, and then appealed to the settling of values on the market to determine what the 'quantity of labour' is, by weighting it by differences in the degree of labour hardship and toil.[18]

Smith tried to escape such circularity by his egalitarian assumption – still held in orthodox neoclassical economics – that all labourers are equal, and that hence wages, at least in the natural long run, will all be equal, or rather will be equal for equal quantities of labour toil among all the workers. According to Smith, competition on the market will tend to equate wages per unit of sacrifice or labour toil. As Douglas put it, 'Smith believed he had established the fact that equal units of labor in the sense of disutility were at any one time compensated for by equal amounts of money wages'.

Thus, Smith opined in an eighteenth century egalitarian way that 'The difference between the most dissimilar characters, between a philosopher and a common street porter, seems to arise, not so much from nature as from habit, custom and education'. There are no unique individuals and irreducible differences between people; in this reductionist view now active again in the twentieth century, the mind of a human being is merely a *tabula rasa* on which external environment fills in the content. Hence, according to Smith, skilled labour earns more than unskilled merely to compensate for years of apprenticeship and training when earnings were much lower: so that their labour hours and toil and hence wages would be equalized over a lifetime. Wages in occupations which are active in only part of the year should be higher to compensate for the fewer days of work – so that annualized incomes would be equal. Other things being equal, furthermore, workers in unpleasant or dangerous occupations would receive higher wages to compensate them for the higher labour sacrifice, while prestigious occupations would receive lower wages since their sacrifice or unpleasantness is lower.

While all these distinctions make some sense and have to be taken into account in any theory of wages, they founder on the *a priori* assumption that every person's mind is a uniform *tabula rasa*. Once enter the realistic assumption of innate differences in talent, and the egalitarian levelling of wage rates to equal units of sacrifice (assuming of course that the latter could be measured) falls to the ground.

As it is, Smith ran into considerable difficulty in explaining why prestigious occupations, far from earning low wages in the real world, actually earn higher wages than the average. When discussing the high-income physician or attorney, for example, he lamely fell back on the implication that they were positions of great trust, and therefore presumably faced onerous and painful responsibilities to their clients and were compensated thereby. His other attempt to rationalize the high incomes of attorneys was to make the dubious assumption that the *average* income in such occupations was *lower* than in others, since a flood of people are attracted by the glittering prizes of very high incomes accruing to the few top people in the profession.

Adam Smith, in addition, muddied the waters still further by putting forward, side by side with the labour-cost theory of value, the very different 'labour-command' theory. The labour-command theory states that the value of a good is determined not by the quantity of labour units contained in it (the labour theory of value), but by the amount of labour that can be purchased by the good. Thus: 'The value of any commodity to the person who possesses it...is equal to the quantity of labour which it enables him to purchase or command'.

If, in the real world, the price of every commodity precisely equalled the amount of labour units 'contained' in its production, then the two quantities – the labour cost and the labour command of a good – would indeed be identical. But if rents and profits (i.e. interest) are included in cost, then the price, or relative purchasing power, of each good would not be equal to the labour cost. Labour cost and labour command for each good would differ.

In his typically purblind way, Adam Smith did not perceive the contradiction between these two labour theories in a world where rent and profits exist (as indeed he did not seem to see the difference between the labour and the cost-of-production theories of value). Ricardo was to see the problem and struggle with it in vain, while Marx tried to resolve it by his theory of 'surplus value' going to the non-workers in the form of rent and profits, a theory that foundered on Marx's attempt to reconcile two contradictory propositions: the labour-cost (or quantity of labour) theory of value, and the acknowledged tendency toward an equalization of profit rates on the market. For, as we shall see further in the treatment of Marx (Chapters 9–13 in Volume II), the 'surplus value' of profits out of labour should be greater in labour-intensive than in capital-intensive industries, and yet profits tend to equalize everywhere. Paul Douglas properly and with rare insight noted that Marx was, in this matter, simply a Smithian–Ricardian trying to work out the theory of his masters:

> Marx has been berated by two generations of orthodox economists for his value theory. The most charitable of the critics have called him a fool and the most severe have called him a knave for what they deem to be transparent contradictions of his theory. Curiously enough these very critics generally commend Ricardo and Adam Smith very highly. Yet the sober facts are that Marx saw more clearly than any English economist the differences between the labor-cost and the labor-command theories and tried more earnestly than anyone else to solve the contradictions which the adoption of a labor-cost theory inevitably entailed. He failed, of course: but with him Ricardo and Smith failed as well... The failure was a failure not of one man but of a philosophy of value, and the roots of the ultimate contradiction made manifest, in the third volume of *Das Kapital*, lie imbedded in the first volume of the *Wealth of Nations*.[19]

Adam Smith also gave hostage to the later emergence of socialism by his repeatedly stated view that rent and profit are deductions from the produce of labour. In the primitive world, he opined, 'the whole produce of labour belongs to the labourer'. But as soon as 'stock' (capital) is accumulated, some will employ industrious people in order to make a profit by the sale of the materials. Smith indicates that the capitalist (the 'undertaker') reaps profits in return for the risk, and for interest on the investment for maintaining the workers until the product is sold – so that the capitalist earns profit for important functions. He adds, however, that 'In this state of things the whole produce of labour does not always belong to the labourer. He must in most cases share it with the owner of the stock who employs him'. By using such phrases, and by not making clear why labourers might be happy to pay capitalists for their services, Smith left the door open for later socialists who would call for restructuring institutions so as to enable workers to capture their 'whole product'. This hostage to socialism was aggravated by the fact that Smith, unlike the later Austrian School, did not demonstrate logically and step by step how industrious and thrifty people accumulate capital out of savings. He was content simply to begin with the alleged reality of a minority of wealthy capitalists in society, a reality which later socialists were of course not ready to endorse.

Smith was even less kindly to the role of landlords, where he recognized no economic function whatever that they might perform. In pungent passages, he writes that 'As soon as the land of any country has all become private property, the landlords like to reap where they never sowed and demand a rent even for its natural produce'. And again: 'as soon as the land becomes private property, the landlord demands a share of almost all the produce which the labourer can either raise or collect from it'. There is no hint of recognition here that the landlord performs the vital function of allocating the land to its most productive use. Instead, these passages were to become understandable red meat for socialists and for Henry Georgists in calls for the nationalizing of land.

As we shall see further below, Smith's labour theory of value did inspire a number of English socialists before Marx, generally named 'Ricardian' but actually 'Smithian' socialists, who decided that if labour produced the whole product, and rent and profit are deductions from labour's produce, then the entire value of the product should rightfully go to its creators, the labourers. Douglas justly concluded that

> It is then from the Whiggish pages of the *Wealth of Nations* that the doctrines of the English Socialists as well as the theoretical exposition of Karl Marx, spring. The history of social thought furnishes many instances where theories elaborated by one writer have been taken over by others to justify social doctrines antagonistic to those to which the promulgator of the theory gave adherence. But had the gift of prevision been granted to those men, few would have been more startled than Adam Smith in seeing himself as the theoretical founder of the doctrines of nineteenth-century socialism.[20]

Modern writers have tried to salvage the unsalvageable labour theory of value of Adam Smith by asserting that, in a sense he did not really mean what he was saying but was instead seeking to find an invariable standard by which he could measure value and wealth over time. But, to the extent that this search was true, Smith simply added another fallacy on top of all the others. For since value is subjective to each individual, there *is no* invariant measure or yardstick of value, and any attempts to discover them can at best distort the enterprise of economic theory and send it off chasing an impossible chimera. At worst, the entire structure of economic theory is permeated with fallacy and error. Professors Robertson and Taylor, indeed, go so far as to call the admitted failure of Adam Smith a grand and noble failure, and one which they assert to be far more inspiring in its essential bankruptcy than if Adam Smith had continued in the subjective value tradition of his forbears. In a bizarre passage, Robertson and Taylor acknowledge the correctness of Professor Kauder's anguished critique of Smith as leading economic theory into a century-long blind alley. But they still laud Smith for his very failure:

> If a true explanation is given here of the reasons for Adam Smith turning from 'scarcity and utility' to a labour theory of value, did he not, in fact, do more for the progress of economics by a grand failure in an impossible but fundamental task, than he would have done, had he been content to add a seventh rung or even to strengthen some of the existing steps in the rickety ladder of subjective-value theory such as, according to Dr. Kauder, it appeared in 1776?[21]

Is it hopelessly banal to counter that truth is always superior to fundamental error in advancing a scientific discipline?

There is a more fundamental and convincing reason for Adam Smith's throwing over centuries of sound economic analysis, his abandonment of utility and scarcity, and his turn to the erroneous and pernicious labour theory of value. This is the same reason that Smith dwelled on the fallacious doctrine of productive versus unproductive labour. It is the explanation stressed by Emil Kauder, and partially by Paul Douglas: Adam Smith's dour Calvinism. It is Calvinism that scorns man's consumption and pleasure, and stresses the importance of labour virtually for its own sake. It is the dour Calvinist who made the extravagant statement that diamonds had 'scarce any value in use'. And perhaps it is also the dour Calvinist who scorned, in the words of Robertson and Taylor, real-world 'market values which depended on monetary whims and fashions on the market', and turned his attention instead to the long-run price where such fripperies played no part, and the grim eternal verities of labour toil seemingly played the decisive economic role. Surely this is a far more realistic view of Adam Smith than the Quixotic romantic in quest of the impossible dream of an invariable measure of value. And while Smith's most famous follower, David Ricardo, was not a Calvinist, his leading immediate disciple, Dugald Stewart, was a Scottish Presbyterian, and the leading Ricardians – John R. McCulloch and James Mill – were both Scottish and educated in Dugald Stewart's University of Edinburgh. The Calvinist connection continued to dominate British – and hence classical – economics.

16.6   The theory of distribution

Adam Smith's theory of distribution was fully as disastrous as his theory of value. Though he was aware of the functions performed by the capitalist, his only venture in explaining the rate of long-run profit was to opine that the greater the 'amount of stock' the lower the rate of profit. He arrived at this highly dubious conclusion from his perfectly valid observation that capitalists tend to move out of low-profit and into high-profit industries, their competition tending to equalize the rates of profit throughout the economy. But more production, lowering selling price and raising costs in a particular industry, is scarcely the same causal claim as more capital throughout the economy lowering profit rates. Indeed, the rate of interest, or long-run rate of profit, is related, not to the quantity of accumulated capital, but to the amount of annual saving, and moreover falling profit rates are not *caused* by increasing saving. On the contrary, as the Austrians would point out, *both* are the results of lower rates of time-preference in the society. It is perfectly possible for a highly capitalized economy to experience rising rates of time-preference, which in turn would bring about higher rates of interest.

Smith saw correctly that increasing capital means an increase in the demand for labour and therefore higher wages, so that an advancing society necessarily means a secular increase in wage rates. Unfortunately, Smith's mechanistic view of the profit rate as being inversely proportional to the total amount of capital led him to believe that wages and profits are always moving inversely to the other – an adumbration of an allegedly inherent class struggle which Ricardo would do much to aggravate.

Moreover, if the supply of labour increases to absorb the increase in demand, wage rates will then fall. At this point, Adam Smith provided the Malthusian hook, for, as we shall see further, the Rev. Malthus was a devoted follower of Adam Smith. Smith, indeed, was picking up a theme common in the eighteenth century: that the population of a species tends to press on the means of its subsistence. As Smith put it: 'Every species of animals naturally multiplies in proportion to the means of its subsistence'. So that Smith saw the secular trend of the economy as capital increasing, wages rising, and the rise in wages calling forth an increase in population:

> The liberal reward of labour, by enabling them to provide better for their children, and consequently to bring up their number, naturally tends to widen and extend those limits [the means of subsistence]... If this demand [for labour] is continually increasing, the reward of labour must necessarily encourage in such a manner the marriage and multiplications of labourers as may enable them to supply that continually increasing demand by a continually increasing population.

In this way, wages tend to settle at the minimum subsistence level for the existing population. A fall in wages below subsistence will forcibly reduce the population and hence the supply of labour, raising wages to the subsistence rate; and if wages should rise above subsistence, the 'excessive multiplication' of workers 'would soon lower it to this necessary rate'.

One of the many problems of this 'Malthusian' approach is that it assumes that human beings will not be able to act on their own to limit population growth in order to preserve a newly achieved standard of living.[22]

In addition to Smith's erroneous Malthusian view that long-run wage rates are at the means of subsistence, he also introduced into economics the unfortunate fallacy that wages, at least in the shorter run, are determined by the relative 'bargaining power' of employers and workers. It was a simple leap from that position to the view that employers have greater bargaining power than workers, thus setting the stage for later pro-union propagandists claiming erroneously that unions can raise overall wage rates throughout the economy.

In his view of rent, Smith characteristically held several unintegrated views running side by side. On the one hand, as we have seen, rent is demanded by landlords who 'reap where they have never sowed'. Why are they able to collect such a rent? Because, now that land has become private property, the labourer 'must pay for the licence' to cultivate the land and 'must give to the landlord a portion of what his labour either collects or produces'. Smith concludes that 'the rent of land therefore...is naturally a monopoly price', since he regards private property in land in the same category as monopolization. Surely, socialist and Henry Georgite calls for land nationalization found here their fundamental inspiration. Smith also sensibly points out that rent will vary according to superior fertility and location of the land. Furthermore, as we have indicated, he attributes rent to the 'powers of nature', which supposedly earns an extra return in agriculture as compared to other occupations.

Smith is also inconsistent on whether land rent is included in cost. At various points he includes land rent in cost and therefore as an alleged determinant of long-run price. On the other hand, he also asserts that high or low rents are the effect of high or low product prices and that since the supply of land is fixed, the full incidence of taxes upon rent will fall on land rather than being shifted. All these inconsistencies can be cleared up if we regard all costs as determined by expected future selling prices, and individual costs to be the opportunity foregone to contribute to expected productive revenue elsewhere. More specifically, while costs do not determine price directly, they do limit supply, and in this sense every expenditure, whether on rent or elsewhere, is definitely a part of cost.

But as we have seen, the greatest of the many defects in Smith's theory was his totally discarding Cantillon's and Turgot's brilliant analysis of the entrepreneur. It was as if these great eighteenth century Frenchmen had never written. Smith's analysis rested solely on the capitalist investing 'stock' and on his labour of management and inspection; the very idea of the entrepreneur as a risk-bearer and forecaster was thrown away and, again, classical economics was launched into another lengthy blind alley. If, of course, one persists in fixing one's vision on the never-never land of long-run equilibrium, where all profits are low and equal and there are no losses, there is no point in talking about entrepreneurship at all.

The political implications of this omission were also not lost on nineteenth century socialists. For if there is no role for entrepreneurial profits in a market economy, then any existing profits must be 'exploitative', far more so than the low, uniform rate existing in long-run equilibrium.

The perceptive Scottish historian of economics, Alexander Gray, wrote of Smith's theory of wages that he presented several theories 'not wholly consistent with each other, [which] lie together in somewhat uneasy juxtaposition'. Gray then slyly added that it is a 'tribute to the greatness of Smith that all schools of thought may trace to him their origin and inspiration'. Other words for such inchoate confusion, for what Gray referred to aptly as a 'vast chaos', come more readily to mind.

16.7   The theory of money

We have seen that David Hume's famous elucidation of the price-specie-flow mechanism in international monetary relations, though attractively written, was itself a deterioration from the pioneering and highly sophisticated analysis of Richard Cantillon. It was, however, better than nothing. Yet, as Jacob Viner put it, 'One of the mysteries of the history of economic thought' is that Adam Smith, though a close friend of Hume for many years, included none of the Humean analysis in his *Wealth of Nations*.[23] Instead, Smith propounded the primitive and erroneous view that every country will have as much specie as it allegedly needs to circulate trade, the surplus overflowing 'channels of circulation...to seek that profitable employment which it cannot find at home'. Gone is any reference whatever to the causal nexus between the quantity of money, price levels, and balances of trade. The mystery deepens when we realize that *The Wealth of Nations* is a grave deterioration even from Smith's own Lectures of over a dozen years earlier. For in those Lectures, unpublished in Smith's own day, we find a clear presentation and summary of the Humean analysis.

Thus, in his Lectures Smith had written that Hume proves

> that when ever money is accumulated beyond the proportion of commodities in any country, the price of goods will necessarily rise; that this country will be undersold in the foreign market, and consequently the money must depart into other nations; but on the contrary whenever the quantity of money falls below the

proportion of goods, the price of goods diminishes, the country undersells others in foreign markets, and consequently money returns in great plenty. Thus money and goods will keep near about a certain level in every country.[24]

Even Smith's modern admirers despair of his confused and scattered, as well as hopelessly inadequate, theory of money and theory of international monetary relations.[25] Professor Petrella tries to explain Smith's later rejection of Hume's specie-flow-price mechanism as a reaction to Hume's giving hostage to the alleged employment benefits of mercantilistic increases in the quantity of money, benefits which Smith was anxious to deny. Petrella cites in support a sentence critical of Hume following the passage from the Lectures just quoted: 'Mr Hume's reasoning is exceedingly ingenious. He seems, however, to have gone a little into the notion that public opulence consists in money...'. But here Petrella attempts to prove too much, for why couldn't Smith simply continue to adopt the specie-flow-price mechanism and then repeat or elaborate on his criticisms of Hume's position, demonstrating the latter's inconsistency?[26]

It seems clear, in contrast, that the mystery of Smith's abandonment of the price-specie-flow mechanism can be solved if we realize that this particular deterioration in his economic analysis was not unique. Indeed, we have noted a similar fatal deterioration in his value theory from the time of the Lectures to the *Wealth of Nations*. It seems plausible that the cause of the decay, in each case, was the same: Smith's shift of concentration from the real world of market prices to the exclusive vision of long-run 'natural' equilibrium. The shift from the real world of market process to focusing on equilibrium states made Smith impatient with the process analysis that was the hallmark and the merit of the specie-flow approach. Instead, Smith treats only a world of pure specie money, and assumes that all countries are always in equilibrium. Moreover, any departures from worldwide monetary equilibrium are eradicated swiftly, leaving the world in a virtually perpetual equilibrium state.[27]

Smith's focus on the long run, in fact, led him to apply his general labour cost-of-production theory of value to the value of money. The value of money, i.e. the value of the metal commodity gold or silver, then becomes the embodiment of the labour cost of producing it. In that way, Smith attempted to integrate the values of money and other goods by assimilating all of them into a labour-cost theory. Thus, Smith wrote, in *The Wealth of Nations*:

Gold and silver, however, like every other commodity, vary in their value, are sometimes cheaper and sometimes dearer... The quantity of labour which any particular quantity of them can purchase or command, or the quantity of other goods which it will exchange for, depends always upon the fertility or barrenness of the mines... The discovery of the abundant mines of America reduced, in the sixteenth

century, the value of gold and silver in Europe to about a third of what it had been
before. As it cost less labour to bring those metals from the mine to the market, so
when they were brought thither they could purchase or command less labour...

Even those few economists who laud Adam Smith as really adopting the
Humean price-specie-flow mechanism concede that he dropped this approach
when considering a mixed monetary system including bank notes or paper
money.[28] Indeed, even though Smith occasionally adhered to the quantity
theory of specie money in its effects on prices, he here throws it over altogether and asserts that convertible bank notes are always equal in value to
gold and hence their quantity will always remain the same. Any increase of
bank notes beyond the total of specie will 'overflow' the 'channel of circulation' and therefore return to the banks in what was later called a 'reflux', in
exchange for specie which immediately flows out of the country. Smith
therefore explicitly denies that an increase in bank notes can raise the prices
of commodities. But why did Smith abandon the quantity theory completely
here, in exchange for such nonsense? Plausibly, because of Smith's need to
integrate all value theory on the basis of the labour cost of production. If he
ever conceded that an increase in the quantity of paper money could affect
values, even temporarily, then Smith would have had to admit an enormous
hole in his labour-cost theory. For the 'labour cost' involved in printing paper
money obviously bears no relation whatever to the exchange value of that
money. Therefore, paper money, including bank paper, had to be assimilated
tightly to the value of specie.

Adam Smith wrote in an eighteenth century Britain where virtually all his
predecessors had denounced the new institution of fractional-reserve banking
as inflationary and illegitimate. His friend David Hume (1752) had called for
the radical repudiation of this institution on behalf of 100 per cent specie-
reserve banking. Other important writers had taken the same position, including Jacob Vanderlint (d. 1740) in his *Money Answers All Things* (1734), and
Joseph Harris (1702–64), master of the Royal Mint, in his *An Essay Upon
Money and Coins* (1757–58). Harris had stated that banks were 'convenient'
so long as they 'issued no bills without an equivalent in real treasure', but
that their increases of credit beyond that limit are inflationary and will eventually endanger the banks' own credit.

If Smith had continued in his predecessors' footsteps, his commanding
authority and prestige might have been able to bring about a fundamental
reform of the fractional-reserve banking system. But, unfortunately, Smith, in
his need to meld all monetary theory into a long-run labour cost of production approach, abandoned the quantity theory and the specie-flow-price mechanism in his discussion of paper money. He thus set economic theory once
again on an erroneous and fateful road by embracing the institution of frac-

tional-reserve credit. No longer holding such credit to be inflationary, Smith went on to adumbrate one of the major defences of paper money, still held to this day: that gold and silver are mere 'dead stock', accomplishing nothing. The banks, by substituting their paper notes for specie, 'enable the country to convert a great deal of this dead stock into active and productive stock...'.

Indeed, so far did Adam Smith rhapsodize about paper money that he likened its accomplishments to providing a sort of highway through the air:

> The gold and silver money which circulates in any country may very properly be compared to a highway, which, while it circulates and carries to market all the grass and corn of the country, produces itself not a single pile of either. The judicious operations of banking, by providing...a sort of waggon-way through the air, enable the country to convert, as it were, a great part of its highways into good pastures and cornfields, and thereby to increase considerably the annual produce of its land and labour.

Adam Smith failed to realize that the stock of gold and silver was far from 'dead'; on the contrary, it performed the vital function of being a money commodity, among other functions providing to every member of society an insurance against paper money inflation, whether launched by government or banks. The stock of gold, in short, performs a 'store of value' service which Smith totally overlooks. Smith's critique of specie as 'dead stock' also stems from his belief that money is not a commodity serving as a medium of exchange, but a claim, a sign, a 'voucher to purchase'. The French economist Charles Rist is justly highly critical of the dead stock approach and its influence on later generations:

> this idea was seized upon with extraordinary alacrity and found high favour...it dominated the thought of English writers in the nineteenth century. The belief that the use of metallic money is a retrograde and costly system, to be discouraged by all possible means, is firmly fixed in British thought on currency and banking. The use of the cheque and the bank-note was for a long time regarded only from this point of view. These two instruments were considered merely as means of economizing money; the idea was taken as the guide to the country's currency policy, and the most disastrous conclusions were drawn from it.[29]

16.8 The myth of *laissez-faire*

If, then, Adam Smith contributed nothing of value to economic thought; if, in fact, he introduced numerous fallacies, including the labour theory of value, and thereby caused a significant deterioration of economic thought from previous French and British economists of the eighteenth century; did he make any positive contribution to economics? A common answer is that the significance of the *Wealth of Nations* was political rather than analytic: that his great achievement was to initiate and take the lead in the advocacy of free trade, free markets, and *laissez-faire*. It is true that Smith articulated the political–economic sentiments of his day. As Joseph Schumpeter wrote: 'Those who extolled A. Smith's work as an epoch-making, original achievement were, of course, thinking primarily of the *policies* he advocated...' Smith's views, Schumpeter added, 'were not unpopular. They were in fashion.' In addition, Schumpeter shrewdly noted that Smith was very much a 'judiciously diluted' Rousseauan in his eighteenth century egalitarianism: 'Human beings seemed to him to be much alike by nature, all reacting in the same simple ways to very simple stimuli, differences being due mainly to different training and different environments.'[30]

But while Schumpeter's explanation of Smith's vast popularity[31] – that he was a plodder in tune with the *Zeitgeist* – holds part of the truth, it still scarcely accounts for the way in which Smith swept the board, blotting out general knowledge of all previous and contemporary economists. This puzzle will be examined further in the next chapter. For the mystery of Smith's total triumph deepens when we realize that he scarcely originated *laissez-faire* thought: as we have seen, he was merely in an eighteenth century tradition flourishing in Scotland and especially in France. Why then were these preceding economists, analytically far superior to Smith and also in the *laissez-faire* framework, so readily forgotten?[32]

Smith's greatest achievement has generally been supposed to be the enunciation of the way in which the free market guides its participants to pursue the good of the consumers by following their own self-interest. As Smith wrote in perhaps his most famous passage: A man

> will be more likely to prevail if he can interest their self-love in his favour, and show that it is for their own advantage to do for him what he requires of them... It is not from the benevolence of the butcher, the brewer, or the baker, that we expect our dinner, but from their regard to their own interest. We address ourselves, not to their humanity, but to their self-love, and never talk to them of our own necessities but of their advantages.

And in an equally famous passage bringing out the general principles of this point:

> As every individual, therefore, endeavours as much as he can both to employ his capital in the support of...industry, and so to direct that industry that its produce may be of the greatest value; every individual necessarily labours to render the annual revenue of the society as great as he can. He generally, indeed, neither intends to promote the public interest, nor knows how much he is promoting it... (B)y directing that industry in such a manner as its produce may be of the greatest value, he intends only his own gain, and he is in this, as in many other cases, led by an invisible hand to promote an end which was no part of his intention.

Smith goes on to caution wisely against alleged aims to promote the 'public good' directly:

> Nor is it always the worse for the society that it was no part of it. By pursuing his own interest he frequently promotes that of the society more effectually than when he really intends to promote it. I have never known much good done by those who affected to trade for the public good.

Hostile critics of *laissez-faire* have latched on to Smith's terminology of the 'invisible hand' to indict him for ostensibly beginning his analysis with a mystical and therefore flagrantly unscientific *a priori* assumption that Providence manipulates people for everyone's good 'by an invisible hand'. Actually, Smith was simply engaging in an *a posteriori* conclusion from his scientific analysis, and from the free market analysis generally, that pursuit of self-interest on the market leads to advancing the interest of all. Similar pursuits in government by no means lead to the same harmonious and happy result, Smith being alive to the pernicious consequences of government's creation of monopolies and its conferring privileges on special interest groups. Smith, a religious man, was simply expressing his quite justified wonderment at the harmonizing influence of the free market, and his 'by an invisible hand' was a metaphor which contained an implicit 'as if' before his use of the phrase.

Despite the undoubted importance of these passages, however, Adam Smith's championing of *laissez-faire* was scarcely consistent. In the first place, Smith retreated from the absolutist, natural law position that he had set forth in his ethical work, *The Theory of Moral Sentiments* (1757). In this book, free interaction of individuals creates a harmonious natural order which government interference can only cripple and distort. In *Wealth of Nations*, on the other hand, *laissez-faire* becomes only a qualified presumption rather than a hard-and-fast rule, and the natural order becomes imperfect and to be followed only 'in most cases'. Indeed, it is this deterioration of the case for *laissez-faire* that German scholars were to label *Das AdamSmithProblem.*

Indeed, the list of exceptions Smith makes to *laissez-faire* is surprisingly long. His devotion to the militarism of the nation-state, for example, induced him to take the lead in the pernicious modern view of excusing any government intervention that might plausibly be labelled for 'the national defence'. On that basis, Smith supported the navigation acts, that bulwark of British mercantilism and systemic subsidy for British shipping. One of Smith's reservations about the division of labour, indeed, is that it leads to a decay of the 'martial spirit', and Smith goes on at length about the decay of the martial spirit in modern times, and about the great importance of restoring and sustaining it. '(T)he security of every society must always depend, more or less, upon the martial spirit of the great body of the people.' It was an anxiety to see government foster such a spirit that led Smith into another important deviation from *laissez-faire* principle: his call for government-run education. It is also important, opined Smith, to have governmental education in order to inculcate obedience to it among the populace – scarcely a libertarian or *laissez-faire* doctrine. Wrote Smith:

> An instructed and intelligent people besides are always more decent and orderly than an ignorant and stupid one. They feel themselves, each individually, more respectable, and more likely to obtain the respect of their lawful superiors, and they are therefore more disposed to respect those superiors. They are...less apt to be misled into any wanton or unnecessary opposition to the measures of government.

In addition to navigation acts and public education, Adam Smith advocated the following forms of government intervention in the economy:

- Regulation of bank paper, including the outlawing of small denomination notes – after allowing fractional-reserve banking.
- Public works – including highways, bridges and harbours, on the rationale that private enterprise would not 'have the incentive' to maintain them properly(!?)
- Government coinage.
- The Post Office, on the simple grounds – which will draw a bitter laugh from modern readers – that it is profitable!
- Compulsory building of fire walls.
- Compulsory registration of mortgages.
- Some restrictions on the export of 'corn' (wheat).
- The outlawing of the practice of paying employees in kind, forcing all payment to be in money.

There is also a particularly lengthy list of taxes advocated by Adam Smith, each of which interferes in the free market. For one thing, Smith paved the way for Henry Georgism and the 'single tax' by urging higher taxes on uncultivated land, displaying his animus against the landlord. He also favoured moderate taxes on the import of foreign manufactures, and taxes on the export of raw wool – thus gravely weakening his alleged devotion to freedom of international trade.

Adam Smith's Calvinist abhorrence of luxury is also seen in his proposals to levy heavy taxes on luxurious consumption. Thus he called for heavier highways tolls on luxury carriages than on freight wagons, specifically to tax the 'indolence and vanity of the rich'. His puritanical hostility to liquor also emerges in his call for a heavy tax on distilleries, in order to crack down on hard liquor and induce people to drink instead the 'wholesome and invigorating liquor of beer and ale'. His devotion to ale, however, was minimal, for Smith also advocated a tax on the retail sale of all liquor in order to discourage the multiplication of small alehouses.

And finally, Adam Smith advocated the soak-the-rich policy of progressive income taxation.

Perhaps Smith's most flagrant violation of *laissez-faire* was his strong advocacy of rigid usury laws, a sharp contrast to the opposition to such laws by Cantillon and Turgot. Smith did not indeed wish to adhere to the medieval prohibition of all credit. Instead, he urged an interest rate ceiling of 5 per cent, slightly above the rate charged to prime borrowers: a 'price which is commonly paid for the use of money by those who can give the most undoubted security'. His reasoning followed his predilection, as we have already noted, for hostility to free market time-preferences between consumption and saving. Driven by Calvinist hostility to luxurious consumption, Smith tried to skew the economy in favour of more 'productive labour' in capital investment and less in consumption. By forcing interest rates below the free market level, Smith hoped to channel credit into the sober hands of prime borrowers, and away from credit into the hands of speculators and of 'prodigal' consumers. As Professor West admits, Adam Smith condemned the demand for loans by 'prodigals and projectors', in which the prodigal 'dissipates in the maintenance of the idle, what was destined for the support of the industrious'. In that way, the ceiling on interest rates, as West notes, 'would reallocate credit into the most productive hands'.

Yet, West, a free market adherent who is generally an uncritical admirer of Smith, then maintains that Smith was curiously inconsistent in not realizing, in this one case, that price controls would create a greater shortage of credit. Here, West echoes the brilliant essay *The Defence of Usury* by the Smithian Jeremy Bentham in accusing the master of inconsistency in his usual advocacy of the free market. But, as Professor Garrison indicates in his comment on West, Smith knew only too well what he was doing. In urging a reallocation of credit by the government 'into the most productive hands', Adam Smith was precisely *trying* to create a shortage of credit for consumers and speculators, and thereby to channel credit into the hands of sober, low-risk businessmen. As Garrison points out,

> Smith was not interested in reducing the cost of borrowing with his credit controls. He was trying to reduce the amount of funds borrowed for certain categories of loans. And his anti-usury scheme was well suited for this. Smith notes that money is lent to the government at three percent, and to sound businessmen at four, and four and a half. Only 'prodigals and projectors', people who are most likely to 'waste and destroy' capital, would be willing to borrow at eight or ten percent. Smith therefore recommended an interest ceiling at five percent. This policy was not aimed at allowing the prodigals and projectors to obtain funds

more cheaply, but at preventing them from obtaining any funds at all. These funds
would be diverted, then, into the hands of those who are more future oriented.

In short, Smith knew full well that a low interest ceiling would not benefit
marginal borrowers by providing them with cheap credit. He knew that usury
laws would dry up credit altogether for marginal borrowers and he sought
precisely that result. For Smith virtually embraced the idea of zero time-
preference as the ideal – the non-time-preference of his mythical 'impartial
spectator' – and, concludes Garrison, 'It is not difficult to see how Smith's
standard of zero time preference coupled with his awareness of sharply
positive time preferences could lead him to make the very policy recommen-
dations that West found to be surprising. He sought to reallocate resources
away from the present and toward the future...'[33]

Perhaps most important of all, how do we square Smith's alleged role as
champion of free trade and *laissez-faire* with his spending the last 12 years of
his life as a commissioner of Scottish customs, cracking down on smugglers
violating Britain's extensive mercantilist laws and evading import taxes? Did
he treat the job as a sinecure? No: recent studies show that his role as a top
enforcer of mercantilist laws and tariffs was active and hard-working. Was he
driven by penury? Hardly, since, with his great reputation, he probably could
have commanded an equivalent sum in a top academic post.[34] Did he suffer
from qualms of conscience? Apparently not, since he not only approached his
job with enthusiasm, but was also particularly, vigilant and hard-nosed in
trying to enforce the onerous restrictions and tariffs to the hilt.

Edwin West, an inveterate admirer of Smith as an alleged devotee of
laissez-faire, speculates that he entered the high customs bureaucracy as a
practical free trader trying to remove or lighten the customs burden on the
Scottish economy. But as Anderson et al. reply, 'If Smith had been deeply
concerned with reducing the cost to the economy resulting from customs, the
most effective strategy at the level of his responsibilities would have been to
reduce the efficiency of the enforcement apparatus. But Smith did not do
this'.[35] On the contrary, Smith showed no appreciation whatever of the social
and economic value of the underground economy or the great British tradition of smuggling. Instead, he tried his best to make enforcement of the
mercantilist laws and burdens as efficient as possible. Neither did he use his
high post to promote reforms in the direction of free trade. On the contrary,
his major 'reform' proposal as commissioner was for compulsory automatic
warehousing of all imports, which would have made inspection and enforcement far easier for the customs officials, at the expense of the smugglers,
international trade and the nation's economy. As Anderson et al. note, 'Smith
was proposing a reform that was likely to increase the costs to the economy
from customs duties'. And finally Smith's correspondence as commissioner

shows no particular desire to cut tariffs or restrictions. In contrast, his dominant emotion seems to have been pride at cracking down on smugglers and thereby increasing government revenue. In December 1785, he writes to a fellow customs official that

> it may, perhaps, give the Gentleman pleasure to be informed that the net revenue arising from the Customs in Scotland is at least four times greater than it was seven or eight years ago. It has been increasing rapidly these four or five years past; and the revenue of this year has overleaped by at least one half the revenue of the greatest former year. I flatter myself it is likely to increase still further.[36]

Well, happy day! *This* from an alleged champion of *laissez-faire*!?

16.9 On taxation

Over the centuries, economists have contributed little of interest or value on the subject of taxation. In addition to describing forms of taxation, they have generally approached the subject from the point of view of the state as a kindly or not so kindly despot, seeking to maximize its revenue while doing minimum harm to the economy. There are variations among the different schools, but the general thrust is the same. Thus, the cameralists (see Chapter 17) were frankly interested solely in maximizing state revenue, as were the French absolutists; the more liberal economists admonished the government to keep tax rates lower than had been customary.

The more liberal economists have tried to strictly demarcate functions which government should and should not perform. By ruling out various kinds of government intervention, the thrust, other things being equal, is to reduce total government taxation and spending. But they have offered us very few guidelines beyond that. If, for example, as in the case of Smith, the government is supposed to supply public works, *how many* should it provide and how much should be spent? There have been almost no preferred criteria, then, for total spending or for overall levels of taxation.

There has been more discussion of the *distribution* of taxation. That is, given, from some arbitrary external dictate, that the *total level* of taxation should be a certain amount, T, there has been considerable discussion of how T should be distributed. In short, the two main problems of taxation are: *how much* should be levied, and *who* should pay? and there has been considerably more thought devoted to the latter question.

But none of this has been very satisfactory. Again, the basic point of view seems to be that of a highwayman or slavemaster, interested in extracting the maximum from his charges while keeping their complaints as minimal as possible. In the discussion in eighteenth century France, there were two favourite tax proposals: proportional income or property taxation, or, as in the case of Marshall Vauban and later the physiocrats, a single tax on land, revenue to a fixed and visible source of income that seems fixed, unchanging, and therefore easy for the state to get at.

Adam Smith's discussion of taxation in the *Wealth of Nations* became, like the rest of his work, a classic setting the central focus for economic thought from that point on. And, like the rest of the work, it was a confused mixture of the banal and the fallacious.[37] Thus, Smith set forth four 'canons' of 'evident justice and utility' in taxation, which were to become famous from then on. Of the four, three are banal: that the tax payment be made as convenient as possible for the payer: that the cost of collection be kept to a minimum since the state does not even benefit from these levies on the taxpayer: and that the tax be certain rather than arbitrary.[38]

The substantive canon was Smith's first in the list: that tax be proportional to incomes. Thus:

> The subjects of every state ought to contribute towards the support of the government, as nearly as possible, in proportion to their respective abilities; that is, in proportion to the revenue which they respectively enjoy under the protection of the state. The expense of government to the individuals of a great nation, is like the expense of a great estate, who are all obliged in proportion to respective interests to the estate.

In the first place, this passage is hopelessly confused in presenting as if they were identical two very different criteria for justice or propriety in taxation: the 'ability-to-pay' and the 'benefit' principles. Smith maintains that people's ability to pay taxes is proportionate to income: and that benefits derived from the state are proportional in the same way. Yet he offers no justification for either of these dubious propositions.

On ability it is by no means clear that people's ability to pay – however that be defined – is proportionate to income. What, for example, of the influence of a person's relative wealth (as contrasted to income), his medical or other expenses, etc.? And one thing is certain; Adam Smith presented no arguments for this bald assertion.

The idea that one's benefit derived from the state is proportional to one's income is even shakier. How precisely do the wealthy, by virtue of that wealth, benefit proportionately from the state as compared to the poor? That would only be true if the government were *responsible* for the wealth, by means of a subsidy, monopoly grant, or some form of special privilege. If not from special privilege, then how do the rich benefit proportionately to their income? Surely not from redistributive measures, by which the state takes money from the wealthy and gives it to bureaucrats or the poor; in that case, it is the latter group who benefit and the rich who suffer from this redistribution. So who then should pay for *such* benefits? The bureaucrats and the poor? And benefits from police protection or the public schools? But surely the wealthy could far more afford to pay for private provision of these services, and therefore the rich benefit *less* than the middle class or certainly than the poor from such expenditures.

Neither would it save the theory to say that since *A*, for example, makes five times as much money as *B*, that *A* therefore benefits five times as much from 'society' and therefore should pay five times the taxes. The fact that *A* makes five times as much as *B* shows that *A*'s services are *individually* worth five times as much as *B* to his fellows on the market. Therefore, since *A* and *B* in truth benefit similarly from the existence of society, the reverse argument would be far more plausible: that the *differential* between *A*'s and *B*'s incomes is due to *A*'s superior productivity, and that 'society', if indeed it can be held to be responsible for anything specific at all, can be held responsible for their equal core incomes, below that differential. The implication of that point would be that both persons, and therefore all persons, should pay an equal tax, that is, a tax equal in absolute numbers.

Finally, whatever society's claim to part of people's incomes may be, society – the division of labour, the body of knowledge and culture, etc. – is in no sense the state. The state contributes no division of labour to the production process, and does not transmit knowledge or carry civilization forward. Therefore, whatever each of us may owe to 'society', the state can hardly claim, any more than any other group in society, to be surrogate for all social relations in the country.

16.10 Notes

1. *Das AdamSmithProblem* referred to only one of the numerous contradictions and puzzles in the Adam Smith saga: the big gap between the natural rights–*laissez-faire* views of his *Theory of Moral Sentiments*, and the much more qualified views of his later and decisively influential *Wealth of Nations*.

2. In an illuminating article on 'Adam Smith's Acknowledgements', Professor Salim Rashid writes: 'It is stated by Schumpeter that this [not acknowledging one's sources] was the practice of the age. This is incorrect. If we turn to some of the works quoted in the *Wealth of Nations*, such as Charles Smith's *Tracts* on the Corn-Trade or John Smith's *Memoirs* on Wool, we shall find them scrupulous in acknowledging their intellectual debts. Among Smith's contemporaries, Gibbon is well-known for the care with which he provided references and the same is true of the best-known agricultural writer of Smith's day, Arthur Young'. Salim Rashid. 'Adam Smith's Acknowledgements: Neo-Plagiarism and the Wealth of Nations', *Journal of Libertarian Studies*, 9 (Autumn 1990), p. 11.

3. The first and most consistent piece of modern Smith revisionism came a year earlier in two excellent and illuminating articles by Emil Kauder: 'Genesis of the Marginal Utility Theory: From Aristotle to the End of the Eighteenth Century', in J. Spengler and W. Allen (eds), *Essays in Economic Thought* (Chicago: Rand McNally and Co., 1960), pp. 277–87; and 'The Retarded Acceptance of the Marginal Utility Theory', *Quarterly Journal of Economics* (Nov. 1953), pp. 564–75. But Schumpeter's revision was far more influential.

4. Unfortunately, since the mid-1970s celebration of Smith's bicentennial, a counter-revisionist trend has set in to try to restore the hagiographical attitude dominant before the 1950s. See our bibliographical essay below.

5. For a new view of Smith's tenure at the customs house based on original investigation into the handwritten minutes of the board of customs commissioners, 1778–90, as well as

on Smith's numerous letters to customs collectors at the outports, see the important article of Gary M. Anderson, William F. Shughart II and Robert D. Tollison, 'Adam Smith in the Customhouse', *Journal of Political Economy*, 93 (August 1985), pp. 740–59.

6. Griping about alienation had begun with the influential *Essay on the History of Civil Society* (1767), written by Smith's friend Adam Ferguson. A similar theme, however, had appeared in Smith's unpublished Glasgow lectures of 1763. On Ferguson's influence, see M.H. Abrams, *Natural Supernaturalism* (New York: W.W. Norton, 1971), pp. 220–21, 508.

7. Quoted in Ronald Hamowy, 'Adam Smith, Adam Ferguson, and the Division of Labour', *Economica* (August 1968), p. 253.

8. Edwin Cannan, *A History of the Theories of Production and Distribution in English Political Economy From 1776 to 1848* (2nd ed., London: P.S. King & Son, 1903), pp. 23–4.

9. Cannan, op. cit., note 8, p. 24.

10. Ingrid Hahne Rima, *Development of Economic Analysis* (3rd ed., Homewood, Ill.: Richard D. Irwin, 1978), p. 79.

11. Edwin G. West, *Adam Smith* (New Rochelle, NY: Arlington House, 1969), p. 173.

12. Also see Nathan Rosenberg, 'Adam Smith on Profits – Paradox Lost and Regained', *Journal of Political Economy*, 82 (Nov./Dec. 1974), pp. 1187–9.

13. J.A. Schumpeter, *History of Economic Analysis* (New York: Oxford University Press, 1954), pp. 324–5.

14. We cannot use the excuse that Smith had developed the utility–scarcity analysis in his lectures and therefore saw no need to repeat it in the *Wealth of Nations*. For the lectures were unpublished and remained so until almost the twentieth century.

15. Paul H. Douglas, 'Smith's Theory of Value and Distribution', in J.M. Clark et al., *Adam Smith, 1776–1926* (Chicago: University of Chicago Press, 1928), p. 80.

16. Emil Kauder, 'Genesis of the Marginal Utility Theory from Aristotle to the End of the Eighteenth Century', in Spengler and Allen, op. cit., note 3, p. 282. Also see H.M. Robertson and W.L. Taylor, 'Adam Smith's Approach to the Theory of Value', in ibid., pp. 293–4.

17. John Locke (1632–1704), the great late seventeenth century English libertarian political theorist, is often erroneously held to have originated the labour theory of value. Actually, Locke was discussing a far different problem from the determination of price. In the first place, he championed the idea of private property in land to the original homesteaders, who took unused land out of the common by 'mixing their labour' with the soil. This is a labour theory of the proper origin of private property rather than a labour theory of value. Second, Locke is trying to demonstrate the unimportance of land – supposedly originally communal – as compared to the importance of human energy and production in determining the value of products or resources. Locke asks us to compare an unused piece of communal land with the difference made by labour in tilling the soil and transforming it into consumer goods. Here Locke is certainly correct in highly valuing the input of human energy, which here includes the creation and the collaboration of capital goods as well as the narrow modern meaning of 'labour'. Human energy, or 'labour' in the broadest sense, has certainly made the crucial difference in the march upwards from penury and barbarism to modern civilization. But this is no 'labour theory of value' in the sense of determining price.

18. Thus Ricardo, following and clarifying Smith, asserted that 'The estimation in which different qualities of labor are held comes soon to be adjusted in the market with sufficient precision for all practical purposes'. And Marx declared that 'the different proportions in which different sorts of labour are reduced to unskilled labour as their standard are established by a social process which goes on behind the backs of the producers'. Cited in Douglas, op. cit., note 15, p. 82n.

19. Douglas, op. cit., note 15, p. 95. Similarly, the astute Alexander Gray wrote that 'through Ricardo, his [Smith's] cost-of-production theory and his emphasis on labour as the source of all value, became one of the cornerstones of the Marxian structure. Indeed, it is a commonplace that Scientific Socialism was arrived at by carrying classical English politi-

cal economy to its logical conclusions'. Alexander Gray, *Adam Smith* (London: The Historical Association, 1948), p. 24.

20. Douglas, op. cit., note 15, pp. 102–3.
21. H.M. Robertson and W.L. Taylor, 'Adam Smith's Approach to the Theory of Value', in Spengler and Allen, op. cit., note 3, p. 301.
22. For a more elaborate critique, see our discussion of Malthus and Malthusianism below (Chapter 17).
23. Jacob Viner, *Studies in the Theory of International Trade* (New York: Harper & Bros, 1937), p. 87.
24. Adam Smith, *Lectures on Justice, Police, Revenue and Arms* (1896, New York: Kelley & Millman, 1956), p. 197.
25. Thus, Douglas Vickers writes, in a volume generally devoted to Smithian apologetics: '...in the matter of the theory of money *The Wealth of Nations* does not deserve very high praise. In the *Wealth of Nations* the theory of money resides at a relative nadir in the swings of its long historical development. Deeper analysis and more extended argument occurred on both sides of the 1776 divide'. Douglas Vickers, 'Adam Smith and the Status of the Theory of Money', in A. Skinner and T. Wilson (eds), *Essays on Adam Smith* (Oxford: The Clarendon Press, 1975), p. 484. Also see W.L. Taylor, *Francis Hutcheson and David Hume as Predecessors of Adam Smith* (Durham, NC: Duke University Press, 1965), p. 132.
26. See Frank Petrella, 'Adam Smith's Rejection of Hume's Price-Specie-Flow Mechanism: A Minor Mystery Revealed', *Southern Economic Journal*, 34 (Jan. 1968), pp. 365–74.
27. Oddly enough, Professor Eagly, in his article allegedly rehabilitating Smith as an adherent of the Humean price-specie-flow theory, demonstrates just the opposite: 'To begin with, Smith assumed the existence of an international purchasing-power-parity for the monetary metals... Whenever and wherever the local price of specie in terms of commodities diverges from the international purchasing-power-parity, specie movements take place immediately. The world demand for specie thus appears to an individual nation as infinitely elastic with respect to its price in terms of commodities. Any small deviation in the domestic commodity price of specie from the international parity results in immediate specie export (or import)'. In short, Smith focuses completely on long-run equilibrium, with process dropping out altogether. Robert V. Eagly, 'Adam Smith and the Specie-Flow Doctrine'. *The Scottish Journal of Political Economy*, 17 (February 1970), p. 64. Bloomfield's apologia for Smith follows Eagly, adding encomiums to Smith's alleged modernity in anticipating Mundellian, neo-monetarist equilibrium economics. Arthur I. Bloomfield, 'Adam Smith and the Theory of International Trade', in Skinner and Wilson, op. cit., note 25, pp. 478–80. J.T. Salerno, 'The Doctrinal Antecedents of the Monetary Approach to the Balance of Payments (doctoral dissertation, Rutgers University 1980), pp. 196–208, also follows Eagly, but admits in the course of his discussion Smith's inconsistencies as well as his stress on long-run equilibrium. Wu, in his generally excellent work, admits that 'Smith said nothing about the intermediate mechanism', but then oddly proclaims that since Smith had approved Hume's analysis in the lectures, 'he could hardly have omitted entirely Hume's doctrine from his celebrated essay'. An unfortunate example of excessive reverence for one's subject leading an author to '*a priori* history', Chi-Yuen Wu, *An Outline of International Price Theories* (London: George Routledge & Sons, 1939), pp. 82–3.
28. See Eagly, op. cit., note 27, pp. 62, 66–8; Salerno, op. cit., note 27, pp. 208–211.
29. Charles Rist, *History of Monetary and Credit Theory: From John Law to the Present Day* (1940, New York: A.M. Kelly, 1966), p. 85.
30. Schumpeter, op. cit., note 13, pp. 184–6.
31. Ibid., p. 181.
32. As Schumpeter notes: the free market principle and the natural law view that the 'free interaction of individuals produces not chaos but an orderly pattern that is logically determined...had been quite clearly enunciated before, for example, by Grotius and Pufendorf'. Ibid., p. 185.
33. In his critique of Smith, Garrison notes that 'Smith's own blueprint for increasing wealth

was...self-defeating, although there is no evidence that this was ever recognized by Smith... In reality credit controls serve only to reduce the gains from intertemporal exchange. Individuals may prefer, say, one unit of a consumption good now to two or even five units of the good next year. If this preference is not allowed to be expressed in the market, then the wealth of the nation, reckoned in terms of present value, i.e. discounted at a rate corresponding to the individuals' true time preference, will actually decrease'. Roger W. Garrison, 'West's "Cantillon and Adam Smith": A Comment', *The Journal of Libertarian Studies*, 7 (Autumn 1985), pp. 291–2. Also see Edwin G. West, 'Richard Cantillon and Adam Smith: A Reappraisal' (unpublished MS), pp. 22–3.

34. See G.M. Anderson et al., 'Adam Smith in the Custom house', *Journal of Political Economy*, 93 (August 1985), p. 751n.

35. Anderson et al., op. cit., note 34, pp. 752–3.

36. Smith to George Chalmers, 22 December 1785, in Ernest C. Mossner and Ian S. Ross (eds), *The Correspondence of Adam Smith* (Oxford: The Clarendon Press, 1977), letter 251, pp. 289–90; quoted in Anderson et al., op. cit., note 34, p. 754.

37. In his canons of taxation, Smith was influenced by his teacher Hutcheson, and by his friend Henry Home, Lord Kames. Smith also may well have been influenced by Carlo Antonio Broggia's (1683–1763) *Tratto de' tributi...*(1743) and Count Pietro Verri's (1728–97) *Meditazione sull' economia politica* (1771). Broggia was a Neapolitan, possibly a retired businessman; Verri was a Milanese who served as an official in the Austrian and also the French administration in Milan.

38. Though these canons may be banal, they are by no means self-evident. Thus, see the critique in Murray N. Rothbard, *Power and Market: Government and the Economy* (Menlo Park, Calif.: Institute for Humane Studies, 1970), pp. 102–3.

17 The spread of the Smithian movement

17.1 The *Wealth of Nations* and Jeremy Bentham

Contrary to received opinion, the *Wealth of Nations* was not an instant success. Of the leading British journals of the day, the *Annual Register* gave it a brief, tepid review, while the *Gentleman's Magazine* ignored it altogether. The most influential journal, the *Monthly Review*, was ambivalent about the book. Indeed, there were no citations to the *Wealth of Nations* in articles on economics for ten years after its publication, and no one mentioned the book in Parliament until 1783. It was only in the 1780s that the book began to roll.

By 1789, the *Wealth of Nations* had already gone into five editions. Between 1783 and 1800, MPs in Britain appealed to the authority of Adam Smith 37 times. The noted English philosopher Jeremy Bentham (1748– 1832), son of a wealthy lawyer, proclaimed himself a fervent disciple of Smith. His first economic work, however, was bold enough to take his master to task for inconsistency in his own free market views by upholding usury laws. In *The Defence of Usury* (1787), Bentham pointed out that usury laws create a scarcity of credit. He also stressed that usury is what would now be called a victimless crime and therefore not really a crime at all. He had noted elsewhere, in a work on morals and legislation, that 'Usury which, if it must be an offence, is an offence committed with consent, that is, with the consent of the party supposed to be injured, cannot merit a place in the catalogue of offences, unless the consent were either unfairly obtained or unfreely; in the first case, it coincides with defraudment; in the other, with extortion'. In short, in the latter cases, no special laws against usury would be needed beyond the common legal prohibitions of force and fraud.

There are hints in Bentham's *Defence of Usury*, for the first time in Britain, that the fundamental cause of interest is time-preference. Thus Bentham refers to lending as 'exchanging present money for future', and also defines a saver as someone who has 'the resolution to sacrifice the present to [the] future'. He also understands that added to pure interest is a risk premium proportionate to the risks a creditor expects to incur in a particular loan.

Some Smith biographers have accepted the legend that Bentham's *Defence of Usury* converted Smith to the free market in lending position, but there is no real evidence to that effect. Moreover, it goes against what we know of Smith's general intractability. A Scottish friend wrote to Bentham that Smith is supposed to have told a third party that he admired the *Defence*, and that he could not complain about the treatment Bentham had accorded to Smith. The friend concluded that Smith had 'seemed to admit that you were right'. On reading this, the eager Bentham wrote to Smith asking him whether he had actually converted him to opposition to usury laws. Smith, however, received the letter virtually on his deathbed, and he could only send Bentham a copy of the *Wealth of Nations*. All this is far too flimsy an evidence of any recantation by Smith.

17.2   The influence of Dugald Stewart

Adam Smith's lectures converted the merchants of Glasgow to a free trade position, but most of his influence was spread through the *Wealth of Nations*. A triumphant *movement* of Smithian disciples really begins only with Dugald Stewart (1753–1828). Stewart was the son of Matthew Stewart, a professor of mathematics at Edinburgh University. Stewart succeeded his teacher Adam Ferguson as professor of moral philosophy at Edinburgh in 1785. Stewart made himself the leading disciple of Smith and, after the death of his master, Stewart became his first biographer, reading his *Account of the Life and Writings of Adam Smith* in 1793 to the Royal Society of Edinburgh. But by this time, Britain was in the throes of a hysterical counter-revolution – a veritable White Terror – against the French Revolution and all its ancillary liberal views. Consequently, Stewart was very circumspect in his memoir, and stayed off any controversial topics, such as the necessity for free markets.

Stewart was a highly prolific writer, and an outstanding and notable orator, but he kept his lectures as well as writings bland and acceptable to the powers-that-be. Thus, in 1794, Stewart recanted his earlier praise of the great French *laissez-faire* liberal and close friend and biographer of Turgot, Marie Jean Antoine Nicolas de Caritat, the marquis de Condorcet (1743–94). This Girondist revolutionary was too hot a topic, and Stewart also made sure to praise the British Constitution in his lectures.

By the turn of the century, however, the worst of the counter-revolutionary hysteria had blown over, and Stewart felt safe enough to propound his true classical liberal views, in books and in lectures. Hence, in 1799–1800, Stewart began to lecture on political economy in addition to his general lectures on moral philosophy. He kept giving these lectures until his retirement from Edinburgh in 1810. His 1800 lectures remained unpublished until printed, as Stewart's *Lectures on Political Economy*, in 1855.

Since the retirement of the great Thomas Reid, founder of the 'common sense' school of philosophy, from his post as professor of moral philosophy at Glasgow in the 1780s and his death a decade later, Dugald Stewart had become the only distinguished philosopher in all of Great Britain. Oxford and Cambridge were still in deep decline. With the European war blocking trips to or from the Continent, it became the fashion for bright young students all over Britain to come to Edinburgh and study under Dugald Stewart.

In this way, and clinging passionately to the Smithian line, Dugald Stewart, in the first decade of the nineteenth century, profoundly influenced and converted a host of future economists, writers and statesmen. These included James Mill, John Ramsay McCulloch, the earl of Lauderdale, Canon Sydney Smith, Henry Brougham, Francis Horner, Francis Jeffrey and the Viscount Palmerston. Economics was thereby developed as a discipline, Stewart giving rise to text writers, publicists, editors, reviewers and journalists. Typical of this illustrious group was the case of Francis Horner (1778–1817), who was born in Edinburgh, the son of a merchant, and studied under Stewart at the university. Returning from England, Horner enrolled in Stewart's new 'special course' in political economy in 1799, where he studied the *Wealth of Nations* and eagerly read Condorcet and Turgot. Horner indeed was so impressed by Turgot that he wanted to translate Turgot's writings into English. Becoming a lawyer shortly thereafter, Horner went to London and became an MP in 1806.

Inspired by Stewart's teachings, his students, Sydney Smith, Henry Brougham, Francis Jeffrey and Francis Horner founded the *Edinburgh Review* in 1802, as a new, scholarly Whig periodical devoted to educating the intelligent public in liberty and *laissez-faire*. This Whig magazine was the only economic journal in Great Britain and as such enjoyed great influence.[1]

The last decade of teaching by Dugald Stewart proved, however, to be the last great burst of the Scottish intellectual ascendancy in Great Britain. For the shades of night were rapidly closing in on the Scottish Enlightenment. In the first place, Tory repression of liberal and Whig ideas during the generation of war with France continued to be far greater in Scotland than in England. More important in the long run was the great revival of militant, evangelical Protestantism that swept western Europe and then the United States in the early years of the nineteenth century. The liberal, moderate and even deistic views that had spread throughout the western world in the last half of the eighteenth century were swept aside by resurgent Christianity. In Scotland, the result was an intellectual counter-revolution against moderate control of the Presbyterian church, and a purging of the Scottish faculties of moral philosophy and theology of moderate, sceptical, and secularist teachings. Smith and Hutcheson were now denounced in retrospect as guilty of a 'refined paganism', and with a resumption of strict theological control of the moral philosophy faculty, Scottish universities lost their pre-eminence in Britain and slid rapidly downhill, intellectually if not theologically. Neither classical liberal social philosophy nor political economy could survive in that kind of academic climate.

As a result, intellectual leadership shifted from Scotland to England, and out of academia altogether for a considerable period. Since English universities were still not hospitable to the new discipline of political economy, the locus of economic thought now shifted from Scottish academics to English businessmen, publicists and government officials. The shift was symbolized by the fact that while the *Edinburgh Review* continued to be published for decades and its nominal home was still Edinburgh, three of its four editors had moved to England within a few months of the start of the publication. One of them, who died at a very young age, was Francis Horner. Moving to

London as an attorney, Horner quickly became a Whig MP, and his expertise on monetary matters made him chairman of the famous bullion committee in 1810 which was to strike a crucial blow for hard money. There he worked closely with David Ricardo. In the first issue of the *Edinburgh Review*, Horner reviewed the famous monetary work of Henry Thornton, as well as a highly important essay by Lord King in a later issue. Horner was a member of prominent Whig clubs in London, the King of Clubs and Brooks', in both of whom he had David Ricardo as a fellow member. Horner also shared scientific interests with Ricardo, and both men were members of the board of the Geological Society of London.

Another illustration of the intellectual shift from Scotland to England is what happened to two bright young Scotsmen who studied under Stewart and were later to become major leaders in British economics. James Mill (1773–1836) was the son of a Scottish shoemaker, who studied under Stewart and was then licensed to preach in the Presbyterian ministry. Failing to find a ministerial post in the increasingly militant Calvinist climate in Scotland, Mill was obliged to move to London, where he became editor of the *Literary Journal*. Eventually, Mill found employment in the London office of the East India Company, which gave him a base to pursue his very active economic and philosophical work in his off hours. The younger John Ramsay McCulloch (1789–1864), who studied with Stewart in his last years, wrote economic articles in *The Scotsman* and the *Edinburgh Review*, and organized an economics lecture series. But despite his obvious merits, McCulloch was unable to find an academic post in Scotland, and finally moved to London to teach political economy at the newly established University of London. But after four years, he spent the rest of his life working as a financial controller in England, again writing and being active in economics in additional to his regular work.

One beneficial result of the Stewart-led sweep of Smithianism in Great Britain is that it swamped the competing strain to 'political economy', the 'political arithmeticians'. These 'political arithmeticians, or statistical collectors', as Stewart contemptuously called them, had formed a competing school in economics since the writings of Sir William Petty (1623–87) and his followers in the late seventeenth century. The arithmeticians generally scorned the classical method of arriving at economic laws deduced from broad insights into human action and the economy. Instead, in a Baconian fashion, they tried in vain to arrive at theoretical generalizations from hodge-podge collections of statistical facts. With little insight into the laws of the free market or the counterproductive nature of government intervention, the political arithmeticians tended to be mercantilists and British chauvinists, proclaiming the economic superiority of their homeland. But this school was demolished by the Smithians, first by Smith himself who declared, in the *Wealth of Nations*, that 'I have no great faith in political arithmetic', and then by Stewart, who engaged in a searching methodological critique of this allegedly 'scientific' school of thought. Stewart wrote: 'The facts accumulated by the statistical collector are merely *particular results*, which other men have seldom an opportunity of verifying or of disproving; and which...can never afford any important information'. In short, in contrast to the replicable quantitative findings of natural science, statistics of human action are mere listings of particular, non-replicable events, rather than the embodiment of enduring natural law. Stewart concluded that 'instead of appealing to political arithmetic as a check on the conclusions of political economy, it would often be more reasonable to have recourse to political economy as a check on the extravagance of political arithmetic'.

After the 1790s, then, Adam Smith held total sway over economic thought in Britain. Amidst a flourishing swarm of views, all the major protagonists in England, as we shall see below, from Bentham to Malthus to Ricardo, considered themselves devoted Smithians, often trying to systematize and clarify the admitted confusions and inconsistencies of their master.

17.3 Malthus and the assault on population

One of the first Smithian economists, and, indeed, a man who was for two decades the only professor of political economy in England, was the Rev. Thomas Robert Malthus (1766–1834). Malthus was born in Surrey, the son of a respected and wealthy lawyer and country gentleman. Malthus graduated from Jesus College, Cambridge, in 1788 with honours in mathematics and five years later became a fellow of that college. During that same year, Robert Malthus became an Anglican curate in Surrey, in the parish where he had been born.

Malthus seemed destined to lead the quiet life of a bachelor curate, when, in 1804, at nearly 40, he married and promptly had three children. The year after his marriage, Malthus became the first professor of history and political economy in England, at the new East India College at Haileybury, a post he retained until his death. All his life, Malthus remained a Smithian, and was to become a close friend, though not disciple, of David Ricardo. His only marked deviation from Smithian doctrine, as we shall see, was his proto-Keynesian worry about alleged underconsumption during the economic crisis after the end of the Napoleonic Wars.

But Malthus was, of course, far more than a Smithian academic, and he gained both widespread fame and notoriety while still a bachelor. For 'Population' Malthus became known worldwide for his famous assault on human population.

In previous centuries, in so far as writers or economists dealt with the problem at all, they were almost uniformly pro-populationists. A large and growing population was considered a sign of prosperity, and a spur to progress. The only exception, as we have seen, was the late sixteenth century Italian absolutist theorist Giovanni Botero, the first to warn that population growth is an ever-present danger, tending as it does to increase without limit, while the means of subsistence grows only slowly. But Botero lived at the threshold of great economic growth, of advances in total population as well as standards of living, and so his gloomy views got very short shrift by contemporaries or later thinkers. Indeed, absolutists and mercantilists tended to admire growing population as providing more hands for production on behalf of the state apparatus as well as more fodder for its armies.

Even those eighteenth century writers who believed that population tended to increase without limit, curiously enough *favoured* that development. This was true of the American Benjamin Franklin (1706–90), in his *Observations Concerning the Increase of Mankind and the Peopling of Countries* (1751). Similarly, the physiocrat leader, Mirabeau, in his famous *L'Ami des Hommes ou traité de la population* (*The Friend of Man or a Treatise on Population* (1756), while comparing human reproduction to that of rats – they would multiply up to the very limit of subsistence like 'rats in a barn' – yet advocated such virtually unlimited reproduction. A large population, said Mirabeau, was a boon and a source of wealth, and it was precisely *because* people will multiply like rats in a barn up to the limit of subsistence that agriculture – and hence the production of food – should be encouraged. Mirabeau had picked up the 'rats in a barn' metaphor from Cantillon, but unfortunately did not inherit Cantillon's highly sensible and sophisticated 'optimum population' realization that human beings will flexibly adjust population to standards of living, and that their non-economic values will help them decide on whatever trade-offs they may choose between a slightly larger population or a smaller population and higher standards of living.

Mirabeau's co-leader of physiocracy, François Quesnay, however, converted him to a gloomy view of the influence of the alleged tendency to unlimited population growth on standards of living. Adam Smith, Malthus's standard-bearer in economics, managed, in typically confused and contradictory fashion, at one and the same time to provide Malthus with all his ammunition for gloom-and-doom while remaining a cheerful proponent of large and growing numbers of people. For on the one hand, Smith opined that people would indeed insist on breeding up to the minimum of subsistence – the essential Malthusian doctrine. But, on the other, Smith asserted cheerfully that 'the most decisive mark of the prosperity of any country is the increase of the number of its inhabitants'.

At about the time that Adam Smith was sinking into confusion and paving the way for the unfortunate anti-population hysteria of Robert Malthus, the unheralded Abate Antonio Genovesi, the first professor of economics on the

Continent (at the University of Naples), was pointing the way to a very different solution to the population question. In his *Lezione di economia civile* (1765), this excellent utility-value theorist was reminiscent of Cantillon's insight about an 'optimum' population. Under any given conditions, he pointed out, population can either be too large or too small for optimum 'happiness' or living standards.

Robert Malthus was moved to consider the population question by wrestling in friendly and repeated argument with his beloved father, Daniel, a fellow country squire in Surrey. Daniel was a bit of a radical, and was influenced by the utopian and even communistic opinions of the day. He was a friend and great admirer of the French radical, Jean Jacques Rousseau.

The 1790s was the era of the outburst of the French Revolution, and it was a decade when ideas of liberty, equality, utopia, and revolution were very much in the air. One of the most popular and influential radical works in England was William Godwin (1756–1836)'s *Enquiry Concerning Political Justice* (1793), which was for a time the talk of England. Godwin, son and grandson of dissenting ministers, had himself been a dissenting minister when he lapsed into secularism and became a radical theorist and writer. In his utopian belief in the perfectibility of man, Godwin has been generally bracketed with the distinguished French philosopher and mathematician, Condorcet, whose great paean to optimism and progress, *Esquisse d'un tableau historique des progrès de l'esprit humain* (*Sketch for an Historical Picture of the Progress of the Human Mind*) (1794) was, remarkably, written while in hiding from the Jacobin Terror and in the shadow of his arrest and death. But the two optimists were very different. For Condorcet, close friend of Turgot and admirer of Adam Smith, was an individualist and a libertarian, a firm believer in free markets and in the rights of private property. William Godwin, on the other hand, was the world's first anarcho-communist, or rather, voluntary anarcho-communist. For Godwin, while a bitter critic of the coercive state, was an equally hostile critic of private property. But in contrast to late nineteenth century anarcho-communists such as Bakunin and Kropotkin, Godwin did not believe in the imposition of rule by a coercive commune or collective in the name of anarchistic 'no-rule'. Godwin believed, not that private property should be expropriated by force, but that individuals, fully using their reason, should voluntarily and altruistically divest themselves of all private property to any passer-by. This system of voluntary abasement, brought about by the perfectibility of human reason, would result in total equality without private property. In his voluntarism, Godwin was thus the ancestor of both the coercive communist and the individualist strains of nineteenth century anarchist thought.

In his way, however, Godwin was every bit as, and even more, appreciative of the benefits of individual freedom and a free society as was Condorcet.

He was sure that population would never grow beyond the limits of the food supply, for he was convinced that 'There is a principle in the nature of human society, by means of which everything seems to tend to its level, and to proceed in the most auspicious way, when least interfered with by the mode of regulation'.

The marquis de Condorcet, sensibly enough, was also not worried about excessive population growth wrecking he future libertarian and free market 'utopia' that he envisaged for the future of man. He was not worried because he believed that on the one hand science, technology and free markets would greatly expand the subsistence available, while reason would persuade people to limit population to numbers that could be readily sustained. William Godwin, however, was not content with this intelligent treatment of the problem. On the contrary, in the first place, Godwin worried, in proto-Malthusian fashion, that population did always tend to press on resources so as to keep living standards down to subsistence level. He believed, however, in some sort of leap in being, a New Godwinian Man, and institutions where 'reason' would instead prevail. It would prevail, in fact, by reason making man master of his passions, to such an extent that sexual passion would gradually become extinct, and advancing health would make man immortal. We would, then, have a future human race of immortal and ever-ageing adults, a utopia that seems impossibly dotty:

> The men therefore...will probably cease to propagate. The whole will be a people of men, and not of children. Generation will not succeed generation, nor truth have, in a certain degree, to recommence her career every thirty years... There will be no war, no crimes, no administration of justice, as it is called, and no government. Every man will seek, with ineffable ardour, the good of all.

William Godwin had learned of the alleged eternal pressure of population down to subsistence from Dr Robert Wallace (1697–1771), a Scottish Presbyterian minister, who had set forth his allegedly utopian government in his *Various Prospects of Mankind* (1761). Wallace's ideal utopia was a world government which imposed totalitarian communism compelling equality and eradicating private property. The state would bring up all children, and all would be taken care of. The fly in the ointment, however, the serpent in Eden, would be population growth. The marvellous conditions provided by world communism would lead to population growing so rapidly that mass misery and starvation would prevail. As Wallace lamented:

> Under a perfect government, the inconveniences of having a family would be so entirely removed, children would be so well taken care of, and every thing become so favourable to populousness, that...mankind would increase so prodigiously, that the earth would at last be overstocked, and become unable to support

its numerous inhabitants…There would not even be sufficient room for containing their bodies upon the surface of the earth.

Hence, utopian communism would have to be abandoned.

William Godwin was too ready to accept Wallace's mechanistic worry about population growth, but thought rather bizarrely that the withering away of sex would provide the cure for Wallace's problem and ensure that egalitarian anarcho-communism would prevail.

Daniel Malthus was just the sort of man to be deeply impressed by the Godwinian utopia, and he and his son Robert spent many happy hours arguing over Godwin's *Political Justice*, its second edition (1796), and his follow-up collection of essays, *The Enquirer* (1797). Robert decided to write a book clobbering these utopian fantasies once and for all, and dredged up the spectre of population growth as the inevitable rock upon which such fantasies would inevitably founder and collapse. Hence the publication in 1798 of the first edition of Malthus's immensely popular and controversial *Essay on the Principle of Population as It Affects the Future Improvement of Society*. The *Essay* went through five more editions in Malthus's lifetime, gained him the nickname of 'Population Malthus', and gave rise to literally millions of words of heated controversy.

There was virtually nothing in Malthus's *Essay* that had not been in Giovanni Botero two centuries earlier – or, for that matter, in Robert Wallace. As in Botero, all improvements in living standards are in vain, giving rise to an immediate and deadly pressure of population growth upon the means of subsistence. Once again, such mechanistic burgeoning of population can only be limited by the 'positive check' of war, famine and pestilence; supplemented by the rather weak 'preventive' check of fewer births spurred by continuing starvation ('preventive or negative' check). There is only one thing that Malthus added to the Botero model: the spurious mathematical precision of his famous statement that population tends to 'go on doubling itself every twenty-five years, or increases in a geometrical ratio', while 'the means of subsistence increase in an arithmetical ratio'.

It is not easy to see why Botero's anti-population hysteria was properly and understandably ignored in an age of joint growth in population *and* living standards, while Malthus, writing in a similar period of growth, should sweep the western world. One reason was undoubtedly the fact that Malthus set himself, with verve and self-assurance, against the highly popular and influential writings of Godwin as well as against the ideals of the French Revolution. Another was the fact that, by the time his *Essay* appeared, British intellectuals and public were turning rapidly away from the French Revolution in a burst of reaction, oppression, and continuing war against France. Malthus had the good fortune of being in tune with the latest twist of the

Zeitgeist. But a third element explained his instant renown: the spurious air of the 'scientific' that his alleged ratios gave to a doctrine in an age that was increasingly looking for models of human behaviour and its study in mathematics and the 'hard' physical sciences.

For spurious Malthus's ratios undoubtedly were. There was no proof whatever for either of these alleged ratios. The absurdly mechanistic view that people, unchecked, would breed like fruit flies, cannot be demonstrated by simply spelling out the implications of the alleged 'doubling itself every twenty-five years', e.g.:

> Taking the population of the world at any number, a thousand millions, for instance, the human species would increase in the ratio of 1, 2, 4, 8, 16, 32, 64, 128, 256, 512, &c, and subsistence as 1, 2, 3, 4, 5, 6, 7, 8, 9, 10, &c. In two centuries and a quarter, the population would be to the means of subsistence as 512 to 10.

In a few more centuries, at the same rate, the 'ratio' of population to subsistence would begin to approach infinity. This is scarcely demonstrable in any sense, certainly not by referring to the actual history of human population which, in most of Europe, remained more or less constant for centuries before the Industrial Revolution.

Still less is there proof of Malthus's proclaimed 'arithmetical ratio', where he simply assumes that the supply of food will increase by the same amount for decade after decade.

Malthus's one attempt at proof of his ratios was extraordinarily feeble. Priding himself on relying on 'experience', Malthus noted that the population of the North American colonies had increased for a long while in the 'geometric ratio' of doubling every 25 years. But this example hardly demonstrates the fearful outstripping by population of the 'arithmetically increasing' food supply. For, as Edwin Cannan astutely notes, 'This population must have been fed, and consequently the annual produce of food must also have increased in a geometrical ratio'. His example proved nothing. Cannan adds that by the sixth chapter of his *Essay*, Malthus 'seems to have had some inkling of this objection to his argument', and he tries to reply in a footnote, that 'In instances of this kind, the powers of the earth appear to be fully equal to answer all the demands for food that can be made up on it by man. But we should be led into an error, if we were thence to suppose that population and food ever really increase in the same ratio'. But since this is precisely what had happened, Malthus is clearly totally unwitting that the second sentence in this note is in flat contradiction to the first.[2]

Malthus's pessimistic conclusion about man thus contrasted with the optimism of his beloved Adam Smith as well as with Godwin. For if the inexorable pressure of population growth is always and everywhere destroying any hope of living standards being above subsistence, then the result is not only gloomy for any communist or egalitarian utopia. It provides an equally gloomy prognosis for the free market society envisioned by Smith, or, far more consistently, by Condorcet. Yet, unfortunately, in his understandable eagerness to demolish the case for egalitarian communism, Malthus threw out the baby with the bath water, and also cast an unnecessary pall on the far more rational 'utopian' prognoses of the free society and private property by Smith and especially Condorcet.

It was easy for Malthus to dismiss brusquely Godwin's absurd reliance on the demise of sex to solve the problem of over population. But his treatment of Condorcet's position was far less cogent. For the sophisticated French aristocrat had strongly implied that birth control played a major role in his optimism about the libertarian future. While modern neo-Malthusians are enthusiastic not only about birth control but also sterilization and abortion as means of family planning, the conservative Malthus drew back in horror from any hint of such measures, which he saw simply as 'vice'. Malthus denounced Condorcet's solution as

> either a promiscuous concubinage, which would prevent breeding, or...something else as unnatural. To remove the difficulty in this way, will, surely, in the opinion of most men,...destroy that virtue, and purity of manners, which the advocates of equality, and of the perfectibility of man, profess to be the end and object of their views.

A sally that might apply neatly to Godwin, but scarcely to Condorcet, for whom 'purity' was scarcely an overriding concern.

In fact, Malthus held out little hope for mankind. His one practical proposal was the gradual abolition of the Poor Law, and especially of the idea of the *right* of the poor to be supported by the state. That would discourage excessive breeding among the poor.

All in all, Schumpeter's scathing assessment of the *Essay* of 1798 was well-deserved. Malthus, he wrote, held

> that population was actually and inevitably increasing faster than subsistence and that this was the reason for the misery observed. The geometrical and arithmetical ratios of these increases, to which Malthus...seems to have attached considerable importance, as well as his other attempts at mathematical precision, are nothing but faulty expressions of this view which can be passed by here with the remark that there is of course no point whatever in trying to formulate independent 'laws' for the behavior of two interdependent quantities. The performance as a whole is deplorable in technique and little short of foolish in substance.[3]

Poor Godwin, however, unfortunately did not come to a similar assessment – at least not immediately. He was, after all, not a scholar of population theory, and he had no immediately effective reply. It took Godwin all of two decades to study the problem thoroughly and come to an effective refutation of his nemesis. In *On Population* (1820), Godwin came to the cogent and sensible conclusion that population growth is not a bogey, because over the decades the food supply would increase and the birth rate would fall. Science and technology, along with rational limitation of birth, would solve the problem.

Unfortunately, Godwin's timing could not have been worse. By 1820, the aging Godwin – along with utopianism and even the French Revolution – had been forgotten in Great Britain. His excellent rebuttal went unread and unsung, while Malthus continued to tower over all as the much admired final word on the population question.

His *Essay* being world-famous, and Godwin and Condorcet as he believed effectively disposed of, Malthus now decided to spend some years actually studying the population problem. Remarkably, Malthus's second edition of the *Essay* in 1803 (on which all five future editions were based) was a very different work. In fact, Malthus's *Essay* is one of the rare works in the history of economic thought whose second edition in effect totally contradicted the first.

The second edition incorporated the fruits of Malthus's study on population through his travels in Europe. Filled with copious statistics, the new edition was fully three times the size of the first. But that was the least of the changes. For whereas in the first edition the 'preventive check' was minor and hopeless, as well as a generally 'vicious' possibility for solution, Malthus now acknowledged that *another* negative, or preventive check, one that entailed neither vice nor misery, was a real possibility for ameliorating or even suspending the eternal pressure of population upon the food supply. This was 'moral restraint', i.e. chastity and restraint from early marriage, which was moral and not 'vicious' because it involved neither birth control nor other forms of 'irregular gratification' or 'improper acts'. Indeed, for Malthus, 'moral restraint' now became the 'most powerful' check on population of them all, more powerful even than vice or the misery and starvation of the previously dominant 'positive check'.

As a result, human beings were no longer viewed as the puppets of inexorable and gloomy forces, which could now be overcome by moral restraint and moral education. In the first edition, indeed, Malthus stood opposed to any growth of leisure or luxury in society, for such increasing ease would eliminate the extreme pressure needed to awaken naturally slothful man into working hard and maintaining maximum production. But now, his view had changed. Now, Malthus realized that if the poor were to acquire the qualities of the middle class, and hence a 'taste for the conveniences and comforts of life', they would be more likely to exercise the moral restraint necessary to maintain that way of life. As Malthus now wrote: 'It is the diffusion of luxury therefore among the mass of the people...that seems to be most advantageous'.

Malthus now emphasized another proposed moral reform in keeping with his new position: that people try to reduce the number of children by marrying at a later date. Such moral restraint, he was now convinced, entailed neither of the two dread checks of vice or misery. Alexander Gray's discussion of this theme is marked by his characteristic insight and wit:

> Contrary to the usual view as to what is involved in Malthusianism, he restricts himself to telling us not to be in too great a hurry to get married, with a special appeal to his women readers, who, 'if they could look forward with just confidence to marriage at twenty-seven or twenty-eight', should (and would) prefer to wait until then, 'however impatiently the privation might be borne by the men'. This is the voice of a dear and kindly old uncle, rather than the monster for whom Malthus has so frequently been mistaken; and it as ineffective as the advice of an uncle in such matters usually is. For even with marriage at twenty-eight there is time for a disconcerting and devastating torrent of children.[4]

Oddly enough, however, Malthus's new view was not very far removed from his enemy Godwin's invocation of 'virtue, prudence, or pride' in limiting the growth of population. Shorn of the nonsense of the withering away of sex, Godwin was now vindicated, and Malthus seemed implicitly to agree by taking the refutation of Godwin and Condorcet – who had now faded from public view – out of the title page of the second edition.

Unfortunately, however, Malthus never acknowledged any change whatever. Godwin rightly complained that Malthus had co-opted his own major criticism without credit or even acknowledging the abandonment of his own views. Malthus maintained from 1803 onwards that his thesis had not at all been changed, but only elaborated and improved. His changes were stuck into the text in passing, while he continued to place great importance upon his arbitrary ratios. His changes were evasive rather than frank; for example, in his second edition, Malthus quietly removed the self-contradictory note in which he denied that food could ever increase 'geometrically', or as much as population. In fact, he virtually admits that food has sometimes increased geometrically in 'new colonies', i.e. in North America. Instead, he now confined his self-confident assertions to prophecy – a prophecy which the growth of living standards in England proved to be wrong within his own lifetime. And yet Malthus continued to write that his ratios were self-evident, even though he conceded that it was impossible to find out what the rate of increase of 'unchecked' population would actually be. In the end, as Cannan justly declares, 'the *Essay on the Principle of Population* falls to the ground as an argument, and remains only a chaos of facts collected to illustrate the effect of laws which do not exist'.[5]

Malthus, in fact, had executed a cunning and successful tactical manoeuvre: he had introduced enough qualifications and concessions to fuzz over his argument. He and his followers could maintain the full arrogance and error of the first edition and then, if challenged, beat a clever retreat by bringing up the qualifications and asserting that Malthus had anticipated and met all the charges against him. He was able to maintain the hard-nosed position of his first edition, while being able to fall back on the cloudy concessions of his second. As Schumpeter writes: 'the new formulation made it indeed possible for adherents to this day to take the ground that Malthus had foreseen, and accounted for, practically everything opponents might say'. He adds that 'this does not alter the fact that all the theory gains thereby is orderly retreat with the artillery lost'. Unfortunately, however, neither Malthus's followers nor even many of his astute critics realized this point. And so, Malthus and his followers had ensconced themselves in the security of a theory that, regardless of the facts, could never be refuted. Or, they could fall back on what Schumpeter calls the 'horrible triviality' that *if* indeed population increased geometrically forever and food barely increased at all, then enormous crowding and misery would result.[6]

Unfortunately, Malthus's own self-serving interpretation of the changes of his second edition was adopted by nearly all his contemporaries – friends and critics alike – as well as by historians until recent years. Most of Malthus's readers, for one thing, had been swept away by the verve and panache of his first edition, and simply didn't bother reading the much longer and stodgier second. Instead, they simply and conveniently interpreted the new material as merely empirical documentation of Malthus's original thesis. Even his more thoughtful readers interpreted moral restraint as just another negative check on population, a mere refinement of the basic theory.

And so, thus protected and interpreted, Malthus's fallacious and inchoate principle of population carried the day and, adopted enthusiastically by Ricardo and his followers, was to become enshrined into British classical economics. As we shall see further in Volume II, even though Nassau W. Senior in effect devastatingly refuted Malthus, his own piety toward Malthus and his image allowed Malthusianism to remain at least officially enshrined in economic thought. It is an unfortunate story. Thus, as Schumpeter writes:

> the teaching of Malthus' *Essay* became firmly entrenched in the system of economic orthodoxy of the time in spite of the fact that it should have been, and in a sense was, recognized as fundamentally untenable or worthless by 1803... It became the 'right' view on population... which only ignorance or obliquity could possibly fail to accept – part and parcel of the set of eternal truth that had been observed once for all. Objectors might be lectured, if they were worthy of the effort, but they could not be taken seriously. No wonder that some people, utterly disgusted at this intolerable presumption, which had so little to back it, began to

loathe this 'science of economics', quite independently of class or party considerations – a feeling that has been an important factor in that science's fate ever
after.[7]

Certainly, the triumph of the Malthusian fallacy played an important role in
the common view that the science of economics itself was and is cold, hard-
hearted, excessively rational, and opposed to the lives and welfare of people.
The idea of economics being anti-human reached a bold and unforgettable
expression in Dickens's Scrooge, the caricature of a Malthusian who cackled
that poverty and starvation would be helpful in 'reducing the surplus population'.

In the last half of the nineteenth century, as Schumpeter writes, 'the interest of economists in the population question declined, but they rarely failed
to pay their respects to the shibboleth'. Then, in the early decades of the
twentieth century, at the very same time as the birth rate in the western world
began to decline sharply, economists revived their interest in Malthusian
doctrine. Schumpeter's irony was properly bitter: 'An ordinary mortal might
have thought that the fall in the birth rate…and the rapidly approaching goal
of a stationary population, should have set worrying economists at rest. But
that mortal would thereby have proved that he knew nothing about economists'. Instead, at the same time that more economists stressed Malthusianism,
others stressed precisely the reverse:

> While some of them were still fondling the Malthusian toy, others zestfully
> embraced a new one. Deprived of the pleasure of worrying themselves and of
> sending cold shivers down the spines of other people on account of the prospec-
> tive (or present) horrors of overpopulation, they started worrying themselves and
> others on account of a prospectively empty world.[8]

By the 1930s, in fact, economists and politicians were howling about the
imminence of 'race suicide', and an excessively falling birth rate. The Great
Depression, as we shall see, was blamed by some economists on a birth rate
which had started falling decades before. Governments such as France, mind-
ful also of their need for cannon fodder, gave bounties to large families.
Then, by the 1960s and 1970s, anti-population hysteria arose again, with ever
more strident calls for voluntary or even compulsory zero population growth,
and countries such as India and China experimented with compulsory sterilization or compulsory abortion. Characteristically, the height of the hysteria,
in the early 1970s, came *after* the 1970 census in the United States noted a
significant decrease in the birth rate and the beginnings of an approach
toward a stationary state of population. It was also observed that various
Third World countries were beginning to see a marked slowing of the birth
rate, a few decades after the fall in death rate due to the infusion of Western

advances in medicine and sanitation. It looked again as if people's habituation to higher living standards will lead them to lower the birth rate after a generation of enjoying the fruits of lower death rates. Population levels will, indeed, tend to adapt to maintain cherished standards of living. It looks as if Godwin was right that given freedom, individuals in society and the marketplace will tend to make the correct birth decisions.

17.4 Resistance and triumph in Germany

In contrast to Great Britain, the German-speaking countries were predictably highly resistant to the spread of Smithian views. They had been ruled, ever since the late sixteenth century, by cameralism. Cameralists, named after the German royal treasure chamber, the *Kammer*, propounded an extreme form of mercantilism, concentrating even more than their confrères in the West on building up state power, and subordinating all parts of the economy and polity to the state and its bureaucracy. Whereas mercantilist writers were generally pamphleteers scrambling for some particular form of state advantage, the cameralists were either bureaucrats in one of the 360 tyrannical German states, or else university professors advising the princes and their bureaucracy how best to maximize their revenue and power. As Albion Small put it: to the cameralists 'the object of all social theory was to show how the welfare of the state might be secured. They saw in the welfare of the state the source of all other welfare. Their key to the welfare of the state was revenue to supply the needs of the state. The whole social theory radiated from the central task of furnishing the state with ready means.'[9]

As professors, the cameralists wrote lengthy tomes cataloguing various parts of the economy and the plans the government should make for each of these parts. The cameralists lauded virtually all forms of government intervention, sometimes to the point of a collectivist welfare–warfare state. They could scarcely be called 'economists', since they had no notion of regular economic law that could reach beyond or nullify the plans of state power.

The first major cameralist was Georg von Obrecht (1547–1612), son of the mayor of Strasbourg, who went on to be a famous professor of law at the university in that town. His lectures were published posthumously (1617) by his son. In the next generation, one important cameralist was Christoph Besold (1577–1638), born in Tübingen, and later a highly influential law professor at the University of Tübingen. Besold wrote over 90 books, all in Latin, of which the *Synopsis politicae doctrinae* (1623) was the most relevant to economics. Another influential cameralist of the early seventeenth century was Jakob Bornitz (1570–1630), a Saxon who was the first systematizer of fiscal policy, and who urged close supervision of industry by the state. Another contemporary who, however, wrote later, in the middle of the seventeenth century, was Kasper Klock (1584–1655), who studied law at Marburg and Cologne and later became a bureaucrat in Bremen, Minden, and finally in Stolberg. In 1651, Klock published the most famous cameralist work to that date, the *Tractus juridico-politico-polemico-historicus de aerario.*

The most towering figure of German cameralism came shortly thereafter. Veit Ludwig von Seckendorf (1626–92), who has been called the father of cameralism, was born in Erlangen, and educated in the University of Strasbourg. He went on to become a top bureaucrat for several German states beginning with Gotha, during which he wrote *Der Teutscher Furstenstaat* (1656). This book, a sophisticated apologia for the German absolutism of the day, went through eight editions, and continued to be read in German universities for over a century. Seckendorf ended his days as chancellor at the University of Halle.

During the late seventeenth century, cameralism took firm hold in Austria. Johann Joachim Becher (1635–82), born in Speyer and alchemist and court physician at Mainz, soon became economic adviser to Emperor Leopold I of Austria, and manager of various state-owned enterprises. Becher, who strongly influenced Austrian economic policy, called for state-regulated trading companies for foreign trade, and a state board of commerce to supervise all domestic economic affairs. A pre-Keynesian, he was deeply impressed by the 'income-flow' insight that one man's expenditure is by definition another man's income, and he called for inflationary measures to stimulate consumer demand. His well-known work was *Politischer Discurs* (1668). Schumpeter described Becher as 'brimming over with plans and projects', but some of these plans did not pan out, as Becher ended up fleeing from the wrath of his creditors. Apparently, his own 'consumer demand' had been stimulated to excess.[10] Becher's brother-in-law, Philipp Wilhelm von Hornigk (1638–1712), was another Mainzer who became influential in Austria. He studied at Ingolstadt, practised law in Vienna, and then entered the government, his Austrian chauvinist tract, *Österreich über Alles, wann es nur will* (*Austria Over All, If She Only Will*) (1684) proving highly popular. Von Hornigk's central theme was the importance of making Austria self-sufficient, cut off from all trade. A third contemporary German cameralist in Austria was Wilhelm Freiherr von Schröder (1640–88). Born in Königsberg and a student of law at the University of Jena, Schröder also became influential as an adviser to Emperor Leopold I of Austria. Schröder managed a state factory, was court financial councillor in Hungary, and set forth his views in his *Fürstliche Schatz und Rentkammer* (1686). Schröder was an extreme advocate of the divine right of princes. His cameralism emphasized the importance of speeding the circulation of money, and of having a banking system that could expand the supply of notes and deposits.

The system of cameralism was set in concrete in Germany by the mid-eighteenth century work of Johann Heinrich Gottlieb von Justi (1717–71).

Justi was a Thuringian who studied law at several universities, and then taught at Vienna and at the University of Göttingen. He then went to Prussia to become director of mines, superintendent of factories, and finally administrator of mines in Berlin.

Justi's work was the culmination of cameralism, including and incorporating all its past tendencies, and emphasizing the importance of comprehensive planning for a welfare state. Characteristically, Justi emphasized the vital importance of 'freedom', but freedom turned out to be merely the opportunity to obey the edicts of the bureaucracy. Justi also stressed the alleged 'alienation' of the worker in a system of factories and an advanced division of labour. Among his numerous works, the most important were *Staatswirthschaft* (1755), the *System des Finanzwesens* (1766), and his two-volume *Die Grundfeste zu der Macht und Glückseeligkeit der Staaten* (*The Groundwork of the Power and Welfare of States*) (1760–61). Justi, however, came a cropper on his own welfare in the welfare state and over his own unwillingness to obey the laws of the realm. Because of irregularities in his accounts as administrator of the Prussian mines, Justi was thrown into jail, where he died.

The other towering figure of eighteenth century German cameralism was a follower of Justi, Baron Joseph von Sonnenfels (1732–1817). Born in Moravia, the son of a rabbi, Sonnenfels emigrated to Vienna where he became the first professor of finance and cameralistics, and became a leading adviser to three successive Austro-Hungarian emperors. An absolutist, mercantilist, and welfare-state proponent, Sonnenfels's views were set forth in his *Grundsätze der Polizei, Handlung, und Finanzwissenschaft* (1765–67). His book, remarkably enough, remained the official textbook of the Austro-Hungarian monarchy until 1848.

In this atmosphere deeply permeated with cameralism it is no wonder that Smith's *Wealth of Nations* made little headway at first in Germany. However, Britain had an important foothold in Germany, for the electorate of Hanover was a continental possession of the British dynasty in the heart of Prussia, and therefore this land was under strong British cultural influence. Hence the first German review of the *Wealth of Nations* appeared in the official journal of the University of Göttingen, in Hanover. The University of Göttingen had developed the most respected department of philosophy, history, and social science in Germany, and by the 1790s it had become a flourishing nucleus of Smithianism in the otherwise hostile German climate.[11]

Taking the lead in introducing Adam Smith into German thought was Friedrich Georg Sartorius, Freiherr von Waltershausen (1765–1828). Sartorius was born in Kassel and studied theology and history at the University of Göttingen. Soon Sartorius taught history at Göttingen, by the 1790s expanding his repertoire to courses in political science and economics. Sartorius published selections of Adam Smith's works, and his *Handbuch der Staatswirthschaft* (Berlin, 1796), was explicitly an economic textbook summarizing the views of Adam Smith. An expanded summary of Smith's work appeared a decade later as the *Von den Elementen des National-Reichthums, und von der Staatswirthschaft, nach Adam Smith* (*Concerning the Elements of National Wealth and State Economy according to Adam Smith*) (1806).

In the same year, however, there appeared another volume which set forth Sartorius' own views, as well as where they differed from the master: *Abhandlungen, die Elemente des Nationalreichthums und die Staatswirthschaft* (*Essays on National Wealth and State Economy*) (1806). Sartorius differs from Smith's odd value theory, and affirms that the main source of value is its use in consumption. The value of labour, too, is determined by its usefulness, and therefore it cannot serve as an invariable measure of value, and neither can money, since money prices are also subject to the changing interplay of supply and demand. Sartorius therefore finds Smith's labour theory of value 'a strange and deceptive conclusion'. Unfortunately, Sartorius' other main deviation from Smith is a great weakening of Smith's already shaky devotion to *laissez-faire*. Sartorius advised frequent interventions by the state.

Sartorius was one of a great quartet of professors who propagated Smithian doctrine in Germany. Another was Christian Jakob Kraus (1753–1807), a distinguished philosopher who was born in East Prussia and studied under Immanuel Kant at the University of Königsberg, later becoming a close friend of Kant. Kraus took his doctorate at the University of Halle, but spent a formative year at Göttingen, where he imbibed a lasting interest in economics. After gaining his doctorate in 1780, Kraus became professor of practical philosophy and cameralia at the University of Königsberg, where he taught not only philosophy, but also the Greek classics, history, English literature and mathematics. By the early 1790s, however, Kraus's interests became entirely devoted to economics. Indeed, Kraus was one of the first persons in Germany to acclaim the *Wealth of Nations*, which he hailed as 'the only true, great, beautiful, just, and beneficial system'. Kraus greeted Adam Smith with none of the deviations or hesitations that had beset Sartorius; in fact, he trumpeted the *Wealth of Nations* as 'certainly one of the most important and beneficial books that have ever been written'. Kraus even dared to liken Smith's book to the New Testament: 'certainly since the times of the New Testament no writing has had more beneficial results than this will have...'.

Curiously enough, for a German academic Kraus published very little during his lifetime. He was, however, a highly influential teacher; his lectures at Königsberg were always crowded and he was considered the most important professor there with the exception of Kant. After his death, Kraus's friends published all his manuscript writings, the most important of which was *Die Staatswirthschaft* (5 vols, Königsberg, 1808–11). The first four volumes of this work were essentially a paraphrase of Smith's *Wealth of Nations*, substituting Prussian for British examples.

The fifth volume of *Die Staatswirthschaft* was by far the most important, for there Kraus presented his own contribution to Smithian economics. Kraus addressed himself to Prussian economic policy, in lecture form. The volume was an incisive call for individualism, free markets, free trade, and a drastic reduction of government intervention. Kraus began with the fundamental insight that every individual wants to improve his lot. ('The desire and effort of each individual to improve his lot is the basis of all state economy, like the force of gravity in the universe.') But if men wish to improve their own lot, then government coercion, requiring certain actions or forbidding others, must necessarily cripple and distort such effort at improvement. For otherwise, why don't individuals do what government wants of their own accord, and without coercion? And since they don't wish to do so, they will seek means of evading the government mandates and prohibitions. In all these cases, and in stark contrast to the cameralists, Kraus puts himself in the point of view of the individuals in society subject to government edicts, and not in the point of view of the officials issuing the decrees.[12]

A charming memorial to Christian Kraus was set forth to a friend by the great statesman of reform, Baron Karl vom Stein (1757–1831). Stein said of his friend and adviser:

> The whole province [Prussia] has gained in light and culture through him, his views forced their way into all parts of life, into the government and legislation. If he has set up no brilliant new ideas, he has at least been no glory-seeking sophist; to have presented the plain truth clearly and purely and correctly expressed, and to have communicated to thousands of auditors successfully, is a greater service than to arouse attention through chatter and paradoxes... Kraus had an unassuming but genial personality, which laid strong hold on its environment, he had flashes of new insight, and great applications, and often astonished us by his unexpected conclusions...Reading his writings, everything there is clear and simple, and at present you need nothing more.[13]

A third member of the Smithian professorial quadrumvirate in Germany was August Ferdinand Lueder (1760–1819). Lueder was also a product of the University of Göttingen, studying there, and becoming professor of philosophy. He was also a history professor and court councillor in Brunswick. Lueder had done a great deal of work in historical and geographical statistics, publishing the statistical compendia, *Historische Portefeuille* (*Historical Portfolio*) (1787–88), and *Repositorium für Geschichte, Staatskunde und Politik* (*Repository for History, Statistics and Policy*) (1802–5). But in the meantime, Lueder read Adam Smith and became an enthusiast, publishing a Smithian work in 1800–2 (*Über Nationalindustrie und Staatswirthschaft*) (*On*

National Industry and State Economy). In addition to a compendium of Smith's views, Lueder provides an impassioned defence of freedom in all its social and political aspects, as well as in the strictly economic sphere. As Lueder wrote in another work, 'I hazarded everything for freedom, truth and justice; for freedom of industry as well as of opinions, of hand as of spirit, of person as well as of property'.

A fascinating aspect of August Lueder is that he was driven both by Smithian methodology and by his devotion to freedom to repudiate his beloved life work, the investigation into national statistics. For not only would statistics mislead government policy makers, but government planners could scarcely hope to plan at all without a raft of statistics at their command. Statistics is not only misleading, therefore; it becomes a necessary condition for the very government intervention which must be repudiated. Lueder levelled his criticisms in two volumes on statistics, *Kritik der Statistik und Politik (Criticism of Statistics and State Policy)* (1812) and *Kritische Geschichte der Statistik (Critical History of Statistics)*. In the preface to his *Kritik*, Lueder wrote movingly:

> On the strongest pillars and the firmest foundation the structure of statistics and policy seemed to me to rest. I had devoted the happiest hours of my life and the greatest part of my time to statistics and policy;…everything in me could not but revolt at the convictions which pressed upon me. But the current of the times flowed too swiftly. Ideas, which had entered my very marrow, had to be reviewed and exchanged for others; one prejudice after another had to be recognized as prejudice; more and more indefensible appeared one rotten prop after another, one rent and tear after the other; finally, to my no small terror, the whole structure of statistics collapsed and with it policy, which can accomplish nothing without statistics. As my insight grew and my viewpoint cleared, the fruits of statistics and policy appeared more and more frightful; all those hindrances which both threw in the path of industry, whereby not only welfare but culture and humanity were hindered; all those hindrances to the natural course of things; all those sacrifices brought to an unknown idol, called the welfare of the state or the commonweal, and bought with ridicule of all principles of philosophy, religion and sound common sense, at the cost of morality and virtue.[14]

With such perceptive insight into the evils of statistics and 'policy', one shudders to think of Lueder's reaction to the current world, where statistics and policy, both then in their infancy, have spread and virtually conquered the earth.

The fourth influential German Smithian academic was Ludwig Heinrich von Jakob (1759–1827). Jakob studied at Halle, and then taught at the University of Kharkov in the Ukraine. As a result, Jakob became a consultant to several commissions at St Petersburg, and helped spread Smithian economics to Russia. But for most of his life Jakob taught political economy and philosophy at the University of Halle, where like Christian Kraus, he combined

Kant and Smith's individualism into an economic and philosophical whole. Like Kraus also, Jakob played an important advisory role in the liberal Stein–Hardenberg reforms in Prussia. His most important work was his *Grundsätze der Nationalökonomie* (*Principles of Economics*) (1805).

At any rate, under the influence of the quadrumvirate of Sartorius, Kraus, Lueder and Jakob, the Smithians rather rapidly took over one economics department after another from the older cameralists, who were pushed back where they more properly belonged, into the departments of law and administration. Smithian views also penetrated the civil service, and were responsible for the important failed liberal reforms, in the early nineteenth century, of Stein and Hardenberg in Prussia. Stein and Hardenberg, it should be added, had both studied at the University of Göttingen. In a little over a decade, Smithianism had triumphed over cameralism in Germany.

17.5   Smithianism in Russia

Smithianism also began to penetrate Russian political culture. Cultural and intellectual life had only begun to flower in that backward and despotic empire in the mid-eighteenth century. The University of Moscow, the first university in Russia, started at the late date of 1755. Enlightenment ideas spread in Russia, and we have seen that Catherine the Great at least flirted briefly with physiocracy. French was the language of the Russian court, and so any ideas prevailing in France, the home of the Enlightenment, had to be taken seriously in Moscow and St Petersburg. In addition, the Scottish version of the eighteenth century Enlightenment was in a sense carried to Russia by the fact that a large number of Scottish professionals – doctors, soldiers, engineers – resided and worked in that country. Scottish Enlightenment books were translated, generally into French, and published in Russia.

In the 1760s, it was the custom of Empress Elizabeth of Russia, the daughter of Peter the Great, to select outstanding students to finish their studies abroad. As a result, the empress made the fateful choice of sending to Scotland in 1761 two men who would be particularly instrumental in spreading Smithian ideas to Russia. The more important of the two was Semyon Efimovich Desnitsky, son of a Ukrainian petty bourgeois, and his lifelong friend and classmate at university, Ivan Andreyevich Tretyakov (1735–76), son of an army officer. The two studied at Glasgow University for six years, studying eagerly under Adam Smith until the latter left his chair at Glasgow in 1764. At Glasgow, Desnitsky and Tretyakov heard Smith's *Wealth of Nations* lectures, and also studied under Smith's colleague and former student John Millar. When the two Russian students were in financial difficulty, Adam Smith lent them money to tide them over. The two Russians returned to Moscow in 1768, imbued with Smithian doctrine, and promptly became the first Russian professors of law at Moscow University. In Moscow, the young Smithians ran into strong faculty hostility. The majority of professors at Moscow University had been German, and the Germans strongly opposed the successful drive by the younger Russians to teach in Russian rather than Latin, and even more were the Germans hostile to the two Smithians' liberal, reformist and anti-clerical views.

Desnitsky and Tretyakov each published a Smithian book in their first year back in Russia. Both books were largely verbatim transcriptions of Smith's lectures, with Desnitsky ghost-writing Tretyakov's volume. Of the two from that point on, Tretyakov was more the faithful Smithian, Desnitsky more the independent thinker. Both men were dominant in the political and law faculty at Moscow University, with Desnitsky becoming known as the outstanding Russian social and political theorist of the second half of the eighteenth century, as well as 'the father of Russian jurisprudence'. Desnitsky also translated the great Blackstone into Russian.

Empress Catherine the Great became interested in the latest intellectual craze, the Scottish Enlightenment and, on Desnitsky's return from Russia, commissioned him to write a Smithian reform plan for Russia, a massive volume – the *Predstavlenie* – which he finished and sent to Catherine in 1768. Its basic thrust was that of moderate political reform; Desnitsky proposed a system of two-house representation, along with independent, life-appointed judges, serving as checks and balances on the executive and legislature. Catherine the Great read the *Predstavlenie*, and incorporated politically trivial suggestions into her famous 1768 reform decree, the *Nakaz*, which was translated into English, French and German.

The *Predstavlenie* itself, however, was far too radical to see the light of day, and it remained unpublished until the revolutionary year of 1905, when it inspired liberal reformers and was reprinted twice in rapid succession.

The influence of Smithianism in Russia was redoubled by the fact that Princess Ekaterina Dashkova resided in Scotland in the late 1770s, while her son studied at Edinburgh University. Dashkova wrote proudly of her close friendship with such 'immortals' as Adam Smith, the Rev. William Robertson, Adam Ferguson, and Hugh Blair.

But despite their eminence, the hostility of the Russian state and Church, seconded by most of the Moscow faculty, to the two jurists' liberal views got them ousted from their university posts. Each was forcibly retired from the university, Tretyakov in 1773, and Desnitsky in 1787, and each died early a few years after their ouster.

Picking up the Smithian torch for the next Russian generation was a German Smithian usually considered a Russian by historians. He was the Baltic German nobleman Heinrich Friedrich Freiherr von Storch (1766–1835). Born in Riga and educated at Jena and Heidelberg, Storch spent his life high up in the Russian civil service, becoming a professor at the Imperial

Cadet Corps at St Petersburg, and educating the future Czar Nicholas I and his younger brother in Smithian political economy. Helping to bring Smithianism to Russia, von Storch wrote, in German, a nine-volume histori-cal and statistical work on Russia at the end of the eighteenth century (1797–1803), and later wrote a treatise on economics in French, *Cours d'économie politique* (1815). The book was published in St Petersburg for the education of the future czar. A moderate Smithian, von Storch sensibly rejected the idea that some labour was 'unproductive', and dabbled in a form of pre-Keynesian income analysis in his last work in 1824.

17.6 The Smithian conquest of economic thought

By the turn of the nineteenth century, the views and doctrines of Adam Smith had swept the board of European opinion, though they had scarcely been embodied in political institutions. Even in France, as will be seen in the second volume of this series, the pre-Smithian subjective utility–scarcity approach to value, as well as the stress on entrepreneurship in the market, continued to be prominent, but only under the cloak of a proclaimed devotion to Adam Smith as the founder of economic theory and free market policy. In the hands of James Mill and Ricardo in England, of J.B. Say in France, and throughout the rest of the Continent, Adam Smith would be treated as the embodiment of the new discipline of 'political economy'.

There were advantages but probably greater disadvantages to this Smithian dominance over economic thought after the 1790s. On the one hand, it meant at least a moderate appreciation of and devotion to freedom of trade at home and abroad. Even more solidly, it meant a keen understanding and a steadfast adherence to the virtues of saving and investment and a refusal to indulge in proto-Keynesian worry about 'hoarding' or underconsumption. Moreover, this adherence to what Schumpeter calls the Turgot–Smith view of saving and investment also meant a determined opposition to wildly inflationary schemes of expansion of money and credit.

On the other hand, there were dire costs to economic thought in this Smithian takeover. Even on the monetary front, Smith had gone against his eighteenth century colleagues in adopting crucial aspects of John Law's inflationary doctrine, in particular praising expansion of bank credit and money within a specie standard framework. In this way, Smith paved the way for later apologetics on behalf of the Bank of England and its generation of credit expansion.

More fatefully, Smith totally set back price and value theory, and led it into a fateful cul de sac, from which it took a century to recover; in some respects, it has never fully recovered. At the root of Smith's drastic changes in theory was undoubtedly his Calvinist contempt for luxury consumer spending. Hence, only work on *material* goods (i.e. material *capital* goods) was productive.

Hence, too, Smith's interventionist call for usury laws to lower the rate of interest so as to ration savings and channel them away from luxurious consumers and speculative 'projectors' to sober prime borrowers. Smith's contempt for consumers also led him to discard the time-honoured subjective utility–scarcity theory of value, and to seek the cause of value not in frivolous consumers but in real cost, or labour pain, embodied into the product. Hence Smith's crucial shift of emphasis in economic theory away from consumer demand and actual market prices, and towards unrealistic, long-run equilibrium. For only in long-run equilibrium does a labour pain, or cost, theory of pricing take on even superficial plausibility. But the exclusive attention to long-run equilibrium led Smith to toss out the entire entrepreneurship-and-uncertainty approach that had been elaborated by Cantillon and Turgot; for in a timeless final equilibrium there is obviously no problem of change or uncertainty.

Smith's labour theory of value led to Marxism and all the horrors to which that creed has given rise; and his exclusive emphasis on long-run equilibrium has led to formalistic neoclassicism, which dominates today's economic theory, and to *its* exclusion from consideration of entrepreneurship and uncertainty.

Smith's stress on the economy-in-perpetual-equilibrium also led him to discard his old friend David Hume's important insight (even if inferior to Cantillon's) into the international specie-flow-price mechanism, and to the important business cycle analysis that lies clearly implicit in that doctrine. For if the world economy is always in equilibrium, then there is no need to consider or worry about increases in money supply causing price rises and outflows of gold or silver abroad, or to consider the subsequent contraction of money and prices.

In essence, then, the common picture of economic thought after Smith needs to be reversed. In the conventional view, Adam Smith, the towering founder, by his theoretical genius and by the sheer weight of his knowledge of institutional facts, single-handedly created the discipline of political economy as well as the public policy of the free market, and did so out of a jumble of mercantilist fallacies and earlier absurd scholastic notions of a 'just price'. The real story is almost the opposite. Before Smith, centuries of scholastic analysis had developed an excellent value theory and monetary theory, along with corresponding free market and hard-money conclusions. Originally embedded among the scholastics in a systematic framework of property rights and contract law based on natural law theory, economic theory and policy had been elaborated still further into a veritable science by Cantillon and Turgot in the eighteenth century. Far from founding the discipline of economics singlehanded, Adam Smith turned his back not only the scholastic and French traditions, but even on his own mentors in the considerably more diluted natural law of the Scottish Enlightenment: Gershom Carmichael and his own teacher Francis Hutcheson.

The most unfortunate aspect of the total Smithian takeover in economics was not so much his own considerable tissue of error, but even more the blotting out of knowledge of the rich tradition of economic thought that had developed before Smith. As a result, the Austrians and their nineteenth century predecessors, largely deprived of knowledge of the pre-Smith tradition, were in many ways forced to reinvent the wheel, to painfully claw their way back to the knowledge that many pre-Smithians had enjoyed long before. Adam Smith and the consequences of Smith is an outstanding example of the Kuhnian case in the history of a science: in all too many cases, the development of knowledge in a discipline is *not* a steady continuous march upward into the light, patiently discarding refuted hypotheses and adding continually to the stock of cumulative knowledge. But rather, the history of the discipline is a zig-zag of great gain and loss, of advances in knowledge followed by decay and false leads, and then by periods of attempts to recapture lost knowledge, trying often dimly and against fierce opposition, to regain paradigms lost.

17.7   Notes

1. A previous embodiment of the *Edinburgh Review* had been founded in 1755 by a group of prominent moderate Presbyterian leaders, including Adam Smith. Only two issues appeared, however. It might be noted that Dugald Stewart was the first biographer of the main Moderate leader and founder of the first *Edinburgh Review*, Principal William Robertson (1721–93).
2. Edwin Cannan, *A History of the Theories of Production and Distribution in English Political Economy from 1776 to 1848* (3rd ed., London: Staples Press, 1917), pp. 110–11.
3. J.A. Schumpeter, *History of Economic Analysis* (New York: Oxford University Press, 1954), p. 579.
4. Alexander Gray, *The Development of Economic Doctrine* (London: Longmans, Green and Co., 1931), pp. 163–4.
5. Cannan, op. cit., note 2, p. 113.
6. Schumpeter, op. cit., note 3, p. 580.
7. Schumpeter, op. cit., note 3, pp. 581–2.
8. Schumpeter, op. cit., note 3, p. 584.
9. Albion W. Small, *The Cameralists* (1909; New York: Burt Franklin, n.d.), p. viii.
10. Oddly enough, while calling for more money, Becher also wrote unknown works, the *Moral Discurs* (1669) and the *Psychosophia* (1678), in which he became one of the earliest communists, calling for the abolition of money. Money, Becher opined, was the primary evil; without it, we would all be forced to work, would enjoy equal incomes, and would therefore be happy.
11. The three most influential German universities of the day were those of Göttingen, Halle in nearby Prussia, and Leipzig.
12. Thus, Christian Kraus writes: 'Whenever it is a question of a law or an arrangement, by which men are to be brought either to do something which they previously did not do, or not to do something which they previously did, then, in the second case, the first question is why people did not cease of their own accord?... Then follows the second question: What will men attempt to do in order to evade the law which conflicts with their interests? Then the third question: How far will that which they undertake in order to evade the law succeed? In the case of the second and third questions many striking views will be gained, which would otherwise have quite escaped us, as soon as we put ourselves entirely in the position of these men and make their situation our own. What has here been said of

ceasing to do is of even greater validity when it is a question of doing; that is, when men are to be brought (enticed or forced) by laws or arrangements to do something which they previously did not want to do'. Quoted in Carl William Hasek, *The Introduction of Adam Smith's Doctrines Into Germany* (New York: Columbia University, 1925), p. 89n.

13. Quoted in ibid., p. 93.
14. Cited in ibid., p. 83.

Bibliographical essay

In a comprehensive history of economic thought, it is clearly impossible for a bibliographical essay to attempt to list, much less annotate, every source for that history, much less for the ancillary fields of history of social, political and religious thought, as well as economic history proper, all of which in my view must be brought into the picture of the development and the clashes in the field of economic thought. The best I can do, then, is to describe and annotate those sources, largely secondary ones, which I found most helpful in working on this study. In that way, the bibliographical appendix may serve as a guide to readers who wish to delve into various topics and areas in this vast and complex field, which in many ways touches on the entire history of western civilization.

Overall bibliographies

By far the most comprehensive bibliographical essay in the history of economic thought is the remarkably full treatment in Henry W. Spiegel, *The Growth of Economic Thought* (3rd ed., Durham, NC: Duke University Press, 1991), which now stretches to no less than 161 pages, and is the most valuable aspect of the book. The four-volume *New Palgrave: A Dictionary of Economics* (London: Macmillan and New York: Stockton Press, 1987), contains a number of excellent essays on particular economists. At the other end of the spectrum, the brief sketches in the unpretentious paperback by Ludwig H. Mai, *Men and Ideas in Economics: A Dictionary of World Economists, Past and Present* (Lanham, MD: Rowman and Littlefield, 1977) are surprisingly useful.

Ancient thought

The only book covering all ancient economic thought in countries including Mesopotamia, India and China is Joseph J. Spengler, *Origins of Economic Thought and Justice* (Carbondale, Ill., Southern Illinois University Press, 1980). Although Professor Spengler probably would not have agreed with this assessment, his book demonstrates that virtually nothing of interest emerged out of the economic thought of these ancient civilizations. The exception is Chinese political philosophy (particularly Taoism), on which the definitive work is the illuminating Kung-chuan Hsiao, *A History of Chinese Political Thought, Vol. One: From the Beginnings to the Sixth Century A.D.* (Princeton, NJ: Princeton University Press, 1979). On a Chinese advocate of *laissez-faire*, see Joseph J. Spengler, 'Ssu-ma Ch'ien, Unsuccessful Exponent of Laissez Faire', *Southern Economic Journal* (Jan. 1964), pp. 223–43.

The only histories of economic thought that do justice to the Greek contribution are Spiegel, *The Growth of Economic Thought* and Barry Gordon, *Economic Analysis Before Adam Smith* (New York: Barnes & Noble, 1975). Spiegel is particularly good on Democritus and Gordon is good on Hesiod and deals extensively with Greek economic thought. Gordon is also unique in dealing fully with Jewish economic thought. His title is misleading, however, since the book stops with the late scholastics, considerably before the time of Adam Smith.

S. Todd Lowry, 'Recent Literature on Ancient Greek Economic Thought', *Journal of Economic Literature*, 17 (March 1979), pp. 65–86, provides a comprehensive annotated bibliographical review of Greek economic thought. Also see Lowry, *The Archaeology of Economic Ideas: The Classical Greek Tradition* (Durham, NC: Duke University Press, 1987). The Oxford W.D. Ross edition of the works of Aristotle is the standard one. On the fascinating controversy on the meaning of Aristotle's equation of exchange, Josef Soudek's lengthy, scholarly, but totally wrongheaded reading of Jevons into Aristotle is in Josef Soudek, 'Aristotle's Theory of Exchange: An Inquiry into the Origin of Economic Analysis', *Proceedings of the American Philosophical Society* 96 (Feb. 1952), pp. 45–75, while Barry Gordon plumps for Aristotle as a proto-Marshallian: 'Aristotle and the Development of Value Theory', *Quarterly Journal of Economics*, 78 (Feb. 1964), pp. 115–28. Far better are two scholars who had the courage to see the equation of exchange as nonsense: the great interpreter of Aristotle, H.H. Joachim, in his *Aristotle: The Nichomachean Ethics* (Oxford: The Clarendon Press, 1951), esp. 148–51, and the ancient historian Moses I. Finley, in his 'Aristotle and Economic Analysis', *Past and Present* (May 1970), pp. 3–25, reprinted in Finley (ed), *Studies in Ancient Society* (London: Routledge & Kegan Paul, 1974), pp. 26–52.

A detailed critique of the various Latin translations of Aristotle's discussion of economic value is in Odd Langholm, *Price and Value in the Aristotelian Tradition* (Bergen: Universitetsforlaget, 1979).

Joseph J. Spengler, in his excellent 'Aristotle on Economic Imputation and Related Matters', *Southern Economic Journal*, 21 (April 1955), pp. 371–89, shows that Aristotle's imputation theory was a forerunner of praxeological and Austrian imputation theory of the nineteenth and twentieth centuries. Spengler himself, however, undervalued the results of his own inquiry, since he didn't realize that Aristotle's imputation theory was an important contribution to action analysis and praxeology even if it did not deal with strictly economic matters.

Also on Aristotle as a pre-Austrian, see Emil Kauder, 'Genesis of the Marginal Utility Theory: From Aristotle to the end of the Eighteenth Century', *Economic Journal*, 43 (Sept. 1953), pp. 638–50.

On Plato as totalitarian, see the hard-hitting and highly influential work by a leading modern philosopher, Karl R. Popper, *The Open Society and Its Enemies* (3rd rev. ed., 2 vols, Princeton, NJ: Princeton University Press, 1957). Unfortunately, Popper confuses the *political* totalitarianism of Plato with the spurious tyranny allegedly implied by the fact that Plato believed in absolute truth and in rational ethics. To a modern, wishy-washy *ad hoc* metaphysician like Popper, *any* firm belief in truth, in black and white, smacks of 'dogmatism' and 'despotism'. Setting the philosophic record straight in defence of Plato, in reply were John Wild, *Plato's Modern Enemies and the Theory of Natural Law* (Chicago: University of Chicago Press, 1953), and Ronald B. Levinson, *In Defense of Plato* (Cambridge: Harvard University Press, 1953). For an attack on Plato's totalitarianism and an exposition of the sophists, the opponents of Socratic philosophy, as classical liberals in politics, see Eric A. Havelock, *The Liberal Temper in Greek Politics* (New Haven: Yale University Press, 1957). On the other hand, for a more recent article confirming the view that the Greek *polis* was inherently statist, had no conception of classical liberalism or individual freedom, and was grounded on the labour of slaves, see Paul A. Rahe, 'The Primacy of Politics in Classical Greece', *American Historical Review* (April 1984), pp. 265–93.

On Plato and the division of labour, see Williamson M. Evers, 'Specialization and the Division of Labor in the Social Thought of Plato and Rousseau', *The Journal of Libertarian Studies*, 4 (Winter, 1980), pp. 45–64; Vernard Foley, 'The Division of Labor in Plato and Smith', *History of Political Economy*, 6 (Summer 1974), pp. 220–42: Paul J. McNulty, 'A Note on the Division of Labor in Plato and Smith', *History of Political Economy*, 7 (Autumn 1975), pp. 372–8; and Foley, 'Smith and the Greeks: A Reply to Professor McNulty's Comments', ibid., pp. 379–89.

On the influence of Plotinus and man's alleged inherent alienation to overcome through history, see the illuminating discussion in Leszek Kolakowksi, *Main Currents of Marxism, I: The Founders* (New York: Oxford University Press, 1981), pp. 11–23.

Cicero's eloquent quotation on the definition of the natural law may be found, among other places, in Michael Bertram Crowe, *The Changing Profile of the Natural Law* (The Hague: Martinus Nijhoff, 1977), pp. 37–8, Crowe including natural law theorists among the Greeks and Romans; and his parable of Alexander and the pirate in Cicero's *On the Commonwealth* (Columbus: Ohio State University Press, 1929), Book III, SIV, p. 210.

Medieval thought
A valuable overall study of medieval economic thought, including that of the early Church Fathers, is in Gordon, *Economic Analysis Before Adam Smith*. Two indispensable articles on the theory of the just price are: Kenneth S. Cahn, 'The Roman and Frankish Roots of the Just Price of Medieval Canon Law', *Studies in Medieval and Renaissance History*, 6 (1969), pp. 3–52, on the early Roman and canon law; and the book-length monograph by John W. Baldwin, 'The Medieval Theories of the Just Price: Romanists, Canonists,

and Theologians in the Twelfth and Thirteenth Centuries', *Transactions of the American Philosophical Society*, 49 (1959). The definitive study of medieval and later theories of usury is John T. Noonan, Jr, *The Scholastic Analysis of Usury* (Cambridge, Mass.: Harvard University Press, 1957).

The conventional neglect and systematic misinterpretation of medieval and late scholastic economic thought began to be rectified in Joseph A. Schumpeter's great *History of Economic Analysis* (New York: Oxford University Press, 1954), especially the first half of Part II, Chapter II. The fullest research for this revision, however, has been provided for us in the extensive writings of Professor Raymond de Roover. De Roover's most important and most anthologized article was his 'The Concept of the Just Price: Theory and Economic Policy', *Journal of Economic History*, 18 (Dec. 1958), pp. 418–34; here de Roover demolishes the historiographic misinterpretation of Heinrich von Langenstein. Also see de Roover, 'Joseph A. Schumpeter and Scholastic Economics', *Kyklos*, 10 (1957–2), pp. 115–46; idem., 'The Scholastics, Usury and Foreign Exchange', *Business History Review*, 41 (Autumn 1967), pp. 257–71: and the collection of essays in Raymond de Roover, *Business, Banking, and Economic Thought; In Late Medieval and Early Modern Europe* (ed. J. Kirshner, Chicago: University of Chicago Press, 1974).

The vital contribution to economic thought of Pierre de Jean Olivi has been finally brought to light by de Roover, in his *San Bernardino of Siena and Sant' Antonino of Florence: The Two Great Economic Thinkers of the Middle Ages* (Boston: Baker Library, 1967), pp. 19–20, 41–2. Also see Julius Kirshner, 'Raymond de Roover on Scholastic Economic Thought', in de Roover, *Business, Banking and Economic Thought*, pp. 28–30. On Olivi as Joachimite and leader of the Spiritual Franciscans, see Malcolm D. Lambert, *Medieval Heresy* (New York: Holmes & Meier, 1977), pp. 182–206. On the Joachimite heresy, also see the vivid work by Norman Cohn, *The Pursuit of the Millennium* (3rd ed., New York: Harper & Bros, 1970), pp. 99ff.

Michael Crowe's *Changing Profile of the Natural Law* is a thorough study of the medieval theorists of natural law. Richard Tuck, *Natural Rights: Their Origin and Development* (Cambridge: Cambridge University Press, 1979), illuminates a crucial distinction between active, or dominion, rights theories, and passive or claim theories.

A scholarly but accessible overall study of European economic history is the paperback, Carlo M. Cipolla (ed.), *The Fontana Economic History of Europe, I: The Middle Ages* (London: Collins/Fontana, 1972), which covers the medieval period. On population changes in that period, see J.G. Russell, 'Population in Europe, 500–1500', in the *Fontana History*, ibid. On the Great Depression of the fourteenth and first half of the fifteenth century, see Robert S. Lopez and Harry A. Miskimin, 'The Economic Depression of the Renaissance', *Economic History Review*, 14 (1962), and Edouard Perroy, 'At the

Origin of a Contracted Economy: the Crises of the 14th Century', in Rondo
E. Cameron, (ed.) *Essays in French Economic History* (Homewood, Ill.:
Richard D. Irwin, 1970), pp. 91–105. A subtle study of the economy of late
medieval/early renaissance Europe is Harry A. Miskimin, *The Economy of
Early Renaissance Europe, 1300–1460* (Englewood Cliffs, NJ: Prentice-Hall,
1969). On the fateful introduction of regular taxation into France, see Martin
Wolfe, 'French Views on Wealth and Taxes from the Middle Ages to the Old
Régime', in D.C. Coleman (ed.), *Revisions in Mercantilism* (London: Methuen
& Co., 1969), p. 190ff.

The late scholastics
For the late scholastics – i.e. in the fourteenth to the sixteenth centuries – the
works of Crowe (natural law), Tuck (natural rights), Gordon and de Roover
(economic thought), and Noonan (usury) continue to be indispensable (see
above). For the *locus classicus* of Crowe's revisionist insights on the
Ockhamite Gregory of Rimini as being actually in favour of an objective
natural law, see Damasus Trapp, 'Augustinian Theology of the 14th Century:
Notes on Editions, Marginalia, Opinions and Book-Lore', in *Augustiniana*, 6
(1956), pp. 146–274; idem, 'Gregory of Rimini, Manuscripts Editions and
Additions', in *Augustiniana*, 8 (1958), pp. 425–43. The key revisionist work
on Gabriel Biel is Heiko A. Oberman, *The Harvest of Medieval Theology:
Gabriel Biel and Late Medieval Nominalism* (Cambridge, Mass.: Harvard
University Press, 1963). More recent confirmation on this revisionism is in
D.E. Luscombe, 'Natural Morality and Natural Law', in N. Kretzmann, et al.
(eds), *The Cambridge History of Later Medieval Philosophy* (Cambridge:
Cambridge University Press, 1982), pp. 705–20. Also see A.S. McGrade,
'Rights, Natural Rights, and the Philosophy of Law', in ibid., pp. 738–56.
    The School of Salamanca was first brought to the attention of economists
in a splendid little book by Marjorie Grice-Hutchinson, *The School of Sala-
manca: Readings in Spanish Monetary Theory, 1544–1605* (Oxford: The
Clarendon Press, 1952). The scope of the book is far wider than the subtitle
implies, and, in addition to a lucid text, it contains English translations of
economic writings from many of the great Salamancans. More on the
Salamancans and other Spanish economists of the period can be found in
Grice-Hutchinson, *Early Economic Thought in Spain, 1177–1740* (London:
George Allen & Unwin, 1978). Also see de Roover, 'Scholastic Economics',
in *Business, Banking, and Economic Thought*, pp. 306–35. Frank Bartholomew
Costello, S.J., *The Political Philosophy of Luis de Molina, S.J.* (Spokane:
Gonzaga University Press, 1974), is a lucid and well-organized work, and
Bernice Hamilton, *Political Thought in Sixteenth-Century Spain* (Oxford:
The Clarendon Press, 1963), studies the legal and political thought of four
Salamancan scholastics: Vitoria, DeSoto, Molina, and Suarez. Insights into

the political philosophy of Suarez and the others can be found in the relevant volume of the mighty work by Frederick Copleston, S.J., *A History of Philosophy, Volume III Ockham to Suarez* (Westminster, Md: The Newman Press, 1959). On the political theory of the Salamancans, see the outstanding work by Quentin Skinner, *The Foundations of Modern Political Thought, Vol. II: The Age of Reformation* (Cambridge: Cambridge University Press, 1978).

On the growth since World War II of the 'revisionist' view of the Spanish and other scholastics presented here, see Murray N. Rothbard, 'New Light on the Pre-history of the Austrian School', in E. Dolan (ed.), *The Foundations of Modern Austrian Economics* (Kansas City: Sheed & Ward, 1976), pp. 52–74.

The most up-to-date and developed work on the Spanish scholastics in Alejandro Chafuen, *Christians for Freedom: Late-Scholastic Economics* (San Francisco: Ignatius Press, 1986). For a contrast between the Salamancan scholastics and the later seventeenth century Spanish mercantilists, see Louis Baeck, 'Spanish Economic Thought: the School of Salamanca and the *Arbitristas*', *History of Political Economy*, 20 (Autumn 1988), pp. 381–408.

Indispensable for the fascinating figure of Juan de Mariana is John Laures, S.J., *The Political Economy of Juan de Mariana* (New York: Fordham University Press, 1928). See also Guenter Lewy, *Constitutionalism and Statecraft During the Golden Age of Spain: A Study of the Political Philosophy of Juan de Mariana, S.J.* (Geneva: Librairie E. Droz, 1960). For Mariana on tyrannicide, along with a discussion of other such sixteenth century and later theorists, see Oscar Jászi and John D. Lewis, *Against the Tyrant: The Tradition and Theory of Tyrannicide* (Glencoe, Ill.: The Free Press, 1957).

A fascinating account of the Jansenist struggle with the Jesuits on casuistry and usury is in J. Brodrick, S.J., *The Economic Morals of the Jesuits* (London: Oxford University Press, 1934). Also useful on both the Jesuits and their Protestant enemies is the informative but sometimes sloppily researched Hector M. Robertson, *Aspects of the Rise of Economic Individualism* (Cambridge: Cambridge University Press, 1933). It is amusing that Brodrick's book was written specifically to refute the thesis of Robertson that Catholic and especially Jesuit thinkers tended to favour the free market, and yet much of the two works confirm each other. Brodrick seems to believe that Robertson is attacking the Jesuits for immorality, whereas in our reading he is simply demonstrating their economic insight and good sense.

For an overall study of the Catholic Counter-Reformation, see Marvin R. O'Connell, *The Counter Reformation: 1559–1610* (New York: Harper & Row, 1974).

On the commercial expansion of the late fifteenth and the sixteenth centuries, see in particular Harry A. Miskimin, *The Economy of Later Renaissance Europe, 1460–1600* (Cambridge: Cambridge University Press, 1977); and also C. Cipolla (ed.), *The Fontana Economic History of Europe, Vol. II, The Sixteenth and Seventeenth Centuries* (London: Collins/Fontana 1974).

Luther and Calvin
An excellent and brief analysis is contained in Gary North, 'The Economic Thought of Luther and Calvin', *The Journal of Christian Reconstruction*, II (Summer 1975), pp. 76–108. Skinner's *Foundations Vol. II*, is excellent on Luther and Calvin's, especially the former's, social and political philosophy, and that of their followers, on which also see the older work by John N. Figgis, *Political Thought from Gerson to Grotius* (1916, New York: Harper & Bros, 1960), especially Ch. III on 'Luther and Machiavelli'. The Weber thesis is argued back and forth in Max Weber, *The Protestant Ethic and the Spirit of Capitalism* (New York: Charles Scribner's, 1930); the Weberian Ernst Troeltsch, *The Social Teaching of the Christian Church*, Vol. II (New York: Macmillan, 1931); Richard H. Tawney, *Religion and the Rise of Capitalism* (1937, New York: New American Library, 1954); and the Robertson and Brodrick books mentioned above. See also the critical study of Kurt Samuelsson, *Religion and Economic Action* (New York: Basic Books, 1961). A fruitful application of the Weber thesis to China and Japan is in Norman Jacobs, *The Origin of Modern Capitalism and Eastern Asia* (Hong Kong: Hong Kong University Press, 1958). De Roover's discovery of the thirteenth century Florentine motto, 'In the name of God and of profit', is in his 'The Scholastic Attitude Toward Trade and Entrepreneurship', in *Business, Banking, and Economic Thought*, p. 345. For Calvin and his followers on usury, see Noonan's great work discussed above.

The brilliant Kauder thesis holds that Calvinism led to the labour theory of value in Britain while Aristotelian Thomism kept France and Italy to a subjective, consumer-oriented theory of value. This thesis may be found in Emil Kauder, *A History of Marginal Utility Theory* (Princeton, NJ: Princeton University Press, 1965), and in Kauder, 'The Retarded Acceptance of the Marginal Utility Theory', *Quarterly Journal of Economics* (Nov. 1953), pp. 564–9. On such tough-minded Calvinists as the English Marian exiles and on the puritan devotion to work, see Michael Walzer, *The Revolution of the Saints: A Study in the Origins of Radical Politics* (Cambridge: Harvard University Press, 1965).

Perhaps the greatest work ever written in the history of economic thought was Eugen von Böhm-Bawerk's *Capital and Interest: Vol. I, History and Critique of Interest Theories* (1921, South Holland, Ill.: Libertarian Press, 1959). Böhm-Bawerk, the first great systematizer of the Austrian School of economics in the 1880s, wrote his survey and critique of preceding theories of interest before proceeding to develop his own theory in later volumes of his masterwork, *Capital and Interest*. While Böhm-Bawerk's treatment of

Salmasius is excellent and appreciative, his discussion of previous writers is greatly marred by his lack of knowledge of the scholastic thinkers, whom he dismisses all too briefly as 'canonists'. The later scholastics have only been resurrected for economists since World War II.

Anabaptist communism
The outstanding work on the totalitarian messianic communism of the coercive wing of the Anabaptists is the brilliant, mordant, and hard-hitting work of Norman Cohn, *The Pursuit of the Millennium* (3rd ed., New York: Harper & Row, 1970). This should be supplemented by the more recent work of Igor Shafarevich, *The Socialist Phenomenon* (New York: Harper & Row, 1980) which, though episodic, also explores socialism in other ages and other climes. All this should be considered in the general framework set forth in the deservedly classic work of Msgr Ronald A. Knox, *Enthusiasm* (1950, New York: Oxford University Press, 1961). A full if schematic account of Anabaptist theologies is in James M. Stayer, *Anabaptists and the Sword* (2nd ed., Lawrence, Kan.: Coronado Press, 1976). Willem Balke's *Calvin and the Anabaptist Radicals* (Grand Rapids, Mich.: William B. Eerdmans, 1981) is an excellent study. George Huntston Williams, *The Radical Reformation* (Philadelphia: The Westminster Press, 1962) is a thorough classic, now a bit outdated by more recent scholarship.

Non-scholastic Catholics
An excellent article on Copernicus' monetary theory is Timothy J. Reiss and Roger H. Hinderliter, 'Money and Value in the Sixteenth Century; the *Monetae Cudendae Ratio* of Nicholas Copernicus', *Journal of the History of Ideas*, 40 (April–June 1979), pp. 293–303. On Copernicus, Oresme, and Aristophanes on Gresham's law, see J. Laurence Laughlin, *The Principles of Money* (New York: Charles Scribner's Sons, 1903), pp. 420ff. The best discussion of Lottini is in Emil Kauder, *A History of Marginal Utility Theory* (Princeton, NJ: Princeton University Press, 1965). Also see Kauder, 'Genesis of the Marginal Utility Theory: From Aristotle to the End of the Eighteenth Century', *The Economic Journal* (Sept. 1953), pp. 638–50. On Lottini's unsavoury activities, see Cecily Booth, *Cosimo I: Duke of Florence* (Cambridge: Cambridge University Press, 1921), pp. 131–2. On Davanzati, see the discussions in Kauder, *History*; Grice-Hutchinson, *Early Economic Thought*; Arthur Eli Monroe, *Monetary Theory Before Adam Smith* (1923, Gloucester, Mass.: Peter Smith, 1965); and Joseph A. Schumpeter, *History of Economic Analysis* (New York: Oxford University Press, 1954).

Monarchomachs: Huguenots and Catholics

Jászi and Lewis, *Against The Tyrant*; and J.W. Allen, *A History of Political Thought in the Sixteenth Century* (1928, 2nd ed., London: Methuen & Co., 1957), serve as useful introductions to the extensive literature on this subject. Skinner, *Foundations*, Vol. II, is excellent on the Huguenots and Buchanan. No one should neglect the only book in English on the Catholic League: Frederic J. Baumgartner, *Radical Reactionaries: The Political Thought of the French Catholic League* (Geneva: Librairie Droz, 1976).

Absolutism and Italian humanism

The best discussion of the political theory of the Italian humanists and its relation to absolutism is in Quentin Skinner, *The Foundations of Modern Political Thought, Volume One: The Renaissance* (Cambridge: Cambridge University Press, 1968). On Diomede Carafa, see Schumpeter, *History of Economic Analysis*, pp. 162–4. On Leon Battista degli Alberti and the Alberti family, see Raymond de Roover, 'The Story of the Alberti Company of Florence, 1302–1348, As Revealed in Its Account Books', in *Business, Banking and Economic Thought* (Chicago: University of Chicago Press, 1974), pp. 39–84.

The clearest and most illuminating discussion of Machiavelli is in Skinner, *Foundations, Volume One*. Also see Isaiah Berlin, 'The Originality of Machiavelli', in M.P. Gilmore (ed), *Studies on Machiavelli* (Florence: G.C. Sansoni, 1972), pp. 147–206.

Absolutism in France

A highly lucid study of absolutist thought in France in the sixteenth century is William Farr Church, *Constitutional Thought in Sixteenth-Century France: A Study in the Evolution of Ideas* (1941, New York: Octagon Books, 1969). Church is particularly good on the absolutists after Bodin. On the influence of humanism in France and on French absolutist thought in general also see the excellent Skinner, *Foundations*, Vols I and II. These should be supplemented by the broader study of French political thought in Nannerl O. Keohane, *Philosophy and the State in France: The Renaissance to the Enlightenment* (Princeton, NJ: Princeton University Press, 1980). Keohane is particularly perceptive on Bodin.

On Montaigne, also see Donald Frame, *Montaigne: A Biography* (New York: Harcourt Brace & World, 1965). On Occitan, see Meic Stephens, *Linguistic Minorities in Western Europe* (Llandysul, Dyfed, Wales: Gomer Press, 1976), pp. 297–308. The literature on the Montaigne fallacy and mercantilism is, surprisingly, virtually non-existent. The classical, though brief, statement is in Heckscher, *Mercantilism*, I, 26. The implications are developed in Ludwig von Mises, *Human Action: A Treatise on Economics* (3rd rev.

ed., Chicago: Henry Regnery, 1966), pp. 664, 687. See also Odd Langholm, *Price and Value in the Aristotelian Tradition: A Study in Scholastic Economic Sources* (Bergen: Universitetsforlaget, 1979), pp. 30, 38n.

Mercantilism

The best introduction to the subject is an excellent work and a marvel of compression: Harry A. Miskimin's *The Economy of Later Renaissance Europe: 1460–1600* (Cambridge: Cambridge University Press, 1977). The great classic work, and deservedly so, is Eli F. Heckscher, *Mercantilism* (2 vols, 1935, 2nd rev. ed., New York: Macmillan, 1955). Heckscher's emphasis on mercantilism as building the nation-state has suffered from unfair criticism in recent years. State-building, and Heckscher's stress on mercantilist ideology, simply need to be supplemented by insight into mercantilism as a system of lobbying for and achieving monopoly and cartel privileges and subsidies from the state in return for political support and/or money to the Crown. I try to begin such a synthesis in my "Mercantilism: A Lesson for Our Time?', *The Freeman*, 13 (Nov. 1963), pp. 16–27, reprinted in *Ideas on Liberty*, Vol. XI (Irvington-on-Hudson: Foundation for Economic Education, 1964). Robert B. Ekelund, Jr and Robert D. Tollison, *Mercantilism as a Rent-Seeking Society: Economic Regulation in Historical Perspective* (College Station, Texas: Texas A&M University Press, 1981) tries to fill the gap left by Heckscher. But while its gloss on Heckscher is sometimes useful, Ekelund and Tollison is excessively schematic, in the public choice tradition, undervaluing the role of ideas in history, especially the role of free market and classical liberal ideology.

John Ulric Nef, *Industry and Government in France and England, 1540–1640* (1940, New York: Russell and Russell, 1968), is an excellent comparative study of the effect of mercantilist policies on industrial development in England and France. For England, S.T. Bindoff, *Tudor England* (Baltimore: Penguin Books, 1950), is trenchant and surprisingly hard-hitting. For France, Charles Woolsey Cole, *Colbert and a Century of French Mercantilism* (2 vols, 1939, Hamden, Conn: Archon Books, 1964), is the classic work on Colbert and on French mercantilism, despite his admiration for both. The post-Colbert French story in the seventeenth century is told in Cole's *French Mercantilism, 1683–1700* (1943, New York: Octagon Press, 1965). Warren C. Scoville, *The Persecution of Huguenots and French Economic Development, 1680–1720* (Berkeley: University of California Press, 1960), presents an interesting revisionist critique of the extent of economic havoc actually wreaked by Louis XIV's revocation of the Edict of Nantes.

On the English monopoly foreign trade companies in the Elizabethan era, see Murray N. Rothbard, *Conceived in Liberty, Vol. I: The American Colonies in the 17th Century* (New Rochelle, NY: Arlington House, 1975).

On absolutism and re-enserfdom in Poland and eastern Europe in the sixteenth century, see Miskimin, *Later Renaissance Europe*, pp. 56–64; and Robert Millward, 'An Economic Analysis of the Origin of Serfdom in Eastern Europe', *Journal of Economic History*, 42 (Sept. 1982), pp. 513–48. For a somewhat similar process in Russia in the third quarter of the sixteenth century, see Alexander Yanov, *The Origins of Autocracy: Ivan the Terrible in Russian History* (Berkeley: University of California Press, 1981); and Aileen Kelly, 'Russia's Old New Right: Review of Yanov, *Origins of Autocracy*', *New York Review of Books*, 30 (17 Feb. 1983), p. 34ff.

On the development of a system of taxation in France, see Martin Wolfe, 'French Views on Wealth and Taxes from the Middle Ages to the Old Regime', in D.C. Coleman (ed.), *Revisions in Mercantilism* (London: Methuen & Co., 1969), pp. 190–209. The classic treatment of the development of taxation under Philip the Fair is Joseph R. Strayer, 'Consent to Taxation Under Philip the Fair', in J.R. Strayer and C.H. Taylor, *Studies in Early French Taxation* (Cambridge, Mass.: Harvard University Press, 1939), pp. 3–108. A discussion of taxation in fifteenth and sixteenth century France, which takes the unconvincing revisionist position that early royal fiscalism differed sharply from the later mercantilism, is in Martin Wolfe, *The Fiscal System of Renaissance France* (New Haven: Yale University Press, 1972). For more on French taxation in the second quarter of the fourteenth century, see John Bell Henneman, *Royal Taxation in Fourteenth Century France: The Development of War Financing 1322–1356* (Princeton, NJ: Princeton University Press, 1971).

For an overview of the history of European banking in this period, see Murray N. Rothbard, *The Mystery of Banking* (New York: Richardson & Snyder/Dutton, 1983). On the Stop of the Exchequer, see the illuminating article by J. Keith Horsefield, 'The Stop of the Exchequer' Revisited', *Economic History Review*, 2nd ser., 35 (Nov. 1982), pp. 511–28.

On the development of the public-debt state in England, see P.G.M. Dickson, *The Financial Revolution in England: A Study in the Development of Public Credit, 1688–1756* (New York: St Martin's Press, 1967). Also see the remarkable revisionist work of John Brewer, *The Sinews of Power: War, Money, and the English State, 1688–1783* (New York: Knopf, 1989). Brewer points out that necessary to the development of the public-debt state was the concomitant growth of the high-tax state, with specific taxes used to back specific long-run public debt in England. In particular, taxation was indirect, especially excise taxes on consumer goods. See also the important article on British taxation by Patrick K. O'Brien, 'The Political Economy of British Taxation, 1660–1815', *Economic History Review*, 2nd ser., 41 (Feb. 1988), pp. 1–32. Also see the revisionist comparison of taxation in Britain and France in this period, demonstrating that the much denounced level of French taxation was considerably lower than in Britain. Peter Mathias and Patrick K. O'Brien, 'Taxation in Britain and France, 1715–1810. A Comparison of the Social and Economic Incidence of Taxes Collected for the Central Governments', *Journal of European Economic History*, 5 (1976), pp. 601–50.

On Parliament's fateful assertion of its authority over the king's revenue in 1690, see Clayton Roberts, 'The Constitutional Significance of the Financial Settlement of 1690', *The Historical Journal*, 20 (1977), pp. 59–76. For an interesting article from a Marxist perspective which includes discussion of the Bank of England, see Marvin Rosen, 'The Dictatorship of the Bourgeoisie: England 1688–1721', *Science and Society*, 45 (Spring 1981), pp. 24–51.

Seventeenth century French mercantilist thought
On the views of the early French mercantilists, particularly Laffemas and Montchrétien, see Charles Woolsey Cole, *French Mercantilist Doctrines Before Colbert* (New York: Richard R. Smith, 1931). Also, on Montchrétien, see the typically incisive and sparkling discussion in Alexander Gray, *The Development of Economic Doctrine* (London: Longmans, Green and Co., 1933), pp. 80–85. On Sully, see David Buisseret, *Sully: and the Growth of Centralized Government in France, 1598–1610* (London: Eyre & Spottiswoode, 1968). On mercantilist thought in the Richelieu, Mazarin, and Colbert eras, see Cole, *Colbert and a Century of French Mercantilism*. On the political thought of Louis XIV, see François Dumont, 'French Kingship and Absolute Monarchy in the Seventeenth Century', and Andrew Lossky, 'The Intellectual Development of Louis XIV from 1661 to 1715', in Raghnild Hatton (ed), *Louis XIV and Absolutism* (London: Macmillan, 1976).

French liberal opposition to mercantilism
On the *Croquants* and other peasant rebellions in seventeenth century France, see Roland Mousnier, *Peasant Uprisings in Seventeenth Century France, Russia, and China* (New York: Harper & Row, 1970). Lionel Rothkrug, *Opposition to Louis XIV: The Political and Social Origins of the French Enlightenment* (Princeton, NJ: Princeton University Press, 1965) is indispensable on the growing liberal and *laissez-faire* opposition to mercantilism. Also highly useful is Nannerl O. Keohane's *Philosophy and the State in France*, particularly on Joly, Vauban, Fénélon, the Burgundy circle, and Boisguilbert. On the latter, see in particular Hazel Van Dyke Roberts, *Boisguilbert: Economist of the Reign of Louis XIV* (New York: Columbia University Press, 1935), and Joseph J. Spengler, 'Boisguilbert's Economic Views Vis-à-Vis those of Contemporary *Réformateurs*', *History of Political Economy*, 16 (Spring 1984), pp. 69–88. Charles Woolsey Cole, *French Mercantilism, 1683–1700* (1943, New York: Octagon Books, 1965), is useful on the merchants and the council of commerce.

English mercantilists: sixteenth and early seventeenth centuries
The indispensable starting-point on the English mercantilists is the classic work of Jacob Viner, *Studies In The Theory of International Trade* (New York: Harper & Bros, 1937), pp. 1–118. Unfortunately, Viner is only the starting-point because of the extreme compression of his study, and because he does not deal with separate individuals or groups or engage in narrative analysis of different time-periods or interactions among the various individuals and groups.

On absolutists in the Tudor and Stuart eras, see W.H. Greenleaf, *Order, Empiricism, and Politics: Two Traditions of English Political Thought* (London: Oxford University Press, 1964). On Sir Robert Filmer, see Peter Laslett (ed.), *Patriarcha and Other Political Works of Sir Robert Filmer* (Oxford: Basil Blackwell, 1949); and Carl Watner, '"Oh, Ye are for Anarchy!": Consent Theory in the Radical Libertarian Tradition', *Journal of Libertarian Studies*, 8 (Winter 1986), pp. 111–37.

For the definitive demonstration that Sir Thomas Smith, not John Hales, was the author of the *Discourse of the Commonweal of this Realm of England*, see Mary Dewar, 'The Authorship of the "Discourse of the Commonweal",' *Economic History Review*, 2nd ser., 19 (August 1966), pp. 388–400. The biography of Smith is Mary Dewar, *Sir Thomas Smith: A Tudor Intellectual in Office* (London: Athlone Press, 1964). The revisionist view that Smith, not Gresham, wrote the famous *Memorandum for the Understanding of the Exchange* is in Mary Dewar, 'The Memorandum "For the Understanding of the Exchange": Its Authorship and Dating', *Economic History Review*, 2nd ser., 17 (April 1965), pp. 476–87. Raymond de Roover, while formally maintaining his original view that Gresham was the author, implicitly throws in the towel in Raymond de Roover, 'On the Authorship and Dating of "For the Understanding of the Exchange"', *Economic History Review*, 2nd ser., 20 (April 1967), pp. 150–52. Daniel R. Fusfeld offers the flimsy thesis that Sir Richard Martin was the author in his, 'On the Authorship and Dating for "For the Understanding of the Exchange"', *Economic History Review*, 2nd ser., 20 (April 1967), pp. 145–52.

For a comprehensive portrayal of Sir Edward Coke as mercantilist and parliamentary statist, see Barbara Malament, 'The "Economic Liberalism" of Sir Edward Coke', *Yale Law Journal* 76 (June 1967), pp. 1321–58. On the early common law not being opposed to monopoly, see William L. Letwin, 'The English Common Law Concerning Monopolies', *University of Chicago Law Review*, 21 (Spring 1954), pp. 355–85.

On Milles, Malynes, Misselden, Mun, and the East India controversy in the first half of the seventeenth century, see Barry E. Supple, *Commercial Crisis and Change In England, 1600–1642* (Cambridge: Cambridge University Press, 1964), pp. 197–224. Also see the insights in Joyce Oldham Appleby,

Economic Thought and Ideology in Seventeenth-Century England (Princeton, NJ: Princeton University Press, 1978). A refreshingly different approach, and closer to the Austrian perspective, may be found in some of the writers in Chi-Yuen Wu, *An Outline of International Price Theories* (London: George Routledge & Sons, 1939), pp. 13–74. Wu's work was a doctoral dissertation under Lionel Robbins during the latter's Austrian period.

Sir Francis Bacon's commitment to English imperialism is examined in Horace B. White, 'Bacon's Imperialism', *American Political Science Review*, 52 (June 1958), pp. 470–89. On Francis Bacon as a Rosicrucian-oriented mystic and purveyor of the pseudo-science of the occult Ancient Wisdom, see Stephen A. McKnight, *Sacralizing the Secular: The Renaissance Origins of Modernity* (Baton Rouge, LA: L.S.U. Press, 1989), pp. 92–7; Frances Yates, 'Francis Bacon "Under the Shadow of Jehova's Wings"', in *The Rosicrucian Enlightenment* (London: Routledge & Kegan Paul, 1972); Frances Yates, 'The Hermetic Tradition in Renaissance Science', in C. Singleton (ed.), *Art, Science and History in the Renaissance* (Baltimore: Johns Hopkins University Press, 1967); and Paolo Rossi, *Francis Bacon: From Magic to Science* (Chicago: University of Chicago Press, 1968).

On the importation of several leading European Baconians to England, by invitation of the puritan country gentry at the start of the English Civil War, see the fascinating article by H.R. Trevor-Roper, 'Three Foreigners and the Philosophy of the English Revolution', *Encounter*, 14 (Feb. 1960), pp. 3–20.

The Baconians, as well as late sixteenth century English mercantilist thought generally, receive an excellent and lively treatment in William Letwin, *The Origins of Scientific Economics* (Garden City, NY: Doubleday, 1965). The most recent major volume dealing with late seventeenth and eighteenth century economic thought overall, though stressing English and Scottish thought, is Terence Hutchison, *Before Adam Smith: The Emergence of Political Economy, 1662–1776* (Oxford: Basil Blackwell, 1988). An early work, but still vitally important for illuminating the anti-working-class views of the English mercantilists and their adherence to 'full employment', is Edgar S. Furniss, *The Position of the Laborer in a System of Nationalism: A Study of the Labor Theories of the Later English Mercantilists* (1920, NY: Kelley & Millman, 1957).

The fullest account of the 'King–Davenant law of demand' is in John Creedy, *Demand and Exchange in Economic Analysis* (Aldershot, Hants: Edward Elgar, 1992), pp. 7–23, as well as in Creedy, 'On the King–Davenant Law of Demand', *Scottish Journal of Political Economy*, 33 (August 1986), pp. 193–212. D.A.G. Waddell, 'Charles Davenant (1656–1714) – A Biographical Sketch', *Economic History Review*, ser. 2, 11 (1958) pp. 279–88, is a convincingly revisionist view of Davenant.

Locke and the Levellers

A pioneering and indispensable work on the libertarian Commonwealthmen of the late seventeenth and eighteenth centuries in Britain is Caroline Robbins, *The Eighteenth-Century Commonwealthman* (Cambridge, Mass.: Harvard University Press, 1959). Directly inspired by Robbins was the outstanding work on the predominant influence of English libertarian thought on the American Revolution, Bernard Bailyn, *The Ideological Origins of the American Revolution* (1967, Cambridge, Mass.: Belknap Press of Harvard University Press, 1992).

Unfortunately, emphasis on the libertarian nature of Lockean influence on the American Revolution quickly became deflected by the 'Pocock thesis', which created an artificial distinction between allegedly 'modern' radical individualists, believers in private property and the free market, as against admirers of 'classical republican virtue' who were basically statists and communitarians who harked back to ancient models. Actually, there is no reason why radical libertarians and free marketers cannot also be opponents of government expenditure and 'corruption'; indeed, the two views usually go together. The major Pocockian work is J.G.A. Pocock, *The Machiavellian Moment* (Princeton, NJ: Princeton University Press, 1975). For critiques of Pocock, in addition to the works of Isaac Kramnick and Joyce Appleby, see in particular the refutation of Pocock's main case: the alleged 'classical virtue' *rather than* libertarianism of the largest single influence on the American revolutionaries: John Trenchard and Thomas Gordon's impressive series of London newspaper articles in the early 1720s: *Cato's Letters*. On *Cato's Letters* as libertarian rather than Pocockian, see Ronald Hamowy, '*Cato's Letters*: John Locke and the Republican Paradigm', *History of Political Thought*, II (1990), pp. 273–94.

The Levellers are presented in collections of their tracts, such as in Don M. Wolfe (ed.), *Leveller Manifestoes of the Puritan Revolution* (1944, New York: Humanities Press, 1967). Also see the editor's lengthy introduction to those tracts. A full treatment of the Levellers is H.N. Brailsford, *The Levellers and the English Revolution* (Stanford, Calif.: Stanford University Press, 1961). One of the best summaries of Leveller doctrine is in C.B. Macpherson, *The Political Theory of Possessive Individualism: Hobbes to Locke* (Oxford: The Clarendon Press, 1962), pp. 137–59.

Richard Ashcraft, *Revolutionary Politics and Locke's Two Treatises of Government* (Princeton, NJ: Princeton University Press, 1986) is excellent on Locke's radicalism and his connection with Leveller ideas. Ashcraft also provides the Shaftesbury explanation for the two Lockes: the early Baconian empiricist and absolutist of the *Essay on Human Understanding*, and the later systematic libertarian theorist. On Locke's early Baconianism, see Neal Wood, *The Politics of Locke's Philosophy: A Social Study of 'An Essay Concerning*

Human Understanding' (Berkeley: University of California Press, 1983); and on Locke's free market views, see Karen I. Vaughn, *John Locke: Economist and Social Scientist* (Chicago: University of Chicago Press, 1980). The definitive edition of Locke's notable *Two Treatises of Government* is the Peter Laslett edition (1960, Cambridge: Cambridge University Press, 2nd ed., 1968); also see Laslett's Introduction.

On Locke's theory of homesteading as the origin of private property and its relation to the Protestant scholastics, see Karl Olivecrona, 'Appropriation in the State of Nature: Locke on the Origin of Property', *Journal of the History of Ideas* (April–June 1974), pp. 211–30. Also see Lawrence C. Becker, *Property Rights: Philosophic Foundations* (London: Routledge & Kegan Paul, 1977), pp. 33–48. For a more recent contribution on Locke's property theory being consistent with free market capitalism, see Neil J. Mitchell, 'John Locke and the Rise of Capitalism', *History of Political Economy*, 18 (Summer 1986), pp. 291–305.

English mercantilists: late seventeenth and eighteenth centuries

For a lengthy discussion of Sir Isaac Newton's role at the Mint, see G. Findlay Shirras and J.H. Craig, 'Sir Isaac Newton and the Currency', *Economic Journal*, 55 (June–Sept. 1945), pp. 217–41.

For the libertarian impact of the satires of Jonathan Swift, see James A. Preu, *The Dean and the Anarchist* (Tallahassee, Fl.: Florida State University Press, 1959). On Swift's *Modest Proposal* as a satire on Pettyism, see Louis A. Landa, 'A *Modest Proposal* and Populousness', in *Essays in Eighteenth-Century English Literature* (1942, Princeton, NJ: Princeton University Press, 1980), pp. 39–48.

On the labour and employment theories in late seventeenth century England, see Theodore E. Gregory, 'The Economics of Employment in England, 1680–1713', in *Gold, Unemployment, and Capitalism* (1921, London: P.S. King & Sons, 1933), pp. 225–44. On the North brothers, see Letwin, *Origins*, pp. 196–220, 271–94.

For contemporary debate on the growth of the public-debt state in England in the first half of the eighteenth century, see P.G.M. Dickson, *The Financial Revolution in England*, pp. 15–33; on Child, Barbon, and the North brothers, see Letwin, *Origins of Scientific Economics*, pp. 3–81, 196–220, 271–94.

On John Law, an older but excellent critique is to be found in Charles Rist, *History of Monetary and Credit Theory from John Law to the Present Day* (1940, New York: M. Kelley, 1966), pp. 43–67. An illuminating study on Law and his influence, as against the hard-money tradition stemming from Turgot, is Joseph T. Salerno, 'Two Traditions in Modern Monetary Theory: John Law and A.R.J. Turgot', *Journal des Économistes et des Études Humaines*, 2, nos 2–3 (June–Sept. 1991), pp. 337–79. A provocative view that Law changed his mind from his *magnum opus* to his Mississippi scheme is in Antoin E. Murphy, 'The Evolution of John Law's Theories and Policies 1707–1715', *European Economic Review*, 35, no. 5 (July 1991), pp. 1109–25.

Bishop Berkeley's inflationist views are celebrated in Hutchison, *Before Adam Smith*, pp. 141–8; and in Salim Rashid, 'Berkeley's *Querist* and Its Influence', *Journal of the History of Economic Thought*, 12 (Spring 1990), pp. 38–60.

The hard-money writers of eighteenth century England are discussed in Hutchison, *Before Adam Smith*, and in the important article of Thomas T. Sekine, 'The Discovery of International Monetary Equilibrium by Vanderlint, Cantillon, Gervaise, and Hume', *Economia Internazionale*, 26 No. 2 (May 1973), pp. 262–82. On Vanderlint and on Joseph Harris, also see Wu, *Outline*, pp. 64–5, 70–71.

Hutchison, *Before Adam Smith*, pp. 229–38, devotes considerable space to Dean Josiah Tucker, but at the cost of greatly overvaluing him; a more sober though slighter account is in Viner, *Studies, passim*. The only book-length study of Tucker is unfortunately padded and diffuse: George Shelton, *Dean Tucker and Eighteenth-Century Economic and Political Thought* (New York: St Martin's Press, 1981).

Professor Salim Rashid has performed the signal service of resurrecting and stressing the importance to mid-eighteenth century English *laissez-faire* thought of Charles the Third Viscount Townshend, not to be confused with his more famous son and namesake, the author of the Townshend taxes on American imports. Salim Rashid, 'Lord Townshend and the Influence of Moral Philosophy on *Laissez Faire*', *The Journal of Libertarian Studies*, 8, no. 1 (Winter 1986), pp. 69–74.

Modern economics: Richard Cantillon: founding father

The year 1931 was a landmark in Cantillon studies, for it saw the first English translation of Richard Cantillon's great *Essai sur la nature du commerce en général*, ed. and trans. by Henry Higgs (1931, New York: A.M. Kelley, 1964). The Higgs Cantillon contains the French text along with the English translation, as well as the 1881 article by W. Stanley Jevons rediscovering Cantillon. Also, in 1931, F.A. von Hayek wrote a comprehensive introduction to the German edition of Cantillon, an introduction that also covers the substantial continental literature.

Until very recently, the only modern comprehensive overview of Cantillon's *Essai* in English has been Joseph J. Spengler, 'Richard Cantillon: First of the Moderns', *Journal of Political Economy*, 62 (August–Oct. 1954), pp. 281–95, 406–24, reprinted in Joseph J. Spengler and William R. Allen (eds), *Essays in Economic Thought: Aristotle to Marshall* (Chicago: Rand, McNally

Co., 1960), pp. 105–40. Also see the classic article by Jevons, 'Richard Cantillon and the Nationality of Political Economy', *Contemporary Review* (January 1881), partially reprinted in Henry W. Spiegel. (ed.), *The Development of Economic Thought: Great Economists in Perspective* (New York: Wiley, 1952), pp. 43–60.

The first biography of Cantillon has finally appeared: Antoin E. Murphy, *Richard Cantillon: Entrepreneur and Economist* (Oxford: The Clarendon Press, 1986). This will long remain the definitive biography of this fascinating figure. Murphy sets us straight on Cantillon's confused and tangled genealogy, family, and date of birth, and for the first time presents vivid details of Cantillon's colourful life, his relationship to John Law, and the overlooked connections between the Mississippi and South Sea bubbles, and he ends with an intriguing mystery story about Cantillon's violent death.

On Cantillon's economics, also see Anthony Brewer, *Richard Cantillon: Pioneer of Economic Theory* (London: Routledge, 1992). Robert Hébert provides a new look at a wholly neglected Cantillon contribution in Robert F. Hébert, 'Richard Cantillon's Early Contributions to Spatial Economics', *Economica*, 48 (February 1981), pp. 71–7.

For the rest, analyses in English concentrate on Cantillon's monetary theory, in particular his pioneering contribution to the theory of international monetary payments and the price-specie-flow mechanism. See in particular, Thomas T. Sekine, 'The Discovery of International Monetary Equilibrium by Vanderlint, Cantillon, Gervaise, and Hume', *Economia Internazionale*, 26, no. 2 (May 1973), pp. 262–82; and Chi-Yuen Wu, *An Outline of International Price Theories* (London: George Routledge & Sons, 1939). Also see Arthur Eli Monroe, *Monetary Theory Before Adam Smith* (1923, Gloucester, Mass.: Peter Smith, 1965); Charles Rist, *A History of Monetary and Credit Theory: From John Law to the Present Day* (1940, New York: A.M. Kelley, 1966); and particularly Douglas Vickers, *Studies in the Theory of Money, 1690–1776* (1959, New York: A.M. Kelley, 1968). Especially outstanding is the unpublished work of Joseph Thomas Salerno, 'The Doctrinal Antecedents of the Monetary Approach to the Balance of Payments' (doctoral dissertation, Rutgers University, 1980).

In August 1980, a Cantillon symposium was held in Pacific Grove, California, which generated a rich supply of Cantillon scholarship. Most of these valuable articles are published in the *Journal of Libertarian Studies*, 7 (Autumn 1985) issue. They include the following: an English translation of F.A. von Hayek's 'Richard Cantillon', introduction of the 1931 edition by Mícheál Ó'Súilleabháin; Vincent Tarascio's 'Cantillon's *Essay*: A Current Perspective', which emphasized Cantillon's insight on the self-regulatory nature of the market economy, his monetary theory, population theory, and stress on uncertainty; David O'Mahony's 'Richard Cantillon – A Man of His Time: A

Comment on Tarascio', who points out Cantillon's pre-Austrian rather than pre-neoclassical theories of price, value and money; Robert F. Hébert, 'Was Cantillon an Austrian Economist?' which points to Cantillon's Austrian approach to uncertainty, entrepreneurship, money and the market; and Roger W. Garrison, 'A Comment on West', who brilliantly demonstrates that Cantillon's hesitancy about the free market economy in matters of *space* was more than matched by Smith's criticism of market choices in matters of *time*. And finally, Antoin E. Murphy, 'Richard Cantillon – Banker and Economist', provides up-to-date information on this fascinating economist's life.

Hébert's subtle analysis of Cantillon as having a pre-Austrian theory of the entrepreneur is elaborated in Robert F. Hébert and Albert N. Link, *The Entrepreneur: Mainstream Views and Radical Critiques* (New York: Praeger Books, 1982), pp. 14–22. Also see Bert F. Hoselitz, 'The Early History of Entrepreneurial Theory', in Spengler and Allen, *Economic Thought*, pp. 234–57.

Early mathematical economists

Daniel Bernoulli's pioneering foray into mathematical economics has been translated into English by Louise Sommer as 'Exposition of a New Theory on the Measurement of Risk', *Econometrica*, 22 (Jan. 1954), pp. 23–36. Good summaries of the theory appear in Schumpeter, *History*, pp. 303–5, and Spiegel, *Growth*, pp. 143–4, but there are no satisfactory critiques; even the normally highly astute Emil Kauder is severely limited by his undue admiration for mathematical economics. See Emil Kauder, *A History of Marginal Utility Theory* (Princeton, NJ: Princeton University Press, 1965), pp. 31–5. For a further critique of mathematical marginal utility theory, see Murray N. Rothbard, *Toward a Reconstruction of Utility and Welfare Economics* (1956, New York: Center for Libertarian Studies, Sept. 1977), pp. 9–12. Also see Harro F. Bernardelli, 'The End of the Marginal Utility Theory?' *Economica* (May 1938), pp. 192–212; Bernardelli, 'A Reply to Mr. Samuelson's Note', *Economica* (Feb. 1939), pp. 88–9; and idem, 'A Rehabilitation of The Classical Theory of Marginal Utility', *Economica* (August 1952), pp. 254–68.

The physiocrats and *laissez-faire*

The best overall survey of the physiocrats and their movement is still Henry Higgs, *The Physiocrats* (1897, New York: The Langland Press, 1952), Valuable also are Joseph J. Spengler, 'The Physiocrats and Say's Law of Markets', and Arthur I. Bloomfield, 'The Foreign-Trade Doctrines of the Physiocrats', reprinted in Spengler and Allen (eds), *Essays*, pp. 161–214, 215–33. Though written from a Marxist perspective, there are some useful insights in Elizabeth Fox-Genovese, *The Origins of Physiocracy: Economic Revolution and Social Order in Eighteenth-Century France* (Ithaca, NY:

Cornell University Press, 1976). Translations from Quesnay as well as his own essays can be found in Ronald L. Meek, *The Economics of Physiocracy: Essays and Translations* (Cambridge, Mass.: Harvard University Press, 1963). A helpful study of the last of the physiocrats in James J. McLain, *The Economic Writings of Du Pont de Nemours* (Newark, Del.: University of Delaware Press, 1977).

A.R.J. Turgot

A collection of all of Turgot's economic writings, newly translated and with an excellent introduction and annotations, is P.D. Groenewegen (ed.), *The Economics of A.R.J. Turgot* (The Hague: Martinus Nijhoff, 1977). Groenewegen, the foremost modern authority on Turgot, offers an illuminating appraisal of his influence in economic thought in 'Turgot's Place in the History of Economic Thought: A Bicentenary Estimate', *History of Political Economy*, 15 (Winter 1983), pp. 585–616. Turgot's lack of influence on Adam Smith is established in Groenewegen, 'Turgot and Adam Smith', *Scottish Journal of Political Economy*, 16 (Nov. 1969), pp. 271–87.

For a detailed analysis and appreciation of Turgot's theory of value and price, see Groenewegen, 'A Reappraisal of Turgot's Theory of Value, Exchange, and Price Determination', *History of Political Economy*, 2 (Spring 1970), pp. 177–96. And on Turgot's theory of capital and interest, see Groenewegen, 'A Re-interpretation of Turgot's Theory of Capital and Interest', *Economic Journal*, 81 (June 1971), pp. 327–40. For Böhm-Bawerk's appraisal of Turgot and a critique of it, see Eugen von Böhm-Bawerk, *Capital and Interest* (South Holland, Ill.: Libertarian Press, 1959), I, pp. 39–45; Frank A. Fetter, *Capital, Interest, and Rent: Essays in the Theory of Distribution* (ed. M. Rothbard, Kansas City: Sheed Andrews and McMeel, 1977), pp. 264–6; Groenewegen, 'Re-interpretation', pp. 327, 337–8. On Turgot's theory of the entrepreneur, see Hébert and Link, *The Entrepreneur*, pp. 27–9. On Turgot's life, see Douglas Dakin, *Turgot and the Ancient Regime in France* (London: Methuen & Co., 1939).

Ferdinando Galiani

On Galiani and Condillac, see the notable article by Emil Kauder, 'Genesis of the Marginal Utility Theory', *Economic Journal* (Sept. 1953), in Spengler and Allen (eds), *Essays*, pp. 277–87. There is no full English translation of either of Galiani's works. There is a partial translation of sections on the theories of value and interest in *Della Moneta* in Arthur Eli Monroe (ed.), *Early Economic Thought* (Cambridge, Mass.: Harvard University Press, 1924), pp. 280–307. An illuminating discussion of Galiani's value theory which unfortunately omits his admittedly less important monetary analysis, is that of Luigi Einaudi: 'Einaudi on Galiani', in Henry W. Spiegel (ed.), *The Devel-*

opment of Economic Thought (New York: Wiley, 1952), pp. 61–82. That gap is made up by Filippo Cesarano, 'Monetary Theory in Ferdinando Galiani's *Della moneta'*, *History of Political Economy*, 81 (Autumn 1976), pp. 380–99.

For the life of Galiani in Paris, see Joseph Rossi, *The Abbé Galiani In France* (New York: Publications of the Institute of French Studies, 1950). Also on Galiani and Genovesi, see Franco Venturi, *Italy and the Enlightenment* (New York: New York University Press, 1972). On Genovesi, Condillac and the utility of exchange, see Oswald St Clair, *A Key to Ricardo* (1957, New York: A.M. Kelley, 1965). On Condillac, see Hutchison, *Before Adam Smith*, pp. 324–31, and Isabel F. Knight, *The Geometric Spirit: The Abbé de Condillac and the French Enlightenment* (New Haven: Yale University Press, 1968).

The Scottish Enlightenment
An illuminating social history of the Scottish Enlightenment and its relation to the moderate Presbyterian clergy is Anand C. Chitnis, *The Scottish Enlightenment: A Social History* (London: Croom Helm, 1976). A trenchant discussion of the moderates as apologists for the Presbyterian state Church Establishment is in Richard B. Sher, *Church and University in the Scottish Enlightenment: The Moderate Literati of Edinburgh* (Princeton, NJ: Princeton University Press, 1985).

On the doctrines and personal interrelationships of the Scottish Enlightenment political economists, see William Leslie Taylor, *Francis Hutcheson and David Hume as Predecessors of Adam Smith* (Durham, NC: Duke University Press, 1965). See also the summary in H.M. Robertson and W.L. Taylor, 'Adam Smith's Approach to the Theory of Value', *Economic Journal* (1957), in Joseph J. Spengler and William R. Allen (eds), *Essays in Economic Thought* (Chicago: Rand McNally, 1960), p. 288ff. The founding father of this group is explored in W.L. Taylor, 'Gershom Carmichael: A Neglected Figure in British Political Economy', *South African Journal of Economics*, 23 (Sept. 1955), pp. 251–5.

For a refutation of the Hayekian view of Bernard Mandeville as exponent of *laissez-faire*, see Jacob Viner, *The Long View and The Short* (1953, Glencoe, Ill.: The Free Press, 1958), pp. 332–42. Von Hayek's attempted rebuttal of Viner rests on von Hayek's failure to comprehend the vital distinction between the 'natural' (the processes and results of voluntary actions), and the 'artificial' (government interventions in such processes), as well as on von Hayek's enchantment with all actions whatsoever that have supposedly yielded 'unintended' results. F.A. von Hayek, 'Dr. Bernard Mandeville', *New Studies in Philosophy, Politics, Economics and the History of Ideas* (1967, Chicago: University of Chicago Press, 1978), pp. 249–66. For an excellent article demonstrating the profound mercantilism and proto-Keynesianism of Mandeville, see Harry Landreth, 'The Economic Thought of Bernard Mandeville', *History of Political Economy*, 7 (1975), pp. 193–208; also see the illuminating article by Salim Rashid, 'Mandeville's *Fable:* Laissez-Faire or Libertinism?' *Eighteenth-Century Studies*, 18 (Spring 1985), pp. 313–30. Landreth shows that, as in the case of other mercantilists, Mandeville was committed to full employment of a large population because he was devoted to maximizing production at low wages. The employment was to be 'full' because forced by the state.

On the influence of Suarez and the Spanish scholastics on Grotius, see José Ferrater Mora, 'Suarez and Modern Philosophy', *Journal of the History of Ideas* (Oct. 1953), pp. 528–47.

David Hume's *Writings on Economics*, ed. E. Rotwein (Madison, Wisc.: University of Wisconsin Press, 1970), provides all Hume's essays on economics and a brief selection of his letters. An illuminating discussion of Hume's neglect of cash balance effects in the balance of payment mechanism is in Sekine, 'Discovery of International Monetary Equilibrium', pp. 274–82. Also see Salerno, 'Doctrinal Antecedents', pp. 150–76. For Hume as inflationist, especially in his later *History of England*, see Constant Noble Stockton, 'Economics and the Mechanism of Historical Progress in Hume's *History*', in D.W. Livingston and J.T. King (eds), *Hume: A Re-Evaluation* (New York: Fordham University Press, 1976), pp. 309–13.

Hume is generally considered the great debunker of natural law, but see A. Kenneth Hesselberg, 'Hume, Natural Law and Justice', *Duquesne Review* (Spring 1961), pp. 45–63, who maintains that Hume eventually slips in a natural law analysis through the back door.

In recent years, it has become fashionable to hold that Sir James Steuart was a sound Keynesian classical liberal, unjustly buried by the success of the *Wealth of Nations*. An excellent article demolishing this position is Gary M. Anderson and Robert D. Tollison, 'Sir James Steuart as the Apotheosis of Mercantilism and His Relation to Adam Smith', *Southern Economic Journal*, 51 (Oct. 1984), pp. 456–68. Anderson and Tollison point out that Steuart was an ardent believer in a totalitarian planned economy, with government regulating and cartellizing all economic activity. Steuart also helped originate the Marxian doctrine of inherent class conflict in society, as well as lauding and wishing to emulate the Spartan economy of totalitarian rule by an élite grounded in a system of slavery. Steuart's *An Inquiry into the Principles of Political Economy* has been republished and edited with an introduction by Andrew S. Skinner (Chicago: University of Chicago Press, 1966).

The celebrated Adam Smith

The writings on Adam Smith stretch almost to infinity, and so we can only try to make a brief and judicious selection here. The definitive collection of all of Smith's writings is now available in the handsome six-volume bicentennial Glasgow edition. The 1976 Glasgow edition of the *Wealth of Nations*, ed. by R.H. Campbell, A.S. Skinner and W.B. Todd, published by the Oxford University Press, has been reprinted in a two-volume soft-cover set by the Liberty Press (Indianapolis: Liberty Classics, 1981). The Campbell–Skinner General Introduction presents the latest scholarship in the field. But the previous state-of-the-art Cannan edition should also be consulted, if only for the healthily critical approach that the great Cannan dares to take toward Adam Smith. (Smith, *Wealth of Nations*, ed. E. Cannan, New York: Modern Library, 1937.)

Still the most lucid and penetrating critique of Adam Smith's confused theories of value and distribution can be found in Paul Douglas, 'Smith's Theory of Value and Distribution', in J.M. Clark et al., *Adam Smith, 1776–1926* (Chicago: University of Chicago Press, 1928), pp. 78–115; reprinted in H.W. Spiegel (ed.), *The Development of Economic Thought* (New York: John Wiley, 1964), pp. 73–102. On the search for an invariable measure of value by Smith and Ricardo, see Richard H. Timberlake, Jr, 'The Classical Search for an Invariable Measure of Value', *Quarterly Review of Economics and Business*, 6 (Spring 1966), pp. 37–44. Edwin Cannan's critique of the classical economics of Smith and Ricardo is subtle and important: Edwin Cannan, *A History of the Theories of Production & Distribution in English Political Economy* (3rd ed. 1917, London: Staples Press, 1953). Cannan's adroit and implicit put-down can be seen in his sesquicentennial summation of Smith's accomplishments: 'Adam Smith as an Economist', *Economica*, 6 (June 1926), pp. 123–34. See also the similar and equally subtle as well as witty put-down by the Scottish historian of economic thought, Alexander Gray, *Adam Smith* (London: The Historical Association, 1948).

Despite these dissenting voices, the hagiographic attitude towards Adam Smith remained generally unbroken until the demolition in the monumental work of Joseph Schumpeter, *History of Economic Analysis* (New York: Oxford University Press, 1954), especially pages 181–94, 323–5, and 557–9. Also see the splendid article by Emil Kauder, 'Genesis of the Marginal Utility Theory', *Economic Journal* (Sept. 1953), pp. 638–50, reprinted in Spengler and Allen, *Essays*, pp. 277–87. Robertson and Taylor, in their comment on Kauder, are more favourable to Smith but fundamentally concede his criticisms: H.M. Robertson and W.L. Taylor, 'Adam Smith's Approach to the Theory of Value', in Spengler and Allen, *Essays*, pp. 288–304.

Unfortunately, the clear-eyed attitude towards Smith engendered by Schumpeterian revisionism has been largely rolled back since the mid-1970s.

Partly this was the consequence of the bicentennial volumes pouring out in admiration of Smith; partly it was due to the influential work of Samuel Hollander, *The Economics of Adam Smith* (Toronto: University of Toronto Press, 1973). In the face of the evidence, Hollander absurdly attempts to torture Smith into the mould of a thoroughly consistent, formalistic proto-Walrasian modern general equilibrium theorist. The large Glasgow edition volume of essays, A. Skinner and T. Wilson (eds), *Essays on Adam Smith* (Oxford: The Clarendon Press, 1975), presents a number of articles in the new Hollanderian mould of hagiography.

However, it is gratifying to find T.W. Hutchison, in his more recent work, acknowledging the grave damage done by Smith in rejecting the entire subjective utility/scarcity tradition he had inherited, as well as Smith's implanting into economics objective-value and labour-value theories. Unfortunately, Hutchison attributes this fateful change to 'unhappy, tiresome, and awkward' confusion on the part of Smith rather than to deeper differences and problems. Hutchison also trenchantly points to Smith's unfortunate abandonment of the insight of previous economists that the division of labour is caused by human diversity, a proposition denied by what Hutchison realizes is the view 'that might be expected...from a social engineer or egalitarian', rather than from Smith as supposed individualist and libertarian. Terence Hutchison, *Before Adam Smith*, pp. 362–6, 370–81.

The standard life of Adam Smith is still John Rae's *Life of Adam Smith*, especially the 1965 edition containing Jacob Viner's searching introductory essay, 'Guide to John Rae's Life of Adam Smith', (New York: A.M. Kelley, 1965). Also see C.R. Fay, *Adam Smith and the Scotland of His Day* (Cambridge: Cambridge University Press, 1956); and William Robert Scott, *Adam Smith as Student and Professor* (Glasgow: Jackson, Son & Co., 1937). The latest concise life of Smith is R.H. Campbell and A.S. Skinner, *Adam Smith* (London: Croom Helm, 1982). For Smith's intellectual milieu, see William Leslie Taylor, *Francis Hutcheson and David Hume as Predecessors of Adam Smith* (Durham, NC: Duke University Press, 1965); and Anand Chitnis, *The Scottish Enlightenment: A Social History* (London: Croom Helm, 1976).

For Adam Smith as someone who failed abysmally to acknowledge the sources for his ideas, see Salim Rashid, 'Adam Smith's Acknowledgements: Neo-Plagiarism and the Wealth of Nations', *The Journal of Libertarian Studies*, 9 (1990), pp. 1–24. On Smith's unjust accusations of plagiarism against his friend, Adam Ferguson, see Ronald Hamowy, 'Adam Smith, Adam Ferguson, and the Division of Labour', *Economica*, 35 (August 1968), pp. 249–59. For an illuminating critique of scholars applying special standards favourable to Adam Smith, see Salim Rashid, 'Does a Famous Economist Deserve Special Standards? A Critical Note on Adam Smith Scholarship', *Bulletin of the History of Economics Society*, 11 (Autumn 1989), pp. 190–

209. On the slowness of the *Wealth of Nations* in achieving renown, see Salim Rashid, 'Adam Smith's Rise to Fame: A Reexamination', *The Eighteenth Century* (Winter 1982), pp. 64–85.

For an illuminating article on Smith as an enthusiastic top customs collector, see Gary M. Anderson, William F. Shughart II, and Robert D. Tollison, 'Adam Smith in the Customhouse', *Journal of Political Economy*, 93 (August 1985), pp. 740–59.

On Adam Smith and his ignorance of the Industrial Revolution going on about him, see R. Koebner, 'Adam Smith and the Industrial Revolution', *Economic History Review*, 2nd ser. 11 (August 1959); and Charles P. Kindleberger, 'The Historical Background: Adam Smith and the Industrial Revolution', in T. Wilson and A.S. Skinner (eds), *The Market and the State: Essays in Honor of Adam Smith* (Oxford: The Clarendon Press, 1976), pp. 1–25. For an up-to-date critique of Smith on this issue, see Salim Rashid, '*The Wealth of Nations* and Historical Facts', *Journal of the History of Economic Thought*, 14 (Autumn 1992), pp. 225–43. For an unconvincing defence of Smith see Ronald Max Hartwell, 'Adam Smith and the Industrial Revolution', in F. Glahe (ed.), *Adam Smith and the Wealth of Nations* (Boulder, Col.: Colorado Associated University Press, 1978), pp. 123–47.

The grave inner contradiction between Smith's favourable and unfavourable views on the division of labour, the latter anticipating Marxian complaints about 'alienation', is admitted by one of Smith's staunchest modern admirers, in Edwin G. West, 'Adam Smith's Two Views on the Division of Labour', *Economica*, n.s. 31 (Feb. 1964), and idem, 'Political Economy of Alienation', *Oxford Economic Papers*, 21 (March 1969), pp. 1–23. Also see idem, 'Adam Smith and Alienation', in Skinner and Wilson (eds), *Essays on Adam Smith*, pp. 540–52. Among other writers pointing to Smith's anticipation of Marxian wailing about 'alienation', see Nathan Rosenberg, 'Adam Smith on the Division of Labour: Two Views or One?', *Economica*, n.s. 32 (May 1965); and Jacob Viner's Introduction to John Rae's *Life of Adam Smith* (1965), p. 35.

On Smith's bias against consumption, see Roger W. Garrison, 'West's Cantillon and Adam Smith: A Comment', *Journal of Libertarian Studies*, 7 (Autumn 1985), pp. 291–2; Cannan, *History of Theories*, pp. 23–4; Ingrid Hahne Rima, *Development of Economic Analysis* (3rd ed., Homewood, Ill.: Richard D. Irwin, 1978), p. 79; Edwin G. West, *Adam Smith* (New Rochelle, NY: Arlington House, 1969), p. 173; Kauder, 'Genesis'; and Gerhard W. Ditz, 'The Calvinism in Adam Smith' (unpublished MS, 1983). The major point of Nathan Rosenberg's 'Adam Smith on Profits – Paradox Lost and Regained', *Journal of Political Economy*, 82 (Nov–Dec. 1977), pp. 1187–8, is that Smith holds high profits to be bad because they induce capitalists to indulge in luxurious consumption.

On Smith's inexplicable failure to carry over Hume's specie-flow-price analysis from his lectures into his *Wealth of Nations*, see the classic critique by Jacob Viner, *Studies in the Theory of International Trade* (New York: Harper & Bros, 1937), p. 87. A realistic assessment of Smith's unsatisfactory theory of money is in Douglas Vickers, 'Adam Smith and the Status of the Theory of Money', surprisingly published in the hagiographical Skinner and Wilson, *Essays*, p. 484. For an unconvincing attempt to explain the deterioration in Smith's monetary theory, see Frank Petrella, 'Adam Smith's Rejection of Hume's Price-Specie-Flow Mechanism: A Minor Mystery Resolved', *Southern Economic Journal*, 34 (Jan 1968), pp. 365–74. Robert V. Eagly tries, in Samuel Hollanderian fashion, to claim Smith's consistency in *really* adopting the Humean view as a proto-Walrasian general equilibrium theorist. Robert V. Eagly, 'Adam Smith and the Specie-Flow Doctrine', *The Scottish Journal of Political Economy*, 17 (Feb. 1970), pp. 61–8. Also, for a critique of Smith's argument on specie as a 'dead stock', see Charles Rist, *History of Monetary and Credit Theory: From John Law to the Present Day* (1940, New York: A.M. Kelley, 1966), p. 85. For a refutation of modern versions of this argument common to Keynesians and monetarists alike, see Roger W. Garrison, 'The "Costs" of a Gold Standard', in Llewellyn H. Rockwell, Jr (ed.), *The Gold Standard: Perspectives in the Austrian School* (1985, Auburn, Ala.: Ludwig von Mises Institute, 1992), pp. 61–79.

On the 'invisible hand' as a metaphor, see William B. Grampp, 'Adam Smith and the Economic Man', *Journal of Political Economy* (August 1948), pp. 319–21. On the first use of the 'invisible hand' concept by the seventeenth century writer Joseph Glanville, and on Smith's similar use of the concept in his philosophic essays, see Spengler, 'Boisguilbert's Economic Views', p. 73.

On Adam Smith as a dubious partisan of *laissez-faire*, see the classic article by Jacob Viner, 'Adam Smith and Laissez-faire', in Clark et al., *Adam Smith, 1776–1926*, pp. 116–79. Also see Joseph M. Jadlow, 'Adam Smith on Usury Laws', *Journal of Finance*, 32 (Sept. 1977), pp. 1195–1200. Oddly, however, Jadlow sees a wise coping with 'externalities' instead of a Calvinist horror of consumption and speculative risk. See also the sensitive discussion in Ellen Frankel Paul, 'Adam Smith: The Great Founder', in *Moral Revolution and Economic Science: The Demise of Laissez-Faire in Nineteenth Century British Political Economy* (Westport, Conn.: Greenwood Press, 1979), pp. 9–44. For a critique of Smith's alleged canons of taxation, see Murray N. Rothbard, *Power and Market: Government and the Economy* (1970, Kansas City, Mo.: Sheed Andrews and McMeel, 1977), pp. 137–8, 144–5.

The spread of the Smithian movement
On the spread of the Smithian movement in Scotland and the influence of
Dugald Stewart, see Jacob H. Hollander, 'The Dawn of a Science', and
especially, 'The Founder of a School', in J.M. Clark et al., *Adam Smith,
1776–1926* (Chicago: University of Chicago Press, 1928). On the founding
of the *Edinburgh Review*, see Anand C. Chitnis, *The Scottish Enlightenment*;
and on Francis Horner, see Frank W. Fetter, 'Introduction', F.W. Fetter (ed.),
The Economic Writings of Francis Horner (London: London School of Economics, 1957). On the spread of Smithianism on the continent of Europe, see
the still indispensable article by Melchior Palyi, 'The Introduction of Adam
Smith on the Continent', in Clark, *Adam Smith*, pp. 180–233. On the spread
of Smithian views into Germany, see Carl William Hasek, *The Introduction
of Adam Smith's Doctrines Into Germany* (New York: Columbia University
Press, 1925). On Ludwig Heinrich von Jakob, see Donald G. Rohr, *The
Origins of Social Liberalism in Germany* (Chicago: University of Chicago
Press, 1963). On the story of, and the problems with, the Stein-Hardenberg
reforms in Prussia, see Walter M. Simon, *The Failure of The Prussian Reform Movement, 1807–19* (Ithaca, NY: Cornell University Press, 1955). On
the German cameralists, who resisted Smithian doctrine, see Lewis H. Haney,
History of Economic Thought (4th ed., New York: Macmillan, 1949), pp. 148–
65. For a detailed portrayal of the cameralists' political views, see Albion W.
Small, *The Cameralists* (1909; New York: Burt Franklin, n.d.). On Johann
Heinrich Gottlieb von Justi's views of alienation of labour in the factories
and under division of labour, and their influence through Sir James Denham
Steuart upon G.W.F. Hegel, see Raymond Plant, *Hegel* (Bloomington, Ind.:
University of Indiana Press, 1973). On the communism of Johann Joachim
Becher, see Eli F. Heckscher, *Mercantilism* (2nd ed., New York: Macmillan,
1955). On Heinrich Friedrich Freiherr von Storch, see Schumpeter, *History*,
pp. 502–3; and Peter Bernholz, 'Inflation and Monetary Constitutions in
Historical Perspective', *Kyklos*, 36, no. 3 (1983), pp. 408–9.

On Semyon Desnitsky and his Smithian influence at the court of Catherine
the Great, see A.H. Brown, 'S.E. Desnitsky, Adam Smith, and the *Nakaz* of
Catherine II', *Oxford Slavonic Papers*, n.s. 7 (1974), pp. 42–59; and idem,
'Adam Smith's First Russian Followers', in Skinner and Wilson (eds), *Essays
on Adam Smith*, pp. 247–73.

Malthus and population
The writings on Malthus and on population are almost infinite; here we can
only suggest any of the numerous reprints of Malthus's first and sixth editions of his *Essay on Population* (see references in Spiegel, *Growth*, pp. 735–
9, 828–9). In addition, there are excellent critiques of Malthus in Schumpeter,
History, pp. 250–58, 578–84, and 889–91; and in Edwin Cannan, *A History*

of the Theories of Production and Distribution in English Political Economy from 1776 to 1848 (3rd ed., London: Staples Press, 1953), pp. 103–114, 132–5. Also see the pungent article by Gertrude Himmelfarb, 'The Specter of Malthus', in her *Victorian Minds* (1968, Gloucester, Mass.: Peter Smith, 1975), pp. 82–110; and the always witty and perceptive Alexander Gray, *The Development of Economic Doctrine* (London: Longmans, Green and Co., 1931), pp. 155–68. It is remarkable that the only extant biography is the useful and extensive but far from deeply analytic Patricia James, *Population Malthus: His Life and Times* (London: Routledge and Kegan Paul, 1979).

Index